P9-BXV-355

THE *SMART*
RETRIEVAL SYSTEM

Experiments in Automatic
Document Processing

Prentice-Hall
Series in Automatic Computation
George Forsythe, editor

GERARD SALTON, *Editor*

Professor of Computer Science
Cornell University

THE SMART RETRIEVAL SYSTEM

Experiments in Automatic Document Processing

PRENTICE-HALL, INC., Englewood Cliffs, New Jersey

© 1971 by Prentice-Hall, Inc.
Englewood Cliffs, N.J.

All rights reserved. No part of this book
may be reproduced in any form or by any
means without permission in writing from
the publisher.

Current printing (last digit):
10 9 8 7 6 5 4 3 2 1

13–81425–3
Library of Congress Catalog Card No. 70–159122

Printed in the United States of America

PRENTICE-HALL INTERNATIONAL, INC., *London*
PRENTICE-HALL OF AUSTRALIA, PTY. LTD., *Sidney*
PRENTICE-HALL OF CANADA, LTD., *Toronto*
PRENTICE-HALL OF INDIA PRIVATE LIMITED, *New Delhi*
PRENTICE-HALL OF JAPAN, INC., *Tokyo*

PREFACE

The automatic SMART document retrieval system was designed at Harvard University between 1961 and 1964, and has been operating on IBM 7094 and 360 equipment both at Harvard and at Cornell University for several years. The system takes documents and search requests in the natural language, performs a fully automatic content analysis of the texts using one of several dozen programmed language analysis methods, matches analyzed documents with analyzed search requests, and retrieves for the user's attention those stored items believed to be most similar to the submitted queries.

Unlike the other computer-based retrieval systems, the SMART system does not rely on manually assigned keywords or index terms for the identification of documents and search requests, nor does it use primarily the frequency of occurrence of certain words or phrases included in the texts of documents. Instead, an attempt is made to go beyond simple word-matching procedures by using a variety of intellectual aids in the form of synonym dictionaries, hierarchical arrangements of subject identifiers, statistical and syntactic phrase generation methods, and the like, in order to obtain content identifications useful for the retrieval process.

By comparing the retrieval performance obtained with the various programmed procedures, the SMART system can be used as a unique experimental tool for the evaluation in a controlled laboratory environment of many fully automatic language analysis methods. In addition, the system

vii

has been used to simulate a user-environment by making it possible for the user to participate in the search process. Specifically, the system utilizes feedback information supplied by the user during the search to construct improved search formulations, and to generate document representations reflecting the interests of the user population. By combining automatic text processing methods with interactive search and retrieval techniques, the SMART system may then lead to the design and implementation of modern information services of the type which may become current in operational environments some years hence.

Most of the documentation pertaining to the SMART system design and to the experimental results obtained with the system over the last few years is contained in a set of book-size scientific reports entitled "Information Storage and Retrieval," known in brief as "the ISR reports." The first ten of these (ISR-1 to ISR-10) were issued at Harvard between November 1961 and March 1966, and the last seven at Cornell. At the time of this writing, the most recent volume issued is ISR-17, dated September 1969.

The ISR reports covering the SMART system are not generally available in the open market; moreover, the information contained in the reports is difficult to assimilate, being dispersed over a large number of volumes including many thousands of pages. For this reason it has seemed advisable to collect in an organized manner, as a single book, the most important contributions contained in the earlier reports.

The present volume thus consists of updated versions of twenty-seven studies taken from the material contained in the ten most recent scientific reports (ISR-8 to ISR-17). Among the material covered are theoretical developments, including the derivation of system evaluation measures, language analysis techniques, document grouping techniques, and adaptive space transformation methods, as well as experimental studies relating to the evaluation of document analysis methods, interactive user feedback procedures, partial document searches based on clustered file organizations, and comparisons between the SMART system and more conventional operational information systems.

The present text is organized into eight major parts, entitled, respectively, The SMART System, Evaluation Viewpoint and Parameters, Language Analysis, Cluster Generation and Search, Basic Feedback Runs, Feedback Refinements, Document Space Transformation, and Operational Comparisons. Each part can be read independently of the remainder, and none of the material requires more than an elementary knowledge of mathematics or computer programming.

The text should be of greatest value as a reference volume for the professional practitioner interested in the design and operations of automatic information systems. It should also be useful as a text of readings in the area of automatic information retrieval for the more mature students enrolled in courses in applied mathematics, computer and information science, or library science. In this latter role, the studies contained in this volume might serve as a point of departure for term projects and for experimental work in modern information processing.

Part I of this volume, consisting of Chapters 1 and 2, covers the basic design of the SMART system. Chapter 1 by G. Salton deals with the background relating to the SMART project and contains a summary of evaluation results already obtained and a report of future plans. Chapter 2 by D. Williamson, R. Williamson, and

M. E. Lesk is a description of the implementation of the SMART system as it is presently operating at Cornell on an IBM 360/65.

The main systems evaluation parameters are covered in Part II, consisting of Chapters 3 to 5. Chapters 3 and 4 by J. J. Rocchio, Jr., contain a derivation of the normalized recall and precision evaluation measures and of the procedures used to obtain average retrieval results valid over many information searches. Chapter 5 by E. M. Keen is a detailed description of the design of a retrieval evaluation system.

The language analysis problems and relevant evaluation results are contained in Part III, consisting of Chapters 6 to 9. Chapter 6 by G. Salton and M. E. Lesk deals with the general problem of language analysis and dictionary construction useful in a content analysis system. Chapter 7 also by G. Salton and M. E. Lesk is a summarization of evaluation results obtained with SMART by processing document collections in the areas of aerodynamics, computer engineering, and documentation. A thorough analysis of the performance of user queries in the area of documentation is contained in Chapter 8 by E. M. Keen. The final chapter of Part III, number 9, by G. Salton covers an extension of the language analysis procedures originally implemented for English items to a collection of German language documents.

Part IV, consisting of Chapters 10 to 13, contains a description of automatic document classification procedures, and of the partial search methods based on document clusters. Chapter 10 by G. Salton is a basic description of cluster searching. Chapter 11 by R. T. Grauer and M. Messier covers the evaluation of a clustering process due to Rocchio. Additional, more efficient methods for automatic document classification are described in Chapter 12 by R. T. Dattola. Finally, Chapter 13 by S. Worona introduces an information search process based on the generation of request, rather than document, clusters.

The standard query transformation process based on user feedback is covered in Part V, consisting of Chapters 14 to 17. The main theoretical considerations relating to the construction of optimal user queries by relevance feedback methods are contained in Chapter 14 by J. J. Rocchio, Jr., and the principal feedback evaluation methods are described in Chapter 15 by G. Salton. A thorough analysis of feedback retrieval is included in Chapter 16 by E. Ide, and the last chapter, number 17, by C. Cirillo, Y. K. Chang, and J. Razon examines a number of novel feedback evaluation methods which circumvent some of the difficulties of the standard feedback evaluation methodology.

Certain refinements of the interactive search process are covered in Part VI of this volume, consisting of Chapters 18 to 22. The main distinctions between positive and negative feedback procedures are described in Chapter 18 by E. Ide and G. Salton; this chapter also contains a discussion of the relevance feedback process in the environment of a clustered information file. A query-splitting procedure, useful when nonhomogeneous sets of retrieved documents are identified as relevant during the search process is evaluated in Chapter 19 by A. Borodin, L. Kerr, and F. Lewis. A novel, experimental procedure for the implementation of negative feedback is contained in Chapter 20 by J. Kelly. Chapter 21 by J. S. Brown and P. D. Reilly deals with refined query modification methods in which the document and query terms receive individual treatment depending on the particular term characteristics. Finally Chapter 22 by D. Michelson, M. Amreich, G. Grissom, and E. Ide describes procedures incorporating author information and bibliographic references into the feedback process.

The use of document, rather than query, transformations, made possible in most interactive retrieval environments is described in Part VII, consisting of Chapters 23 and 24. A procedure for document space transformation is introduced in Chapter 23 by S. R. Friedman, J. A. Maceyak and S. F. Weiss; a brief evaluation of the suggested procedure is also given. A modification of the transformation process covered in Chapter 23 is examined in detail in Chapter 24 by T. L. Brauen, and a thorough evaluation is presented both for the positive and the negative space modification processes.

The last part, number VIII, consists of Chapters 25 to 27, and covers various aspects connected with the operational evaluation of the SMART system. The use of a large variety of information displays of the kind presently available in an interactive retrieval environment with graphic or typewriter console equipment is described and evaluated in Chapter 25 by M. E. Lesk and G. Salton. Chapter 26 by M. E. Lesk and G. Salton covers an experiment designed to determine the importance of user relevance assessments for retrieval evaluation. Finally, in Chapter 27 by G. Salton a preliminary comparison is made between the retrieval effectiveness of the fully automatic SMART system, and the well-known MEDLARS system operating at the National Library of Medicine in Washington.

Readers wishing a quick overall view might restrict their attention to Parts I and III, and possibly to the operational problems described in Part VIII. The problems of content analysis are covered in detail in parts I, II, III and also VIII, whereas the interactive search procedures are contained in Parts IV, V, VI and VII. Readers interested in the problems of automatic language analysis should thus concentrate on the first set of chapters, while persons concerned with problems of file organization and file search should study the other half (Parts IV to VII).

The SMART system consisting of dozens of programmed routines and several hundred thousand machine instructions could not have been implemented without the help of the many programmers, analysts, and students who over the years have participated in the project, both at Harvard and at Cornell. Among those particularly instrumental who have extensively contributed to the design and programming phases are Dr. E. H. Sussenguth, Jr., now at IBM Corporation, Dr. J. J. Rocchio, Jr., now with International Computing Company, Dr. M. E. Lesk, now at Bell Telephone Laboratories; Mr. E. M. Keen, now at the College of Librarianship in Aberystwyth, Wales; and Mr. Robert E. Williamson, a graduate student at Cornell University. A number of other present or former students have performed important evaluation studies, including, in particular, T. Brauen, R. Dattola, and E. Ide.

To all these individuals, and to past and future users of the system, I am indebted for help and advice, and for extraordinary patience in bearing with the imperfections of an experimental system. I also wish to thank the McGraw-Hill Book Company for permission to include certain tabular material in Chapters 6 and 7. Finally, I am particularly grateful to the National Science Foundation whose continuous support over many years made it possible to design the system and to perform the research leading to the present implementation of the SMART system.

Ithaca, New York   GERARD SALTON

CONTENTS

PART I
THE SMART SYSTEM

The SMART *automatic document retrieval system is introduced, and the main experimental results obtained with the system are reviewed. Some new experiments to be carried out with the system are then described, including tests in the areas of text analysis, and in adaptive search methods. Also, a proposed real-time implementation of* SMART *is mentioned briefly.*

1

THE *SMART* PROJECT— STATUS REPORT and PLANS†

G. SALTON

1-1 INTRODUCTION

The SMART document retrieval system has been operating on an IBM 7094 computer since the end of 1964 and on an IBM 360/65 since 1968. The system takes documents and search requests in English, performs a fully automatic content analysis of the texts, matches analyzed documents with analyzed search requests, and retrieves those stored items believed to be most similar to the queries. Among the language analysis procedures incorporated into the system are word suffix cutoff methods, thesaurus lookup procedures, phrase generation methods, statistical term associations, syntactic analysis, hierarchical term expansion, and others. These analysis methods are used to reduce document and query texts into a form actually utilized during the search and retrieval process.

The system has been used largely as an experimental tool for the evaluation of the effectiveness of many different types of analysis and search procedures. Thus, the potential benefits, as well as the complications which would have arisen from an operational implementation in a user environment were

†An earlier version of this report was published as Section I in *Scientific Report ISR-12*, June 1967.

initially given up in favor of a system that could be operated in a controlled laboratory environment. As a result, it has been possible to conduct several hundred analysis and search experiments, using document collections in the areas of computer science, documentation, aerodynamics, and medicine, and considerable information is now known about the effectiveness of fully automatic retrieval procedures and the design of automatic information systems.

Even though the original SMART experiments were conducted in a laboratory environment, the basic aim of eventual conversion of the system into a prototype for future fully automatic information systems has been pursued for the following reasons:

1. Some criticisms concerning the value of experimental results can be dispelled only by demonstrations in an operational environment.

2. The effectiveness of the automatic search and analysis methods is likely to be improved if the user can be made to participate in the search process, since it then becomes possible to generate a search strategy geared to the information needs of individual users.

3. The development of equipment organizations, which make it possible, more or less simultaneously, to provide service to a number of different users who may be located far away from the central equipment, offers reasonable prospects for an early implementation of real-time information systems.

Accordingly, an increasingly large number of search experiments have been performed in which a user environment is simulated by running iterative searches based on user feedback. Specifically, search strategies have been developed which use feedback information obtained as a result of an initial search, to alter the search requests so as to bring them in close correlation with the user's needs. Then these new requests can be altered as before by new feedback information, and the procedure can be iterated as many times as required.

Since the user is responsible for providing the information to be returned to the system and therefore is expected to be present during a search, it is obviously not possible to perform a full search of all stored items, except where very long search times are tolerable. Therefore fast cluster search strategies have been implemented and tested, based on a document-grouping method, which restrict the actual search to only certain document groups for each given request.

The main experimental results are summarized in the remainder of this chapter, and future plans and projects are outlined.

1-2 EXPERIMENTAL RESULTS

The SMART experiments have all been performed using one or more of the following document collections: a collection of 780 abstracts of documents in the computer literature (IRE-3), collections of 1400 and 200 abstracts in aerodynamics

(CRAN-1), a collection of 1200 documents in documentation (Ispra), a collection of 82 short papers in the field of documentation (ADI), and a collection of about 270 documents in medicine (Medlars). Manually assigned keyword lists were available in addition to the abstracts for the collections in aerodynamics and medicine, and the ADI collection was available in full text as well as in abstract form. Most experiments were run in parallel over all collections, except, of course, the comparisons with the manual indexing and the full text processes which could be performed only for the specific collections for which the necessary input was available.

Except for certain minor deviations, a ranking of various analysis and search procedures in decreasing order of effectiveness produces the same output for all collections. That is, methods which are effective in one context are effective also in the others, and contrariwise; the less effective procedures turned out to be less effective generally. Specifically, procedures based on synonym recognition, weighted content identifiers, cosine correlation to match documents and search requests, and document abstract processing are *always* more effective than methods using simple word stem matches (without synonym detection), nonweighted terms, correlation methods based only on the number of matching terms, and analysis procedures which consider only the titles of the documents being examined.

The following specific conclusions appear to hold generally for technical document collections and are not likely to be reversed by future tests with larger collections in different environments:

(a) *Document length:* document abstracts are more effective for automatic content analysis purposes than are document titles alone; further improvements appear possible when abstracts are replaced by larger text portions; however, the increase in effectiveness is not large enough to warrant the conclusion that full text processing is always superior to abstract processing.

(b) *Term weights and matching functions:* weighted content identifiers are more effective for content description than nonweighted ones, and the cosine correlation function is more useful as a measure of document-request similarity than the overlap function; service can be improved by using sophisticated request-document matching functions.

(c) *Word normalization* procedures are most effective if the vocabulary is redundant and relatively nontechnical.

(d) Dictionaries providing *synonym recognition* produce statistically significant improvements in retrieval effectiveness compared with word stem matching procedures; the improvement is largest for dictionaries obeying certain principles with regard to the word groupings which are incorporated.

(e) Phrase generation methods, whether implemented by dictionary lookup or by *statistical association processes*, appear to offer improvements in retrieval effectiveness for some recall levels by introducing new associated information identifiers not originally available; the improvement is not, however, sufficiently general or substantial, when averages over many search requests are considered, to warrant incorporation into automatic systems, except under special circumstances where suitable control procedures can be maintained.

(f) The average performance of most *hierarchy procedures* does not appear to be sufficiently promising to make it reasonable to advocate their immediate incorporation in an analysis system for automatic document retrieval.

(g) Fully automatic text processing is not substantially inferior to *manual-indexing* methods; for large and heterogeneous collections, a clear advantage should result for the automatic text analysis, because of indexer variability and the difficulties of ensuring a uniform application of a given set of indexing rules to all documents; the computer process in such cases does not necessarily decay as the collections grow larger.

(h) The order of merit of the tested procedures is approximately as follows:
  i. Most effective: abstract processing with phrase and synonym recognition.
  ii. Next most effective: weighted word stem matching and statistical word associations using abstracts for analysis purposes.
  iii. Less effective: logical word stem matching disregarding term weights.
  iv. Least effective: title processing using only document titles for analysis purposes, and document-request matching based on overlap function.

(i) *Feedback procedures* based on relevance judgments submitted by the users as a result of an initial search operation appear effective in producing large-scale increases in performance during subsequent search iterations.

(j) *Partial cluster searches* using an examination of selected document groupings only, rather than a complete match with all stored items, seem to promise drastic reductions in search time, at only minor costs in recall and precision.

In the next few pages, plans are outlined for the implementation of additional search and retrieval experiments, using the laboratory environment provided by the SMART system. Furthermore, new design features are suggested which will make it possible to implement the automatic analysis and search system under conditions which closely approximate the presently accepted standards for operational information systems.

1-3 FUTURE PLANS

1-3-A Text-Processing Experiments

The validity of the evaluation results outlined previously is difficult to challenge on strictly technical grounds because of the controlled conditions under which the analysis and testing was carried out, and also because of the relative universality of the results over all the collections used. Criticism may, however, be based on more formal grounds: the small size of the test collections, the artificial preparation of some of the requests, or the output results based on the relative merit of two or more processing methods, rather than on any absolute performance measurement.

For this reason additional language-processing experiments are planned based on the processing of document collections of larger size than those used up to now. New comparisons between the SMART system and more conventional, operating retrieval systems are also under way, using collections tied to operational environments. Finally, experiments are planned with collections in the less technical subject areas to ascertain whether retrieval performance in fact degrades as the subject field becomes more heterogeneous or less technical.

Each of the following proposed investigations, listed under six main headings, would answer some pending questions relating to the operational implementation of fully automatic retrieval systems:

i. *Automatic dictionary construction.* The more effective analysis methods incorporated into the SMART system make use of various types of thesauri and synonym dictionaries. Several automatic procedures for constructing such thesauri, starting with a representative sample document collection in the subject area under investigation, have been studied, and a number of automatic dictionaries, involving various degrees of mechanization, are available for the ADI collection. A test is proposed, comparing a manually constructed thesaurus with thesauri obtained by automatic term grouping, as well as with dictionaries using term grouping supplemented by frequency constraints on the terms within the groups. Such an experiment should demonstrate whether it is possible to eliminate the manual dictionary construction problem before implementing automatic retrieval systems.

ii. *Use of bibliographic citations for content identification.* In addition to abstracts and texts, most documents carry bibliographic citations in the form of references to or from other items in the literature. A test is under way to compare the use of such citations for purposes of document indexing with other more conventional indexing procedures. Specifically, citations are available for a collection of documents in aerodynamics; these can be added to the normal terms which identify each item. The query representations can be lengthened similarly by addition of citations from the respective query source documents. The experiment then consists in comparing the retrieval effectiveness of citations only, index terms only, and citations added to index terms.

iii. *Effect of generality change.* One of the open questions in retrieval testing is the effect of changes in the size of the collections used on the effectiveness of automatic retrieval systems. Specifically, it is important to show that results obtained for small collections can be extended to the larger collections which would be required under operational conditions. The Cranfield collection in aerodynamics can be used for a partial test by processing the same request set first against the small collection of 200 documents, and then against the larger collection of 1400 documents—the main change being a change in generality—that is, the number of relevant items compared with the total number of items in the collection.

iv. *Comparison with operational systems.* An in-house evaluation of the Medlars system currently operating at the National Library of Medicine has been undertaken at NLM. As a result, a large number of user queries actually processed by Medlars has been evaluated fully. By keypunching the abstracts of documents processed at Medlars, it then becomes possible to compare the automatic SMART analysis methods using abstracts with the semi-automatic Medlars system using manually assigned keywords. Some preliminary experiments have already been performed with a small collection of medical documents. It is proposed to extend these to larger document collections and to additional analysis methods, first using only word stem matching, then thesaurus-type dictionaries in the medical field, and finally phrase procedures.

v. *Comparison with classical subject index.* A collection of documents consisting of short articles (approximately 400 words each) published in *Time* magazine is available on tape. These documents are normally used by Time Inc. as part of a retrieval system designed to answer queries from a variety of sources. The tool used by *Time* to decide on relevance is the published *Time Subject Index*. An experiment is proposed to test the effectiveness of the automatic analysis methods using text search in comparison with the *Time Subject Index* used as a search tool. This experiment is of value for two further reasons: the *Time* collection is the first one available which uses long (400-word) abstracts, and it is the first one in a nontechnical subject field. It is important to determine whether performance degrades for nontechnical subject areas.

vi. *Foreign language input problem.* One of the practical problems which militates against the use of automatic text-processing methods in information retrieval is the fact that many documents are likely not to be available in English, in which case the English language rules available in SMART do not apply. It is, however, worthwhile to determine whether a somewhat simple-minded, word-for-word translation of the English language tools into a foreign language might produce for foreign language documents results comparable with those now produced for English. German and French document collections in the area of documentation are now available from Euratom in Ispra, and a translation of the English documentation thesaurus into German has been prepared. Preliminary retrieval results are already available which compare the performance of English queries and English documents against that of German queries and German documents, on the one hand, and English queries and German documents, on the other. Since the thesaurus translation appears to operate satisfactorily for German, tests are planned for the French collection also. This will permit an assessment of the effect of the thesaurus translation from one language to another.

1-3-B User Feedback and Document-Clustering Experiments

Further experiments are also planned in the areas of user feedback procedures and partial searches of the stored collection with fast response times. The cluster searches in which the matching operation between documents and search requests is confined to a few document groups only (namely, those whose centroids are sufficiently close to each given search request) are important because rapid responses are obtained for the user population. The feedback procedures, on the other hand, have been shown to lead to large-scale improvements in retrieval effectiveness, beyond that obtainable by one-shot searches carried out without user assistance.

The following main experiments in adaptive search methodology are planned:

i. *Cluster searching.* An attempt must be made to determine optimal strategies both for cluster generation and for searching. In particular, it is unclear how many document groups should be examined in each case; whether it is advantageous to group the document groups themselves into larger supergroups and then to conduct a "three-level" rather than a "two-level" search; whether incoming requests should be accumulated, and request groups should be constructed so that incoming requests could be compared first against the existing request groups rather than against existing document groups. Most of the presently used document-grouping methods require a similarity matrix giving a correlation coefficient between each pair of documents; the construction of such a matrix requires of the order of n^2 operations. Some new, simpler grouping procedures have been proposed by Needham, Doyle, and others, which are not based on a similarity matrix and require fewer operations. It is important to investigate their use in information retrieval.

ii. *User feedback runs.* The previously mentioned document-grouping methods are expected to be useful in an operational situation when utilized in conjunction with user feedback procedures. A large number of experimental feedback procedures have been tested already. Some of the outstanding problems include the question of deciding on the number of documents to be returned to the user in each case; the problem of what to do with feedback information which is wholly negative, that is, where the user is dissatisfied with every item he receives; the question of ambiguous requests where relevant documents pertaining to several distinct concept groupings are retrieved, and queries must be broken up into two or more subqueries before the feedback process can be used; the combination into a single operation of cluster searches with user feedback. Investigations are also under way to determine the type of information best used for feedback purposes, such as relevance judgments for documents retrieved previously, citations to stored documents known to be relevant to a given query, or dictionary excerpts of terms similar to query terms already used, and so on.

Eventually, one can visualize a retrieval system in which fully automatic analysis procedures are coupled with adaptive search methods in such a way that information provided by the user population during and after the search serves to alter and refine not only the query formulations but also the document analysis itself. This may lead to document and query representations which improve in time and to the identification of retrieval methodologies tailored to specific user classes and responsive to special user interests.

1-3-C   Real-Time Operating System

The SMART system, presently operating under a batch-processing monitor on an IBM 7094 and an IBM 360/65, was designed as an experimental tool and includes programs which are deliberately experimental in nature. Initially in fact, it was believed more important to analyze the main search results in detail and to understand the retrieval situations pertaining to many different types of running conditions, than to concentrate on problems relating to real-life situations which are less well understood (such as retrieval costs and user satisfaction).

While the current analysis tasks cannot as yet be considered to be terminated, as shown in the preceding paragraphs, the time is nevertheless at hand when a batch-processing type system should be supplemented by a system capable of furnishing real-time responses to user requests and individualized service to each user. In addition to furnishing an automatic retrieval tool which corresponds more directly to the type of situation which users may face in the not too distant future, an automatic real-time system will make it possible to carry out a number of new studies which cannot be superimposed easily onto the current SMART operating system. The following features, in particular, depend to some extent on real-time capabilities:

(a) The implementation of a limited conversational system which would enable the users to supply information relating to user needs and the system to respond to user indications by performing appropriate tasks and returning appropriate comments.

(b) The implementation of a display system capable of furnishing to the user selected portions of the stored files, including dictionary excerpts and excerpts of the stored document information, to be used during the search and retrieval operation.

(c) The monitoring of system parameters which are likely to influence operating strategies and costs, such as the response time, the fraction of time devoted usefully to retrieval tasks by the users and by the computer, the fraction of time spent by the users waiting at the consoles, and so on.

(d) The simultaneous accommodation of several users, some of whom may be located at some distance from the central equipment, and all of whom may require access to the same central data store.

(e) The processing of background retrieval tasks, for example, in the form of standing requests, or standing user profiles, as required in a system for the selective dissemination of information.

(f) The provision of limited facilities for question answering (fact retrieval) in addition to document retrieval, for example, in the form of stored tables of data and facilities for handling requests answered by the tabular information.

These tasks can be implemented even without full time-sharing capabilities, by providing a small number of appropriate input–output stations and facilities for attaching these stations to the central equipment. Initially, only one user might be

serviced at any one time, depending on the particular scheduling algorithm in use. The file storage could be implemented initially by disk files, for document collections of limited size, and might be expanded eventually to a tape strip store (such as, for example, a data cell), providing access times on the order of one minute to document files for from 50,000 to 100,000 items.

If the initial implementations prove viable, the real-time system could be expanded eventually to a full time-sharing facility, where several different user classes receive more or less simultaneous service, while sharing all computer facilities including memory space, stored files, input–output consoles, and the like. In that case, a special monitor system must be provided to serve as an interface between the user consoles and the normal SMART executive routines. Two main system routines are required by the real-time system: a *console* monitor which locates any console requiring attention and identifies the required task in each case, and a *cycling* routine which cycles among SMART procedures and provides service (by calling the SMART executive) to all consoles requesting the task carried out at any given instant within a processing cycle. Such a systems organization leads effectively to a batching of procedures for all consoles situated in the same phase within the retrieval cycle.

With the real-time implementation of the automatic SMART analysis and retrieval procedures, it should be possible to transform the present experimental laboratory system into a prototype automatic information-handling facility designed for operational use in the not too distant future.

*The systems organization of the SMART programs is discussed as implemented
for operation in a batch-processing mode on the IBM 360/65. Covered in
particular are the basic input and text analysis routines, the document-clustering
programs, the search routines, and the feedback operations. Sample computer output
is shown in each case to illustrate the operations.*

2

THE CORNELL IMPLEMENTATION OF THE SMART SYSTEM†

D. WILLIAMSON, R. WILLIAMSON, and M. LESK

2-1 INTRODUCTION

The SMART system is designed for the exploration, testing, and measurement of proposed algorithms for document retrieval. The system takes
documents and search requests in English, performs a fully automatic content
analysis of the texts, matches analyzed documents with analyzed search
requests, and retrieves those stored items believed to be most similar to the
queries. The request authors (users) can submit information to improve
their queries (relevance feedback), and this information is used by several
experimental procedures to improve search results. The time required to
match large collections of documents with the requests can be reduced by
grouping these documents (clustering) and matching requests against a representative sample of the entire group of documents. Finally, exhaustive
evaluation procedures can be used to ascertain the effectiveness of various
methods used in searching.

Several important criteria are incorporated in the implementation
of the SMART system [1]. The requirement for mixing different processing

†This study was first issued as Section I in *Scientific Report, ISR-16*, October 1969.

12

methods, such as clustering, relevance feedback, and searching, implies that the programming system should be written in terms of many small blocks, in such a way that any one process would be synthesized by assembling several blocks into one unit. In this manner, not only can a process be carried out using many different combinations of methods, but a change in any part of the system does not require major alterations of the other parts of the system. In addition, processing speed is enhanced by making it possible to operate on several queries in parallel.

2-2 BASIC SYSTEM ORGANIZATION

The SMART information retrieval process can be divided into five basic sections: (1) input of printed text, (2) grouping of documents for searching purposes (clustering), (3) selection of a group of documents to be searched, (4) searching of the document group, and (5) evaluation of the search. The printed text specifying the queries and documents must be converted into a form handled more easily by a computer. For this purpose various automatic language analysis devices can be used which reduce each query and document to "concept vector" form.

Fast search algorithms are obtained by grouping documents into classes of similar documents. The grouping (clustering) consists of placing documents containing similar concepts together into the same group and constructing a representative central item (centroid) for each group. Given such a clustered document file, the search of a document group (cluster) is performed by first matching requests against the central items of each cluster. Certain clusters are then selected as most likely to contain documents of interest. These documents are then searched in the normal manner, one item at a time. After seeing some retrieved documents, the requestor can modify his request, either by changing it physically or by furnishing relevance assessments for some of the retrieved items (to be used later for automatic query modification).

Several measures of retrieval performance are computed to help in evaluating each search. The sign test, *t* test, and Wilcoxon rank sum test are also used to determine the significance of the evaluation measurements.

2-2-A Input of Printed Text

The first section involves the reading of text (e.g., abstracts and queries) and the conversion of a given text into numeric concept vectors with weights. The conversion process may involve the use of suitable dictionaries and other language normalization aids. At present, a relatively simple PL/1 program is used to implement this section. A more flexible Fortran IV program is planned for later implementation as described in report ISR-14 [2]; a system flow chart for the future text conversion system is also included in Sec. 2-4.

The presently available text-handling program, LOOKUP, is a procedure which performs dictionary lookups by accepting a dictionary, suffix list, and input texts and producing concept vectors for the texts. Words missing from the dictionary are processed properly as well. The algorithm is essentially that of Sussenguth [3], although the tree structure storage format is not used. LOOKUP is designed primarily for ease of programming and is coded entirely in PL/1.

The overall operation of LOOKUP is divided into three parts. First, the dictionary and suffix list are read into memory, the lists are sorted alphabetically, and the necessary initialization is performed. Second, the text is read in and divided into words, and the words are looked up in the dictionary and suffix lists. Third, the concept numbers derived by dictionary lookup from the words in each document are sorted and condensed into a properly weighted vector. The vector can be printed and/or stored in machine-readable form. The lookup program finds a match between an input word and a dictionary entry under the following conditions:

1. The word matches exactly a dictionary entry.

2. It matches a dictionary entry with a final "e" dropped and a suffix beginning with a vowel added.

3. It matches a dictionary entry plus a suffix.

4. It matches a dictionary entry with a final "y" changed to "i" and a suffix added.

5. It matches a dictionary entry, with a final consonant doubled and a suffix added.

When several possible matches are found, the match involving the longest stem is preferred; within stems of the same length, preference is in numerical order as above. Thus, if "cop", "cope", and "copy" are all stems in the dictionary, and all normal English suffixes are included in the suffix list, "cops" is found from "cop" under rule 3; "copes" or "coping" is found from "cope" under rule 2; "copying" from "copy" under rule 3; "copies" from "copy" under rule 4; "copper" from "cop" under rule 5. Other morphological features of English are not recognized. Such word pairs as "mouse" and "mice", "sing" and "sung", "fight" and "fought", or "court-martial" and "courts-martial" must be entered explicitly in the dictionary if both members are to be recognized. Special rules exist which specify that all stems must be at least three letters long (to avoid, for example, finding "wing" from "we" under rule 2 or "inning" from "in" under rule 5). Furthermore, all words are truncated at 24 characters.

The program can distinguish titles from the body of the text, if asked. And it may either split the weight of an ambiguous word among its concept numbers or weight all concept occurrences equally. The suffix list may be omitted from the lookup, in which case only words that match exactly a dictionary entry can be found. And the programmer may choose whether hyphenated words are to be considered as a unit or as separate words. As in the previous SMART implementation, concept numbers of zero or concept numbers of 32000 or more are considered to be nonsignificant and are dropped from the vector.

Figure 2-1 shows a typical output of LOOKUP. First the title is given and then the text of the document (or query in this case). The resulting numeric concept vector is printed next. This consists of pairs of concept numbers followed by the respective

```
LISTING OF INPUT TEXT, MISSING WORDS, AND VECTORS   PAGEL08

*FIND QA7PAPERS
DESCRIBE PRESENTLY WORKING AND PLANNED SYSTEMS FOR PUBLISHING
AND PRINTING ORIGINAL PAPERS BY COMPUTER, AND THEN SAVING THE
BYPRODUCT, ARTICLES CODED IN CATA-PROCESSING FORM, FOR FURTHER
USE IN RETRIEVAL .

VECTOR:    927/ 12/, 2574/ 12/, 3509/ 12/, 4087/ 12/, 4989/ 12/, 4999/ 12/,
          5068/ 12/, 5253/ 12/, 5432/ 12/, 5440/ 12/, 5469/ 12/, 5516/ 12/,
          5543/ 12/, 5554/ 12/, 5569/ 12/, 5576/ 12/, 5602/ 12/, 5605/ 12/,
            0/  0/,

  1007
*FIND QA8INDEXING
DESCRIBE INFORMATION RETRIEVAL AND INDEXING IN OTHER LANGUAGES . WHAT
BEARING DOES IT HAVE ON THE SCIENCE IN GENERAL .QUE

VECTOR:   3931/ 12/, 4369/ 12/, 4762/ 12/, 4989/ 12/, 4999/ 12/, 5372/ 12/,
          5489/ 12/, 5598/ 12/, 5606/ 12/,   0/  0/,

  1008
*FIND QA9ANALYSIS
WHAT POSSIBILITIES ARE THERE FOR AUTOMATIC GRAMMATICAL AND
CONTEXTUAL ANALYSIS OF ARTICLES FOR INCLUSION IN AN INFORMATION
RETRIEVAL SYSTEM .QUE

VECTOR:   3338/ 12/, 4821/ 12/, 4916/ 12/, 4999/ 12/, 5469/ 12/, 5474/ 12/,
          5511/ 12/, 5605/ 12/, 5606/ 12/,   0/  0/,

  1009
*FIND QA10GROUP
THE USE OF ABSTRACT MATHEMATICS IN INFORMATION RETRIEVAL,
E.G. GROUP THEORY .

VECTOR:   2883/ 12/, 4999/ 12/, 5491/ 12/, 5555/ 12/, 5602/ 12/, 5606/ 12/,
            0/  0/,
```

Fig. 2-1 Sample text lookup.

concept weights (for example, concept 927 with weight 12, concept 2574 with weight 12, etc.). Concepts are listed in the vector in increasing numeric order.

2-2-B Document-Clustering for Search Purposes

At present two clustering algorithms are in operation—CLUSTR, which uses Rocchio's clustering algorithm [4], and DCLSTR, a variation of Doyle's clustering algorithm [5].

Rocchio's clustering algorithm is based on the following methodology. First an unclustered document is selected as a possible cluster center. Then, all of the other unclustered documents are correlated with it, and the document is subjected to a density test to see if a cluster should be formed around it. The density test specifies that at least N_1 documents should have correlations higher than a specified parameter p_1 with the document in question, and that at least N_2 documents should have correlations higher than p_2 (p_2 is generally larger than p_1). This test ensures that documents on the edge of large groups do not become cluster centers. If the document passes the density test, thus becoming a cluster center, a cutoff correlation, p_{min}, is determined from the cluster size limits and the distribution of correlation values. The cutoff correlation becomes p_1 if fewer documents than the minimum cluster size (M_1) have correlations above p_1. If more such documents exist, the cutoff correla-

$N_1 \geq N_2$

?

(#documents w/correlation $> p_1$) $> M_1$

tion is chosen at the greatest correlation difference occurring within the first M_2 adjacent documents, where M_2 is the maximum cluster size.

Centroid formation

A classification vector is then formed by taking the centroid of all the document vectors having correlations above $p_{\min}$. This centroid vector is matched against the entire collection, and the cutoff parameters for cluster size are recalculated to create an altered cluster.

As a result of this process, some documents may appear in more than one cluster; some which were in a cluster when the centroid was formed originally may not remain in any cluster. These documents, as well as those which failed the density test, are termed "loose", and those within the cluster are termed "clustered".

This entire procedure is repeated with all unclustered documents; first pass terminates when all items are either clustered or loose. Figures 2-2, 2-3, and 2-4 illustrate the formation of a cluster. Document 2 is correlated first with all previously unclustered documents in the collection (9 documents of the 82 documents in the

CLUSTERING ABOUT DOCUMENT   2

RANK	DOC	CORR	RANK	DOC	CORR	RANK	DOC	CORR
1	2	1.0000	2	64	0.4002	3	27	0.3631
6	68	0.2512	7	61	0.2475	8	18	0.2367
11	12	0.1990	12	55	0.1867	13	14	0.1961
16	34	0.1697	17	33	0.1689	18	22	0.1634
21	50	0.1445	22	82	0.1420	23	48	0.1400
26	19	0.1239	27	6	0.1235	28	30	0.1006
31	77	0.0934	32	81	0.0934	33	32	0.0921
36	53	0.0854	37	78	0.0748	38	25	0.0729
41	26	0.0583	42	58	0.0578	43	38	0.0539
46	42	0.0460	47	15	0.0454	48	49	0.0437
51	21	0.0394	52	35	0.0385	53	54	0.0374
56	43	0.0337	57	36	0.0335	58	44	0.0283
61	0	0.0000	62	0	0.0000	63	0	0.0000
66	0	0.0000	67	0	0.0000	68	0	0.0000
71	0	0.0000	72	0	0.0000	73	0	0.0000

RANK	DOC	CORR	RANK	DOC	CORR
4	39	0.3466	5	41	0.2628
9	29	0.2258	10	71	0.2174
14	66	0.1749	15	73	0.1715
19	16	0.1515	20	69	0.1511
24	9	0.1257	25	23	0.1257
29	8	0.0934	30	65	0.0934
34	67	0.0891	35	17	0.0880
39	75	0.0691	40	24	0.0665
44	7	0.0511	45	10	0.0467
49	80	0.0432	50	79	0.0417
54	63	0.0353	55	59	0.0347
59	0	0.0000	60	0	0.0000
64	0	0.0000	65	0	0.0000
69	0	0.0000	70	0	0.0000

DOCUMENT   2 HAS PASSED THE DENSITY TEST.
CUTOFF WILL BE CHECKED.

Fig. 2-2 The testing of document 2 as a possible cluster center.

CORRELATIONS FOR CENTROID   2

RANK	DOC	CORR	RANK	DOC	CORR	RANK	DOC	CORR
1	2	0.7221	2	64	0.5501	3	27	0.5252
6	68	0.4657	7	18	0.4358	8	29	0.4343
11	30	0.3859	12	55	0.2971	13	66	0.2784
16	33	0.2591	17	22	0.2467	18	23	0.2458
21	17	0.2326	22	9	0.2258	23	69	0.2253
26	34	0.2090	27	14	0.2054	28	58	0.1937
31	28	0.1862	32	8	0.1857	33	78	0.1595
36	77	0.1485	37	53	0.1480	38	80	0.1473
41	63	0.1384	42	79	0.1281	43	82	0.1237
46	44	0.1190	47	42	0.1138	48	21	0.1131
51	36	0.1027	52	67	0.0988	53	49	0.0945
56	10	0.0902	57	7	0.0872	58	20	0.0849
61	54	0.0638	62	37	0.0637	63	60	0.0573
66	45	0.0526	67	4	0.0519	68	76	0.0516
71	13	0.0385	72	31	0.0382	73	74	0.0179

RANK	DOC	CORR	RANK	DOC	CORR
4	39	0.5177	5	71	0.4965
9	61	0.4333	10	41	0.4082
14	16	0.2655	15	12	0.2624
19	6	0.2366	20	73	0.2339
24	65	0.2149	25	15	0.2117
29	48	0.1910	30	19	0.1901
34	26	0.1567	35	75	0.1544
39	81	0.1459	40	50	0.1455
44	32	0.1204	45	38	0.1195
49	25	0.1057	50	43	0.1054
54	24	0.0944	55	57	0.0936
59	46	0.0743	60	59	0.0730
64	35	0.0547	65	5	0.0541
69	72	0.0432	70	3	0.0418

Fig. 2-3   The correlation of centroid 2 with all unclustered documents.

collection had previously been clustered around document 1). The correlations are ranked, and the ranks, document numbers, and correlation coefficients are listed in Fig. 2-2. In the example, at least 10 documents (N_1) must have a correlation greater then 0.15 (p_1), and at least 5 documents (N_2) must have a correlation greater than 0.25. The correlation of document 2 is larger than 0.15 for 19 other documents, and for 5 other documents the correlation exceeds 0.25. Document 2 therefore passes the density test. M_1 in this example is 5, and therefore p_{min} is calculated by finding the greatest correlation difference between adjacent documents, starting with the document of rank 5 (at least M_1 documents must be included) and checking differences up to M_2 documents (in this case 15 documents). The largest gap occurs between ranks 7 and 8; therefore p_{min} is taken to be 0.2475.

The centroid vector is formed by merging the document vectors of documents having correlations above p_{min} (0.2475). The centroid, composed of concepts and weights, is shown in Fig. 2-4. This centroid is then correlated with all previously unclustered documents (Fig. 2-3). A second cutoff correlation p_{min} is calculated to deter-

ITEM 2 CENTROID00000002 ACIABTH CCCS COCCUOO2

CON	WT	CON	WT	CON	WT	CON	WT	CON	WT
1	24	3	24	4	60	5	144	7	36
19	84	20	12	21	18	22	30	23	18
36	12	37	12	41	12	42	24	43	12
54	12	57	12	61	132	62	12	63	12
77	36	81	48	85	12	87	24	91	24
126	24	128	12	129	72	135	24	136	12
147	24	150	12	155	12	158	12	162	12
193	12	196	12	199	24	212	24	213	12
231	12	232	12	243	12	248	12	259	12
282	12	284	12	286	24	287	48	291	24
321	12	444	12	455	36	481	6	530	12

CON	WT	CON	WT	CON	WT	CON	WT
8	120	12	60	13	24	17	48
25	48	26	12	32	48	33	72
46	24	48	60	50	12	51	72
64	12	66	48	67	24	7?	36
98	36	99	12	115	12	116	108
138	12	140	12	141	1?	143	12
171	12	180	60	184	12	191	12
217	12	219	36	223	12	225	12
266	24	267	12	271	36	275	12
293	12	294	12	296	12	315	12

THE 95 CONCEPTS ABOVE HAVE A SUM OF ABSOLUTE WEIGHTS = 2640

WITH A ROOT SUM OF SQUARED WEIGHTS = 377.00

THE 11 RELEVANT -- 2 64 27 39 71 68 18 29 61 41 30

Fig. 2-4 The completed cluster 2.

note that formation of clusters is not deterministic i.e. depends on order in which documents are in

mine which documents belong in cluster 2. Here the greatest correlation difference (starting at M_1 and checking until M_2) occurs between the documents ranked 11 and 12. Therefore $p_{\min}$ becomes 0.3859, and the top 11 documents are included in cluster 2. These documents are listed as the "11 Relevant" in Fig. 2-4.

another clustering alg.

DCLSTR uses a variation of Doyle's algorithm. The following description of the algorithm covers the main points [5]. Assume that the document set is partitioned arbitrarily into m clusters, where S_j is the set of documents in cluster j. Associated with each set S_j is a corresponding concept vector C_j and a frequency vector F_j. The concept vector consists of all the concepts occurring in the documents of S_j, and the frequency vector specifies the number of documents in S_j in which each concept occurs.

Every concept in C_j is assigned a rank according to its frequency; that is, concepts with the highest frequency have a rank of 1, concepts with the next highest frequency receive a rank of 2, and so on. Given an integer b (*base value*), every concept in D_j is assigned a *rank value* equal to the base value minus the rank of that concept. The vector of rank values is called the *profile* P_j of the set S_j. Figure 2-5 illustrates the concept and frequency vectors and the corresponding profiles for a sample document collection.

Starting from a partition of the document set into m clusters, the profiles are generated as described. Every document d_i in the document space is now scored against each of the m profiles by a *scoring function* g, where $g(d_i, P_j)$ equals the sum of

d_1	d_2	d_3	d_4	d_5	d_6	d_7
c_1	c_1	c_1	c_1	c_1	c_3	c_6
c_2	c_2	c_7	c_2	c_8		c_8
c_5	c_4	c_8	c_3			
	c_5		c_5			

(a)

S_1	C_1	F_1	P_1	S_2	C_2	F_2	P_2	S_3	C_3	F_3	P_3
d_1	c_1	3	5	d_2	c_1	2	5	d_6	c_3	1	5
d_3	c_2	1	3	d_4	c_2	2	5	d_7	c_6	1	5
d_5	c_5	1	3		c_3	1	4		c_8	1	5
	c_7	1	3		c_4	1	4				
	c_8	2	4		c_5	2	5				

(b)

Document	Profile of Highest Score	Score
d_1	2	15
d_2	2	19
d_3	1	12
d_4	2	19
d_5	1	9
d_6	3	5
d_7	3	10

(c)

S'_1	S'_2	S'_3	L
d_3	d_1	d_7	d_5
	d_2		d_6
	d_4		

(d)

Fig. 2-5 One iteration of Doyle's classification algorithm (cutoff = 10): (a) document concept vectors; (b) initial clusters, profiles, and frequencies (profile construction using base value = 6); (c) document scoring; (d) resulting clusters.

the rank values of all the concepts from d_i which occur in C_j. Figure 2-5 shows the results of scoring the documents in the sample collection against the profiles from Fig. 2-5.

A new partition of the document set into $m + 1$ clusters is then made by the following formula:

$$S_j = \{d_i \mid g(d_i, P_j) \geq T_i\}, \quad 1 \leq j \leq m,$$

$$T_i = \begin{cases} H_i - [a \cdot (H_i - T)], & \text{if } H_i > T, \\ T, & \text{otherwise,} \end{cases}$$

where

$$H_i = \max [g(d_i, P_j)],$$
$$0 \leq a \leq 1,$$
$$T = a \text{ is the given cutoff value.}$$

Those documents which do not fall into any of the m clusters S_j are called *loose documents*, and they are assigned to a special class L. The process is now repeated after replacing P_j by P'_j. The iteration continues until S_j satisfies the termination condition that $S'_j = S_j$ (actually $S_j^{*'} = S_j^*$, where S_j^* is the subset of S_j consisting of all those documents that score highest against profile P_j).

Basically, this algorithm matches documents to existing clusters by computing a document-cluster score for each document with respect to each cluster and placing a document into those clusters for which a sufficiently high score is obtained. The clusters are then updated to include the new documents. In each iteration all the documents are correlated with all the clusters, and the clusters are updated until further updating does not alter the group of documents in each cluster. This updating is shown in list form in Figs. 2-6 and 2-7. The 12 profiles (clusters) of Fig. 2-6 are matched against the documents and are updated to become the profiles of Fig. 2-7.

```
           THE  DOCUMENTS  IN  PROFILE    1  ARE
    67    71     80      81      82      83      84     87     100    102    128

           THE  DOCUMENTS  IN  PROFILE    2  ARE
    20    64     65      66      68      70      85     86     103    122    124    169    196

           THE  DOCUMENTS  IN  PROFILE    3  ARE
    45    74     75      76      77      79     112    135     154    161

           THE  DOCUMENTS  IN  PROFILE    4  ARE
     9    17     23      62     116     117     134    146     147    151    180    197

           THE  DOCUMENTS  IN  PROFILE    5  ARE
     3    61     90      93      94     110     113    120     181

           THE  DOCUMENTS  IN  PROFILE    6  ARE
    18    25     41      63      69     111     114    115     121    183    192    193    195

           THE  DOCUMENTS  IN  PROFILE    7  ARE
     2    19     39     101

           THE  DOCUMENTS  IN  PROFILE    8  ARE
     4    30     31      57      58     187     188

           THE  DOCUMENTS  IN  PROFILE    9  ARE
    23    28     29      43      72      78      91     92      95     104    118    132    133
   149   152    153     155     156     158     159    179     185

           THE  DOCUMENTS  IN  PROFILE   10  ARE
    13    15     16      56      59      60     136    141     150    160    176    182    184
   189   198

           THE  DOCUMENTS  IN  PROFILE   11  ARE
     8   162    163     164     165     166     167    168

           THE  DOCUMENTS  IN  PROFILE   12  ARE
    46    47     48      49      50      52
```

Fig. 2-6   Original profiles (clusters).

It should be noted that the document-clustering process can be extended to the clustering of clusters. That is, if one of the two clustering algorithms generates m groups of documents, these m groups could be grouped together, as if they were documents, into n clusters, where $1 \leq n \leq m$. These n clusters could then be grouped together, and so on, until a hierarchical cluster tree is formed as shown in Fig. 2-8. At present no routines for automatically constructing such multilevel cluster trees exist in the SMART system, although such an algorithm is planned for implementation in the near future. Both CLUSTR and DCLSTR generate the first level of the cluster trees, thus representing special cases of more general tree construction routines.

```
       THE DOCUMENTS IN PROFILE  1 ARE
67     71     81     83     84     87     100     128

       THE DOCUMENTS IN PROFILE  2 ARE
64     65     66     70     86     124

       THE DOCUMENTS IN PROFILE  3 ARE
74     75     76     77     112     154     161

       THE DOCUMENTS IN PROFILE  4 ARE
9      62     116     147     151     197

       THE DOCUMENTS IN PROFILE  5 ARE
5      61     90     110     113     120     181

       THE DOCUMENTS IN PROFILE  6 ARE
18     25     41     114     115     121     183     192     195

       THE DOCUMENTS IN PROFILE  7 ARE
2      19     39

       THE DOCUMENTS IN PROFILE  8 ARE
4      31     57     58     187     188

       THE DOCUMENTS IN PROFILE  9 ARE
28     95     132     133     158     159     179     185

       THE DOCUMENTS IN PROFILE 10 ARE
58     60     150     160     182     184     189     198

       THE DOCUMENTS IN PROFILE 11 ARE
8      162     163     164     165     166     167     168

       THE DOCUMENTS IN PROFILE 12 ARE
46     47     48     49
```

Fig. 2-7 Updated profiles (clusters).

□ Cluster root
◇ Centroid
d Document

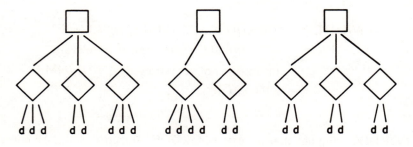

Fig. 2-8 A hypothetical cluster tree.

2-2-C   The Selection of Documents to be Searched

The search process takes place in four steps. First a search query is defined, either by using the author's original query, or a modification of the original query, in numeric concept vector form. One important query alteration is obtained by using documents judged relevant by the author to modify the original query vector. This process is known as relevance feedback and is discussed in Sec. 2-2-D.

Once a search query is defined, the set of documents to be correlated with the query is selected. SMART provides two options; either a *full search* or a *tree search* may be made. In a full search every document in the retrieval base is correlated with the query. In this case the selection of the documents to be searched is trivial—all documents in the collection are searched.

In the tree search [6], a set of documents is selected by a cyclic process, using a tree such as that pictured in Fig. 2-9. At any one time, a set of active nodes exists in the tree; initially this is the set of roots (the highest level of clusters). Each node in the active set is compared with the search query. A score, called the "goodness" of each node, is then computed using the relatedness of a query to a node, as well as other information about the structure of a tree; the nodes of the "active" set are then ordered by this value of the "goodness". A subset of active nodes is selected as being most promising. The corresponding nodes are deleted from the active set, and the sons of these nodes (if centroids) are correlated with the query and become a part of the active set. Those sons which represent documents are then entered into a list of documents to be used in subsequent correlations with the query. The active set is reordered cyclically, and another group of nodes is selected for examination until some desired number of documents are located. The process used to obtain a list of specific documents to be compared directly to a query is represented in Fig. 2-9.

The listing reproduced in Fig. 2-10 shows an example of the input to the cluster-searching routine. The first iteration (run 0) uses a full search instead of a tree search. The second iteration (run 1) represents a tree search on the cluster collection "CENTROID NO MORE" using the "COSINE" correlation. The desired number of documents to be selected for correlation with the query is given by "WANTED", where "WANTED" is defined as

$$\text{WANTED} = \text{"CORDOC"} + \text{"TIMALL"} * \text{"ALLOF"}$$
$$+ \text{"TIMREL"} * (\text{the number of relevant}$$
$$\text{documents not yet retrieved}) + \text{"TIMNMR"}$$
$$* \text{"NOMOR"},$$

where

CORDOC   implies that at least "CORDOC" documents will be correlated in this iteration.

TIMALL   "TIMALL" times "ALLOF" (for this iteration) documents are correlated additionally in this iteration.

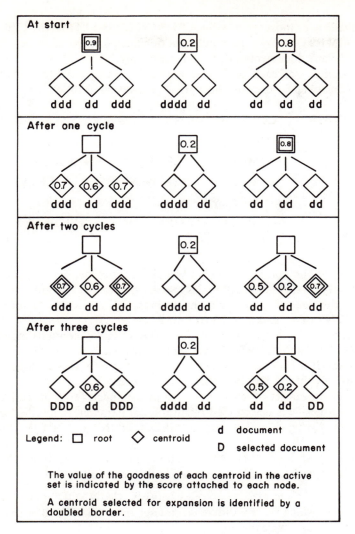

Fig. 2-9 Searching a hypothetical tree.

TIMREL   "TIMREL" times the number of relevant documents not yet retrieved are correlated additionally in this iteration.

TIMNMR   "TIMNMR" times "NOMOR" (for this iteration) documents are
correlated additionally in this iteration.

"ALLOF" and "NOMOR" are user-supplied constants indicating how many documents are used in relevance feedback. Therefore the second and fourth terms of the
parameter "WANTED" are constants, like "CORDOC", for a given iteration. These
constants are expressed by three parameters (rather than being lumped into one)

for user convenience; most users will set "TIMALL" and "TIMNMR" to zero. The parameter "TIMREL" allows the number of documents searched to be related to the number of relevant documents not found previously.

The "goodness" of each node (the parameter value used to rank the nodes) may also be controlled by the user through 17 parameters as follows.

$$\text{"GOODNESS"} = \text{"COEF"} + \text{"MCN"} * \text{"CROWN"}^{\text{"PCN"}} + \text{"MLV"}$$
$$+ \text{"LEVEL"}^{\text{"PLV"}}$$
$$+ \text{"MCFCN"} * \text{"COEF"}^{\text{"PFCFCN"}} * \text{"CROWN"}^{\text{"PNCFCN"}}$$
$$+ \text{"MCNLV"} * \text{"CROWN"}^{\text{"PNCNLV"}} * \text{"LEVEL"}^{\text{"PVCNLV"}}$$
$$+ \text{"MCFLV"} * \text{"COEF"}^{\text{"PFCFLV"}} * \text{"LEVEL"}^{\text{"PVCFLV"}}$$
$$+ \text{"MALL"} * \text{"COEF"}^{\text{"PALLCF"}} * \text{"CROWN"}^{\text{"PALLCN"}}$$
$$* \text{"LEVEL"}^{\text{"PALLLV"}},$$

where "COEF" is the correlation value (usually cosine) between the node and the query, "CROWN" is the number of nodes that are the sons of the node, and "LEVEL" is the level of the node. For example, the node in Fig. 2-9 with a "goodness" of 0.9 has a "CROWN" of 11 and a "LEVEL" of 3.

It should be noted that the formula for "GOODNESS" contains many combinations of "CROWN" and "LEVEL", making the formula extremely flexible for experimental purposes. It is expected that most users will use only two or three terms, most parameters in "GOODNESS" being set usually to zero.

The size of the subset of active nodes to be expanded (after all active nodes are ranked by "goodness") is determined by additional parameters specified by the user, as printed in the listing (Fig. 2-10) under "SELECTION" and "REJECTION".

MINNOD MAXNOD	At least "MINNOD" nodes and not more than "MAXNOD" nodes are to be expanded in this iteration.
GAP	If there exist two nodes between "MINNOD" and "MAXNOD" which have a difference greater than "GAP", all nodes above that gap are expanded.
EPSLON	Any nodes within "EPSLON" of the last node selected for expansion are also to be expanded.
MNGOOD	Any node with a "GOODNESS" of less than "MNGOOD" is not to be retained for expansion.
MNCORR	Any node with a correlation less than "MNCORR" with the query is not retained for expansion.
PERCOL	Only nodes whose combined "CROWN" is greater than "PERCOL" per cent of the size of the collection being searched need be retained for expansion.

PARAMETERS FOR TREE SEARCHING

ITERATION 0   A FULL SEARCH RATHER THAN A TREE SEARCH IS BEING DONE.

ITERATION 1

	COLLECTION		CENTROID NO MORE		CORRELATION		COSINE	
WANTED	CORDOC	2	TIMALL	2	TIMREL	2	TIMNMR	0
GOODNESS	MCN	1.00	PCN	-1.00	MLV	0.10	PLV	1.00
	MALL	0.0	PALLDF	0.0	PALLCN	0.0	PALLLV	0.0
	MCFCN	0.0	PFCFCN	0.0	PNCFCN	0.7		
	MCNLV	0.0	PNCNLV	0.0	PVCNLV	0.0		
	MCFLV	0.0	PFCFLV	0.0	PVCFLV	0.0		
SELECTION	MINNOD	1	MAXNOD	3	GAP	0.10	EPSLON	0.05
REJECTION	MNGOOD	0.10	MNCORR	0.05	PERCOL	0.0 %	TIMMAX	0.0

Fig. 2-10 Parameters for tree searching.

TIMWAN   Only nodes whose combined "CROWN" is greater than "TIM-WAN" times the number of documents to be correlated with are retained for expansion.

The selection of the documents using the parameters from Fig. 2-10 is shown in Figs. 2-11, 2-12, and 2-13. The queries are processed as a batch, and queries 31, 32, 33, and 34 are shown as examples. The queries are first matched against the "roots" of the centroid tree consisting of centroids 1, 2, and 3. The results of the matching and other useful statistics are shown in Fig. 2-11. The query number, iteration number, number of documents wanted and found, centroid used to match, "goodness" of the matching, statistics of the centroid, and the cosine correlation are given for each query match against all the roots. The "REJECTION" parameters are used here to eliminate centroids before any ranking is done on "goodness". A "MNGOOD" of 0.10 causes centroid 2 to be dropped from the active set of query 33 and centroid 3 to be dropped from the active set of queries 31 and 32. Similarly, a "MNCORR" of 0.05 causes centroid 1 and centroid 3 to be dropped from the active set of query 33. The centroids remaining in the active set of each query are then ranked, and the "SELECTION" parameters are used to select those nodes to be expanded (Fig. 2-11). Note that query 33 has no active set remaining and therefore is dropped from further searching (a more careful set of parameters for "goodness" would have eliminated this problem).

The "SELECTION" parameters indicate that at least one centroid should be expanded, and up to three centroids may be expanded until a gap of 0.10 in "goodness" occurs. Query 34 exhibits such a gap between centroids 3 and 2; hence only centroid 3 is selected for expansion.

The expansion of centroids is shown in Fig. 2-12. Both query 31 and 32 now have an active set of six centroids; query 34 has three centroids in its active set. Again the active sets are matched against their respective queries, and the "REJECTION" parameters are applied. This time one centroid (centroid 4) is dropped from the active set of query 31, four centroids (centroids 5, 6, 7, and 9) are dropped from the active set of query 32, and no centroids are dropped from the active set of query 34.

Figure 2-13 shows the selection of centroids to be expanded from among the active sets. Again applying the "SELECTION" parameters, no gap greater than 0.1 occurs within the first three centroids (centroids 7, 9, and 5) for query 31; furthermore, centroids 6 and 10 have a goodness within the "EPSLON" of 0.05 and, hence, are also selected for expansion. A gap greater than 0.1 occurs between the first and second centroids (centroids 10 and 4) for query 32; therefore only centroid 10 is to be expanded. Query 34 has a gap in goodness greater than 0.1 between centroids 2 and 8; thus only centroids 11 and 12 are expanded.

The expansion for query 31 produces 43 document sons, easily satisfying the need for 12 documents. Query 32 finds 14 document sons during expansion, and the need for 12 documents is satisfied again. Query 34, however, finds only 8 document sons and 3 centroid sons on expansion; thus it becomes necessary to search further to find an additional 4 documents. The selection and expansion of a third set of nodes

TREE SEARCHING -- SELECTING THE DOCUMENTS WITH WHICH 17 QUERIES WILL BE CORRELATED.

AUTHOR	QUERY	ITER	DOCUMENTS WANT	HAVE	NEED	CENTROID	GOODNESS	CROWNS CROWN	LEVEL	CORRELATION	
BATCH	31-1	1	12	0	12	1	0.2375	26.	2.00	0.2375	
BATCH	32-1	1	12	C	12	1	0.1039	26.	2.00	0.1039	
BATCH	33-1	1	12	C	12	1		26.	2.00	0.C	TO BE DROPPED (BY MINCOR)
BATCH	34-1	1	12	C	12	1	0.1419	26.	2.00	0.1419	
BATCH	31-1	1	12	C	12	2	0.2540	41.	2.00	0.2540	
BATCH	32-1	1	12	C	12	2	0.1111	41.	2.00	0.1111	
BATCH	33-1	1	12	C	12	2	0.0222	41.	2.00	0.0222	TO BE DROPPED (BY MNGOOD)
BATCH	34-1	1	12	C	12	2	0.2842	41.	2.00	0.2842	
BATCH	31-1	1	12	C	12	3	0.0689	25.	2.00	0.0689	TO BE DROPPED (BY MNGOOD)
BATCH	32-1	1	12	C	12	3	0.0502	25.	2.00	0.0502	TO BE DROPPED (BY MNGOOD)
BATCH	33-1	1	12	0	12	3		25.	2.00	0.0	TO BE DROPPED (BY MINCOR)
BATCH	34-1	1	12	C	12	3	0.5314	25.	2.00	0.5314	

AUTHOR	QUERY	ITER	DOCUMENTS WANT	HAVE	NEED	CENTROID	GOODNESS	CROWNS NODES	EST.CUM	
BATCH	31-1	1	12	0	12	2	0.2540	41	41	TO BE EXPANDED
						1	0.2375	26	67	TO BE EXPANDED
BATCH	32-1	1	12	0	12	2	0.1111	41	41	TO BE EXPANDED
						1	0.1039	26	67	TO BE EXPANDED
BATCH	34-1	1	12	0	12	3	0.5314	25	25	TO BE EXPANDED
						2	0.2842	41	66	TO BE RETAINED
						1	0.1419	26	92	TO BE RETAINED

Fig. 2-11 First selection of nodes to be expanded.

AUTHOR	QUERY	ITER	WANT	HAVE	NEED	CENTROID		SON	SON	SON	SON	SON	SON
BATCH	31-1	1	12	0	12	1	3 CENTROID SONS -	-7	-6	-4			
BATCH	32-1	1	12	0	12	1	3 CENTROID SONS -	-7	-6	-4			
BATCH	31-1	1	12	0	12	2	3 CENTROID SONS -	-10	-9	-5			
BATCH	32-1	1	12	0	12	2	3 CENTROID SONS -	-10	-9	-5			
BATCH	34-1	1	12	0	12	3	3 CENTROID SONS -	-12	-11	-8			

TO BE DROPPED (BY MNGOOD)
TO BE DROPPED (BY MNGOOD)
TO BE DROPPED (BY MNGOOD)
TO BE DROPPED (BY MNGOOD)

AUTHOR	QUERY	ITER	DOCUMENTS			CENTROID	GOODNESS	CROWNS	CORRELATION
			WANT	HAVE	NEED			CROWN LEVEL	
BATCH	31-1	1	12	0	12	4	0.0462	10. 1.00	0.0462
BATCH	32-1	1	12	0	12	4	0.1048	10. 1.00	0.1048
BATCH	31-1	1	12	0	12	5	0.2480	21. 1.00	0.2480
BATCH	32-1	1	12	0	12	5	0.0380	21. 1.00	0.0380
BATCH	31-1	1	12	0	12	6	0.2472	6. 1.00	0.2472
BATCH	32-1	1	12	0	12	6	0.0865	6. 1.00	0.0865
BATCH	31-1	1	12	0	12	7	0.3085	10. 1.00	0.3085
BATCH	32-1	1	12	0	12	7	0.0734	10. 1.00	0.0734
BATCH	34-1	1	12	0	12	8	0.2180	7. 1.00	0.2180
BATCH	31-1	1	12	0	12	9	0.2688	6. 1.00	0.2688
BATCH	32-1	1	12	0	12	9	0.0581	6. 1.00	0.0581
BATCH	31-1	1	12	0	12	10	0.2240	14. 1.00	0.2240
BATCH	32-1	1	12	0	12	10	0.2078	14. 1.00	0.2078
BATCH	34-1	1	12	0	12	11	0.6764	8. 1.00	0.6764
BATCH	34-1	1	12	0	12	12	0.2084	12. 1.00	0.2084

Fig. 2-12 Expansion of first set of active nodes.

First table

AUTHOR	QUERY	ITER	WANT	HAVE	NEED	CENTROID	GOODNESS	NODES	EST.CUM	
BATCH	31-1	1	12	0	12		7	0.3085	10	10	TO BE EXPANDED
							9	0.2698	6	16	TO BE EXPANDED
							5	0.2440	21	37	TO BE EXPANDED
							6	0.2472	6	43	TO BE EXPANDED
							10	0.2740	14	57	TO BE EXPANDED
BATCH	32-1	1	12	0	12		10	0.2078	14	14	TO BE EXPANDED
							4	0.1048	10	24	TO BE RETAINED
BATCH	34-1	1	12	0	12		11	0.6764	8	8	TO BE EXPANDED
							2	0.2842	41	49	TO BE EXPANDED
							8	0.2180	7	56	TO BE RETAINED
							12	0.2084	10	66	TO BE RETAINED
							1	0.1419	26	92	TO BE RETAINED

Second table

AUTHOR	QUERY	ITER	WANT	HAVE	NEED	CENTROID		SCN	SON	SON	SON	SON	SON
BATCH	34-1	1	12	0	12	2	3 CENTROID SONS –	-10	-9	-5			
BATCH	31-1	1	12	21	-9	5	21 DOCUMENT SONS –	2	4	7	8	19	9
								11	12	17	8	19	23
								24	25	38	40	40	42
								46	48	67	69	69	70
								71					
BATCH	31-1	1	12	27	-15	6	6 DOCUMENT SONS –	1	14	27	37	37	65
								80					
BATCH	31-1	1	12	37	-25	7	10 DOCUMENT SONS –	5	13	24	52	52	53
								56	59	67	79	79	81
BATCH	31-1	1	12	43	-31	9	6 DOCUMENT SONS –	1	18	33	55	55	73
								77					
BATCH	32-1	1	12	14	-2	10	14 DOCUMENT SONS –	1	2	11	16	16	22
								29	32	39	47	47	50
								51	63	66	82	82	
BATCH	34-1	1	12	8	4	11	8 DOCUMENT SONS –	6	15	28	30	30	34
								41	58	61			

Fig. 2-13 Selection of second set of nodes to be expanded and expansion of these nodes.

for query 34 is shown in Fig. 2-14. Here, expansion of centroid 5 produces 21 document sons for query 34, thus filling the total requirement of 12 documents.

It should be noted that the selection of documents to be searched is not equivalent to final searching. For example, query 31 must still be processed in a regular search against the 43 selected documents. The averaged results of the searching runs are presented in Sec. 2-2-E.

2-2-D   The Searching of the Document Groups

Once the documents to be searched in a given iteration are selected, the query used in the search process is constructed. The search query is generated using concept numbers from four distinct sources: the author's original query, documents which the author considers relevant before the search is started, specific concepts and weights which the author would like to add to the query, and relevance feedback information from previous search iterations (if available). Information from the first three sources is contained for iteration 0 (first search, hence no feedback information) in Fig. 2-15. The following information is given for each query: the author, the query number, the iteration number, the sources of the query and the corresponding document numbers, multipliers for these documents (all weights of concepts in a given document are multiplied by the specified multiplier), and the query concept numbers and their weights. For example, query 1 uses the concepts from the original query (with all weights multiplied by one), plus all the concepts from documents 3 and 10 (all weights in both documents being multiplied by 2), plus concept 12 with a weight of 14. Query 1 is then defined by the combination of all these concepts and their weights.

Following the initial search query set up, further modifications can be made before the search is started. The user specifies the type of modification to be made by introducing parameters as shown in Fig. 2-16.

The options for the query modification are listed in Fig. 2-16, one section being devoted to each iteration. The parameters are defined as follows:

ORIG MULT   Multiplier of original query.

PREV MULT   Multiplier of query used for previous iteration.

MIN CORR   Parameter-controlling retrieval. Any document with a correlation less than (or equal to) "MIN CORR" is not shown to the user and is deleted from the recovered list prior to sorting into correlation order. The higher this value, the faster will be the resulting query-document correlation. If punched, the field must include a decimal point. As usual, a blank field is equivalent to zero.

TYPE CORR   The type of correlation to be used. If blank, the correlation of the previous iteration is used. If blank for the zeroth iteration, 'COSINE' is substituted. At present, "COSINE" is the correlation normally used.

```
                         DOCUMENTS                                       CROWNS
AUTHOR     QUERY   ITER  WANT HAVE NEED   CENTROID  GOODNESS  CROWN  LEVEL  CORRELATION

 BATCH      34-1    1     12    8    4          5    0.3157   21.     1.CO    C.3157



AUTHOR     CUERY   ITER  WANT HAVE NEED   CENTROID                      SON    SON    SON    SON    SON

BATCH      34-1    1     12   29   -17         5
                                                   21 DOCUMENT SONS -   2      4      7      8      9
                                                                       11     12     17     19     23
                                                                       24     25     38     40     42
                                                                       46     48     67     69     70
                                                                       71
```

Fig. 2-14 Selection and expansion of third set of nodes for query 34.

```
AUTHOR    QUERY#  ITER  SOURCE              DOC#  MULT   DOC#  MULT   DOC#  MULT   DOC#  MULT   DOC#  MULT

BATCH       1-1   0
                        ORIGINAL QUERY        (     1)
                        AUTHOR SUPPLIED      3(     2)   10(     2)
                        USER SUPPLIED       CON#  WGHT   CON#  WGHT   CON#  WGHT   CON#  WGHT   CON#  WGHT
                           CONS&WGHTS        2(    14)
BATCH       2-1   0
                        ORIGINAL QUERY        (     1)
                        AUTHOR SUPPLIED     12(     2)   29(     3)   47(     2)   61(     2)   76(     2)

                        USER SUPPLIED       CON#  WGHT   CON#  WGHT   CON#  WGHT   CON#  WGHT   CON#  WGHT
                           CONS&WGHTS        2(    79)
BATCH       3-1   0
                        ORIGINAL QUERY        (     1)
                        AUTHOR SUPPLIED     10(     2)
                        USER SUPPLIED       CON#  WGHT   CON#  WGHT   CON#  WGHT   CON#  WGHT   CON#  WGHT
                           CONS&WGHTS        1(    12)    2(    12)    3(    12)
```

Fig. 2-15 First construction of search queries.

SEARCH--CHECKING AND PRINTING OF CONTROL CARDS FOR SEARCH PARAMETERS.

OPTIONS FOR SEARCH   0 ARE:

ORIG MULT	PREV MULT	MIN CORR	TYPE CORR	NORMAL	ITEMS&MULTS	CONS&WGHTS	FREEZE/FLUID	UNITVC	WGHTS DRPED	PER DRPED
1	0	0.0150	COSINE	ABNORMAL	YES	YES	FLUID	BY WORD	POS.AVE.	99.90

POS MULT	NEG MULT	POS RANK CUT	NEG RANK CUT	POS CORR CUT	NEG CORR CUT	POS ATLEST	NEG ATLEST	POS NOMORE	NEG NOMORE
0	0	0	0	1.0000	1.0000	0	0	0	0

UNLESS	STOPALL	PREC CUTOFF	PDEFIN
0	NO	0.0	ILS

OPTIONS FOR SEARCH EHW   1 ARE:

ORIG MULT	PREV MULT	MIN CORR	TYPE CORR	NORMAL	ITEMS&MULTS	CONS&WGHTS	FREEZE/FLUID	UNITVC	WGHTS DRPED	PER DRPED
0	1	0.0	COSINE	ABNORMAL	NO	NO	FLUID	BY WORD	POS.NON.	0.0

POS MULT	NEG MULT	POS RANK CUT	NEG RANK CUT	POS CORR CUT	NEG CORR CUT	POS ATLEST	NEG ATLEST	POS NOMORE	NEG NOMORE
1	-1	5	2	1.0000	1.0000	0	0	5	2

UNLESS	STOPALL	PREC CUTOFF	PDEFIN
2	YES	0.0	ILS

Fig. 2-16 Options for searching.

NORMAL — If this field contains the word 'NORMAL' for each definition, "RMULT" is divided by the number of relevant items used in that definition. "NMULT" is likewise divided by the number of nonrelevant documents used during feedback.

ITEMS & MULTS — This field contains 'YES' if specific items and multipliers are given for each and every query in this iteration.

CONS & WGHTS — This field contains 'YES' if a specific vector of concepts and weights is supplied for each and every query in this iteration.

FREEZE/ FLUID — If this field contains 'FREEZE', the items previously seen by the user and included in the query are frozen in the order seen. Otherwise, all rank positions are available, and all documents are correlated.

UNITVC — If this field contains the words "BY WORD", the weights of a given vector are not normalized. If this field contains the word 'COSINE', all weights in a given vector are normalized according to the cosine correlation prior to being added to the composite for the new query. This is accomplished by multiplying each weight by a suitable multiplier and dividing by the square root of the sum of squared weights of the vector being added. To prevent weights from disappearing (due to integer arithmetic), the multipliers must be set at a high value when using this feature. If this field contains the word 'LINEAR', normalization is accomplished by dividing by the sum of absolute values of all weights in the vector being added.

WGHTS DRPED — This field is of the form 'XXXXYYYY'. If 'XXXX' is 'NEG.', negative weights are permitted; otherwise only positive weights will be kept after definition. 'YYYY' can be either '   ', 'ABS.', or 'AVE.'. If 'YYYY' is blank, only concepts with weight zero are deleted from the new query. (This obviously does not change the correlations.) If 'YYYY' is 'ABS.', all concepts with weight less than "PERDRP" are deleted. If 'YYYY' is 'AVE.', then all concepts with absolute weight less than ("PERDRP" * the sum of absolute weights)/(100 * the number of unique concepts) are deleted. The former method is used to delete weights less than a specific value, let us say 12. The latter method permits dropping all weights less than a certain percentage of the average weight. For example, if all concepts less than 90% of the average weight are dropped from normal composites, 75% of the concepts are deleted, but only 40% of the weight of the composite is lost.

PER DRPED — (See above. This is a floating-point number and must be punched with a decimal point.)

FOR COMPOSITE   1, WEIGHTS WERE DROPPED BY (POS.AVE., 99.9), ORIGINALLY, 23 CONCEPTS HAD A WEIGHT SUM OF   962.
                    WEIGHTS WERE TESTED AGAINST 40.   THERE ARE NOW   6 CONCEPTS AND A WEIGHT SUM OF   600.

ITEM   1   A01 TITLES PROB IN MAKING DESCRIPT - DIFF IN AUTO RETR   R

```
CON  WT    CON  WT    CON  WT    CON  WT    CON  WT    CON  WT
  1 168     10 120     11  48     15  72     93  72    533 120
```

THE   6 CONCEPTS ABOVE HAVE A SUM OF ABSOLUTE WEIGHTS = 600 WITH A ROOT SUM OF SQUARED WEIGHTS = 264.00

FOR COMPOSITE   2, WEIGHTS WERE DROPPED BY (POS.AVE., 99.9), ORIGINALLY, 61 CONCEPTS HAD A WEIGHT SUM OF 2971.
                    WEIGHTS WERE TESTED AGAINST 47.   THERE ARE NOW 22 CONCEPTS AND A WEIGHT SUM OF 1987.

ITEM   2   A02 FACT   PERTINENT DATA RETR. AUTO IN RESPONSE TO REQ E

```
CON  WT    CON  WT    CON  WT    CON  WT    CON  WT    CON  WT    CON  WT    CON  WT    CON  WT
  1 204      2  79      4  72      5 132      8  72      9  96     11  72     18  96     19 132
 46  72     48 132     81 144    116 192    126  48    134  48    135  48    147  48    154  48
180  72    291  60    304  48    530  48
```

THE 22 CONCEPTS ABOVE HAVE A SUM OF ABSOLUTE WEIGHTS = 1987 WITH A ROOT SUM OF SQUARED WEIGHTS = 474.01

FOR COMPOSITE   3, WEIGHTS WERE DROPPED BY (POS.AVE., 99.9), ORIGINALLY, 11 CONCEPTS HAD A WEIGHT SUM OF   444.
                    WEIGHTS WERE TESTED AGAINST 39.   THERE ARE NOW   4 CONCEPTS AND A WEIGHT SUM OF   300.

ITEM   3   A03 INFORM WHAT IS 1 SCIENCE - GIVE DEFINITIONS

```
CON  WT    CON  WT    CON  WT    CON  WT
  1  96     10  84     15  48     93  72
```

THE   4 CONCEPTS ABOVE HAVE A SUM OF ABSOLUTE WEIGHTS = 300 WITH A ROOT SUM OF SQUARED WEIGHTS = 154.14

Fig. 2-17 The construction of the vectors for the first iteration.

The second line of Fig. 2-16 covers parameters used only for relevance feedback and not for the initial iteration, although the values are printed. Definitions for the second and third lines are covered in the discussion describing the second iteration.

For query 1, the user-supplied parameters call for a multiplier of the query of 1, nonnormalized vectors, additional items and multipliers, additional concepts and weights, no normalizing of weights ("UNITVC" = "BY WORD"), and dropping of all concepts whose absolute weight is less than

$$\frac{99.9 * \text{sum of the absolute weights}}{100.0 * \text{the number of unique concepts}}$$

In query 1, concepts with a weight smaller than 40 are dropped in accordance with the specifications of Fig. 2-16. The display of Fig. 2-17 for query 1 shows that the original 23 concepts (formed by combining the concept vectors of the original query plus author-supplied documents and author-supplied concepts and weights) are reduced to the six concepts shown in the figure.

These modified queries are then correlated with every document in the group selected previously (in this case, a full search of the entire collection is made). After the queries are correlated with all the documents, documents having a correlation greater than 0.015 ("MIN CORR" for this iteration) are ranked. The top 30 documents retrieved are listed in Fig. 2-18. The first two lines of the listing contain the titles for the iteration, the query title, and the relevant items for the query. (At present, the document relevance is prejudged and held constant for all runs using a given query collection.) The major section of Fig. 2-18 contains the correlation and rank of the documents retrieved for each iteration. The recall and precision values (defined in Sec. 2-2-E) obtained after retrieval of the given document are also given. For example, document 69 is the first document retrieved for query 1 in the first iteration (iteration 0). The correlation coefficient of this document with the query is 0.3924, and the recall and precision values after the retrieval of document 3 are 0.0 and 0.0, respectively. Similarly, document 17, a relevant document, is retrieved with rank 2, and its correlation with the query is 0.3430. The recall and precision values after retrieval of document 17 are 0.333 and 0.333, respectively. The last section of Fig. 2-18 contains various statistics for the run. These are defined as follows:

DOC CORR — The total number of document-query correlations performed in the given iteration.

CENT CORR — The total number of centroid-query correlations performed in the given iteration.

DROP DOC — The number of documents with a query-document correlation of less than "MIN CORR".

CORR RANK — The number of documents with a query-document correlation of greater than or equal to "MIN CORR".

LEGEND   RUN 0 - SCH1   RUN 1 - SCH2   RUN 2 - SCH3   RUN 3 - SCH4

QUERY   1 - AOI TITLES PROB IN MAKING DESCRIPT - DIFF IN AUTO RETR R   THE   3 RELEVANT ITEMS BEING   17   46   62

CORRELATIONS 0	CORRELATIONS 1	RANK	DOCUMENTS 0	DOCUMENTS 1	RECALL 0	RECALL 1	PRECISION 0	PRECISION 1
0.3924	0.9259	1	69	17R	0.0	0.333	0.0	1.000
0.3430	0.3250	2	17R	4	0.333	0.333	0.500	0.500
0.3087	0.2577	3	4	40	0.333	0.333	0.250	0.333
0.2858	0.2561	4	27	71	0.333	0.333	0.250	0.250
0.2654	0.2407	5	11	46R	0.333	0.667	0.200	0.400
0.2259	0.2331	6	71	69	0.333	0.667	0.167	0.333
0.2146	0.2250	7	47	25	0.333	0.667	0.143	0.286
0.2123	0.2169	8	46R	68	0.667	0.667	0.750	0.250
0.1945	0.2117	9	57	30	0.667	0.667	0.222	0.222
0.1788	0.2085	10	19	47	0.667	0.667	0.200	0.200
0.1778	0.1978	11	62R	11	1.000	0.667	0.273	0.182
0.1742	0.1963	12	23	66	1.000	0.667	0.250	0.167
0.1742	0.1865	13	30	24	1.000	0.667	0.231	0.154
0.1617	0.1853	14	81	56	1.000	0.667	0.214	0.143
	0.1852	15	2	26	1.000	0.667	0.200	0.133
0.1358	0.1838	16	70	1	1.000	0.667	0.188	0.125
0.1345	0.1797	17	1	43	1.000	0.667	0.176	0.118
0.1324	0.1787	18	39	12	1.000	0.667	0.167	0.111
0.1286	0.1771	19	22	16	1.000	0.667	0.158	0.105
0.1213	0.1771	20	75	49	1.000	0.667	0.150	0.100
0.1196	0.1718	21	15	22	1.000	0.667	0.143	0.095
0.1180	0.1702	22	14	45	1.000	0.667	0.136	0.091
0.1151	0.1679	23	77	59	1.000	0.667	0.130	0.087
0.1078	0.1657	24	64	28	1.000	0.667	0.125	0.083
0.0990	0.1622	25	34	19	1.000	0.667	0.120	0.080
0.0980	0.1622	26	25	81	1.000	0.667	0.115	0.077
0.0947	0.1571	27	61	53	1.000	0.667	0.111	0.074
0.0857	0.1558	28	28	23	1.000	0.667	0.107	0.071
0.0835	0.1411	29	55	21	1.000	0.667	0.103	0.069
0.0808	0.1382	30	51	38	1.000	0.667	0.100	0.067
0.0797	0.1361	56		62R		1.000		0.054
0.0768								

	DOC.CORR	CENT.CORR	DROP DOC	CORR.RANK	OLD.DOC	OLD RELDOC	NEW DOC	POS.FEED	NEG FEED	QUERY CORR	REC.CEIL
RUN 0	82	0	23	59	0	0	0	1	0	1.0000	0.0
RUN 1	82	0	5	77	0	0	5	2	1	0.5336	0.3333

Fig. 2-18   Retrieval results for query 1.

OLD DOC	The total number of documents seen previously by the user.
OLD RELDOC	The total number of relevant documents seen previously by the user.
NEW DOC	The total number of documents (relevant and nonrelevant) shown to the user in this iteration.
POS FEED	The number of items in the definition of the query with a positive multiplier for feedback.
NEG FEED	The number of items in the definition of the query with a negative multiplier for feedback.
QUERY CORR	The correlation of the query used in the present iteration with the original user query.
REC CEIL	The recall ceiling seen by the user.

The listing of the retrieved relevant documents completes the first iteration of the search. At this point, the user makes relevance judgments, or alternatively, prejudged relevance decisions are registered, and a new search query is constructed using information about the retrieved documents. The user-supplied instructions specifying what information is to be used and how the new query is to be constructed are taken from the input parameters (shown in Fig. 2-16 in the second set of two lines under options for SEARCH 1). The definitions of the parameters are as follows:

POS MULT	All weights of the relevant documents used in feedback are multiplied by this number.
NEG MULT	All weights of the nonrelevant documents used in feedback are multiplied by this number. To signify that negative feedback is not desired, "NEG MULT" is blank or zero.
POS RANK CUT	All relevant items with iteration ranks above "POS RANK CUT" according to the ordering of the previous iteration are used in defining the new query.
NEG RANK CUT	All nonrelevant items with iteration ranks above "NEG RANK CUT" according to the ordering of the previous iteration are used in defining the new query.
POS CORR CUT	All relevant items with a correlation above this value are also used. (This value must include a decimal point.) If "POS CORR CUT" is zero or blank, no relevant are selected by this parameter.
NEG CORP CUT	All nonrelevant items with a correlation above this value are also used.
POS ATLEST	At least "POS ATLEST" relevant will be fed back (if they exist—implying that more remain to be found).

NEG ATLEST | At least "NEG ATLEST" nonrelevant will be fed back.

POS NOMOR | However, no more than "POS NOMOR" items will be searched to provide the "POS ATLEST" relevant documents.

NEG NOMOR | However, not more than "NEG NOMOR" nonrelevant will be used. Note that only documents scanned in an attempt to locate relevant documents for positive feedback are used in attempting to find nonrelevant for negative feedback.

UNLESS | Negative feedback is done except when "UNLESS" relevant documents are found. If "UNLESS" are found, no negative feedback at all is done. To signify that no negative feedback is desired, "NEW MULT" should contain blanks or a zero. Should 'UNLESS' be left blank or set to zero, negative feedback is attempted regardless of the number of relevant actually used in positive feedback.

STOPALL | "STOPALL" is set to 'YES' if the user wishes to stop considering documents for feedback once all the relevant documents have been found. If set to 'NO,' documents will be considered until the specifications of the other feedback parameters have been satisfied. The default is 'NO'.

PREC CUTOFF | If the precision after "POS RANK CUT" documents is over "PREC CUTOFF," and if the precision after more items are judged drops below "PREC CUTOFF", the judging of documents ceases.

POEFIN | 'SILENT' if search queries are not to be printed;
'STANDARD' if search queries are to be printed;
'DETAILS' if details of the search query definition process are to be printed (used only for debugging).

Using iteration 2 as an example, the new search query Q_{i+1} is defined by the following equation:

$$Q_{i+1} = (1)Q_i + (1)\sum_{j=1}^{n_r} (r_i)_j - (1)\sum_{j=1}^{n_s} (s_i)_j,$$

where $(r_i)_j$ designates the concepts and weights of relevant document r_j, $(s_i)_j$ designates the concepts and weights of nonrelevant document s_j, Q_i is the previous query (for iteration i), and n_r and n_s are defined by the number of relevant documents retrieved and the number of nonrelevant documents retrieved, respectively.

In iteration 2, $n_r \leq 5$; therefore, only the top five documents are retrieved, and not all of them will be relevant (in most cases). If at least two relevant documents are retrieved among the top five documents, no negative feedback will be done ($n_s = 0$). If fewer than two relevant documents are found, any nonrelevant retrieved among the top two documents will be used for feedback ($n_s \leq 2$). This condition is stipulated by an "UNLESS" of 2 and a "NEG RANK CUT" of 2.

The newly defined search queries are shown in Fig. 2-19. For query 1, one relevant and four nonrelevant documents are retrieved in the top five. The relevant document (17) and the only nonrelevant in the top two retrieved (69) are used to construct the new query. Query 2 retrieves one relevant, but the top two retrieved are both nonrelevant, so both (27 and 33) are used, together with the one relevant found during feedback. Query 3 finds three relevant in the top five retrieved; hence no negative feedback is used. The new query vectors (Fig. 2-20) are used for searching, and the results are shown in Fig. 2-18, second iteration (run 1).

2-2-E   Search Evaluation

Several different evaluation measures are used in the SMART system, all based on the concepts of recall and precision. The definitions of these measures are the following:

$$\text{Recall} = \frac{a}{b},$$

and

$$\text{Precision} = \frac{a}{c},$$

where

$a =$ number of relevant documents retrieved,

$b =$ number of relevant documents in the collection,

$c =$ number of documents retrieved.

These measures are usually computed at a specified point during retrieval, either after a given number of documents has been retrieved, or after a given recall has been obtained.

Two types of averaging graphs and four types of overall recall and precision averages are generated by the SMART system and are listed in Figs. 2-21, 2-22, 2-24, and 2-25. Figure 2-21 shows one type of graph and all four overall averages. At the top of the listing the runs being evaluated are identified [in this case a full search run (run 0) and a centroid search run (run 1)]. The recall levels being used are listed below as is the precision achieved at each recall level. The number of queries used in the averaging at each point is also given. For example, at recall level 0.10, run 0 shows a

AUTHOR	QUERY#	ITER	SOURCE	DOC#	MULT	DOC#	MULT	DOC#	MULT
BATCH	1-1	1	PREVIOUS QUERY						
			REL & NON-REL USED	69(	1)	17(	1)		
BATCH	2-1	1	PREVIOUS QUERY						
			REL & NON-REL USED	27(	-1)	33(	-1)	71(	1)
BATCH	3-1	1	PREVIOUS QUERY						
			REL & NON-REL USED	60(	1)	43(	1)	3(	1)

Fig. 2-19 Redefinition of search query.

ITEM 1 A01 TITLES PROB IN MAKING DESCRIPT - DIFF IN AUTO RETR R

CON	WT	CON	WT	CON	WT	CON	WT	CON	WT	CON	WT	CON	WT	CON	WT	CON	WT
1	12	5	12	6	12	9	12	21	36	22	6	23	18	25	24	59	12
67	12	72	12	78	12	104	12	115	12	156	12	171	12	185	12	228	12
229	24	276	24	277	24	297	24	529	12								

THE 23 CONCEPTS ABOVE HAVE A SUM OF ABSOLUTE WEIGHTS = 336 WITH A ROOT SUM OF SQUARED WEIGHTS = 76.37

ITEM 2 A02 FACT PERTINENT DATA RETR. AUTO IN RESPONSE TO REQ E

CON	WT	CON	WT	CON	WT	CON	WT	CON	WT	CON	WT	CON	WT	CON	WT	CON	WT
3	12	5	12	8	12	17	36	21	30	25	12	26	12	36	12	41	12
43	12	62	12	63	12	64	12	72	12	158	12	171	12	193	12	196	12
223	12	266	12	271	12	284	12	291	12	294	12	444	12	481	6		

THE 26 CONCEPTS ABOVE HAVE A SUM OF ABSOLUTE WEIGHTS = 360 WITH A ROOT SUM OF SQUARED WEIGHTS = 77.30

ITEM 3 A03 INFORM WHAT IS I SCIENCE - GIVE DEFINITIONS

CON	WT	CON	WT	CON	WT	CON	WT	CON	WT	CON	WT	CON	WT	CON	WT	CON	WT
1	144	5	12	9	36	10	108	11	24	15	12	22	12	26	12	31	24
34	36	38	12	52	12	58	12	108	12	134	12	162	12	163	12	171	12
193	12	195	12	211	12	217	12	225	24	240	24	253	12	260	12	274	12
291	12	363	12	427	36	465	12	533	72								

THE 32 CONCEPTS ABOVE HAVE A SUM OF ABSOLUTE WEIGHTS = 780 WITH A ROOT SUM OF SQUARED WEIGHTS = 215.67

Fig. 2-20 Construction of the vectors for the second iteration.

```
LEGEND:  RUN   0 --   35 QUERIES (PLUS     0 NULLS) -- SMART     FULL SCH
                                                        DOCUMENTATION RUN
         RUN   1 --   35 QUERIES (PLUS     0 NULLS) -- SMART     CENT SCH
                                                        DOCUMENTATION RUN
```

	RUN 0			RUN 1	
RECALL	NQ	PRECISION		NQ	PRECISION
0.0	0	0.4948		0	0.4813
0.05	1	0.4948		1	0.4813
0.10	2	0.4948		1	0.4803
0.15	5	0.4734		4	0.4620
0.20	13	0.4282		11	0.4197
0.25	18	0.4222		12	0.4148
0.30	18	0.4179		12	0.4073
0.35	24	0.3812		16	0.3797
0.40	24	0.3791		15	0.3680
0.45	24	0.3690		15	0.3599
0.50	31	0.3666		19	0.3599
0.55	31	0.2901		15	0.2900
0.60	31	0.2876		15	0.2895
0.65	31	0.2661		15	0.2800
0.70	30	0.1961		13	0.2154
0.75	29	0.1946		13	0.2154
0.80	29	0.1918		13	0.2102
0.85	25	0.1756		13	0.2102
0.90	24	0.1636		13	0.2034
0.95	24	0.1636		13	0.2034
1.00	28	0.1636		14	0.2034

```
NORM  RECALL          0.7024              0.4920
NORM  PRECISION       1.0000              1.0000
RANK  RECALL          0.2014              0.2208
 LOG  PRECISION       0.3435              0.3458
```

```
SYMBOL KEYS:  NQ  = NUMBER OF QUERIES USED IN THE AVERAGE
                    NOT DEPENDENT ON ANY EXTRAPOLATION.
            NORM  = NORMALIZED.
```

Fig. 2-21 Recall-level averages.

precision of 0.4948, but for only two queries a relevant document had been retrieved at that recall level.

Below the recall-level averages are listed the four overall averages. These are described more extensively in Chapter 8, reference [3] and are defined briefly below [7]:

$$\text{Normalized recall} = 1 - \frac{\sum_{i=1}^{n} r_i - \sum_{i=1}^{n} i}{n(N-n)},$$

$$\text{Normalized precision} = 1 - \frac{\sum_{i=1}^{n} \log r_i - \sum_{i=1}^{n} \log i}{\log \frac{N}{(N-n)!\,n!}},$$

$$\text{Rank recall} = \frac{\sum_{i=1}^{n} i}{\sum_{i=1}^{n} r_i},$$

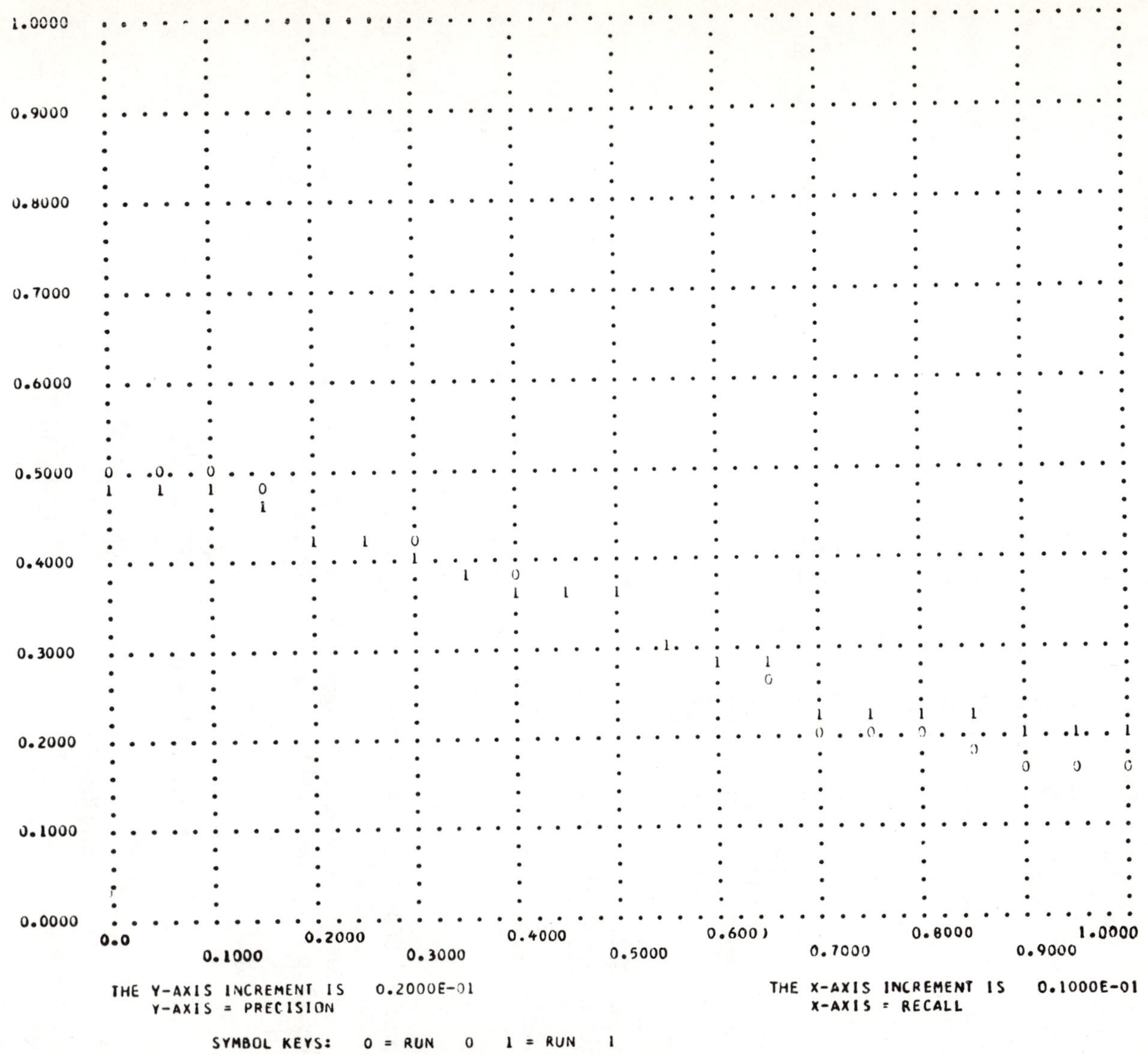
1.0000
0.9000
0.8000
0.7000
0.6000
0.5000
0.4000
0.3000
0.2000
0.1000
0.0000
0.0
0.1000
0.2000
0.3000
0.4000
0.5000
0.600)
0.7000
0.8000
0.9000
1.0000
THE Y-AXIS INCREMENT IS 0.2000E-01
Y-AXIS = PRECISION
THE X-AXIS INCREMENT IS 0.1000E-01
X-AXIS = RECALL
SYMBOL KEYS: 0 = RUN 0 1 = RUN 1

Fig. 2-22 Recall-level graph.

and

$$\text{Log precision} = \frac{\sum_{i=1}^{n} \log i}{\sum_{i=1}^{n} \log r_i},$$

where

$n =$ number of relevant documents,

$N =$ number of documents in collection,

$r_i =$ rank of ith relevant document,

$i =$ ideal rank positions for the ith relevant item.

Figure 2-22 shows a computer-generated graph of the recall and precision averages given previously in Fig. 2-21. In this type of graph, the precision is recorded along the ordinate for each given recall level shown along the abscissa. For example, at a recall of 0.10 (10% of the relevant documents retrieved), run 0 shows a precision of 0.4948, and run 1 shows a precision of 0.4803. These precision values are the averages of the precision, at a given recall level, for all the queries searched. It should be noted that interpolation methods are needed to produce the averages, since all queries do not possess an exact precision value at each given recall level.

The graph of Fig. 2-23 shows the necessary interpolation for a hypothetical query with four relevant items. The relevant documents are assumed to be retrieved

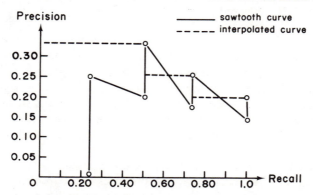

Fig. 2-23 An illustration of the interpolation method used by the "neo-Cleverdon" recall-precision averages.

with ranks of 4, 6, 12, and 20. Thus, at 25% recall, the precision is 0.25; at 50% recall, the precision is 0.33, and so on. However, these values correspond actually to the highest possible precision points for a given recall level, since they are calculated just after a relevant document is retrieved. In this example, after three documents are retrieved, the precision is 0, after five documents, the precision is 0.20, and so on. The range of precision for each recall level is indicated by the top and bottom points of the vertical segments of the sawtooth curve. The solid sawtooth line connecting these points is intended to indicate the drop in precision between the actual recall levels for this query, as more nonrelevant documents are retrieved.

The interpolation method used by the SMART system is based on the dashed lines shown in Fig. 2-23 where a horizontal line is led leftward from each peak point of precision, up to a point where a higher point of precision is encountered. This new curve (the dashed line in Fig. 2-23) does *not* lie above the sawtooth curve at all points. When the precision drops from one recall level to the next, an immediate drop in precision occurs from the first point to the level of the next point indicated. For example, in Fig. 2-23 the precision value at 0.50 recall is 0.33; at 0.55 recall, the interpolated value used for the new averages is 0.25 precision. When the precision rises from one recall level to the next, however, the first precision point actually achieved is ignored for purposes of interpolation. The achieved precision of 0.25 at 0.25 recall in the example of Fig. 2-23 is ignored, and an interpolated precision of 0.33 is used for the averages for all recall levels from 0 to 0.50.

The second kind of average graph also generated is shown in Figs. 2-24 and 2-25. In this graph, the recall and precision are recorded and averaged after the retrieval of a given number of documents. For example, after one document has been retrieved for each query in run 0, the average recall (over all the queries) is 0.0903, and the average precision is 0.3714. The recall and precision values are averaged for 24 different cutoff points, and for 6 different percentage points, such as after 10% of the collection has been retrieved, and so on. Three other statistics (besides the recall and precision) are measured and listed for each cutoff point. The first is the number of relevant documents (NR) retrieved at the given cutoff, and the second is the cumulative number of relevant documents (CNP) retrieved by this point. These values are included to aid in the proper evaluation of runs, since the document-level averages are not plotted at equal levels of recall for each query (as are the recall-level graphs). Also listed is the number of queries used to obtain the average at each point.

The final part of the evaluation process consists of tests of the significance of the differences between runs. Three basic statistical tests, the sign test, the *t* test, and the Wilcoxon signed rank test, are calculated for each pair of search runs. All three statistical tests indicate whether a given difference in two averages is likely to have occurred by chance.

A one-sided test is designed to compare a supposedly better sample B with a given standard sample A. Specifically, one proposes two hypotheses H_0 and H_1. H_0 states that two samples A and B are produced by the same distribution; H_1 states that sample B is statistically better than sample A. H_1 is accepted if it is unlikely, under H_0, that a difference between samples as great as, or greater than, that observed would occur by chance.

Similarly a two-sided test compares two samples under the same H_0, but with the alternate hypothesis H_1 being that samples A and B are from different distributions. Here again H_1 is accepted if the probability, under H_0, is low that a difference between

LEGEND: RUN 0 -- 35 QUERIES (PLUS 0 NULLS) -- SMART   FULL SCH
                                                 DOCUMENTATION RUN
         RUN 1 -- 35 QUERIES (PLUS 0 NULLS) -- SMART   CENT SCH
                                                 DOCUMENTATION RUN

			RUN 0					RUN 1	
RANK	NR	CNR	NQ	RECALL	PRECISION	NR	CNR	NQ	RECALL	PRECISION
1	13	13	35	0.0903	0.3714	13	13	24	0.0903	0.3714
2	11	24	35	0.1927	0.3429	11	24	24	0.1927	0.3429
3	7	31	33	0.2265	0.3095	7	31	21	0.2265	0.3095
4	4	35	33	0.2389	0.2714	4	35	21	0.2389	0.2714
5	7	42	33	0.2831	0.2657	7	42	21	0.2831	0.2657
6	4	46	33	0.2977	0.2476	5	47	19	0.2986	0.2524
7	4	50	33	0.3170	0.2347	5	52	18	0.3236	0.2429
8	3	53	33	0.3258	0.2214	2	54	17	0.3315	0.2276
9	1	54	33	0.3315	0.2048	3	57	17	0.3417	0.2188
10	1	55	33	0.3324	0.1914	2	59	17	0.3457	0.2090
11	6	61	33	0.3674	0.1935	7	66	17	0.3887	0.2139
12	1	62	32	0.3710	0.1853	3	69	13	0.4066	0.2117
13	2	64	32	0.3783	0.1805	3	72	11	0.4247	0.2103
14	5	69	32	0.4018	0.1826	4	76	11	0.4397	0.2111
15	4	73	32	0.4336	0.1824	4	80	10	0.4556	0.2124
16	2	75	31	0.4717	0.1791	4	84	9	0.4692	0.2141
17	4	79	30	0.4950	0.1796	1	85	7	0.4739	0.2105
18	2	81	29	0.5015	0.1774	3	88	6	0.4918	0.2105
19	4	85	29	0.5238	0.1784	0	88	4	0.4918	0.2069
20	1	86	28	0.5286	0.1752	2	90	4	0.4997	0.2066
30	20	106	24	0.6571	0.1657	3	93	0	0.5243	0.1953
50	28	134	13	0.8120	0.1626	0	93	0	0.5243	0.1835
75	21	155	2	0.9430	0.1603	16	109	0	0.5434	0.1837
100	15	170	0	1.0000	0.1636	61	170	0	1.0000	0.2034
	0	170				0	170			
10.0%	53	53	33	0.3258	0.2214	54	54	17	0.3315	0.2276
25.0%	33	86	28	0.5286	0.1752	36	90	4	0.4997	0.2066
50.0%	38	124	16	0.7576	0.1643	3	93	0	0.5243	0.1874
75.0%	22	146	6	0.8862	0.1619	0	93	0	0.5243	0.1803
90.0%	7	153	2	0.9145	0.1601	12	105	0	0.5364	0.1826
100.0%	17	170	0	1.0000	0.1636	65	170	0	1.0000	0.2034

SYMBOL KEYS: NR = NUMBER OF RELEVANT.
              CNR = CUMULATIVE NUMBER OF RELEVANT.
              NQ = NUMBER OF QUERIES USED IN THE AVERAGE
                   NOT DEPENDENT ON ANY EXTRAPOLATION.
              % = PERCENT OF TOTAL NUMBER OF ITEMS IN COLLECTION.

Fig. 2-24 Document-level averages.

two samples as great as, or greater than, that observed would occur by chance.

The t test assumes that the differences d_i between the two sets of sample values, a_i and b_i, are distributed normally. Explicitly, it is assumed that d_i has mean $\bar{d}$ and standard deviation σ_d. Note that $\bar{d}$ and σ_d are computable for any distribution, including also the normal distribution. In particular, it is known that many sets of differences are not normally distributed. (For further discussion of the t test and sign test, see reference [7] and Chapter 8, reference [3].)

The sign test assumes that a result is equally likely to favor either sample A or sample B (only the signs of the differences are recorded). Thus, it measures the probability of a distribution favoring either A or B, according as the differences in sample values are mostly positive or negative.

The Wilcoxon signed rank test postulates that a greater difference between paired samples is more significant, but only as the numbers affect the ranking of the dif-

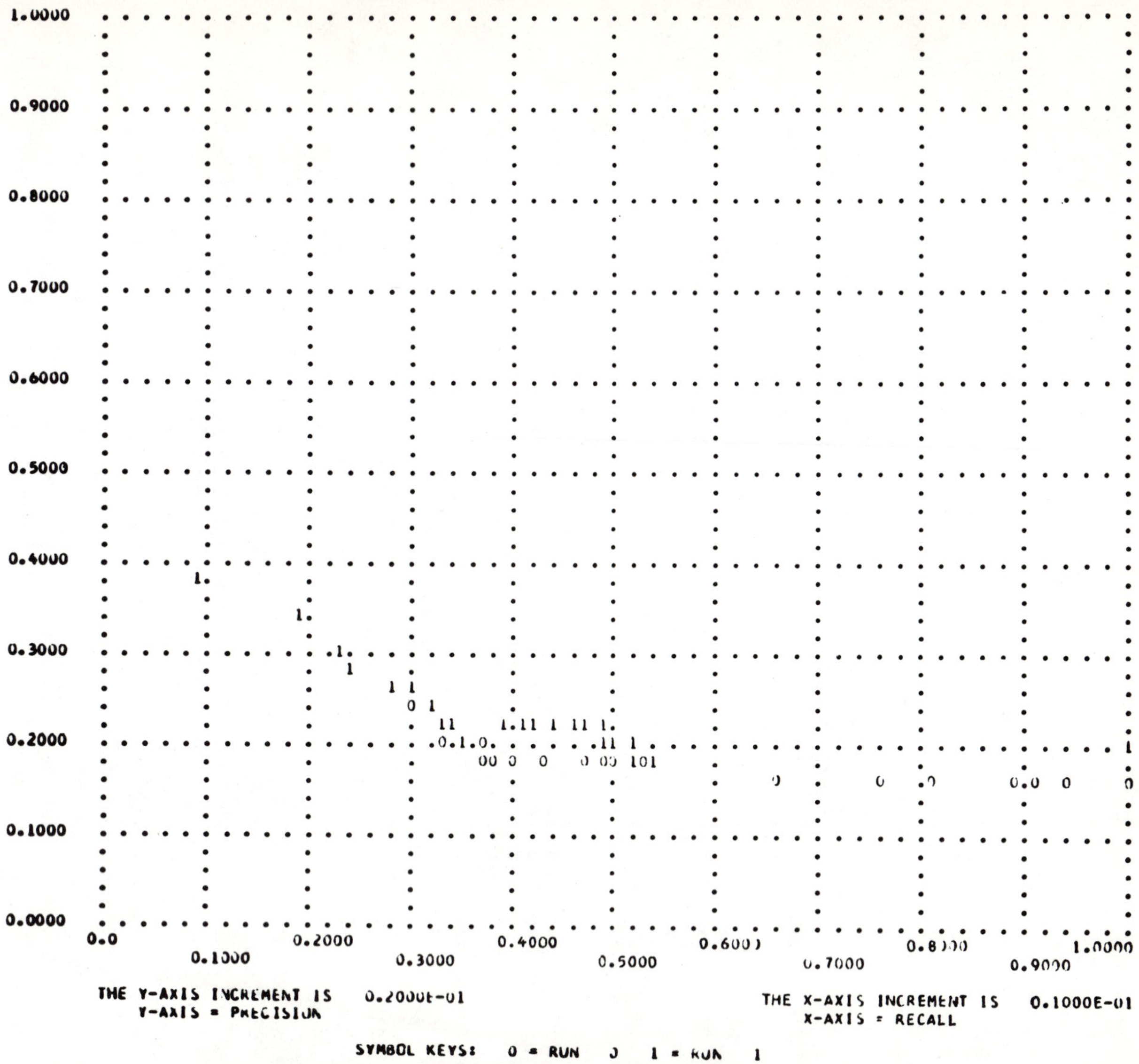

THE Y-AXIS INCREMENT IS   0.2000E-01
Y-AXIS = PRECISION

THE X-AXIS INCREMENT IS   0.1000E-01
X-AXIS = RECALL

SYMBOL KEYS: 0 = RUN 0   1 = RUN 1

Fig. 2-25 Document-level graph.

ferences. For example, differences of $-1, 2, -3, 4$, and 20 are equivalent to differences of $-1, 2, -3, 4$, and 5, since only the rank of the ordered differences favoring a sample is important (not the actual values of the differences). The Wilcoxon test assumes that the two samples come from the same family of distributions, that is, either two normal distributions, or two binomials, and so on.

The three tests are performed for 11 points of the recall-level averages, and for the 4 overall measures of recall and precision of the document level averages; in addition, the tests are also performed for 17 cost statistics. The three listings for the three different test procedures (Figs. 2-26 through 2-28) cover only the first option (11 points of the recall-level averages plus the 4 overall measures).

For the t test (Fig. 2-26), the following values are given for each of the 15 statistics: the mean and standard deviation of the statistic for each of the two searches (A and B); the mean and standard deviation of the differences between the statistics for A and B; a value T, which is defined as

$$T = \frac{(\bar{A} - \bar{B}) * \sqrt{N}}{\sigma_{A-B}},$$

where N is the number of degrees of freedom (which is one less than the number of queries being tested). The one-sided and two-sided probabilities (indicating whether a difference between the two samples as great as, or greater than, that observed would occur by chance) is also listed. Finally, the 15 one-sided tests are combined statistically into a single measure also listed.

The sign test (Fig. 2-27) gives the number of queries favoring search A, favoring search B, and tied; the normal deviate ignoring ties (computed by using the binomial normal approximation); the one-sided and two-sided probabilities for the test ignoring ties. The normal deviate and the one-sided probability using ties (based on a method described by Cathy May [8]) are also computed and listed. The one-sided tests are again statistically combined into overall figures.

The Wilcoxon signed rank test (Fig. 2-28) gives the sum of ranks favoring search A and favoring search B; the number of degrees of freedom (specifically, the number of untied pairs); the normal deviate (computed using the Wilcoxon normal approximation); the resulting one-sided and two-sided probabilities. A statistically combined significance value is also listed.

2-3 ACCESS TO THE SMART SYSTEM

The SMART system exists at Cornell University as a private library system. It is located on a disk which is accessible by reading in sets of control cards. When the SMART programs are loaded, a routine called EXEC receives control. This routine interrogates control cards in the data stream to ascertain which routines are desired and transfers control of those routines in the sequence requested.

T E S T

TESTING COLLECTION B FOR PERFORMANCE BETTER THAN COLLECTION A (1-SIDED) OR UNEQUAL TO COLLECTION A (2-SIDED)
A (FILE 0), 42 QUERIES: CRN2ST   FULL   FEEDBACK SEARCHES ON CRANFIELD 200 COMBINATION OF WORDFORM AND THESAURUS
B (FILE 1), 42 QUERIES: CRN2ST   FEED1   FEEDBACK SEARCHES ON CRANFIELD 200 COMBINATION OF WORDFORM AND THESAURUS

ON OPTION 1, 15 MEASURES -- RANK RECALL, LOG PRECISION, NORMALIZED RECALL, NORMALIZED PRECISION, AND RECALL LEVEL AVERAGES

STATISTICS	MEAN A	SD A	MEAN B	SD B	MEAN A-B	SD A-B	T	1-SIDED PROB	2-SIDED PROB
RANK R	0.8778	0.1358	0.9184	0.1142	-0.0407	0.0788	-3.3437	0.0003	0.0007
LOG P	0.7035	0.2168	0.7448	0.2026	-0.0413	0.0771	-3.4713	0.0001	0.0003
NORM R	0.3231	0.3233	0.3757	0.3046	-0.0526	0.1348	-2.5273	0.0058	0.0116
NORM P	0.4961	0.2647	0.5304	0.2618	-0.0343	0.0739	-3.0063	0.0015	0.0029
R-L-A .0	0.6541	0.3735	0.6676	0.3622	-0.0135	0.0434	-2.0238	0.0213	0.0426
REC 0.1	0.6541	0.3735	0.6676	0.3622	-0.0135	0.0434	-2.0238	0.0213	0.0426
0.2	0.6131	0.3678	0.6330	0.3563	-0.0199	0.0583	-2.2116	0.0133	0.0267
0.3	0.5626	0.3697	0.5952	0.3550	-0.0325	0.0758	-2.7820	0.0029	0.0057
0.4	0.5439	0.3668	0.5800	0.3509	-0.0361	0.0805	-2.9061	0.0020	0.0040
0.5	0.5028	0.3612	0.5486	0.3372	-0.0458	0.0994	-2.9829	0.0016	0.0032
0.6	0.4095	0.3481	0.4974	0.3245	-0.0879	0.1483	-3.8414	0.0003	0.0006
0.7	0.3690	0.3386	0.4190	0.3222	-0.0499	0.1569	-2.0633	0.0193	0.0387
0.8	0.3150	0.3198	0.3551	0.3022	-0.0401	0.1462	-1.7787	0.0376	0.0751
0.9	0.2784	0.3202	0.3305	0.3041	-0.0521	0.1288	-2.6205	0.0045	0.0090
1.0	0.2774	0.3205	0.3305	0.3041	-0.0530	0.1299	-2.6461	0.0042	0.0084

COMBINED SIGNIFICANCE -- TOTAL CHI SQUARE WITH 30 DEGREES OF FREEDOM
THE PROBABILITY OF A CHI SQUARE LARGER THAN THE OBSERVED 170.5000 IS 0.0000

SYMBOL KEYS: SD -- STANDARD DEVIATION

Fig. 2-26 t test.

SMART--FEEDBACK SEARCHES ON CRANFIELD 200 WORDFORM PAGE 66 09/10/69 23:53:16.10 87.1600

S I G N T E S T

TESTING COLLECTION B FOR PERFORMANCE BETTER THAN COLLECTION A (1-SIDED) OR UNEQUAL TO COLLECTION A (2-SIDED)
A (FILE 0), 42 QUERIES: CRN2ST FULL FEEDBACK SEARCHES ON CRANFIELD 200 COMBINATION OF WORDFORM AND THESAURUS
B (FILE 1), 42 QUERIES: CRN2ST FEED1 FEEDBACK SEARCHES ON CRANFIELD 200 COMBINATION OF WORDFORM AND THESAURUS

ON OPTION 1, 15 MEASURES -- RANK RECALL, LOG PRECISION, NORMALIZED RECALL, NORMALIZED PRECISION, AND RECALL LEVEL AVERAGES

STATISTICS	FAVORING METHOD A	FAVORING METHOD B	TIED	NORM DEV IGN TIES	1-SIDED PROB	2-SIDED PROB	NORM DEV USING TIES	1-SIDED PROB
RANK R	7	19	16	2.3534	0.0153	0.0306	-0.6172	0.7800
LOG P	8	18	16	1.9612	0.0387	0.0774	-0.9258	0.8598
NORM R	7	19	16	2.3534	0.0153	0.0306	-0.6172	0.7800
NORM P	8	18	16	1.9612	0.0387	0.0774	-0.9258	0.8598
R-L-A .0	1	7	34	2.1213	0.0385	0.0770	-4.3205	1.0000
REC 0.1	1	7	34	2.1213	0.0385	0.0770	-4.3205	1.0000
0.2	1	8	33	2.3333	0.0226	0.0451	-4.0119	1.0000
0.3	1	13	28	3.2071	0.0018	0.0036	-2.4689	0.9955
0.4	1	15	26	3.5000	0.0006	0.0011	-1.8516	0.9778
0.5	2	17	23	3.4412	0.0007	0.0014	-1.2344	0.9174
0.6	3	20	19	3.5447	0.0004	0.0007	-0.3086	0.6784
0.7	8	16	18	1.6330	0.0767	0.1534	-1.5430	0.9552
0.8	9	17	16	1.5689	0.0851	0.1702	-1.2344	0.9174
0.9	8	18	16	1.9612	0.0387	0.0774	-0.9258	0.8598
1.0	8	18	16	1.9612	0.0387	0.0774	-0.9258	0.8598
COMBINED	73	230	327	9.0194	0.0000	0.0000	-6.7730	1.0000

COMBINED SIGNIFICANCE -- TOTAL CHI SQUARE WITH 30 DEGREES OF FREEDOM
IGNORING TIES -- THE PROBABILITY OF A CHI SQUARE LARGER THAN THE OBSERVED 131.4126 IS 0.0000
USING TIES -- THE PROBABILITY OF A CHI SQUARE LARGER THAN THE OBSERVED 3.4689 IS 1.0000

SYMBOL KEYS: NORM DEV IGN TIES -- STANDARD NORMAL DEVIATE CALCULATED IGNORING TIES
NORM DEV USING TIES -- STANDARD NORMAL DEVIATE CALCULATED USING TIES

Fig. 2-27 Sign test.

SMART--FEEDBACK SEARCHES ON CRANFIELD 200 WORDFORM PAGE 67 09/10/69 23:53:16.24 87.3000

W I L C O X O N   S I G N E D - R A N K   T E S T

TESTING COLLECTION B FOR PERFORMANCE BETTER THAN COLLECTION A (1-SIDED) OR UNEQUAL TO COLLECTION A (2-SIDED)
A (FILE 0), 42 QUERIES: CRN2ST FULL FEEDBACK SEARCHES ON CRANFIELD 200 COMBINATION OF WORDFORM AND THESAURUS
B (FILE 1), 42 QUERIES: CRN2ST FEED1 FEEDBACK SEARCHES ON CRANFIELD 200 COMBINATION OF WORDFORM AND THESAURUS

ON OPTION 1, 15 MEASURES -- RANK RECALL, LOG PRECISION, NORMALIZED RECALL, NORMALIZED PRECISION, AND RECALL LEVEL AVERAGES

STATISTICS	SUM OF RANKS FAVORING A	SUM OF RANKS FAVORING B	NDF	NORMAL DEVIATE	1-SIDED PROB	2-SIDED PROB
RANK R	51.5	299.5	26	3.1494	0.0009	0.0019
LOG P	55.0	296.0	26	3.0605	0.0013	0.0026
NORM R	72.0	279.0	26	2.6287	0.0045	0.0091
NORM P	57.0	294.0	26	3.0097	0.0015	0.0030
R-L-A .0	4.5	31.5	8	1.8904	0.0342	0.0685
REC 0.1	4.5	31.5	8	1.8904	0.0342	0.0685
0.2	4.5	40.5	9	2.1325	0.0189	0.0378
0.3	10.0	95.0	14	2.6680	0.0043	0.0086
0.4	12.0	124.0	16	2.8957	0.0022	0.0045
0.5	23.0	167.0	19	2.8974	0.0022	0.0044
0.6	23.0	253.0	23	3.4977	0.0001	0.0002
0.7	93.0	207.0	24	1.6286	0.0533	0.1066
0.8	108.0	243.0	26	1.7144	0.0444	0.0888
0.9	80.0	271.0	26	2.4255	0.0079	0.0157
1.0	80.0	271.0	26	2.4255	0.0079	0.0157

COMBINED SIGNIFICANCE -- TOTAL CHI SQUARE WITH 30 DEGREES OF FREEDOM
THE PROBABILITY OF A CHI SQUARE LARGER THAN THE OBSERVED 157.3448 IS 0.0000

SYMBOL KEYS: NDF -- NUMBER OF DEGREES OF FREEDOM

Fig. 2-28 Wilcoxon signed-rank test.

A typical deck setup for the system is reproduced as follows:

Initiates SMART routines.	[//JOB ....(parameters)...... [/*SMART
Sets up document groups for a collection already on file.	{ CLUSTR ......(parameters)...... { ....(parameters)...... { . { .
Performs retrieval runs using methods called for by the parameter cards.	{ SEARCH ......(parameters)...... { ....(parameters)...... { . { .
Performs statistical averages for the previous search.	{ AVERAG ......(parameters)...... { ....(parameters)...... { . { .
Signals end of job.	[STOP

2-4 BASIC SMART SYSTEM FLOWCHART

The SMART routines fall into two categories: routines that can be called with control cards and routines that can only be called by other routines. The latter set is interconnected by means of complex internal vectors, designed to make the most efficient use of in-core storage. A set of flow charts is included in Figs. 2-29 through 2-34. The routines which can be called by control cards are enclosed by boxes.

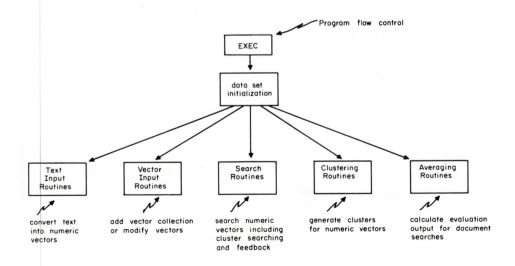

Fig. 2-29 SMART system chart.

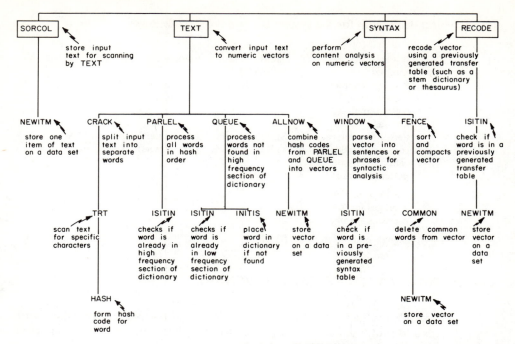

Fig. 2-30   SMART system chart—text input routines.

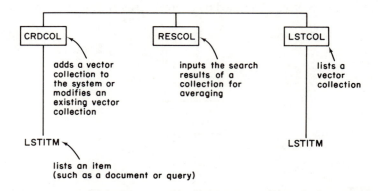

Fig. 2-31   SMART system chart—vector handling routines.

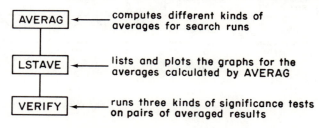

Fig. 2-32   SMART system chart—averaging routines.

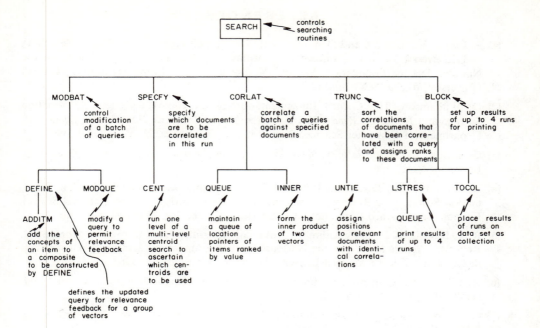

Fig. 2-33 SMART system chart—search routines.

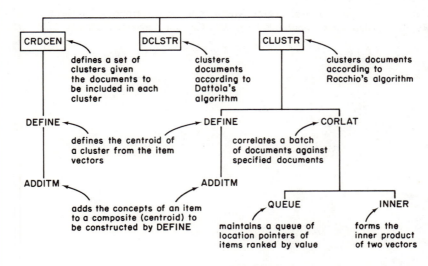

Fig. 2-34 SMART system chart—clustering routines.

REFERENCES

[1] E. Ide, R. Williamson, and D. Williamson, The Cornell Programs for Cluster Searching and Relevance Feedback, Information Storage and Retrieval, *Report ISR-12* to the National Science Foundation, Section IV, Department of Computer Science, Cornell University, Ithaca, N.Y. June 1967.

[2] D. Williamson, The Cornell Implementation of the SMART System, Information Storage and Retrieval, *Report ISR-14* to the National Science Foundation, Section II, Department of Computer Science, Cornell University, Ithaca, N. Y. October 1968.

[3] G. Salton, *Automatic Information Organization and Retrieval*, Chap. 8, McGraw-Hill, Inc., New York, 1960.

[4] J. J. Rocchio, Jr., Document Retrieval Systems—Optimization and Evaluation, Information Storage and Retrieval, Doctoral thesis, *Report ISR-10* to the National Science Foundation, Harvard Computation Laboratory, Cambridge, Mass. March 1966.

[5] R. T. Dattola, A Fast Algorithm for Automatic Classification, Information Storage and Retrieval, *Report ISR-14* to the National Science Foundation, Section V, Department of Computer Science, Cornell University, Ithaca, N.Y., October 1968.

[6] R. Williamson, Centroid Searching (Tree Searching), Unpublished notes, Cornell University, Ithaca, N.Y., May 1968.

[7] G. Salton and M. E. Lesk, Computer Evaluation of Indexing and Text Processing, Information Storage and Retrieval, *Report ISR-12* to the National Science Foundation, Section III, Department of Computer Science, Cornell University, Ithaca, N.Y., June 1967; also Chap. 7 of this volume.

[8] Cathy May, Evaluation of Search Methods in an Information Retrieval System, Term Report written for *Computer Science 435*, Cornell University, Ithaca, N.Y., May 1968.

PART II

EVALUATION PARAMETERS

The SMART *system is designed to provide a flexible test bed for evaluating a variety of potentially useful methods of automatic content analysis in information retrieval.* SMART *is primarily a document retrieval system; however, many of the analysis techniques employed are also applicable to other phases of information retrieval, including fact retrieval and question-answering systems. This chapter introduces a generalized model of the system and derives several evaluation indices which can be used to determine the influence of the various system parameters.*

3

PERFORMANCE INDICES FOR DOCUMENT RETRIEVAL SYSTEMS †

J. J. ROCCHIO, JR.

3-1 THE MODEL

A document retrieval system employing fully automatic indexing may be characterized by the following elements:

(a) A set of reference documents in the natural language D.

(b) A set of retrieval requests in the natural language Q.

(c) An index language L.

(d) A transformation T from the natural language to the index language which operates on members of the set D.

(e) A transformation T' (possibly the same as T) which maps retrieval requests to the index language L.

(f) A search function S whose domain is the cardinal product of elements of

†This study was first published as Section III in *Scientific Report ISR-8*, December 1964.

57

the set Q with those of the set D, and whose range is such that S induces at least a partial order on the set D.

In the SMART system the index language L may be considered to be a property space. The transformations T and T' may take several forms. For example, natural language word stems may be mapped one-to-one into elements of L or alternatively, T may be a composite transformation resulting from a many-to-many mapping of word stems to elements of L (thesaurus transformation) followed by mappings from L to L (hierarchy). In addition, the resulting image of a document $d_i \in D$ under a given transformation T can be either a binary property vector in L or a numeric vector. The search function S used in SMART may also be controlled, but it is characterized basically by a correlation process involving a request image and the set of reference document images.

A retrieval operation in terms of this model consists in applying the search function S to the cardinal product $T(D) \times T(q)$, $q \in Q$. One may consider the ordering induced on D from the range of S to be the result of the retrieval operation, or one may introduce a decision function C whose domain is the range of S and whose range is the positive integers. Such a decision function partitions D into disjoint subsets, normally consisting of a retrieved subset and its complement with respect to D. In the general case, C may, however, introduce a multilevel classification.

To evaluate the effectiveness of a retrieval operation, it is necessary to introduce a subjective element. Let us assign to each request q, a subset D_q of D which is the set of reference documents "relevant" to q. In general the specification of this subset for a given q may be an ill-defined process. In an operational framework, D_q is that subset of R which the originator of the request q would choose if he were given the opportunity of making an exhaustive search on D. Alternatively, one may consider that corresponding to each request q, an ordering of D is defined which reflects the "degree of relevance" of each document in R to the request. In this case one may still identify a relevant subset D_q by considering those members of D for which the degree of relevance exceeds a given threshold.

Assume for the present that for each q in Q a subset D_q of relevant documents is known or, alternatively, a partial ordering of D exists which reflects the degree of relevance. The object of the document retrieval system is to produce a subset D'_q (or induce a partial order on D) which is identical to D_q (that is, equivalent to the partial order determined by the degree of relevance). Evaluation of a retrieval system then requires a determination of how each of the system elements affects the degree to which this objective is met for all members of Q.

The most commonly used performance indices of document retrieval systems are the recall and precision ratios introduced by Cleverdon in connection with the Aslib–Cranfield project [1]. These measures are based on having an objective set D_q of relevant documents for each query presented to the system. After a retrieval operation, which produces a two-way classification of D into a retrieved subset D_a and its complement with respect to D, the following parameters are obtained:

$n(D_q)$ = total number of relevant documents;

$n(D_a)$ = total number of retrieved documents;

$n(D_q \cap D_a)$ = total number of relevant retrieved documents.

Using these parameters one can define:

$$\text{Recall} = \frac{n(D_q \cap D_a)}{n(D_q)},$$

and

$$\text{Precision} = \frac{n(D_q \cap D_a)}{n(D_a)}.$$

Clearly, recall as defined by Cleverdon is a measure of the inclusiveness of the set D_a with respect to the set D_q, while precision is a measure of the exclusiveness of the set D_a with respect to the complement of D_q. It should be noted that the joint behavior of these parameters is required to judge performance intuitively; that is, a recall of 1 or a precision of 1 alone does not imply satisfactory performance: however, if both recall and precision are 1, then $D_a = D_q$.

It must be noted also in connection with these parameters that the decision function C of the model is required to specify the retrieved subset D_a. In many respects this is undesirable because an additional variable is then introduced into the system. In fact, when evaluating the various content analysis techniques, including the structure of the index language L and of the transformations T and T', it is desirable to introduce as few extraneous constraints as possible. This suggests that one should deal directly with the search function S. Another justification for doing so is the fact that the decision function is usually determined subjectively, in the sense that in practice the needs of a particular user dictate its characteristics.

In practice, the decision function C can be eliminated easily, because the search function S can be used to induce a partial ordering on D directly. A user could then request that the results of the retrieval operation be presented to him in this induced order. If this were done, the user could examine any desired subset of this ordered set, specifying in effect the "retrieved subset" a posteriori by the number of documents examined.

In view of these considerations a set of performance indices has been developed which may be applied directly to the ordering induced on D by a retrieval search S.

3-2 EVALUATION INDICES

Under the assumption that the ordering induced on the set of reference documents by the search process S is the principal result of a retrieval operation and that a set of relevant documents D_q is available corresponding to each request q, the objective of a retrieval operation may be recast in the following form: a retrieval operation with respect to a request q is expected to produce an ordering on the reference collection D, such that every member of the set D_q is ranked above all members of the complement of D_q with respect to $D(\bar{D}_q)$.

Note that in this formulation no emphasis is placed on any relative order among the members of the set D_q of relevant documents. While such an ordering might in theory seem desirable, the determination of an unordered set D_q is difficult enough by itself, so that imposition of an additional ordering criterion may be impractical. A partial order within D_q may, however, have some significance and in fact has been employed in some of the Aslib–Cranfield experiments to specify degrees of relevance. These in turn lead to the definition of different subsets D_q, but not to the specification of retrieval order with respect to relevance order.

Given the previously stated definition of the objective of a retrieval operation, two functions of the ordering induced on D may be defined which are related to the recall and relevance (precision) of Cleverdon. Consider an ordering induced on D by S such that a one-to-one mapping exists from D to the dense set of integers from 1 to $n(D)$; increasing rank order in the set of integers then reflects decreasing connection between the request image and document image.

In this case, define:

$$r^*(i) = \begin{cases} \dfrac{i}{n_0} & \text{for } 1 \leq i \leq n_0, \\ 1 & \text{for } n_0 \leq i \leq N, \end{cases}$$

and

$$p^*(i) = \begin{cases} 1 & \text{for } 1 \leq i \leq n_0, \\ \dfrac{n_0}{i} & \text{for } n_0 \leq i \leq N, \end{cases}$$

where

$n_0 = n(D_q)$, the number of relevant documents to the query under consideration;

$N = n(D)$, the number of documents in the reference collection;

i = the rank index induced on D.

The function $r(i)$ is viewed as the number of relevant documents having rank order less than or equal to i divided by the total number of relevant documents. Thus, it is Cleverdon's recall as a function of the order induced on D by a retrieval operation. Clearly, $r^*(i)$ is the recall function which pertains when the retrieval operation produces an ideal ordering on D. Similarly, $p(i)$ is the number of relevant documents having rank order less than or equal to i divided by i, with $p^*(i)$ defined for the case when all members of D_q have a rank index less than every member of $\bar{D}_q$. Hence for each query q, $r_q^*(i)$ and $p_q^*(i)$ define a desired (or objective) recall function and a desired precision function.

Since it has been assumed that S induces only an ordering on D, as opposed to a metric, these functions are defined strictly only for discrete values of the rank index i. As it is intended to extend these functions to a continuous independent variable—that is, to define a function $r^*(x)$ equivalent to $r^*(i)$—a possible anomaly is noted. This arises from the fact that it is possible within the framework of the system, for S to produce a mapping from elements of $\{q \times D\}$ to the real line. This, in fact, occurs when S is a correlation process which correlates a query image with the set of document images viewed as vectors in some abstract space. The process of inducing an ordering from this mapping and then treating this ordering as a function of a continuous real variable gives the impression of coming full circle. In fact, there is clearly a loss of information involved because relative distance between the images of d_i and d_j is not preserved by this process. The justification for making this transformation from the domain of S to an ordering index lies in the assumption that the order so derived has significance of and by itself.

The extension then to functions of a real variable is accomplished by defining two function $r^*(x)$ and $p^*(x)$ such that:

$$\left. \begin{aligned} r^*(x) &= r^*(i) \\ p^*(x) &= p^*(i) \end{aligned} \right\} \quad \text{for } x = i,\, i = 1, 2, \ldots, N,$$

and further that:

$$r^*(x) = \begin{cases} \dfrac{j}{n_0} & \text{for } j \leq x \leq j + 1 \\ & \qquad j \text{ integral and less than } n_0, \\ 1 & \text{for } x > n_0, \end{cases}$$

and

$$p^*(x) = \begin{cases} \dfrac{j}{x} & \text{for } j \leq x < j + 1 \\ & \qquad j \text{ integral and less than } n_0, \\ \dfrac{n_0}{x} & \text{for } x > n_0. \end{cases}$$

At this point, recall and precision functions may be defined for the results of a retrieval operation with respect to a particular query. In particular, let the ranks of each member of the set of relevant documents D_q resulting from applying S to $\{q \times D\}$ be specified as:

$$0(i) \quad \text{for } i = 1, 2, \ldots, n_0,$$

where $0(i + 1) > 0(i)$. In this case:

$$r_q(x) = \begin{cases} 0 & \text{for } 1 \leq x \leq 0(1), \\ \dfrac{i}{n_0} & \text{for } 0(i) \leq x < 0(i + 1), \\ 1 & \text{for } x \geq 0(n_0), \end{cases}$$

and

$$p_q(x) = \begin{cases} 0 & \text{for } 1 \le x \le 0(1), \\ \dfrac{i}{x} & \text{for } 0(i) \le x < 0(i+1), \\ \dfrac{n_0}{x} & \text{for } x \ge 0(n_0). \end{cases}$$

At this point, a recall error and a precision error may be defined by considering:

$$\text{Recall error} = \int_{x=1}^{N} [r^*(x) - r_q(x)] \, dx,$$

and

$$\text{Precision error} = \int_{x=1}^{N} [p^*(x) - p_q(x)] \, dx.$$

Since $r^*(x)$ is an upper bound to $r(x)$ and, similarly, for $p^*(x)$ and $p(x)$, these errors are always greater or equal to zero.

To compute these integrals we introduce the unit step function $U_{-1}(x)$ defined by

$$U_{-1}(x) = \begin{cases} 1 & \text{for } x \ge 0, \\ 0 & \text{for } x < 0, \end{cases}$$

and note that:

$$\int_{-\infty}^{b} U_{-1}(x) \, dx = b.$$

Now $r^*(x)$ can be expressed as:

$$r^*(x) = \frac{1}{n_0}[U_{-1}(x-1) + U_{-1}(x-2) + \ldots + U_{-1}(x-n_0)],$$

and

$$r(x) = \frac{1}{n_0}\{U_{-1}[x - 0(1)] + U_{-1}[x - 0(2)] + \ldots + U_{-1}[x - 0(n_0)]\}.$$

Therefore,

$$\int_{1}^{N} [r^*(x) - r(x)] \, dx = \frac{1}{n_0} \sum_{i=1}^{n_0} \int_{1}^{N} \{U_{-1}(x-i) - U_{-1}[x - 0(i)]\} \, dx,$$

$$= \frac{1}{n_0} \sum_{i=1}^{n_0} [0(i) - i],$$

$$= \frac{1}{n_0} \sum_{i=1}^{n_0} 0(i) - \frac{1}{n_0} \sum_{i=1}^{n_0} i,$$

or

$$\text{Recall error} = \bar{0} - \frac{n_0 + 1}{2}.$$

That is the integral of the difference between the recall function for perfect retrieval and the recall function which results from an actual retrieval is simply the difference between the average rank $\bar{0}$ induced on the members of the set of relevant documents D_q by the retrieval operation and the mean of the ranks which a perfect retrieval would induce.

To normalize this parameter to the range 0–1, consider the case for which the rank of every member of the set D_q is greater than every member of $\bar{D}_q$. This is clearly the case of maximum error; hence:

$$\text{Max recall error} = \frac{1}{n_0} \sum_{i=1}^{n_0} N - (i - 1) - \frac{n_0 + 1}{2},$$

$$= \frac{1}{n_0} \left[\frac{n_0}{2}(N + N - n_0 + 1) \right] - \frac{n_0 + 1}{2},$$

$$= N - n_0.$$

Therefore,

$$\frac{\bar{0} - [(n_0 + 1)/2]}{N - n_0}$$

is a normalized index of overall recall error. As this index is measuring recall error, it is desirable to reverse it. Hence:

$$1 - \left[\frac{\bar{0} - [(n_0 + 1)/2]}{N - n_0} \right]$$

will be the index of recall performance.

The precision error can be expressed in terms of the unit step function as follows:

$$p^*(x) = \frac{1}{x}[U_{-1}(x - 1) + U_{-1}(x - 2) + \cdots + U_{-1}(x - n_0)],$$

and

$$p(x) = \frac{1}{x}\{U_{-1}[x - 0(1)] + U_{-1}[x - 0(2)] + \cdots + U_{-1}[x - 0(n_0)]\}.$$

Now,

$$\int_{-\infty}^{b} U_{-1}(x - a) \frac{dx}{x} = \int_{a}^{b} \frac{dx}{x} \ln b - \ln a.$$

Therefore,

$$\text{Precision error} = \int_1^N [p^*(x) - p(x)]\, dx$$

$$= \sum_{i=1}^{n_0} \int_1^N \frac{dx}{x} [U_{-1}(x - i) - U_{-1}(x - 0(i))]$$

$$= \sum_{i=1}^{n_0} \ln 0(i) - \ln i$$

$$= \sum_{i=1}^{n_0} \ln 0(i) - \sum_{i=1}^{n_0} \ln i,$$

or

$$\text{Precision error} = \ln \prod_{i=1}^{n_0} 0(i) - \ln n_0!$$

Again, by the same consideration, this index may be normalized to lie in the range 0–1 by dividing by the maximum precision error. This error must be:

$$\text{Max precision error} = \ln \prod_{i=1}^{n_0} N - i + 1 - \ln n_0!$$

$$= \ln \frac{N!}{N - n_0!} - \ln n_0!$$

$$= \ln \binom{N}{n_0}.$$

Therefore the normalized index of precision error is

$$pe = \frac{\ln \prod_{i=1}^{n_0} 0(i) - \ln n_0!}{\ln \binom{N}{n_0}}.$$

Again, since this is an index of error, an index of performance is obtained by considering $1 - pe$,

$$1 - \frac{\ln \prod_{i=1}^{n_0} 0(i) - \ln n_0!}{\ln \binom{N}{n_0}}$$

will be the index of overall precision performance.

Since both these indices reflect overall performance, a value of 1 for either implies a value of 1 for the other, in opposition to the conventional recall and precision ratios The difference between these two overall measures lies in the weighting given to the relative position of the relevant documents in the retrieved rank list. The recall index weights rank order uniformly because it is sensitive to each relevant document. The precision index, however, weights initial ranks more strongly because it is sensitive to having a high percentage of relevant documents in the initial part of the retrieved list.

The recall and precision indices derived here depend on the assumption that the ordering induced on D by S is a full order; that is, it can be represented by a one-to-one mapping from D to the integers from 1 to $n(D)$. As this may not be true in general, since a partial order rather than a full order may result, a method for defining document rank in this case is required.

The most natural way of treating documents which are equivalent under a partial order induced by S is to give each member of the equivalent set the average of the ranks which would apply to the set members if they were differentiable. Hence, if S induces the partial order $d_1 > d_2 > \{d_3, d_4, d_5\} > d_6$, on a set $D = \{d_1, d_2, d_3, d_4, d_5, d_6\}$, and $D_q = \{d_1, d_5, d_6\}$, the rank assigned to d_1 would be 1, to d_5 would be 4, and to d_6 would be 6.

In addition, these performance indices may be extended to the case in which there is a partial ordering of the set of relevant documents D_q. In this case, the objective of a retrieval operation would need to be redefined to take account of this partial ordering. Assume that a set of relevant documents D_q for a query q is defined, and that, further, a partial ordering on D_q is specified which reflects degree of relevance; that is,

$$D_{q_1} > D_{q_2} > \cdots > D_{q_k},$$

where $D_{q_i} \in D_q$ and $>$ implies "more relevant than." In this case, one may define the objective of a retrieval operation as follows: a retrieval operation with respect to a query q and a partially ordered set of relevant documents D_q is expected to produce an ordering on the reference collection D, such that every member of the set D_{q_i} is ranked higher than $D_{q_{i+1}}$, and that all members of D_q are ranked higher than $\bar{D}_q$.

Corresponding to this definition, expressions for $r^*(x)$, $p(x)$, $r_q(x)$, and $p_q(x)$ could be defined in a manner analogous to those defined above. The development of the indices for this case is more cumbersome than the case considered previously and will not be presented here. The only significant difference which arises is due to the fact that a relevant document d_i in subset D_{q_i} may have lower retrieval rank than a document d_i in subset D_{q_j}, where the partial ordering on D_q is such that $D_{q_j} > D_{q_i}$. This necessitates considering only the positive differences between the retrieval ranks of the relevant documents and the corresponding ideal retrieval ranks. To illustrate, consider a case in which

$$D_q = \{d_1, d_2, d_3, d_4, d_5, d_6\},$$

and

$$D_{q_1} = \{d_1, d_2, d_3\} > D_{q_2} = \{d_4, d_5, d_6\}.$$

Let the retrieval order be $d_1, d_5, d_3, d_4, d_2, d_6, \ldots$ Then

$$\sum_{i=1}^{n(D_{q_1})} 0(i) - i + \sum_{i=n(D_{q_1})+1}^{i=n(D_{q_1})+n(D_{q_2})} 0(i) - i = (1+5+3) - (1+2+3)$$

$$+ (4+2+6) - (4+5+6) = 3 + (-3) = 0,$$

even though there is clearly a departure from ideal retrieval. By considering only positive differences, the result would be a retrieval error of 3. The same observations apply to the precision index.

3-3   EXPERIMENTAL USE

These indices have been used to evaluate the results of a variety of experiments conducted with the SMART system. As one might expect from the formulation, the range of the recall index is rather limited; that is, a random retrieval would produce a recall index of 0.5. Hence one would suspect observed results to be near 1.0. In fact, the observed range is from about 0.9–1.0 with the average probably close to 0.97. The precision index, however, has a reasonable range for the requests examined to date and typically varies from 0.6–1.0. In practice, then, one is forced to expand the scale of the recall index, so that a range 0–1 is no longer maintained. For the results obtained to date a scale expansion of 5, introduced so as to maintain an upper value of 1.0, produces a range for the recall index similar to that of the precision index. Therefore the scaled recall index has been defined as:

$$1.0 - 5(1.0 - x),$$

where x is the normalized recall index.

Two related performance indices may be derived from the two which have been considered. These are useful in the case where a particular query is subjected to a set of retrieval operations which are to be compared.

It may be remembered that the recall error was found as:

$$\text{Recall error} = \bar{0} - \frac{n_0 + 1}{2}.$$

Since $\bar{0}_{max} = (n_0 + 1)/2$, an index with a maximum value of 1 may be defined as:

$$\text{Rank recall} = \frac{(n_0 + 1)/2}{\bar{0}}.$$

A similar observation for the case of the derived precision error produces a precision index:

$$\text{Log precision} = \frac{\log n_0!}{\log \prod_{i=1}^{n_0} 0(i)}.$$

The advantage of these indices lies in the fact that they are simpler and, therefore, easier to compute than the normalized indices, and that the rank recall takes on a wider range for the results which have been observed. The disadvantages of both these measures is their dependence on n_0, the number of relevant documents for the query in question. This dependence makes it impossible to average these indices over a set of queries, and thus their usefulness is limited.

REFERENCE

[1] C. W. Cleverdon, Report on the Testing and Analysis of an Investigation into the Comparative Efficiency of Indexing Systems, *Aslib–Cranfield Research Report*, Cranfield, England, October 1962.

The fundamental concepts involved in measuring the performance of a document retrieval system are examined, and the conclusion is reached that two different viewpoints may be taken depending on one's basic assumptions. The rationale for each of these is examined, and the differences between them is discussed. Some illustrations are given with respect to the effect of the evaluation viewpoint on precision and recall measures.

4

EVALUATION VIEWPOINTS IN DOCUMENT RETRIEVAL †

J. J. ROCCHIO, JR.

4-1 INTRODUCTION

A document retrieval system operating on a retrieval request produces a partition of a source doucment collection into two disjoint subsets, the retrieved subset and the nonretrieved subset. The basis for judging the performance of the system is a comparison between this partition and the one which the originator of the query would produce if he were to examine every source document. In most cases such a direct comparison is not feasible, and thus various artifacts (such as sampling, use of contrived queries, etc.) are used to approximate the ideal case. However in all instances the underlying basis for system evaluation remains the same.

In some retrieval systems a retrieval operation may produce a ranking or even a metric ordering of source documents with respect to the input query. In these cases questions of "degree of relevance" can be avoided by inducing a partition from the ordering using a cutoff criterion, or by requiring that each relevant document (one which the user would retrieve) be ranked above every member of the nonrelevant set. In this latter case then, the basis for evaluation is a comparison between the ordering induced by the system

†This study was published as Section XXI in *Scientific Report ISR-9*, August 1965.

and the ordering induced by the user rather than between the respective partitions.

In either case, if we assume that the set of documents relevant to each input query is both known and fixed, any performance evaluation is a measure of (1) the indexing transformation which produces the images manipulated by the system, (2) the query image (since we assume that the query structure for a fixed relevant set may vary), and (3) the search or matching function which operates on these images to produce an effective partition of the source document collection.

While the paragraph above outlines the basic mechanics of retrieval system evaluation, it neglects an important aspect of evaluation which has often been overlooked, namely the evaluation viewpoint. Under the above assumptions about the system model there still remains an important choice to be made by the evaluator. Since the notion of relevance is so complex and so dependent on personal factors, any system evaluation must clearly be based statistically. Thus, in effect, any evaluation of a document retrieval system must in fact be an estimate of the degree to which the systems ability to detect relevance matches that of humans'.

The validity of such an estimate based on the system performance with respect to some finite sample set of queries depends on how representative the sample set is of the real-life environment of the system. It is not, however, this question to which we address ourselves but rather to a related one, namely whether the evaluation viewpoint considers retrieval queries as atomic, or whether the relation between a relevant document and the set of nonrelevant documents (implicitly defined by each query for all members of the document set relevant to that query) is considered atomic. Both these alternative evaluation viewpoints, called macro and micro evaluation, respectively, are tenable and in fact have been compared one against the other without the comparers' appreciation of the distinction.

4-2 MACRO EVALUATION

Macro evaluation is a query-oriented viewpoint, and as such, any performance index formulated on this basis would be query distributed or averaged on a per-query basis. The justification for considering queries as atomic is simply that this corresponds to the viewpoint of the system user. The user interacts with the retrieval system via his retrieval request and would thus judge the usefulness of the system on the basis of its performance with respect to his request. The sample mean of an evaluation parameter obtained by averaging over the total number of queries represents an estimate of the worth of the system to the average user. An underlying assumption of this approach is of course that the distribution of results over the sample set of queries allows a meaningful average performance per query to be produced. If the performance distribution is too wide, one might try to categorize requests in some fashion so as to produce a meaningful performance estimate for each category. Of course this would still be done on a query-average basis.

4-3 MICRO EVALUATION

Micro evaluation is produced by a document-oriented viewpoint, in which one assumes that the determining element of system behavior is the relation between a relevant document and the set of nonrelevant documents. With this viewpoint each query provides a set of samples of this relation, and thus any performance index is document distributed or averaged on a per-document basis. This approach makes it necessary to justify that the set of samples provided by a single request are independent and reflect the relevance relation which pertains in general. If this is not true, the micro evaluation viewpoint will weight any performance index so derived heavily towards the systems behavior for those requests having a large number of relevant documents, thus distorting the statistical validity of the estimate. It is not, however, the primary purpose of this discussion to establish which of these evaluation orientations has more merit, but rather to point out the differences so that the implications of each are understood clearly.

4-4 EXAMPLE

As an illustration of the effect of the evaluation viewpoint on performance indices we consider now the precision-recall curve of Cleverdon which has been perhaps the most widely used evaluation tool for document retrieval systems. As Cleverdon has conceived and used this measure, it is a micro evaluation performance index.

Define recall as the number of relevant documents retrieved divided by the total number of relevant documents, and define precision as the number of relevant documents retrieved divided by the total number of documents retrieved. Clearly these parameters of a retrieval operation assume that the matching function of the system induces a dichotomous partition of the source document set. Each ratio is indicative of a different aspect of how this partition induced by the system compares with that induced from the users' relevance judgments. The recall ratio measures the inclusiveness of the retrieved subset with respect to the relevant set, and the precision measures the exclusiveness of the retrieved set with respect to the nonrelevant set. Cleverdon's approach was to plot these ratios, one versus the other, with a parameter of the matching function (cutoff criterion) providing different points.

Clearly the evaluation of a single request by this means is unambiguous. However, the evaluation of system behavior with respect to a sample set of N queries can be produced from either the micro or the macro viewpoint.

Assume that for a particular cutoff (which specifies a partition of the source collection), the total number of retrieved documents for the ith query is t_i, and the number both relevant and retrieved is r_i. Further let the total number of documents which are relevant to request i be n_i.

Under these conditions a single point on the precision-recall curve is defined according to the micro viewpoint as

$$\text{Micro recall} = \frac{\sum_{i=1}^{N} r_i}{\sum_{i=1}^{N} n_i}, \quad \text{Micro precision} = \frac{\sum_{i=1}^{N} r_i}{\sum_{i=1}^{N} t_i}.$$

Thus the micro recall is the number of relevant documents retrieved per relevant document, and micro precision is the number of relevant documents retrieved per retrieved document. Unless the variation of both n and t over all sample requests is small, these parameters do not reflect the behavior of an average request.

From a query-oriented point of view, the conditions above define N rather than one point in the precision-recall plane. This set of points can be represented by a single average point defined by:

$$\text{Macro recall} = \frac{1}{N} \sum_{i=1}^{N} \frac{r_i}{n_i}, \quad \text{Macro precision} = \frac{1}{N} \sum_{i=1}^{N} \frac{r_i}{t_i}.$$

Thus the macro recall is just the average recall over the query sample, while the macro precision is the corresponding average precision.

It is interesting to note that if the number of relevant documents per query is constant or the number of retrieved documents per query is constant then the micro and macro recall or precision are identical, respectively. This of course is expected because in this event the micro statistic merely weights the performance of each query equally and therefore is identical to the macro statistic.

A numerical example may serve to illustrate the differences in these approaches more concretely. Consider a set of two queries for which the following table describes the hypothetical system behavior.

Table 4-1

HYPOTHETICAL RETRIEVAL RESULTS FOR
A SAMPLE OF TWO QUERIES

QUERY	n	CUTOFF 1		CUTOFF 2	
		t	r	t	r
1	10	3	2	20	6
2	3	3	2	60	2

For the above retrieval results, the recall-precision figures of Table 4-2 indicate the micro and macro parameter values.

From Table 4-2 it can be noted that at Cutoff 1 micro recall is significantly lower, which reflects the fact that the request having the large number of relevant documents

(1) has much lower recall than request (2). Similarly at Cutoff 2, micro precision is lower because in this case the request having more retrieved documents (2) has lower precision.

Table 4-2

Comparison of Micro and Macro Precision-Recall Points

	CUTOFF 1		CUTOFF 2	
	Micro	*Macro*	*Micro*	*Macro*
Recall	0.31	0.43	0.62	0.63
Precision	0.66	0.66	0.1	0.17

A comparison between query-averaged and document-averaged precision versus recall curves for a sample set of 24 queries is shown in Fig. 4-1. The results were obtained from experiments run on the SMART system. Since the matching function in SMART produces a ranked output, cutoff points were chosen by the following method. Let the user examine the retrieved list in order until he encounters *n* consecutive nonrelevant documents; this defines a cutoff point, By varying *n*, a series of points on the precision versus recall curve can be produced. Note that although this method

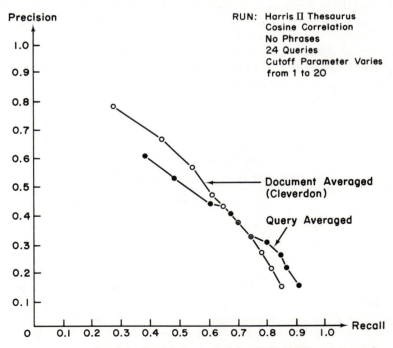

Fig. 4-1   Precision vs. recall for 24 SMART system queries.

of specifying a cutoff is not ideal, because it ignores any metric information contained in the retrieved ordering, it might correspond quite closely to the way a user would react in practice to the system.

4-5   CONCLUSION

The only generalization which can be made with respect to the effect of these alternative viewpoints on a precision versus recall curve is that recall results derived from the micro viewpoint will be more representative of the system behavior on queries having a large number of relevant documents, and that micro precision will be more representative of the system behavior on queries having a large number of retrieved documents. Without evidence that this in fact is not biasing the performance estimate for the retrieval system, it would seem that the macro viewpoint has more merit.

Evaluation of the SMART system is based on techniques for the measurement of retrieval performance. This chapter discusses many aspects of retrieval performance measurement in general, describes several of the measures used by SMART, and gives a detailed account of the way in which results of individual requests are processed in order to present averaged results. Several measures professed by other researchers in the area are examined and evaluated, and some considerations relating to future testing are made.

5

EVALUATION PARAMETERS†

E. M. KEEN

5-1 *PURPOSES, VIEWPOINTS, AND PROPERTIES OF PERFORMANCE MEASURES*

Since performance measures are used for different purposes according to test objectives, a division into three types is suggested. First, there is the need for measures with which to make merit comparisons within a single test situation, that is, to make "internal" comparisons only. In tests of this type the document collections, search requests, and relevance decisions are held constant while some system variable is altered, and this procedure has been used for almost all of the SMART experiments [1]. Such situations are best characterized in terms of performance measurement, by saying that comparisons are made in situations of constant generality, and a "generality number" may be computed in such cases [2]:

$$G = \frac{\text{Total relevant in collection} \times 1000}{\text{Total documents in collection}}$$

Although generality tends to vary between requests, an average value for a set of requests serves to characterize a particular series of experiments.

†This study was published as Section II in *Scientific Report, ISR-13*, December 1967.

A second purpose of performance measurement is that of making "external" comparisons between results obtained in different situations, in which generality is expected to differ. Such comparisons may be made even within an experimental test environment if different request sets or collection sizes are introduced and compared.

A third purpose that may be distinguished is a specific need to interpret experimental results in terms of expected real-life merit, rather than merely comparing different techniques in a laboratory. Experimental tests of the kind conducted by SMART are simulation tests, and any conclusions drawn from the results may need to be presented in a way that would be typical of the performance if the system were being used operationally.

The choice of performance measures is also affected by viewpoint, either the viewpoint of the user, or of a researcher seeking fundamental insight into retrieval capability. User satisfaction depends mainly on document sets a, b, and c in Fig. 5-1, since a user is interested in examining as few nonrelevant items as possible and as many relevant items as he wishes to see, but he is not concerned about d or about the total collection size. From a system efficiency viewpoint, which is important in some types of research, the value of d, and the collection size are needed. For example, test comparisons in situations of differing generality require measures that include d if a strict comparison of efficiency is the object.

Documents	Relevant	Nonrelevant	
Examined	a	b	$a + b$
Not Examined	c	d	$c + d$
	$a + c$	$b + d$	$a + b + c + d$

$$\text{Recall} = \frac{a}{a + c} \qquad \text{Cut-off} = \frac{a + b}{a + b + c + d}$$

$$\text{Precision} = \frac{a}{a + b} \qquad \text{Generality number} = \frac{(a + c)1000}{a + b + c + d}$$

$$\text{Fallout} = \frac{b}{b + d}$$

Fig. 5-1 Evaluation measures derived from 2 × 2 contingency table.

Still more sophisticated techniques may be needed, when large heterogeneous collections are used, because an evaluation of system efficiency may then require adjustment for differing concentrations of documents by subject in different collections. This allows the actual collection size to be replaced by the real number of documents within the subject areas covered by a set of requests. No suitable method of achieving this type of comparison has been developed yet, but it is crucial to further research in this area if accurate comparisons between heterogeneous collections are to be achieved.

Four desirable properties of retrieval performance measures are suggested by

John Swets [3], namely that the measure should be

1. Able to measure retrieval effectiveness alone, separately from other criteria such as cost.
2. Independent of any particular cutoff.
3. A single number.
4. On a number scale to give absolute and relative values.

Swets, however, does not recognize the possibility that different purposes and measurement viewpoints may be important, and the resulting measure proposed takes no account of the user viewpoint in a directly meaningful way. From matters discussed already, several other properties appear desirable:

1. Ability to reflect success of the system in meeting needs of different types, such as high precision or high recall.
2. Ability to interpret measures directly in terms of a user's experience; for example, 0.2 precision at 0.5 recall means that the user has examined half the relevant documents available, while at the same time four nonrelevant document items were looked at for every one relevant.
3. Ability to compare systems of differing generality.

Other properties can be suggested, but the purposes and viewpoints specified here should override such properties as the "single number" or "absolute and relative scales," which are desirable perhaps but not essential. The purposes, viewpoints, and properties discussed are summarized in Fig. 5-2.

(A) *Purposes*
   1. 'Internal' test comparisons, "G" constant
   2. 'External' test comparisons, "G" varies
   3. Interpretation of merit in simulated real-life terms

(B) *Viewpoints*
   1. System efficiency
   2. User satisfaction

(C) *Properties*
   1. Retrieval effectiveness alone
   2. Independent of cut-off
   3. Single number
   4. Absolute and relative values
   5. Differing user needs
   6. Interpretation in user terms
   7. Comparisons involving "G" changes

Fig. 5-2   Factors affecting the choice of performance measures.

5-2   MEASURES FOR RANKING SYSTEMS

The provision of a ranked output, in which documents are ordered according to the magnitude of their correlation coefficient with the search request, makes it possible to use evaluation measures of many types, since a direct evaluation of the rank positions occupied by the relevant documents may be made, or a series of cutoffs may be applied according to many different criteria. The performance measures used by SMART are now described briefly, and some additional suggested measures are noted. The primary purposes of measurement in SMART have been that of internal comparisons (Purpose 1, Fig. 5-2) and that of the viewpoint of user satisfaction (Viewpoint 2, Fig. 5-2).

5-2-A   Single Number Measures

Sets of measures known as *rank recall* and *log precision* and *normalized recall* and *normalized precision* are in use and have been described [1], [4], [5], [6]. These measures are cutoff independent in that the rank positions of all the relevant documents to a request are compared with the ideal positions resulting from a perfect system. Results presented in other sections of this report employ the two normalized measures. The formulas are repeated for convenience:

$$\text{Normalized recall} = 1 - \frac{\sum\limits_{i=1}^{n} r - \sum\limits_{i=1}^{n} i}{u\,(N-n)},$$

$$\text{Normalized precision} = 1 - \frac{\sum\limits_{i=1}^{n} \log r_i - \sum\limits_{i=1}^{n} \log i}{\log N!/(N-n)!\,n!}$$

where
$n =$ number of relevant documents,
$N =$ number of documents in collection,
$r_i =$ rank of ith relevant document,
$i =$ ideal rank position for the ith relevant item.

The result obtained from one individual search request is given in Fig. 5-3, and both

RELEVANT DOCUMENTS		
Rank	*Number*	*Correlation*
1	588	.5764
2	589	.5477
4	590	.3833
6	592	.3523
13	772	.2092

$$\text{Normalized recall} = 1 - \frac{\sum 1, 2, 4, 6, 13 - \sum 1, 2, 3, 4, 5}{5(200-5)} = 0.9887$$

$$\text{Normalized precision} = 1 - \frac{\sum \log 1, 2, 4, 6, 13 - \sum \log 1, 2, 3, 4, 5}{\log \dfrac{200!}{(200-5)!\,5!}} = 0.9238$$

Fig. 5-3   Result of Cran-1 individual request Q268, Thesaurus-2, showing evaluation using the normalized measures.

the normalized measures are computed. Normalized recall gives as equal "weight" to documents with high rank positions as to documents with low rank positions, but normalized precision gives stronger weight to the initial section of the retrieval list—to those with high rank positions.

An attempt to derive a single number measure of a quite different type is reported by John Swets [3]. Single-number measures are different from the measures used by SMART because they are not based directly on the ranked output list but use, in the first place, performance curves similar to those discussed in the Sec. 5-2-B; examination of these measures are thus deferred. The normalized "sliding ratio" measure proposed by Giuliano and Jones [8] appears to be designed for use at one selected cut-off point and so again differs from the SMART measures.

5-2-B Varying Cutoff Performance Curves

The most common measures of retrieval performance are the precision and recall ratios derived from the retrieval table, given in Fig. 5-1. These measures are desirable even with a ranking system, since they alone seem capable of representing a user's viewpoint (Viewpoint 2, Properties 5 and 6, Fig. 5-2.). It is a simple matter to construct performance curves of this type from a ranked output, since a series of cutoff points may be chosen, precision and recall calculated, and the points joined to form a curve.

A precision versus recall curve for an individual request is presented in Fig. 5-4, using the familiar graph and showing the shape of the curve when a cutoff is established after each document. Results for a single request always exhibit the step pattern, but interpolation and extrapolation techniques to be described in Sec. 5-3 produce a smoother curve. The practice, as with the normalized measures, is to present results averaged over a whole set of search requests. Figure 5-5 shows an example of some averages for two retrieval runs in the form of a tabular computer printout, and a graph of the precision versus recall curves.

A quite similar "performance characteristic" curve is proposed for use with ranking systems by Giuliano and Jones [8]; it seems to offer no advantage over the precision versus recall curve. It is advocated for another reason to be discussed in Sec. 5-4. The normalized sliding ratio measure also proposed by Giuliano and Jones uses either the recall or precision ratios at each cutoff point. The equation given and the example calculated in Fig. 5-6 show that, up to a cutoff equal to the number of relevant items, this measure is the precision ratio; at higher cutoffs, the measure equals recall. While it is true that a perfect result would produce a perfect measure of performance, it would do so at every cutoff point, which would not seem to be a desirable result. In the perfect case, a user who wanted high recall, not knowing how many relevant items the system contained, might suggest a cutoff too "early" in the list and would miss some relevant items; yet this measure would show a perfect result at that cutoff point. Other similar examples can be constructed, and the conclusion is that the normalized sliding ratio measure does not include many valuable features.

The "operating characteristic" curves used by John Swets [3] and drawn on a

RECALL-PRECISION AFTER RETRIEVAL OF *n* DOCUMENTS			
n	*Number (x = Relevant)*	*Recall*	*Precision*
1	588 x	0.2	1.0
2	589 x	0.4	1.0
3	576	0.4	0.67
4	590 x	0.6	0.75
5	986	0.6	0.60
6	592 x	0.8	0.67
7	984	0.8	0.57
8	988	0.8	0.50
9	578	0.8	0.44
10	985	0.8	0.40
11	103	0.8	0.36
12	591	0.8	0.33
13	772 x	1.0	0.38
14	990	1.0	0.36

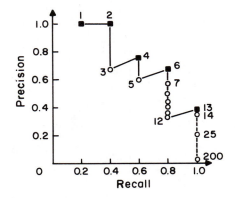

Fig. 5-4 Result of Cran-1 individual request Q268, Thesaurus-2, showing evaluation using a graph of precision versus recall.

graph of the recall ratio and the fallout ratio are described by him in terms of probabilities. The fallout ratio has been used in previous experiments [2] and is discussed in Sec. 5-5. Swets uses this measure because the operating characteristic curves may be examined in terms of statistical decision theory, and hopefully, a single number measure may be derived to represent the whole curve, if the curves follow some suitable theoretical model. Results from SMART and other experimental systems are used by Swets, but the resulting fit with the model curves is only partially successful, in that an s value as well as an E value are required strictly to characterize an operating characteristic curve, as shown in Fig. 5-7. It should be noted that although this kind of measure is suitable for reflecting the system efficiency viewpoint and meets almost perfectly Properties 1, 2, 3, 4, and 7, it does not and cannot display user satisfaction in terms of precision and therefore does not meet Properties 5 and 6 (Fig. 5-2).

ADI ABSTRACTS COLLECTION, AVERAGES OVER 35 REQUESTS			
STEM		THESAURUS	
REC.	PREC.	REC.	PREC.
0.1	0.7963	0.1	0.8788
0.2	0.6350	0.2	0.7567
0.3	0.5283	0.3	0.6464
0.4	0.4603	0.4	0.5577
0.5	0.4051	0.5	0.4912
0.6	0.3699	0.6	0.4470
0.7	0.3383	0.7	0.3893
0.8	0.2996	0.8	0.3287
0.9	0.2568	0.9	0.2726
1.0	0.2018	1.0	0.2093
RNK REC = 0.2415		RNK REC = 0.2534	
LOG PRE = 0.3587		LOG PRE = 0.3837	
NOR REC = 0.7652		NOR REC = 0.8045	
NOR PRE = 0.5339		NOR PRE = 0.6075	

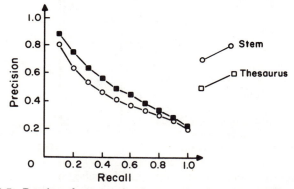

Fig. 5-5 Results of two retrieval runs, showing the averages produced.

5-2-C   Comparison of Single Number and Curve Measures

The relationship between the single number normalized measures on the one hand and the precision-recall curve on the other has not yet been established theoretically. Both types of measures are obtained for every retrieval run, and in the vast majority of cases the two types of measure give the same merit when two runs are being compared for effectiveness. For example, the two average sets of results given in Fig. 5-5 show that both normalized recall and normalized precision favor the abstracts–

Normalized "Sliding Ratio" Statistic:

$$\mu(n) = \frac{f(n)}{f^*(n)}$$

where n = Rank position

f = Number of relevant examined in ideal result

f^* = Number or relevant actually examined.

Example using Cran-1 Request Q268, with Ranks of Five Relevant 1, 2, 4, 6, 13

Rank(n)	f	f*	μ
1	1	1	1.00
2	2	2	1.00
3	3	2	0.67
4	4	3	0.75
5	5	3	0.60
6	5	4	0.80
7	5	4	0.80
.	.	.	.
.	.	.	.
.	.	.	.
13	5	5	1.00
14	5	5	1.00
.	.	.	.
.	.	.	.
.	.	.	.

Fig. 5-6 Result of Cran-1 individual request Q268, Thesaurus-2, showing evaluation using the normalized "sliding ratio" statistic proposed by Giuliano and Jones [8].

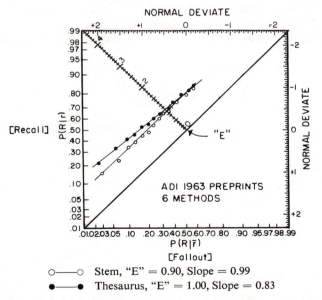

○——○ Stem, "E" = 0.90, Slope = 0.99

●——● Thesaurus, "E" = 1.00, Slope = 0.83

ADI abstracts, "pseudo-Cranfield" cut-off, micro evaluation of 35 requests

Fig. 5-7 Two "operating characteristic" curves of fallout versus recall and "E" values obtained, as suggested by Swets [3].

thesaurus option, and the same result is given by the precision-recall curve, since the curve for abstracts-thesaurus is closer to the 1.0 precision at 1.0 recall corner over the whole of its range than the curve for abstracts-stem.

A minority of results do not show such complete agreement, and a comparison presented in Fig. 5-8 shows that only above 0.9 recall does the curve merit agree with merit assigned by the normalized measures. Two individual requests from the request set used are given in Fig. 5-9, showing that although in both requests the normalized measures strongly favor the Cosine Logical option, some portions of the precision-recall curve favor Cosine Numeric. In request QA12 the ranks of the last two relevant documents favor cosine numeric, but the normalized measures are more directly influenced by the larger rank changes at the top rank positions that favor cosine logical. In request QA4 the same effects cause the high precision end of the curve to favor cosine numeric. Clearly single-number measures cannot reflect the crossing of performance curves, unless the measures are designed specifically to reflect merit that exists at a particular point on the curve. But this possibility is not met by the normalized measures, and it is not always correct to say that normalized recall reflects merit at the high recall end of the curve, and normalized precision does so at the high precision end. For example, Fig. 5-10 shows a result in which the average curve for First Iteration is at all points better than Initial Search, yet normalized recall indicates that the latter appears to be better. This occurs because the First Iteration result improves the ranks of quite a few documents that were already quite highly ranked in Initial Search (thus the normalized precision is best for First Iteration), but at the same time some other relevant documents that were poorly ranked on Initial Search are worsened by quite large amounts in First Iteration, thus causing normalized recall to drop, without affecting the curve appreciably.

The examples given are practically the only such observed in over 100 perfor-

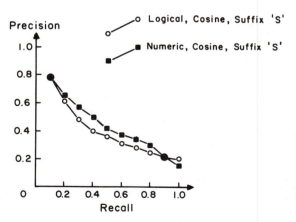

ADI, text, 35 requests

	Normed. Recall	Normed. Precision
Logical, Cosine	.7768	.5462
Numeric, Cosine	.7520	.5308

Fig. 5-8 Comparison of merit assigned by precision recall curve and normalized measures in run case of poor agreement.

Request QA12   5 Relevant Documents

    Cosine Numeric—Ranks of Relevant   1, 3, 14, 17, 18
    Cosine Logical—Ranks of Relevant   1, 2, 3, 18, 23

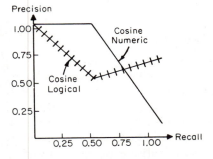

	Cosine Numeric	Cosine Logical
Normed. Recall	.9013	.9169
Normed. Precision	.7270	.8230

Request QA4   2 Relevant Documents

    Cosine Numeric—Ranks of Relevant   1, 15
    Cosine Logical—Ranks of Relevant   2, 3

	Cosine Numeric	Cosine Logical
Normed. Recall	.9188	.9875
Normed. Precision	.7515	.8645

NOTE: Precision Recall curves are extrapolated to 1.0 Precision 0.0 Recall, as discussed in Sec. 5-3-C.

Fig. 5-9 Results of two individual requests from the ADI text, suffix 's', Cosine numeric versus logical runs, showing merit assigned by normalized measures and precision-recall curves.

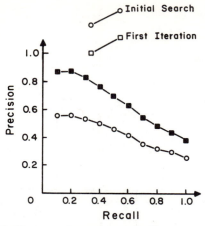

Cran-1, Thesaurus-3, averages over 42 requests

Normed. Recall	Normed. Precision
.8772	.6815
.8680	.7622

Fig. 5-10   Results of two searches in a relevance feedback evaluation run, comparing merit assigned by the normalized measures with the precision-recall curve.

mance comparisons and thus are definitely the exception rather than the rule. The reasons for the discrepancies lie in the way in which the different measures apply different weight to different distributions of the relevant documents.

5-3 THE CONSTRUCTION OF AVERAGE PRECISION VERSUS RECALL CURVES

In the context of the SMART experiments, the construction of a precision versus recall curve for a set of search requests requires techniques for averaging over individual requests, choosing cutoff points to construct curves, and coping with problems that arise because individual requests have differing numbers of relevant documents. Different methods of meeting these three problems are suggested, and these methods are divided into those that are suitable only for test comparisons (Purposes 1 and 2, Fig. 5-2), and those that satisfy the need to accurately simulate the result experienced by real users (Purpose 3, Fig. 5-2). An additional problem that arises only for the fast cluster searches is also discussed.

5-3-A Averaging Techniques

The two main alternative averaging techniques have been described as micro evaluation and macro evaluation [1, 5, 6]. The micro method requires the computation over all requests of the number of documents both retrieved and relevant (for a given cutoff) so that one final precision recall pair can be calculated, whereas the macro method requires the computation of precision-recall pairs for each request with the final precision-recall pair obtained by averaging, using the arithmetic mean. The macro method is preferred generally because it provides both adequate comparisons for test purposes and meets the need of indicating a user-oriented view of the result; the micro method on the other hand tends to give undue weight to requests that have many relevant documents. As Salton and Rocchio have shown [1, 5], the macro method produces somewhat better precision-recall curves, but the difference between the two methods with current collections and requests is near to or less than 5%, as seen in the comparison of Fig. 5-11. The use of the micro method usually gives the same performance merit when two options are compared, so that this issue does not affect comparative test results at all.

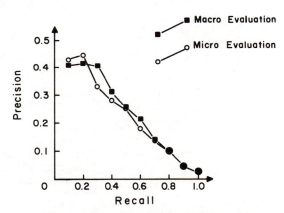

Cran-1, abstracts, thesaurus-3, "pseudo-Cranfield averages over 42 requests

Fig. 5-11 Retrieval comparison of the macro and micro averaging methods.

Further work on the averaging problem may reveal that the arithmetic mean is not the only suitable method to use. Averaging is a problem simply because of the extreme variance in individual results, as can be seen from the plot of individual precision-recall curves for 22 requests given in Fig. 5-12. The macro evaluation curve for these 22 requests is given in Fig. 5-13, together with a curve based on the median, rather than the mean. The scatter of results raises the question of statistical significance; this matter is discussed in an article by Salton and Lesk [9].

5-3-B Cutoff Techniques

Cutoff techniques in conventional manual and mechanized retrieval systems usually depend on the search terms used, with specified term matches establishing the cutoff points. The equivalent in SMART is the use of the correlation coefficient that is obtained between the request and each document, but the provision of ranked

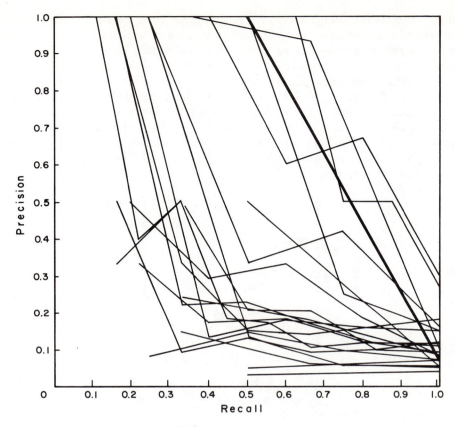

ADI, abstracts, thesaurus

Fig. 5-12   Individual precision-recall curves for 22 requests, showing the wide scatter of individual results.

output permits other cutoff criteria to be used, specifically related to the exact number or the acceptablity of the documents as they are examined. Cutoff techniques for experimental purposes must be based on methods applicable to all requests, regardless of variations in the number of relevant items. For this reason only the ranked output list is used, and no account is taken for cutoff purposes of the correlation, although one study using correlation magnitudes has been made [10].

By using the precision-recall pairs that can be computed as each document in the output list is examined (Fig. 5-4), three cutoff methods seem feasible. The first method is to obtain average curves from all requests just as drawn in Fig. 5-4, by computing mean precision-recall pairs for each document cutoff level. If done by hand, the cutoff points may be recorded on the curve as in Fig. 5-14(a), or a computer-produced average may be used which produces precision at ten recall levels for plotting convenience, Fig. 5-14(b). This technique is referred to as the *pseudo-Cranfield*

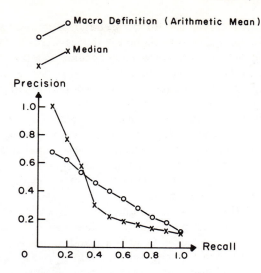

ADI, abstracts, thesaurus, averages of 22 requests

Fig. 5-13 Comparison of average results using mean and median of the individual requests.

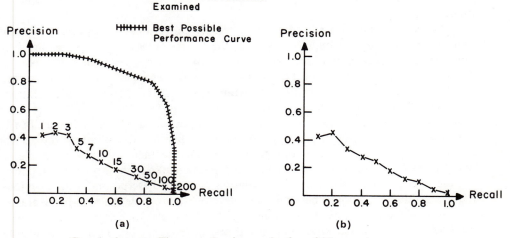

Cran-1, abstracts, Thesaurus-3, micro evaluation of 42 requests

Fig. 5-14 An illustration of the document cut-off or "pseudo-Cranfield" method: (a) document cut-off "pseudo-Cranfield" computed by hand; (b) document cut-off "pseudo-Cranfield" as computed by evaluation routines at ten recall levels.

method, and although it is available for many runs, it is not used generally for SMART evaluations. One advantage of this method is that is seems to be fully user oriented, since the plot of Fig. 5-14(a) shows how many documents a typical user must examine to get x recall. Another advantage is that computation does not depend on the interpolation and extrapolation techniques that are required for the other methods to be described. A disadvantage stems from the fact that the requests vary according to the number of relevant items, so that if one of the requests has only a single relevant document, any cutoff made at two or more documents will not give 1.0 precision even if all requests have a quite perfect performance. One simple solution to this is to give the theoretical best possible curve for a given set of requests, as is done in Fig. 5-14(a). It is a simple matter to use this cutoff method with macro evaluation; the macro curve in Fig. 5-11 was obtained in this way.

The second and third cutoff techniques use, respectively, precision and recall ratios to determine the cutoff points at which averages will be computed. A set of precision or recall values are picked in advance, and requests are averaged essentially at the cutoff points at which the required precision or recall ratios are reached. The use of precision values, although theoretically possible, has not been tested. This is primarily because recall is more suitable for this, since precision does not decrease monotonically with rank (the upward sloping "steps" in Fig. 5-4 indicate that more than one cutoff can produce a given precision). Although recall does increase monotonically, there is still one problem that requires solution. The vertical segments of the "step" curve for an individual request (Fig. 5-4) show that at some recall points, more than one cutoff point may exist from which to choose, each giving a different precision ratio.

At least five possible solutions are available concerning the choice of a cutoff, namely, that having the highest precision, the lowest precision, the precision of the "middle" document, a precision ratio computed from the average precision over all cutoff points, or a precision ratio computed as the average of the top and bottom points only. Figure 5-15 indicates an example of each of these possible solutions.

There is a further question, relating to the precision values to be used at recall points where no vertical part of the step is encountered, such as at 0.5 recall in Fig. 5-4. It is possible, for example, by using one of the five possible points at the vertical segments, to join up the chosen points on the vertical segment by a new interpolation line. Figure 5-16(a) shows that, when the cutoff having the highest precision is chosen for use at the vertical segments, interpolation between these points of an individual request produces a smooth performance curve, which is quite suitable for averaging over sets of requests. This example in Fig. 5-16(a) is the one used most frequently by SMART, and the description appeared first in reference [4]. This type of average curve normally uses ten recall levels, 0.1, 0.2, and so on, and is referred to as the *quasi-Cranfield* method. Its advantage is that it can be interpreted quite simply by noting that a cutoff is established immediately when a relevant document is encountered in each output list. It very effectively reflects merit at the high recall end of the plot, since the lowest precision ratio for any individual request is computed when a recall of 1.0 is reached, unlike the pseudo plot which continues making

Ranks	Recall	Precision
5	.6	.6000
6	.8	.6667
7	.8	.5714
8	.8	.5000
9	.8	.4444
10	.8	.4000
11	.8	.3636
12	.8	.3333
13	1.0	.3846

Choices of Precision to Use at .8 Recall:

1. Document with highest precision, rank 6, precision .6667
2. Document with lowest precision, rank 12, precision .3333
3. Document in 'middle' position, rank 9, precision .4444
4. Documents at all ranks, average precision .4685
5. Documents at best and worst ranks, average precison .5000.

Fig. 5-15 Calculation examples of five choices of precision to be used at constant recall, using one vertical "step" of the precision-recall curve from Figure 5-4.

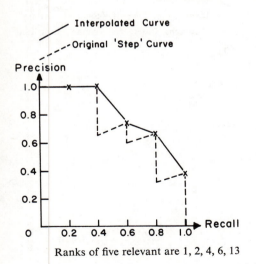

Ranks of five relevant are 1, 2, 4, 6, 13

(a)

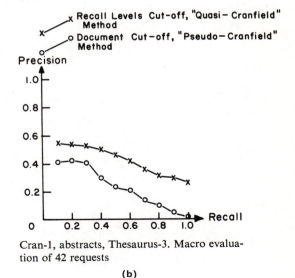

Cran-1, abstracts, Thesaurus-3. Macro evaluation of 42 requests

(b)

Fig. 5-16 Illustrations of the recall levels cut-off—"quasi-Cranfield" method: (a) curve for individual request Q268, Cran-1, Thesaurus-2, using recall levels cut-off—"quasi-Cranfield" method; (b) average curves to compare cut-offs.

cutoffs until the last document in the collection is reached. This technique is quite adequate for making comparisons within SMART, but a possible disadvantage in some circumstances is that the curve is not typical of a real user environment because it produces too optimistic a result. Figure 5-16(b) compares a pseudo and a quasi curve for the same set of averaged results.

A modification to the technique is being tested, in which the cutoff having the highest precision at each vertical segment is still used, but the interpolation lines are altered to produce what is believed to represent the best possible curve that a user could achieve, assuming that almost optimum choices of cutoff are made. Figure 5-17(a) gives an example of this method. The reason for this type of extrapolation line which retains constant precision resides in the fact that user requirements would ask for the best possible precision above x recall. Whatever the value of x, the best possible precision is always the next peak in the step curve, so a line of constant precision leading to that peak is thought to give the required result. A slight modification, yet to be made, is that sometimes the next peak encountered above x recall is eclipsed by a higher peak at still greater recall (occurring, for example, when one relevant document is followed by another in the rank list). Thus the line should be connected to the highest peak. This technique is known as the *semi-Cranfield* method; an average curve of this method is presented in Fig. 5-17(b), together with curves of the other two types. The comparison is affected slightly by a different tied rank pro-

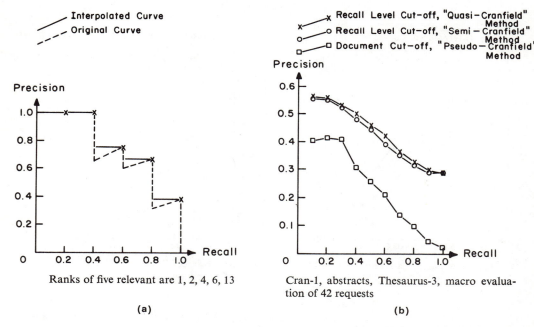

Ranks of five relevant are 1, 2, 4, 6, 13

(a)

Cran-1, abstracts, Thesaurus-3, macro evaluation of 42 requests

(b)

Fig. 5-17   Illustrations of the recall levels cut-off—"semi-Cranfield" method: (a) curve for individual request Q268, Cran-1, Thesaurus-2, using recall levels cut-off—"semi-Cranfield" method; (b) average curves to compare cut-offs.

cedure used for the semi-Cranfield curve, but any differences due to this effect are very small indeed. In fact the quasi-Cranfield and semi-Cranfield methods result in a quite similar performance curve, but the latter does give the theoretical maximum performance that a user could achieve. Other choices of cutoff to be used at the vertical segments would produce curves positioned lower on the graph than for these two methods and would probably reflect a performance that is more typical of user experience. However, for experimental test comparisons, the procedures used are completely adequate.

5-3-C Extrapolation Techniques for Request Generality Variations

Discussion of the recall level cutoff techniques suggests consideration of one further problem, caused by the variation in numbers of relevant documents for different requests. The problem is that requests having few relevant documents cannot exhibit low recall values and therefore have shorter precision-recall curves than those that have many relevant documents. The extreme example is furnished by a request with only one relevant document, where the performance on a graph is reflected by only a single point on the graph, somewhere at 1.0 recall. The question arises as to whether the performance of such a request should still be incorporated in the average results at recall levels lower than 1.0, and five possible methods are suggested.

The first method is to use individual precision-recall curves only at points where they can in fact be drawn by methods discussed in Sec. 5-3-B; at low recall values, only those requests having many relevant documents will then enter into the averages. Figure 5-18 gives an example based on 42 requests, where the numbers of requests that would enter into the averages are given at each of 10 recall levels. Although

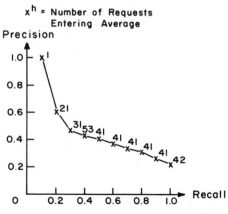

Cran-1, abstracts, stem, "quasi-Cranfield" cutoff, macro evaluation of 42 requests

Fig. 5-18 Illustration of first method of averaging where individual requests have varying amounts of relevant documents.

this method is quite simple to use and gives quite acceptable results for "internal" test comparisons, any attempts to compare dissimilar request sets are complicated by different request generality distributions.

All the other suggested methods use some technique of extrapolation, so that all requests have full length precision-recall curves that extend from 0.0 to 1.0 recall. The second method involves extrapolation of the beginning of all curves to 0.0 precision at 0.0 recall. Four examples using different numbers of relevant and different rank positions are given in Fig. 5-19. This method is justified mathematically, since if no documents are retrieved (case a and c), recall is 0, and precision is strictly zero; if the first document retrieved is nonrelevant, recall is zero, and precision zero ($0/\geqq 1 = 0$). The disadvantage of this method is that the intermediate values introduced by the extrapolation lines do not make much sense.

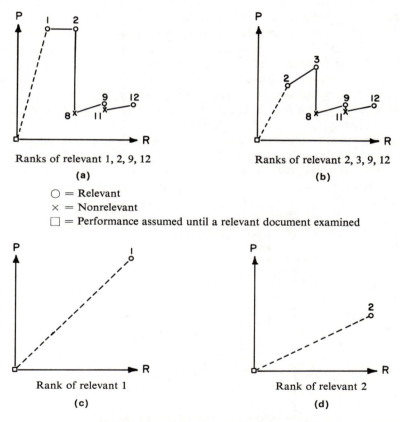

Ranks of relevant 1, 2, 9, 12

(a)

Ranks of relevant 2, 3, 9, 12

(b)

○ = Relevant
× = Nonrelevant
□ = Performance assumed until a relevant document examined

Rank of relevant 1

(c)

Rank of relevant 2

(d)

Fig. 5-19 Illustrations of second method of "left end extrapolation": (a) first document relevant, total relevant > 1; (b) first document nonrelevant, total relevant > 1; (c) total relevant 1, first document relevant; (d) total relevant 1, first document nonrelevant.

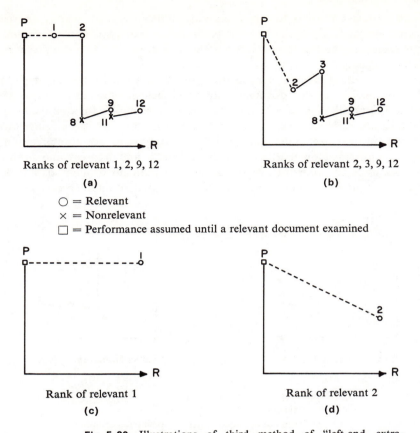

Ranks of relevant 1, 2, 9, 12

(a)

Ranks of relevant 2, 3, 9, 12

(b)

○ = Relevant
× = Nonrelevant
□ = Performance assumed until a relevant document examined

Rank of relevant 1

(c)

Rank of relevant 2

(d)

Fig. 5-20 Illustrations of third method of "left-end extrapolation": (a) first document relevant, total relevant > 1; (b) first document nonrelevant, total relevant > 1; (c) total relevant 1, first document relevant; (d) total relevant 1, first document nonrelevant.

The third method uses extrapolation of all curves to 1.0 precision at 0.0 recall and is used normally by SMART together with the quasi-Cranfield recall level cutoff. Figure 5-20 reproduces the four previous examples processed in the indicated manner. In documentary terms when no documents are examined (cases a and c), precision may in a sense be regarded as perfect, hence the 1.0 precision point is used. Cases b and d pose a problem for the precision ratio, since retrieval of only nonrelevant documents normally indicates zero precision, but the 1.0 precision ratio is used here for these cases for reasons of simplicity as well. As with the second method, the primary disadvantage is that intermediate values introduced by the extrapolation lines have no user-oriented meaning.

The fourth method is proposed in an attempt to reflect more correctly precision in cases b and d, where only nonrelevant documents are retrieved. Thus if no documents are retrieved at all, a 1.0 precision and 0.0 recall is used; if only nonrelevant documents are retrieved first, then 0.0 precision at 0.0 recall is used. Figure 5-21 gives the examples, but this hybrid combination of methods 2 and 3 still provides poor meaning to a user.

The fifth method uses an extrapolation at constant precision; that is, the precision ratio of the first relevant document retrieved is held constant as the curve is extrapolated to 0.0 recall. Figure 5-22 includes the four examples for this method. This method has the best documentary interpretation from a user viewpoint, since intermediate points on the extrapolated part of the curve do give an accurate precision ratio that can be achieved at low recall value in cases a and b, and in cases c and d this extrapolation seems to be fairer for averaging purposes than any of methods 2 to 4. This does mean that the precision value at low recall is dependent on the precision achieved

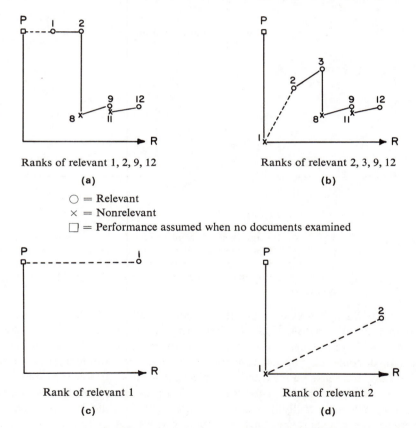

Ranks of relevant 1, 2, 9, 12

(a)

Ranks of relevant 2, 3, 9, 12

(b)

○ = Relevant
× = Nonrelevant
□ = Performance assumed when no documents examined

Rank of relevant 1

(c)

Rank of relevant 2

(d)

Fig. 5-21 Illustrations of fourth method of "left end extrapolation": (a) first document relevant, total relevant > 1; (b) first document nonrelevant, total relevant > 1; (c) total relevant 1, first document relevant; (d) total relevant 1, first document nonrelevant.

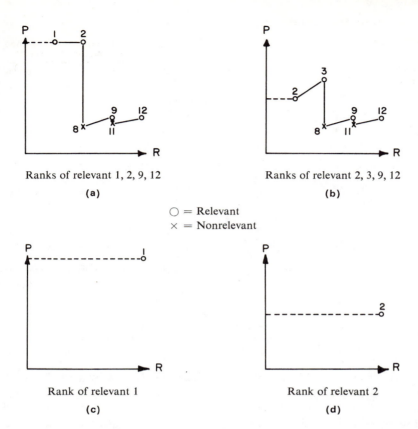

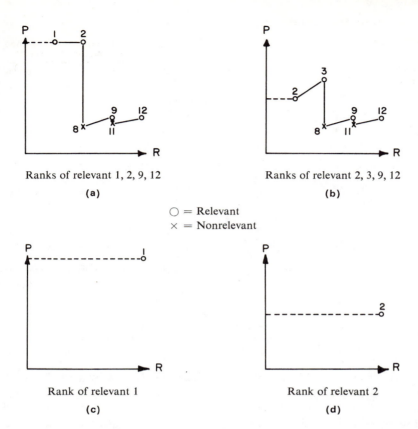

Ranks of relevant 1, 2, 9, 12

(a)

Ranks of relevant 2, 3, 9, 12

(b)

○ = Relevant
× = Nonrelevant

Rank of relevant 1

(c)

Rank of relevant 2

(d)

Fig. 5-22 Illustrations of fifth method of "left end extrapolation": (a) first document relevant, total relevant > 1; (b) first document nonrelevant, total relevant > 1; (c) total relevant 1, first document relevant; (d) total relevant 1, first document nonrelevant.

when the first relevant document is encountered, and a later relevant document may give slightly higher precision (as in Fig. 5-22, case b); usually, the extrapolation is sensible.

The foregoing discussion of different techniques for extrapolation is partly an academic one, since in the test comparisons made within SMART comparative merit will not be affected by choice of extrapolation method when the request set is unaltered. Method 3, which has been used in runs made at Harvard, does not correctly indicate merit at the left end of the curve, if comparisons involving changes in request sets or average generality are to be made. For example, three hypothetical requests with differing numbers of relevant items are seen in Fig. 5-23(a) to be served badly by this method at, let us say, 0.2 recall, where merit of the three requests is really the reverse of the fact. For this reason, it is preferable that in further work extrapolation method 5 be used. A comparison of methods 3 and 5 is made in Fig.

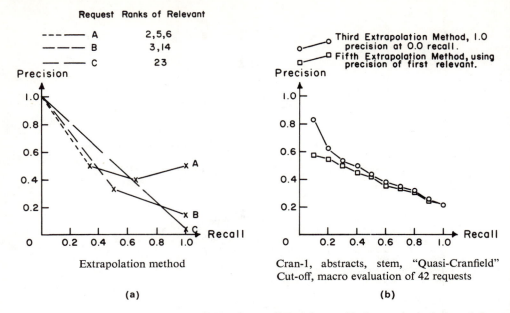

Extrapolation method

(a)

Cran-1, abstracts, stem, "Quasi-Cranfield"
Cut-off, macro evaluation of 42 requests

(b)

Fig. 5-23 Comparisons of extrapolation methods three and five:
(a) three individual requests using 1.0 precision at 0.0 recall; (b)
comparison of two extrapolation methods using averaged results.

5-23(b), which shows that the difference in curves averaged by a recall level (quasi-Cranfield) cutoff, is quite small except at the high precision end. If it were important to know, at each recall level on the curve, how many of the requests are averaged using an extrapolated part of the individual curves, and how many have enough relevant items to actually enter the average without extrapolation, then this information can be recorded at the ten recall levels on the curve, as was done in Fig. 5-18.

5-3-D Extrapolation Techniques for Evaluation of Cluster Searching

Experiments on cluster searching, many of which are described in other chapters of this book, raise an additional problem when precision-recall curves of cluster results are to be averaged. The difficulty arises because, when only certain clusters of documents are searched, rather than the total collection, some of the relevant documents are frequently not examined, so that no rank positions exist for these relevant documents. This phenomenon is both an expected and an important one, since this "recall ceiling" is one of the measures used to evaluate cluster searching. An ideal precision curve that would result from a cluster search averaged over many requests would commence in the usual manner at the high precision end but would go only as far as the recall ceiling, thus allowing a comparison with the ordinary full search curve only up to that recall ceiling.

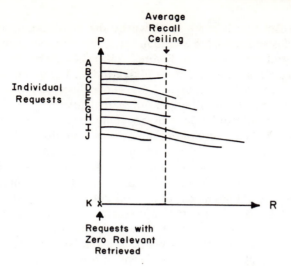

Fig. 5-24 Representation of the cluster search evaluation problem.

The problem is illustrated in Fig. 5-24 for some hypothetical individual requests. There it is seen that some requests naturally do not reach the average recall ceiling, some exceed it, and others are not included on the plot at all, since no relevant documents at all are found in the cluster search. One solution would be to include in the average curve only those requests which supply some results, so that as the average curve approaches the recall ceiling it would be based on fewer than the total requests. Other methods can also be suggested which employ extrapolation techniques so that every request enters into the whole of the average curve.

The first additional suggested extrapolation technique has been used exclusively in test results obtained so far with the SMART system. As Fig. 5-25 shows for three individual requests, the recall ceiling reached by the search results (0.4 in cases b and c) is extrapolated linearly to the 1.0 recall points, using the precision gained in the full

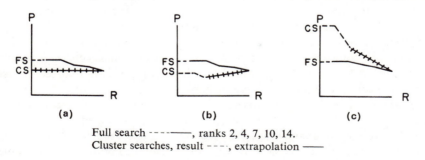

Full search - - - - ——, ranks 2, 4, 7, 10, 14.
Cluster searches, result - - - -, extrapolation ——

Fig. 5-25 The extrapolation technique used to construct average precision-recall curves for cluster searches: (a) cluster ranks— none; (b) cluster ranks—3, 7; (c) cluster ranks—1, 3.

search. Since the full search curve is drawn by the quasi-Cranfield cutoff method, this means that cluster results are extrapolated to the precision achieved by the last relevant document in the full search. Figure 5-25(a) shows what happens to a cluster result in which no relevant documents at all are found. Using the left-end extrapolation method recommended in Sec. 5-3-C, the whole cluster curve is an extrapolation from the chosen point at 1.0 recall in the full search curve.

Extrapolation could also be done by assigning to those relevant documents not found in the cluster search a random rank position, bounded by the rank of the last document recovered by the cluster search and the total collection size. It would be feasible also to extrapolate by use of the precision achieved if the relevant documents not found were ranked in the worst possible positions, that is, assuming that recall 1.0 is obtained only as the last document in the collection is examined. A further suggestion is to use the full search curve before it reaches 1.0 recall and use some method of joining the end of the cluster curve to some point along the full search curve. No comparison of these methods has yet been made because the present technique is as satisfactory conceptually as any of the other suggestions.

5-4 MEASURES FOR VARYING RELEVANCE EVALUATION

Although the rendering of relevance decisions is a task quite separate from the considerations which go into the construction of performance measures reflecting system effectiveness, it may be desirable to use performance measures based on grades of relevance rather than on binary decision of "relevant" or "nonrelevant" alone. The performance characteristic curve suggested by Giuliano and Jones [8] is designed to use spectra of relevance; in their view the usual precision and recall can be used only in situations where relevance decisions are black or white. An example of a performance characteristic curve using relevance grades is given in Fig. 5-26(a). The CRAN-1 collection is used because grades of relevance on a scale of four are available for these relevance decisions; thus a "point score" is assigned to those requests, giving a score of four to the most relevant documents, three to the next, and two and one to the final two grades. Figure 5-26(a) then uses these cumulated relevance points on the *y* axis as indicating a type of recall and uses rank positions (cutoff ratio) on the *x* axis. Two dictionaries are compared, and the best possible performance curve is displayed.

However, as has been demonstrated in reference [2], it is not correct to assume that precision and recall are incapable of handling relevance grades. Figure 5-26(b) uses the same data and displays two precision-recall graphs, where recall is based on the relevance points score rather than on the more usual document score. In fact, the merit of the two options compared is quite identical—and must be so mathematically— so that the curves cross at the same point. Furthermore, the rank position value can be indicated on the precision-recall graph as shown. The performance characteristic curve does not give any directly visible information about the amount of nonrelevant material being retrieved; the conclusion is then that precision is of value here.

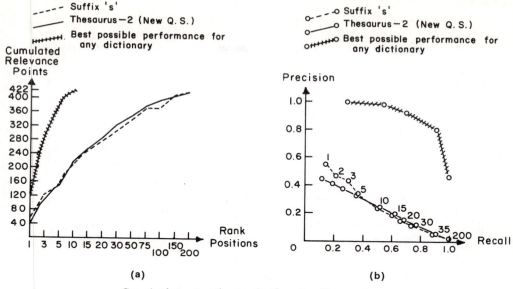

Cran-1, abstracts, micro evaluation over 42 requests

Fig. 5-26 Performance curves that are based on grades of relevance: (a) performance characteristic curve using relevance points; (b) precision-recall curve, with recall based on relevance points, "pseudo-Cranfield" cut-off.

It is also quite simple to modify the single number measures to incorporate grades of relevance. For example, using the normalized recall measure, a *weighted normalized recall* may be defined as

$$\text{Weighted normalized recall} = 1 - \frac{\sum_{i=1}^{n} (r_i \, w_i) - \sum_{i=1}^{n} (i w_i)}{n \, (N - n)},$$

where

n = number of relevant documents,

N = number of documents in collection,

r_i = rank of ith relevant document,

w_i = weight score derived from relevance grade of ith relevant document.

This equation therefore uses the sum of the products of the ranks and the weight scores of the relevant documents, rather than the sum of the ranks alone as in conventional normalized recall. Some examples given in Fig. 5-27 will clarify the use of this measure.

Figure 5-27(a) illustrates a perfect case, where the four relevant documents are given relevance grade weights of 4 (most highly relevant), 3, 2, and 1 (least relevant).

	RELEVANCE	
Rank	*Grade*	*Products*
1	4	4
2	3	6
3	2	6
4	1	4
	Sum of Products 20	
	Weighted Normed. Recall 1.000	

(a)

	RELEVANCE	
Rank	*Grade*	*Products*
1	1	1
2	2	4
3	3	9
4	4	16
	Sum of Products 30	
	Weighted Normed. Recall .9872	

(b)

	RELEVANCE	
Rank	*Grade*	*Products*
1	4	4
3	3	9
4	2	8
9	1	9
	Sum of Products 30	
	Weighted Normed. Recall .9872	

(c)

	RELEVANCE	
Rank	*Grade*	*Products*
3	3	9
13	2	26
19	4	76
41	2	82
	Sum of Products 193	
	Weighted Normed. Recall .7844	

(d)

Fig. 5-27 Examples of use of weighted normalized recall: (a) perfect ranks and perfect relevance grade order; (b) perfect ranks and worst relevance grade order; (c) less than perfect ranks and perfect relevance grade order; (d) actual performance of Cran-1 request Q167, suffix "s" dictionary.

Performance in rank position is perfect, as is the order in which the relevant documents are ranked, so a weighted normalized recall of 1.0 results. Figures 5-27(b) and (c) show cases of less than optimum relevance grades and ranks, respectively, although both have equal merit in weighted normalized recall. This illustrates the fact that a different range of weights assigned to the relevance grades could be used to adjust the relative effect of ranking and relevance grade ordering. An actual result is given in Fig. 5-27(d).

5-5 MEASURES FOR VARYING GENERALITY COMPARISONS

The generality number defined in Sec. 5-2 reflects the concentration of relevant documents in a given collection. From a user viewpoint, the greater the number of relevant documents in a system, the higher the probability is of finding relevant documents at a given cutoff point. Comparing the ADI and CRAN-1 collections, for example, although the average request has a similar number of relevant documents in both collections (4.9 ADI, 4.7 CRAN-1), the differing collection sizes (82 ADI, 200 CRAN-1) show that the concentration of relevant items favors the ADI collection. This may be observed by imagining a user, who examines every document in both collections in order to be certain of gaining 1.0 recall, and who will finally end up with a precision ratio of 0.0592 in ADI and 0.0236 in CRAN-1 (at this cutoff point, the precision ratio becomes the generality number itself). Thus higher precision ratios are expected with higher generality numbers at all cutoff points in the curve, unless some other factors such as subject language or request and relevance decisions causes some strong effect over the low and middle recall regions of the curve.

Figure 5-28(a) includes a comparison of this type using the ADI (documentation) and CRAN-1 (aerodynamics) collections, where the expected merit is found above 0.7 recall; below that point, the ADI collection falls below CRAN-1. The reasons for this result are not important to the present discussion relating to measurements. From the user viewpoint, the comparison in Fig. 5-28(a) reflects merit accurately, but from a system viewpoint, the change in generality number makes the ADI collection more hospitable to good retrieval than CRAN-1; thus a measure is needed to take this into account.

As was suggested in Sec. 5-1, the value of d (Fig. 5-1, total nonrelevant items not examined) is needed for system comparisons; Fig. 5-1 also defines the fallout ratio as used in the Cranfield Project [2]. Figure 5-28(b) gives a fallout recall graph of the ADI and CRAN-1 results, which shows that CRAN-1 is now correctly superior over the whole performance range, except at 1.0 recall where both curves meet. It is also possible to represent this system viewpoint result in a precision-recall graph, since an equation to adjust precision for generality is given in reference [2]; namely,

$$\text{Adjusted precision ratio} = \frac{R_1 \times G}{(R_1 \times G) + F_1 (1000 - G)},$$

where

R_1 = recall ratio at a given cutoff point,

F_1 = fallout ratio at a given out-off point,

G = generality number (1000 $\times$ total relevant)/(collection size) to which it is desired to alter the results.

Thus, in Fig. 5-28(c), the ADI recall and fallout ratios are recorded as R_1 and F_1 for a series of cutoff points, and G is set to 23.6 in order to adjust the generality of ADI to fit the generality of CRAN-1. The adjusted precision versus recall curve is given in Fig. 5-28(c). It should be noted that the precision for ADI does not now represent a user-oriented evaluation but has been adjusted artificially to give a system-oriented evaluation. A series of tables appears in reference [2] in which the fallout values for ranges of recall and precision values have been computed for a range of generality numbers, primarily to permit quick calculation of adjusted precision ratios. It should be emphasized, however, that the ordinary precision-recall curve still gives a valid and

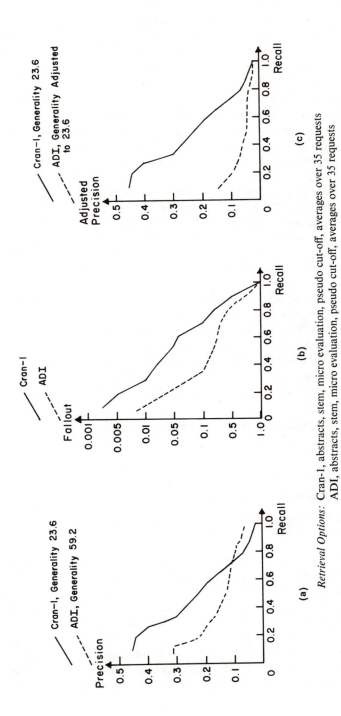

Retrieval Options: Cran-1, abstracts, stem, micro evaluation, pseudo cut-off, averages over 35 requests
ADI, abstracts, stem, micro evaluation, pseudo cut-off, averages over 35 requests

Fig. 5-28 Techniques for performance comparison in situations of different generality: (a) precision-recall, with variation in generality; (b) fallout-recall, which allows for generality; (c) precision-recall with adjustment giving constant generality.

useful user-oriented result, and it is in experimental test comparisons only that the two viewpoints for evaluation (Fig. 5-2) give different and complementary results.

5-6 TECHNIQUES FOR DISSIMILAR SYSTEM COMPARISONS AND OPERATIONAL TESTING

Comparisons between systems of a semiautomatic nature, such as SMART, with more conventional mechanized or manual systems, such as the Medlars system, introduce many theoretical and practical problems. Although direct comparisons of such dissimilar systems are almost impossible to make, one small part of the problem concerning performance measurement can be discussed. This relates to the ability to compare the retrieval performance of a system that produces a ranked output, such as SMART, with a system that conventionally uses a search term-matching cutoff, retrieving unordered sets of documents of generally uncontrollable numbers.

For experimental systems that use search term-matching cutoffs, such as the Cranfield Project which uses techniques of "coordination levels," it is possible to obtain full precision versus recall curves if very exhaustive search programs are used to establish many cutoff points; the resulting curves can then be compared to the curves produced by SMART. If a direct comparison of this sort is not possible, then an alternative is to apply to the nonranking system a simple random-ranking technique that places relevant documents in random positions in each of the large sets of retrieved documents, as has been done at Cranfield.

For operational system comparisons, however, such exhaustive searching is rarely possible, and tests of such systems usually produce just one precision-recall pair, or at the most, three or four quite closely positioned pairs. In such cases, a comparison may be made by making the SMART results fit in with those of the non-ranking system. This is accomplished by choosing cutoffs in SMART searches that are in some way identical to the cutoffs made in the nonranking system. In a rather simple test comparison, for example, the 35 ADI requests were hand searched in a KWIC type concordance of the ADI–abstracts collection, and the result compared with the SMART abstracts–thesaurus retrieval run. The hand searches were based on four or five keywords for each request, and the final performance of what was intended to be a medium precision at medium recall search was 0.22 precision at 0.72 recall. Comparison with SMART requires an examination of each individual hand-searched request to see how many documents were retrieved, followed by the generation of a cutoff in the SMART ranked output at an identical point to obtain one comparable precision recall pair. The SMART result produced 0.16 precision at 0.64 recall. Naturally the hand search benefited from the free choice that was allowed for any synonyms known to the searcher, and higher recall in the hand search would have required choices of further keywords. SMART's fully ranked output would allow high precision at low recall (0.31 precision, 0.31 recall, and cutoff 4 documents), or high recall (0.84 recall, 0.11 precision, and cutoff 33 documents) simply by examining more or less of the output. Techniques of this type have been used in comparisons of SMART and Medlars searches using a common set of documents and requests.

A final consideration for evaluation of operational tests pertains to the appropriate measures to be used. So far experimental tests of the SMART system have measured the recall ratio on the basis of the total relevant items in the collection. Although this accurately simulates users with a high recall requirement, those users with a high precision requirement are probably not served too well by the high precision end of the same curve. The reason is that at least some users wanting high precision are not at all concerned about getting high recall, and since they wish only to see, let us say, one, two, or three relevant items, they are clearly satisfied on the recall side long before 100% recall of the total relevant items in the collection is achieved. It is suggested that in semi-operational tests which will be made in SMART in the future, a *relative recall* be computed:

$$\text{Relative recall} = \frac{\text{Total relevant examined}}{\text{Total relevant user would like to examine}}.$$

This ratio is relative to user satisfaction rather than to total system resources. Several adjustments might be made for actual tests, since some users would perhaps examine more relevant than they intended (1.5 recall would not be very useful for evaluation purposes), and other users might wish to see more relevant than were available in the system at all (an acquisitions, rather than retrieval failure).

5-7 THE COMPARISON OF SPECIFIC AND GENERAL REQUESTS AND THE VIEWPOINTS OF THE HIGH PRECISION AND HIGH RECALL USER

The comparison of a set of "specific" requests with a set of "general" requests provides an environment of acute change in request generality. Isolation of specific from general requests is carried out by dividing a given request set into equal or nearly equal groups according to the numbers of documents in the collection that are relevant. The comparison of the specific and general request sets then involves a very large change in average generality, although the collection size is unaltered. To illustrate the problems caused by this type of comparison further, the set of 21 specific requests will be compared with the 21 general requests in the CRAN-1 aerodynamics collection, using the stem dictionary results.

Since the generality change suggests that fallout should be used in place of precision, a fallout versus recall plot is given in Fig. 5-29(a). Apart from a slight crossing of the curves between 0.8 and 0.9 recall, the specific requests are seen to have a superior performance, from the point of view of system efficiency. The precision versus recall plot, however, will reflect a direct performance comparison ignoring the generality change, so a plot of this type is given in Fig. 5-29(b), where it is now seen that except between 0.25 and 0.4 recall the general requests have a superior performance. It should be noted that a pseudo-Cranfield type of cutoff is used here for comparison of specific

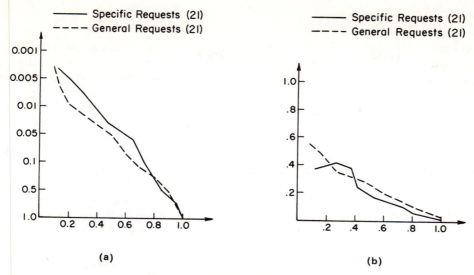

(a)

(b)

Fig. 5-29 Cran-1 abstracts stem, micro evaluation, pseudo-Cranfield cut-off, averages over 21 requests: (a) system efficiency evaluation; (b) user satisfaction evaluation.

and general requests, since a plot of the quasi-Cranfield type as used in reference [4] gives a large bias in favor of the specific requests. This occurs because the specific requests all require greater lengths of left-end extrapolation, and the technique used for extrapolating to 1.0 precision at 0.0 recall (method 3, Sec. 5-3-C, Fig. 5-20) produces specific requests with falsely high precision values at low recall for the specific requests.

A partial explanation of the data contained in Fig. 5-29 is given in Fig. 5-30.

Perfor-mance	SPECIFIC REQUESTS (63 relevant) Cutoff, n documents					GENERAL REQUESTS (135 relevant) Cutoff, n documents				
	$n=1$	2	3	4	5	$n=1$	2	3	4	5
Total retrieved	21	42	63	84	105	21	42	63	84	105
Relevant retrieved	8	17	24	25	26	11	20	27	33	38
Nonrelevant retrieved	13	25	39	59	79	10	22	36	51	67
Recall	.13	.27	.38	.40	.41	.08	.15	.20	.24	.28
Fallout	.00314	.00604	.00943	.01426	.00910	.00246	.00541	.00886	.01255	.01648
Precision	.38	.41	.38	.30	.25	.52	.48	.43	.39	.36

Fig. 5-30 Details of comparison of specific and general requests at the first five document cutoffs (Cran-1 collection, abstracts, stem dictionary, macro average over 21 specific and 21 general requests).

At each of the cutoff points shown, the general requests produce a greater number of relevant and a smaller number of nonrelevant than the specific requests. But also at each cutoff, the recall ratios favor the specific requests, and both fallout and precision ratios favor the general requests. The recall merit is explained by noting that the smaller number of total relevant in the specific requests makes each one "count" for more in recall, since one relevant found in the specific requests increases recall by 0.016, and one relevant found in the general requests increases recall by 0.008. Clearly the fallout and precision merit is affected by the higher concentration of relevant documents found in the general requests. It is not clear that fallout is free from the effects of generality in this sense, and therefore it is not certain that the fallout versus recall plot truly reflects system effectiveness when a generality change of this type is encountered. Also, since recall is affected here by the difference in request generality, it is not certain that recall accurately reflects user satisfaction, although it obviously does measure what the user examines.

This last difficulty arises because it is not really clear just how the positions should be weighted when specific and general requests are compared. Six examples for comparison are given in Fig. 5-31; if some rational hand ranking of the merit of these six requests is not possible, then no satisfactory performance measure to compare specific and general requests can be derived. One obvious solution is to recognize formally what has often been stated, namely, that user needs differ considerably and that the two ends of the spectrum may be represented by the high recall need and the high precision need. For example, if the high precision need is defined to mean that the best precision should be obtained in the process of finding just two relevant documents only, then the cases A, D, and F, in Fig. 5-31 are superior to B, E, and C. Also, if the high recall need is defined to mean that a full 1.0 recall is required, then the best performance will be achieved when perfect recall is reached quickly and has high precision, so that in Fig. 5-31 cases A, D, and B are superior to C, F, and E. Making the further distinction that A, B, and C are specific and D, E, and F are general requests, this hypothetical example shows that the high precision user is served best on the average by the general requests, and the high recall user is served best by the specific requests.

The cases in Fig. 5-31 are chosen to be typical of the results obtained in the CRAN-1 request sets being used. One method of presenting average results that

Generality	Request	Ranks of Relevant
Specific {	A	1, 2, 10
	B	3, 4, 17
	C	7, 21, 45
General {	D	1, 2, 5, 7, 8, 9, 14, 15
	E	3, 7, 10, 22, 33, 37, 49, 51
	F	1, 2, 8, 10, 11, 29, 36, 47

Fig. 5-31 Rank positions of the relevant documents for six hypothetical requests.

| SPECIFIC REQUESTS | | | GENERAL REQUESTS | | |
| Average Rank of: | | | Average Rank of: | | |
First Relevant	Second Relevant	Third Relevant	First Relevant	Second Relevant	Third Relevant
11.1	18.0	48.8	4.6	8.2	95.3

Cran-1 Abstract, Stem Dictionary

Fig. 5-32 Comparison of specific and general requests using the average rank position of the first, second, and last ranked relevant documents.

reflects the success achieved in meeting the two different types of user need is given in Fig. 5-32. The high precision and high recall needs are based on the definitions given in the previous paragraph. An average rank position is thus calculated for the first- and second-ranked relevant documents (for a high precision merit), and for the last-ranked relevant document (for a high recall merit). It can now be concluded that the high precision user is served best by the general requests, and the high recall user by the specific requests. However, the computation of the arithmetic mean rank is sometimes a poor representation of the data, since the variance can be large, and one or two very bad requests can unduly influence the average. Some type of histogram would solve this problem but at the cost of a somewhat more complex presentation. One compromise solution is suggested by Fig. 5-33, where information on the rank of the first relevant is rearranged to show the numbers of search requests that produce a given rank (in three ranges) for the first relevant.

This comparison of specific and general requests on behalf of both high precision and high recall users requires more experimental work, since it is expected that there may also be some correlation between user needs and request generality, with high precision users tending to pose general requests, and high recall users tending to pose specific requests. Further work is required to develop methods of constructing plots of the precision versus recall type to represent high precision and high recall

| | NUMBER OF REQUESTS WITH RANK OF FIRST RELEVANT = | | |
Request sets	1–2	3–10	>10
Specific	10	8	3
General	14	4	3

Cran-1, Abstract, Stem Dictionary

Fig. 5-33 Comparison of specific and general requests showing the numbers of requests that rank the first ranked relevant document in three ranges.

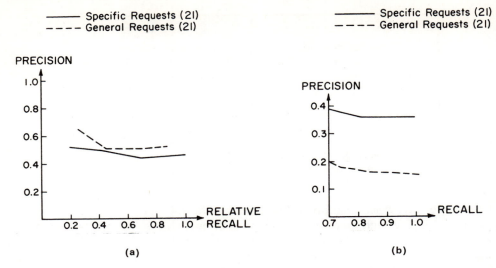

Fig. 5-34   Cran-1 abstracts stem, micro evaluation, pseudo cut-off with final cut-off at last relevant, average over 21 requests: (a) evaluation from viewpoint of user satisfaction for high precision users; (b) evaluation from viewpoint of user satisfaction for high recall users.

runs, both separately and in one combined plot. A suggestion for two individual plots is made in Fig. 5-34 where the CRAN-1 results are used again. Evaluation for the high precision user is made in Fig. 5-34(a) by use of standard precision versus "relative recall" (defined in Sec. 5-6), with relative recall here based on retrieval of just two relevant documents for each request. This plot assumes that the searches will make a final cutoff after the second relevant document is reached; for several reasons the totalling procedure is basically the pseudo-Cranfield one. Figure 5-34(b) reflects the interests of the high recall user, and standard recall commences measurement on the plot at a recall of 0.7. This plot is less satisfactory than the other because a search strategy and cutoff that would be adopted by a user wanting high recall is not easy to simulate. Thus a cutoff is established at the last relevant document using the pseudo-Cranfield totalling method in order to show the maximum difference in precision that could occur at 1.0 recall comparing the specific and general requests, and assuming that an optimum cutoff were chosen.

The suitability of the normalized meures for comparison of specific and general requests needs to be investigated further. Since both the equations used contain N, the collection size, some allowance is made for generality, and in seven out of eight cases observed so far, both the normalized measures provide the same merit between specific and general requests as that shown by the fallout versus recall plot. This means that the normalized measures tend to reflect the merit experienced by a high recall user.

5-8 THE PRESENTATION OF DATA AS INDIVIDUAL REQUEST MERIT

Evaluation methodology using averaged measures always suppresses some data, and when the variance of individual requests is large, the arithmetic mean may be a poor measure of merit. For this reason, presentation of results using averages should be followed in each case by data on the individual requests. For example, if normalized recall averaged over 12 requests shows one option to be quite superior to another, individual request examination might reveal that six of the requests favored the option that was superior on average, four favored the other option, and two had an identical performance on both options. The tables used to present this type of data usually give both the numbers of requests favoring each option together with those equal on both options; in addition, percentages are produced to aid speedy interpretation. Several ways of computing the percentages are possible, and six methods are illustrated in Fig. 5-35. Percentages including the equal cases are needed when the number of such cases is large and may be given either in the form of row 3 or 4. The "superiority percentage" has the advantage of a single number presentation.

An extension of this type of comparison is the presentation of the magnitudes of the differences in the merit of individual requests. A set of nine hypothetical request results is given in Fig. 5-36, comparing three options. A table of the numbers of requests preferring options I and II would show that 66.7% prefer option II, and 33.3% prefer option I. However, since the average normalized recall values given in Fig. 5-36(a) show that options I and II have almost identical merit, it is clear that the three requests preferring I over II do so by quite large amounts, and the six preferring II over I by smaller amounts. The magnitude difference plot in Fig. 5-36(b) is designed to show this situation visually. The requests favoring each option are arranged in decreas-

	NUMBER AND PERCENTAGES OF INDIVIDUAL REQUESTS			
	Option I	*Option II*	*Both Options Equal*	*"Superiority" Percentage*
1. Numbers	6	4	2	
2. Percentages ignoring equal cases	60%	40%	–	20%
3. Percentages including equal cases	50%	33%	17%	17%
4. Percentages adding equal cases to both options	67%	50%	–	17%

Fig. 5-35 Illustration of methods of computing percentages of the numbers of requests favoring given options.

	NORMALIZED RECALL		
Req.	*Option I*	*Option II*	*Option III*
A	.8125	.8000	.8135
B	.8250	.8000	.8135
C	.8010	.8000	.7810
D	.8000	.8100	.7850
E	.8000	.8080	.7900
F	.8000	.8060	.7950
G	.8000	.8040	.7990
H	.8000	.8020	.8080
I	.8000	.8010	.8150

(a)

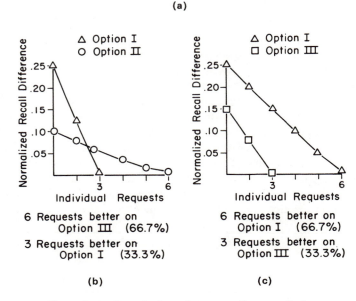

6 Requests better on
Option III (66.7%)

3 Requests better on
Option I (33.3%)

(b)

6 Requests better on
Option I (66.7%)

3 Requests better on
Option III (33.3%)

(c)

Fig. 5-36 Illustration of method used to compile magnitude difference plot: (a) results of nine hypothetical requests; (b) plot of differences comparing options I and II; (c) plot of differences comparing options I and III.

ing order of their performance differences across the plot, and since the areas underneath both curves are nearly equal, this reflects the fact that both options have nearly identical averages. Further, since the option I curve terminates some way short of the option II curve on the x axis, this indicates that more individual requests favor II. Another comparison is given in Fig. 5-36(c), where option I is seen to be superior to option II both in the averages and in the individual requests.

REFERENCES

[1] G. Salton, The Evaluation of Computer-Based Information Retrieval Systems, *Proceedings 1965 International FID Congress*, Spartan Books, New York, 1966.

[2] C. Cleverdon and M. Keen, Factors Determining the Performance of Indexing Systems, *Test Results*, Vol. 2, Aslib–Cranfield Research Project, Cranfield, England, 1966.

[3] J. A. Swets, Effectiveness of Information Retrieval Methods, *Report No. 1499, Bolt, Beranek, and Newman, Inc.*, Cambridge, Mass., Draft, April 1967; also in *American Documentation*, Vol. 20, No. 1, January 1969.

[4] G. Salton, The Evaluation of Automatic Retrieval Procedures—Selected Test Results Using the SMART System, *American Documentation*, Vol. 16, No. 3, July 1965 (Also *Report ISR-8*, Section IV).

[5] J. J. Rocchio, Jr., Evaluation Viewpoints in Document Retrieval, Information Storage and Retrieval, *Report ISR-9* to the National Science Foundation, Section XXI, Harvard Computation Laboratory, Cambridge, Mass., August 1965; also Chap. 4 of this volume.

[6] J. J. Rocchio, Jr., Document Retrieval Systems—Optimization and Evaluation, Doctoral thesis, *Report ISR-10* to the National Science Foundation, Harvard Computation Laboratory, Cambridge, Mass., April 1966.

[7] J. A. Swets, Information Retrieval Systems, *Science*, Vol. 141, July 19, 1963.

[8] V. E. Giuliano and P. E. Jones, Study and Test of Methodology for Laboratory Evaluation of Message Retrieval Systems, *Report ESD-TR-66-405*, Little, Brown & Company, Boston, August 1966.

[9] G. Salton and M. E. Lesk, Computer Evaluation of Indexing and Text Processing, *Report ISR-12* to the National Science Foundation, Section III, Cornell University, Ithaca, N.Y., June 1967; also in *Journal of the ACM*, Vol. 15, No. 11, January 1968, pp. 8–36; also Chap. 7 of this volume.

[10] S. J. Sillers, Distinguishing Retrieved from Nonretrieved Information: The Cut-off Problem, Information Storage and Retrieval, *Report ISR-9* to the National Science Foundation, Section XXII, Harvard Computation Laboratory, Cambridge, Mass., August 1965.

PART *III*

LANGUAGE ANALYSIS

The role of dictionaries and authority lists in an information retrieval environment is examined. A variety of dictionary types are described with emphasis on their use as part of a system for natural language analysis. Several methods are also suggested for the automatic or semiautomatic dictionary construction.

6

INFORMATION ANALYSIS and DICTIONARY CONSTRUCTION†

G. SALTON and M. E. LESK

6-1 INTRODUCTION

The basis of any information system is believed generally to consist of a system of information analysis, used to decide what a given information item or a given search request is all about. In a conventional library system, this analysis may be performed by a human agent who uses established classification schedules to decide what category, or categories, will fit a given item most reasonably. In certain other well-known indexing systems, keywords or index terms may be assigned manually to documents and search requests, to be used for the identification of information content.

Regardless of what type of analysis is performed and, in particular, regardless of whether the analysis is done manually or automatically, it is necessary to start with a set of carefully prepared instructions which specify the allowable steps and set forth in detail the meanings and implications of choosing one or another of the permissible alternatives. These instructions are often collected in the form of dictionaries of various types, listing the allowable information identifiers and giving a definition for each which regularizes and

†This study was published originally as Section II of *Scientific Report ISR-11*, June 1966; a somewhat altered version was published under the title Information Dissemination and Automatic Information Systems, *Proc. IEEE*, Vol. 54, No. 12, December 1966.

controls its use. As will be seen, such dictionaries may take a variety of forms, including almost always so-called "see" references which provide links for entries to be replaced by other preferred terms, and "see also" references which designate cross-references applicable to the dictionary items. Negative dictionaries may also exist, containing terms or categories which should not be used for purposes of information identification.

In view of the importance of the initial information analysis and classification—all later search and retrieval operations are of course of no avail in the absence of a careful and consistent determination of information content—it is appropriate to examine in detail the problems connected with the generation and use of dictionaries. Accordingly, the present study specifies the form of a variety of dictionaries which have been found useful in information analysis and examines some of the principles of dictionary construction. Emphasis is placed on those dictionaries which can be used for natural language analysis, since many of the information items and of the search requests to be stored may be expected to be expressed by words or word strings in the natural language. Performance characteristics are given, based on search results obtained with various dictionaries, and several methods are suggested for the construction of dictionaries by semiautomatic means.

6-2 LANGUAGE ANALYSIS

Consider the problem of taking a document or search request in the natural language and of attempting to use some automatic procedure to generate content identifications for the input texts. Such a task immediately raises many difficulties brought about by the complexity of the language and by the irregularities which govern the syntactic and semantic structure. The following principal problems must be dealt with [1]:

1. Words which carry out syntactic functions but which do not contribute directly to the specification of information content must often be eliminated (but some words, such as "can" may occur both as significant and nonsignificant words).

2. Many distinct words may be used to supply the same or related meanings; such synonymous words or expressions must be recognized if an accurate content analysis of documents and search requests is to be undertaken.

3. Many words can be used in several different senses depending on the context (for example, "base" may variously represent military bases, lamp bases, bases in baseball, and so on); it is important to identify such homographs and, if possible, to recognize the proper meaning in a given context.

4. Many types of syntactic equivalences occur in the language, where completely different constructions are used to represent the same general idea; as an extension of the overall synonym problem, it is important to recognize at least the principal types of syntactic paraphrasing.

5. The use of indirect references is prevalent in the natural language, where pronouns, collective names, and other particles are used to refer to entities known presumably by the context; the identification of the proper antecedents of such pronouns is difficult, particularly for cases where many different words can operate as antecedents.

6. Relations may exist between words which are not contained in the text explicitly but which can be deduced from the context, or from other texts previously analyzed; the identification of such relations requires deductive capabilities of considerable power.

7. The meaning of many words may change with time, or contrariwise, new words may be created to refer to entities referred to previously in different terms (for example, the unit of time previously known as "millimicrosecond" is now generally known as "nanosecond").

   If the natural language is used as primary input to an information system, any content analysis system will have to include methods for consistent language normalization. One of the most effective ways for providing such a normalization is by means of suitably constructed dictionaries. The following types of dictionaries appear to be of interest in this connection:

1. A *negative dictionary* containing terms whose use is proscribed for content analysis purposes.

2. A *thesaurus,* or synonym dictionary, which specifies for each dictionary entry one or more synonym categories or concept classes; ambiguous entries are then replaced by many concepts, and many different words (synonyms) may map into the same concept category; a thesaurus is then used to perform a many-to-many mapping from word entries to concept classes.

3. A *phrase dictionary* may be used to specify the most frequently used word or concept combinations (called phrases); such a phrase dictionary can often increase the effectiveness of a content analysis by assigning for content identification a relatively unambiguous phrase instead of two or more ambiguous components (for example, the terms "program" and "language" are more ambiguous, standing alone, than the phrase "programming language").

4. A *hierarchical* (tree-like) *arrangement* of terms or concepts, similar to a standard library classification schedule which makes it possible, given a certain dictionary entry, to find more general concepts by going up in the hierarchy, or to find more specific ones by going down (for example, from a concept such as "syntax", one can obtain the more general "language" or the more specific "punctuation".

   Dictionaries do not, of course, eliminate language ambiguities completely, but they can serve to reduce the effects of many irregularities by using appropriate dictionary-mapping algorithms. For example, a correspondence between a word and a single concept may receive a higher weight than one between a word and a multiplicity of concepts, since the former presumably implies a unique meaning for that word, while the latter implies ambiguity.

Even if almost all terms used in a given context are inherently ambiguous, the juxtaposition of many multiple mappings can often identify the appropriate concept classes with reasonable accuracy. The relevant categories will be reinforced normally, since they apply to many terms, while the extraneous categories will be distributed randomly.

Consider, for example, the set of terms "base", "bat", "glove", and "hit". Each term is ambiguous, and a given multiple thesaurus mapping may specify the correspondences shown in Table 6-1. In that table, three categories are shown for the word "base", and two categories are shown for each of the other terms. Despite the apparent ambiguities, a document identified by the four original terms can nevertheless be assigned to the "baseball" class with reasonable expectation of success, since the other categories occur more or less at random for the given terms, whereas the "baseball" class is always present.

Table 6-1

SAMPLE THESAURUS MAPPING

| ORIGINAL TERMS | CONCEPT CLASSES | | | | |
	Lamps	*Games (Baseball)*	*Animals*	*Military Usage*	*Clothing*
Base	✓	✓		✓	
Bat		✓	✓		
Glove		✓			✓
Hit		✓		✓	

The principal advantages of synonym and phrase dictionaries for purposes of content identification may then be summarized as follows:

1. They permit a consistent assignment of concept classes to items of information thereby replacing either keywords and index terms assigned to documents and search requests, or the words occurring in them.

2. They can often be used to resolve ambiguities by looking at the pattern of occurrence of the concepts.

3. They can serve for the analysis of many different subject fields and for different types of usage, since it is possible to adapt the dictionary to the particular search environment.

On the negative side, dictionaries are often difficult to construct, particularly if the environment within which they are expected to operate is subject to change. Furthermore most dictionaries are useless unless their mode of usage is consistent for all operations. Obviously if a dictionary is used in one way for information classification and in another for information searching, an effective result cannot be guaranteed.

Various types of thesauri are examined in more detail in the next few paragraphs.

6-3 DICTIONARY CONSTRUCTION

6-3-A The Synonym Dictionary (Thesaurus)

As explained previously a thesaurus is a grouping of words, or word stems, into certain subject categories, hereafter called concept classes. A typical example is shown in Fig. 6-1, where the concept classes are represented by three-digit numbers, and the individual entries are shown under each concept number. In Fig. 6-2, a similar thesaurus arrangement is shown in alphabetical order of the words included. The concept numbers appear in the middle column of Fig. 6-2 (concept numbers over 32,000 are attached to "common" words which are not accepted as information identifiers); the last column consists of one or more three-digit syntax codes attached to the words to be used for purposes of syntactic analysis.

```
408  DISLOCATION            413  CAPACITANCE
     JUNCTION                    IMPEDANCE-MATCHING
     MINORITY-CARRIER            IMPEDANCE
     N-P-N                       INDUCTANCE
     P-N-P                       MUTUAL-IMPEDANCE
     POINT-CONTACT               MUTUAL-INDUCTANCE
     RECOMBINE                   MUTUAL
     TRANSITION                  NEGATIVE-RESISTANCE
     UNIJUNCTION                 POSITIVE-GAP
                                 REACTANCE
409  BLAST-COOLED                RESIST
     HEAT-FLOW                   SELF-IMPEDANCE
     HEAT-TRANSFER               SELF-INDUCTANCE
                                 SELF
410  ANNEAL
     STRAIN                 414  ANTENNA
                                 KLYSTRON
411  COERCIVE                    PULSES-PER-BEAM
     DEMAGNETIZE                 RECEIVER
     FLUX-LEAKAGE                SIGNAL-TO-RECEIVER
     HYSTERESIS                  TRANSMITTER
     INDUCT                      WAVEGUIDE
     INSENSITIVE
     MAGNETORESISTANCE      415  CRYOGENIC
     SQUARE-LOOP                 CRYOTRON
     THRESHOLD                   PERSISTENT-CURRENT
                                 SUPERCONDUCT
412  LONGITUDINAL                SUPER-CONDUCT
     TRANSVERSE

                            416  RELAY
```

Fig. 6-1 Thesaurus excerpt in concept number order.

	CONCEPT NUMBERS			SYNTAX CODES
BLOCK	663			070043040
BLUEPRINT	58			070043
BOMARC	324			070
BOMBARD	424	0343		043
BOMBER	346			070
BOND	105			070043
BOOKKEEPING	34			070
BOOLEAN	20			001
BORROW	28			043
BOTH	32178			008080012
BOUND	523	0105		070043134135
BOUNDARY	524			070
BRAIN	404	0235		070
BRANCH	48	0042		070042
BRANCHPOINT	23			070
BREAK	380			043040070
BREAKDOWN	689			070
BREAKPOINT	23			070
BRIDGE	105	0458	0048	070043
BRIEF	32232			001043071
BRITISH	437			001071
BROAD-BAND	312			001071
BROKE	380			134104
BROKEN	380			135105
BUFFER	24			070043
BUG	69			070
BUILD	80			043
BUILT	80			134135
BULK	558			070
BURNOUT	69			070
BUS	61			070
BUSINESS	472			070
BUT	32027			091012
BY	32020			074013
BYTE	31			070
C-1100	155			070
CALCULATE	605			043040
CALCULATOR	237			070
CALCULUS	506			070
CALL	32283			070043045040
CAMBRIDGE	444			070
CAN	32118			009
CANCEL	385			043
CANNED	182			134135
CANNING	182			136137071001
CANNOT	32102			009
CANONICAL	706			001
CANS	182			133
CAPABILITY	32269			070
CAPABLE	32269			001071
CAPACITANCE	413			070
CAPACITOR-DIODE	228			071001
CAPIT	340	0213		043
CARD	27			070
CARE	32186			070040
CARGO	331			070
CARRIER	316	0061		070
CARRY	28			070043040

Fig. 6-2 Thesaurus excerpt in alphabetic order.

When constructing a thesaurus to be used for vocabulary normalization, one immediately faces three types of problems. First, what words should one include in the thesaurus. Second, what type of synonym categories should one use (that is, should one aim for broad, inclusive concept classes, or should the classes be narrow and specific). Third, where should each word appear in the thesaurus structure (that is, to which concept classes should a given word be assigned).

Consider first the words to be included. Usually there is not much question about the fact that common function words (e.g., "and", "or", and "but") should not appear in the synonym dictionary, since these words provide no indication of subject matter out of context. A significant problem does arise, however, in connection with very frequent words. These may be nontechnical words in the general vocabulary such as "discuss" and "make", or they may be technical words which, in their particular environment, are in effect reasonably common. For example, in a collection dealing with computer science, such words as "machine", "computer", or "automatic" are in effect common words with reasonably high frequency. If such frequent words are included in a synonym dictionary, most documents will exhibit occurrences of these words, and therefore significant matching coefficients may be obtained between documents and requests, even though the technical texts may be really quite dissimilar (except for the fact that they may deal with computers). If on the other hand these words are excluded, then it becomes possible that one or another document cannot be retrieved when in fact it is pertinent. Obviously some compromise must be made between one's interest in retrieving everything even remotely useful (that is, between the necessity of obtaining high "recall") and the need not to obtain too much extraneous material (the need for high "precision").

A similar problem arises in connection with very low-frequency words. For example, if a term such as "Morse Code" is excluded from the dictionary, then the very few documents dealing with this type of code may not be retrievable. On the other hand, if "Morse Code" appears in a thesaurus category together with many other types of coding systems, then a request for "Morse Code" could also produce many other documents dealing with coding systems, but *not* with the specific system wanted.

Once the words to be included in the dictionary are chosen, the second main problem arises. This deals with the type of synonym categories to be created. It is clear that if very broad and somewhat fuzzy categories are desired, such that a given category includes both somewhat specific terms and also somewhat broader ones, then the resulting dictionary will in general interpret a question in a reasonably broad sense, and as a result the recall which is the proportion of relevant documents retrieved, is likely to be rather high. At the same time the precision may be low, since it must be expected that much irrelevant material will also be produced in the process.

If on the other hand the categories are very specific, the chance of picking up irrelevancies is much smaller, and the precision is increased. The recall may suffer, however, since relevant matter is likely to be missed at the same time. In either case, that is, whether the categories used are broad or specific, problems will arise if words with very different frequency characteristics are included in the same category.

Obviously the effectiveness of the specific terms is much smaller, if these terms are in fact considered equivalent to broader terms of higher frequency by the applicable thesaurus mapping.

This discussion then raises the possibility of providing different thesauri for different types of questions. Specifically, if it is expected that the user is interested in resaonably complete retrieval, including almost everything that is likely to be useful, then the thesaurus with broad categories which provides high recall and low precision should be used. On the other hand if only a few items are to be retrieved, but the user insists that these items must be relevant, then the specific thesaurus categories will prove more useful. This then confirms the well-known fact that any kind of retrieval tool must be constructed with the retrieval environment in mind in which it is expected to operate.

The problem of where a given term is to be put within a given thesaurus organization depends largely on the type of user which may be expected to avail himself of the retrieval systems. For example, dictionaries constructed for a population of students may be expected to require an organization somewhat different from that which would be useful to advanced research scientists. The latter might, for example, be interested in the specific physical characteristics of certain devices, while the former would be more interested in the uses of the devices. A "transistor" could then appear in a category under "three-terminal switching devices" if the users were to be engineers, but it would appear under "computer components" for a user population consisting of computer programmers.

The following principles of thesaurus construction may then be enunciated:

1. No very rare concepts should be included in the thesaurus since these could not be expected to produce many matches between documents and search requests.

2. Very common high-frequency terms should also be excluded from the dictionary, since these produce too many matches for effective retrieval (it is in fact possible to replace individual high-frequency terms by much more specific compound or hyphenated terms; for example, terms such as "computer" or "control" might well be eliminated in favor of a term such as "computer control", since the former is clearly ambiguous in many contexts whereas the latter is much more specific).

3. Nonsignificant words should be studied carefully before any are included in the list of words to be eliminated (for example, a term such as "hand" should be included in a thesaurus dealing with biology, but it should not be included if its high-frequency count is due to expressions such as "on the other hand").

4. Ambiguous terms should be coded only for those senses which are likely to be present in the document collections to be treated (for example, at least two category numbers must be shown for the term "field", corresponding on the one hand to the notion of subject area, and on the other hand to its technical sense in algebra; however, no category number need be shown to cover the notion of "a patch of land" if the dictionary deals with the mathematical sciences or related technical fields).

5. Each concept class should only include terms of roughly equal frequency so that the matching characteristics are approximately the same for each term within a category.

In the SMART system it was found useful to operate with a reasonably large number of concept classes (on the order of 700 for a given restricted subject field), and also to use a large list of nonsignificant words to be excluded from the content indications. In particular this list includes verbs such as "begin", "contain", "indicate" "call", "designate", and so forth, which could not be depended upon to provide safe content indications. It was also found useful to isolate high-frequency terms into separate categories so that these terms would not impair the retrieval effectiveness of other more specific terms.

An example of the kind of analysis normally necessary for dictionary construction is the concept number 101 representing the notion of "tag". The word list attached to this concept originally included terms such as "call", "designate", "identify", "identifier", "identification", "index", "indicate", "label", "mark", "name", "point", "signal", "sign", subscript", and "tag". The concept occurred in 94 documents out of some 500, with the following distribution of significant terms:

Term	Frequency	Number of Documents
Index	17	7
Signal		
(pulse)	20	14
Identify	6	4

All other terms under concept 101, which occurred a total of 91 times, were accounted for almost exclusively by the terms "pointed out", "indicated", and "call". As a result of the analysis, the words "indicate", "call", "name", and "designate" were removed from category 101 and were included in the list of common words. The words "sign" and "signal" were also removed from category 101 because they seemed to occur in the document collection only in the sense of "pulse signal" and therefore not in the sense of "tag". Words with stem "identi", accounting for "identifier", "identification", "identify", and so on, were moved to a new concept number representing the idea of recognition. At the end only the terms "index", "label", "subscript", and "tag" remained under category 101.

6-3-B The Word-Stem Thesaurus and Suffix List

One of the earliest ideas in automatic information retrieval was the suggested use of words contained in documents and search requests for purposes of content identification. Then no elaborate content analysis is required, and the similarity between different items can be measured simply by the amount of overlap between the respective vocabularies. While one should not expect that word-matching techniques alone will normally provide adequate retrieval performance, it is useful to consider a word-matching technique as part of a retrieval system, since this provides a standard against which various types of dictionary procedures may be measured. This was one of the reasons for including in the SMART system the so-called *word stem thesaurus* [2], [3].

The word stem thesaurus consists simply of a list of word stems, constructed by using the words included in a typical document collection, each distinct word stem being furnished with a different sequence number. The sequence numbers in the stem thesaurus are then equivalent to the concept numbers included in the regular thesaurus with the exception that each sequence number, of course, has only a single correspondent (word or word stem) in the stem thesaurus which is then equivalent to the multiple correspondences in the regular thesaurus. A typical sample from a stem thesaurus is shown in Fig. 6-3, where the word stems are listed in the order of increasing frequency of occurrence within a document collection, rather than in the usual alphabetic order.

Clearly, the operation, which consists in using the sequence numbers obtained from a stem thesaurus for purposes of document and request identification, leads effectively to a word-matching technique for document retrieval, since sequence numbers and text words are in effect isomorphic. The main virtues of the stem thesaurus per se result from the fact that the dictionary lookup routine programmed for the regular thesaurus will serve also for the stem thesaurus (because the structure of the two thesauri is the same). Also, the stem thesaurus permits the word-matching operation to be confined to only those words actually included in the thesaurus (because the others will not have an assigned sequence number).

This raises a question about the type of stem thesaurus which should be used as a standard for the word-matching operations. The following alternatives appear of principal importance in this connection:

1. The stem thesaurus can include complete English words, or alternatively, can be made up of *word stems* obtained from the original words by a suffix cutoff process.

2. An entry can be included in the stem thesaurus for each text word included in a certain document collection, or expected to be important in a given topic area; or alternatively, function words and other words not easily used for content identification may be excluded or marked with a special identifying code.

3. All noncommon words or word stems may be used, or only those words which have certain predetermined frequency characteristics (for example, words occurring more than 5 times but less than 100 times in a given document collection).

In the SMART system, all dictionaries (including regular and stem thesauri) are based on word stems rather than original words. Furthermore, common words appear on an exclusion list and are thus not included in any of the dictionaries. Experiments were conducted with the SMART system, using both unrestricted vocabularies (*full stem* thesaurus), as well as frequency restricted entries (*partial stem*). A sample set of document abstracts of some 50,000 total running words would

FRE- QUENCY	STEM	SUFFIX	SEQUENCE NUMBER
11	MODULE	S	2099
11	PLACE	S	2100
11	RESPONSE		2101
11	RF		2102
11	SOURCE		2103
11	THICK		2104
11	TRUNC	ATION	2105
11	WAVE		2106
11	WHEREB	Y	2107
11	WIR	ING	2108
12	ALPHABET	ICAL	2109
12	BASE		2110
12	CAP	ABLE	2111
12	CENT		2112
12	CONCEPT		2113
12	DECIS	ION	2114
12	DEPCSIT	ED	2115
12	DUE		2116
12	ECCNOM	ICAL	2117
12	ESAKI		2118
12	EXAMIN	ED	2119
12	FUNCTICN	AL	2120
12	GRAPH		2121
12	HAV	ING	2122
12	IMPROVE	MENT	2123
12	IMPROV	ED	2124
12	INDIVIDU	AL	2125
12	LEAST		2126
12	MAGNETIZ	ATION	2127
12	MAIN		2128

FRE- QUENCY	STEM	SUFFIX	SEQUENCE NUMBER
12	MANIPUL	ATION	2129
12	MECHAN	ISM	2130
12	MODUL	ATION	2131
12	MUCH		2132
12	OSCILL	ATORS	2133
12	PHYS	ICAL	2134
12	PREV	IOUS	2135
12	RANGE		2136
12	RECCRD		2137
12	RELAX	ATION	2138
12	REPCRT	ED	2139
12	REVERS	ED	2140
12	RULE	S	2141
12	SATIS	FY	2142
12	SHCW		2143
12	STUC	Y	2144
12	SYSTEMAT	ICALLY	2145
12	TREE	S	2146
12	TUNNEL		2147
13	10		2148
13	650		2149
13	ANISOTRCP	Y	2150
13	ASSUM	ED	2151
13	CARRI	ER	2152
13	CAR	RY	2153
13	COMP	ON	2154
13	COMPUNIC	ATIONS	2155
13	COMPOS	ITION	2156
13	DEPCNSTR	ATE	2157
13	DEAS	ITY	2158

Fig. 6-3 Word stem frequency list (stem thesaurus).

typically produce a full stem thesaurus of about 2800 distinct word stems and a partial stem dictionary of about 900 stems (assuming a frequency of at least four occurrences for each entry listed). If it is desired to list word stems, rather than full words, these must of course first be generated by a suffix cutoff system. To this end, a suffix dictionary is built.

Typically, each suffix is listed with a sequence number and with one or more syntactic codes. The latter may be used if subsequently it becomes necessary to recombine stems and suffixes into complete, acceptable words, as may be required for example to carry out a syntactic analysis. A representative suffix dictionary for English suffixes may contain about 200 entries. To simplify the lookup algorithm, noun suffixes may be entered in the plural as well as singular forms, and adjectival suffixes may also be listed in the adverbial form. Verb suffixes should include the common endings "ed", "ing", and "s", as well as true verb suffixes such as "fy" with their inflected forms. (Multiple suffixes, such as "fying" could be detected by a dual scanning of the suffix list, looking first for "ing" and then for "fy"; a dual scan is avoided if such multiple suffixes are also entered in the suffix dictionary.)

In general, it is possible to encode word stems and suffixes in such a way so that no ambiguity results when the fragments are combined into full words. For example, the stem "recti" is coded as a potential verb because it can form "rectify"; the stem "reduct", on the other hand, is carried without syntax codes, since it can be combined only with common suffixes such as "ion" and "ible" which by themselves are carried as complete homographs, representing respectively "noun singular" and "adjective."

In a limited number of cases, partial syntactic coding may introduce an ambiguity; for example, if the word "capital" is coded as a potential verb to accept the suffix "ize", the plural noun "capitals" will receive the extraneous coding of a verb in the third person singular. This difficulty may be prevented by entering the stem "capit" with a partial verb code. The suffix "als" properly carries with it only the plural noun code, and "capitalize" can then be found by a double scan of the suffix list [2].

6-3-C   The Phrase Dictionaries

Both the regular as well as the stem thesauri are based on entries corresponding either to single words or to single word stems. In attempting to perform a subject analysis of written text, it is possible however to go further by trying to locate "phrases" consisting of sets of words which are judged to be important in a given subject area.

Phrases can be used for subject identification by building phrase dictionaries which help to locate combinations of concepts, rather than individual concepts alone. Such phrase dictionaries would then normally include pairs, triples, or quadruples of words or concepts, corresponding in written texts to the more likely noun and prepositional phrases which may be expected to indicate the subject content in a given topic area.

Many different strategies can be used in the construction of phrase dictionaries. For example, it is possible to base phrase dictionaries on combinations of high-frequency words or word stems occurring in documents and search requests; alternatively, one may want to use a thesaurus before an appeal is made to a phrase dictionary. Under those circumstances, the phrase dictionary would then be based on combinations of concept categories included in the thesaurus, rather than on combinations of words.

Furthermore, given the availability of a phrase dictionary, one can recognize the presence of phrases in a given text under a variety of circumstances. For example, the existence of a phrase may be recognized whenever the phrase components are present within a given document, regardless of any actual syntactic relation between the components. Alternatively, the presence of a phrase may be inferred whenever the components are located within the same sentence of a given document, rather than merely within the boundaries of the same document. Finally, even more stringent restrictions can be imposed before a phrase is actually accepted, by checking that a preestablished syntactic relation actually exists between the phrase components in the document under consideration.

In the SMART system, the phrase dictionaries are based on co-occurrences of thesaurus concepts, rather than text words, and two principal strategies are used for phrase detection. (1) The so-called "statistical phrase" dictionary is based on a phrase detection algorithm which takes into account only the co-occurrence characteristics of the phrase components; specifically a statistical phrase is recognized, if and only if all phrase components are present within a given document or within a given sentence of a document, and no attempt is made to detect any particular syntactic relation between the components. (2) The "syntactic phrase" dictionary includes not only the specification of the particular phrase components which are to be detected, but also information about the permissible syntactic dependency relations which must obtain if the phrase is to be recognized. Thus, if it were desired to recognize the relationship between the concept "program" and the concept "language", any possible combination of these two concepts such as, for example, "programming language", "languages and programs", and "linguistic programs", would be recognized as proper phrases in the statistical phrase dictionary. In the syntactic dictionary, however, an additional restriction would consist in requiring that the concept corresponding to "program" be syntactically dependent on the concept "language". This eliminates phrases such as "linguistic programs" and "languages and programs", but would permit the phrases "programming languages" or "programmed languages".

A typical excerpt from a statistical phrase dictionary used in connection with the SMART system is shown in Fig. 6-4. It may be seen that up to six phrase components are permitted in a given phrase, but that the usual phrase specification consists of two, or at most three, components. With each phrase included in Fig. 6-4 is listed a phrase concept number which replaces the individual component concepts in a given document specification whenever the corresponding phrase is detected by the phrase-processing algorithm in use. For example, the first line of Fig. 6-4 shows that a phrase with concept number 543 is detected whenever the concepts 544 and 608 are jointly present in the document under consideration. Whenever such a phrase concept is attached to a given document specification, the weight of the phrase concept can be increased over and above the original weight of the component concepts to give the phrase specification added importance.

PHRASE CONCEPT	COMPONENT CONCEPTS					
543	544	608	−∩	−∩	−∩	−∩
282	280	281	−∩	−∩	−∩	−∩
282	306	281	−∩	−∩	−∩	−∩
280	69	648	−∩	−∩	−∩	−∩
280	69	215	−∩	−∩	−∩	−∩
694	1285	1284	−∩	−∩	−∩	−∩
291	265	290	−∩	−∩	−∩	−∩
291	265	496	−∩	−∩	−∩	−∩
422	646	185	−∩	−∩	−∩	−∩
640	309	290	−∩	−∩	−∩	−∩
294	21	293	−∩	−∩	−∩	−∩
393	21	635	−∩	−∩	−∩	−∩
393	635	106	−∩	−∩	−∩	−∩
294	21	245	−∩	−∩	−∩	−∩

Fig. 6-4 Excerpt from statistical phrase dictionary.

Since the phrase components used in the SMART system represent concept numbers rather than individual words, a given phrase concept number then in fact represents many different types of English word combinations depending of course on the number of word stems assigned to each component concept by the original thesaurus mapping.

The syntactic phrase dictionary has a more complicated structure as shown by the excerpt reproduced as Fig. 6-5. Here, each syntactic phrase, also known as a "criterion tree" or "criterion phrase", consists of a specification of the component concepts, syntactic indications, and syntactic relations which may obtain between the included concepts. For example, the first phrase shown in Fig. 6-5 carries the

NAME OF TREE	OUTPUT CON-CEPT	FIRST NODE CONCEPTS	SECOND NODE	TYPE 7 SERIAL 143	TYPE 15 SERIAL 398	TYPE 16 SERIAL 399

```
MAGSWI=422(185,624)/(225)$7/143,15/398,16+
MANMCH=517(600)/(516)$7/144,15/400
MANROL=286(290)/(113)$7/145,5+,15/401,16+,19+
MATHOP=594(615)/(7,116,376)$7/147
MCHBKD=69(689)/(600)$1/148
MCHCOD=304(102,281)/(14,41,600,601)$1/149,15/404
MCHOPE=93(615)/(600)$7/150
MCHORI=41(513)/(600,601)$7/151,15/405
MCHTIM=691(617)/(152,600,601,605,1281)$7/152
MCHTIM=691(617)/(72,615)$1/153
MCHTRA=303(98)/(119,600)$1/154,4+,5+,6+,10+,15/406,16+,19+
MFMACC=593(672)/(121)$1/159,15/409
MFMCOR=557(669)/(121)$7/137,15/395
MFMFFF=284(64)/(121)$1/160,6+,15/410
MFMSPA=552(212)/(121)$1/162,13+,15/411
```

Fig. 6-5 Excerpt from criterion tree dictionary.

concept number 422 as well as the mnemonic indicator MAGSWI to indicate that this phrase deals in one way or another with magnetic switches. Figure 6-5 also shows that the first component of the phrase must consist either of concepts 185 or 624, while the second phrase component must represent concept 225. The indicators after the dollar sign in the output of Fig. 6-5 carry the syntactic information. In particular, the information given for the phrase MAGSWI indicates that this particular phrase must be of syntactic types 7, 15, or 16.

More specifically, four main classes of syntactic specifications exist which correspond, respectively, to noun phrases, subject-verb relations, verb-object relations, and subject-object relations. In turn the four syntactic classes are subdivided into approximately 20 syntactic types, each of which specifies a particular syntactic relation between the components. The particular relations which apply to a sample phrase, which is labeled SYNTAX, are shown in Fig. 6-6. It may be seen in the figure that the first component of the phrase must correspond either to concepts 11 or 158, whereas the second component corresponds to concepts 102, 188, or 170. Also specified in Fig. 6-6 are the four allowable format types, namely 1, 3, 4, and 13. These formats are specified in the center of Fig. 6-6 in the form of syntactic dependency trees.

Dependency trees are characterized by the fact that vertical displacement along a given path of the tree denotes syntactic dependence, the dependent structures always being listed below the corresponding governing structures. This can be illustrated by using the example of Fig. 6-6, where the format type 1 specifies that the second com-

PHRASE SPECIFICATION:

SYNTAX (11, 158) / (102, 188, 170) $ 1, 3, 4, 13

CONCEPT NODE 1   CONCEPT NODE 2   FORMATS

NODE 1	NODE 2	FORMATS	SAMPLE PHRASES
11 ANAL SYNTHESIS SYNTHES SYNTHET	102 INTERLINGU LANGUAGE 170 PHRASE SENTENCE	1	1 SYNTACTIC ANALYSIS PHRASE RELATIONS ANALYSIS OF SENTENCES
		3	3 WE CAN ANALYZE THE LANGUAGE ... SYNTHESIZE A SYNTAX
158 CLASS CORRESPOND GROUP INDEPEND RELATE	SUBJECT WORD 188 GRAMMAR SYNTAX SYNTACTIC	4	4 THE GRAMMAR IS NOW AVAILABLE FOR ANALYSIS
		13	13 THIS ANALYSIS IS APPLICABLE TO RUSSIAN GRAMMAR

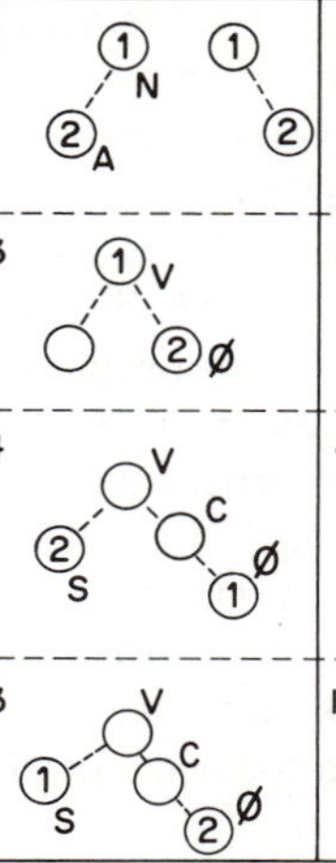

Fig. 6-6 Criterion phrase specification.

ponent, corresponding in this case to either concept numbers 102, 188, or 170, be dependent syntactically on the first component corresponding to concept 11 or 158; furthermore, the second component is specified as an adjective, while the first component is specified as a noun. Examples corresponding to each of the syntactic format frames listed are shown on the right-hand side of Fig. 6-6. For instance, the first tree of format-type 1 might correspond to English phrases such as "syntactic analysis", "syntactic synthesis", "phrase relations", "subject correspondence", and so on. Because of the multiple assignment of concepts to phrase components and the multiplicity of syntactic format types specified for each phrase, a given criterion phrase generally represents many hundreds of English phrases or sentences. This feature is used to match the many sentence parts in the language which are semantically similar but syntactically quite distinct.

Since the syntactic dependency specifications are always directed from a dependent component to a governing component, the grammatical structure of a syntactic phrase, unlike that of a statistical phrase, is well determined. For the first example of Fig. 6-6 (format-type 1) the string "phrase relations" is an acceptable interpretation; "relational phrase" is not. Similarly for format-type 13, an acceptable interpretation is "this analysis is applicable to Russian grammar", but the transposed "this grammar is applicable to Russian analysis" would not be acceptable.

6-3-D   The Concept Hierarchy

Hierarchical arrangements of subject headings have been used for many years in library science and related documentation activities. In general, such arrangements make it possible to classify more specific topics under more general ones and to formulate a search request by starting with a general formulation and progressively narrowing the specification down to those areas which appear to be of principal interest. Thus, one can start with a topic area such as "mathematics" and from there proceed to "algebra", which is a subdivision of mathematics, where one can go in turn to "graph theory", which then leads to "tree structures", from which finally one can obtain the "syntactic dependency trees" illustrated previously in Fig. 6-6.

In a content analysis system, a hierarchical arrangement of words or word stems can be used both for information identification and for retrieval purposes. Thus, if a given search request is formulated in terms of "syntactic dependency trees", and it is found that not enough useful material is actually obtained, it is possible to "expand" this request to include all tree structures or indeed all abstract graphs, by using a hierarchical subject classification.

A hierarchy of concept numbers is included in the SMART system, and it is assumed that a thesaurus lookup operation precedes any hierarchical expansion operation. A typical example from the SMART concept hierarchy is shown in Fig. 6-7. The broad, more general concepts appear on the left side of the figure, corresponding to the "roots" of the hierarchical tree; the more specific concepts appear further to the right. For example, concept 270 is the root of a subtree; this concept has four sons on the next lower level: concepts 224, 471, 472, and 488. Concept 224 in turn has two

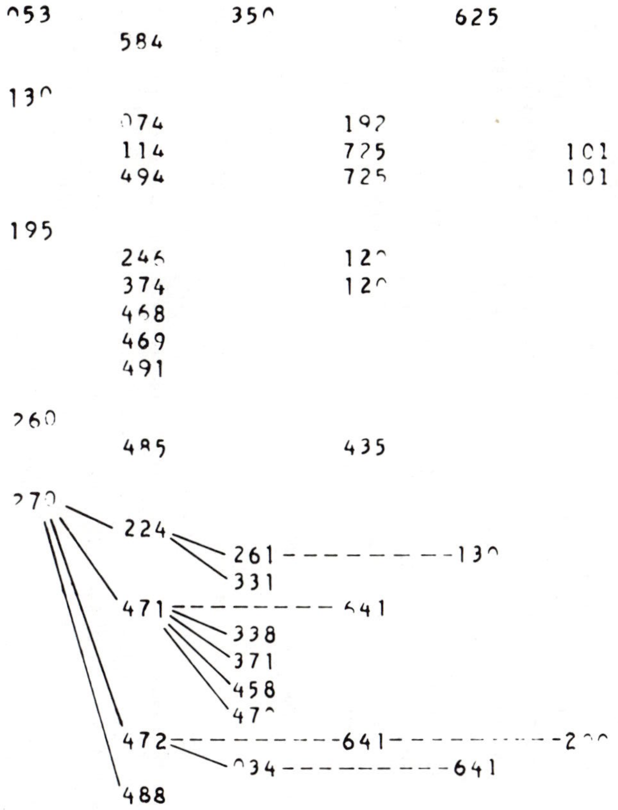

CONCEPT SEQUENCE
NUMBER NUMBER

CONCEPT NUMBER	SEQUENCE NUMBER
53	1
584	2
-0	3
130	4
74	5
114	6
494	7
-0	8
195	9
246	10
374	11
468	12
469	13
491	14
-0	15
260	16
485	17
-0	18
270	19
224	20
261	21
331	22
471	23
338	24
371	25
458	26
470	27
472	28
34	29
488	30
-0	31

Fig. 6-7 Hierarchy excerpt.

131

sons, labeled 261 and 331; similarly, concept 471 has four sons, including 338, 371, 458, and 470. It may be seen from Fig. 6-7 that the sons of a concept, representing more specific terms, are shown below their parents and further to the right.

The hierarchy of Fig. 6-7 also provides for the inclusion of cross references from one concept to another, which are connected to the original concept by broken lines. Such cross references represent general, unspecified types of relations between the corresponding concepts and receive in general a different interpretation than the generic inclusion relations normally represented by the hierarchy.

It would be nice if it were possible to give some generally applicable algorithm for constructing hierarchical subject arrangements. This is, in fact, a topic which has preoccupied many people including mathematicians, philosophers, and librarians for many years. In general, one can say that broad concepts should be near the top of the tree, while specific concepts should be near the bottom. Furthermore there appears to be some relationship between the frequency of occurrence of a given concept in a document collection and its place in the hierarchy. More specifically those concepts which exhibit the highest frequency of occurrence in a given document collection, and which by this very fact appear to be reasonably common, should be placed on a higher level than other concepts whose frequency of occurrence is lower.

Concerning the specific place of a given concept within the hierarchy, this should be made to depend on the user population and on the type of expansion which is most often requested. Thus, a concept corresponding to "syntactic dependency tree" would appear most reasonably under the broader category of "syntax", which in turn could appear under the general class of "language", assuming that the user population consists of linguists or grammarians. On the other hand, if the users were to be mathematicians or algebraists, then the "syntactic dependency trees" should probably appear under "abstract trees", which in turn would come under "graph theory", a branch of algebra. It does not appear reasonable to expect that a hierarchical arrangement of concepts will serve equally well for all uses under all circumstances. Rather, any hierarchy will serve its function, if it can be counted upon to suggest ways of broadening or narrowing a given search request or a given interpretation of the subject matter under most of the circumstances likely to arise in practice.

6-4 AUTOMATIC THESAURUS CONSTRUCTION

Under normal circumstances, the task of constructing a subject dictionary for a given topic area is one which demands many skills, including a great deal of persistence and tenacity. It is not usually enough to be a subject expert in a given area; training is also normally expected in linguistics and philosophy. Futhermore, since the task is of large proportions, a committee is often appointed to thrash out controversial questions and eventually produce a suggested standard dictionary. Such a committee-produced standard ends frequently by satisfying no one, despite the enormous effort that goes into its construction.

Clearly, if it were necessary to follow this particular pattern in order to build a useful dictionary for retrieval purposes, then any saving which might result from automatic search and retrieval methodology might be promptly lost through the elaborate preparations required to build dictionaries.

This situation has led to many efforts calculated to produce dictionaries either full automatically or at least by more systematic procedures than a committee-controlled process. Any reasonably standardized method for dictionary construction not only saves time and decreases costs but also permits a great deal more latitude in the type of retrieval procedures which can be implemented. The following principal advantages are evident:

1. The retrieval procedures can be extended to collections in many different areas, since the dictionary problem no longer constitutes an impediment.

2. Differences in vocabulary between different subject areas can be investigated— for example, the frequently heard assertion that the vocabulary in some subject areas is "soft" (that is, not well standardized and ambiguous), whereas in other areas it is "hard".

3. It removes any possible differences in retrieval effectiveness between different subject areas due to disturbances introduced by varying methods of thesaurus construction.

4. The retrieval effectiveness of a variety of thesauri for a given collection can be investigated; this includes variations in the thesaurus size, in the number of concept classes, and in the correspondents assigned to each class.

No matter what particular method of thesaurus construction is adopted, the main virtue of an automatic process is to eliminate the human element, either completely if a fully automatic method can be found, or partially if the process is semiautomatic. In the latter case, it is desirable to restrict the human activities to questions which require only local decisions within the given subject area, rather than global considerations involving linguistic knowledge and experience in subject classification and indexing.

Some systematic procedures for thesaurus construction are described in the next few paragraphs, and a simplified example of one particular semiautomatic process is given.

6-4-A Fully Automatic Methods

Most automatic methods for thesaurus construction are based on the vocabulary contained in a sample document collection assumed to be typical for a given subject area [4], [5], [6]. In particular, a frequency count is made of the words contained in a set of documents, and each document is identified by certain high-frequency words included in it. The choice of these words may be based strictly on frequency characteristics, or alternatively, on more complicated properties of the word distribution for the given collection. In any case, the sample collection is represented initially

	terms assigned to documents						
	T_1	T_2	T_3	T_4	T_5	T_6	$T_7 \cdots$
D_1	3	0	0	2	0	6	1
document $\quad D_2$	0	0	1	3	2	0	2
vectors $\quad D_3$	0	2	3	0	4	0	0
D_4	1	2	1	0	3	1	0

(a)

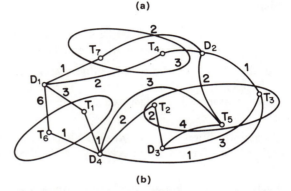

(b)

Fig. 6-8 Term-document graphs and matrices: (a) term-document matrix showing frequency of terms assigned to documents; (b) term-document graph for matrix of Fig. 6-8(a).

by a term-document matrix, or a term-document graph as shown in Fig. 6-8. The matrix element at the intersection of row i and column j of the matrix represents the weight of term j in document i; this same weight is represented in the graph of Fig. 6-8(b) by the labeled branch between nodes T_j and D_i.

Given such a term-document matrix or graph, it is now possible, by well-known statistical association methods, to compute similarity coefficients between terms, based on co-occurrence characteristics of the terms in the documents of the collection. Then the similarity coefficient between each pair of terms can be made to depend on the frequency with which the terms are jointly assigned to the documents of a collection. In Fig. 6-8, for example, it may be noted that both terms T_1 and T_6 are assigned to documents D_1 and D_4 (although with differing weights), while they are both *not* assigned to documents D_2 and D_3. As a result, the term association process may assign these two terms to a common thesaurus category.

For the example of Fig. 6-8 an associative procedure might result in the formation of three-term (thesaurus) groups, consisting respectively of terms T_1 and T_6 (because of joint assignment to documents D_1 and D_4), terms T_7 and T_4 (because of joint assignment to D_1 and D_2), and finally terms T_2, T_3, and T_5 (because of joint assignment to D_3 and D_4). The result of a term association process may then be displayed as an association map, in which the terms are represented by nodes and term relations, or alternatively, thesaurus groupings by appropriate branches between nodes [4], [7], [8].

6-4-B Semiautomatic Methods

The methods outlined in the preceding section are based on the assumption that term co-occurrences in documents, or joint assignment of terms to documents, are indicative of term similarity or relatedness. This assumption may not always hold, and if it holds, its applicability may be restricted to a given document collection rather than to a complete subject field. For this reason, it is also of interest to consider somewhat less radical procedures which require a certain amount of human judgment. Generally these methods are based on various automatic aids but use subject experts for the basic task of defining the meaning of each term which is introduced into the thesaurus [9], [10], [11], [12].

The basic idea is to start, as before, with a word frequency list for the words included in the given document collection. In addition, it is also useful to have an available listing which exhibits the words in context, so that a distinction may be made between individual word uses for ambiguous terms. For example, a word such as "base" may be broken down into "$base_1$", "$base_2$", and "$base_3$", to represent, respectively, "army base", "lamp base", and "baseball base" (assuming that those three uses of the term are in fact present in a given collection). A standard "keyword-in-context" (KWIC) list may be prepared automatically to permit a human observer to ascertain the individual word uses for the terms included in a collection. An example of a typical KWIC index list, used in conjunction with the SMART system, is shown in Fig. 6-9 [13].

Figure 6-9 shows that the term "spectral" is used in the given collection in only one sense, namely that of a "spectral norm", the term "square" is, however, used in two senses in the concordance excerpt, first as a rectangle of equal sides (square matrix), and then as a power of two (square root). The list of word uses to be constructed would then include a single instance of the term "spectral" but two separate examples of "square".

After the list of word uses to be included in the thesaurus is available, it becomes necessary to group them into thesaurus classes. This can be done in various ways:

1. An informal judgment can be made for each pair of word uses to decide whether, in the subject area under consideration, they are synonymous, and if so, they can be grouped in the same thesaurus class.

2. A set of "syntactic frames" can be used, and those word uses which fit into the same frames can be collected in the same thesaurus group, or equivalently, a decision is made based on whether term A can always replace term B in a given context X [9]. Of course this decision is not mechanized, but the dictionary maker is faced only with local choices within certain narrow limits.

3. A set of questions can be prepared which is designed to elicit answers about the terms to be grouped, and each term can be identified by the set of answers obtained in response to the proposed questions; for example, one might ask "does this term represent a physical object or process, does it represent an abstraction, or is this question inapplicable"; a score of 1 may then be assigned for a physical object, 2 for an abstraction, and 3 if the question is not applicable.

TEST RUN CF SCCCER   C9/C7/65   PAGE 56

DOCUMENT NUMBER

SPECIFIED
BY ANY SIMPLE EXTENSION CF THE METHODS USED FOR COMPLETELY | SPECIFIED | FUNCTIONS . AN ANALYSIS CF THE PROBLEM IS PRESENTE — 90
NUMBER CF CCCURRENCES 2

SPECTRAL
WA MERGING TECHNIQUE . SEVERAL EXAMPLES ARE GIVEN . ON THE | SPECTRAL | NORMS CF SEVERAL ITERATIVE PROCESSES — 178
RMS CF SEVERAL ITERATIVE PROCESSES . THE | SPECTRAL | NORM CF A SQUARE SYMMETRIC POSITIVE DEFINITE MATRIX — 179
TIVE METHOD CF MATRIX INVERSION IS DERIVED IN TERMS OF THE | SPECTRAL | NORM . VARIOUS THEOREMS CONCERNING THE SPECTRAL NOR — 182
RMS OF THE SPECTRAL NORM . VARIOUS THEOREMS CONCERNING THE | SPECTRAL | NORM ARE PROVED THE RESULTS OBTAINED ARE APPLIED TO — 183
NUMBER CF CCCURRENCES 4

SPLITTING
TORED INITIALLY CN THE P.IST TAPE . AN ITERATIVE SCHEME OF | SPLITTING | BLOCKS CF DATA WHOSE DESIGNATION HAS THE HIGHEST N — 24
NO WRITING IN THE REVERSE DIRECTION ANY GROUP REQUIRED FOR | SPLITTING | IS ALWAYS UNDER THE HEAD CF THE APPROPRIATE TAPE U — 29
NUMBER CF CCCURRENCES 2

SQUARE
ATIVE PROCESSES . . THE SPECTRAL NORM OF A | SQUARE | SYMMETRIC POSITIVE DEFINITE MATRIX IS DEFINED AS THE — 179
METRIC POSITIVE DEFINITE MATRIX IS DEFINED AS THE POSITIVE | SQUARE | ROOT OF A COMPLEX NUMBER — 180
ORGANIZE SUCH A CALCULATION IS FLOWCHARTED . CN TAKING THE | SQUARE | ROOT OF A COMPLEX NUMBER . ONE SOLUTION IS T — 214
TC CANCELLATION RESULTING FROM A SUBTRACTION IN TAKING THE | SQUARE | ROOT CF A COMPLEX NUMBER IS NOTED . ONE PER IS T — 216
LEX NUMBER IS NOTED . ONE SOLUTION IS TC TAKE INTERMEDIATE | SQUARE | ROOTS TO DOUBLE LENGTH ACCURACY ANOTHER IS TC FIND TH — 217
NUMBER CF CCCURRENCES 5

ST
ESCRIBED . THE UNSORTED CATA IS STORED INITIALLY ON THE P.IST TAPE . AN ITERATIVE SCHEME CF SPLITTING BLOCKS OF CATA WH — 24
NUMBER CF CCCURRENCES 1

STAGE
DYNAMIC PROGRAMMING SHOW HOW TC PROCEED OPTIMALLY FROM CNE | STAGE | TO THE NEXT WITH THE NUMBER CF COMPUTATIONS INCREASING — 243
NUMBER CF CCCURRENCES 1

STAGES
F COMPUTATIONS INCREASING CNLY LINEARLY WITH THE NUMBER OF | STAGES | CONSIDERED . THE GENERAL PRINCIPLES ARE ILLUSTRATED B — 245
NUMBER CF CCCURRENCES 1

STARTING
QLENTIAL MACHINES | STARTING | FROM MEALY S MODEL CF A SEQUENTIAL MACHINE A CONNEC — 144
NUMBER CF CCCURRENCES 1

STATE
MBERS ARE SUGGESTED FCR FUTURE CATA PROCESSING COMPUTERS. | STATE | LOGIC RELATIONS IN AUTONOMOUS SEQUENTIAL NETWORKS — 51
SSED . THE RELATIONSHIP BETWEEN THE INTERNAL LCCIC AND THE | STATE | SEQUENTIAL BEHAVIOR OF SUCH NETWORKS IS EXAMINED THROU — 93
CONDITIONS FCR THE NETWORK TC BE NEASIANGULAR I.E. TO HAVE A | STATE | DIAGRAM WHICH IS DETERMINISTIC EVEN IN REVERSE TIME A — 56
SIGULARITY CONDITION ARE DEMONSTRATED . THE EFFECTS CN THE | STATE | DIAGRAM OF SEVERAL KINDS CF CONSTRAINTS IMPOSED CN THE — 58
NUMBER CF CCCURRENCES 4

STATES
FUNCTIONS IS TAKEN INTO ACCOUNT . MINIMIZING THE NUMBER OF | STATES | IN INCOMPLETELY SPECIFIED SEQUENTIAL SWITCHING FUNCTI — 84
LY DESCRIBES THE MACHINE IS DEVELOPED . THE EQUIVALENCE OF | STATES | OF A SEQUENTIAL MACHINE IS ANALYZED SYSTEMATICALLY BY — 146
NUMBER CF CCCURRENCES 2

STATISTICAL
ATICN CF AN ADDRESS FUNCTION IS DESCRIBED . USUALLY ONLY A | STATISTICAL | APPROXIMATION TC THE ACCESS FUNCTION IS KNOWN . — 9
NUMBER CF CCCURRENCES 1

Fig. 6-9 Concordance excerpt.

At the end of such a procedure, each term is then identified by a set of properties (in the form of contexts which fit a given term, or in the form of answers to questions about the terms), and the complete vocabulary may be represented by a property matrix, as shown in simplified form in Fig. 6-10. It remains, then, to find the semantic distance between terms by comparing the rows of properties representing the respective word uses.

		P_1	P_2	P_3	P_4	P_5	P_6	
	T_1	1	0	0	2	1	0	0 property inapplicable
	T_2	0	1	0	1	0	1	1 property applies,
word-uses	T_3	2	0	1	1	2	0	somewhat
obtained	T_4	1	2	0	1	0	1	2 property applies
from collection									strongly

Fig. 6-10 Typical term-property matrix.

Specifically, rows which are completely identical can be coalesced into a single group immediately; terms which are not identical may be grouped by judiciously eliminating certain properties (certain columns in the property matrix); alternatively, terms which have been grouped already may be split apart by introducing new properties to differentiate them. For example, if property P_3 were removed from the property matrix of Fig. 6-10, terms T_1 and T_3 will both exhibit the same set of assigned properties (although with differing weights) and may therefore be grouped. Similarly, the removal of property P_1 results in the grouping of terms T_2 and T_4.

In practice, it may be useful to consider more formal methods, first for comparing the rows of the property matrix (that is, for computing a similarity coefficient between each pair of terms) and then for generating term clusters.

6-5 SEMIAUTOMATIC HIERARCHY FORMATION

The need for a hierarchical arrangement of terms, or concept classes, as part of an information retrieval system is by no means obvious, although it is easy to find useful applications for a well-constructed hierarchy, particularly when the search strategies considered are designed to proceed from more general to more specific search formulations or vice versa.

It has been seen in this connection that, when words or word uses of unequal frequency are included in a thesaurus or represented on an association map, a hierarchical arrangement results almost inevitably, since frequent words can be made into categories, and words of lesser frequency can be made into subcategories [4]. Hierarchical association maps have in fact been constructed, using the frequency character-istics of the words as a criterion [14], [15]. In any case, no matter what procedure is actually adopted, it would seem that a useful hierarchy which places general concepts near the top of the tree and specific ones near the bottom must exhibit the expected frequency characteristics which generally hold between broad and specific terms.

Since the construction of a complete hierarchy without any guidelines is at best a thankless task, and at worst an impossible one, methods must be investigated to generate hierarchical arrangements semiautomatically. Three different procedures are outlined, all of which are based on a term-property matrix of the type shown in Fig. 6-10 or a term-document matrix as shown in Fig. 6-8(a).

The first process directly uses the questions also used for thesaurus construction and breaks down the initial vocabulary as a function of the responses elicited. First an initial question is asked, and classes of word uses are formed based on the responses to this question; the next question is then applied to each of the resulting word classes which are thereby broken down again, and so on, until the subdivision is sufficiently fine.

The process is applied to a sample vocabulary, and the resulting hierarchy is shown in Fig. 6-11, where the word use frequency is attached to each node. A typical Question *B* is applied first to the complete vocabulary, thus forming two groups of "physical objects" and "abstractions or processes", with a frequency of 1119 and 1079

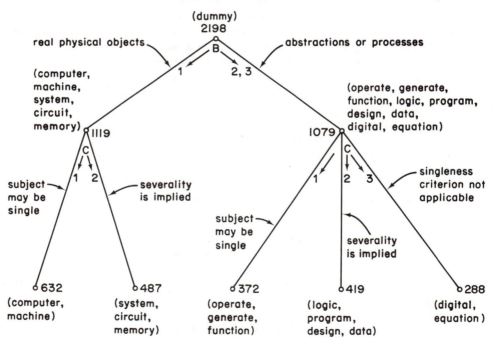

Fig. 6-11   Hierarchy construction by property separation (word use frequencies are shown).

respectively. Question C is then used to furnish the five classes already shown in Fig. 6-11 [14].

A somewhat different process operates directly from the word use frequencies and is therefore not based on the thesaurus groupings as is the previous method. Instead, the hierarchy is constructed first, and the thesaurus is based later on the previously available hierarchy. A start is made as before, with a concordance and a word frequency list, and the word uses are selected for inclusion in the hierarchy. The two-way hierarchy is now started by choosing the word use with highest frequency, let us say, word T_i, and letting one node represent word T_i plus all words like it, the second branch representing all "other" words not related to T_i. The word goup of highest total frequency is now chosen, and its high-frequency word is used again as a criterion for partitioning; this procedure continues until all word groups are small enough to be entered as concept classes into the thesaurus.

At each point in the partitioning process the following local decisions must be made:

1. The highest-frequency word in the high-frequency word goup is chosen, and it is used as the "central" word of the subbranch; then the other words in the same word group are examined to see if they fall into the same subbranch by being related in one way or another to the central word; no relations need exist among the words which form the "other", unrelated class.

2. If a given word cannot be placed properly in one of the two categories (either related to the central word or unrelated), it is left at the present level as a parent of the words in the subbranches.

3. If all words in a given word group are being placed in the same branch with the high-frequency word, this word belongs one level up as a parent of all the remaining words.

Consider again the vocabulary of Fig. 6-11. The highest-frequency word is "computer" (frequency 508). First, two classes are formed of words like "computer" and the "other" words (see Fig. 6-12). The high-frequency class contains the term "computer", so that it is subdivided again using the word "computer" as a criterion. Then this produces two classes consisting, respectively, of "computer", "program", "digital", and "memory" and "system", "circuit", and "data"; the term "machine" which is generic to the whole class remains on the second level. The original "other" category can be subdivided also, using the included high-frequency word "operate" as a guide and producing the complete hierarchy shown in Fig. 6-12.

A comparison of the hierarchies of Figs. 6-11 and 6-12 reveals that the word groups produced by the thesaurus question method of Fig. 6-11 may be more reasonable; however, the frequency procedure is more systematic and may conceivably be easier to apply.

The last hierarchy formation process is also based on a term-document or a term-property matrix. In this case, however, the process of forming the hierarchy is completely automatic, even though the original property matrix may have been con-

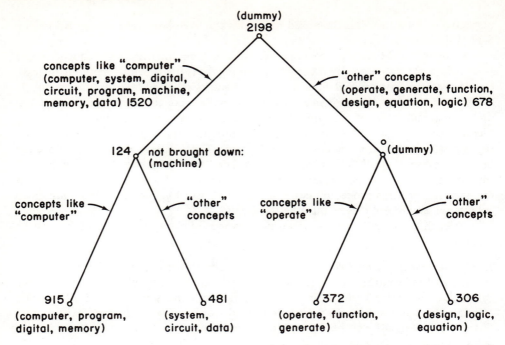

Fig. 6-12 Hierarchy construction by frequency algorithm.

structed by hand. Consider two arbitrary terms identified by weighted property vectors. The following conditions may then be obtained:

1. Terms *A* and *B* are identified by different properties, and as such are not related.

2. Terms *A* and *B* are identified by the same properties, and the weights of the properties are reasonably similar for both terms, so that neither term dominates the other, and they are placed in the same concept class.

3. Terms *A* and *B* are identified by the same properties, but the property weights are higher for term *A* than for term *B*; then *A* may be said to dominate *B* and may be placed on a higher level in the hierarchy.

4. Terms *A* and *B* are identified by the same properties, and *B* dominates *A*.

In order to make a decision concerning the similarity between two property vectors, it is necessary to compute a similarity coefficient between them. In the present context, it is best to use an asymmetric coefficient such that the similarity between term *i* and term *j* is not necessarily the same as between term *j* and term *i*. Given property vectors $\mathbf{v}^i$ and $\mathbf{v}^j$, representing terms T_i and T_j, respectively, a possible similarity measure is

$$\mathbf{c}_{ij} = \frac{\sum\limits_k \min\,(\mathbf{v}^i_k,\,\mathbf{v}^j_k)}{\sum\limits_k \mathbf{v}^i_k}.$$

Using this measure, a term-term correlation matrix can now be constructed, giving for each pair of terms the similarity measure c. It may be noticed, that if the two vectors $\mathbf{v}^i$ and $\mathbf{v}^j$ are identical, then $\mathbf{c}_{ij}$ equals 1, and when $\mathbf{v}^i$ and $\mathbf{v}^j$ have no common properties, then $\mathbf{c}_{ij}$ equals 0. A cutoff value K may now be applied to the similarity coefficients, and a hierarchy may be formed based on the following algorithm [11]:

1. If $\mathbf{c}_{ij}$ and $\mathbf{c}_{ji}$ are both below the cutoff value K, then terms i and j are unrelated.

2. If $\mathbf{c}_{ij}$ and $\mathbf{c}_{ji}$ are both above cutoff, then terms i and j are synonymous and are placed in the same thesaurus category.

3. If $\mathbf{c}_{ij}$ is below cutoff and $\mathbf{c}_{ji}$ is above cutoff, then term i is a parent of term j in the hierarchical arrangement.

4. If $\mathbf{c}_{ij}$ is above cutoff and $\mathbf{c}_{ji}$ is below cutoff, then term j is a parent of term i.

This system may not generate a true tree structure, since a given term may have more than one assigned parent. The method is, however, fully automatic, and a manual revision after the initial generation can be used to modify the resulting hierarchy to make it acceptable. This can be accomplished, for example, by introducing cross references between terms in the hierarchy to replace the connections which are not compatible with the tree organization.

Various procedures have been suggested for updating hierarchies and dictionaries by addition of new terms and deletion of old ones [11], [12]. These must be used in conjunction with the dictionary lookup operations in any operating situation.

REFERENCES

[1] G. Salton, Automatic Phrase Matching, in *Readings in Automatic Language Processing*, D. G. Hays, ed., American Elsevier Publishing Co., Inc., New York, 1966, pp. 169–188.

[2] C. Harris, Dictionary and Hierarchy Formation, Information Storage and Retrieval, *Report ISR-7* to the National Science Foundation, Section III, Harvard Computation Laboratory, Cambridge, Mass., June 1964.

[3] C. Harris, Dictionary Construction and Updating, Information Storage and Retrieval, *Report ISR-8* to the National Science Foundation, Section VII, Harvard Computation Laboratory, Cambridge, Mass., December 1964.

[4] L. B. Doyle, Is Automatic Classification a Reasonable Application of Statistical Analysis of Text, *Journal of the ACM*, Vol. 12, No. 4, October 1965.

[5] S. F. Dennis, The Construction of a Thesaurus Automatically from a Sample of Text, *Proceedings Symposium on Statistical Association Methods for Mechanized Documentation, Miscellaneous Publication 269*, National Bureau of Standards, Washington, D.C., 1965, pp. 61–148.

[6] G. Salton, Data Manipulation and Programming Problems in Automatic Information Retrieval, *Communications of the ACM*, Vol. 9, No. 3, March 1966.

[7] L. B. Doyle, Semantic Road Maps for Literature Searchers, *Journal of the ACM*, Vol. 8, No. 4, October 1961.

[8] L. Rolling, Euratom Thesaurus—Keywords Used within Euratom's Nuclear Energy Documentation Project, *Report EUR 500.e*, Euratom Center for Information and Documentation, Brussels, 1964.

[9] K. Sparck Jones, Experiments in Semantic Classification, *Mechanical Translation*, Vol. 8, No. 3–4, October 1965.

[10] F. Lévery, Organisation et consultation d'un thesaurus, *Proceedings 1965 International FID Congress*, Spartan Books, New York, October 1965.

[11] C. T. Abraham, Techniques for Thesaurus Organization and Evaluation, in *Information Science*, M. Kochen, ed., Scarecrow Press, Inc., 1965.

[12] P. Reisner, Semantic Diversity and a Growing Man-machine Thesaurus, in *Information Science*, M. Kochen, ed., Scarecrow Press, Inc., 1965.

[13] Guy T. Hochgesang, SOCCER—A Concordance Program, Information Storage and Retrieval, *Report ISR-11* to the National Science Foundation, Section III, Cornell University, Ithaca, N.Y. 1966.

[14] M. Lesk, Semi-automatic Semantic Classification Systems, Unpublished manuscript, Harvard Computation Laboratory, Cambridge, Mass., 1965.

[15] L. B. Doyle, Expanding the Editing Function in Language Data Processing, *Communications of the ACM*, Vol. 8, No. 4, April 1965.

This study provides a summary of the SMART *system organization with emphasis on the evaluation procedures incorporated into the system. Experimental retrieval results are then given using document collections in the areas of computer science, documentation, and aerodynamics. In particular, the retrieval effectiveness of the following system parameters is covered: demand length, query-document matching functions, term weights, word stem generation methods, synonym recognition use, phrase recognition procedures, and hierarchical expansion methods. The evaluation results are used to derive design criteria for modern information systems.*

7

COMPUTER EVALUATION OF INDEXING AND TEXT PROCESSING †

G. SALTON and M. E. LESK

7-1 INTRODUCTION

Throughout the technical world, a growing interest is evident in the design and implementation of mechanized information systems. Over the last few years, the general feeling that something should be done to help organize and store some of the available information resources has given way to the widespread impression that modern computing equipment may in fact be capable of alleviating and solving to some extent the so-called information problem. Specifically, it is believed that the required capacity to store many data or document collections of interest does exist, that procedures are available for analyzing and organizing the information in storage, and that real-time software and hardware can be used to ensure the retrieval of stored information in response to requests from a given user population in a convenient form and at little cost in time and effort [1], [2], [3].

Before investing the necessary resources required for the implementation of sophisticated information services, it is necessary to generate the

†This study was published as Section III in *Scientific Report ISR-12*, June 1967. It also appeared in *Journal of the ACM*, Vol. 15, No. 1, January 1968, pp. 8–36.

detailed systems specifications and to determine which of many possible alternative design features should in fact be implemented. This, in turn, must be made to depend on experimentation in a controlled environment to test and evaluate the effectiveness of various possible search and analysis procedures. The SMART document retrieval system, which has been operating on an IBM 7094 for over two years, has been used extensively to test a large variety of automatic retrieval procedures, including fully automatic information analysis methods, automatic procedures for dictionary construction, and iterative search techniques based on user interaction with the system [4], [5], [6], [7].

The present study summarizes the results obtained with the SMART system over a two-year period starting in 1964 and presents evaluation output based on the processing of three document collections in three different subject fields. Conclusions are drawn concerning the most likely analysis methods to be implemented in an operational environment. The emphasis throughout is on text analysis procedures because they form an important part of a document-handling system. Several operational problems, including the actual network implementation of a retrieval system are not covered; cost and timing estimates are also excluded because these are tied directly to the specific environment within which a given system actually operates.

First, the basic features of the SMART system are described, and then the design of the main experiments is outlined; this includes the statistical procedures used to test the significance of the evaluation output obtained. Then the principal evaluation results are presented, and tentative conclusions are reached concerning the effectiveness of automatic text analysis procedures as part of future information systems. The results derived from the present experiments are also compared briefly with the output obtained with several other testing systems.

7-2 THE SMART SYSTEM

7-2-A Basic Organization

The SMART system is a fully automatic document retrieval system operating on the IBM 7094. The system does not rely on manually assigned keywords or index terms for the identification of documents and search requests, nor does it use primarily the frequency of occurrence of certain words or phrases included in the document texts. Instead, the system goes beyond simple word-matching procedures by using a variety of intellectual aids in the form of synonym dictionaries, hierarchical arrangements of subject identifiers, phrase-generating methods, and the like, in order to obtain the content identifications useful for the retrieval process.

The following facilities incorporated into the SMART system for purposes of document analysis are of principal interest:

(a) A system for separating English words into stems and affixes which can be used to reduce incoming texts into *word stem* form.

(b) A synonym dictionary, or thesaurus, which replaces significant word stems by *concept numbers*, each concept representing a class of related word stems.

(c) A *hierarchical arrangement* of the concepts included in the thesaurus which makes it possible, given any concept number, to find its "parent" in the hierarchy, its "sons," its "brothers," and any of a set of possible cross references.

(d) *Statistical association* methods which compute similarity coefficients between words, word stems, or concepts, based on co-occurrence patterns between these entities in the sentences of a document or in the documents of a collection; associated items can then serve as content identifiers in addition to the original ones.

(e) *Syntactic analysis* methods which permit the recognition and use, as indicators of document content, of phrases consisting of several words or concepts where each element of a phrase must hold a specified syntactic relation to each other element.

(f) *Statistical phrase* recognition methods which operate like the preceding syntactic procedures by using a preconstructed phrase dictionary, except that no test is made to ensure that the syntactic relationships between phrase components are satisfied.

(g) *Request-document matching* procedures which make it possible to use a variety of different correlation methods to compare analyzed documents with analyzed requests, including concept weight adjustments and variations in the length of the document texts being analyzed.

Stored documents and search requests are processed by the system without any prior manual analysis using one of several hundred automatic content analysis methods; those documents which most nearly match a given search request are identified. Specifically, a correlation coefficient is computed to indicate the degree of similarity between each document and each search request, and documents are then ranked in decreasing order of the correlation coefficient [4], [5], [6]. Then a cutoff can be selected, and documents above the chosen cutoff can be withdrawn from the file and turned over to the user as answers to the search request.

The search process may be controlled by the user in that a request can be processed first in a standard mode. After analysis of the output which is produced, feedback information can then be returned to the system where it is used to reprocess the request under altered conditions. The new output can be examined again, and the search can be iterated until the right kind and amount of information are obtained [7], [8].

The SMART systems organization makes it possible to evaluate the effectiveness of the various processing methods by comparing the output obtained from a variety of different runs. This is achieved by processing the *same* search requests against the *same* document collections several times, while making selected changes in the analysis procedures between runs. By comparing the performance of the search requests under different processing conditions, it is then possible to determine the relative effectiveness of the various analysis methods. The evaluation procedures actually used are described in the next section.

7-2-B   Evaluation Process

The evaluation of an information search and retrieval system can be carried out in many different ways depending on the type of system considered—operational, experimental with user populations, or laboratory—on the viewpoint taken—the user, the manager, or the operator—and on other factors—such as the special aims of the evaluation study. A large number of different variables may affect the results of any evaluation process. These include the kind of user population, the type and coverage of the document collection, the indexing tools, the analysis and search methods incorporated into the system, the input–output equipment, the operating efficiency, cost and time lag, and many others.

In the present context, the user's viewpoint is taken, and the overriding criterion of systems effectiveness is taken to be the ability of the system to satisfy the user's information need. Management criteria such as cost are not considered, even though in the final analysis the problem is of primary importance; the most effective system will not be of use if the operations are too costly to be performed. However, costs are difficult to measure in an experimental situation where unusual fluctuations may occur because of many extraneous factors. Furthermore, the immediate need is for a measurement of the effectiveness of the intellectual tools used to analyze and search the stored information, since these are responsible in large part for the retrieval results. Costs can be taken into account later, for example, by providing several classes of service at varying cost.

The evaluation measures actually used are based on the standard *recall* and *precision* measures. In an operational situation, where information needs may vary from user to user, some customers may require high recall—the retrieval of almost everything that is likely to be of interest—while others may prefer high precision—the rejection of everything likely to be useless. Everything else being equal, a perfect system is one which exhibits both a high recall and a high precision.

If a cut is made through the document collection to distinguish retrieved items from nonretrieved on the one hand, and if procedures are available for separating relevant items from nonrelevant ones on the other hand, the standard recall R and standard precision P may be defined as follows:

$$R = \frac{\text{Number of items retrieved and relevant}}{\text{Total relevant in collection}},$$

and

$$P = \frac{\text{Number of items retrieved and relevant}}{\text{Total retrieved in collection}}.$$

The computation of these measures is straightforward only if exhaustive relevance judgments are available for each document with respect to each search request, and if the cutoff value which distinguishes retrieved from nonretrieved material can be determined unambiguously [8], [9], [10].

In the evaluation work carried out with the SMART system, manually derived, exhaustive relevance judgments are used because all the document collections processed are relatively small. Moreover, the choice of a unique cutoff is avoided by computing the precision for various recall values and exhibiting a plot showing recall against precision. An example of such a graph is shown in Fig. 7-1 for query

RELEVANT DOCUMENTS		
Rank	Number	Correlation
1	80	.5084
2	102	.4418
3	81	.4212
10	82	.2843
11	193	.2731
14	83	.2631
15	87	.2594
20	88	.2315
40	86	.1856
50	109	.1631
69	84	.1305
78	85	.1193

(a)

RECALL-PRECISION AFTER RETRIEVAL OF X DOCUMENTS		
X	Recall	Precision
1	0.0833	1.0000
2	0.1667	1.0000
3	0.2500	1.0000
9	0.2500	0.3333
10	0.3333	0.4000
11	0.4167	0.4545
13	0.4167	0.3846
14	0.5000	0.4286
15	0.5833	0.4667
19	0.5833	0.3684
20	0.6667	0.4000
39	0.6667	0.2051
40	0.7500	0.2250
49	0.7500	0.1837
50	0.8333	0.2000
68	0.8333	0.1470
69	0.9167	0.1594
77	0.9167	0.1428
78	1.0000	0.1538

(b)

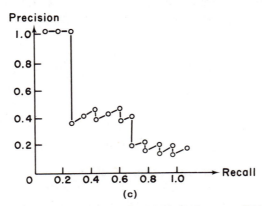

(c)

Fig. 7-1 Performance characteristics for query Q145 (Cranfield-1, word stem run): (a) list of relevant documents; (b) recall-precision table; (c) recall-precision plot.

Q145, processed against a collection of 200 documents in aerodynamics. A total of 12 documents in the collection were judged relevant to the request, the relevance judgments being performed by a subject expert independently of the retrieval system. The ranks of the relevant documents produced by the search system after ordering of the documents in decreasing correlation order are shown in Fig. 7-1(a). For the retrieval process illustrated in Fig. 7-1, these ranks range from 1 for the relevant document with the highest request-document correlation to 78 for the relevant item with the lowest correlation. By choosing successive cutoff values after the retrieval of 1, 2, 3, . . . , n documents, and computing recall and precision values at each point, a recall-precision table can be constructed, as shown in Fig. 7-1(b). The recall-precision graph obtained from this table is represented in Fig. 7-1(c).

Recall-precision graphs, such as that of Fig. 7-1(c), have been criticized because a number of parameters are obscured when plotting recall against precision—for example, the size of the retrieved document set and the size of the collection [11]. Such plots are, however, effective in summarizing the performance of retrieval methods averaged over many search requests, and they can be used advantageously to select analysis methods which fit certain specific operating ranges. Thus, if it is desired to select a procedure which favors the retrieval of *all* relevant material, then one must concentrate on the high recall region; similarly, if *only* relevant material is desired, the high precision region is of importance. In general, it is possible to obtain high recall only at a substantial cost in precision and vice versa [8], [9], [10].

In addition to the standard recall and standard precision measures, whose values depend on the size of the retrieved document set, it is also possible to use indicators which are independent of the retrieved set. In particular, since the SMART system produces ranked document output in decreasing order of correlation between documents and search requests, evaluation measures can be generated based on the ranks of the set of relevant documents, as determined by the automatic retrieval process, compared with the ranks of the relevant documents for an ideal system where all relevant items are retrieved before any nonrelevant ones are retrieved.

Two particularly attractive measures with this property are normalized recall and normalized precision, which are defined as follows [7], [9]:

$$R_{\text{norm}} = 1 - \frac{\sum_{i=1}^{n} r_i - \sum_{i=1}^{n} i}{n(N-n)},$$

and

$$P_{\text{norm}} = 1 - \frac{\sum_{i=1}^{n} \log r_i - \sum_{i=1}^{n} \log i}{\log N!/(N-n)!\, n!}$$

where n is the size of the relevant document set, N is the size of the total document collection, and r_i is the rank of the ith relevant document when the documents are arranged in decreasing order of their correlation with the search request.

These measures range from 1 for a perfect system, in which all relevant items are placed at the top of the retrieved list, to 0 for the worst case where all nonrelevant items are retrieved before any relevant ones. Furthermore under certain circumstances, the normalized measures can be shown to be closely related to the standard measures as follows [12]:

$$R_{\text{norm}} \approx \frac{1}{N} \sum_{i=1}^{n} R(i),$$

when the number of relevant documents n is small compared to the collection size N, and

$$P_{\text{norm}} \approx \frac{1}{N} \sum_{i=1}^{n} P(i)$$

for large N and not too small n. $R(i)$ and $P(i)$ correspond, respectively, to the standard recall and precision values after the retrieval of i documents.

Two further overall measures of retrieval effectiveness, analogous to the normalized measures but somewhat simpler to compute, are the "rank recall" and "log precision" measures, defined as

$$\text{Rank recall} = \frac{\sum_{i=1}^{n} i}{\sum_{i=1}^{n} r_i},$$

and

$$\text{Log precision} = \frac{\sum_{i=1}^{n} \log i}{\sum_{i=1}^{n} \log r_i},$$

where again n is equal to the number of relevant documents, and r_i is the rank (in decreasing correlation order) of the ith relevant document. Like the normalized measures, rank recall and log precision are functions of the rank of the relevant documents, but contrary to the earlier situation, these measures do not take into account the collection size N.

Under normal circumstances, the results of a systems evaluation must reflect overall system performance, rather than the performance for individual requests only. In these circumstances, it is convenient to process many search requests and to use an average performance value as a measure of retrieval effectiveness [12]. For the overall evaluation measures (normalized recall, normalized precision, rank recall, and log precision), the averaging process presents no problem because only a single set of values is obtained in each case for each request. The averaging method is more complex for the standard recall-precision graph, since a continuous set of values is involved, and the number of relevant documents differs from request to request. In the SMART system, the averaging process for the recall-precision graph corresponding to many search requests is performed as follows:

(a) Ten specified standard recall values are selected ranging from 0.1 to 1.0.

(b) For each recall level, the number of documents which must be retrieved in order to obtain the specified level is determined.

(c) Using the cutoff value calculated in this manner for the number of retrieved documents, the precision value is generated corresponding to the specified recall.

(d) The precision values obtained for a given recall value are averaged over a number of search requests, and the resulting point is added to the recall-precision plot.

(e) The ten individual points on the plot are joined to produce an average recall-precision curve.

Averaged evaluation results are presented for three different document collections in Sec. 7-3.

7-2-C   Significance Computations

For each search request and each processing method, the evaluation procedure incorporated into the SMART system produces 14 different statistics, including 4 global statistics (rank recall, log precision, normalized recall, and normalized precision), and 10 local statistics (standard precision for 10 recall levels). A problem then arises concerning the use of these 14 statistics for the assessment of systems performance. In theory, comparisons between different processing methods are easy to make by contrasting, for example, the recall-precision plots obtained in each case. In practice, it is difficult to draw "hard" conclusions because the variation in performance between individual requests is large, because the 14 measures have different ranges, and because it is unclear a priori whether the magnitude of a given recall or precision value is significant or not. In particular, given a specified recall or precision value, it is of interest to determine whether values as large, or larger, as the given one could be expected under random circumstances, or whether on the contrary the probability of obtaining a given specified value for an average system is very small.

Because of the large request variance and the differences in the range of the various parameters, the significance computations incorporated into the SMART system are based on *paired comparisons* between the request performance using processing method *A*, and the performance using method *B*. In particular, the difference in magnitude is computed for each of the 14 pairs of statistics obtained for each request for each pair of processing methods. These differences are then averaged over many requests, and statistical computations are used to transform the averaged differences into probability measurements. Each of the 14 values obtained in this manner represents the probability that if the performance level of the two methods *A* and *B* were in fact equally high for the given statistic (except for random variations in the test results), then a test value as large as the one actually observed would occur for a system. A probability value of 0.05 is usually taken as an upper bound in judging whether a deviation in test values is significant or not. Using this probability value as a limit, the corresponding test difference would in fact be significant 19 times out of 20; only 1 time out of 20 would two equally effective systems be expected to produce as large a test difference.

Because it is difficult to judge systems performance by using 14 different probability values corresponding to the 14 evaluation measures, an *aggregate probability value* is computed from 14 individual probabilities. The significance of this aggregate depends on the independence of the various individual tests.

Two separate testing procedures are incorporated into the SMART system. The first one uses the well-known *t test* based on Student's *t* distribution [13]. This test requires an underlying normal distribution of the data used in the test process, as well as the independence among the search requests processed against the document collections. The *t* test process takes into account the actual magnitude of the differences for the statistics being calculated, and the resulting probabilities are considered to be reliable indicators of system differences.

A less demanding testing procedure is furnished by the *sign test*, where the magnitude of the differences in the statistics is not taken into account, but the sign of the differences is (that is, an indication of whether method *A* provides a larger test result than *B* or vice versa) [14]. An attractive feature of the sign test is that normality of the input data is not required, and since this normality is generally hard to prove for statistics derived from a request-document correlation process, the sign test probabilities may provide a better indicator of system performance than the *t* test.

The *t* test computations are performed as follows: let m_{ijA} be the value of statistic *i* for request *j*, using method *A* (for example, the value of the rank recall or the normalized recall). Then, given two processing methods *A* and *B*, and a set of *k* requests, the average of the differences for statistic *i* are computed. Specifically,

and

$$d_{ij} = m_{ijA} - m_{ijB},$$

$$D_i = \frac{1}{k} \sum_{j=1}^{k} d_{ij}.$$

The difference computations for two statistics (rank recall and log precision) are shown in Table 7-1. The average differences are then used to obtain the standard deviation of the differences $(SD)_i$ and the *t* test values T_i, where

$$T_i = \frac{D_i}{(SD)_i} k.$$

The *t*-test values T_i are now converted to probabilities P_{ti} using Student's *t* distribution with *k* degrees of freedom.

The probabilities derived from the 14 statistics are then used to compute an aggregate probability by first converting the two-tailed *t* test to a one-tailed test, changing each probability to chi-square, adding the chi-square values, and finally reconverting to a probability P_t, using a chi-square distribution with 28 degrees of freedom [13]. Specifically, let *s* be the sign of the sum of the differences D_i, or

$$s = \text{sign}\left(\sum_i D_i\right).$$

Then

$$\text{if sign } D_i = s \Rightarrow P'_{ti} = \tfrac{1}{2} P_{ti},$$

Table 7-1

COMPUTATION OF RECALL AND PRECISION DIFFERENCES
FOR INDIVIDUAL REQUESTS

(Method A: Stem Concon; Method B: Thesaurus)

REQUEST NAME	RANK RECALL		DIFFERENCE	LOG PRECISION		DIFFERENCE
	Method A	*Method B*		*Method A*	*Method B*	
AUTOMATA PHR	0.5238	0.9649	−0.4411	0.7126	0.9881	−0.2755
COMP SYSTEMS	0.0725	0.1228	−0.0503	0.3783	0.4806	−0.1023
COMPS-ASSEMB	0.3714	0.7428	−0.3714	0.8542	0.9453	−0.0911
CORE MEMORY	0.0691	0.1064	−0.0373	0.3157	0.3695	−0.0538
DIFFERNTL EQ	0.5298	0.7574	−0.2276	0.8620	0.9219	−0.0599
ERROR CONTRL	0.1460	0.1875	−0.0415	0.5342	0.5972	−0.0630
M10-COUNTERS	0.8182	0.7347	0.0835	0.8682	0.8599	0.0083
M2-TRANSMIT	0.0522	0.0963	−0.0441	0.2819	0.4698	−0.1879
M3-INFORM	0.1968	0.3134	−0.1166	0.6300	0.7666	−0.1366
M8-STORAGE	0.0375	0.2763	−0.2388	0.2670	0.4666	−0.1996
MISSILE TRAK	1.0000	0.7500	0.2500	1.0000	0.6309	0.3691
MORSE CODE	1.0000	1.0000	0.0000	1.0000	1.0000	0.0000
PATTERN RECG	1.0000	1.0000	0.0000	1.0000	1.0000	0.0000
RANDOM NUMBS	0.0517	0.2000	−0.1483	0.1750	0.3408	−0.1658
SOLSTAT CIRC	0.2766	0.3402	−0.0636	0.6921	0.7912	−0.0991
SWITCH FUNCS	0.3529	0.4444	−0.0915	0.7416	0.8005	−0.0589
THIN FILMS	0.2157	0.8462	−0.6305	0.6294	0.9242	−0.2948
Total	6.7142	8.8833	−2.1691	10.9422	12.3531	−1.4109
Average value over 17 requests	0.3950	0.5225	−0.1276	0.6437	0.7267	−0.0830

alternatively

$$\text{if sign } D_i \neq s \Rightarrow P'_{ti} = 1 - \tfrac{1}{2}P_{ti}.$$

The chi square of the sum is now obtained such that

$$\chi^2 = -\sum_{i=1}^{14} -2 \log P'_{ti}.$$

Finally, this value is converted to the desired probability P_t.

The t-test computations are shown for two sample analysis methods A and B in Table 7-2. The values in the first two columns of Table 7-2 represent averages over 17 search requests for each of the 14 evaluation measures. The final probabilities P_{ti} range from a high of 0.107 for the standard precision at recall value 1, to a low of 0.0007 for the normalized precision. The final probability value P_t is smaller than 1.10^{-4}, thus indicating that the combination algorithm concentrates on the significant tests, while ignoring the less significant ones. The validity of the process depends on

Table 7-2

t-TEST COMPUTATIONS FOR 14 DIFFERENT RECALL AND PRECISION MEASURES

(Averages over 17 requests, Method *A*: Stem Concon; Method *B*: Thesaurus)

	EVALUATION MEASURE	AVERAGE VALUE		DIFFERENCE OF AVERAGE	STANDARD DEVIATION	*t*-TEST VALUE	PROBABILITY
		Method A	*Method B*				
1.	Rank recall	0.3950	0.5225	−0.1276	2.07E−01	2.54E 00	0.0219
2.	Log precision	0.6437	0.7267	−0.0830	1.47E−01	2.33E 00	0.0334
3.	Normed recall	0.9233	0.9675	−0.0442	5.35E−02	3.41E 00	0.0036
4.	Normed precision	0.7419	0.8639	−0.1219	1.20E−01	4.19E 00	0.0007
5.	0.1	0.7385	0.9735	−0.2351	2.88E−01	3.37E 00	0.0039
6.	0.2	0.6544	0.8973	−0.2428	2.82E−01	3.55E 00	0.0026
7.	0.3	0.5844	0.8245	−0.2401	2.51E−01	3.95E 00	0.0011
8.	Precision Graph 0.4	0.5326	0.7551	−0.2226	2.39E−01	3.84E 00	0.0014
9.	(Precision for 0.5	0.5187	0.7146	−0.1959	2.00E−01	4.04E 00	0.0009
10.	ten recall levels) 0.6	0.5035	0.6499	−0.1464	1.59E−01	3.79E 00	0.0016
11.	0.7	0.4452	0.6012	−0.1561	1.79E−01	3.59E 00	0.0024
12.	0.8	0.4091	0.5514	−0.1423	2.24E−01	2.62E 00	0.0184
13.	0.9	0.3794	0.4973	−0.1179	2.29E−01	2.12E 00	0.0499
14.	1.0	0.3106	0.4118	−0.1012	2.44E−01	1.71E 00	0.1070

Combined Significance: Total Chi Square: 1.67E−02
Total probability of *B* over *A*: 0.0000

an assumption of independence among the 14 measures, which is true to a limited extent for the measures used.

The sign test uses the binomial instead of the t distribution to produce a probability value. Specifically, given two processing methods for which the null hypothesis applies (that is, two equivalent methods), each d_{ij} has an equal chance of being positive or negative; moreover, since the search requests are assumed unrelated (independent) and randomly distributed, the signs of the differences are unrelated. The number, let us say M, of positive signs is accordingly distributed binomially with P equal to one-half and k equal to the number of requests.

M can then serve as a statistic to test the null hypothesis by taking large values of M as significant evidence against the equivalence of the two methods tested. Obviously, a test based on rejecting the equivalence hypothesis for large values of M is equivalent to a test based on rejection for small values of M', the number of negative signs. As before, a probability of 0.05 may be taken as an upper limit for rejecting the equivalence assumption.

Since the sign test does not depend on the magnitudes of the differences, the number of positive or negative signs can be cumulated directly. In particular, the number of requests preferring method A is summed over all measures, as well as the number of requests preferring method B. These totals are then subjected to the same testing process, as follows. Let t be a tolerance value, taken as 0.001 for the present test; further, for each statistic i, let

$$k_{ai} = \text{number of } d_{ij} \ (j = 1, \ldots, k) \text{ exceeding } +t,$$

$$k_{bi} = \text{number of } d_{ij} \text{ smaller than } -t,$$

and

$$k_{ci} = \text{number of } d_{ij} \text{ such that } |d_{ij}| \leq t,$$

where the number of requests $k = k_{ai} + k_{bi} + k_{ci}$.

The sign test probability for statistic i is now computed as follows: Let

$$k_{vi} = k_{ai} + k_{bi},$$

and

$$k_{wi} = \min (k_{ai}, k_{bi}).$$

Then

$$P_{si} = \sum_{j=1}^{k_{wi}} \frac{k_{vi}!}{j! \, (k_{vi} - j)!} \, 2^{-k_{vi}+1}.$$

The overall probability P_s can be cumulated directly for the 14 evaluation measures. Specifically, if

$$k_a = \sum_i k_{ai},$$

$$k_b = \sum_i k_{bi},$$

$$k_v = k_a + k_b,$$

and

$$k_w = \min (k_a, k_b),$$

then

$$P_s = \sum_{j=1}^{k_w} \frac{(k_v)!}{j! \, (k_v - j)!} \, 2^{-k_v + 1}.$$

The sign test computations are shown in Table 7-3 for the same processing methods and search requests used previously as examples in Tables 7-1, 7-2, and 7-3. The individual probabilities P_{si} range in values from 0.0010 to 0.1185. Again the overall probability is smaller than $1 \cdot 10^{-4}$; this is also reflected by the fact that method B is preferred 165 times, while A is superior only 26 times, with 47 ties.

Since the 14 statistics used may not be fully independent, a question arises concerning the interpretation of the cumulated t-test probability P_t, and the cumulated sign test probability P_s. As a general rule, the equality hypothesis between two given methods A and B can be rejected safely when both probabilities P_s and P_t do not exceed 0.001 in magnitude, implying that most of the individual probabilities P_{si} and P_{ti} are smaller than 0.05, and when the same test results are obtained for all document collections being tested. If, on the other hand, the values of the final prob-

Table 7-3

SIGN TEST COMPUTATIONS FOR 14 DIFFERENT RECALL
AND PRECISION MEASURES

(Averages over 17 Requests, Method A: Stem Concon; Method B: Thesaurus)

EVALUATION MEASURE		NUMBER OF REQUESTS SUPERIOR (METHOD A)	NUMBER OF REQUESTS SUPERIOR (METHOD B)	NUMBER OF REQUESTS EQUAL (A AND B)	PROBABILITY (B OVER A)
Rank recall		2	13	2	0.0074
Log precision		2	13	2	0.0074
Normed recall		2	13	2	0.0074
Normed precision		2	13	2	0.0074
Recall-precision graph	0.1	0	9	8	0.0039
	0.2	0	11	6	0.0010
	0.3	1	12	4	0.0034
	0.4	1	11	5	0.0036
	0.5	0	13	4	0.0002
	0.6	3	11	3	0.0574
	0.7	2	12	3	0.0129
	0.8	3	12	2	0.0352
	0.9	4	11	2	0.1185
	1.0	4	11	2	0.1185
Combined significance for 14 measures		26	165	47	0.0000

abilities are larger, or if the test results differ from one collection to the next, additional tests would seem to be required before a decision can be made.

7-3 EXPERIMENTAL RESULTS

7-3-A Test Environment

The principal parameters controlling the test procedure are listed in Tables 7-4, 7-5, and 7-6, respectively. The main properties of the document collections and search requests are shown in Table 7-4. Specifically, results are given for three document collections in the following subject fields:

(a) Computer Science (IRE-3): a set of 780 abstracts of documents in the computer literature, published in 1959–1961 and used with 34 search requests.

Table 7-4

DOCUMENT COLLECTION AND REQUEST CHARACTERISTICS

	Characteristics		IRE-3	CRAN-1	ADI
	Number of documents in collection		780	200	82
	Average number of words (all words) per document	full text	–	–	1380
		abstract	88	165	59
		title	9	14	10
Document collection	Average number of words (common words deleted) per document	full text	–	–	710
		abstract	49	91	35
		title	5	11	7
	Average number of concepts per analyzed document	full text	–	–	369
		abstract	40	65	25
		title	5	9	6
	Number of search requests		34	42	35
	Average number of words per request (all words)		22	17	14
Search requests	Request preparation (a) short paragraphs prepared by staff members for test purposes		✓		✓
	(b) short paragraphs prepared by subject experts previously submitted to operational system			✓	

Table 7-5

Characteristics	IRE-3	CRAN-1	ADI
Preparation of relevance judgments			
(a) dichotomous prepared by staff experts based on abstracts using full relevance assessment	✓		
(b) dichotomous prepared by subject experts based on abstracts and full text (full relevance assessment)		✓	
(c) dichotomous prepared by staff experts based on full text using full relevance assessment			✓
Number of relevant documents per request (all requests)			
(a) range	2–65	1–12	1–33
(b) mean	17.4	4.7	4.9
(c) generality (mean divided by collection size)	22.2	23.6	59.2
Number of relevant documents per specific request			
(a) number of specific requests	17	21	17
(b) mean number of relevant	7.5	3.0	2.1
Number of relevant documents per general request			
(a) number of general requests	18	21	18
(b) mean number of relevant	25.8	6.4	7.4

Table 7-6

General Test Environment

Characteristics	IRE-3	CRAN-1	ADI
User population			
(a) 10 students and staff experts	✓		✓
(b) 42 subject experts		✓	
Number of retrieved documents per request	all	all	all
Number of indexing and search programs used			
(a) matching algorithms	2	2	2
(b) term weight adjustment	2	2	2
(c) document length variation	3	4	3
(d) basic dictionaries (suffix "s", stem, thesaurus, stat. phrases, hierarchy, syntax)	6	5	5
(e) concept-concept association dictionaries	2	3	1
(f) total basic options	144	240	60

(b) Documentation (ADI): a set of 82 short papers, each an average of 1380 words in length, presented at the 1963 Annual Meeting of the American Documentation Institute and used with 35 search requests.

(c) Aerodynamics (CRAN-1): a set of 200 abstracts of documents used by the second Aslib–Cranfield Project [15] and used with 42 search requests.

Each of these collections belongs to a distinct subject area, thus permitting the comparison of the various analysis and search procedures in several contexts. The ADI collection in documentation is of particular interest because full papers are available rather than only document abstracts. The Cranfield collection, on the other hand, is the only one which is also manually indexed by trained indexers, thus making it possible to perform a comparison of the standard keyword search procedures with the automatic text-processing methods.

The procedure used to collect relevance assessments and the related statistical information concerning the average number of relevant documents per request are summarized in Table 7-5. Exhaustive procedures were used to assess the relevance of each document with respect to each search request. Only one person (the requestor) was asked to collect the judgments for each request, and dichotomous assessments were made to declare each document as either relevant or not. In the words of a recent study on evaluation methodology, the process used consists of "multiple events of private relevance" [17].

Additional data concerning the user population and the number of search programs employed are given in Table 7-6. In each case, the user population consisted of volunteers who were asked to help in the test process. Several hundred analysis and search methods incorporated into the SMART system were used with the three document collections. Results based on about 60 of these processing methods are exhibited in the present study.

The methods chosen are generally useful in answering a number of basic questions affecting the design of automatic information systems. For example, can automatic text-processing methods be used effectively to replace a manual content analysis? If so, what part or parts of a document should be incorporated in the automatic procedure? Is it necessary to provide vocabulary normalization methods to eliminate ambiguities caused by homographs and synonymous word groups? Should such a normalization be handled by means of a specially constructed dictionary, or is it possible to replace thesauri completely by statistical word association methods? Which dictionaries can be used most effectively for vocabulary normalization? What should the role of the user be in formulating and controlling the search procedure? These and other questions are considered in the evaluation process described in the remainder of this chapter.

7-3-B   Document Length

A primary variable of interest is the *length* of each document to be used for content analysis purposes. This fundamental question enters into many of the arguments between advocates of automatic systems and others who hold that manual content analysis methods are essential, because in an automatic environment, it is not normally possible to process the full text of all documents.

In Fig. 7-2, three analysis systems based only on document titles are compared with systems based on the manipulation of complete document abstracts. In each case, weighted word stems, extracted either from the titles or from the abstracts of the documents, are matched with equivalent indicators from the search requests. Figure 7-2 exhibits recall-precision graphs, averaged respectively over 34, 42, and 35 search requests for the computer science, aerodynamics, and documentation collections. In every case, the abstract process is found to be superior to the "title only" option, particularly at the high recall end of the curve, since the abstract curve comes closest to the upper right-hand corner of the graph where both recall and precision are equal to 1. [For an ideal system which retrieves all relevant items before any irrelevant ones, the recall-precision curve shrinks to a single point with coordinates (1, 1)].

The significance output for the graphs shown in Figs. 7-2 through 7-9 is collected in Table 7-7. In each case, reference is made to the graphs being compared, and the combined probability values P_s and P_t are listed with an indicator specifying the preferred method. The superiority of the abstract-stem process of Fig. 7-2 is reflected in the significance output of Table 7-7. The probability of a correct null hypothesis is smaller than 1.10^{-4} for both the sign and the t tests, thus showing that document titles are definitely inferior to doument abstracts as a source of content indicators.

The ADI documentation collection was used to extend the analysis to longer document segments. The results of a comparison between document abstract processing (60 words) and full text processing (1400 words) show that the full text process is superior to the abstract process. The improvement in performance appears smaller than that shown in Fig. 7-2 for the title-abstract comparison. In particular, the t-text probabilities for the abstract—full text comparisons are too large to permit an unequivocal rejection of the null hypothesis in this case.

In summary, document abstracts are more effective for content analysis purposes than are document titles alone; further improvements appear possible when abstracts are replaced by large text portions; however, the increase in effectiveness is not large enough to reach the unequivocal conclusion that full text processing is always superior to abstract processing.

7-3-C   Matching Functions and Term Weights

It is easy in an automatic text-processing environment to differentiate among individual content indicators by assigning weights to the indicators in proportion to their presumed importance. Such weights can be derived in part by using the frequency of occurrence of the original text words which give rise to the various indicators, and in part as a function of the various dictionary-mapping procedures. Thus, ambiguous terms which in a synonym dictionary would normally correspond to many different thesaurus classes, can be weighted less than unambiguous terms. The SMART system includes procedures for testing the effectiveness of such weighted (numeric)

Table 7-7

Combined Significance Output

RETRIEVAL METHODS BEING COMPARED	CORRESPONDING GRAPH NUMBER	DOCUMENT COLLECTION					
		IRE-3		CRAN-1		ADI	
		P_s	P_t	P_s	P_t	P_s	P_t
Title stem (A)	Fig. 7-2	0.0000 (B > A)	0.0000 (B > A)	0.0000 (B > A)	0.0000 (B > A)	0.0000 (B > A)	0.0000 (B > A)
Abstract stem (B)							
Abstract stem (A)		–	–	–	–	0.1420 (B > A)	0.0892 (B > A)
Full text stem (B)							
Abstract thesaurus (A)		–	–	–	–	0.0064 (B > A)	0.0987 (B > A)
Full text thesaurus (B)							
Numeric stem (A)	Fig. 7-3	0.0000 (A > B)	0.0000 (A > B)	0.0000 (A > B)	0.0000 (A > B)	0.3736 (A > B)	0.0040 (A > B)
Logical stem (B)							
Cosine logical stem (A)	Fig. 7-4	0.0000 (A > B)	0.0000 (A > B)	0.0000 (A > B)	0.0000 (A > B)	0.0891 (A > B)	0.0148 (A > B)
Overlap logical stems (B)							
Overlap numeric stem (A)		–	–	0.3497 (B > A)	0.1427 (B > A)	–	–
Overlap logical stem (B)							
Overlap numeric stem (A)		–	–	0.0000 (B > A)	0.0000 (B > A)	–	–
Cosine numeric stem (B)							
Word stem (A)		0.0000 (A > B)	0.0000 (A > B)	0.0000 (B > A)	0.0000 (B > A)	0.0000 (A > B)	0.0000 (A > B)
Suffix "s" (B)							
Thesaurus (A)	Fig. 7-5	0.0000 (A > B)	0.0000 (A > B)	0.0020 (A > B)	0.1483 (A > B)	0.0000 (A > B)	0.0000 (A > B)
Word stem (B)							
Old thesaurus (A)	Fig. 7-6	0.0000 (B > A)	0.0000 (B > A)	0.0000 (B > A)	0.0000 (B > A)	–	–
New thesaurus (B)							

Table 7-7—Cont.

RETRIEVAL METHODS BEING COMPARED	CORRESPONDING GRAPH NUMBER	DOCUMENT COLLECTION					
		IRE-3		CRAN-1		ADI	
		P_s	P_t	P_s	P_t	P_s	P_t
Thesaurus (A) / Phrases, weight 1.0 (B)		1.0000 (A > B)	0.8645 (B > A)	0.0001 (A > B)	0.1120 (A > B)	0.0391 (B > A)	0.1171 (B > A)
Word stem (A) / Stem concon (B)	Fig. 7-7	0.1948 (A > B)	0.0566 (A > B)	0.0086 (B > A)	0.0856 (B > A)	0.4420 (B > A)	0.6521 (B > A)
Concon all, 0.60 (A) / Concon 3–50, 0.60 (B)		—	—	0.0000 (B > A)	0.0525 (B > A)	—	—
Concon 3–50, 0.60 (A) / Concon 6–100, 0.45 (B)		—	—	0.0001 (B > A)	0.0991 (B > A)	—	—
Thesaurus (A) / Hierarchy parents (B)	Fig. 7-8	0.1047 (A > B)	0.1676 (A > B)	—	—	—	—
Thesaurus (A) / Hierarchy brothers (B)	Fig. 7-8	0.0000 (A > B)	0.0000 (A > B)	—	—	—	—
Thesaurus (A) / Hierarchy sons (B)		0.0000 (A > B)	0.0000 (A > B)	—	—	—	—
Thesaurus (A) / Hierarchy cross ref. (B)		0.0000 (A > B)	0.0000 (A > B)	—	—	—	—
Index stem (A) / Abstract stem (B)	Fig. 7-9	—	—	0.0465 (A > B)	0.0415 (A > B)	—	—
Index stem (A) / Stem concon (B)	Fig. 7-9	—	—	0.0020 (A > B)	0.0176 (A > B)	—	—
Index new thesaurus (A) / Abstract, new thesaurus (B)	Fig. 7-9	—	—	0.0019 (A > B)	0.0001 (A > B)	—	—

161

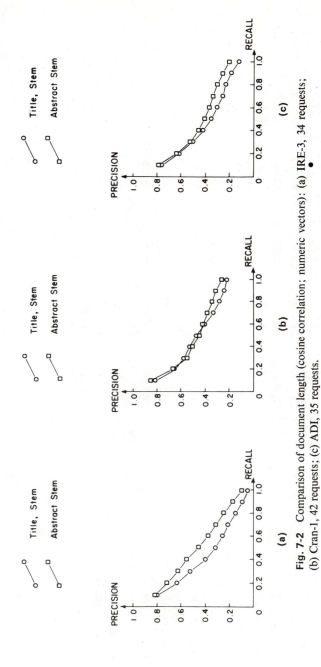

Fig. 7-2 Comparison of document length (cosine correlation; numeric vectors): (a) IRE-3, 34 requests; (b) Cran-1, 42 requests; (c) ADI, 35 requests.

content indicators compared with nonweighted (logical) indicators, where all term weights are either 1 or 0 (1 if a given term is assigned to a given document, and 0 if it is not).

The recall-precision graphs for the three collections used previously are shown in Fig. 7-3, and the corresponding significance output is reproduced in Table 7-7. In each case, weighted word stems extracted from document abstracts or full text are compared with nonweighted (logical) stems. The results are clearly in favor of the weighted process for all three collections, the largest performance differences being registered for the IRE collection in computer science. The recall-precision graph for the ADI collection also appears to show a considerable advantage for the weighted process, and this is reflected in the *t*-test probability of 0.0040. However, when the magnitudes of the results are disregarded, it is found that nearly as many evaluation parameters favor the nonweighted process as the weighted one for the documentation collection. Therefore the test results are not wholly significant for that collection. On the whole, it appears that weighted content indicators produce better retrieval results than nonweighted ones, and that binary term vectors should therefore be used only if no weighting system appears readily available.

Another variable affecting retrieval performance which can be incorporated easily into an automatic information system is the correlation coefficient used to determine the similarity between an analyzed search request and the analyzed documents. Two of the correlation measures which have been included in the SMART system are the cosine and overlap correlations which are defined as follows:

$$\text{Cos}(\mathbf{q}, \mathbf{d}) = \frac{\sum_{i=1}^{n} \mathbf{d}_i \mathbf{q}_i}{\sqrt{\sum_{i=1}^{n} (\mathbf{d}_i)^2 \times \sum_{i=1}^{n} (\mathbf{q}_i)^2}},$$

and

$$\text{Ovlap}(\mathbf{q}, \mathbf{d}) = \frac{\sum_{i=1}^{n} \min(\mathbf{q}_i, \mathbf{d}_i)}{\min\left(\sum_{i=1}^{n} \mathbf{q}_i, \sum_{i=1}^{n} \mathbf{d}_i\right)},$$

where $\mathbf{q}$ and $\mathbf{d}$ are considered to be n-dimensional vectors of terms representing an analyzed query $\mathbf{q}$ and an analyzed document $\mathbf{d}$, respectively, in a space of n terms assignable as information identifiers.

Both the cosine and the overlap functions range from 0 for no match to 1 for perfect identity between the respective vectors. The cosine correlation is more sensitive to document length, that is, to the number of assigned terms because of the factor in the denominator and tends to produce greater variations in the correlations than the overlap measure.

A comparison of cosine and overlap-matching functions is shown in the output of Fig. 7-4. In each case, logical (nonweighted) vectors are used with either of the two correlation methods. The results are clearly in favor of the cosine-matching function,

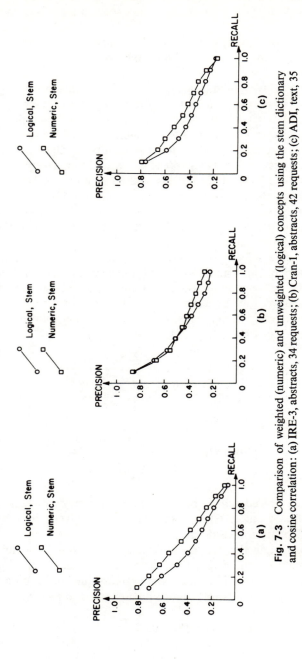

Fig. 7-3 Comparison of weighted (numeric) and unweighted (logical) concepts using the stem dictionary and cosine correlation: (a) IRE-3, abstracts, 34 requests; (b) Cran-1, abstracts, 42 requests; (c) ADI, text, 35 requests.

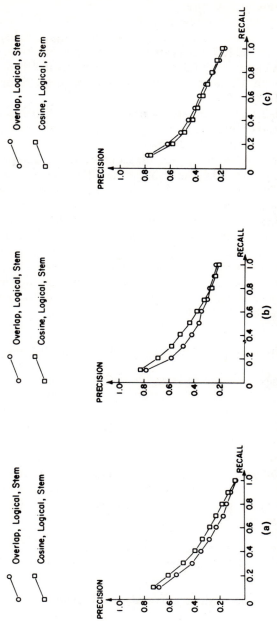

Fig. 7-4 Comparison of overlap and cosine matching functions: (a) IRE-3, abstracts, 34 requests; (b) Cran-1, abstracts, 42 requests; (c) ADI, text, 35 requests.

165

although the sign test result for the ADI collection is not sufficiently one-sided to reach a hard conclusion in that case.

The combined effect of parameter adjustment in both the weighting and the correlation method can be studied by combining the output of Figs. 7-3 and 7-4. The significance data of Table 7-7 indicate that the weakest method appears to be the combination of logical vectors with the overlap correlation, and the most satisfactory results are obtained with the numeric (weighted) term vectors and the cosine correlation.

It should be noted that the overlap-logical process corresponds to the standard keyword-matching method used in almost all operational, semimechanized retrieval situations. In such cases, nonweighted keywords assigned to each document are compared with keywords attached to the search requests, and a count is taken of the number of overlapping keywords. The resulting coefficient is then equivalent to a non-normalized overlap function. It would appear from the results of Figs. 7-3 and 7-4, that standard keyword-matching systems can be improved by the simple device of using a better matching function and assigning weights to the keywords.

To summarize: weighted content identifiers are more effective for content description than nonweighted ones, and the cosine correlation function is more useful as a measure of document-request similarity than the overlap function; therefore advantage can be taken of the computational facilities incorporated into many mechanized information systems, and service can be improved by using more sophisticated request-document matching methods.

7-3-D   Language Normalization—The Suffix Process

If natural language texts are to form the basis for an automatic assignment of information identifiers to documents, then the question of language normalization is of primary concern. Indeed, no human intermediaries exist who could resolve some of the ambiguities inherent in the natural language itself, or some of the inconsistencies introduced into written texts by the authors or writers responsible for the preparation of the documents.

A large number of experiments have been conducted therefore with the SMART system, using a variety of dictionaries for purposes of language normalization in each of the three subject fields under study. The performance of the following dictionaries is studied in particular:

(a) *Suffix "s"* process, where words differing by the addition of a terminal "s" are recognized as equivalent (for example, the words "apple" and "apples" are assigned a common identifier, but not words "analyzer" and "analyzing".

(b) The *word stem dictionary*, where all words which exhibit a common word stem are treated as equivalent; for example, "analysis", "analyzer", "analyst", and so on.

(c) The *synonym dictionary*, or thesaurus, where a set of synonymous, or closely related terms are all placed into a common thesaurus class, thus ensuring that common identifiers are derived from all such terms.

(d) The *statistical phrase dictionary* which makes it possible to recognize "phrases" consisting of the juxtaposition of several distinct concepts; thus if a given document contains the notion of "program", as well as the notion of "language", it could be tagged with the phrase "programming language"; the statistical phrase dictionary incorporated into the SMART system is manually constructed and contains a large variety of common noun phrases for each of the subject areas covered.

(e) The *concept association method* where concepts are grouped not by reference to a preconstructed dictionary but by using statistical co-occurrence characteristics of the vocabulary under investigation.

A comparison of the suffix "s" dictionary with a complete word stem dictionary is illustrated in the output of Table 7-7. In the former case, the texts of documents and search requests are looked up in a table of common words so as to delete function words and other text items not of immediate interest for content analysis purposes; the final "s" endings are then deleted so as to confound words which differ only by a final "s." In the latter case, a complete suffix dictionary is also consulted, and the original words are reduced to word stem form before request identifiers are matched with document identifiers.

The results obtained from the experiments are contradictory, in the sense that for two of the collections used (IRE-3 and ADI) the more thorough normalization inherent in the word stem process, compared with suffix "s" recognition alone, improves the search effectiveness; for the third collection (Cranfield), the reverse result appears to hold. For none of the collections is the improvement of one method over the other really dramatic, so that in practice either procedure might be used reasonably.

The discrepancy between the IRE and ADI results, on the one hand, and the Cranfield results, on the other, may be caused by differences in the respective vocabularies. Specifically, the Cranfield texts are substantially more technical in nature, and the collection is more homogeneous than is the case for the other collections. In order to differentiate between the various document abstracts, it is then important to maintain finer distinctions for the Cranfield case than for ADI and IRE, and these finer differences are lost when several different words are combined into a unique class through the suffix cutoff process. The argument can be summarized by stating that dictionaries and word normalization procedures are most effective if the vocabulary is redundant and relatively nontechnical; in the reverse case, such procedures may not in fact result in processing advantages.

7-3-E Synonym Recognition

One of the perennial problems in automatic language analysis is the question of language variability among authors and the linguistic ambiguities which result.

Therefore several experiments have been performed using a variety of synonym dictionaries for each of the three subject fields under study (*Harris-2* and *Harris-3* dictionaries for the computer literature, *quasi-synonym* or *QS* lists for aeronautical engineering, and a regular thesaurus for documentation). Use of such a synonym dictionary permits the replacement of a variety of related terms by similar concept identifiers, thereby ensuring the retrieval of documents dealing with the "manufacture of transistor diodes" when the query deals with the "production of solid state rectifiers".

The output of Fig. 7-5 which represents a comparison of the word stem matching procedure with a process including a thesaurus lookup operation for the recognition of synonyms shows that considerable improvements in performance are obtainable by means of suitably constructed synonym dictionaries. The improvement is again smallest for the Cranfield collection in part for the reasons stated already in Sec. 7-3-D, and in part because the dictionary available for this collection was not constructed originally to mesh in with the SMART retrieval programs. However in the present case, the synonym recognition seems to benefit the Cranfield material also. The significance output for Fig. 7-5 shows that all thesaurus improvements are fully significant, with the exception of the *t* test for the Cranfield collection. The null hypothesis can therefore be rejected unequivocally for all collections except Cranfield.

The differences observed in the performance of the various synonym dictionaries suggest that not all dictionaries are equally useful for the improvement of retrieval effectivenes. The experiments conducted with the SMART system in fact led to the principles of dictionary construction outlined previously in Chapter 6 and reference [17].

The differences in search effectiveness for two sets of two synonym dictionaries are shown in Fig. 7-6. The less effective dictionaries (Harris-2 for the IRE collection, and "old " quasi-synonym for the Cranfield) were in each case constructed manually by specialists using ad hoc procedures set up for the occasion. The other two dictionaries are improved versions obtained manually by using some of the dictionary construction principles listed previously. The significance output shows that fully significant improvements are obtained from one dictionary version to the next. It may be noted in this connection that the synonym recognition results of the main Cranfield experiments [18] were obtained with the "old", less effective synonym dictionary, rather than with the new one.

In summary, it appears that dictionaries providing synonym recognition produce statistically significant improvements in retrieval effectiveness compared with the word stem matching process; the improvement is largest for dictionaries obeying certain principles with regard to the word groupings which are incorporated.

7-3-F Phrase Recognition

The SMART system makes provision for the recognition of "phrases" to identify documents and search requests, rather than only individual concepts alone. Phrases can be generated using a variety of strategies. For example, a phrase can be assigned

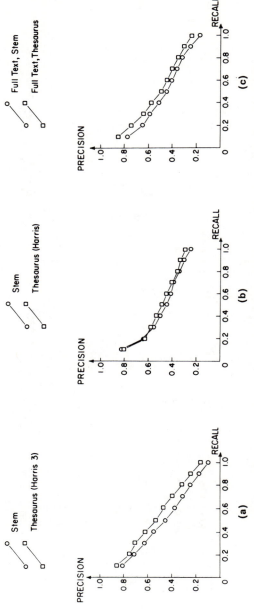

Fig. 7-5 Comparison of synonym recognition (thesaurus) with word stem matching process: (a) IRE-3, 34 requests; (b) Cran-1, abstracts, 42 requests; (c) ADI, full text, 35 requests.

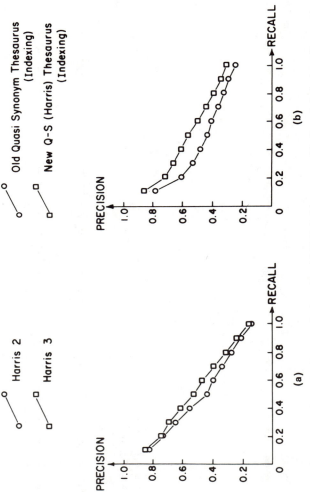

Fig. 7-6 Comparison of thesaurus dictionaries: (a) IRE-3, 34 requests; (b) Cran-1, indexing, 42 requests.

any time the specified components co-occur in a given document or in a given sentence of a document; alternatively, more restrictive phrase generation methods can be used by incorporating a syntactic recognition routine into the phrase generation process to check the syntactic compatibility between the phrase components before a phrase is actually accepted [19].

In the SMART system, the normal phrase process uses a preconstructed dictionary of important phrases, and simple co-occurrence of phrase components, rather than syntactic criteria, is used to assign phrases to documents. Phrases seem to be particularly useful as a means of incorporating into a document representation those terms whose individual components are not always meaningful by themselves. For example, "computer" and "control" are reasonably nonspecific, while "computer control" has a much more definite meaning in a computer science collection.

The results of the phrase lookup procedure compared with the equivalent process using only a synonym dictionary indicate that for two of the collections the phrase dictionary offers improvements in certain ranges of the recall and precision curve. The output of Table 7-7 shows, however, that the improvements are not significant, and on the whole the phrase dictionary does not appear to offer any real help in the middle recall range. Whether this result is due to the recognition of false phrases where phrase components are all present in the text but do not really belong together (such as in the phrase "solid state" in the sentence "people whose knowledge is solid state that computer processing is efficient") remains to be seen. The available evidence would seem to indicate that the presence of such false phrases is quite rare and that a more serious deficiency is the small size of the statistical phrase dictionary from which many potentially useful phrases may be absent.

Phrases can also be recognized by using the statistical properties of the words in a text, rather than a preconstructed dictionary of phrase components. Specifically, if two given terms co-occur in many of the documents of a collection, or in many sentences within a given document, a nonzero correlation coefficient can be computed as a function of the number of co-occurrences. If this coefficient is sufficiently high, the two terms can be grouped and can be assigned jointly to documents and search requests. Associative methods are therefore comparable to thesaurus procedures except that the word associations reflect strictly the vocabulary statistics of a given collection, whereas a thesaurus grouping may have more general validity [20, 21].

Many possible methods exist for the generation of statistical word associations. Specifically, by varying several parameters suitably, a number of different types of term associations can be recognized; furthermore, once an association between term pairs is introduced, it is possible to assign to it a smaller or a greater weight. Two main parameters that can be used in this connection are the cutoff value K in the association coefficient below which an association between terms is not recognized and the frequency of occurrence of the terms being correlated. When all terms are correlated, no matter how low their frequency in the document collection, a great many spurious associations may be found; on the other hand, some correct associations may not be observable under any stricter conditions. Increasingly more restrictive association procedures, applied first only to words in the frequency range 3 to 50 and then

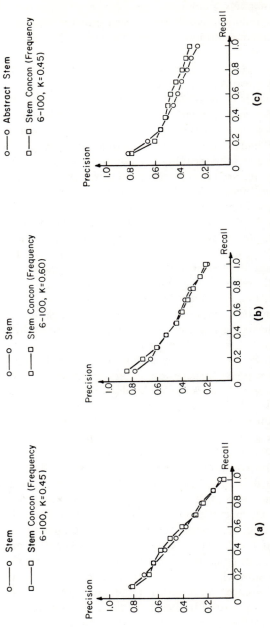

Fig. 7-7 Comparison of word stem dictionary with addition of statistical word-word association (stem concon): (a) IRE-3, 34 requests; (b) Cran-1, abstracts, 42 requests; (c) ADI, full text, 35 requests.

in the frequency range 6 to 100, eliminate many spurious associations but also some correct ones.

Figure 7-7 shows a comparison of the word-stem matching process with the statistical term-term association method (labeled "stem concon" in Fig. 7-7 to indicate a concept-concept association in which word stems are manipulated). The applicable frequency restrictions for the concept pairs and the cutoff values K are also included in Fig. 7-7. The output of Fig. 7-7 and the corresponding significance computations indicate that for the Cranfield collections, in particular, the term associations provide some improvement over the word stem process; local improvements for certain recall ranges are also noticeable for the ADI and IRE collections. Only for Cranfield does the sign test appear to be of some statistical significance, so that based on the present tests, no strong claims of overall effectiveness can be made for the association process.

The conclusion is reinforced by performing a comparison between the thesaurus lookup process and the word stem association method. Table 7-7 shows that the advantage is clearly and significantly with the more powerful thesaurus method for both the ADI and IRE collections. For Cranfield, the advantage is still slightly with the word stem association process particularly at the high recall end, where the more exhaustive indexing procedures represented by the stem associations supplies additional useful information identifiers and serves therefore to maintain the finer distinctions among the Cranfield documents. However, the superiority of the association method is not statistically significant for Cranfield, so that the conclusion reached previously must stand.

Table 7-7 also includes a comparison of various word stem association strategies performed for the Cranfield collection. The output suggests that the more restrictive association processes are more effective as a retrieval aid than the more general ones. Specifically, as the number of generated association pairs grows, too many of them appear to become spurious, thus depressing the retrieval performance. In practice, limitations should be imposed on the number and types of associated terms actually used.

To summarize, the phrase generation methods, whether implemented by dictionary lookup or by statistical association processes, appear to offer improvements in retrieval effectiveness for some recall levels by introducing new associated information identifiers not originally available; the improvement is not, however, sufficiently general or substantial, when averages over many search requests are considered, to warrant incorporation into automatic information systems, except under special circumstances where suitable control procedures can be maintained.

7-3-G   Hierarchical Expansion

Hierarchical arrangements of subject identifiers are used in many standard library classification systems and are also incorporated into many nonconventional information systems. Subject hierarchies are useful for the representation of generic inclusion relations between terms, and they also serve to broaden, narrow, or otherwise "expand" a given content description by adding hierarchically related terms to

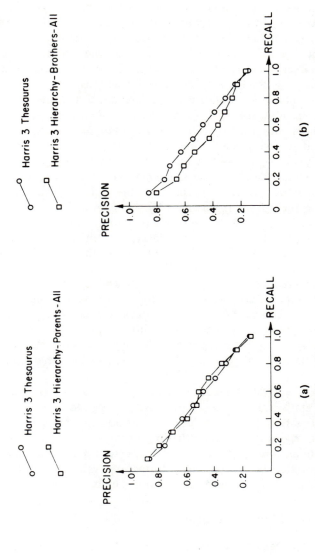

Fig. 7-8 Sample hierarchy procedures (IRE-3, 34 requests): (a) hierarchy expansion by parents; (b) hierarchy expansion by brothers.

those originally available. Specifically, given an entry point in the hierarchy, it is possible to find more general terms by going "up" in the hierarchy (expansion by parents), and more specific ones by going "down" (expansion by sons); related terms which have the same parent can also be obtained (expansion by brothers); finally any available cross references between individual entries can be identified (expansion by cross references).

A hierarchical arrangement of thesaurus entries was used with the IRE collection to evaluate the effectiveness of the hierarchical expansion procedures. In the test process carried out with the SMART system, the concepts present in both the document and request vectors were looked up in the hierarchy, and appropriately related hierarchy entries were added to the original content identifiers. The expanded document vectors which resulted were then matched with the requests, and documents were arranged in decreasing correlation order as usual. A comparison of the standard thesaurus process with two of the four hierarchical expansions described previously is shown in Fig. 7-8, and the corresponding significance output is included in Table 7-7.

In each case it is seen that the standard thesaurus process alone is superior; moreover, the equality hypothesis can be rejected unequivocally for the expansions by brothers, sons, and cross references. A question exists only for the expansion by parents, where more general terms are added to the original identifiers. Figure 7-8(a) shows, in particular, that this expansion process does in fact improve retrieval performance for certain recall levels.

Of course many alternative methods exist for using a hierarchy. It is possible, for example, to expand requests without expanding the documents or vice versa; terms obtained from the hierarchy can also *replace* the original content identifiers instead of being added to them. In general, the expansions tend to produce large-scale disturbances in the information identifiers attached to documents and search requests. Occasionally, such a disturbance can serve to crystallize the meaning of a poorly stated request, particularly if the request is far removed from the principal subjects covered by the document collection. More often, the change in direction specified by the hierarchy option is too violent, and the average performance of most hierarchy procedures does not appear to be sufficiently promising to advocate their immediate incorporation in an analysis system for automatic document retrieval.

7-3-H   Manual Indexing

The Cranfield collection was available for purposes of experimentation both in the form of abstracts and in the form of manually assigned index terms. The indexing performed by trained indexers is extremely detailed, consisting of an average of over 30 terms per document. As such, the indexing performance may be expected to be superior to the subject indexing normally used for large document collections. Therefore a meaningful comparison with standard manual keyword indexing systems may not be possible. A comparison of index term performance with certain automatic procedures using document abstracts is represented in Fig. 7-9, together with the corresponding significance output in Table 7-7. Figures 7-9(a) and 7-9(b) show that the

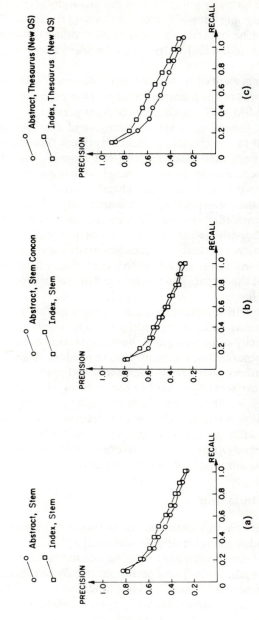

Fig. 7-9 Comparison of manual indexing with text processing (Cranfield-1, 42 requests): (a) manual indexing vs. abstract (word stem process); (b) manual indexing (stem) vs. abstract (word-word association); (c) manual indexing vs. abstract, thesaurus.

overall performance of a straight index term match is only slightly superior to a match of word stems abstracted from the document abstracts; for certain recall ranges, the automatic word-word association method in fact proves to be more effective than a manual index term match. In any case, Table 7-7 shows that the null hypothesis which postulates equivalence cannot be rejected in that instance.

When the index terms are looked up in the thesaurus and a comparison is made with the thesaurus process for the document abstracts, a clearer advantage is apparent for the indexing; that is, the identification of synonyms and related terms inherent in the thesaurus process seems of greater benefit to the indexing than to the automatic abstract process. Even there, however, the advantage for the index term process is not fully significant.

Based on those results, it is not possible therefore to say that the automatic text processing is substantially inferior to the manual-indexing method; indeed, one is tempted to say that the efforts of the trained indexers may well have been superfluous for the collection at hand, since equally effective results could be obtained by simple word-matching techniques. Such a result appears even more probably in the case of larger or less homogeneous collections, where the manual indexing tends to be less effective because of the variabilities among indexers and the difficulties of ensuring a uniform application of a given set of indexing rules to all documents. The computer process in such cases does not necessarily decay as the collections grow larger, and the evaluation output may then be more favorable for the automatic procedures.

7-4 CONCLUDING COMMENTS

A summary of the main evaluation output is contained in Table 7-8, where eight processing methods are presented in order for the three document collections used. The measure used to rank the output is a combined coefficient consisting of the sum of the normalized recall and the normalized precision. The following principal conclusions can be drawn from the data of Table 7-8:

(a) The order of merit for the eight methods is generally the same for all three collections, with the possible exception of the suffix "s" method which performs better than average for CRAN-1 and worse than average for ADI.

(b) The performance range of the methods used is smaller for the Cranfield collection than for the other two collections.

(c) The use of logical vectors (disregarding term weight), overlap correlation, and titles only is always less effective than the use of weighted terms, cosine correlation, and full document abstracts.

(d) The thesaurus process involving synonym recognition always performs more effectively than the word stem or suffix "s" methods when synonyms are not recognized.

Table 7-8

OVERALL MERIT FOR EIGHT PROCESSING METHODS USED
WITH THREE DOCUMENT COLLECTIONS

	IRE–3			CRAN–1			ADI		
ORDER	D*	*Method*	M†	D	*Method*	M	D	*Method*	M
1	D4	stat. phrase	1.686	D3	thesaurus	1.579	D4	stat. phrase	1.456
2	D3	thesaurus	1.665	D1	suffix "s"	1.574	D3	thesaurus	1.448
3	D2	stems	1.570	D4	stat. phrase	1.566	D5	concon	1.367
4	D5	concon	1.559	D5	concon	1.556	D2	stems	1.335
5	D1	suffix "s"	1.530	D2	stems	1.535	D2	no weights	1.294
6	D2	no weights	1.494	D2	no weights	1.477	D2	title only	1.293
7	D2	overlap	1.455	D2	title only	1.430	D1	suffix "s"	1.283
8	D2	title only	1.369	D2	overlap	1.407	D2	overlap	1.241
Range		0.317			0.172			0.215	

*D: Dictionary used—D1: Suffix "s"; D2: Word Stem; D3: Thesaurus; D4: Stat. Phrase; D5: Word-Word Association.

†M: Merit measure (normalized recall plus normalized precision).

(e) The thesaurus and statistical phrase methods are substantially equivalent; other dictionaries perform less well (with the exception of suffix "s" for Cranfield).

These results indicate that, in automatic systems, weighted terms should be used, derived from document excerpts whose length is at least equivalent to that of an abstract; furthermore, synonym dictionaries should be incorporated wherever available. Other local improvements may be obtained by incorporating phrases, hierarchies, and word-word association techniques. The Cranfield output shows that the better automatic text-processing methods (abstracts—thesaurus) may not be substantially inferior to the performance obtained with manually assigned index terms.

A comparison of the test results obtained here with other related studies is difficult to perform. For the most part, only fragmentary results exist which do not lend themselves to a full analysis [16], [22]. The Cranfield project studies contain the only available extensive test results, including the performance of manually assigned index terms, phrases, and dictionary concepts together with a wide variety of "recall devices" (procedures that broaden or generalize the meaning of the terms) and "precision devices" (procedures that add discrimination and narrow the coverage of the terms) [18]. The principal conclusions reached by the Cranfield project are also borne out by the SMART studies: that phrase languages are not substantially superior to single terms as indexing devices, that synonym dictionaries improve performance, but that other dictionary types, such as hierarchies, are not as effective as expected.

Further experiments leading to the design of automatic information systems should be performed in different subject areas with larger document collections. Furthermore, it becomes increasingly important to evaluate also the search procedures likely to be used in an automatic systems environment, particularly those real-time search methods where the user can control the search strategy to some exent, by providing suitable feedback information. Work in this direction is continuing [7], [23], [24].

Acknowledgement: The assistance of Mr. Cyril Cleverdon and Mr. Michael Keen in making available the documents and dictionaries used by the Aslib–Cranfield Research Project is gratefully acknowledge. Mr. Keen was also instrumental in preparing many of the output graphs included in this study.

REFERENCES

[1] Committee on Scientific and Technical Information (COSATI), Recommendations for National Document Handling Systems, *Report PB 168267*, distributed by the Clearinghouse for Federal, Scientific and Technical Information, Springfield, Va., November 1965.

[2] M. Rubinoff, ed. *Toward a National Information System*, Spartan Books, New York, 1965.

[3] G. S. Simpson and C. Flanagan, Information Centers and Services, in *Annual Review of Information Science and Technology*, C. Cuadra, ed. Chap. XII, John Wiley & Sons, Inc., New York, 1966.

[4] G. Salton, A Document Retrieval System for Man-machine Interaction, *Proceedings of the ACM 19th National Conference*, Philadelphia, 1964.

[5] G. Salton and M. E. Lesk, The SMART Automatic Document Retrieval System—An Illustration, *Communications of the ACM*, Vol. 8, No. 6, June 1965.

[6] G. Salton, Progress in Automatic Information Retrieval, *IEEE Spectrum*, Vol. 2, No. 8, August 1965.

[7] J. J. Rocchio, Jr. and G. Salton, Information Search Optimization and Iterative Retrieval Techniques, *Proceedings of the AFIPS Fall Joint Computer Conference*, Las Vegas, Nev., November 1965, Spartan Books, New York, 1965.

[8] J. J. Rocchio, Jr., Document Retrieval Systems—Optimization and Evaluation, Doctoral thesis, *Report ISR-10* to the National Science Foundation, Harvard Computation Laboratory, Cambridge, Mass., March 1966.

[9] C. W. Cleverdon, The Testing of Index Language Devices, *Aslib Proceedings*, Vol. 5, No. 4, April 1965.

[10] G. Salton, The Evaluation of Automatic Retrieval Procedures—Selected Test Results Using the SMART System, *American Documentation*, Vol. 16, No. 3, July 1965.

[11] R. A. Fairthorne, Basic Parameters of Retrieval Tests, *1964 ADI Annual Meeting*, Philadelphia, October 1964.

[12] G. Salton, Evaluation of Computer-Based Retrieval Systems, *Proceedings 1965 International FID Congress*, Spartan Books, New York, 1966.

[13] R. A. Fisher, *Statistical Methods for Research Workers*, Hafner Publishing Company, New York, 1954.

[14] J. L. Hodges and E. L. Lehmann, *Basic Concepts of Probability and Statistics*, Holden-Day, Inc., San Francisco, 1964.

[15] C. W. Cleverdon, J. Mills, and M. Keen, Factors Determining the Performance of Indexing Systems, *Design*, Vol. 1, Aslib–Cranfield Research Project, Cranfield, England, 1966.

[16] V. E. Giuliano and P. E. Jones, Study and Test of a Methodology for Laboratory Evaluation of Message Retrieval Systems, *Report ESD-TR-66-405* Little, Brown & Company, Boston, August 1966.

[17] G. Salton, Information Dissemination and Automatic Information Systems, *Proc. IEEE*, Vol. 54, No. 12, December 1966.

[18] C. W. Cleverdon and M. Keen, Factors Determining the Performance of Indexing Systems, *Test Results*, Vol. 2, Aslib–Cranfield Research Project, Cranfield, England, 1966.

[19] G. Salton, Automatic Phrase Matching, in *Readings in Automatic Language Processing*, D. Hays, ed., American Elsevier Publishing Company, Inc., New York, 1966.

[20] L. B. Doyle, Indexing and Abstracting by Association, *American Documentation*, Vol. 13, No. 4, October 1962.

[21] V. E. Giuliano and P. E. Jones, Linear Associative Information Retrieval, in *Vistas in Information Handling*, P. Howerton, ed., Spartan Books, New York, 1963.

[22] B. Altman, A Multiple Testing of the Natural Language Storage and Retrieval ABC Method: Preliminary Analysis and Test Results, *American Documentation*, Vol. 18, No. 1, January 1967.

[23] E. M. Keen, Semi-Automatic User Controlled Search Strategies, *Proceedings of the Fourth Annual National Colloquium on Information Retrieval*, A. B. Tonik, ed., Int. Information Inc., Philadelphia, 1967, pp. 141–154.

[24] G. Salton, Search Strategy and the Optimization of Retrieval Effectiveness, *Report ISR-12* to the National Science Foundation, Department of Computer Science, Cornell University, Ithaca, N.Y., 1967; also in *Mechanized Information Storage, Retrieval, and Dissemination*, K. Samuelson, ed., North Holland Publishing Co., Amsterdam, 1968, pp. 73–107.

The conclusions reached as a result of the experimental work performed with the SMART system have been derived generally from the average system performance for a given set of search requests. The present study examines the search requests used experimentally in greater depth in an attempt to obtain detailed performance characteristics, which in turn may lead to improvements in the automatic processing system. The 35 queries associated with the collection of 82 papers in documentation are chosen for investigation.

8

AN ANALYSIS OF THE DOCUMENTATION REQUESTS†

E. M. KEEN

8-1 REQUEST PREPARATION

In Chapter 7, a brief description of the ADI documentation collection, requests, and relevance decisions is given. The collection consists of 82 documents, both in abstract and short text form. Requests were prepared by two nonusers of the system; also the relevance decisions were made by these persons by examining every document for potential relevance.

The two request preparers (an engineer and an applied mathematician) were graduate students at Harvard University. Since neither person was familiar with the subject field of documentation, it was suggested that some familiarity with the subject would be gained by looking at the document texts in the collection. The task of request preparation should then follow. Specifically, requests thought likely to be asked by workers in the field should be devised, but these requests should not be based on any particular documents in the collection. No suggestions were made regarding request length. An examination of all documents in the collection should follow, and every document should be judged not relevant or relevant to each given query. Neither person was familiar with the SMART system.

†This study was published as Section X of *Scientific Report ISR-13*, December 1967.

181

The full text of the 82 documents was supplied in the form of computer printout, and none of the KWIC indexes or subject categories printed in the published volume were supplied. Both preparers worked independently, one producing 17 requests and the other 18 requests. The task appears to have been carried out as instructed, except that some requests might have been prompted by particular documents in the collection. This factor is not necessarily a weakness, since full relevance decisions were obtained, so that the test is not based on the "source document" technique which has often been criticized. Additional comments in this area will be made when discussing "Unclear Requests" (Sec. 8-2-D) and "Relevance Decisions" (Sec. 8-3).

8-2 CHARACTERISTICS OF THE REQUESTS

8-2-A Length

Excluding nonsubject words contained in the standard "common" word list used by SMART, the stem dictionary gives an average of 8.0 stems per request, and the thesaurus dictionary reduces this to 5.1 concept numbers per request. The eight thesaurus concepts used most frequently are given in Table 8-1, together with the

Table 8-1

QUERY CONCEPTS USED WITH FREQUENCY DATA

TERM (STEM)	THESAURUS CONCEPT NUMBER	NUMBER OF REQUESTS			FREQUENCY IN COLLECTION	
		Total	*A**	*B**	*Stem†*	*Rank†*
Information	1	24	11	13	998	1
Retrieval	5	14	12	2	255	14
Automat	19	14	7	7	86	86
Comput	3	7	2	5	326	8
Dissemination	108	6	3	3	47	124
Article	21	6	5	1	86	86
Index	4	5	1	4	424	3
Scienc	10	5	4	1	300	9

*Requests prepared by Persons *A* and *B*.
†Frequency is based on word stems; therefore "Information" is the most frequent stem (Rank 1) and is used 998 times.

number of requests and frequency of use in the collection. More than half the 35 requests use one or more of these 8 concepts. Comparison of request length between the two different preparers shows that person *A* constructed longer requests than person *B*; this matter is considered in Sec. 8-4-C.

8-2-B   Important Request Words

Since the requests are fairly short, it must be expected that some requests would contain one or two quite important words that are vital to the request demand. For example, request *A*15 reads "How much do information retrieval and dissemination systems cost?"; request *B*4 reads "Automated information in the medical field". The words "cost" and "medical" are very important in the request statements and render otherwise general requests much more specific. Since SMART assigns a weight to each request word in part on the basis of frequency of occurrence in the request and collection, these important words are liable not to receive the desired weight; this problem is taken up again in Sec. 8-4-D.

8-2-C   Multiple Need Requests

Nearly all requests express the need as a single topic; two requests, however, demand documents on two topics. Request *B*1 asks for information on both coding and matching in machine systems, and request *A*1 requires information on "titles"—meaning journal titles, organization names, and presumably their abbreviations—and also "titles"—meaning the subject statement as applied to scientific papers. There is nothing inherently wrong in using multiple need requests; for test purposes, however, such requests sometimes cause difficulties when binary relevance decisions are used. For example, of the three documents assessed as relevant to request *A*1, two clearly answer only the first part of the request, and one answers only the second part of the request. Thus it is never possible, even for a perfect system, to establish a complete match between the request and the relevant documents. It is believed that where multiple needs are expressed, separate search requests will give superior results.

8-2-D   Unclear Requests

Two requests in particular are unclear. In request *A*1, does the phrase "approximate titles" mean abbreviated titles? Does request *A*8 ask for documents in information retrieval as practiced in countries other than those speaking English, or is it asking about information retrieval (practiced anywhere) of documents written in languages other than English? The full request statements are contained in the Appendix of this Chapter.

Several other requests also perpetuate the unclear terminology that abounds in the field of documentation. Request *B*2 asks what does an "automated" information system include and exclude? Request *B*3 requires documents either describing the shortages that exist of information personnel, or some solutions to the problem such as the need to provide suitable training. Request *B*11 uses the words "index system", and since only one document on the cataloging of books is judged relevant, "index system" has been taken to be synonymous with book cataloging only.

Such requests would, in an operating situation, be clarified by interaction with the questioner; this advantage is, however, denied to the SMART tests which are not based on feedback methods. It is surprising to note that the five requests quoted do perform quite well for retrieval purposes; of the total of 13 relevant documents involved, only 3 receive consistently poor rank positions (below 15) on all search options.

8-2-E Difficult Requests

Of considerable interest in the analysis of a system such as SMART is the identification of requests that may be quite reasonable in themselves, but that nevertheless create problems due to some system weakness. Six examples are given.

Request $A2$ contains the following negative statement: ". . . as opposed to references or entire articles themselves . . .". SMART cannot recognize the significance of the negation, and a search will be made for the ideas as stated. Unless rules to recognize negative statements can be added to the system, users or request preparers must be advised to avoid negatives.

In request $A8$, "other languages" is a very important part of the request, but the idea of "languages other than English" is another negative statement which cannot be handled. Even if "other" were replaced by "foreign", correct matches with relevant documents would be difficult to achieve because a thesaurus concept that links "foreign" with all possible named languages or countries might work well for this particular request, but would at the same time provide an unhelpful grouping for other requests asking for one language in particular.

Request $A10$ contains the homonym "abstract", used here in the sense of "abstract mathematics" rather than in the sense of a summary of a document. The use of phase recognition could cope with this problem, except that the phrase list in use does not contain the required phrase. A synonym problem also exists because none of the relevant documents use the phrase "abstract mathematics". In only one case was "abstract" used in a sense other than "document summary", namely, in "abstract trees". Interaction with the requestor seems necessary here in such a case.

Request $A11$ reveals the problem of ordinarily common words being used in a technical sense. Words such as "evaluation" and "need" are relegated to the common word list when the thesaurus is used, thus leaving a request specification only in terms of high-frequency words in the collection. The stem dictionary uses both words and gives a better performance result. However, because such words frequently occur in nontechnical senses, two of the four relevant documents receive poor (lower than 15) rank positions. There seems to be no way of coping with such problems, except to get the requestors to supply alternative and less ambiguous words where possible.

Another example of this kind is in request $A13$, in which "criteria", "objective", and "evaluation" appear. In this case inclusion of these request words in the stem dictionary results in good rank positions for 5 of the 6 relevant documents. Where several such ambiguous words occur, the co-occurrence of all of them in a document in the incorrect sense is less likely; an improved type of phrase dictionary may overcome the problem.

A problem of synonym recognition is raised by request $B13$. The phrase "physical sciences" is really ambiguous and not very well chosen, since examination of the relevant documents reveals that it covers notions such as "materials", "chemistry", "engineering", technology", "missiles and space technology", and "environmental engineering". The use of such wide-ranging relations in a thesaurus category would be reflected by a concept number with a great many corresponding words; this would not serve all types of requests equally well and would in any case require some recognition of phrases rather than single words.

These examples of difficult requests point to two areas in which future work is required. The first is the problem of ambiguity caused by natural language, which may be handled partially by sophisticated recognition procedures (to include negative statements, for example), but may in other cases only be handled by introducing constraints to the free statement of the request. The second problem is that of making synonym connections in cases where a generic term is used. A possible solution is the provision of more than one synonym dictionary, which would include one dictionary containing some quite large groupings of many words into few concepts to handle the difficult cases.

8-3 RELEVANCE DECISIONS

Since both request preparers alone were responsible for the requests and relevance decisions produced, no possibility for disagreement arose during the setting up of the test. Evidence suggests that a consistent and conscientious job was done, although one could argue that the judges were not competent, or that real information needs did not arise, and so on. Measurement of the accuracy with which this procedure can simulate real user requests, needs, and relevance decisions awaits a carefully controlled comparative test. To submit the actual judgments made to a panel of judges for their opinion would undoubtedly reveal disagreements with the request preparers, and probably among the judges themselves; such a procedure, then, would serve no real purpose at the present time. A cursory look at the decisions has been taken, and some discrepancies are noted in order to illustrate the problems connected with the relevance judgments.

The discussion of unclear requests in Sec. 8-2-D is closely linked to the relevance decisions, since as J. O'Connor shows [1], relevance disagreements are often due to unclear request forms; furthermore, since many requests that are thought to be clear turn out not to be so in fact, one is led to different request interpretations and hence to different relevance decisions. Probably more examples than the five given in Sec. 8-2-D exist, but by the stringent criteria for clarity suggested by O'Connor, many real user requests would be regarded as unclear also.

Several of the requests deal with quite similar topics and sometimes do not have as many relevant documents in common as the requests suggest. Examples are requests $A15$ and $B8$, $B1$ and $B16$, $B9$ and $B11$, and $A5$, $B3$, and $B6$. A clear error of judgment is seen for document 7, where the photo composition method that is described for producing NASA's "Scientific and Technical Aerospace Reports" is thought relevant to request *A*7, which demands documents on systems for producing original papers by computer. The request preparer probably did not realize that NASA STAR is not a series of original reports. No specific examples have been found of documents that should have been recognized as relevant, except in those cases where two or more requests seem very similar, as noted.

8-4 REQUEST PERFORMANCE

8-4-A General Performance Analysis Methods

It was intended to divide the individual requests into three groups, namely:

(a) Requests which perform badly on all processing options.

(b) Requests which perform well on some options and badly on others.

(c) Requests which perform well on all options.

Definitions of good and bad performance are arbitrary, but it is thought that good performance requires rank positions for relevant documents of at least 15;

Table 8-2

RANK POSITIONS OF THE TWO DOCUMENTS RELEVANT TO
REQUEST A9

(Comparing three dictionaries, two document lengths, and three matching functions)

DOCUMENT LENGTH CORRELATION FUNCTION	DICTIONARY					
	STEM		THESAURUS 1		THESAURUS 2 (HASTIE)	
	Doct. 82	*Doct. 50*	*Doct. 82*	*Doct. 50*	*Doct. 82*	*Doct. 50*
Text: overlap logical	60	43	59	36	40	65
Text: cosine logical	9	44	[7]	24	①	57
Text: cosine numeric	63	52	29	61	14	⑤
Title: Cosine numeric	67	[8]	41	38	49	22

◯ Relevant document having best rank.

▢ Relevant document having second best rank.

⊏⊐ Request having best performance.

⌐¬ Request having second best performance.

any relevant item positioned lower than this indicates a poor result. Any requests which fall into groups (a) and (c) were thought to be particularly useful for analysis; in practice, however, all 38 requests fall into group (b). Requests *B*6 and *B*14 perform well on nearly all options, but occasionally one of the relevant documents falls below rank position 10. A surprisingly large amount of change in the ranks of the relevant is found when different options are tested; Table 8-2 gives an example for one request and two relevant documents. For this request, all those options found on average to be the poorest (such as titles only, the use of cosine logical, and the "Hastie" Thesaurus) give the best results.

Since the division into groups by achieved performance does not assist in the analysis, another method of analysis is suggested: this consists of looking for strong correlation between measurable request characteristics and the use of particular performance options. A summary of possible request characteristics is given in Table 8-3. These can now be used to look for direct correlation between characteristics and performance, as attempted in Sec 8-4-B, 8-4-C, and 8-4-D.

Table 8-3

OBJECTIVE AND SUBJECTIVE QUERY
EVALUATION CHARACTERISTICS

Request Characteristics	*Objective*	*Subjective*
1. Number of documents judged relevant in test collection or request generality.	✓	
2. Length of request, using all words, subject words only, or dictionary concept numbers.	✓	
3. Clarity of request demand and quality of relevance decisions.		✓
4. Request processing in the system used, such as SMART. Factors such as quality of dictionaries used and frequency of use in the request words.	✓	✓
5. Test environment variables, such as the use of several personnel to prepare requests.		✓

8-4-B Variation in Generality, Length, and Concept Frequency

Request generality refers to the number of documents in the collection that are relevant; using this principle, the request set may be divided into specific and general requests. With the 35 requests divided into sets of 17 and 18, request generality data is given in Table 8-4 together with evaluation results of normalized recall and precision, comparing the stem and thesaurus dictionaries. As has been observed previously [2], the specific requests give a better performance than the general ones, although normalized precision shows only a small difference. There is no correlation at all between request generality and dictionary in these results.

Table 8-4

PERFORMANCE RESULTS FOR TWO DICTIONARIES
AND SEVERAL QUERY TYPES

Dictionary	Evaluation Measure	All: 35 Requests 1–33 Relevant (Mean 4.9)	Specific: 17 Requests 1–3 Relevant (Mean 2.1)	General: 18 Requests 4–33 Relevant (Mean 7.4)
Stem	Normalized recall	0.7601	0.8018	0.7209
	Normalized precision	0.5326	0.5358	0.5295
Thesaurus 1	Normalized recall	0.8016	0.8482	0.7576
	Normalized precision	0.6069	0.6126	0.6016

Request length results are given in Table 8-5, with the requests again divided into two sets. The long requests perform better than the short ones, but they do so by a much greater amount with the stem dictionary than the thesaurus dictionary, so that for the long requests, normalized recall shows the stem to be slightly superior to the thesaurus. This correlation suggests that the generally inferior stem dictionary may be adequate for long requests.

Table 8-5

PERFORMANCE RESULTS FOR VARYING QUERY LENGTHS

Dictionary	Evaluation Measure	All: 35 Requests 4–18 Concepts (Mean 8.0)	Long: 17 Requests 8–18 Concepts (Mean 10.8)	Short: 18 Requests 4–7 Concepts (Mean 5.4)
Stem	Normalized recall	0.7601	0.8363	0.6883
	Normalized precision	0.5326	0.6191	0.4509
Thesaurus 1	Normalized recall	0.8016	0.8352	0.7699
	Normalized precision	0.6069	0.6353	0.5801

Requests may also be characterized by the frequency of use in the collection of the request concepts. Two methods of obtaining averages for the 35 requests are given in Table 8-6, each method supplying an arithmetic mean and a median value. The average frequency per average request concept has been found to be the more satisfactory of the two, and requests are again divided into two sets by this principle in Table 8-7. Requests having low frequencies per average concept are seen to perform best, with no real differences between stem and thesaurus dictionaries.

It is to be expected that these three characteristics of generality, length, and concept frequency are strongly interconnected, since specific requests are probably often long ones, and also probably have low average concept frequencies. A visual

Table 8-6

METHODS OF COMPUTING AVERAGE FREQUENCY OF USE
OF QUERY CONCEPTS (STEM DICTIONARY)

Average Frequencies	Mean	Median
Average total frequency per request (i.e., sum of concept frequencies)	1542	1605
Average concept frequency (overall concepts per request)	220	220

Table 8-7

PERFORMANCE RESULTS FOR QUERIES OF
VARYING CONCEPT FREQUENCY

Dictionary	Evaluation Measure	All: 35 Requests Freq. 26–483 (Mean 220)	Low Frequency: 17 Requests Freq. 26–218 (Mean 130)	High Frequency: 18 Requests Freq. 223–483 (Mean 305)
Stem	Normalized recall	0.7601	0.8154	0.7080
	Normalized precision	0.5326	0.5671	0.5000
Thesaurus 1	Normalized recall	0.8016	0.8527	0.7533
	Normalized precision	0.6069	0.6717	0.5457

representation of the correspondence between the three characteristics is given in
Fig. 8-1. Table 8-8 shows that 19 of the 35 requests fall exactly into the two expected

Table 8-8

QUERY CLASSIFICATION ACCORDING TO LENGTH,
GENERALITY, AND CONCEPT FREQUENCY

CLASSIFICATION (FREQUENCY)		LONG		SHORT		TOTAL (FREQUENCY)
		Low Freq.	High Freq.	Low Freq.	High Freq.	
Specific	Low Freq.	9		2		11
	High Freq.		2		4	6
General	Low Freq.	4		2		6
	High Freq.		2		10	12
Classification (Total)		13	4	4	14	35

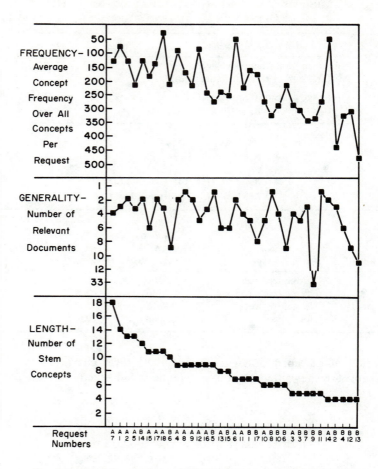

Fig. 8-1   Data for the 35 individual requests showing visually the correspondence between length, generality and average concept frequency.

combinations of three characteristics each. These characteristics seem to be the only available objective means of stating whether requests are broad or narrow in a subject field sense; although perfect correspondence is not obtained, there is possibly a strong correlation between these characteristics and real breadth of requests. The superiority

Table 8-9

PERFORMANCE COMPARISON FOR QUERIES WITH EXPECTED
CORRELATION IN LENGTH, GENERALITY,
AND CONCEPT FREQUENCY

Dictionary	Evaluation Measure	Specific, Long, and Low Frequency (9 Requests)	General, Short, and High Frequency (10 Requests)
Stem	Normalized recall	0.8309	0.5812
	Normalized precision	0.6085	0.4072
Thesaurus 1	Normalized recall	0.8617	0.7247
	Normalized precision	0.6702	0.5870

of the specific, long, and low-frequency requests is seen again in performance figures for the 19 requests that fall exactly into the expected combinations as seen in Table 8-9. The thesaurus dictionary is seen, as expected, to give the most improvement to the general short- and high-frequency requests. Further analysis of this type awaits suitable computer programs because the hand analysis methods used are too time consuming.

8-4-C   Comparison of Requests of the Two Preparers

Since two persons were responsible for request preparation, any variation in the measurable characteristics of generality, length, and frequency noted already may be correlated with the different preparers. Tables 8-10, 8-11, and 8-12 show that a quite strong correlation does exist, since the requests from preparer *A* are on average more specific and longer, and hence have lower mean frequencies than requests from preparer *B* (Table 8-10). Table 8-11 repeats the data of Table 8-8, adding the request preparer distinction. Table 8-12 shows that if the eight sets of results in Table 8-11 are divided into two sets of four each by the diagonal line in Table 8-11, correspondence is quite marked and is probably statistically significant.

Table 8-10

QUERY CHARACTERISTICS ACCORDING TO PREPARER

Generality, Length, and Frequency	All 35 Requests	Preparer A (18 Requests)	Preparer B (17 Requests)
Generality (Mean relevant)	4.9	3.3	6.5
Length (mean concepts)	8.0	9.6	6.3
Frequency (mean frequency)	220	157	287

Table 8-11

DATA FOR THE 35 INDIVIDUAL REQUESTS GIVEN IN TABLE 8-8
DIVIDED INTO THE REQUESTS OF THE TWO PREPARERS

REQUESTS (FREQUENCY)		LONG		SHORT	
		Low Freq.	*High Freq.*	*Low Freq.*	*High Freq.*
Specific	Low Freq.	A8 B1		A2 B0	
	High Freq.		A1 B1		A0 B4
General	Low Freq.	A3 B1		A0 B2	
	High Freq.		A1 B1		A3 B7

Table 8-12

CORRELATION BETWEEN REQUEST PREPARERS AND
REQUEST TYPE, WHERE "BROAD" IS THE SUM OF THE
FOUR CATEGORIES TO THE LEFT OF THE DIAGONAL IN
TABLE 8-11, AND "NARROW" IS THE SUM OF THE
OTHER FOUR

CATEGORIES	PREPARER		TOTAL
	A	*B*	
Broad $\geq \frac{2}{3}$	14	3	17
Narrow $\geq \frac{2}{3}$	4	14	18
Total	18	17	35

The previously examined subject request characteristics such as studies of unclear requests, requests having a multiple need, and requests containing identifiable important words (see Sec. 8-4-D) are divided almost equally among requests of the two preparers. Thus, although the requests prepared by person *A* are expected to give the better performance, it is not correct to assume that *A* did a better quality job than *B*. The six requests judged difficult for the system (Sec. 8-2-E) comprise five *A* requests and one *B*, but as has been noted, only three of these requests actually performed poorly (two *A* and one *B*).

The performance results in Figure 8-2 compare the *A* and *B* requests for two dictionary runs each made on two different document lengths—text and abstracts. The expected superiority of the *A* requests is seen in the stem dictionary results, but with the thesaurus, the *B* requests perform slightly better. Since the *B* requests are quite inferior to *A* with the stem dictionary, this leaves a greater opportunity for

Input and Dictionary	Evaluation Measure	"A" Requests	"B" Requests
Text, Stem	Normed. Recall	.8028	.7516
	Normed. Precision	.5917	.5209
Text, Thesaurus-1	Normed. Recall	.8124	.8294
	Normed. Precision	.6041	.6519
Abstract, Stem	Normed. Recall	.7830	.7358
	Normed. Precision	.5403	.5244
Abstract, Thesaurus-1	Normed. Recall	.8000	.8033
	Normed. Precision	.5826	.6327

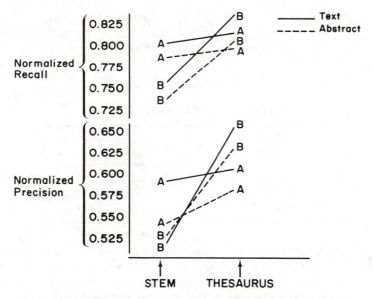

Fig. 8-2 Comparison of "A" and "B" requests for two dictionaries and two document lengths.

improvement using the thesaurus; the initial inferiority on stem requires an explanation, however, as does the fact that the thesaurus does not much improve the *A* requests. It is difficult to isolate any fundamental reasons for this result, because individual problems with both the stem and thesaurus dictionaries seem primarily to be the cause, as the following example shows.

Request *B*10, with a normalized recall of 0.8205 with thesaurus and 0.3718 with stem, has four documents assessed as relevant, and the thesaurus produces improvements in rank positions of 22, 26, 32, and 60 compared with stem. Reasons for the superiority of thesaurus in this case are:

(a) The thesaurus provides additional matching concepts between the request and all four relevant documents, including the important concept "computer."

The stem dictionary fails to match this concept, because the suffix routine used does not conflate all word forms, and "computation" is separated from "compute" and "computer."

(b) The thesaurus does not contain "system" but regards it as a common word to be ignored, and although the stem dictionary uses it and establishes matches with all four relevant documents, this high-frequency word also establishes matches with many nonrelevant documents.

(c) The very important request concept "chemistry" is grouped with synonyms in the thesaurus which successfully increase the weight given to this concept compared with stem, producing increases of 1 to $18\frac{1}{2}$, 2 to $11\frac{1}{2}$, 3 to 25, and 4 to $11\frac{1}{2}$.

These three reasons for the superiority of the thesaurus process are thought to be typical for other requests also. There is also a strong correlation of reasons (a) and (b) between the A and B requests, since as Table 8-13 shows, the concepts "com-

Table 8-13

OCCURRENCE OF TWO-QUERY CONCEPTS

TERM (STEM)	REQUESTS OF PREPARER	
	A	*B*
Computer	2	5
Stem	4	11

puter" and "system" appear a total 16 times in the B requests, and only 6 times in the A requests. This gives the B requests greater opportunity to benefit from the superior handling of these concepts in the thesaurus. This treatment of the different sets of requests constitutes only a first step of the problem and points mainly to some of the factors known to be involved.

8-4-D   The Recognition of Important Request Words

The presence of quite specific and important single request words and the problem of giving them a weight in proportion to their importance was noted in Sec. 8-2-B. In order to discover whether increases in the weight of such important words does improve retrieval performance, the 35 requests were examined (without knowledge of search results, relevant documents, or concept frequency) to see whether such important concepts could easily be identified. Seventeen requests were found to possess such important concepts, and each of the concepts was tripled in weight. These decisions are recorded in the Appendix. This simulates a rather feasible requestor rule which would ask for any important concepts to be underlined in the request statement, and which could be recognized by the system, producing a corresponding increase in weight by some factor. Six requests in addition to the 17 were also slightly modified. Request $A1$ was divided into two as suggested by Sec. 8-2-C; in request $A2$ the negative statement was removed; in requests $A8$ and $B11$ the difficulties caused by common words used in a technical sense prompted selection of one or two synonyms for the given words; in two requests, keypunching errors which preserved hyphenated words were corrected. These six modifications are all thought to represent reasonable demands that would be made to users of an operational system.

These 24 requests are now processed together with the 12 requests for which no modification was made; they are described as "Hand Modified"; a total of 36 results because request $A1$ is split into two. Comparison of retrieval performance of the modified with the original unmodified requests is made for six retrieval runs in Fig. 8-3 and 8-4. All precision-recall curves for the hand-modified requests show them to be superior over the whole performance range, with increases in precision at most recall values of more than 5% and in the middle recall ranges of nearly 10%.

Using the abstract-thesaurus result for analysis, the six requests that were quite severely modified did not perform very well; only $B11$ was notably improved, and

Table 8-14

RESULTS OF FOUR REQUESTS IN WHICH MANUAL
MODIFICATION BY IMPORTANT TERM WEIGHTING
IMPROVES PERFORMANCE

REQUEST	RELEVANT DOCUMENT NUMBER	RANKS OF RELEVANT AND NORMALIZED MEASURES	
		"Original"	"Modified"
Request $A9$ (2 relevant)	82	33	1
	50	50	27
		NR 0.5000	NR 0.8438
		NP 0.1718	NP 0.6780
Request $B2$ (3 relevant)	80	5	1
	65	17	2
	27	42	42
		NR 0.7553	NR 0.8354
		NP 0.4392	NP 0.7683
Request $B10$ (4 relevant)	9	1	2
	48	2	1
	69	19	3
	70	27	4
		NR 0.8750	NR 1.0000
		NP 0.7387	NP 1.0000
Request $B11$ (1 relevant)	36	21	1
		NR 0.7531	NR 1.0000
		NP 0.3091	NP 1.0000

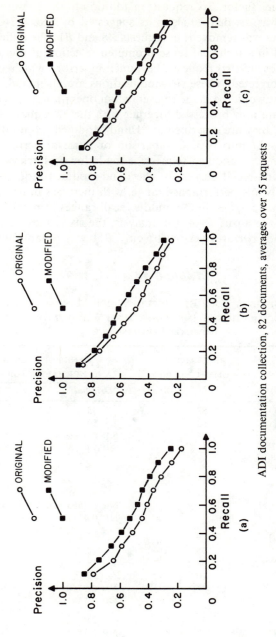

Fig. 8-3 Performance comparisons between requests as received (original) and manual modification by important "key" term weight increases: (a) full text, stem; (b) full text, thesaurus; (c) full text, thesaurus and phrases.

ADI documentation collection, 82 documents, averages over 35 requests

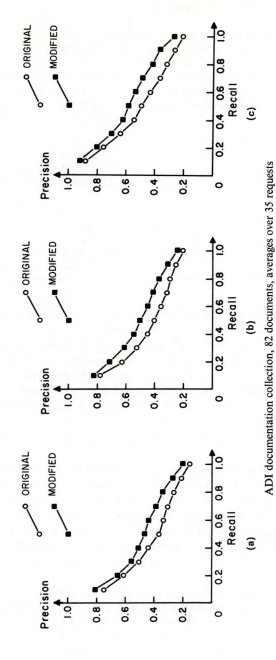

ADI documentation collection, 82 documents, averages over 35 requests

Fig. 8-4 Performance comparisons between requests as received (original) and manual modification by important "key" term weight increases: (a) abstracts, suffix 's'; (b) abstracts, stem; (c) abstracts, thesaurus.

197

Table 8-15

RESULTS OF TWO REQUESTS IN WHICH MANUAL
MODIFICATION BY IMPORTANT TERM WEIGHTING
DOES NOT IMPROVE PERFORMANCE

REQUEST	RELEVANT DOCUMENT NUMBER	RANKS OF RELEVANT AND NORMALIZED MEASURES	
		Original	*Modified*
Request *A*4 (2 relevant)	29	1	1
	63	30	43
		NR 0.8250	NR 0.7437
		NP 0.6660	NP 0.6216
Request *A*7 (4 relevant)	19	1	2
	7	6	14
	9	8	16
	40	25	19
		NR 0.9038	NR 0.8686
		NP 0.7279	NP 0.5916

some of the others received a worse performance. Of the seventeen requests that had triply weighted important words, ten were improved, five has a worse performance, and two remained unaffected. Four of the ten that were improved are shown in Table 8-14, and the two that were worsened by the greatest amounts are given in Table 8-15, with rank positions for all the relevant and normalized measures.

It is interesting to note that at present these hand modifications do produce a superior result to the relevance feedback process described elsewhere [3], [4], [5]. Further work on relevance feedback is expected to result in improvements, but for high precision requirements, hand-modified requests may always be superior (at the cost of increased user effort).

The treatment of important request words might be made more drastic, for example by the use of an "essential" word rule, which would only present to the searcher documents that contain the noted important words. This strategy could in fact be achieved by assigning very high weights to the important concepts (weights of several hundred would be needed in text runs); alternatively, modifications could be made to the search algorithm. It is almost certain that this procedure would imply that some relevant documents would never be found, although large increases in precision might be possible.

For example, for seven requests containing important concepts chosen at random, only 9% of the relevant items would be lost, and although actual precision results cannot be calculated, of the 86 nonrelevant documents that were given rank positions above 16 in the output, 32 would be excluded by this rule. Other requests subsequently examined occasionally produce a much greater recall ceiling and also a greater precision improvement, so that this procedure is worth further experimentation.

8-5 PERFORMANCE EFFECTIVENESS AND SEARCH PROCEDURES

A comparison of the retrieval results obtained in the documentation collection with the performance of the aerodynamics and computer science collection shows the documentation results to be quite inferior. Several factors in the text environments differ between the collections, and matters such as the quality of terminology in the subject language, as well as the testing of techniques used for collection gathering, request preparation, and relevance decisions all contribute to the differences observed in unknown proportions.

It seems likely that the imprecise terminology encountered in documentation which appears in both the documents and requests is a major cause of the poor performance. In order to overcome these problems, extra human intellect may be needed in the system. It may not be possible to build synonym dictionaries that will provide for this entirely, but good dictionaries together with a good choice of search strategy is likely to improve performance considerably. Some proof of the value of carefully chosen search words is given in Figure 8-5, where a hand search of the KWIC-type concordance to the abstracts is compared with a SMART abstracts-thesaurus result. The hand searcher chose up to five keywords for each request and was allowed to use any words that might be considered useful as suggested by the request statement. A comparison with SMART in Fig. 8-5(a) is made after fitting the SMART results to the hand searches by making cutoffs in the SMART-ranked output in such a way that the number of documents retrieved for each request is identical to the hand-searched results. Fig. 8-5(b) shows two fuller SMART curves obtained by making a series of cutoffs after one document, two documents, and so on, up to the last document in the collection. It is not surprising that the hand searches work better, since the free choice of synonyms made on an individual request basis should work better than the obligatory use of the preconstructed set of synonyms contained in the thesaurus. The hand searches do not use any feedback to obtain a fair comparison, since the search keywords were chosen before any reference was made to the KWIC concordance. The result of SMART using the hand-modified "important" concept with increased weights is included in Fig. 8-5(b); the curve now lies much closer to the hand result. Naturally a hand system permitting coordinate keyword searches would extend the hand curve to higher precision values, and choices of more than five keywords per request would enable higher recall ratios to be reached.

This result does not reflect unfavorably on the automatic indexing procedures, because hand searches are less easy to conduct in the sort of situation in which SMART would operate, such as a large file of individually long document surrogates. It is clear also that in an operational use of SMART search strategies employing several dictionaries in a variety of possible ways could be used, and for users willing to employ some intellect to interact strongly with the system, quite large performance gains may be expected. A system might in fact operate in the following ways: the

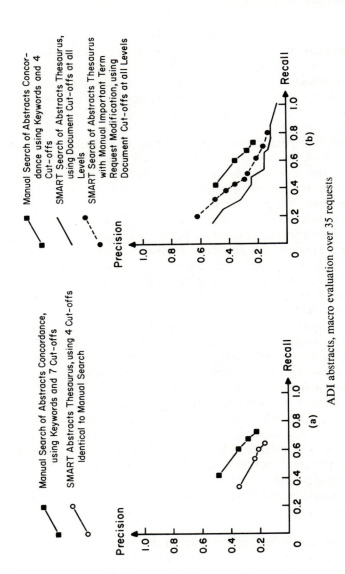

Fig. 8-5 Comparisons of a hand search in the KWIC concordance with SMART searches using abstracts thesaurus.

ADI abstracts, macro evaluation over 35 requests

(a)

Manual Search of Abstracts Concordance, using Keywords and 7 Cut-offs

SMART Abstracts Thesaurus, using 4 Cut-offs Identical to Manual Search

(b)

Manual Search of Abstracts Concordance using Keywords and 4 Cut-offs

SMART Search of Abstracts Thesaurus, using Document Cut-offs at all Levels

SMART Search of Abstracts Thesaurus with Manual Important Term Request Modification, using Document Cut-offs at all Levels

use of several dictionaries successively, until the required performance is reached; the use of several dictionaries with "merged" output results [6]; the use of a manual or automatic method of making an accurate presearch best dictionary choice, yet to be developed; the use of dictionary display methods to allow users willing to interact strongly to delete or add synonyms; the use of relevance feedback methods to iterate searches and improve performance.

Of these suggestions the idea of making a presearch dictionary choice has been explored but with no success so far. If, for example, long requests work better with the stem dictionary, and short requests need the thesaurus, then a simple automatic choice could be made by the system. Using the abstract-stem versus abstract-thesaurus result, Table 8-16 shows that none of the factors of generality, length, or concept frequency are correlated with either dictionary, and even the requests made up by the two preparers do not markedly prefer particular dictionaries. Other criteria may be discovered to aid such a presearch choice, and if a perfect choice were achieved, the result would be as given in Figure 8-6, where the curve based on choice of the best dictionary is seen to be better than the use of either dictionary exclusively.

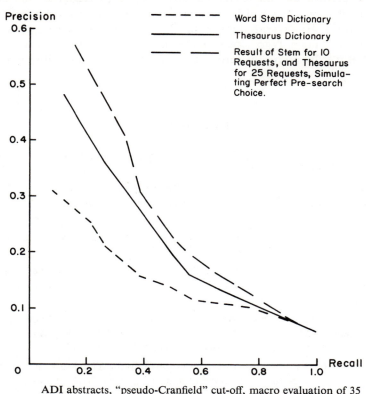

ADI abstracts, "pseudo-Cranfield" cut-off, macro evaluation of 35 requests.

Fig. 8-6 Comparison of perfect pre-search choice of two dictionaries with each dictionary used exclusively.

Table 8-16

GENERALITY, LENGTH, AND FREQUENCY CHARACTERISTICS
USING PRESEARCH DICTIONARY FOR TWO DICTIONARIES

REQUEST	GENERALITY		LENGTH		FREQUENCY		PREPARER	
	Specific	*General*	*Long*	*Short*	*Low*	*High*	*A*	*B*
Stem (10 requests)	4	6	6	4	4	6	6	4
Thesaurus (25 requests)	13	12	11	14	13	12	12	13

The possibility of achieving a satisfactory automatic subject recognition is considered in an extensive analysis performed by J. O'Connor [7]. It seems certain that some loss of performance due to an inability to correctly recognize and match with ideas asked for in requests will be experienced unless very sophisticated procedures can be developed. However, failure in matching occurs also in manual systems due both to errors and inability to cope with the tasks of manual indexing and vocabulary control. Thus it is by no means certain that automatic systems will in practice prove inferior.

REFERENCES

[1] J. O'Connor, Relevance Disagreements and Unclear Request Forms, *American Documentation*, Vol. 18, No. 3, July 1967.

[2] G. Salton, The Evaluation of Automatic Retrieval Procedures—Selected Test Results using the SMART System, *American Documentation*, Vol. 16, July 1965.

[3] J. J. Rocchio, Jr. and G. Salton, Information Search Optimization and Iterative Retrieval Techniques, *Proceedings of the AFIPS Fall Joint Computer Conference*, Las Vegas, Nev., November 1965, Spartan Books, New York, 1965.

[4] E. M. Keen, User Controlled Search Strategies, in *Proceedings of the Fourth Annual National Colloquium on Information Retrieval*, A. B. Tonik, ed., Int. Information Inc., Philadelphia, 1967, pp. 141–154.

[5] H. A. Hall and N. H. Weiderman, The Evaluation Problem in Relevance Feedback Systems, *Report ISR-12* to the National Science Foundation, Section XII, Computer Science Department, Cornell University, Ithaca, N.Y., June 1967.

[6] J. J. Rocchio, Jr., Combinations of Analysis Methods—The Merged Output Results, *Report ISR-9* to the National Science Foundation, Section XIX, Harvard Computation Laboratory, Cambridge, Mass. August 1965.

[7] J. O'Connor, Automatic Subject Recognition in Scientific Papers: An Empirical Study, *Journal of the ACM*, Vol. 12, October 1965.

APPENDIX

Request Texts

The text of each request constituting the set of 35 used in the tests on the ADI documentation collection is listed. All tests use the requests exactly as stated, except for the hand modification runs described in Sec. 8-4.

Original Query		*Modified Query*	
QA1	What problems and concerns are there in making up descriptive titles. What difficulties are involved in automatically retrieving articles from approximate titles. What is the usual relevance of the content of articles to their titles.	QA1	What problems and concerns are there in making up descriptive titles, that is, in devising names and abbreviations for journals and organizations. What is the usual relevance of the content of articles to their titles.
QA2	How can actually pertinent data, as opposed to references or entire articles themselves, be retrieved automatically in response to information requests.	QA2	How can actually pertinent data be retrieved automatically in response to information requests.
QA3	What is information science. Give definitions where possible.		
QA4	Image recognition and any other methods of automatically transforming printed text into computer-ready form.	QA4	Image recognition and any other methods of automatically transforming printed text into computer ready form.
QA5	What special training will ordinary researchers and businessmen need for proper information management and unobstructed use of information retrieval systems. What problems are they likely to encounter.	QA5	What special training will ordinary researchers and businessmen need for proper information management and unobstructed use of information retrieval systems. What problems are they likely to encounter. Researchers, researchers, businessmen, businessmen.
QA6	What possibilities are there for verbal communication between computers and humans, that is, communication via the spoken word.		
QA7	Describe presently working and planned systems for publishing and printing original papers by computer, and then saving the byproduct. Articles coded in data-processing form, for further use in retrieval.	QA7	Describe presently working and planned systems for publishing and printing original papers by computer, and then saving the byproduct. Articles coded in data processing form, for further use in retrieval.

Original Query	*Modified Query*
QA8 Describe information retrieval and indexing in other languages. What bearing does it have on the science in general.	QA8 Describe information retrieval and indexing in foreign languages. What bearing does it have on the science in general.
QA9 What possibilities are there for automatic grammatical and contextual analysis of articles for inclusion in an information retrieval system.	QA9 What possibilities are there for automatic grammatical and contextual analysis of articles for inclusion in an information retrieval system. Grammatical, grammatical, contextual, contextual.
QA10 The use of abstract mathematics in information retrieval, e.g., group theory.	
QA11 What is the need for information consolidation, evaluation, and retrieval in scientific research.	
QA12 Give methods for high speed publication, printing, and distribution of scientific journals.	
QA13 What criteria have been developed for the objective evaluation of information retrieval and dissemination systems.	QA13 What criteria have been developed for the objective evaluation of information retrieval and dissemination systems.
QA14 What future is there for automatic medical diagnosis.	QA14 What future is there for automatic medical diagnosis. Medical, medical, diagnosis, diagnosis.
QA15 How much do information retrieval and dissemination systems, as well as automated libraries, cost. Are they worth it to the researcher and to industry.	QA15 How much do information retrieval and dissemination systems, as well as automated libraries, cost. Are they worth it to the researcher and to industry. Cost, cost.
QA16 What systems incorporate multiprogramming or remote stations in information retrieval. What will be the extent of their use in the future.	
QA17 Means of obtaining large volume, high speed, customer usable information retrieval output.	QA17 Means of obtaining large volume, high speed, customer usable information retrieval output. Output, output.
QA18 What methods are there for encoding, automatically matching, and automatically drawing structures extended in two dimensions, like the structural formulas for chemical compounds.	
QB1 Techniques of machine matching and machine searching systems. Coding and matching methods.	QB1 Techniques of machine matching and machine searching systems. Coding and matching methods. Coding, coding, matching, matching.
QB2 Testing automated information systems.	QB2 Testing automated information systems. Testing, testing.

Original Query	*Modified Query*
QB3 The need to provide personnel for the information field.	QB3 The need to provide personnel for the information field. Personnel, personnel.
QB4 Automated information in the medical field.	QB4 Automated information in the medical field. Medical, medical.
QB5 Amount of use of books in libraries. Relation to need for automated information systems.	QB5 Amount of use of books in libraries. Relation to need for automated information systems. Book, book, use, use.
QB6 Educational and training requirements for personnel in the information field. Possibilities for this training. Needs for programs providing this training.	
QB7 International systems for exchange and dissemination of information.	QB7 International systems for exchange and dissemination of information. International, international.
QB8 Cost and determination of cost associated with systems of automated information.	CB8 Cost and determination of cost associated with systems of automated information. Cost, cost.
QB9 Computerized information retrieval systems. Computerized indexing systems.	
QB10 Computerized information systems in fields related to chemistry.	QB10 Computerized information systems in fields related to chemistry. Chemistry, chemistry.
QB11 Specific advantages of computerized index systems.	QB11 Specific advantages of computerized index systems for book indexing and book catalogs.
QB12 Information dissemination by journals and periodicals.	
QB13 Information systems in the physical sciences.	QB13 Information systems in the physical sciences. Physical, physical, sciences, sciences.
QB14 Attempts at computerized and mechanized systems for general libraries. Problems and methods of automated general author and title indexing systems.	QB14 Attempts at computerized and mechanized systems for general libraries. Problems and methods of automated general author and title indexing systems. General, general, libraries, libraries.
QB15 Retrieval systems which provide for the automated transmission of information to the user from a distance.	
QB16 Methods of coding used in computerized index systems.	QB16 Methods of coding used in computerized index systems. Coding, coding.
QB17 Government agencies and projects dealing with information dissemination.	QB17 Government agencies and projects dealing with information dissemination. Government, government.

Experiments conducted over the last few years with the SMART document retrieval
system have shown that fully automatic text-processing methods using relatively
simple linguistic tools are as effective for purposes of document indexing,
classification, search, and retrieval as the more elaborate manual methods normally
used in practice. Up to now, all experiments were carried out entirely with
English language queries and documents.
The present study describes an extension of the SMART procedures to German
language materials. A multilingual thesaurus is used for the analysis of documents and
search requests, and tools are provided which make it possible to process English
language documents against German queries and vice versa. The methods are
evaluated, and it is shown that the effectiveness of the mixed language processing
is approximately equivalent to that of the standard process operating within a single
language only.

9

AUTOMATIC PROCESSING OF FOREIGN LANGUAGE DOCUMENTS†

G. SALTON

9-1 INTRODUCTION

For some years, experiments have been under way to test the effectiveness of automatic language analysis and indexing methods in information retrieval. Specifically, document and query tests are processed fully automatically, and content identifiers are assigned using a variety of linguistic tools, including word stem analysis, thesaurus lookup, phrase recognition, statistical term association, syntactic analysis, and so on. The resulting concept identifiers assigned to each document and search request are then matched, and the documents whose identifiers are sufficiently close to the queries are retrieved for the user's attention.

The automatic analysis methods can be made to operate in real-time—while the customer waits for an answer—by restricting the query-document comparisons to only certain document classes; interactive user-controlled search methods can be implemented which adjust the search request during

†An earlier version of this study was presented at the International Conference on Computational Linguistics, Sanga–Saby, Sweden, September 1969. It is also included in *Scientific Report ISR-16*, Section IV, October 1969 and in *Journal of the ASIS*, Vol. 21, No. 3, May–June 1970.

the search in such a way that more useful, and less useless, material is retrieved from the file.

The experimental evidence accumulated over the last few years indicates that retrieval systems based on automatic text-processing methods—including fully automatic content analysis as well as automatic document classification and retrieval—are not in general inferior in retrieval effectiveness to conventional systems based on human indexing and human query formulation.

One of the major objections to the practical utilization of the automatic text-processing methods has been the inability to handle automatically foreign language texts of the kind normally stored in documentation and library systems. Recent experiments performed with document abstracts and search requests in French and German appear to indicate that these objections may be groundless.

In the present study, the SMART document retrieval system is used to carry out experiments using foreign language documents and queries as input. The foreign language texts are automatically processed using a thesaurus (synonym dictionary) translated directly from a previously available English version. Foreign language query and document texts are looked up in the foreign language thesaurus, and the analyzed forms of the queries and documents are then compared in the standard manner before retrieving the highly matching items. The language analysis methods incorporated into the SMART system are first reviewed briefly. Then the main procedures used to process the foreign language documents are described, and the retrieval effectiveness of the English text-processing methods is compared with that of the foreign language material.

9-2 THE EVALUATION OF LANGUAGE ANALYSIS METHODS

SMART is a fully automatic document retrieval system operating on the IBM 7094 and IBM 360/65. Unlike other computer-based retrieval systems, the SMART system does not rely on a manual content analysis of documents and search requests. Instead, queries and documents are processed without any prior manual analysis by one of several hundred automatic content analysis methods, using as basic input the query and document texts in the natural language, or alternatively, document texts, abstracts, or summaries.

The following language analysis procedures included in the SMART system are of principal interest for document analysis purposes: (1) a system for separating English words into stems and suffixes (the stem-thesaurus method); (2) a synonym dictionary, or thesaurus, used to recognize synonyms; (3) a hierarchical arrangement of terms which permits "expansion" in various ways of the document and query texts; (4) statistical procedures to compute association coefficients between terms based on their statistical co-occurrence in the documents of a collection; (5) syntactic analysis methods which can be used to recognize syntactically valid phrases in queries and documents; (6) statistical phrase methods in which the phrase recognition is based on a preconstructed phrase dictionary.

The SMART systems organization makes it possible to evaluate the effectiveness of the various processing methods by comparing the outputs produced by a variety of different runs. This is achieved by processing the same search requests against the same document collections several times and making judicious changes in the analysis procedures between runs. In each case, the search effectiveness is evaluated by presenting paired comparisons of the *average* performance over many search requests for two given search and retrieval methodologies [1, 2].

Many different criteria may suggest themselves for measuring the performance of an information system. In the evaluation work carried out with the SMART system, the effectiveness of an information system is assumed to depend on its ability to satisfy the users' information needs by retrieving the material desired, while rejecting unwanted items. Two measures have been used widely for this purpose—*recall* and *precision* which represent, respectively, the proportion of relevant material actually retrieved and the proportion of retrieved material actually relevant [3]. (Ideally, all relevant items should be retrieved, while at the same time, all nonrelevant items should be rejected, as reflected by perfect recall and precision values equal to 1.)

It should be noted that both the recall and precision figures which can be achieved by a given system are adjustable, in that a relaxation of the search conditions often leads to high recall, while a tightening of the search criteria leads to high precision. Unhappily, experience has shown that, *on the average*, recall and precision tend to vary inversely because the retrieval of more relevant items also leads normally to the retrieval of more irrelevant ones. In practice, a compromise is usually made, and a performance level is chosen such that much of the relevant material is retrieved, while the number of nonrelevant items which are also retrieved is kept within tolerable limits.

In theory, one might expect that the performance of a retrieval system would improve as the language analysis methods used for document and query processing become more sophisticated. In actual fact, this turns out not to be the case. A first indication of the fact that retrieval effectiveness does not vary directly with the complexity of the document or query analysis was provided by the output of the Aslib–Cranfield studies. The researchers on this project tested a large variety of indexing languages in a retrieval environment and came to the astonishing conclusion that the simplest type of indexing language would produce the best results [4]. Specifically, three types of indexing languages were tested: (1) *single terms* (i.e., individual terms or concepts assigned to documents and queries); (2) *controlled terms* (i.e., single terms assigned under the control of the well-known *EJC Thesaurus of Engineering and Scientific Terms*); (3) *simple concepts* (i.e., phrases consisting of two or more single terms). The results of the Cranfield tests indicated that single terms are more effective for retrieval purposes than either controlled terms or complete phrases [4].

These results might be dismissed as being due to certain peculiar test conditions if it were not for the fact that the results obtained with the automatic SMART retrieval system substantially confirm the earlier Cranfield output [3]. Specifically, the following basic conclusions can be drawn from the main SMART experiments:

(a) The simplest automatic language analysis procedure, consisting of the assignment to queries and documents of weighted word stems contained originally in these documents, produces a retrieval effectiveness almost equivalent to that obtained by intellectual indexing carried out manually under controlled conditions [3], [5].

(b) Use of a thesaurus lookup process, designed to recognize synonyms and other term relations by replacing the original word stems with the corresponding thesaurus categories, improves the retrieval effectiveness by about 10% in both recall and precision.

(c) Additional, more sophisticated language analysis procedures, including the assignment of phrases instead of individual terms, the use of a concept hierarchy, the determination of syntactic relations between terms, and so on, *do not*, on the average, provide improvements over the standard thesaurus process.

An example of a typical recall-precision graph produced by the SMART system is shown in Fig. 9-1, where a statistical phrase method is compared with a syntactic phrase procedure. In the former case, phrases are assigned as content identifiers to documents and queries whenever the individual phrase components are all present within a given document; in the latter case, the individual components must also exhibit an appropriate syntactic relationship before the phrase is assigned as an identifier. The output of Fig. 9-1 shows that the use of syntax degrades performance (the ideal performance region is in the upper right-hand corner of the graph where both the recall and the precision are close to 1). Several arguments may explain the output of Fig. 9-1:

(a) The inadequacy of the syntactic analyzer used to generate syntactic phrases.

(b) The fact that phrases are often appropriate content identifiers even when the phrase components are not syntactically related in a given context (e.g., the sentence "people who need information require adequate retrieval service" is

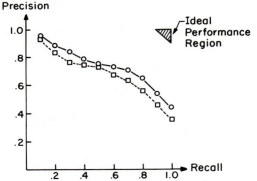

Recall	Precision	
	o——o	□-----□
0.1	.960	.938
0.3	.834	.776
0.5	.769	.735
0.7	.706	.625
0.9	.546	.467

Fig. 9-1 Comparison between statistical and syntactic phrases (averages over 17 queries).

identified adequately by the phrase "information retrieval", even though the components are not related in the sentence).

(c) The variability of the user population which makes it unwise to overspecify document content.

(d) The ambiguity inherent in natural language texts which may work to advantage when attempting to satisfy the information needs of a heterogeneous user population with diverse information needs.

Most likely, a combination of some of the above factors is responsible for the fact that relatively simple content analysis methods are generally preferable in a retrieval environment to more sophisticated methods. The foreign language processing to be described in the remainder of this chapter must be viewed in the light of the foregoing test results.

9-3   MULTILINGUAL THESAURUS

The multilingual text-processing experiment is motivated by the following principal considerations:

(a) In typical American libraries up to 50% of the stored materials may not be in English; about 50% of the material processed in a test at the National Library of Medicine in Washington was not in English (of this, German accounted for about 25%, French for 23%, Italian for 13%, Russian for 11%, Japanese for 6%, Spanish for 5%, and Polish for 5%) [6].

(b) In certain statistical text-processing experiments carried out with foreign language documents, the test results were about equally good for German as for English [7].

(c) Simple text-processing methods appear to work well for English, and there is no a priori reason why they should not work equally well for another language.

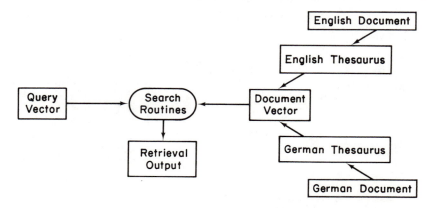

Fig. 9-2   Foreign language text processing system.

The basic multilingual system used for text purposes is outlined in Fig. 9-2. Document (or query) texts are looked up in a thesaurus and reduced to "concept vector" form. Query vectors and document vectors are then compared, and document vectors sufficiently similar to the query are withdrawn from the file. In order to ensure that mixed language input is processed properly, the thesaurus must assign *the same* concept categories, no matter what the input language. The SMART system, therefore, utilizes a multilingual thesaurus in which one concept category corresponds both to a family of English words, or word stems, as well as to their German translation.

A typical thesaurus excerpt is shown in Fig. 9-3, giving concept numbers, English word class, and corresponding German word class, respectively. This thesaurus was produced by manually translating into German an originally available English version. Table 9-1 shows the results of the thesaurus lookup operation for the English and Ger-

```
230  ART                      ARCHITEKTUR

231  INDEPEND                 SELBSTAENDIG
                              UNABHAENGIG

232  ASSOCIATIVE

233  DIVIDE

234  ACTIVE                   AKTIV
     ACTIVITY                 AKTIVITAET
     USAGE                    TAETIGKEIT

235  CATHODE                  DIODE
     CRT                      VERZWEIGER
     DIODE
     FLYING-SPOT
     RAY
     RELAIS
     RELAY
     SCANNER
     TUBE

236  REDUNDANCY
     REDUNDANT

237  CHARGE                   EINGANG
     ENTER                    EINGEGANGEN
     ENTRY                    EINGEGEBEN
     INSERT                   EINSATZ
     POST                     EINSTELLEN
                              EINTRAGUNG

238  MULTI-LEVEL
     MULTILEVEL

239  INTELLECT                GEISTIG
     INTELLECTUAL
     INTELLIG
     MENTAL
     MIND
     NON-INTELLECTUAL

240  ACTUAL                   PRAXIS
     PRACTICE
     REAL
```

Fig. 9-3 Excerpt from multi-lingual thesaurus.

```
*FIND Q13BAUTHORS

   IN WHAT WAYS ARE COMPUTER SYSTEMS BEING
APPLIED TO RESEARCH IN THE FIELD OF THE
BELLES LETTRES ? HAS MACHINE ANALYSIS OF
LANGUAGE PROVED USEFUL FOR INSTANCE, IN
DETERMINING PROBABLE AUTHORSHIP OF
ANONYMOUS WORKS OR IN COMPILING
CONCORDANCES ?
```

```
   DANS QUEL SENS LES CALCULATEURS
SUNT-ILS APPLIQUES A LA RECHERCHE DANS
LE DOMAINE DES BELLES-LETTRES ? EST-CE
QUE L'ANALYSE AUTOMATIQUE DES TEXTES A
ETE UTILE, PAR EXEMPLE, POUR DETERMINER
L'AUTEUR PROBABLE D'OUVRAGES ANONYMES OU
POUR FAIRE DES CONCORDANCES ?
```

```
   INWIEWEIT WERDEN COMPUTER-SYSTEME ZUR
FORSCHUNG AUF DEM GEBIET DER SCHOENEN
LITERATUR VERWENDET ? HAT SICH
MASCHINELLE SPRACHENANALYSE ALS
HILFREICH ERWIESEN, UM Z.B. DIE
VERMUTLICHE AUTORENSCHAFT BEI ANONYMEN
WERKEN ZU BESTIMMEN ODER UM KONKORDANZEN
ZUSAMMENZUSTELLEN ?
```

Fig. 9-4   Query QB13 in three languages.

man versions of query QB 13. The original query texts in three languages (English, French, and German) are shown in Fig. 9-4. It may be seen that seven out of nine "English" concepts are common with the German concept vector for the same query. In view of this, one may expect that the German query, processed against the German thesaurus, could be matched against English language documents as easily as the English version of the query. Table 9-1 also shows that more query words were not found during lookup in the German thesaurus than in the English one. This is due to the fact that only an incomplete version of the German thesaurus was available at run time.

9-4   FOREIGN LANGUAGE RETRIEVAL EXPERIMENT

To test the simple multilingual thesaurus process, two collections of documents in the area of library science and documentation (the Ispra collection) were processed

Table 9-1

THESAURUS LOOKUP FOR QUERY QB13

ENGLISH			GERMAN		SAMPLE THESAURUS ENTRIES
Concept	*Weight*		*Concept*	*Weight*	
3	12	√*	3	12	Computer, processor
19	12	√	19	12	Automatic, semiautomatic
			21	4	Artikel, Presse, Zeitschrift
33	12	√	33	6	Analyze, analyzer, analysis, etc.
			45	4	Herausgabe, Publikation
49	12				Compendium, compile, deposit
			64	4	Buch, Heft, Werk
65	12	√	65	12	Authorship, originator
			68	12	Literatur
147	12	√	147	6	Discourse, language, linguistic
207	12	√	207	12	Area, branch, subfield
267	12	√	267	12	Concordance, keyword-in-context, KWIC
345	12				Bell
Not found					Anonymous, letters
			Not found		Schoenen, hilfreich, vermutlich
					Anonymen, zusammenzustellen

*English concepts in common with German concepts for same query.

against a set of 48 search requests in the documentation area. The English collection consisted of 1095 document abstracts, whereas the German collection contained only 468 document abstracts. The overlap between the two collections included 50 common documents. All 48 queries were originally available in English; they were translated manually into German by a native German speaker. The English queries were then processed against both the English and the German collections (runs E-E and E-G), and the same was done for the translated German queries (runs G-E and G-G, respectively). Relevance assessments were made for each English document abstract with respect to each English query by a set of eight American students in library science; the assessors were not the same as the users who submitted the search requests originally. The German relevance assessments (German documents against German queries), on the other hand, were obtained from a different, German-speaking assessor.

The principal evaluation results for the four runs using the thesaurus process are shown in Fig. 9-5, averaged over 48 queries in each case. It is clear from the output of Fig. 9-5 that the cross language runs, E-G (English queries–German documents) and G-E (German queries–English documents), are not substantially inferior to the corresponding output within a single language (G-G and E-E, respectively), the difference being of the order of 0.02 to 0.03 for a given recall level. On the other hand, both runs using the German document collection are inferior to the runs with the English collection.

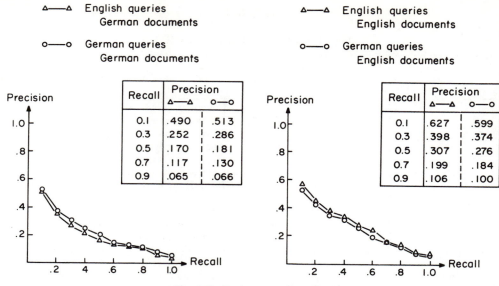

Fig. 9-5 Basic comparison English vs. German queries (thesaurus process).

The output of Fig. 9-5 leads to the following principal conclusions:

(a) Query processing is comparable in both languages; if this were not the case, then one would expect one set of query runs to be much less effective than the other (that is, either E-E and E-G, or else G-G and G-E).

(b) Language-processing methods (that is, thesaurus categories, suffix cutoff procedures, etc.) are equally effective in both cases; if this were not the case, one would expect one of the single language runs to come out very poorly, but neither E-E, nor G-G came out as the poorest run.

(c) Cross language runs are performed properly; if this were not the case, one would expect E-G and G-E to perform much less well than the runs within a single language. Since this is not so, the principal conclusion is then obvious that *documents in one language can be matched against queries in another nearly as well as documents and queries in a single language.*

(d) Runs using the German document collection (E-G and G-G) are less effective than those performed with the English collection. The indication is apparent then that some characteristic connected with the German document collection itself— for example, the type of abstract, the language of the abstract, or the relevance assessments—requires improvement; the effectiveness of the cross language processing, however, is not at issue.

The foreign language analysis is summarized in Table 9-2.

Table 9-2

ANALYSIS OF FOREIGN LANGUAGE PROCESSING

Translation Problem	*Corresponding Observation**	*Observation Confirmed*
Poor query processing or poor translation	E–E and E–G much better than G–E and G–G, or vice versa	No
Poor language processing	Either E–E or G–G much poorer than cross language runs	No
Poor cross language processing	Both E–G and G–E poorer than other runs	No
Poor processing of one document collection	Either E–G and G–G, or else G–E and E–E simultaneously poor	Yes

*E–E : English queries–English documents.
 E–G : English queries–German documents.
 G–E : German queries–English documents.
 G–G : German queries–German documents.

9-5 FAILURE ANALYSIS

Since the query processing operates equally well in both languages, while the German document collection produces a degraded performance, it becomes worthwhile to examine the principal differences between the two document collections.

Table 9-3

CHARACTERISTICS OF DOCUMENT COLLECTIONS

CHARACTERISTIC OF COLLECTIONS	DOCUMENT COLLECTION	
	English	*German*
Number of document abstracts	1095	468
Number of documents common to both collections	50	50
Number of queries used in test	48	48
Number of relevance assessors	8	1
Number of common relevance assessors	0	0
Generality of collection (number of relevant documents over total number of documents in collection	0.013	0.029
Average number of word occurrences not found in the thesaurus during lookup of document abstracts	6.5	15.5

These are summarized in Table 9-3. The following principal distinctions arise:

(a) The organization of the thesaurus used to group words or word stems into thesaurus categories.

(b) The completeness of the thesaurus in terms of words included in it.

(c) The type of document abstracts included in the collection.

(d) The accuracy of the relevance assessments obtained from the collections.

It does not appear that any essential difficulties arise with regard to the organization of the multilingual thesaurus. This is confirmed by the fact that the cross language runs operate satisfactorily. It is also substantiated by the output of Fig. 9-6,

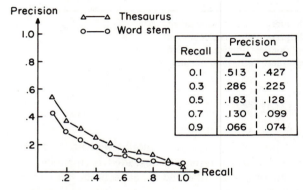

Recall	Precision	
	△—△	○—○
0.1	.513	.427
0.3	.286	.225
0.5	.183	.128
0.7	.130	.099
0.9	.066	.074

Fig. 9-6   Thesaurus comparison for German queries and German documents.

comparing a German word stem run (using standard suffix cutoff and weighting procedures) with a German thesaurus run. It is seen that the German thesaurus improves performance over word stems for the German collection in the same way as the English thesaurus was seen earlier to improve retrieval effectiveness over the English word stem analysis [2], [3].

The other thesaurus characteristic—that is its completeness—appears to present a more serious problem. Table 9-3 shows that only approximately 6.5 English words per document abstract were not included in the English thesaurus, whereas over 15 words per abstract were missing from the German thesaurus. Obviously, if the missing words turn out to be important for content analysis purposes, the German abstracts will be more difficult to analyze than their English counterpart. A brief analysis confirms that many of the missing German words, which do not therefore produce concept numbers assignable to the documents, are indeed important for content identification. Figure 9-7, listing the words not found for document 005, shows that 12 out of 14 missing words appear to be important for the analysis of that document. Therefore it would seem essential that a more complete thesaurus be used under operational conditions and for future experiments.

68   PAGE 483   NOVEMBER 8, 1968   PAGE 484   00001

*TEXT 00501063 ZUR KOMPILATION VON THESAURI

WORD NOT FOUND	KIND	LOC	NUM	SENTENCE AND WORD NUMBERS	
KOMPILATION	SUFFIX	2	1	1,	2
THESAURUSELEMENTE	SUFFIX	4	1	2,	5
GEBRAUCHT	SUFFIX	1	1	2,	13
SCHLAGWORTES	SUFFIX	2	1	3,	11
HOMONYME	SUFFIX	2	1	4,	4
SYNONYME	SUFFIX	2	1	4,	6
VERVOLLSTAENDIGUNG	SUFFIX	4	1	5,	3
VERWEISSYSTEMS	SUFFIX	4	1	5,	8
VORORDNUNG	SUFFIX	2	1	5,	13
HAUPTLISTE	SUFFIX	2	1	5,	15
HILFSLISTEN	SUFFIX	2	1	5,	19
UNERLAESSLICH	SUFFIX	6	1	5,	20
GEBRAUCH	SUFFIX	1	1	6,	11
KONKORDANZEN	SUFFIX	2	1	6,	15

Fig. 9-7   List of words not found in thesaurus for document 005.

The other two collection characteristics, including the type of abstract and the accuracy of the relevance judgments are more difficult to compare because the two collections under consideration are not identical. In an attempt to obtain a valid assessment of the differences in relevance assessments and abstract characteristics, a retrieval run was made for that part of the two collections common to both the English and German versions. This subcollection consisted of 50 documents and 11 queries (only those queries could be used for which the set of relevant documents included at least 1 of the common 50—not necessarily the same one—for both the German and the English assessments).

The output of Fig. 9-8 shows that the German abstracts were not of the same quality as the English ones. Specifically, keeping the English relevance assessments constant, it is seen that the English version abstracts are superior to the German (curves 1 and 3); the same is true using the German relevance assessments (curves 4 and 2). The relevance assessments themselves can be compared by keeping query and collection language invariant and by varying the relevance judgments. A comparison of curves 1 and 4 for the English abstracts, or curves 3 and 2 for the German ones, shows that the performance obtained by using the English abstracts to assess relevance (English relevance assessments) is much superior to that obtained with the German assessments.†

Although, the qualities of the German abstracts and of the relevance assessor do not appear to match the respective English counterparts, thus accounting for the

---

†An earlier study showed that recall-precision results are not affected by ordinary differences in the relevance assessments obtained from different judges for *the same* collection [8]. This result is not applicable here, since the abstract collections used in making the assessments are distinct in the present case. Furthermore for the present collection, it is difficult to say whether it is the lack of informative abstracts in the German collection which is chiefly responsible for the performance difference, or the lack of adequate relevance assessments. Obviously, these two factors are closely related.

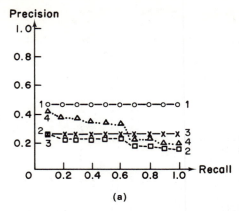

(a)

Queries Documents Relevance	English English (English)	English German (German)	English German (English)	English English (German)
Symbol	○——○	□- - -□	×——×	△·······△
Recall	*Precision*			
0.1	.468	.282	.244	.445
0.3	.468	.223	.244	.385
0.5	.468	.223	.244	.370
0.7	.468	.187	.244	.210
0.9	.468	.174	.244	.185

(b)

Fig. 9-8 Recall-precision results for common documents (11 queries, 50 documents).

inferior performance of the German subcollection, the basic results pertaining to the cross language processing described previously are in no way affected.

9-6 CONCLUSION

An experiment using a multilingual thesaurus in conjunction with two different document collections, in German and English, respectively, has shown that cross language processing (for example, German queries against English documents) is nearly as effective as processing within a single language. Furthermore, a simple translation of thesaurus categories appears to produce a document content analysis which is equally effective in English as in German. In particular, differences in morphology (for example, in the suffix cutoff rules) and in language ambiguities do not seem to cause a substantial degradation when moving from one language to another. For these reasons, the automatic retrieval methods used in the SMART system for English appear to be applicable also to foreign language material.

Future experiments with foreign language documents should be carried out using a thesaurus that is reasonably complete in all languages and with identical query and document collections for which the same relevance judgments may then be applicable across all runs.

REFERENCES

[1] G. Salton and M. E. Lesk, The SMART Automatic Document Retrieval System—An Illustration, *Communications of the ACM*, Vol. 8, No. 6, June 1965.

[2] G. Salton, *Automatic Information Organization and Retrieval*, McGraw-Hill, Inc., New York, 1968.

[3] G. Salton and M. E. Lesk, Computer Evaluation of Indexing and Text Processing, *Journal of the ACM*, Vol. 15, No. 1, January 1968; also Chap. 7 of this volume.

[4] C. W. Cleverdon and E. M. Keen, Factors Determining the Performance of Indexing Systems, *Design*, Vol. 1, *Test Results*, Vol. 2, Aslib–Cranfield Research Project, Cranfield, England, 1966.

[5] G. Salton, A Comparison Between Manual and Automatic Indexing Methods, *American Documentation*, Vol. 20, No. 1, January 1969; also Chap. 27 of this volume.

[6] F. W. Lancaster, Evaluation of the Operating Efficiency of Medlars, Final Report, National Library of Medicine, Washington, D.C., January 1969.

[7] J. H. Williams, Computer Classification of Documents, *FID–IFIP Conference on Mechanized Documentation*, Rome, June 1967; included in *Mechanized Information Storage, Retrieval and Dissemination*, K. Samuelson, ed., North Holland Publishing Co., Amsterdam, 1968.

[8] M. E. Lesk and G. Salton, Relevance Assessments and Retrieval System Evaluation, *Information Storage and Retrieval*, Vol. 4, No. 4, October 1968; also Chap. 26 of this volume.

PART IV

CLUSTER GENERATION
AND SEARCH

Future real-time information retrieval systems may be expected to utilize automatic text analysis procedures, for the preparation of analyzed search requests, and user feedback information, for the generation of a useful search strategy. The analysis procedures and the search strategies to be used will vary to some extent with the equipment used in the system, with the type of service to be furnished, and with the user population. If the user population is large, and service is to be rendered simultaneously to many users, then it is not possible to process each search request against an entire collection of stored items. Instead, a number of partial searches may by used to replace a single full search of the collection.
In the present study, various partial search strategies are described, based on available document and request groupings. The SMART *system is used to evaluate these strategies and to postulate an efficient, real-time, user-controlled search strategy.*

10

CLUSTER SEARCH STRATEGIES AND THE OPTIMIZATION OF RETRIEVAL EFFECTIVENESS†

G. SALTON

10-1 INTRODUCTION

Presently operating mechanized information systems are based on mechanized information files which can be searched mechanically. All other operations, including particularly the input operations, the indexing and analysis operations, and the processing of the final output, are normally carried out with the help of human experts. In the foreseeable future such mechanized systems may be modified in two important respects. First, the analysis of incoming documents and search requests may be carried out automatically, instead of manually, using for this purpose a variety of stored dictionaries and tables, as well as statistical and syntactic text analysis methods. Second, the operations may be based on time-sharing equipment, where access to the central store can be provided to a number of different users, more or less simultaneously by means of special input–output consoles.

A great deal of work has been done over the last few years in the area of automatic indexing in an attempt to generate indexing methods which could

†An earlier version of this study was included in *Mechanized Information Storage, Retrieval and Dissemination*, K. Samuelson, ed., North Holland Publishing Co., Amsterdam, 1968. It was also issued as Section V in *Scientific Report, ISR-12*, June 1967.

223

be incorporated into operating information systems [1], [2]. Several evaluation studies have also been carried out to determine the effectiveness of many kinds of automatic text analysis procedures, and tentative conclusions have been reached concerning the relative effectiveness of the analysis methods under consideration [3], [4], [5], [6], [7].

The area dealing with search strategies and with procedures designed to make the user participate in the search process has received much less attention. Instead, even in the experimental situations, searches are carried out in such a way that each analyzed search request is compared in turn against each analyzed document. Documents, or citations which exhibit a sufficiently high-matching coefficient with a search request, are then withdrawn from the file and handed to the appropriate user. The user population does not in general participate in the search process over which it has no real control.

When time-sharing equipment becomes available in operational situations, the search process described previously can no longer be carried out efficiently. In those circumstances the search and retrieval system must overcome two substantial constraints of the existing time-sharing organizations:

(a) The small amount of internal storage which can normally be allocated to any given user (users must compete for memory space with many other users).

(b) The rudimentary nature of the input–output console equipment likely to be made available to each user, which permits the introduction or withdrawal of only limited amounts of information.

At the same time, the information system should profit from the fact that the customer can now be made a part of the system, by asking him periodically to provide feedback information designed to clarify his information need.

The limitations inherent in the restricted available storage space and in the simple typewriter-like input-output devices may be overcome by fast search algorithms, confined to only small subsections of the stored file, and by limited interactions with the user. Such fast search algorithms are described in the next few sections, and evaluation results obtained by using the SMART automatic retrieval system are given to illustrate the effectiveness of the various search and retrieval procedures [8], [9].

10-2   CLUSTER SEARCH PROCESS

10-2-A   Overall Process

In a traditional library environment, answers to information requests are not usually obtained by conducting a search through an entire document collection. Instead, the items are classified first into subject areas, and a search is restricted to items within a few chosen subject classes. This same device can also be used in a mechanized system by constructing groups of related documents and confining the search to certain groups only. Specifically, the following overall strategy can be used:

(a) Groups or clusters of related documents are constructed by comparing the identifiers for a given document with the identifiers of all other documents, and by grouping those documents whose sets of identifiers are sufficiently similar.

(b) For each such document group, a representative element, also known as the *centroid vector*, is chosen; then this centroid vector is used to represent the whole document set in that group.

(c) The search proceeds in two steps: a given search request is compared first against the centroids of all document groups; then a second search is used to match the request against the individual documents located in groups with highly matching centroids.

A stylized picture of such a two-level cluster search is shown in Fig. 10-1, where each document is represented by a small square, and each search request is represented by a triangle. It is seen that requests *A* and *C* lie close to the centroid vectors of two of the document clusters; the similarity coefficient between the requests and the corresponding centroids may therefore be expected to be large, and the document search is then confined to documents in the two respective groups only. Request *B*, on the other hand, lies close to the centroid of four clusters, thus necessitating a detailed search of these four groups.

Obviously, the two-level search can be extended to a three-level, or even higher-level, search by grouping the centroid vectors themselves into broader groups of larger coverage, followed by a grouping of these broader groups into still broader ones, and so on. In that case, a search is first made of the centroids for the highest-

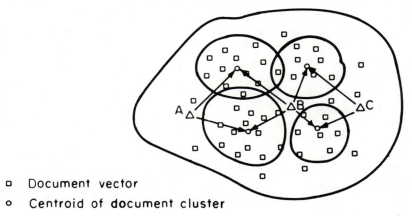

□   Document vector

o   Centroid of document cluster

△   Request vector

Fig. 10-1   Sample clustered document space.

level groups; this isolates some centroid groups on the next lower level; a search of these identifies certain groupings on the next lower level, and so on down, until some document clusters are found which must be searched individually.

The efficiency of such a *multilevel* or *cluster search* varies with the clustering process used and with the collection under consideration. It is greatest when the collection can be subdivided into nonoverlapping groups of approximately identical size. It diminishes as the amount of overlap between groups increases and as the size of the groups begins to deviate from a common ideal value. Obviously, a cluster search will not be workable if the documents of interest to the user are not included in the groups which are to be searched individually, since such relevant documents are not then retrievable. This will be discussed in greater detail in Sec. 10-2-C.

10-2-B   Cluster Generation

The problem of taking sets of items identified by certain properties and grouping them in such a way so that items identified by a common property set are placed into a common class is well known in many fields. A number of mathematical techniques have been used in the past with varying degrees of success in the implementation of a clustering program, including matrix eigenvalue analysis, factor analysis, latent class analysis, and others. Some of these techniques have also been applied to the documentation area, where the items to be grouped are documents, and the properties used to effect the grouping are keywords or index terms attached to the documents [10], [11], [12].

The process to be described here was developed by Rocchio. It differs from some of the others in that the number of clusters to be generated can be controlled, as can the cluster size and the amount of overlap between clusters [13]. Such controlled clusters may be more useful in an application to documentation than clusters which are subject to large size variations and to a great degree of overlap.

All documents are considered initially to be unclustered, and each document is first subjected to a region *density test* to determine whether a sufficient number of other documents are located in the same vicinity. This test specifies that more than n_1 items should have a correlation higher than some parameter p_1 with the candidate, and that more than n_2 items should have correlations higher than p_2. The test ensures that items on the edge of large groups do not become centers of groups, and that annular regions where items are concentrated in a ring-like area around the candidate item are not accepted as clusters. An example of a density test failure is shown in Table 10-1, where an attempt is made to select document 13 as a cluster center. In the example, the requirement that at least five documents have a correlation greater than 0.25 with document 13 is not met, since the fifth highest correlation (with document no. 19) is only 0.1979. Items which fail the density are considered to be "loose" and are not chosen again as potential cluster centers.

If a document passes the density test, a cutoff value is chosen as a function of the preestablished minimum and maximum number of permissible items per cluster, and items whose correlation with the central document is larger than the cutoff value are

Table 10-1

DENSITY TEST FAILURE

(Less than five documents exhibit correlation greater than 0.25)

Document Rank	Document Number	Correlation
1	13	1.0000
2	24	0.3664
3	26	0.3071
4	74	0.2643
5	19	0.1979
6	22	0.1453
7	59	0.1248
8	45	0.1172
9	78	0.1166
10	38	0.1161
11	46	0.1077
12	75	0.0882
13	17	0.0844
14	23	0.0722
15	36	0.0641
16	4	0.0640
17	63	0.0507
18	81	0.0447
19	55	0.0447
20	35	0.0369
21	57	0.0358
22	80	0.0207
23	16	0.0181
24	25	0.0175
25	77	0.0149
26	44	0.0135
27	82	0.0000
28	73	0.0000
29	69	0.0000
30	54	0.0000
31	50	0.0000
32	14	0.0000

used to define a cluster. In the example of Table 10-2, items are grouped around document 7, which previously passed the density test, and the six top documents (nos. 7, 42, 9, 20, 32, and 31) with a correlation above cutoff define an initial cluster. The cutoff is picked at the point of maximum correlation difference between two adjacent documents to produce the shortest boundary between identified subset and neighboring unclustered items.

Given the set of documents D defining a cluster, the centroid vector is chosen as the center of gravity of the set of document vectors derived from the elements of D.

Table 10-2

CORRELATION OF TOP 15 DOCUMENTS WITH DOCUMENT NO. 7

	Document Rank	Document Number	Correlation
	1	7	1.0000
	2	42	0.4352
	3	9	0.3935
	4	20	0.3541
	5	32	0.3002
	6	31	0.2789
Cutoff →			
	7	25	0.2374
	8	22	0.2130
	9	73	0.1984
	10	57	0.1949
	11	81	0.1826
	12	55	0.1826
	13	75	0.1801
	14	78	0.1705
	15	36	0.1527

Specifically, if each document is identified by a property, or keyword vector **d**, the centroid vector is defined as

$$C = \sum_{d^{(i)} \in D} d^{(i)}.$$

The centroid vector C_1, which results from the addition of the six document vectors identified in Table 10-2, is shown in Table 10-3. The documents defining the group are listed at the top of the figure, and the centroid vector itself consists of 65 concepts (represented by three-digit numbers) each with a specified weight.

The centroid vector thus derived is now matched against the *entire* document collection, and the cutoff parameters on category size are reapplied to create an altered cluster. The results of this matching operation are show in Table 10-4 for the centroid C_1 of Table 10-3. The cutoff again falls between the sixth and seventh documents, and the resulting cluster identified in the example of Table 10-4 is the same as that which originally defined the cluster in Table 10-2. Such a result is of course not necessarily obtained in all cases.

This clustering process is now repeated with all unclustered items; the first pass ends when all items are either clustered or loose. Since the centroid vectors are correlated against the entire collection, some items may of course end up in several different clusters. If the number of categories formed is less than the number originally specified, a second pass could be made with relaxed density conditions. Alternatively,

Table 10-3

FORMATION OF CENTROID C_1 USING DOCUMENTS
7, 9, 20, 31, 32, AND 42

Concept Numbers	Weights	Concept Numbers	Weights	Concept Numbers	Weights	Concept Numbers	Weights
1	24	3	120	5	12	6	24
7	12	8	24	10	24	19	24
23	24	24	36	28	12	30	24
32	24	33	34	40	48	43	12
44	36	47	24	50	12	54	6
57	12	58	36	67	12	70	24
71	12	72	12	73	24	76	48
78	12	79	36	87	12	89	24
95	12	103	24	108	12	113	12
114	24	122	12	130	78	134	12
149	12	152	12	172	12	180	12
181	12	205	12	207	24	211	12
222	12	246	36	258	72	259	12
261	12	262	12	278	12	285	12
291	12	298	12	322	12	323	12
349	12	532	12	594	24	600	6

Table 10-4

CORRELATION OF TOP 15 DOCUMENTS WITH CENTROID C_1

(Cluster contains documents 7, 9, 20, 31, 32, and 42)

	Document Rank	Document Number	Correlation
	1	7	0.7853
	2	42	0.7028
	3	9	0.5593
	4	20	0.5497
	5	31	0.5007
	6	32	0.4425
Cutoff →	7	73	0.3518
	8	40	0.3049
	9	56	0.2957
	10	75	0.2950
	11	1	0.2685
	12	51	0.2516
	13	25	0.2473
	14	57	0.2468
	15	55	0.2463

the density test could be made more restrictive, or the category size limits could be increased.

At the end of this initial clustering operation, a relatively large number of items might remain loose. Furthermore, the amount of overlap between clusters might be considerable. Under these circumstances, it is possible to use an additional optional clustering pass based on the formation of a partition class for each centroid vector. Specifically each document is assigned to that centroid with which it exhibits the highest correlation, and the document groups so obtained are used to define a new centroid. For the centroid C_1 of Table 10-3, this maximum correlation partition specifies documents 9, 20, 31, 32, and 42. These five documents in turn define the new centroid C_2 shown in Table 10-5.

Table 10-5

FORMATION OF NEW CENTROID C_2 FROM
MINIMUM CORRELATION PARTITION

(Using documents 9, 20, 31, 32, and 42)

Concept Numbers	Weights	Concept Numbers	Weights	Concept Numbers	Weights	Concept Numbers	Weights
1	24	3	84	5	12	6	12
7	12	8	24	10	12	19	12
22	6	23	24	24	36	28	12
30	24	32	24	33	24	40	36
44	24	47	12	50	12	54	6
58	24	67	12	70	24	71	12
72	12	73	24	76	36	78	12
79	24	87	12	89	24	103	24
108	12	113	12	114	24	172	12
180	12	181	12	205	12	207	12
222	12	246	36	258	48	259	12
261	12	262	12	278	12	285	12
291	12	322	12	349	12	532	12
594	24	600	6				

It may be noted that document no. 7 which was used originally as the center for the clustering operation given in the example is no longer present, since its highest centroid correlation occurs with a centroid other than C_1. The centroid C_2 of Table 10-5 lacks some of the concepts originally present in C_1, and the weights are generally lower.

The new centroid is now correlated against the complete document collection as before, and a cutoff determines a new cluster, consisting, for the case used as an example, of documents 7, 9, 20, 31, and 42, as shown in Table 10-6. A "blending" routine is now used to assign loose documents to that group with which they exhibit

Table 10-6

CORRELATION OF TOP 15 DOCUMENTS WITH CENTROID C_2

	Document Rank	Document Number	Correlation
	1	42	0.7271
	2	7	0.6246
	3	20	0.5647
	4	9	0.5609
	5	31	0.5298
Cutoff →	6	32	0.4482
	7	73	0.3712
	8	75	0.3061
	9	56	0.2746
	10	40	0.2701
	11	49	0.2649
	12	1	0.2502
	13	55	0.2438
	14	78	0.2400
	15	57	0.2400

Table 10-7

FINAL CLUSTER AROUND CENTROID C_2 AFTER BLENDING

Cluster	Document Rank	Document Number	Correlation
Original documents	1	42	0.7271
	2	7	0.6246
	3	20	0.5647
	4	9	0.5609
	5	31	0.5298
Loose documents added by "blending" routine	6	32	0.4482
	7	73	0.3712
	8	75	0.3061
	9	78	0.2400
	10	25	0.2252
	11	54	0.2044
	12	38	0.1790
	13	63	0.1592

the highest correlation. For the example given in Tables 10-2 through 10-6, the results of the blending operation are shown in Table 10-7.

To summarize, the complete process consists of three grouping operations: the first around the initial items which pass the density test, the second around the centroids of the clusters previously generated, and the third around the new centroids obtained after partition of the previous sets. For the example, the changes in the generated cluster are summarized in Table 10-8.

Table 10-9 lists the parameters which enter into the cluster generation process, including density control parameters and cluster size parameters. These parameters are used to control the number of clusters and amount of overlap desired and also to exclude certain items from the clustering process, or to delete concepts of low weight from the document and centroid vectors.

Figure 10-2 shows in summary form the results of a clustering operation for a collection of 82 documents in the documentation area. Each cluster is identified by a different numeric digit, ranging from 1 for the first cluster to 7 for the last. In each case, the correlation coefficient of a given document with its respective centroid can be read off on the ordinate, and the number of documents in each cluster is given by the abscissa of the right-most entry for the given cluster. Thus Fig. 10-2 shows, for

Table 10-8

SUMMARY OF GENERATION PROCESS FOR TYPICAL CLUSTER

Generator	*Resulting Cluster*
1. Document 7	7, 9, 20, 31, 32, 42
2. Centroid C_1	7, 9, 20, 31, 32, 42
3. Minimum correlation partition	9, 20, 31, 32, 42
4. Centroid C_2	7, 9, 20, 31, 42
5. Centroid C_2 with blending	7, 9, 20, 25, 31, 32, 38, 42, 54, 63, 73, 75, 78.

Table 10-9

CLUSTERING PARAMETERS

Type of Control	*Function*
Master	Use of maximum correlation partition to redefine clusters.
	Placement of loose documents in clusters.
	Documents to be included in clustering process.
Density test	Minimum number of documents with correlation exceeding p_1.
	Minimum number of documents with correlation exceeding p_2.
	Minimum significant correlation.
	Documents to be considered as cluster roots.
Cluster size	Type of correlation coefficient.
	Minimum number of documents per cluster.
	Maximum number of documents per cluster.
	Minimum significant correlation difference.
	Correlation difference sufficient to force a break between clusters.
	Weight of concept to be deleted from vector.
	Type of centroid definition.

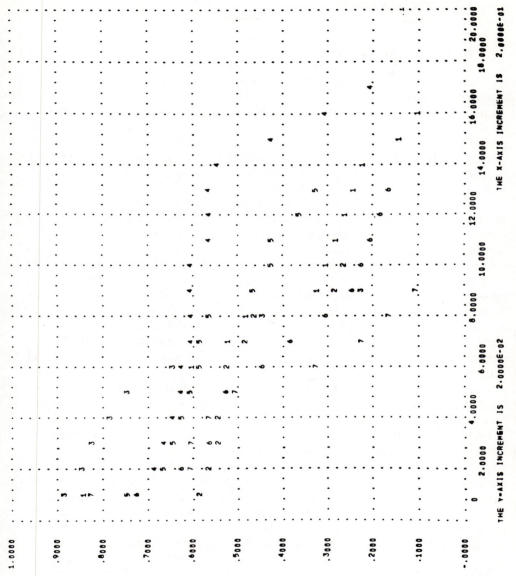

Fig. 10-2 Correlation of clustered documents with their respective centroid vectors (82 documents—7 clusters—5 overlapping documents).

233

example, that cluster 4 contains 17 documents, while cluster 2 contains only 10. The more useful clusters are generally those where all documents have high correlations with their respective centroid.

10-2-C   Cluster Searching and Evaluation

After a given document collection is available in clustered form, the search operation can be conducted in two steps. First an incoming request is correlated with the centroid vectors of all the clusters. For the collection of 82 documents used previously as an example in Fig. 10-2, this requires seven comparisons for each request. This preliminary operation is followed by a match of each search request with the individual documents included in the n clusters exhibiting the highest correlation with the given request, or alternatively, with the documents in all clusters for which the centroid-request correlation exceeds a given threshold.

A typical cluster match is shown in Fig. 10-3 for the collection of 82 documents in documentation processed against request QB17. The ordinate corresponds to the correlation coefficient between the request and each of the seven centroid vectors, labeled from A to G for centroids 1 to 7, respectively. Thus, the highest correlation with the request (0.42) was obtained for centroid 4 (labeled D), the next highest (0.38) for centroid 7 (labeled G), and so on. The abscissa represents the correlation coefficient between the request and each of the individual documents within the various clusters. Documents which are relevant to the given request, as determined outside of the system by human subject experts, are identified by an asterisk in the graph of Fig. 10-3. Thus, there are four relevant documents in cluster D (the cluster with the highest correlating centroid with the request), and two additional ones in cluster G (the cluster with the next highest correlation).

Assuming that the search strategy chosen requires that clusters with a centroid correlation exceeding 0.30 be individually examined, the 7 centroid comparisons must then be followed by 17 comparisons for cluster D, plus 9 comparisons for cluster G (only 12 characters appear in Fig. 10-3 for cluster D, and only 7 for cluster G, since several documents with identical correlation coefficients are represented by a single character). Documents included in clusters other than D and G are never examined, thus reducing the search time to a fraction of that needed for the "full" search which consists in an examination of every document in the collection. At the same time, the partial search limits the number of relevant documents actually retrievable to those included in the first two clusters—a total of 6 out of 8 relevant for query QB17 as shown in the example. This accounts for the *recall ceiling*, or limitation in the amount of retrievable relevant material, inherent in all partial search algorithms. Clearly, relevant items which are never examined in the first place can, of course, never be retrieved.

The evaluation of the effectiveness of the cluster search algorithm can be based on the standard *recall* and *precision* measures, where recall is defined as the proportion of relevant matter retrieved and precision as the proportion of retrieved material

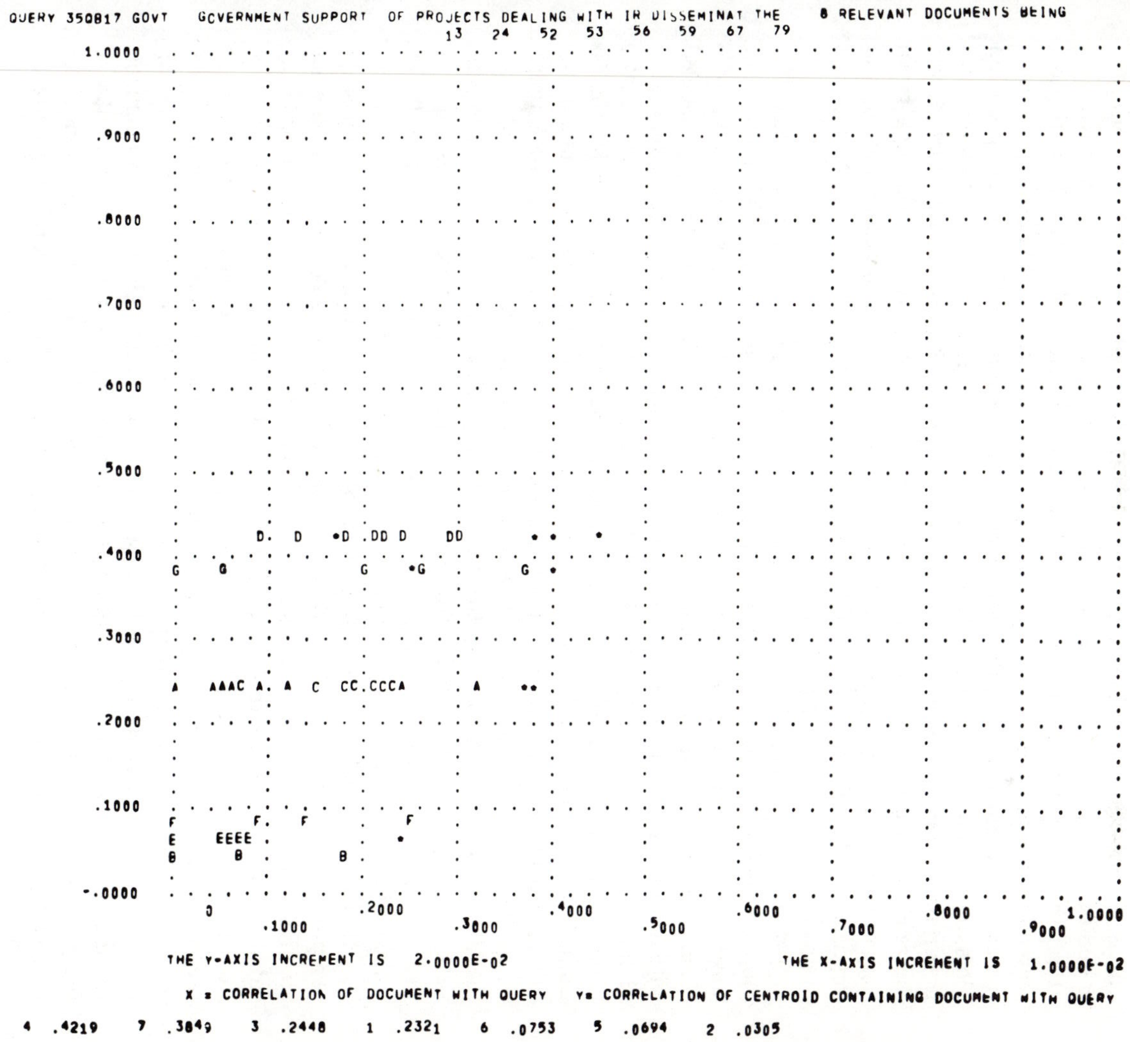

QUERY 350817 GOVT GCVERNMENT SUPPORT OF PROJECTS DEALING WITH IR DISSEMINAT THE 8 RELEVANT DOCUMENTS BEING

1.0000

.9000

.8000

.7000

.6000

.5000

.4000   D   D   •D .DD D   DD   •
               G   G   G •G   G •   •
.3000   •G

.2000   A   AAAC A. A   C CC.CCCA   A   ••
                                                  A

.1000   F   F   F   F
               E   EEEE   •
               B   B   B

-.0000 F
        E
        B

        0   .1000   .2000   .3000   .4000   .5000   .6000   .7000   .8000   .9000   1.0000

THE Y-AXIS INCREMENT IS 2.0000E-02   THE X-AXIS INCREMENT IS 1.0000E-02

X = CORRELATION OF DOCUMENT WITH QUERY   Y= CORRELATION OF CENTROID CONTAINING DOCUMENT WITH QUERY

4   .4219   7   .3849   3   .2448   1   .2321   6   .0753   5   .0694   2   .0305

Fig. 10-3   Cluster correlation with query QB17 (*Relevant documents).

13   24   52   53   56   59   67   79

235

actually relevant. As in the other evaluation work carried out with the SMART system [6], [7], manually derived, exhaustive relevance judgments are used in which the relevance of each document is determined with respect to each of the search requests. By varying the cutoff used to produce a variable number of retrieved documents, a number of recall-precision pairs are obtained which can then be displayed as a graph showing recall against precision. The recall-precision plots for the individual search requests can then be averaged, and a single curve can be obtained representing the average performance of the system over many search requests. Recall-precision plots are particularly useful if it is desired to select search and analysis methods to fit certain operating ranges. Thus, if it is desired to select a procedure which favors the retrieval of *all* relevant material, then one must concentrate on the high recall region; similarly, if *only* relevant material is desired, the high precision region is of importance. (In general, it is possible to obtain high recall only at a substantial cost in precision and vice versa [4] [6] [7].)

A typical recall-precision plot is shown for query QB17 in Fig. 10-4. Recall is plotted along the abscissa and precision along the ordinate. Figure 10-4 contains four superimposed curves: the curve labeled with 1's and single hyphens corresponds to a cluster search in which only a single cluster is examined (cluster *D*); the curve labeled with 2's and double hyphens represents the cluster search based on the examination of the two top clusters (clusters *D* and *G*); similarly, the curve labeled with 3's or triple hyphens is produced by an examination of the three clusters with the highest centroid correlations (*D*, *G*, and *C*). For purposes of comparison, the results of the full search, in which all documents are examined, is also shown in Fig. 10-4, represented by *F*'s and asterisks. When several of the curves have identical values and ought therefore to be superimposed in the output of Fig. 10-4, only the curve of highest rank is shown, the ranking going from *F* to 1, 2, and 3 in that order. For example, in Fig. 10-4, all four curves exhibit the same recall performance up to a value of 0.375. This accounts for the single curve labeled with 3's in that region.

It may be noted that the curve corresponding to a single-cluster search stops at a point where the recall is 0.5 and the precision 0.23; these values are obtained when all 17 documents in the first cluster are examined. Higher recall, or lower precision values are not possible in this case, since cluster *D* does not contain additional items. For the two-cluster search, the limits are reached when the recall is 0.75 and the precision 0.24. Finally, for the three-cluster search, the values are 0.875 and 0.2188, respectively. The full search, corresponding to an exhaustive examination of the collection, is not subject to any recall ceiling below 1 because all relevant documents can then be compared with the request and retrieved. For the full search, the value of the precision is 0.2286 at recall 1. In the example of Fig. 10-4, the precision of the three-cluster search is actually equal or superior to that of a full search up to a recall of 0.75.

Performance figures for the cluster searches are shown averaged over 35 search requests in the output of Fig. 10-5. The curves labeled with 1's, 2's, and 3's again represent one-cluster, two-cluster, and three-cluster searches, and *F*'s are used for the

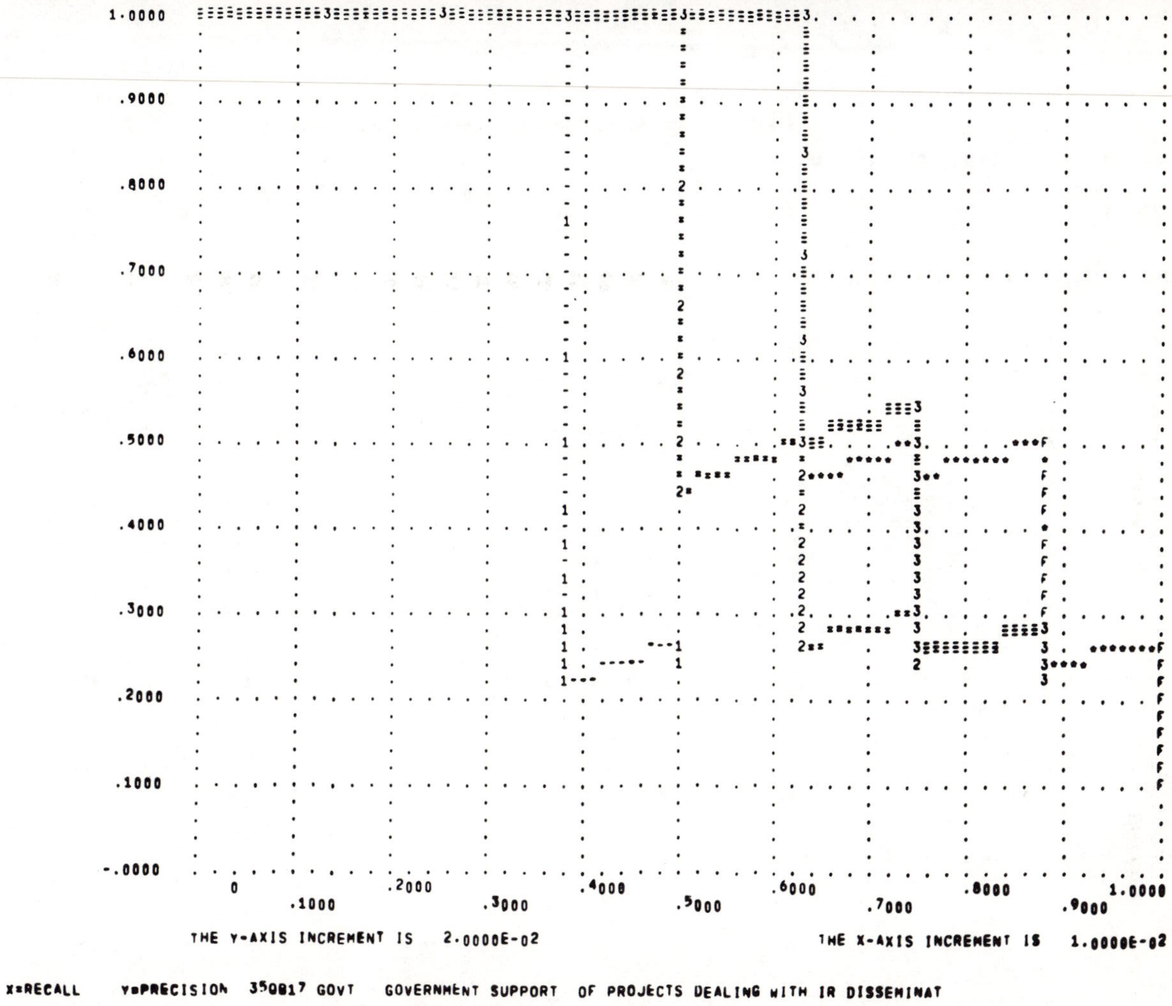
1.0000
.9000
.8000
.7000
.6000
.5000
.4000
.3000
.2000
.1000
-.0000
0
.1000
.2000
.3000
.4000
.5000
.6000
.7000
.8000
.9000
1.0000
THE Y-AXIS INCREMENT IS 2.0000E-02
THE X-AXIS INCREMENT IS 1.0000E-02
X=RECALL Y=PRECISION 35QB17 GOVT GOVERNMENT SUPPORT OF PROJECTS DEALING WITH IR DISSEMINAT

Fig. 10-4 Recall-precision plot for cluster search query QB17.

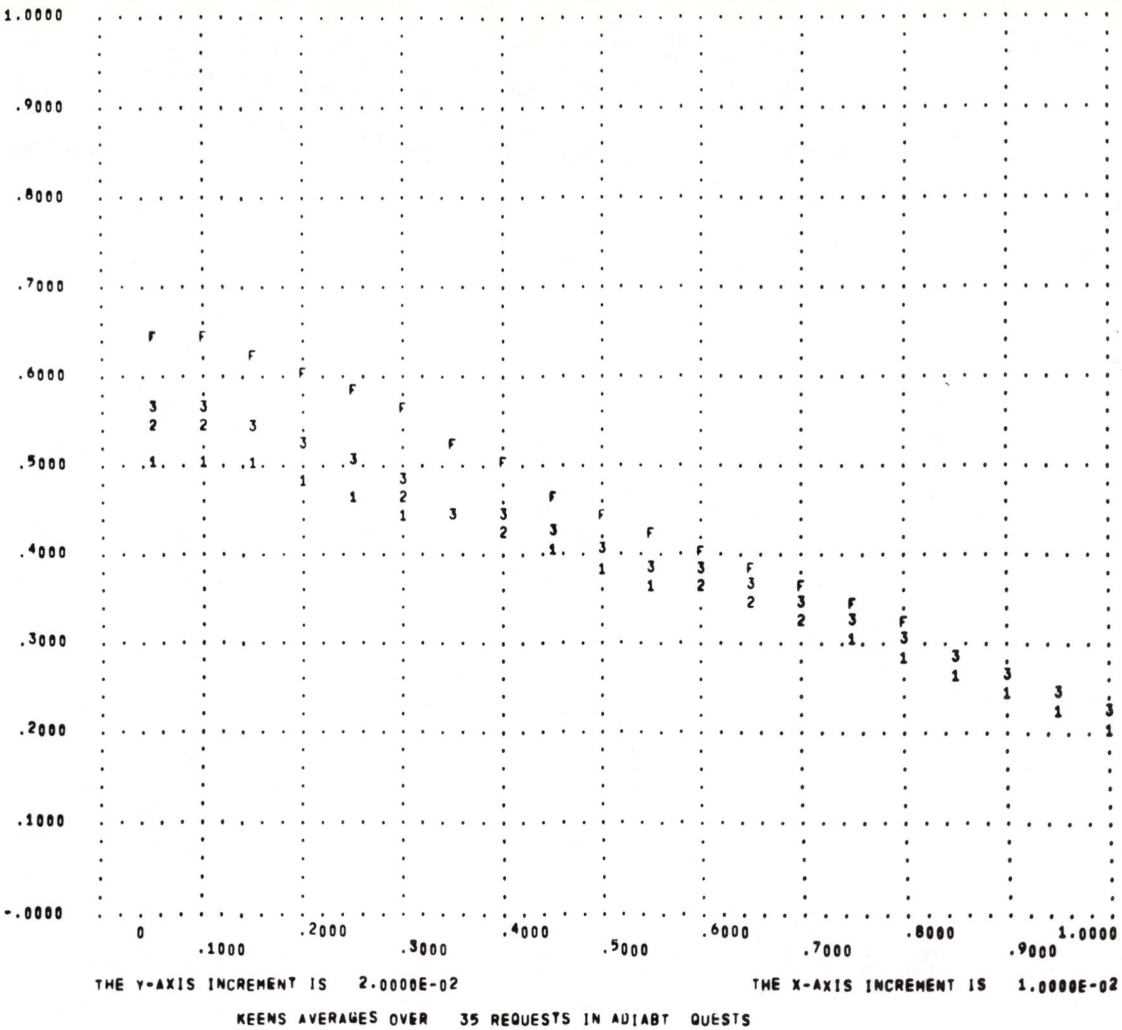

Fig. 10-5 Averaged recall-precision of cluster search showing comparison with full search (averages over 35 requests).

238

full search. It may be noted that the precision difference between three-level and full search amounts to less than 10% for most recall levels and actually becomes much smaller than that for high recall values. The average maximum precision difference between the one-cluster and full searches is only about 15% (at recall of 0.10) and diminishes for higher recall values. Obviously, the performance of the cluster search improves when additional clusters (beyond the first) are examined, but the improvement is modest for the collection used in the example.

The output graph of Fig. 10-5 may not be directly usable for the evaluation of systems performance, since the recall ceiling is not shown for the cluster searches. The curves, in fact, represent averages over a variable number of requests, depending on the recall level considered. A more useful evaluation output is shown in Fig. 10-6 for two collections of 82 documents in documentation and 200 documents in aerodynamics, respectively. An *n*-cluster search is represented by a curve labeled *n*, and the curves for the cluster searches terminate at their respective recall ceilings. For the documentation collection, the average recall ceilings are 0.31, 0.47, and 0.64 for the one-, two-, and three-cluster searches, respectively.

It is clear from the output of Fig. 10-6, that nothing but a full search will avail, if very high recall is demanded. On the other hand for average recall levels, a two- or three-cluster search, involving only about one fifth of the number of matches compared with those needed in a full search, appears to result in very little less in precision (for the aerodynamics collection a six-cluster search, involving about 31% of the total collection, is actually found to be superior to a full search); for low recall levels, the precision of a one-cluster search is from 5 to 15% smaller than that of a full search.

If these results are taken as typical for document collections in other technical areas as well, cluster searching appears to offer large savings in search time, at no substantial loss in recall and precision for all searches not requiring either a very high recall performance or a very high precision.

The preceding discussion, based on preconstructed document clusters, can be extended to partial searches involving other types of clustering strategies. If, for example, the document collection under consideration changes very rapidly, and the retrieval system is very active, it may not be useful to operate with standard document clusters, since the quality of these clusters is then bound to deteriorate as time goes on. In such a case it may be more appropriate to operate with *clusters of requests* processed previously by the system, rather than with document clusters. Such a situation is pictured in Fig. 10-7 where the cross-hatched request clusters are superimposed on the document cluster space. A document cluster is then assumed to exist in association with each request cluster, consisting of documents previously found useful in answering the corresponding requests. A two-level search can then be performed in the following manner:

(a) A new incoming request is compared first with the centroid vectors of all request clusters.

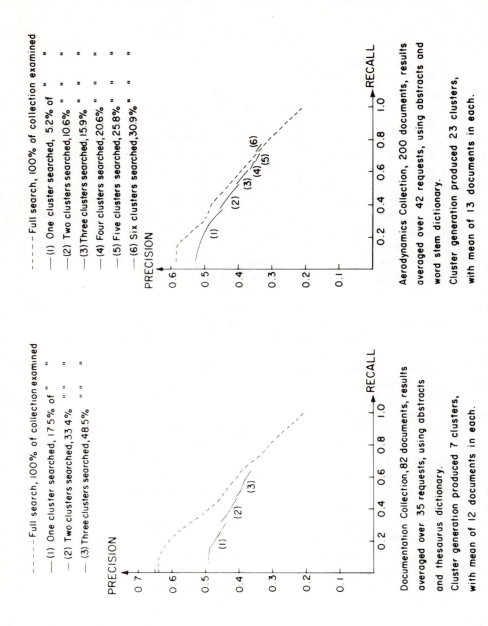

Fig. 10-6 Cluster search evaluation.

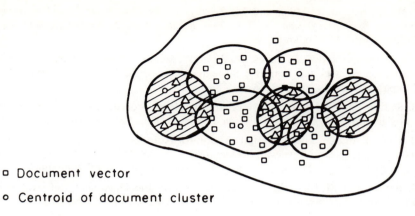

□ Document vector

○ Centroid of document cluster

△ Request vector

/// Query clusters

Fig. 10-7 Clustered document space with request clusters.

(b) The documents associated with the highest-matching request clusters are then compared individually with the new requests, and documents with a sufficiently high correlation coefficient are retrieved as before.

The request-clustering process may be expected to be particularly efficient in situations where a homogeneous user population is to be serviced, in which case, new incoming requests might be similar in nature to requests handled previously for other customers. If, on the other hand, the set of request clusters used produces the same configuration in the document space as the original set of document clusters—a situation which does not obtain in the example of Fig. 10-7—then the request clustering method will not offer advantages. The request clustering method remains to be fully evaluated [14].

REFERENCES

[1] M. E. Stevens, Automatic Indexing: A State of the Art Report, *Monograph 91*, National Bureau of Standards, Washington, D.C., 1965.

[2] M. E. Stevens, V. E. Giuliano, and L. B. Heilprin, ed., Statistical Association Methods for Mechanized Documentation, *Publication 269*, National Bureau of Standards, Washington, D.C. 1965.

[3] M. M. Henderson, *Bibliography on Evaluation of Information Systems*, National Bureau of Standards, Washington, D.C., July 1965.

[4] C. W. Cleverdon, J. Mills, and M. Keen, Factors Determining the Performance of Indexing Systems, *Design*, Vol. 1, *Test Results*, Vol. 2, Aslib–Cranfield Research Project, Cranfield, England, 1966.

[5] V. E. Giuliano and P. E. Jones, Study and Test for a Methodology for Laboratory Evaluation of Message Retrieval Systems, *Report ESD-TR-66-405*, Little, Brown & Company, Boston, August 1966.

[6] G. Salton, The Evaluation of Automatic Retrieval Procedures—Selected Test Results Using the SMART System, *American Documentation*, Vol. 16, No. 3, July 1965.

[7] M. E. Lesk and G. Salton, Design Criteria for Automatic Information Systems, Information Storage and Retrieval, *Report ISR-11* to the National Science Foundation, Dept. of Computer Science, Cornell University, Ithaca, N.Y., June 1966.

[8] G. Salton and M. E. Lesk, The SMART Automatic Document Retrieval System— An Illustration, *Communications of the ACM*, Vol. 8, No. 6, June 1965.

[9] G. Salton et al., Information Storage and Retrieval, Reports ISR-7, ISR-8, ISR-9, and ISR-11, the National Science Foundation, Harvard University, Cambridge, Mass., and Cornell University, Ithaca, N.Y., 1964–1966.

[10] R. E. Bonner, On Some Clustering Techniques, *IBM Journal of Research and Development*, Vol. 8, No. 1, January 1964.

[11] H. Borko and M. D. Bernick, Automatic Document Classification, *Journal of the ACM*, Vol. 10, No. 2, April 1963.

[12] R. M. Needham and K. Sparck Jones, Keywords and Clumps, *Journal of Documentation*, Vol. 20, No. 1, March 1964.

[13] J. J. Rocchio, Jr., Document Retrieval System—Optimization and Evaluation, Doctoral thesis, *Report ISR-10* to the National Science Foundation, Harvard Computation Laboratory, Cambridge, Mass., March 1966.

[14] V. R. Lesser, A Modified Two-Level Search Algorithm Using Request Clustering, *Report ISR-11* to the National Science Foundation, Section VII, Dept. of Computer Science, Cornell University, Ithaca, N.Y., June 1966.

*This report evaluates the performance of a clustering algorithm developed by
J. J. Rocchio, Jr. It also contains a brief description of the algorithm obtained from
Scientific Report ISR-IO [1]. Results of 16 computer runs are presented in
tabular form. These runs are subdivided into smaller groups (according to the
values of the input parameters) for the purpose of detailed analysis. Complete
discussions are given for six of these groups. Precision-recall plots are included for
each of the above mentioned test runs.*

11

*AN EVALUATION OF ROCCHIO'S
CLUSTERING ALGORITHM*†

ROBERT T. GRAUER and MICHEL MESSIER

11-1 INTRODUCTION

The basic classification problem consists in subdividing a given set of
documents into a reasonable number of smaller sets in such a way that
the documents within each subgroup are sufficiently similar to justify ignoring the individual differences between them. That is, one seeks to represent
each individual document of a subgroup or cluster by a typical document of
that cluster. Document clusters are usually formed to facilitate the matching
process between search requests and the given document collection. One
seeks to maximize search efficiency and at the same time to minimize the
loss of relevant documents retrieved in the search. The objective of this
project is to evaluate the success of a clustering algorithm developed by
J. J. Rocchio, Jr. using for this purpose a program written by Robert Williamson.

†This study was published originally as Section VI in *Scientific Report ISR-12*,
June 1967.

11-2   A DESCRIPTION OF ROCCHIO'S ALGORITHM

In Rocchio's algorithm all items are considered first as unclustered, and from here they pass into one of two states—clustered or loose. An unclustered item is selected as a possible cluster center and is subjected to a density test which requires that at least n_1 documents have a correlation of at least p_1, and that at least n_2 documents have a correlation of at least p_2 with the document in question. This ensures that items on the edge of large groups are not chosen as centers of groups or that annular regions are accepted as clusters.

annular region

If a given document fails to pass the density test, it is considered loose, and another unclustered document is considered as a potential center. If a document does pass the density test, a cutoff correlation p_{min} is determined as a function of the category size limits and the correlation distribution. Documents with a correlation above p_{min} are automatically placed above the cutoff. If correlations fall below p_{min} before the size limit is exceeded, the cutoff is chosen at the greatest correlation difference between adjacent documents.

A classification vector is then formed; it is defined as the *centroid* of all items belonging to the cluster at this time. The centroid is matched against the entire collection, and the cutoff parameters on category size are reapplied to create an altered cluster. Each document is then placed into one of three categories as follows:

1. The correlation coefficient of the item may exceed the cutoff value but may at the same time be below p_{min}. Such a document is marked loose to prevent its subsequent choice as a possible cluster center.

2. Documents with a correlation coefficient below the cutoff are unclustered.

3. Items above p_{min} are clustered.

This process is repeated with all unclustered items until every document is either clustered or loose. It is quite possible for a document to end up in two or more clusters because each centroid vector is matched against every document in the collection.

Since no simple way exists of determining in advance how many categories will be formed in this manner, a second pass may be made which will alter the number of clusters formed by altering the density test parameters.

A third pass is used to cluster any documents which are still unclustered after passes one and two. One option is to place these documents in the cluster with whose centroid vectors they correlate best. The third pass also redefines the centroid vector and resulting clusters via a correlation partition routine which reduces the number of duplications. This routine seeks to eliminate the type of situation illustrated in Fig. 11-1, where two documents, denoted by X and located in the intersection of the two groups, correlate more highly with centroid B, even though they were assigned originally to the A group. The partition routine then reassigns these two items to the B

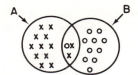

Fig. 11-1 Typical document groups.

group. Following the reassignments, new centroids are created which are then matched against all documents in the collection to yield new document clusters.

11-3 EXPERIMENTAL PROGRAM

In the present section, the required input parameters for the program are detailed, and several relevant questions relating to a clustering methodology are treated. Because of restrictions on the available computer time, no results are available for some of the questions on the list. However, it is felt that every parameter mentioned here merits consideration, and a complete report on clustering requires answers to all questions. The authors feel that subsequent work should be undertaken to supplement the present report. The program requires specification of the following parameters:

1. Cluster generation starting point.
2. Minimum and maximum number of documents per cluster.
3. Lower bound on the correlation between an item and a cluster classification vector below which an item will not be placed in a given cluster.
4. Removal of low-weighted concepts from centroid vector.
5. Density test parameters.
6. Cutoff criteria.
7. Blending.
8. Correlation coefficient used.

Several other problems are also of interest. In evaluating the results of a cluster generation, the question of the number of clusters to be examined by the user arises. Examining all the documents in the three most relevant clusters will undoubtedly yield higher recall than an examination of only those items in the single most relevant cluster. However, it is not clear where the point of diminishing returns actually lies. Similarly, it is unclear whether better results are to be expected if one examines ten documents in the cluster which correlates most highly with the query, or alternatively, five documents in each of the two most highly correlated clusters.

The question of overlap between clusters also arises. Are better results achieved with substantial duplication (the same document appearing in more than one cluster) or with a minimum of duplication? Then there is the question of the cutoff criteria. Should cutoff occur at the greatest difference in correlation coefficients, at a point where the first difference in coefficients exceeds *p*, or after the first *n* documents?

Documents clustered after the first pass are not considered in subsequent density tests. Because of this, a change in the order in which the documents are examined may yield different clusters. If, however, all documents are considered in all density tests, the order in which documents are examined would have considerably less influence. This procedure would increase the number of clusters obtained, since each potential cluster center then has more available documents on which the density test can be applied, thereby producing a higher probability for a successful density test. The program allows initially unclustered documents to be blended into the cluster with whose centroid vector they correlate best. However, the best correlation may be as low as 0.10 in some cases. It is possible that these low-correlated documents have a detrimental effect on precision. The effect of not blending all such documents, or not blending a percentage of such documents, merits consideration.

After a set of "optimal" values has been obtained for these parameters using the first test collection, the same "optimal" values might be run with another collection to see if the optimal results are reproduced. That is, one would like to determine whether an "optimal" set of parameters for one collection is also optimal for another, or whether different parameters are needed under different circumstances—for example by those users seeking high recall and by those users seeking high precision.

11-4 EVALUATION SYSTEM

Some fundamental definitions are required.

$$\text{Recall} = \frac{\text{No. of relevant documents retrieved}}{\text{No. of relevant documents in collection,}}$$

$$\text{Precision} = \frac{\text{No. of relevant documents retrieved}}{\text{Total no. of documents retrieved,}}$$

$$\text{User percentage scanned} = \frac{\text{No. of documents scanned by user}}{\text{Total no. of documents in collection,}}$$

$$\text{Machine percentage scanned} = \frac{\text{No. of documents scanned by machine + no. of clusters}}{\text{Total no. of documents in collection,}}$$

Recall ceiling = Maximum recall that can be obtained by searching all the documents in a cluster set.

Several methods can be used in any proposed evaluation. A precision-recall plot is useful because it gives the user an oriented view of the performance results while also affording a direct comparison with the results of a full search. It is deficient in that it does not show the effect of the percentage of the collection scanned by the machine.

A plot of machine percentage of the scanned collection versus the recall ceiling is deficient in that it neglects the effects of the user percentage of the collection scanned. It also obscures the actual search results. For example, if run *A* yields a recall ceiling of 0.2500 and the machine scans 30% of the collection, whereas run *B* yields a recall ceiling of 0.3500 and the machine scans 40% of the collection, it is unclear which run is actually better. This method is also deficient in that comparisons with a full search are meaningless here. A plot of user percentage of the scanned collection versus the recall ceiling poses similar difficulties. Ideally a three-dimensional plot could be used, but the difficulties of construction eliminate this from consideration. An alternative is the computation of a "value" of the run according to:

$$\text{Value} = \alpha(\text{recall ceiling}) + \beta(\text{user percentage}) + \gamma(\text{machine percentage})$$

where the value of α, β, and γ are determined arbitrarily. Different users would require different sets of coefficients. For example, a user who required high recall and is unconcerned about the proportion of the collection to be scanned might use $\alpha = 0.8$, $\beta = 0.2$, and so on.

Since it is difficult to ascertain suitable values of α, β, and γ, it is proposed to do an analogous type of evaluation in which three different sets of optimum parameters will be determined for different user and machine requirements:

1. One set to yield maximum recall ceiling given that the percentage the user will scan is at most 20%, and that the machine is to scan at most 40%.

2. A second set to minimize the percentage the user will scan (disregarding the percentage the machine is to scan) at a recall ceiling of at least 0.4000.

3. A third set to minimize the percentage the machine will scan (disregarding the percentage the user will scan) at a recall ceiling of at least 0.2500.

4. A further quantity to be examined when evaluating output is the time used by the computer for cluster generation.

Note that in the evaluation section of this report all precision-recall plots are collected at the conclusion of section *B*. These plots reflect performance for a search of one, two, and three clusters. The graphs for two and three clusters could be extrapolated back to low values of recall, but such an extrapolation would clutter up the plot, making it difficult to scan.

11-4-A Tabulation of Results

This section contains the complete tabulation of machine results for ADI runs 1 to 16 inclusive.† Six tables of data are presented in the following order:

†This ADI collection consists of 82 documents in documentation and 35 search requests.

Table 11-1

CLUSTER PARAMETERS FOR RUNS 1 TO 8 INCLUSIVE

CLUSTER PARAMETERS	RUN NUMBER							
	1	2	3	4	5	6	7	8
1. Amount of collection used in clustering.	The entire collection of 82 documents. A constant parameter in all runs.							
2. First document used in clustering.	Document no. 1. A constant parameter in all runs.							
3. Density test.	$5 \geq 0.25$, $10 \geq 0.15$ A constant parameter in all runs.							
4. Minimum and maximum number of documents per cluster.	5,15	5,15	0,–	5,15	5,15	5,15	2,15	2,15
5. Correlation coefficient.	Cosine coefficient.							
6. Difference in correlation to force break.	Maximum difference between adjacent documents. A constant parameter in all runs.							
7. Is centroid vector redefined?	No. A constant parameter in all runs.							
8. Concepts deleted in centroid vector.	–	Wt. ≤ 12	–	Wt. ≤ 24	–	Wt. $\leq 1\%$	–	–
9. Is maximum correlation partitioning used?	Yes	Yes	No	Yes	No	Yes	Yes	Yes
10. Are loose documents blended?	Yes	Yes	Yes	Yes	Yes	Yes	Yes	Yes
11. Is entire collection used in all density tests?	No	No	No	No	No	No	No	Yes

Table 11-1. Cluster parameters for runs 1 to 8.

Table 11-2. Cluster parameters for runs 9 to 16.

Table 11-3. Cluster characteristics for runs 1 to 8.

Table 11-4. Cluster characteristics for runs 9 to 16.

Table 11-5. Evaluation parameters of user percentage and machine percentage for runs 1 to 16.

Table 11-6. Evaluation parameters of recall ceiling and machine time required for cluster generation for runs 1 to 16.

For the complete evaluation of these tables, the reader is referred to Sec. 11-4-B in which detailed studies are made of selected groups of runs. The following comparisons were made in particular:

Table 11-2

CLUSTER PARAMETERS FOR RUNS 9 TO 16 INCLUSIVE

CLUSTER PARAMETERS	RUN NUMBER							
	9	10	11	12	13	14	15	16
1. Amount of collection used in clustering.	The entire collection of 82 documents. A constant parameter in all runs.							
2. First document used in clustering.	Document no. 1. A constant parameter in all runs.							
3. Density test.	5 > 0.25, 10 > 0.15 Constant for runs 9–14						10 > 0.25 5 > 0.40 20 > 0.15 10 > 0.20	
4. Minimum and maximum number of documents per cluster.	5,15	7,15	5,15	5,15	7,15	10,15	2,15	2,15
5. Correlation coefficient.	Cosine coefficient.							
6. Difference in correlation to force break.	Maximum difference between adjacent documents. A constant parameter in all runs.							
7. Is centroid vector redefined?	No	No	No	Yes	No	No	No	No
8. Concepts deleted in centroid vector	–	–	Wt ≤ 36	–	–	–	–	–
9. Is maximum correlation partitioning used?	Yes	Yes	Yes	Yes	Yes	Yes	Yes	Yes
10. Are loose documents blended?	Yes	Yes	Yes	Yes	Yes	Yes	Yes	Yes
11. Is entire collection used in all density tests?	Yes	No	No	No	Yes	Yes	Yes	Yes

Table 11-3

CLUSTER CHARACTERISTICS FOR RUNS 1 TO 8

CLUSTER CHARACTERISTICS	RUN NUMBER							
	1	2	3	4	5	6	7	8
1. Collection size.	82	82	82	82	82	82	82	82
2. Number unclustered before blending.	34	32	48	31	27	34	43	29
3. Number clustered before blending.	48	50	34	51	55	48	39	53
4. Number duplications.	5	8	0	5	8	4	3	28
5. Number clusters.	7	8	34	7	7	7	14	28
6. Mean documents per cluster.	12.4	11.3	2.4	12.4	12.9	12.3	6.1	3.9
7. Mean documents per cluster without blended documents.	7.6	7.3	1.0	8.0	7.9	7.6	3.0	2.9

Table 11-4

CLUSTER CHARACTERISTICS FOR RUNS 9 TO 16

CLUSTER CHARACTERISTICS	RUN NUMBER							
	9	10	11	12	13	14	15	16
1. Collection size.	82	82	82	82	82	82	82	82
2. Number unclustered before blending.	22	26	31	30	19	17	41	54
3. Number clustered before blending.	60	56	51	52	63	65	41	28
4. Number duplications.	57	6	3	6	34	51	18	4
5. Number clusters.	17	7	7	7	11	10	19	8
6. Mean documents per cluster.	8.2	12.5	12.1	12.6	10.5	13.7	5.3	10.7
7. Mean documents per cluster without blended documents.	6.9	8.9	7.7	8.3	8.8	11.6	2.2	3.5

Table 11-5

EVALUATION PARAMETERS OF USER PERCENTAGE
AND MACHINE PERCENTAGE FOR RUNS 1 TO 16

RUN NUMBER	MACHINE PERCENTAGE			USER PERCENTAGE		
	1	2	3	1	2	3
1	26.1	42.0	57.1	17.5	33.4	48.5
2	24.4	38.2	51.8	14.4	28.4	42.1
3	44.5	47.4	50.0	3.0	5.8	8.5
4	26.5	43.2	60.5	17.9	34.7	52.1
5	26.0	43.2	59.0	17.5	34.6	50.5
6	25.8	41.4	56.2	16.2	31.8	46.3
7	25.2	33.6	41.2	8.2	16.5	24.1
8	40.0	46.0	51.7	5.9	11.8	17.5
9	32.3	43.6	52.8	11.6	23.0	33.4
10	25.2	40.6	55.4	16.7	32.1	46.8
11	26.3	42.7	59.6	17.8	34.3	51.0
12	26.3	41.1	58.2	17.1	32.6	49.5
13	25.9	38.1	49.8	12.5	24.7	36.3
14	28.5	45.0	61.2	16.3	32.8	49.1
15	31.2	38.9	47.0	8.1	15.8	23.8
16	25.7	42.0	54.3	17.2	32.3	44.6

Table 11-6

EVALUATION PARAMETERS OF RECALL CEILING
AND MACHINE TIME REQUIRED FOR CLUSTER
GENERATION FOR RUNS 1 TO 16

RUN NUMBER	AVERAGE RECALL CEILING			MACHINE TIME
	1	2	3	(Mins)
1	0.3117	0.4656	0.6434	6.52
2	0.2991	0.3955	0.5733	7.15
3	0.1573	0.2568	0.3192	14.37
4	0.3431	0.5035	0.6692	7.01
5	0.2595	0.4880	0.6517	6.28
6	0.2990	0.4727	0.6259	7.20
7	0.2007	0.3725	0.5129	10.58
8	0.2097	0.3817	0.4305	14.56
9	0.3079	0.4546	0.5920	9.02
10	0.3163	0.4546	0.6358	6.38
11	0.3085	0.4912	0.6317	6.41
12	0.2466	0.4871	0.6571	7.55
13	0.3565	0.5033	0.5825	8.23
14	0.3843	0.5405	0.6074	8.30
15	0.2237	0.3384	0.3833	15.17
16	0.2941	0.5194	0.6223	11.38

Study 1. Many clusters with few documents per cluster versus few clusters with many documents per cluster.

Study 2. Consideration of entire collection in all density tests.

Study 3. Variation of density test parameters.

Study 4. Deletion of low-weighted concepts from centroid vector.

Study 5. Redefinition of the centroid vector.

Study 6. Deletion of the maximum correlation partition routine.

11-4-B Detailed Analysis

Study 1. This study was made to determine if superior results are obtained with many clusters of relatively few documents or fewer clusters with relatively many documents. The problem is attacked in runs 1, 3, 7, and 10 in which the input parameter denoting the minimum number of documents per cluster is varied. All other parameters are kept constant.

This particular study serves as an illustrative example of the method of evaluation employed in all other studies. The manner in which conclusions are reached for the three different user specifications is shown in detail together with relevant result data extracted from the complete tables found in the preceding section. For the other studies only the conclusions are shown.

Example. The data given below are used to determine the run which yields a maximum recall ceiling given that the user percentage scanned is 20% at most and that the machine is to scan 40% at most.

Any of the percentages in the set of user percentages enclosed in the dashed lines of Table 11-7 meets the required specification; similarly, the machine percentages are also shown in dashed lines. The intersection of these two sets is the smaller set drawn in dotted lines in Table 11-8 from which one selects a maximum recall ceiling of 0.3725 obtained from scanning two clusters in run 7.

Table 11-7

USER AND MACHINE PERCENTAGES FOR STUDY 1

RUN NUMBER	MACHINE SCANNING (%)			USER SCANNING (%)		
	1	2	3	1	2	3
3	44.5	47.4	50.0	3.0	5.8	8.5
7	25.2	33.6	41.2	8.2	16.5	24.1
1	26.1	42.0	57.1	17.5	33.4	48.5
10	25.2	40.6	55.4	16.7	3.21	46.8

Table 11-8

RECALL CEILING FOR STUDY 1

RUN NUMBER	MINIMUM DOC./CLUS.	RECALL CEILING		
		1	2	3
3	0	0.1573	0.2568	0.3192
7	2	0.2007	0.3725	0.5129
1	5	0.3117	0.4056	0.6434
10	7	0.3163	0.4546	0.6358

Similarly in meeting the second set of specifications (i.e., to minimize the percentage the user will scan and to yield a recall ceiling of at least 0.4000), one would scan the documents in the three most relevant clusters of run 7 obtaining an average recall ceiling of 0.5129 with the user scanning 24.1%. For the third set of specifications (to minimize the percentage the machine will scan and still yield an average recall ceiling at of least 0.2500), one would search the documents in the first cluster of run 10. One obtains an average recall ceiling of 0.3163, and the machine scans 25.2% of the collection.

Conclusions.

1. Based on the precision-recall plot of Fig. 11-2, one may construct the summary graph of Fig. 11-3 in which the run yielding the optimum precision-recall plot is typed above the appropriate recall range. Run 3 is clearly best up to its recall ceiling. Run 7 is best to a recall ceiling of 0.3750. From this point on there is little difference between all runs valid over an appropriate range. It is not surprising that run 3 yields the best precision-recall plot in its range. This run contains a very large number of clusters (34) and very few documents per cluster (2.4). One would guess intuitively that such an arrangement would yield comparatively high precision values because each retrieved cluster contains very few documents each of which correlates highly with the cluster centroid and thus also with the particular query. However, since so few documents

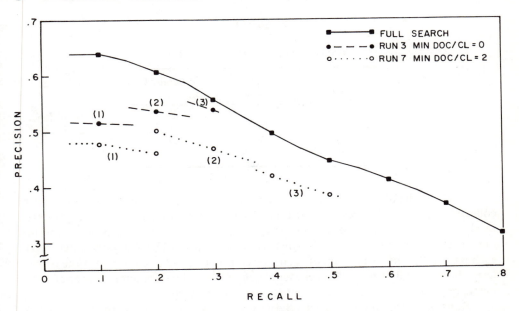

Fig. 11-2 *Study 1.* The effect of average cluster size on recall and precision; (*n*) number of clusters examined.

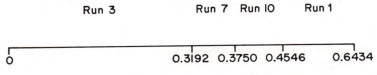

Fig. 11-3 Optimum performance for corresponding recall ranges.

are found in each retrieved cluster, one expects the recall ceiling to be very low.

2. For the user interested in a low-user percentage, many clusters with few documents give better results. This is an obvious conclusion because fewer documents per cluster retrieved means fewer documents to be searched by the user.

3. For the user interested in a low machine percentage, many clusters with few documents per cluster also appear to be best. However, there should not be as many clusters as the case in which user percentage is minimized; in that latter case, the large number of clusters increases the machine percentage considerably.

4. The user who is interested only in high recall requires many documents per cluster. Both user and machine percentages are then high because more documents are being searched. Runs 1 and 10 appear equivalent.

5. The data of Table 11-9 show that precision-recall plots improve with an increase in the number of clusters examined. Unfortunately, the generation of more clusters increases the amount of computer time required. This problem is treated in Study 3.

Table 11-9

TIMING CHART FOR RUNS OF STUDY 1

Run Number	Number of Clusters	Time Required (Mins/Sec)
3	34	14.37
7	14	10.58
1	7	6.52
10	7	6.38

Study 2. The objective here was to determine whether it is better to use the entire collection for all density tests rather than to delete those documents already clustered in all subsequent density tests. The study consists of comparisons between the following groups of runs: runs (1,9), runs (7,8) and runs (10,13). The only difference in each pair is that the second run of each pair considers all 82 documents for the density test, whereas the first run deletes clustered documents. The minimum number of documents required per cluster is different for each of the three pairs.

Runs 8, 9, 13, and 14 collectively may serve as a supplement to the previously raised question of the minimum number of documents to be included per cluster. In the latter group of runs, the minimum number of documents required per cluster is respectively 2, 5, 7, and 10, but in each run all 82 documents must be used in all density tests. The output is shown in Fig. 11-4.

Conclusions.

1. Based on the three precision-recall plots of Figs. 11-5, 11-6, and 11-7 (one for each pair), it is seen that by using the entire collection results are at least as good and in most cases better than the partial runs which include deletions of documents.

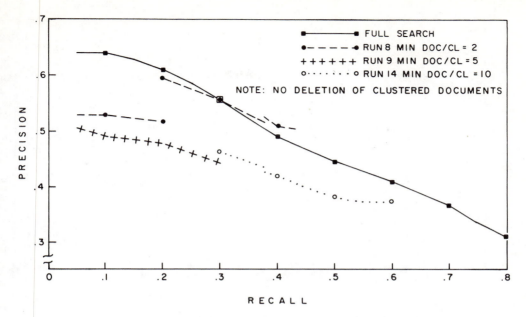

Fig. 11-4 *Study 2.* The effect of average cluster size on recall and precision (note: no deletion of clustered documents).

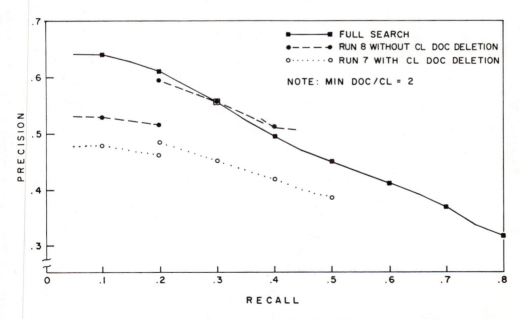

Fig. 11-5 *Study 2.* The effect of deleting clustered documents from subsequent density tests (runs 8 and 7).

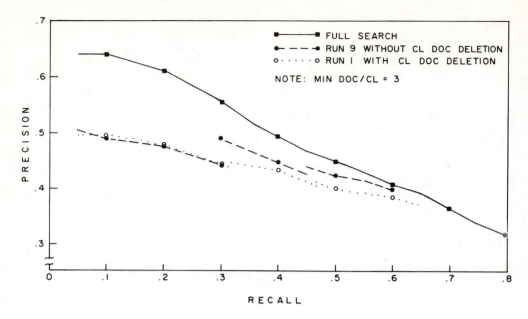

Fig. 11-6 *Study 2.* The effect of deleting clustered documents from subsequent density tests (runs 9 and 1).

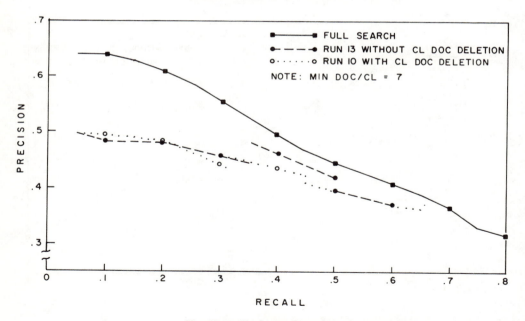

Fig. 11-7 *Study 2.* The effect of deleting clustered documents from subsequent density tests (runs 13 and 10).

(In each of the three plots, the dashed line indicates the run in which the entire collection is considered for all density tests.) The only exceptions occur for the first cluster in the graphs for (1,9) and (10,13) (Figs. 11-6 and 11-7). These results deviate by a maximum of only 0.01. Thus one may feel justified in reaching the overall conclusion that considering all documents in all density tests yields decidedly better precision-recall plots. Run 8 is especially worthy of mention, since it is the only run which surpasses the results of the full search run.

These results are not unexpected. Using the entire collection in all density tests will obviously increase the number of clusters and correspondingly decrease the number of documents per cluster. As was explained in the previous study, this situation is conducive to high precision.

2. Based on the single precision-recall plot for runs 8, 9, 13, and 14, the conclusion of the previous study is substantiated; that is, the runs with the greatest number of clusters and fewest documents per cluster yield the best plots.

3. Conclusions may be drawn from a comparison of the average recall ceiling with the user percentage scanned for each pair as shown in Table 11-10. For each pair the run which considers the entire collection is designated with an asterisk in Table 11-10.

Note that for one and two clusters in all pairs, the recall ceilings are approximately equal, yet the user percentages are substantially reduced when all 82 documents are considered. In the third cluster the recall ceiling is reduced as well, but the user percentages are down proportionately more. (A decrease of 0.0824 in recall ceiling corresponds to a decrease of 6.6% in user percentage; a decrease of 0.0514 in recall ceiling corresponds to a decrease of 15.1% in user percentage; a decrease of 0.0533 in recall ceiling corresponds to a decrease of 10.5% in user percentage.)

Based on the data of Table 11-10, the user interested in a low-user percentage would want the entire collection to be used in all density tests. This is to be expected, since consideration of the entire collection in all density tests increases the number of clusters, decreases the documents per cluster, and therefore decreases user percent-

Table 11-10

RECALL CEILING AND USER-SCANNING PERCENTAGE
FOR RUNS OF STUDY 2

RUN NUMBER	RECALL CEILING			USER SCANNING (%)			AVERAGE DOCS./CLUS.
	1	2	3	1	2	3	
7	0.2007	0.3725	0.5129	8.2	16.5	24.1	6.1
*8	0.2097	0.3817	0.4305	5.9	11.8	17.5	3.9
1	0.3117	0.4656	0.6434	17.5	33.4	48.5	12.4
*9	0.3079	0.4546	0.5920	11.6	23.0	33.4	8.2
10	0.3163	0.4546	0.6358	16.7	32.1	46.8	12.5
*13	0.3565	0.5033	0.5825	12.5	24.7	36.3	10.5

age (fewer documents are listed in each retrieved cluster). Unfortunately examination of machine percentage versus recall ceiling does not produce such a well-defined pattern.

4. A determination of the optimum runs for the different user specifications yields the following results. User 1 may obtain a recall of 0.3565 with the machine having to scan 25.9% and the user searching 12.5% of the collection. This result is a slight improvement over the results obtained by this user in the previous study in which a recall ceiling of 0.3725 was obtained with the machine scanning 33.6% and the user scanning 16.5%. Users 2 and 3 obtain almost identical results in both studies. Unfortunately, no strong conclusions may be drawn from these parameters.

5. As was also true in the previous study, the runs with the largest number of clusters yield the optimum precision-recall plots. These runs also exhibit the largest cluster generation times. (Run 8 with 28 clusters required 14 minutes, 56 seconds, whereas run 13 required 8 minutes, 23 seconds for 7 clusters.) The following study attempts to retain the high precision-recall plots of the runs having many clusters, while simultaneously decreasing the computer time required for generation.

Study 3. This was run to determine the effect of varying the density test parameters. From Studies 1 and 2 it is concluded that the best precision-recall plots are obtained for those runs in which there are a large number of clusters and few documents per cluster. Unfortunately, these runs are also characterized by large cluster generation times. Run 8 of Study 2 is especially important in that its precision-recall plot surpasses that of a full search. In an effort to keep the excellent plot and simultaneously reduce the cluster generation time, the density test parameters for run 8 are rendered more rigid. It is hoped that the number of documents per cluster will remain low (consequently maintaining the high precision-recall), and that, simultaneously, the number of clusters will decrease thereby reducing the time required for cluster generation. Apparently these two conditions are incompatible. Note, however, that there is a large amount of overlap between clustered documents (28 duplications) in run 8. If this overlap can be reduced, then both conditions may be met simultaneously. The data of Table 11-11 are useful in reaching conclusions.

Conclusions.

1. Run 15 increases rather than decreases the cluster generation time. Evidently, the time involved to impose a more rigid density test is greater than the time saved by

Table 11-11

CLUSTER GENERATION PARAMETERS FOR STUDY 3

Run Number	Density Test	Number of Clusters	Number of Duplications	Documents per Cluster	Time
8	$5 \geq 0.25$, $10 \geq 0.15$	28	28	3.9	14.56
15	$10 \geq 0.25$, $20 \geq 0.15$	19	18	5.3	15.17
16	$5 \geq 0.40$, $10 \geq 0.20$	8	4	10.7	11.38

generating fewer clusters. Run 16 does manage to reduce the generation time, but its density test parameters are too rigid, as only 8 clusters are formed. A compromise between the two runs is suggested, but time did not permit other runs to be made.

2. The precision-recall plot of run 15 (Fig. 11-8) is as good as that of run 8 using

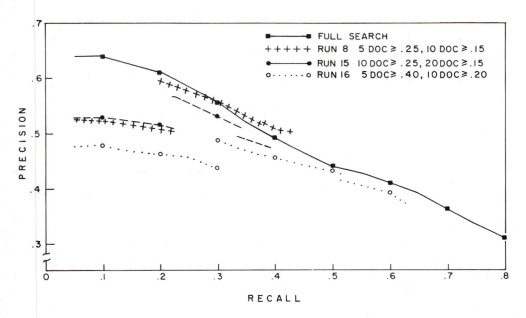

Fig. 11-8 *Study 3.* The effect of density test parameters on recall and precision.

one cluster. When two and three clusters are used, run 8 is decidedly better. However, the plot of run 15 is a good plot and is better than that obtained in any of 14 other runs, excluding part of run 3. The plot of run 16 is clearly inferior to the other two.

3. The data relating to machine and user percentages and to recall ceiling included in Table 11-12 show that machine percentage is reduced for run 16. This is

Table 11-12

PERFORMANCE PARAMETERS FOR STUDY 3

RUN NUMBER	MACHINE PERCENTAGE			USER PERCENTAGE			RECALL CEILING		
	1	2	3	1	2	3	1	2	3
8	40.0	46.0	51.7	5.9	11.8	17.5	0.2097	0.3817	0.4305
15	31.2	38.9	47.0	8.1	15.8	23.8	0.2237	0.3384	0.3833
16	25.7	42.0	54.3	17.2	32.3	44.6	0.2941	0.5194	0.6223

expected because of the few clusters present in this run. User percentage increases with increases in the cluster size.

4. Very definite effects can be obtained by varying density parameters. It is felt that this area is one of the most promising, and considerable study should be devoted to it.

Study 4. This was developed to determine the effects of deleting low-weighted concepts from the centroid vector. It was believed that low-weighted concepts detract from the true picture of the centroid vector. Moreover by deleting such concepts, it might be possible to save considerable computer time and/or storage space.

Consider first the centroid generation. In general, the weights of concepts in the constituent documents are summed over all documents, the resulting vector of sums being equal to the centroid vector. The following is a typical example:

Document 1	0	12	0	24	0	0
Document 2	36	0	48	0	0	48
Document 3	12	12	0	12	12	12
Sum is centroid vector	48	24	48	36	12	60

The weighting scheme used is arbitrary. In the runs described in this report, the weighting was performed as follows: If a concept appeared once in a document, it was assigned a weight of 12, twice a weight of 24, and so on.

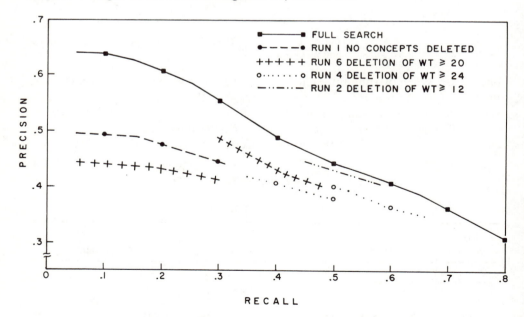

Fig. 11-9 *Study 4.* The effect of deleting low-weighted concepts from centroid vector.

Conclusions.

1. By studying the precision-recall plot of Fig. 11-9, it is seen that there is no single run which is consistently best. Thus, the deletion of low-weighted concepts appears to have little or no effect on a precision-recall plot.

2. Based on the figures in Table 11-13, one finds that it is possible to delete low-weighted concepts with apparently no effect on recall ceiling, user percentage, or machine percentage. (Note that in the runs where the recall ceiling is low, as in run 2, the scanning percentages are proportionately lower as well.)

Table 11-13

PERFORMANCE PARAMETERS FOR STUDY 4

RUN NUMBER	WEIGHT DELETION	RECALL CEILING			MACHINE SCANNING (%)			USER SCANNING (%)		
		1	2	3	1	2	3	1	2	3
1	0	0.3117	0.4656	0.6434	26.1	42.0	57.1	17.5	33.4	48.5
2	≤ 12	0.2991	0.3955	0.5783	24.4	38.2	51.8	14.4	28.4	42.1
6	$\leq 1\% \simeq 21$	0.2990	0.4727	0.6259	25.8	41.4	56.2	16.2	31.8	46.3
4	≤ 24	0.3431	0.5035	0.6692	26.5	43.2	60.5	17.9	34.7	52.1
11	≤ 36	0.3085	0.4912	0.6317	26.3	42.7	59.6	17.8	34.3	15.0

3. An examination of the times required for cluster generation fails to yield a definite relationship between deletion of weights and times required for generation. In conclusion, the writers feel that it is possible to delete low-weighted concepts without either a beneficial or detrimental effect in recall ceiling, machine percentage, user percentage, the precision-recall plot, or cluster generation times. The question of whether core storage is actually saved by the deletion remains open. Excluding the latter possibility, it appears that nothing is to be gained or lost by deletion of low-weighted concepts from the centroid vector.

Study 5. This was developed to determine the effect of redefining the centroid vector. Remember that Rocchio's algorithm specifies that after the centroid vector has been generated it is matched against all documents in the collection, and that a set of documents is then chosen to be included in a cluster. It is possible that the set of documents chosen to go into the cluster differs slightly from the set used originally to constitute the centroid. The present study investigates the effects resulting from a redefinition of the centroid vector in such a way that it consists only of the set of documents actually contained in the cluster. Such a redefinition has a great deal of intuitive appeal. In the subsequent discussion, run 12 is the run in which the centroid vector has been redefined. Run 1 has identical input parameters, but its centroid vector remains constant. The output is shown in Fig. 11-10.

Conclusions.

1. Run 1 (the run in which the centroid vector is not redefined) gives a better precision-recall plot a greater percentage of the time. The writers are unable to explain this result.

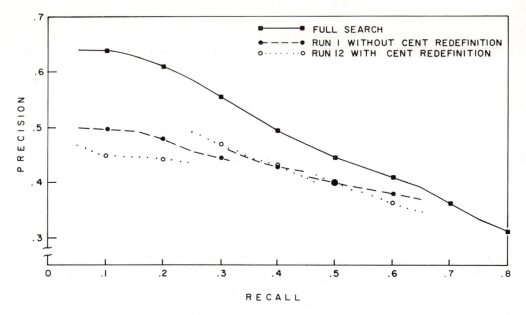

Fig. 11-10   *Study 5.*   The effect of centroid vector redefinition on recall and precision.

2. Both the machine and user percentages are extremely close using one, two, and three clusters in both runs. The average recall ceiling is decidedly better using one cluster in run 1 and very slightly better for two and three clusters in run 12.

3. Obviously when the centroid vector is redefined, one expects the cluster generation time to increase. This expectation is verified experimentally. Run 1 required 6 minutes, 52 seconds. Run 12 required 7 minutes, 55 seconds.

4. Based on these observations, it would appear that the benefits to be derived from redefinition are not sufficient to merit the increase in computer time required for cluster generation. A possible, additional investigation would be a redefinition of the centroid vector immediately after the blended documents have been added into appropriate clusters.

Study 6. The objective was to determine the effects of eliminating the maximum correlation partition routine. (The function of this routine was described in Section 11-2.) Run 5 is identical to run 1 except that the former omits the partition routine. Results are shown in Fig. 11-11.

Conclusions.

1. The precision-recall plot appears to be better for run 1 a greater percentage of the time. One might expect this result intuitively. The maximum correlation partition routine places a document into the centroid with which it correlates best. Hence, the retrieved clusters, which were generated under this routine, are apt to include documents with higher correlations than those clusters generated without the routine. Thus, one expects improved precision.

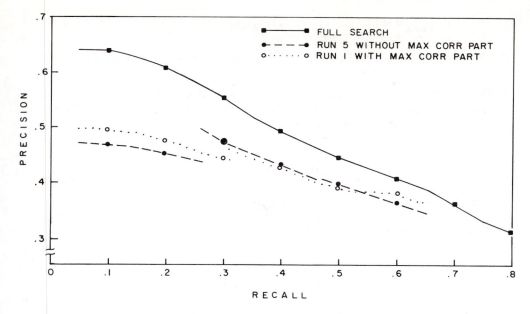

Fig. 11-11 *Study 6.* The effect of the maximum correlation partition on recall and precision.

2. The user and machine percentages are very close using one, two, and three clusters for both runs. The recall ceiling is decidedly better using one cluster for run 1 (as expected from the precision-recall plot); little difference is found for three clusters.

3. As expected, run 1 has a larger cluster generation time (6 minutes, 52 seconds) than does run 5 (6 minutes, 28 seconds).

4. The writers are unable to decide at this time whether the maximum correlation partition routine is worth the extra one-half minute of computer time. Further investigation of this topic is suggested.

11-4-C   Conclusions and Remaining Questions

It is felt that studies one, two, and four of this report are complete and resolve the following questions:

1. Use of many clusters with few documents versus few clusters with many documents.

2. Consideration of the entire collection in all density tests.

3. Deletion of low-weighted concepts from the centroid vector.

The investigations of studies three, five, and six are only partially complete and should be pursued further. Among the problems untouched by this report, the following three appear to be most interesting.

1. Determination of search parameters; that is, how many clusters are to be searched and how many documents are contained in each cluster?

2. Effects of not blending all unclustered documents or of blending only a percentage of unclustered documents.

3. Establishment of a cutoff criterion to decide whether cutoff should occur after the greatest difference in correlation coefficients, after the first difference which exceeds p, or after the first n documents?

REFERENCE

[1] J. J. Rocchio, Jr., Document Retrieval Systems—Optimization and Evaluation, doctoral thesis, *Report ISR-10* to the National Science Foundation, Harvard Computation Laboratory, Cambridge, Mass., March 1966.

An algorithm for classifying items in a collection automatically is described as follows. The necessary time is proportional to $N \cdot p \cdot log_m p$, where N is the number of items in the collection, m is the final number of clusters desired, and p is the number of clusters produced at each level of the algorithm. Clusters are produced for two different document collections, and the results are evaluated by performing centroid searches on the clustered collection. Finally, a new evaluation measure is defined, and comparisons are made with clusters produced by other automatic methods.

12

EXPERIMENTS WITH A FAST ALGORITHM FOR AUTOMATIC CLASSIFICATION†

R. T. DATTOLA

12-1 INTRODUCTION

In order to use real-time automatic document retrieval systems on a very large data base, it is necessary to classify the documents so as to avoid searching the entire collection. However, the classification of a document collection containing more than a few thousand items is not feasible with most procedures for automatic classification. A method is needed which can classify hundreds of thousands of items into useful clusters in a reasonable amount of time.

The method presented in this study is an outgrowth of earlier attempts at fast procedures for automatic classification [1] [2]. The algorithm is first presented in a general form, and a proof is given which describes how the time needed to classify a given collection is related to the number of documents in the collection. Then the algorithm as implemented is described in detail, and experiments in classification and evaluation are discussed.

†This study was published originally as Section XIII in *Scientific Report ISR-16*, October 1969.

12-2   GENERAL DESCRIPTION

Consider a document collection consisting of N documents with an average of r concepts per document. Assume that the document collection is partitioned into p equal-sized clusters, where S_j is the set of documents in cluster j. Associated with each set S_j is a corresponding profile vector P_j, consisting of the rank values of all the concepts from the documents in S_j. The rank value is equal to a constant (base value) minus the rank of the concept, where concepts are ranked in decreasing order of the number of documents in the cluster in which they occur.

A cycle of the algorithm is defined as follows:

(a) Each document d_i in the collection is scored against each of the p profiles by a scoring function $g(d_i, P_j)$.

(b) Let $H_i = \max\limits_{1 < j < p} [g(d_i, P_j)]$, (i.e., H_i is the highest score of d_i over all the profiles), and let

$$K_i = \begin{cases} H_i - a\cdot(H_i - K), & \text{if } H_i > K, \\ K, & \text{otherwise,} \end{cases}$$

where $0 < a < 1$, and K is a specified cutoff score. Then define new clusters $S'_j = \{d_i / g(d_i, P_j) \geq K_i\}$.

(c) All documents d_i such that $H_i < K$ are assigned to a set L' of *loose documents*.

(d) Test for convergence; that is, test if $S_j^* = S_j^{*\prime}$ and if $L' = L$, where $S_j^* = \{d_i / d_i \in S_j$, and $g(d_i, P_j)$ is the highest score of $d_i\}$.

If the convergence test fails, the cycle is repeated with the new clusters S'_j and the new profiles P'_j. If the test succeeds, then an *iteration* of the algorithm has been completed. Since the algorithm is not guaranteed to terminate, an arbitrary upper bound B is placed on the maximum number of cycles allowed per iteration. [1].

Additional iterations of the algorithm can be performed by lowering the cutoff value K, thereby reducing the number of loose documents. One *level* of the algorithm is completed when the number of loose documents is less than a specified constant. Additional levels of the algorithm are executed by treating each of the p clusters as a separate collection and classifying each of these into p additional clusters. Thus, at the end of the first level, the document collection has been classified into p clusters, at the end of the second level into p^2 clusters, and so on.

In order to compute the time required for the algorithm, assume that m final clusters are desired, where $m = p^x$ for some positive integer x. An assumption is made that the time needed to compute the scoring function $g(d_i, P_j)$ is independent of the length of P_j and depends only on the number of concepts in d_i. (This assumption is valid for the scoring function that has been implemented.) Since a document contains on the average r concepts, the time required for the computation of $g(d_i, P_j)$ is proportional to r.

In the following computation, it is assumed that the parameter a in step (b) of the cycle description is 0. As will be shown later, this specifies the overlap to be 0; that is, documents cannot occur in more than one cluster. If the overlap is not 0, the computation time is increased because the average number of documents per cluster is greater. However, the increase in time depends only on the overlap and not on the number of documents in the collection. For example, if a document occurs on the average in two clusters instead of just one, then the computation time is doubled independently of N. Also, it is assumed that the average document size r is independent of N. For these reasons, overlap and documents size will be included in k, the constant of proportionality.

On the first level of the algorithm, each of the N documents is compared against p profiles. The number of iterations and cycles required depend on the parameters B and K and, again, are independent of N. Thus, for the first level,

$$T = k \cdot N \cdot p.$$

On the second level, each of the p clusters now contains on the average N/p documents. These are compared against p new profiles, and this is repeated for each of the p clusters. Thus,

$$T = k \cdot \frac{N}{P} \cdot p \cdot p = k \cdot N \cdot p.$$

Similarly for all the other levels, $T = k \cdot N \cdot p$. At the end of the x'th level, there are p^x clusters. Thus, x levels must be executed to obtain $p^x = m$ clusters. Therefore, the total time required is $T = k \cdot N \cdot p \cdot x$, where

$$p^x = m,$$
$$log \ p^x = \log m,$$
$$x \cdot \log p = \log m,$$

and

$$x = \frac{\log m}{\log p}.$$

Taking logarithms to base p yields

$$T = k \cdot N \cdot p \cdot \log_p m.$$

Given a collection of N documents, if m final clusters are to be produced, what is the value of p which minimizes T? This is solved by setting $dT/dp = 0$. Since $k \cdot N$ is a constant with respect to p, dT'/dp can be used, where $T' = p \cdot \log_p m$, such that

$$\frac{dT'}{dp} = p \cdot \frac{d \log_p m}{dp} + \log_p m,$$

where

$$\log_p m = \frac{\log_m m}{\log_m p} = \frac{1}{\log_m p} \text{ (change of base formula)}.$$

$$\frac{dT'}{dp} = p \cdot \frac{d(1/\log_m p)}{dp} + \frac{1}{\log_m p},$$

$$= \frac{-p \cdot d(\log_m p)/dp}{(\log_m p)^2} + \frac{1}{\log_m p},$$

$$= \frac{-p \cdot \log_m e}{p \cdot (\log_m p)^2} + \frac{1}{\log_m p},$$

$$= \frac{-\log_m e}{(\log_m p)^2} + \frac{\log_m p}{(\log_m p)^2},$$

$$= \frac{(\log_m p - \log_m e)}{(\log_m p)^2}$$

$$= \frac{\log_m (p/e)}{(\log_m p)^2}.$$

Thus, $dT'/dp = 0$ when $\log_m (p/e) = 0$ and $p/e = 1$. Therefore, T is minimized for $p = e$. Rounding off to the nearest integer gives $p = 3$.

Although the computation time is minimized for $p = 3$, in practice it might not be useful to form only three clusters at every level. However, since T has only one minimum point, the time increases monotonically as p increases.

The algorithm as described can be used to generate multilevel clusters. However, it is generally more effective not to equate one level of the algorithm with one level of a multilevel classification scheme. For example, suppose a set of 10^6 documents is to be classified into two levels, with 100 centroids on the first level and 10,000 centroids on the second level. This can be done directly with two levels of the algorithm where $p = 100$. In this case

$$T = k \cdot 10^6 \cdot 10^2 \cdot \log_{100} 10^4 = k \cdot 10^6 \cdot 10^2 \cdot 2 = 2k \cdot 10^8.$$

However, the specifications can also be satisfied by using four levels of the algorithm instead of only two, where the results of the second and fourth levels are used as the two levels of clusters. In this case, $p = 10$ and

$$T = k \cdot 10^6 \cdot 10 \cdot \log_{10} 10^4 = k \cdot 10^7 \cdot 4 = 4k \cdot 10^7.$$

12-3 IMPLEMENTATION

In this section the algorithm is described in detail exactly as programmed. The major change from the general description is that only one level of the algorithm has been implemented. Thus, in all the experiments, $p = m$ and

$$T = k \cdot N \cdot m \cdot \log_m m = k \cdot N \cdot m.$$

In addition, this section describes several alternate methods for generating the initial clusters that are necessary to start the algorithm; a formal definition of overlap is given as well.

The algorithm is designed to control three basic parameters: number of clusters, amount of overlap, and size of clusters. The number of clusters and amount of overlap are input parameters, while the size of clusters is fixed internally to vary no more than one-half to twice the average cluster size. In addition to these, several other parameters are controlled as explained throughout this section.

12-3-A Initial Clusters

In order to execute the classification algorithm, it is necessary to designate initial clusters. Four different methods of initial cluster generation are implemented; they are referred to as the *correlation, similarity correlation, frequency*, and *random* methods. All of the methods involve choosing only one document per cluster that is used as a seed to start the algorithm.

The correlation method uses the cosine correlation to locate documents that are highly correlated with many other documents.

1. Randomly select $\sqrt{N}$ documents from the collection but exclude those documents that have already been defined as cluster seeds.

2. Compute the *global average cosine correlation* (GAVG) and standard deviation (STD) for the sample.
   (a) Start with the first document in the sample and compute the cosine correlation between this document and all other documents in the sample.
   (b) Calculate the mean value (MEAN) of the correlations computed in step (a).
   (c) Repeat steps (a) and (b) for all documents in the sample.
   (d) Define GAVG as the mean value of all the values computed in step (b).
   (e) calculate STD for step (d).

3. Use the chosen documents as cluster seeds if MEAN $\geq$ GAVG + STD. Assuming a normal distribution, approximately 16% of the documents in the sample are used as seeds.

4. Repeat steps 1–3 until the number of seeds = m. Use each seed as an initial cluster.

The similarity correlation is identical to the previous method except that step 3 is changed as follows:

> Use the chosen documents as cluster seeds if MEAN $\geq$ GAVG + STD *and* if the correlation of this is *below* a specified cutoff with each of the documents already defined as seeds.

This additional condition prevents two very similar documents from being used as seeds for different clusters.

The frequency method does not use random samples or correlation coefficients but directly locates documents which have many concepts in common with other documents.

1. Calculate the frequency score (FS) for every document in the collection.
   (a) For every concept in the document calculate its frequency f, where $f =$ the number of documents in the collection in which the concept occurs.
   (b) FS $=$ the sum of the frequencies of all the concepts divided by the number of concepts in the documents.
2. Rank the documents in order of decreasing frequency scores and pick the top m documents as cluster seeds.

Finally, the random method simply picks out m random documents from the collection to be used as cluster seeds.

12-3-B Overlap

The coefficient used to measure the overlap between clusters is an m-dimensional extension of Tanimoto's two-dimensional correlation coefficient. The most obvious way to measure overlap is to simply compute the average number of clusters per document. When this number is 1, there is no overlap between clusters. However, the main problem with this measure is that the upper bound depends on the number of clusters; for example, for 10 clusters, the upper bound is 10, for 100 clusters the upper bound is 100. Of course, the upper bound is reached when every document occurs in every cluster; that is each cluster is equivalent to the entire collection.

The generalized form of Tanimoto's coefficient has a lower bound of 0 and an upper bound of 1 independent of the number of clusters. Let $S_i =$ a binary vector of length N specifying the documents in cluster i; that is,

$$S_i(j) = \begin{cases} 1, & \text{if document } j \text{ is in cluster } i, \\ 0, & \text{otherwise.} \end{cases}$$

Let

$$\#S_i = \sum_{k=1}^{N} S_i(k)$$

that is, $\#S_i$ is the number of documents in cluster i. Let $I_{i,j} = S_i \cap S_j$. Then $I_{i,j}$ is the number of documents occurring in both cluster i and cluster j. Tanimoto's two-dimensional coefficient is:

$$T = \frac{\#I_{i,j}}{(\#S_i + \#S_j - \#I_{i,j})}.$$

Extending this to m dimensions yields:

$$\phi = \frac{\sum\limits_{i=1}^{m-1} \sum\limits_{j=i+1}^{m} \#I_{i,j}}{(m-1)\sum\limits_{i=1}^{m} \#S_i - \sum\limits_{i=1}^{m-1} \sum\limits_{j=i+1}^{m} \#I_{i,j}}$$

From now on, the numerator of ϕ will be referred to by NUM.

Theorem. ϕ has a minimum value of 0 and a maximum value of 1. Furthermore, it attains these bounds if and only if there is no overlap or if all clusters are identical, respectively.

Proof:

(a) Clearly ϕ is 0 when $S_i \cap S_j = 0$ for all i and j, $i \neq j$, since $\#I_{i,j}$ is always 0. On the other hand, ϕ can only be negative or undefined if

$$(m-1)\sum_{i=1}^{m} \#S_i \leq \text{NUM}.$$

However, this is impossible since

$$(m-1)\sum_{i=1}^{m} \#S_i = \sum_{j=1}^{m-1} \sum_{i=1}^{m} \#S_i > \sum_{j=1}^{m-1} \sum_{i=j+1}^{m} \#S_i$$

and

$$\#S_i \geq \#I_{i,j}.$$

(b) Let $S_1 = S_2 = \cdots = S_m$. Then $\#S_i = \#S_1$, and $I_{ij} = I_{1,1} = S_1$. This implies $\#I_{i,j} = \#S_1$ for all i. Therefore,

$$\phi = \frac{\text{NUM}}{(m-1)\sum\limits_{i=1}^{m} \#S_1 - \text{NUM}}$$

But

$$\text{NUM} = \sum_{i=1}^{m-1} \sum_{j=i+1}^{m} \#S_1.$$

Therefore

$$\phi = \frac{[(m-1) + (m-2) + \cdots + 1] \cdot \#S_1}{(m-1) \cdot m \#S_1 - [(m-1) + \cdots + 1] \cdot \#S_1}$$

$$= \frac{m(m-1)\#S_1/2}{m(m-1)\#S_1 - m(m-1)\#S_1/2}$$

$$= \frac{m(m-1)\#S_1}{2m(m-1)\#S_1 - m(m-1)\#S_1}$$

$$= \frac{m(m-1)\#S_1}{m(m-1)\#S_1}$$

$$= 1.$$

ϕ can only be greater than 1 if NUM is greater than the denominator. If so, then

$$\text{NUM} > (m-1)\sum_{i=1}^{m} \#S_i - \text{NUM},$$

which implies

$$2\,\text{NUM} > (m-1)\sum_{i=1}^{m} \#S_i$$

$$= [(\#S_2 + \cdots + \#S_m) + \#S_1] + [(\#S_3 + \cdots + \#S_m)$$
$$+ (\#S_1 + \#S_2)] + \cdots + [\#S_m + (\#S_1 + \cdots + \#S_{m-1})]$$

$$= \sum_{i=1}^{m-1}\sum_{j=i+1}^{m} \#S_j + (m-1)\#S_1 + (m-2)\#S_2 = \cdots + \#S_{m-1}$$

$$= \sum_{j=1}^{m-1} \#S_1 + \cdots + \sum_{j=m-1}^{m-1} \#S_{m-1} + \sum_{i=1}^{m-1}\sum_{j=i+1}^{m} \#S_j$$

$$= \sum_{j=2}^{m} \#S_1 + \cdots + \sum_{j=m}^{m} \#S_{m-1} + \sum_{i=1}^{m-1}\sum_{j=i+1}^{m} \#S_j$$

$$= \sum_{i=1}^{m-1}\sum_{j=i+1}^{m} \#S_j + \sum_{i=1}^{m-1}\sum_{j=i+1}^{m} \#S_j$$

$$= 2\sum_{i=1}^{m-1}\sum_{j=i+1}^{m} \#S_j.$$

But this is impossible because $S_j \geq I_{i,j}$.

12-3-C Algorithm

After the initial clusters are generated, there exist m clusters with one document in each cluster. The cutoff point for loose documents K is now set so that at the end of the first cycle each cluster will average five documents. At the end of each iteration, K is reset so that x percent of the loose documents will be clustered at the end of the next cycle, where x is an input parameter. The iterations continue until less than y percent of the documents remain loose, where y is also an input parameter. Finally, an option is provided to allow the loose documents to be assigned to the cluster against which they score highest (blending), or to simply group them all together into an additional cluster.

So far nothing has been said about the choice of the base value that is used in calculating the rank values of concepts in profiles. As discussed elsewhere [1], the base value should be set a little above the average cluster size at the beginning of each iteration. The purpose of this is two-fold: first, to prevent the rank values from dropping below 1, and second, to allow documents to move freely between clusters. If the base value is too low, many rank values drop below 1, and all are reset to 1 even though the concepts have different frequencies. Table 12-1 illustrates a case where the base value is too low. For present experiments the base value is set to twice the average

Table 12-1

EXAMPLE OF LOW BASE VALUE

(Base value $= 5$)

Concept	Frequency	Rank	Rank Value
c_1	7	1	3
c_2	5	2	3
c_3	4	3	1
c_8	2	5	1
c_9	3	4	1
c_{10}	1	6	1
c_5	1	6	1
c_4	1	6	1

cluster size at the beginning of each iteration, but experiments have shown that this is probably too high. Even in the largest clusters, the lowest rank values do not come close to 1.

Another parameter which is controlled is the size of the clusters. This is accomplished by deleting those clusters whose size falls below one-half the average and by breaking up those clusters whose size exceeds twice the average. These checks are made at the end of every *cycle* of the algorithm. Clusters which get too large are broken up into two nonoverlapping clusters by the following algorithm:

1. Select a random sample from among the documents in the cluster and generate seeds as in steps 1–3 of the correlation method for initial cluster generation.

2. Select those two documents from the seeds that correlate *lowest* with one another and use these two documents as cluster centers for the two new clusters.

3. Assign the documents in the original cluster to the cluster center to which they correlate highest.

Consider step (b) in the general description of the algorithm in Sec. 12-2. The parameter a is used to control the overlap, where $0 < a < 1$. However, a does not correspond to the actual overlap between clusters as computed by ϕ. After every cycle of the algorithm, the overlap is computed and compared with the input parameter OVER, which is the requested amount of overlap. The parameter a is then adjusted so that the value of ϕ approaches OVER. However, when loose documents are blended into the nearest cluster at the end of the algorithm, the amount of overlap between clusters decreases because each loose document is assigned to only one cluster. But as the percent of loose documents at the end of the algorithm is an input parameter, the effect of blending on the overlap can be predicted beforehand. Instead of adjusting a so that ϕ approaches OVER, ϕ should approach XOVER so that ϕ equals OVER *after* blending.

The change in ϕ after blending occurs only in the term

$$(m - 1) \sum_{i=1}^{m} \#S_i,$$

since some clusters increase in size. The change is

$$(m - 1) \cdot \left(\sum_{i=1}^{m} \#S_i + y \cdot N \right),$$

where y is the percent of documents loose at the end of the algorithm. After blending ϕ should equal OVER, where

$$\text{OVER} = \frac{\text{NUM}}{(m - 1) \cdot \left(\sum_{i=1}^{m} \#S_i - y \cdot N \right) - \text{NUM}}.$$

Before blending,

$$\text{XOVER} = \frac{\text{NUM}}{(m - 1) \cdot \sum_{i=1}^{m} \#S_i - \text{NUM}}.$$

XOVER must be expressed in terms of OVER. Rewriting OVER,

$$\text{OVER} = \frac{\text{XOVER}\left[(m - 1) \cdot \sum_{i=1}^{m} \#S_i - \text{NUM} \right]}{(m - 1) \cdot \sum_{i=1}^{m} \#S_i - \text{NUM} + (m - 1) \cdot y \cdot N}.$$

Solving for XOVER,

$$\text{XOVER} = \frac{\text{OVER}\left[(m - 1) \sum_{i=1}^{m} \#S_i - \text{NUM} + (m - 1) \cdot y \cdot N \right]}{(m - 1) \sum_{i=1}^{m} \#S_i - \text{NUM}},$$

and

$$\text{XOVER} = \frac{\text{OVER}[1 + (m - 1) \cdot y \cdot N]}{(m - 1) \sum_{i=1}^{m} \#S_i - \text{NUM}}.$$

After every cycle, XOVER is reset by the above formula, and a is adjusted as follows:

1. If $\phi < \text{XOVER}$, set $a = a + (1 - a) \cdot (\text{XOVER} - \phi)$.
2. If $\phi > \text{XOVER}$, set $a = a + a \cdot (\text{XOVER} - \phi)$.

The quantity $(\text{XOVER} - \phi)$ is the difference between the required overlap and the actual overlap, and $(1 - a)$ or a represents the maximum amount that a can be changed in the proper direction.

One final input parameter controls the centroid definition. Cluster centroids are defined by a profile of concepts, and the corresponding rank values define the weights. An input parameter z is provided which determines what percent of the concepts in the profile will be used to define the centroid. The concepts in each profile are sorted in decreasing order by rank values, and the top z percent of the concepts are used to define the centroid. Normally more than z percent are actually used, since the last concept in the top z percent may have several ties, and all ties are also taken.

12-4   EVALUATION

The final evaluation of the clusters can only be made by performing centroid searches on the classified collection. Two separate types of evaluation are possible—internal and external. The internal evaluation attempts to determine how variations in the parameters of the classification algorithm affect the search results. The external evaluation compares the retrieval results from clusters produced by this algorithm with other algorithms and with a full search.

12-4-A   Evaluation Measures

Standard recall-precision curves that are used to evaluate full searches are not satisfactory for centroid search evaluation. The problem is that recall-precision curves do not take into consideration the amount of work which must be done by the retrieval system. Since the main advantage in centroid searching is a reduction in the number of query-document correlations, it is important to include the amount of work performed in any evaluation.

The total number of correlations in a centroid search is equal to the number of query-centroid correlations plus the number of query-document correlations. Dividing this number by the total number of correlations necessary for a full search N, yields a fraction which compares the amount of work in a centroid search to a full search. This fraction is referred to as the *correlation percentage (CP)* [3]. One way of representing the results is to include the correlation percentage along with the standard recall-precision measures. However, experiments have shown that the standard recall-precision measures improve as the CP increases, even when comparing the results from different sets of clusters. It is difficult to decide whether a cluster set that produces a normalized recall of 0.75 and a normalized precision of 0.60 with a CP of 0.20 is better or worse than another set of clusters producing a normalized recall of 0.70 and a normalized precision of 0.55 with a CP of 0.15. The CP can be controlled to some extent during the centroid search, but quite often it varies by 10% or more from the desired value. This is due to the difference in sizes of the clusters and cannot be avoided as long as all the documents in the selected clusters are correlated against the query.

A method is proposed which modifies the recall-precision curve by taking into account the value of the correlation percentage. Consider a query Q which has two relevant documents, R_1 and R_2. Assume, for example, that the total number of documents in the collection is 20. Table 12-2(a) shows the results of a possible centroid search where one cluster containing five documents is selected. Table 12-2(b) shows

<table>
<tr><td colspan="4" align="center">**Table 12-2(a)**</td><td colspan="4" align="center">**Table 12-2(b)**</td></tr>
<tr><td colspan="4" align="center">STANDARD EVALUATION MEASURE</td><td colspan="4" align="center">STANDARD EVALUATION MEASURE</td></tr>
<tr><td colspan="4" align="center">(Comparison of five documents)</td><td colspan="4" align="center">(Comparison of ten documents)</td></tr>
<tr><td>*Rank*</td><td>*Document*</td><td>*R*</td><td>*P*</td><td>*Rank*</td><td>*Document*</td><td>*R*</td><td>*P*</td></tr>
<tr><td>1</td><td>R_1</td><td>0.5</td><td>1.0</td><td>1</td><td>R_1</td><td>0.5</td><td>1.0</td></tr>
<tr><td>2</td><td>N</td><td>0.5</td><td>0.5</td><td>2</td><td>N</td><td>0.5</td><td>0.5</td></tr>
<tr><td>3</td><td>N</td><td>0.5</td><td>0.33</td><td>3</td><td>N</td><td>0.5</td><td>0.33</td></tr>
<tr><td>4</td><td>R_2</td><td>1.0</td><td>0.5</td><td>4</td><td>R_2</td><td>1.0</td><td>0.5</td></tr>
<tr><td>5</td><td>N</td><td>1.0</td><td>0.5</td><td>5</td><td>N</td><td>1.0</td><td>0.5</td></tr>
<tr><td>6</td><td>N</td><td>1.0</td><td>0.5</td><td>6</td><td>N</td><td>1.0</td><td>0.5</td></tr>
<tr><td>7</td><td>N</td><td>1.0</td><td>0.5</td><td>7</td><td>N</td><td>1.0</td><td>0.5</td></tr>
<tr><td>8</td><td>N</td><td>1.0</td><td>0.5</td><td>8</td><td>N</td><td>1.0</td><td>0.5</td></tr>
<tr><td>9</td><td>N</td><td>1.0</td><td>0.5</td><td>9</td><td>N</td><td>1.0</td><td>0.5</td></tr>
<tr><td>10</td><td>N</td><td>1.0</td><td>0.5</td><td>10</td><td>N</td><td>1.0</td><td>0.5</td></tr>
<tr><td>11</td><td>N</td><td>1.0</td><td>0.5</td><td>11</td><td>N</td><td>1.0</td><td>0.5</td></tr>
<tr><td>12</td><td>N</td><td>1.0</td><td>0.5</td><td>12</td><td>N</td><td>1.0</td><td>0.5</td></tr>
<tr><td>13</td><td>N</td><td>1.0</td><td>0.5</td><td>13</td><td>N</td><td>1.0</td><td>0.5</td></tr>
<tr><td>14</td><td>N</td><td>1.0</td><td>0.5</td><td>14</td><td>N</td><td>1.0</td><td>0.5</td></tr>
<tr><td>15</td><td>N</td><td>1.0</td><td>0.5</td><td>15</td><td>N</td><td>1.0</td><td>0.5</td></tr>
<tr><td>16</td><td>N</td><td>1.0</td><td>0.5</td><td>16</td><td>N</td><td>1.0</td><td>0.5</td></tr>
<tr><td>17</td><td>N</td><td>1.0</td><td>0.5</td><td>17</td><td>N</td><td>1.0</td><td>0.5</td></tr>
<tr><td>18</td><td>N</td><td>1.0</td><td>0.5</td><td>18</td><td>N</td><td>1.0</td><td>0.5</td></tr>
<tr><td>19</td><td>N</td><td>1.0</td><td>0.5</td><td>19</td><td>N</td><td>1.0</td><td>0.5</td></tr>
<tr><td>20</td><td>N</td><td>1.0</td><td>0.5</td><td>20</td><td>N</td><td>1.0</td><td>0.5</td></tr>
</table>

similar results for a different set of clusters where one cluster containing ten documents is searched. In both cases the two relevant documents are retrieved at the same ranks, so the recall-precision figures are identical.† However, if there are four clusters in both cases, then CP = 9/20 for case (a), while CP = 14/20 for case (b). Thus, the evaluation measure should rate case (a) better than case (b), since the same retrieval results are obtained with less work.

Consider now a method in which the precision is *not* held constant after a recall of 1, but instead is allowed to drop until the rank is equal to the total number of

---

†In the present SMART evaluation system, the precision is held constant after *all* the relevant documents are retrieved.

query-centroid plus query-document correlations that have been made. Table 12-3 illustrates the recall-precision results for the previous example using this new method of evaluation.

Another problem occurs when some of the relevant documents are not retrieved. Suppose as in the previous example, that there are two relevant documents but only

Table 12-3(a)				Table 12-3(b)			
NEW EVALUATION MEASURE				NEW EVALUATION MEASURE			
(Comparison of five documents)				(Comparison of ten documents)			
Rank	*Document*	*R*	*P*	*Rank*	*Document*	*R*	*P*
1	R_1	0.5	1.0	1	R_1	0.5	1.0
2	N	0.5	0.5	2	N	0.5	0.5
3	N	0.5	0.33	3	N	0.5	0.33
4	R_2	1.0	0.5	4	R_2	1.0	0.5
5	N	1.0	0.4	5	N	1.0	0.4
6	N	1.0	0.33	6	N	1.0	0.33
7	N	1.0	0.29	7	N	1.0	0.29
8	N	1.0	0.25	8	N	1.0	0.25
9	N	1.0	0.22	9	N	1.0	0.22
10	N	1.0	0.22	10	N	1.0	0.2
11	N	1.0	0.22	11	N	1.0	0.18
12	N	1.0	0.22	12	N	1.0	0.17
13	N	1.0	0.22	13	N	1.0	0.15
14	N	1.0	0.22	14	N	1.0	0.14
15	N	1.0	0.22	15	N	1.0	0.14
16	N	1.0	0.22	16	N	1.0	0.14
17	N	1.0	0.22	17	N	1.0	0.14
18	N	1.0	0.22	18	N	1.0	0.14
19	N	1.0	0.22	19	N	1.0	0.14
20	N	1.0	0.22	20	N	1.0	0.14

one of them is retrieved. Table 12-4 illustrates these results where both sets of clusters retrieve the relevant document at the same rank.† Once again the recall-precision results are identical, even though case (a) proved as effective as (b) at less cost.

Instead of assigning all the unrecovered relevant documents to the lowest ranks, they are distributed uniformly throughout the ranks, starting with a rank exceeding by one the total number of correlations performed and ending with the rank equal to the collection size. The first unrecovered relevant is always assigned the middle rank, and the others are spaced uniformly above and below it. Table 12-5 illustrates this assignment for the sample case. Since case (a) did less work, the unrecovered relevant is assigned a higher rank than in case (b). A graph which plots recall versus

†Relevant documents which are not retrieved are assigned to the lowest possible ranks in SMART.

Table 12-4(a)

STANDARD EVALUATION MEASURE

(Comparison of five documents)

Rank	Document	R	P
1	R_1	0.5	1.0
2	N	0.5	0.5
3	N	0.5	0.33
4	N	0.5	0.25
5	N	0.5	0.2
6	N	0.5	0.17
7	N	0.5	0.14
8	N	0.5	0.13
9	N	0.5	0.11
10	N	0.5	0.10
11	N	0.5	0.09
12	N	0.5	0.08
13	N	0.5	0.08
14	N	0.5	0.07
15	N	0.5	0.07
16	N	0.5	0.06
17	N	0.5	0.06
18	N	0.5	0.06
19	N	0.5	0.05
20	R_2	0.5	0.1

Table 12-4(b)

STANDARD EVALUATION MEASURE

(Comparison of ten documents)

Rank	Document	R	P
1	R_1	0.5	1.0
2	N	0.5	0.5
3	N	0.5	0.33
4	N	0.5	0.25
5	N	0.5	0.2
6	N	0.5	0.17
7	N	0.5	0.14
8	N	0.5	0.13
9	N	0.5	0.11
10	N	0.5	0.10
11	N	0.5	0.09
12	N	0.5	0.08
13	N	0.5	0.08
14	N	0.5	0.07
15	N	0.5	0.07
16	N	0.5	0.06
17	N	0.5	0.06
18	N	0.5	0.06
19	N	0.5	0.05
20	R_2	0.5	0.1

Table 12-5(a)

NEW EVALUATION MEASURE

(Comparison of five documents)

Rank	Document	R	P
1	R_1	0.5	1.0
2	N	0.5	0.5
3	N	0.5	0.33
4	N	0.5	0.25
5	N	0.5	0.2
6	N	0.5	0.17
7	N	0.5	0.14
8	N	0.5	0.13
9	N	0.5	0.11
10	N	0.5	0.1
11	N	0.5	0.09
12	N	0.5	0.08
13	N	0.5	0.08
14	N	0.5	0.07
15	R_2	1.0	0.13
16	N	1.0	0.13
17	N	1.0	0.13
18	N	1.0	0.13
19	N	1.0	0.13
20	N	1.0	0.13

Table 12-5(b)

NEW EVALUATION MEASURE

(Comparison of ten documents)

Rank	Document	R	P
1	R_1	0.5	1.0
2	N	0.5	0.5
3	N	0.5	0.33
4	N	0.5	0.25
5	N	0.5	0.2
6	N	0.5	0.17
7	N	0.5	0.14
8	N	0.5	0.13
9	N	0.5	0.11
10	N	0.5	0.1
11	N	0.5	0.09
12	N	0.5	0.08
13	N	0.5	0.08
14	N	0.5	0.07
15	N	0.5	0.07
16	N	0.5	0.06
17	N	0.5	0.06
18	R_2	1.0	0.11
19	N	1.0	0.11
20	N	1.0	0.11

precision at every rank (*document level*), using the modified results, reflects the superiority of case (a) as illustrated in Fig. 12-1. A graph which plots recall versus precision at selected recall points (*recall level*) is not used in the evaluation, because only the highest precision for a given recall is used in such a graph. Notice that in cases where all the relevant have not been retrieved, the precision is held constant after the assigned rank of the last relevant, since the CP is already taken into account during the assignment of the unretrieved relevant documents.

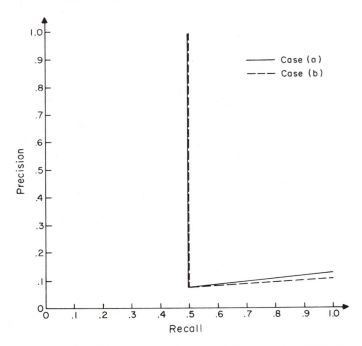

Fig. 12-1   Document level graph for example of Table 5.

In order to illustrate the effects of the new evaluation process on an actual collection, a set of ADI clusters called BASE is considered using both evaluation measures. Four centroid searches are performed on the base set of clusters: BASE2, BASE3, BASE4, and BASE5. BASE2 searches the top two centroids, BASE3 searches the top three centroids, and so on. Figure 12-2 shows the search results using the standard recall-precision measure, and Fig. 12-3 shows the results using the new evaluation measure. Also included in each graph are the results of a full search.

For the highest-ranked documents, both curves are almost identical because the new adjustments usually do not affect the high ranks. However, at the lower ranks the new adjustments favor the searches with the lower correlation percentage. The high recall end of Fig. 12-2 clearly illustrates the superiority of those searches with a high CP. This is to be expected because more relevant documents are retrieved with higher CP searches.

In Fig. 12-3 searches with the highest correlation percentages are still better at the high recall end, but the difference is much smaller than in Fig. 12-2. In fact, there

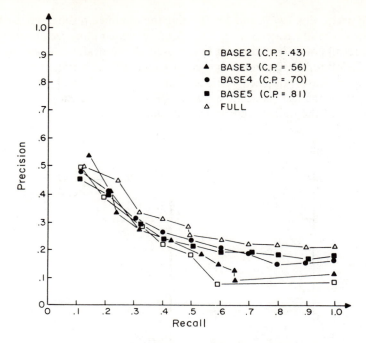

Fig. 12-2 Evaluation using standard measure.

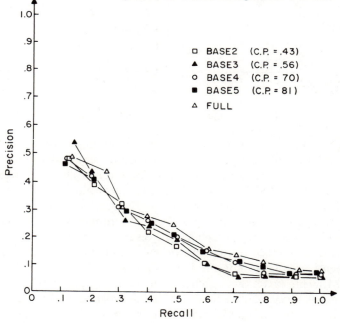

Fig. 12-3 Evaluation using new measure.

is very little difference between BASE4, BASE5, and FULL, and between BASE2 and BASE3. Also, the difference between the BASE2 curve and the FULL curve are much less.

When comparing the search results obtained from different sets of clusters, an attempt is made to keep the CP's as equal as possible, even though the new evaluation measure adjusts for differences. However, when the CP's differ by as much as 0.15 (BASE4 compared to BASE3), the graph for the higher CP search can be expected to be higher.

12-4-B   Internal Evaluation

The purpose of the internal evaluation is to investigate how changes in the input parameters affect the multilevel search results. All the experiments are conducted on the 82 document ADI collection and the 200-document Cranfield thesaurus collection. The following parameters are investigated:

1. Initial cluster generation.
   (a) Correlation.
   (b) Similarity correlation.
   (c) Frequency.
   (d) Random.
   (e) Results from a one-pass algorithm [5].
2. Number of clusters.
3. Overlap between clusters.
4. Cutoff; that is, percent of documents allowed to be loose at the end of the classification.
5. Percent loose clustered on the next iteration.

In addition to evaluating the retrieval results, the internal evaluation should determine how close the classification comes to satisfying the input parameters. However, it is probably better not to "force" a classification algorithm to satisfy exactly input parameters such as the number of clusters and amount of overlap. The algorithm should allow some variation in these parameters depending on the collection use. For example, suppose a collection consists of repetitions of three distinct documents. Then, clearly, three clusters at most should be produced, no matter how many are requested. On the other hand, it is difficult to obtain experimental conclusions if the parameters are not controlled. Therefore, the algorithm is designed to keep the parameters within fairly small boundaries. In practice it might be better to relax some of these restrictions a little.

Experiments are performed by varying one of the five parameters and comparing the results with those obtained with a base classification [4]. The parameters for the base classification usually fall somewhere near the middle of the two extremes. Table 12-6 lists the classification parameters for the ADI collection, and Table 12-7 illustrates

Table 12-6

ADI Clusters

RUN	NUMBER OF CLUSTERS		PERCENT OVERLAP		CUTOFF (% LOOSE)		PERCENT LOOSE	APPROX. TIME TAKEN (MIN.)	NUMBER OF ITERATIONS	NUMBER OF CYCLES
	In	*Out*	*In*	*Out*	*In*	*Out*				
BASE	10	9	5	0.3	10	12	40	1.1	3	6
CLUST5	5	4	5	1.2	10	13	40	1.0	5	12
CLUST15	15	15	5	0.4	10	4	40	0.8	1	4
OVRO	10	9	0	0	10	12	40	0.7	3	5
OVR10	10	9	10	0.3	10	12	40	0.8	3	7
OVR15	10	8	15	13.3	10	12	40	1.3	4	12
CUTO	10	10	5	0.1	0	2	40	1.0	5	9
CUT20	10	9	5	0.2	20	23	40	0.7	2	5
CUT30	10	9	5	0.2	30	23	40	0.7	2	5
LSE20	10	9	5	0.2	10	12	20	1.0	5	9
LSE60	10	9	5	0.4	10	3	60	0.8	3	6
LSE80	10	9	5	0	10	6	80	0.8	2	5
BASEFREQ	10	10	5	0	10	12	40	1.0	3	6
OVROFREQ	10	10	0	0	10	12	40	1.0	2	6
BASESIM	10	9	5	0	10	11	40	0.9	4	9
OVROSIM	10	9	0	0	10	11	40	0.9	4	9
FREQ	9	8	5	0.5	5	7	25	1.7	7	17
CORR2	9	7	5	0.2	5	7	25	1.3	6	17
CORR1	9	8	5	1.1	5	8	25	1.1	6	13
SIM	9	9	5	1.0	10	11	25	1.4	6	14
RANDOM	9	11	5	2.2	5	4	25	1.4	4	15
ROCCHIO	–	7	–	1.5	–	–	–	–	–	–
BEST	10	9	2	0	10	3	60	0.7	3	6
FASTO	9	11	5	3.3	5	8	25	1.4	3	13
FASTD	9	11	0	0	5	5	25	1.0	3	7
MDJ	–	14	–	0	–	–	–	–	–	–

Table 12-7

CRANFIELD CLUSTERS

RUN	NUMBER OF CLUSTERS		PERCENT OVERLAP		CUTOFF (% LOOSE)		PERCENT LOOSE TAKEN (Taken)	APPROX. TIME (MIN.)	NUMBER OF ITERATIONS	NUMBER OF CYCLES
	In	Out	In	Out	In	Out				
BASE	15	12	5	5.4	10	13	40	6.2	6	47
CLUST10	10	9	5	6.1	10	13	40	2.7	3	26
CLUST20	20	20	5	1.7	10	14	40	3.9	3	20
OVRO	15	13	0	0	10	9	40	2.5	5	17
OVR10	15	14	10	15.1	10	8	40	5.6	4	31
OVR15	15	14	15	15.3	10	8	40	6.0	4	35
CUTO	15	13	5	6.2	0	3	40	6.6	4	37
CUT20	15	13	5	6.4	20	16	40	4.5	4	29
CUT30	15	14	5	1.1	30	27	40	2.4	3	17
LSE20	15	13	5	4.1	10	11	20	9.1	9	69
LSE60	15	13	5	1.5	10	11	60	2.3	3	14
LSE80	15	15	5	1.3	10	9	80	2.0	2	10
BASEFREQ	15	13	5	3.8	10	9	40	3.5	5	24
OVROFREQ	15	12	0	0	10	10	40	2.4	4	13
BASESIM	15	13	5	5.7	10	12	40	4.4	4	30
OVROSIM	15	15	0	0	10	13	40	2.8	3	13
RANDOM	15	18	5	7.1	10	13	40	6.4	3	30
CORR	15	10	5	3.5	5	8	50	4.2	4	25
FREQ	15	13	5	8.8	5	4	50	6.0	4	35
ROCCHIO	–	18	–	2.9	–	–	–	–	–	–
BEST	15	15	2	0.5	10	16	60	3.6	3	23
RANCLUST	–	15	–	3.2	–	–	–	–	–	–

the same parameters for the Cranfield collection. The first two columns specify the number of clusters requested (In) and the number actually produced (Out); the next two columns show the percent of overlap requested and the percent produced, and the next two columns specify the percent of documents loose at the end of the algorithm. "Percent loose taken" specifies the percent of loose documents clustered at the end of each iteration. The results of the experiments are shown as document-level recall-precision graphs using the new evaluation measure; the CP figures are included when available.

12-4-C Initial Clusters

The initial cluster evalution includes several sets of cluster generation and centroid searches. For the ADI collection, the following experiments are performed:

1. 25% loose, $\leq .5\%$ overlap (Fig. 12-4).
   (a) FREQ (frequency).
   (b) CORR2 (correlation).
   (c) FASTD (input from one-pass algorithm, 0% overlap).
2. 25% loose, 1–3% overlap (Fig. 12-5).
   (a) CORRI (correlation).

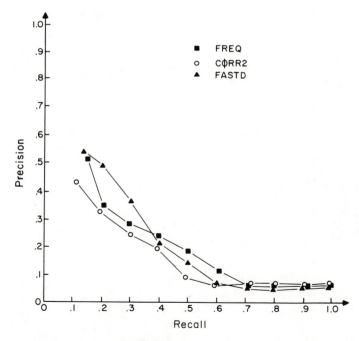

Fig. 12-4 ADI initial clusters (25% loose, $\leq$.5% overlap).

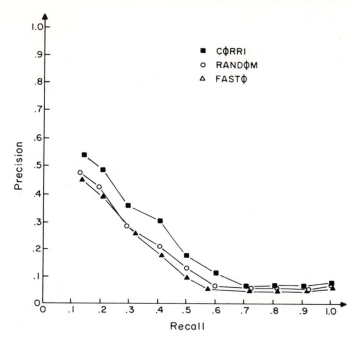

Fig. 12-5 ADI initial clusters (25% loose, 1–3% overlap).

  (b) RANDOM (random).
  (c) FASTO (input from one-pass algorithm, overlapping clusters).

3. 40% loose, 0% overlap (Fig. 12-6).
  (a) OVRO (correlation).
  (b) OVROSIM (similarity correlation).
  (c) OVROFREQ (frequency).

  With the exception of experiment 1(c) (0% overlap requested), within each of the three experiments, all of the input parameters are identical. The only difference is the method used to generate the initial clusters. All evaluations are made by visual inspection of the document-level recall-precision curves. The following notation is used to indicate the results:

(a) $=$ Two methods give approximately similar results, or it is impossible to determine from the graphs which method is better.

(b) $>$ The first method is better than the second.

(c) $\gg$ The first method is much better than the second.

  The results of the three ADI experiments with initial clusters are as follows:

1. (FREQ = FASTD) > CORR2.

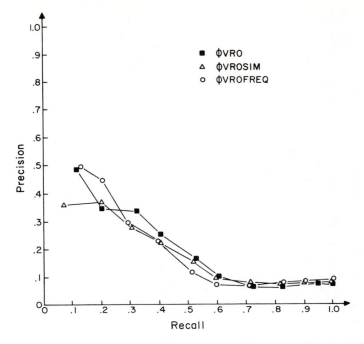

Fig. 12-6   ADI initial clusters (40% loose, 0% overlap).

2. CORR1 > (RANDOM = FASTO).

3. OVRO = OVROSIM = OVROFREQ.

Unfortunately, the results do not show that any method is consistently better than any other. The only conclusion is that the frequency, the similarity correlation, and the use of disjoint clusters from a one-pass algorithm never perform worse than any other method, while the random method and overlapping clusters place last in their only test.

The following initial cluster experiments are performed with the Cranfield collection:

1. 40% loose, 4–7% overlap.
   (a) BASE (correlation).
   (b) BASESIM (similarity correlation).
   (c) BASEFREQ (frequency).
   (d) RANDOM (random).

2. 40% loose, 0% overlap.
   (a) OVRO (correlation).
   (b) OVROSIM (similarity correlation).
   (c) OVROFREQ (frequency).

The results of these two initial cluster experiments are

1. (RANDOM = BASEFREQ) > (BASE = BASESIM).

2. OVRO $\gg$ OVROFREQ > OVROSIM.

Once again the results are inconclusive. The correlation method performs better than the other two methods in the nonoverlapping case, but it does not do as well as the random or frequency methods in the first experiment. Surprisingly, the random method actually performs better than the correlation or similarity correlation methods. This indicates that the algorithm is insensitive to the type of initial clusters used, or that none of the methods used so far is very good. Additional experiments must be carried out using different methods of initial cluster generation. One method which can be tried involves running the algorithm twice. The first time, the initial clusters are generated using the random method. The clusters produced by this run are then used as the initial clusters for the second run.

12-4-D   Number of Clusters

In the remainder of the experiments, the "correlation" method of initial cluster generation is used, and unless otherwise specified, all other parameters are identical to the BASE run. For any given collection, the number of clusters can be chosen to minimize the search time, assuming that all clusters contain the same number of documents. This assumption is reasonably valid because the cluster sizes are maintained between one-half and twice the average cluster size.

Consider a collection of N documents classified into m clusters, where each cluster contains on the average n documents. For a centroid search which looks at the documents in the top q clusters, the search time is $ST = m + q \cdot n$. Assuming $\phi = 0$, then $n = N/m$ and $ST = m + q \cdot N/m$. The search time is minimized for $d\mathrm{ST}/dm = 0$.

$$\frac{d\mathrm{ST}}{dm} = \frac{1 - q \cdot N}{m^2}.$$

When $d\mathrm{ST}/dm = 0$, then $m = \sqrt{q \cdot N}$.

For the ADI collection, ST is minimized with $\sqrt{82} = 9$ clusters if one centroid is searched, and with $\sqrt{164} = 13$ clusters if two centroids are searched. Of course, there is no guarantee that optimizing the search time yields the best results. The following experiments are performed with the ADI collection (Fig. 12-7):

1. BASE (9 clusters).

2. CLUST5 (4 clusters).

3. CLUST15 (15 clusters).

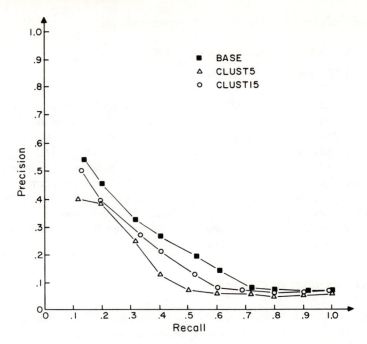

Fig. 12-7 ADI number of clusters.

The parameters for the centroid search allow the number of centroids searched per query to vary for different queries. A specified minimum is always searched for each query, but additional centroids may also be searched if the query-centroid correlation is close enough to the correlations of the centroids already chosen. Thus, the average number of centroids searched is usually higher than the minimum. In experiment 1 a minimum of two centroids is searched, while in experiment 2 one centroid is searched, and in experiment 3 three centroids are searched. The minimum number of centroids searched is chosen to keep the search times approximately equal. The approximate search times for each experiment are:

1. $ST = 9 + 2 \cdot 82/9 = 9 + 164/9 = 9 + 18 = 27.$

2. $ST = 4 + 1 \cdot 82/4 = 4 + 21 = 25.$

3. $ST = 15 + 3 \cdot 82/15 = 15 + 246/15 = 15 + 16 = 31.$

The results of the experiment show that BASE > CLUST15 > CLUST5.

For the Cranfield collection, a similar set of experiments was performed as follows:

1. BASE (12 clusters).

2. CLUST10 (9 clusters).

3. CLUST20 (20 clusters).

All of these searches are made using a minimum of one centroid, so the approximate search times may be quite different. Fortunately, the actual CP's are available, and they can be compared with the ST figures:

1. $ST = 12 + 1 \cdot 200/12 + 17 = 29.$
   $CP = 0.26 \longrightarrow ST'$ (actual search time) $= 0.26 \cdot 200 = 52;$
2. $ST = 9 + 1 \cdot 200/9 = 9 + 22 = 31,$
   $CP = 0.34 \longrightarrow ST' = 0.34 \cdot 200 = 68;$
3. $ST = 20 + 1 \cdot 200/20 = 20 + 10 = 30,$
   $CP = 0.25 \longrightarrow ST' = 0.25 \cdot 200 = 50.$

All the ST values are lower than the actual search time, but this is mainly due to the fact that more than one centroid is often used, and the overlap is not 0.

The results indicate that (BASE = CLUST10) > CLUST20. Unlike the ADI results, the search with the smallest number of clusters does better than the search with the largest number. This is probably due to the larger number of clusters used with the ADI CLUST15. At any rate, both the ADI and Cranfield results indicate that the middle number of clusters does best. Notice that both sets of BASE clusters contain very close to $\sqrt{N}$ clusters ($\sqrt{82} = 9$, $\sqrt{200} = 14$).

12-4-E Overlap

An inspection of Tables 12-6 and 12-7 shows that the amount of overlap produced is very often much different from the amount requested. The requested overlap is varied from 0% to 15% in steps of 5%, but in both collections, several of the specifications were not met. However, the following comparisons can be made for the ADI experiments (Fig. 12-8):

1. BASE (.3%).
2. OVRO (0%).
3. OVR15 (13.5%).

The results indicate that BASE > (OVRO = OVR15). Thus, for the ADI collection a small amount of overlap performs better than a large amount of overlap and better than 0 overlap.

The following experiments are performed for the Cranfield collection:

1. BASE (5.4%),
2. OVRO (0%),
3. OVR15 (15.3%).

The results obtained indicate that OVRO ≫ BASE > OVR15. Once again the clusters with a very large amount of overlap perform poorly, even though the CP for OVR15

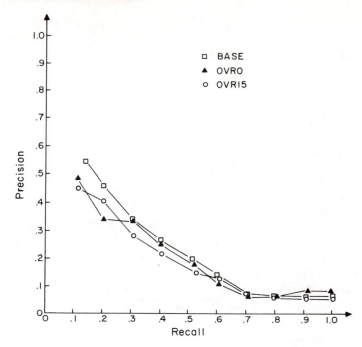

Fig. 12-8 ADI overlap.

is about twice as great as the CP for BASE and for OVRO. However, a surprising result is the better performance of the clusters with 0% overlap compared to those with 5% overlap. Since the best ADI results are obtained with only .3% overlap, the conclusion is that a very small amount of overlap is helpful, but more than 5% is too much. More experiments needs to be run using an overlap between 0–5%. It appears that the best results should be obtained in this range.

12-4-F Cutoff

The value of the cutoff determines how many documents are left loose at the end of the algorithm. In all cases, the loose documents are blended into the nearest cluster. The following experiments are compared for the ADI collection (Fig. 12-9):

1. BASE (12% loose).
2. CUTO (2.5% loose).
3. CUT20 (23% loose).

The main advantage of a high cutoff is that it allows the algorithm to terminate faster. The cutoff should be chosen as high as possible to shorten the cluster time,

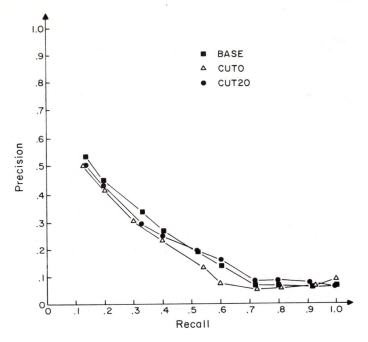

Fig. 12-9 ADI cutoff.

without seriously affecting the search results. The ADI results show that (BASE = CUT20) > CUTO. This is surprising, since it is expected that the lower cutoff would produce better results.

The analogous experiments are run on the Cranfield collection:

1. BASE (13% loose).
2. CUTO (3.0% loose).
3. CUT20 (16% loose).
4. CUT30 (27% loose).

The overlap for CUT30 is only 1.1%, while for the other runs it is 5–6%. The experiments on overlap indicate that 1% is probably better than 5–6%. Thus, CUT30 might do well because of its overlap. The results show that (BASE = CUTO) > CUT30 > CUT20.

The Cranfield results favor the lower cutoff values, and it is possible that CUT20 would have done better than CUT30 if their overlaps were equal. However, the experiment with 3% loose does not do better than the run with 13% loose. Since the lower cutoffs do not perform as well in the ADI experiments, the best cutoff appears to be 12–13%.

12-4-G Percent Loose Clustered

This parameter controls the percentage of loose documents that are clustered at the beginning of the next iteration. Thus, 40% means that 40% of the remaining loose documents are assigned to clusters after the first cycle of the next iteration. The following experiments are performed for both the ADI and Cranfield collections:

1. BASE (40%).

2. LSE20 (20%).

3. LSE60 (60%).

4. LSE80 (80%).

The Cranfield results are reproduced in Fig. 12-10. For the ADI, (BASE = LSE60 = LSE80) > LSE20 and for the Cranfield, LSE60 ≫ BASE > (LSE80).

In both cases LSE20 is poorest, but LSE60 is much better than the others for the Cranfield results; therefore, 60% loose gives the best results over both collections.

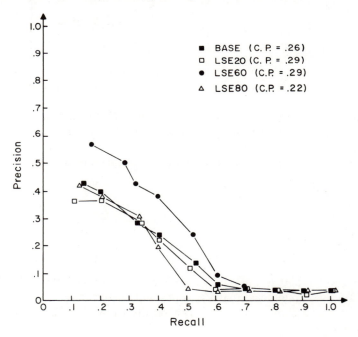

Fig. **12-10** Cranfield percent loose clustered.

12-4-H External Evaluation

On the basis of the internal evaluation results, the following conclusions are made regarding the "best" input parameters for the classification algorithm:

1. Initial clusters—no conclusion (correlation used).

2. Number of clusters—approximately $\sqrt{N}$ clusters; for example, the best results are obtained with 9 clusters for the ADI collection and 13 for the Cranfield collection.

3. Overlap—probably somewhere between 1–3% (2% used).

4. Cutoff—10%.

5. Percent loose clustered—60%.

An additional run called BEST is made using the above parameters as input. Unfortunately, all of the output parameters did not satisfy their input requests; for example, the overlap is 0% for the ADI and .5% for the Cranfield. However, LSE60 for the Cranfield clusters matches the input parameters almost exactly—13 clusters, 1.5 overlap.

Figure 12-11 shows the recall-precision curves for BEST, LSE60, and FULL

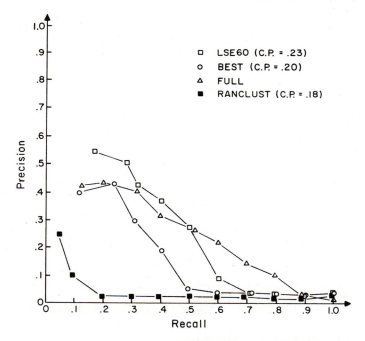

Fig. 12-11 Cranfield full search comparison.

for the Cranfield collection. Also included in Fig. 12-11 are the results of a random clustering of the collection. In the ADI case, BEST and OVRO have 0% overlap, and the results obtained show that FULL > BEST > OVRO. In the Cranfield results, the surprising fact is the poor showing of BEST. However, the run which actually contains the desired output parameters, LSE60, performs better than the full search up to 50% recall. Thus,

$$(\text{FULL} = \text{LSE60}) \gg \text{BEST} \gg \text{RANCLUST}.$$

Comparisons can also be made with cluster results from Rocchio's classification algorithm [6]. Several sets of clusters are available as output from Rocchio's algorithm, and those which yield the *best* retrieval results are chosen for comparison. These clusters are called ROCCHIO in Table 12-6 and Table 12-7. The Rocchio clusters are compared against those runs which most closely match the number of clusters and overlap of ROCCHIO. Thus, SIM is used for the ADI results, and RANDOM is used from the Cranfield results. The search parameters are adjusted so that *exactly* two centroids are chosen for every query. The results of Fig. 12-12 indicate that SIM $\gg$

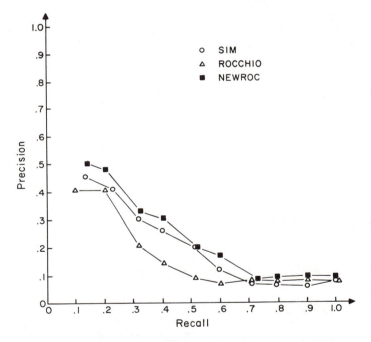

Fig. 12-12   ADI Rocchio comparison.

ROCCHIO, and RANDOM2 $\gg$ ROCCHIO. However, another run called NEWROC is made by using Rocchio's clusters with the same centroid definition also used for SIM and RANDOM2.

The centroids for Rocchio's clusters are defined by using all the concepts and by taking the sum of the weights; that is, if concept i occurs in two documents within the cluster with weights of x_1 and x_2, then its weight in the centroid is $x_1 + x_2$. The centroids for the clusters in this study are defined as the top y percent of the concepts included in the profile vector, where the weight of each concept is defined as its rank value. For the ADI experiments a minimum of 50% of the concepts are used. The rank value differs from Rocchio's weights in two important respects:

1. The weight of a concept *within* a particular document is ignored in computing the rank value; that is, all concepts in a document are assigned the same weight.

2. The *magnitude* of the difference in the number of documents within the cluster in which a concept occurs is ignored; that is, if concept i is ranked first and occurs in ten documents, and concept j is ranked second, then it does not matter if concept j occurs in nine documents or only two documents; its rank value is still one less than the rank value of concept i.

Figure 12-12 shows that NEWROC > SIM ≫ ROCCHIO, while for the Cranfield output, RANDOM2 > NEWROC ≫ ROCCHIO. Thus, in both cases the results improve greatly over the Rocchio clusters simply by changing the centroid definition. However, the present classification algorithm still performs better than NEWROC for the Cranfield results, although NEWROC does better for the ADI results.

The final external evaluation is made by comparison with the results from a one-pass clustering algorithm. A description of the algorithm and the results are presented by Marathe and Rieber [5]. The best set of one-pass clusters is chosen (MDJ–0% overlap) and plotted against OVRO using the new evaluation measure. Fig. 12-13 shows that OVRO = MDJ. However, CP = 0.50 for OVRO, and CP =

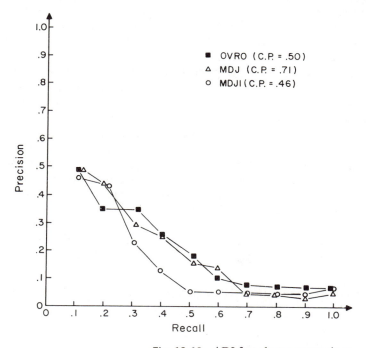

Fig. 12-13 ADI fast cluster comparison.

0.71 for MDJ. Both searches are made using a minimum of two clusters per query. The very high correlation percentage for the one-pass clusters is due to the size of the clusters. MDJ contains 14 clusters, but the three largest clusters, which are usually chosen in the search, contain 72% of the documents; 7 of the clusters contain only 1 document. Another run is made called MDJ1 where exactly one cluster is chosen per query. Even in this case CP is quite high (0.46), but now OVRO > MDJ1. It is clear that the one-pass algorithm needs to be modified so that the size of the clusters does not vary so much. Perhaps an additional pass should be made to break up large clusters and to merge smaller clusters.

12-5 CONCLUSION

The multilevel classification algorithm presented in this study runs in time $T = k \cdot N \cdot p \cdot \log_p m$, where k is a constant, N is the number of documents in the collection, m is the final number of clusters desired, and p is the number of clusters produced at each level of the algorithm. It is shown that the closer p is to e, the faster the algorithm will operate. The complete multilevel algorithm is not yet implemented, so that all the experiments are run with $p = m \rightarrow T = k \cdot N \cdot m$. With $m = \sqrt{N}$, $T = k \cdot N^{3/2}$. This is, of course, much better than classification methods that run in time proportional to N^2, but it is still not satisfactory for very large collections. For these collections it is necessary to implement the entire algorithm and to run with small values of p. With $N = 10^6$, it is theoretically possible for T to equal $k \cdot 10^6 \cdot 3 \cdot \log_3 m$, where $p = 3$. If once again $m = \sqrt{N}$, then $T = k \cdot 10^6 \cdot 3 \cdot \log_3 10^3 = k \cdot 10^6 \cdot 3 \cdot 6.3 = k \cdot 10^6 18.9 = 2k \cdot 10^7$. This is much better than using only one level, where $p = m$, and $T = k \cdot 10^6 \cdot 10^3 = k \cdot 10^9$.

Fortunately, many of the input parameters which yield the best search results also help to lower the constant of proportionality k. Table 12-7 shows that LSE60, the best cluster run, took approximately 2.3 minutes for the 200-document Cranfield collection, while LSE20 took over 9 minutes! Both the high percent of loose clustered and the low amount of overlap reduce the clustering time.

One of the major problems with the algorithm is its failure to satisfy the requested amount of overlap. This is due to the fact that the parameter a is not changed enough after each cycle. Recall that a is reset to $a + (1 - a) \cdot (\text{XOVER} - \phi)$, if $\phi < \text{XOVER}$, and reset to $a + a \cdot (\text{XOVER} - \phi)$, if $\phi > \text{XOVER}$. One possible improvement consists in introducing a parameter b such that,

$$a = \begin{cases} a + b \cdot (1 - a) \cdot (\text{XOVER} - \phi), & \text{if} \quad \phi < \text{XOVER}, \\ a + b \cdot a \cdot (\text{XOVER} - \phi), & \text{if} \quad \phi > \text{XOVER}. \end{cases}$$

The parameter b is set to 1.0 at the beginning of each iteration. After every cycle, b is reset as follows:

$$b = b \cdot (1 + |\text{XOVER} - \phi|).$$

Thus, b ranges between 1.0 and 2.0.

A comparison with Rocchio's algorithm shows that the method used to define centroids is very important. Certainly the rank values prove to be better than the sum of the weights. However, it is not clear whether the rank values are better because they ignore weights within documents, or because they ignore the *magnitude* of differences in the number of documents in which each concept occurs. This can be decided by summing the weights as Rocchio does, but instead of using this sum as the weight, by ranking the concepts according to their sum and then calculating the rank values to be used in the centroid definition.

All the evaluations performed in this study are done by visual inspection of the document level recall-precision graphs. This rather inexact method can be improved by using statistical tests such as the sign test and the *t*-test to compare two curves. Routines are being prepared to perform such tests, and they will be used in the future.

Finally, all of the conclusions and evaluations are based on results from an 82-document and a 200-document collection, containing 35 and 42 queries, respectively. These results should be supplemented by experiments run on the 424-document Cranfield collection containing 155 queries and eventually on the 1400-document Cranfield collection.

REFERENCES

[1] R. T. Dattola, A Fast Algorithm for Automatic Classification, *Report ISR-14* to the National Science Foundation, Section V, Department of Computer Science, Cornell University, Ithaca, N.Y., October 1968.

[2] L. B. Doyle, Breaking the Cost Barrier in Automatic Classification, *SDC Paper SP-2516*, System Development Corp., Santa Monica, Calif., July 1966.

[3] S. L. Worona, Query Clustering in a Large Document Collection, *Report ISR-16* to the National Science Foundation, Section XV, Department of Computer Science, Cornell University, Ithaca, N.Y., September 1969; also Chap. 13 of this volume.

[4] K. S. Jones and D. Jackson, The Use of Automatically Obtained Keyword Classifications for Information Retrieval, Information Storage and Retrieval, Vol. 5, pp. 175–201, Pergamon Press, 1970.

[5] V. P. Marathe and S. L. Rieber, A One-Pass Clustering Algorithm, *Report ISR-16* to the National Science Foundation, Section XIV, Department of Computer Science, Cornell University, Ithaca, N.Y., September 1969.

[6] J. J. Rocchio, Jr., Document Retrieval Systems—Optimization and Evaluation, *Report ISR-10* to the National Science Foundation, Harvard University, Cambridge, Mass., March 1966.

The Cranfield 424-document collection is clustered using queries and known relevance judgments. This clustering method is compared to a full search of the collection and several searches using a standard clustering technique. Several new evaluation parameters are defined and applied to the experiment.

13

QUERY CLUSTERING IN A LARGE DOCUMENT SPACE†

S. WORONA

13-1 INTRODUCTION

One of the most important aspects of any information retrieval system is time—how quickly a user's request can be processed, the specified information generated, and the output returned to the user. This is especially true in a real-time system, where the optimum time is measured in seconds. For a large-sized document collection, search time—the time spent scanning and correlating against the members of the collection—is critical. It can become excessive because it often varies with the size of the collection. Because of this, various techniques have been developed to shorten search time. "Batching", that is, searching the document collection only once for serveral queries, has proven effective in reducing per-query search time. This must be considered unworkable, however, in a real-time system, when only single queries are available. "Clustering" techniques, which use one "centroid" to represent many documents, also lower search time and are, in addition, well suited for single query real-time systems. Clustering is the operation which consists of dividing a

---

†This study was published originally as Section XV in *Scientific Report ISR-16*, October 1969.

document space into several groups, each of which is considered as a unit. Each cluster is represented by a centroid, similar in form to the documents it represents. On the surface, then, a collection of centroids is no different from a normal document collection.

All clustering operations can be divided into two parts. The first controls how the clusters are to be generated from the document collection and how centroids are to be assigned to the clusters. The second determines a search scheme by which the collection of centroids is scanned and certain clusters are chosen for expansion. In addition, the final ranking of retrieved documents and the subsequent use of relevance feedback techniques [2, 8] may become part of a clustering system. These last considerations, however, are not peculiar to clustering and are not discussed in this chapter.

13-2   GENERATING CLUSTERS

Several methods of generating document clusters are being used currently in experimental systems; those developed by Bonner, Rocchio, and Dattola [3], [4], [5], [6], [7]. Most of these systems make use of correlations between the documents to be clustered, grouping those which correlate highest, and then forming each cluster centroid from the concept vectors of the documents included in that cluster. Thus, these techniques produce clusters of documents whose concept vectors are highly related to each other, each cluster being represented by another vector which is a mathematical combination of the documents it represents. Parameters for these clustering routines include the number of clusters desired, the number of loose documents permitted, the level of correlation between cluster members, and the degree of "overlap" of the clusters.

In reference [1], Lesser suggests that a different clustering method be used. His method is a two-pass algorithm, consisting of the following steps. First all *queries* processed previously by a system are clustered by a standard method. The resulting query clusters are used to cluster the document collection in one of three ways:

1. All documents correlating highly with the centroid of a query-cluster form a cluster.

2. All documents correlating highly with one or more queries of any one query cluster form a cluster.

3. All documents judged relevant to one or more queries of any one query cluster form a cluster.

The centroids of the resulting document clusters are the centroids of the corresponding query clusters. In this way, each document is represented in its cluster by a centroid formed from queries rather than documents. According to Lesser, this process is effective, since incoming queries are more likely to be similar to past queries than to documents. Thus, Lesser believes, new queries are less likely to fall between query clusters than between document clusters (see Fig. 13-1).

In addition to this property, the query-clustering method, especially when performed with relevance judgments, may enable a retrieval system to "mature" as more and more queries are entering into the system. As in all clustering schemes, updating the clusters would be periodical, depending both on the number of queries processed and on the number of new documents received.

    x   Document
    o   Query
——   Standard document cluster
- - - -   Query cluster with associated documents
    □   "New" query falling <u>within</u> query cluster,
          but <u>between</u> document clusters

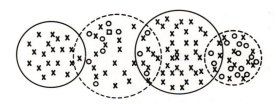

Fig. 13-1   Query-document space (from [1]).

13-3 SEARCHING CLUSTERED COLLECTIONS

In general, collections of centroids can themselves be clustered to form "super centroids", and so on. With each new clustering, another "level" is added to the degree of the required search. Only simple centroids of level two are considered here.

When searching such centroids, one parameter is crucial—the number of clusters to be expanded. Of course, numerous other considerations are also important, including the method of determining the "goodness" of the centroids searched. These are, however, superseded in importance by the former, which controls the portion of the collection that is to be used in the search. If this portion is too large, the search is likely to be successful, but the resulting saving in search time may be insignificant. On the other hand, taking too small a piece of the document collection may produce poor, although rapidly obtained, results.

13-4 PARAMETERS FOR EVALUATING
CLUSTER SEARCHES

As in any search attempt, it is important to determine the recall and precision of a clustered search. However, other considerations also enter the picture, as full searches are replaced by centroid matches. Perhaps the most important, and possibly the most difficult to measure, is the amount of savings in machine time offered by the centroid search. All other values used to decide the effectiveness of a search must be considered in combination with the statistics of how much time is saved. In this paper, no attempt is made to combine such time considerations with any other parameters. Rather, all parameters are presented separately. This is done because no acceptable method of combining these parameters has been decided upon. Indeed, the desired results may vary with the application. Given the following conditions to decide whether a search retrieving 45% of all relevant documents while scanning 45% of a collection is better or worse than one retrieving 30% while using only 30% of the collection, different users would undoubtedly give different answers.

The factor used in this chapter to measure time savings is *correlation percentage*, that is, the ratio of the number of documents *and centroids* scanned to the number of documents in the collection. This will, in most applications, be a number between 0 and 1, with a full search always evaluated at 1.

Given any particular query, it is reasonable to ask how different cluster-generating procedures rate as creators of good "targets" for a search. For example, a scheme generating clusters, none of which contain a large number of the relevant documents for that query, will yield poor results no matter what the search technique, because several clusters must then be expanded before all the relevant documents are retrieved, thus destroying the effectiveness of clustering. It is then necessary to examine the "target value" of the tested clustering schemes. For a given query, the "target clusters" are those n clusters which, between them, contain the largest number of relevant documents, where n is the number of clusters to be expanded. Given two clusters with equal numbers of relevant documents, the smaller is chosen. When more than 1 cluster is to be expanded, the target clusters are those which have the smallest total of (different) documents, while still containing the most relevant possible. The target value of a clustering scheme for a particular query is the ratio of the number of relevant documents in the target clusters to the number of relevant for that query.

The ideal system is one in which the target value for all queries is 1, and the correlation percentage is minimized. This alone, however, will not assure good results. After ideal clusters have been formed for each query, it is necessary that they correlate in the proper way. The "aim" is then defined as a measure of how well a centroid was assigned to each cluster. The "aim clusters" of a given query are those n clusters which are expanded during a search. As with "target value", the "aim value" is the ratio of relevant documents in the aim clusters to the total number of relevant for the query. This should not be confused with the "recall ceiling", a similar concept, but one which yields different results. (The recall ceiling does not take into account relevant documents dropped because they did not correlate highly enough with the query.)

Although this chapter does not deal with a wide enough range of experimental data to make full use of aim and target values, these concepts make it possible to separate judgments on clustering from those on centroid assignment and may be valuable in an in-depth study of clustering techniques.

Perfect values for aim and target should do much to optimize a search scheme and, when combined with low correlation percentages, may be even more effective. One more consideration is important, however. Take, for example, a collection of clusters, all of which contain all the relevant documents for a particular query. Another set of clusters may contain only one cluster including all such documents. Quite conceivably, aim, target, and correlation percentage values may be identical for the two schemes on the given query; yet, the two schemes may be quite different. The former may have a great deal of "wasted" documents where they are not needed by the query. The term "rejection" is used to refer to the tendency of a clustering scheme to "reject" relevant documents from all but the target cluster(s) of a given query. It is defined as the ratio of occurrences (not necessarily different) of relevant documents in the target clusters to occurrences (not necessarily different) of relevant documents throughout the clustered collection. Again, a value of 1 is optimal.

13-5 THE EXPERIMENT

Lesser's attempt to demonstrate the effectiveness of query clustering yielded encouraging results. The limitations of the experiment, however, put the results on a less-than-solid basis. Since the most damaging of these limitations was the small size of the collection used (only 35 queries and 82 documents), it was decided that an experiment on a larger collection was in order. In the present experiment, the Cranfield 424 collection, containing 424 documents and 155 queries, is used. As in Lesser's approach, the procedure is in two phases—first query clusters are formed, and then document clusters are generated from these. Unlike Lesser, who associated documents in a cluster if they correlated highly with one or more queries in any one query cluster, the current experiment uses relevance judgments to form document clusters.

The 155 queries are split into two groups, one of 130 and one of 25, by choosing every sixth query for the smaller group. (This process is used because the collection is arranged in order of subject area, so that taking any continuous subgroup would destroy generality.) The 130 queries were clustered using Dattola's clustering algorithm [7], producing 11 clusters with an overlap of 13.9%. Clusters range in size from 17 to 37 queries, with an average of 28. Queries in this collection have from 3 to 22 relevant documents, averaging 6.5. Document clusters are then formed by replacing the list of queries with a list of relevant documents for each cluster. Since this experiment is being done using Cornell University's SMART system, each centroid is easily associated with a different collection. Both documents and queries are specified generally by a four-digit integer, and both have the same general appearance. It is thus possible to use documents and queries interchangeably in almost all applications.

The resulting document collection is described in Table 13-1. Overlap was not calculated for this collection, although it is estimated to be about 20–40%. Statistics are available giving the number of times a document appears in a given number of collections (for example, only 102 out of 424 documents appear in exactly 1 cluster), from which the overlap is estimated.

It is interesting to note that a collection of query clusters with an overlap of only 14% is turned into document clusters with an overlap nearly twice as high. The reasons for this include the fact that many documents are relevant to a great many queries, and that sets of co-relevant documents are common.

In a clustering algorithm, the question of "loose documents" must be considered. Loose documents are those which, at some point in the clustering procedure, belong to no cluster. If such documents are not "blended in" in one way or another, subsequent queries are likely to have artificially low recall ceilings. After associating all of the relevant documents with the queries of the initial query collection, it is found that some 29 documents remain loose. Fifteen of these documents are found to be relevant to one or more of the 25 queries, so these documents can be blended in. This is done by correlating all 15 documents with all 11 centroids and including each document in the 2 clusters, whose centroids are closest to the documents. In addition, each document is also included in any cluster for which the centroid-document correlation is 0.15 or higher. The parameters specifying two clusters and 0.15 correlation are chosen to maintain the characteristic overlap of the collection at its original level and are, for the most part, a product of intuition.

Since a clustered search is inherently different from a full search, it is desirable that other clustering methods be used for comparison. Thus, the Cranfield 424-document collection was itself clustered using Dattola's algorithm. The results of this operation appear in Table 13-1. Notice, in particular, the great difference in the number of concepts appearing in an average cluster for the two cluster schemes. This points up the fact that Dattola's algorithm produces clusters with document-related centroids, while query-clustering techniques produce centroids resembling queries rather than documents.

Four test searches are made, each with the same initial parameters. All documents

Table 13-1

STATISTICS OF CLUSTERED COLLECTIONS

PARAMETER	CLUSTERING METHODS	
	Document Clusters Generated by Dattola's Algorithm	*Document Clusters Generated using Query Clusters and Relevance Judgments*
Number of clusters	21	11
Number of documents in largest cluster	124	160
Percent of collection in largest cluster	29	38
Number of documents in smallest cluster	25	52
Percent of collection in smallest cluster	6	12
Number of documents in average cluster	81	119
Percent of collection in average cluster	19	28
Percent of overlap in clusters	18.5	(See text)
Number of concepts in average clusters	374	127

correlating greater than 0 are considered; all other values are set at default conditions. One full search, one clustered search using clusters generated by query clustering, and two clustered searches using Dattola's algorithm to generate clusters are made. The first of these two calls for only one cluster to be expanded for each query, while the second calls for two clusters. (A trial was made on which three clusters were to be expanded for each query, but this run failed because insufficient space was available on the program disc storage unit.) Complete statistics are available (including aim, target, and rejection values—see the appendix of this chapter—where applicable) for the full search, query-clustered search, and the first of the two normally clustered searches. Statistics for the remaining clustered search are limited to recall and precision values shown in Table 13-2.

Table 13-2

RESULTS OF FOUR SEARCHES

(n = Number of clusters expanded)

	PARAMETER				
SEARCH METHOD	*Normalized Recall*	*Normalized Precision*	*Rank Recall*	*Log Precision*	*Average Correlation Percentage*
Full search	0.8258	0.5968	0.1920	0.4327	100
Clustered search using query clusters	0.5538	0.4500	0.0621	0.3328	31.2
Clustered search using Dattola's algorithm, $n = 1$	0.3378	0.3040	0.0179	0.2712	21.2
Clustered search using Dattola's algorithm, $n = 2$	0.6072	0.4893	0.1034	0.3665	38.8

13-6   RESULTS

As the graph of Fig. 13-2 indicates, the query-clustered search results in recall-precision values rivaling a full search and surpassing it at one point, up to a recall level of 0.40. The search with normal clusters, setting $n = 2$, passes the query cluster graph at recall 0.30 and remains close to the full search graph from that point on. The standard clusters with $n = 1$ generate values quite a bit lower than the others.

A preliminary observation is that these results follow directly the correlation percentages of Table 13-2: the higher the CP, the better the results on the graph of Fig. 13-2. Of course, this relationship is not linear, as the full search is only slightly better than both the query cluster search and the standard cluster search with $n = 2$; the full search has however a CP nearly three times the size of the others. Obviously, other factors are involved here.

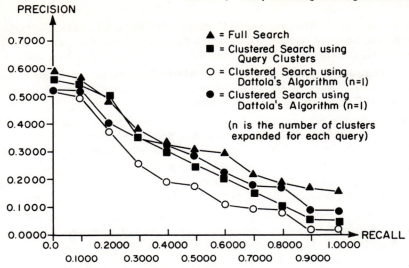

PRECISION

▲ = Full Search
■ = Clustered Search using
     Query Clusters
○ = Clustered Search using
     Dattola's Algorithm (n=1)
● = Clustered Search using
     Dattola's Algorithm (n=1)

(n is the number of clusters
expanded for each query)

Recall-Level Averages for Clustered Search

Fig. 13-2   Recall-level averages for clustered search.

It is suggested that, with "good" enough clusters and centroids, a clustered search need not lose a great deal of the recall compared with a full search. Notice in the figures of the appendix that the $n = 1$ normal cluster search has a very low aim value, completely cancelling out the high target value. Thus, although for most queries there is a cluster which "suits" it very well, that cluster is seldom found in the search. The problem might be in the construction of the centroid. On the other hand, the query-clustered documents maintain both high aim and target values and achieve markedly better results. Of course, these differences are not independent of the correlation percentage. Yet, it is questionable whether document clusters may be constructed with high aim and target values and at the same time low correlation percentages. For several queries, it appears that normal document clustering is inferior to query clustering, even with similar correlation percentages (queries 6, 8, 20, 24, and 25). On the other hand, other queries show the opposite trend (queries 7, 9, and 22). Additional results are needed, particularly of query-clustering methods generating relatively small clusters. Until such tests are carried out, the present results must remain inconclusive.

REFERENCES

[1] V. R. Lesser, A Modified Two-Level Search Algorithm Using Request Clustering, *Report ISR-11* to the National Science Foundation, Section VII, Department of Computer Science, Cornell University, Ithaca, N.Y., June 1966.

[2] W. Riddle, T. Horwitz, and R. Dietz, Relevance Feedback in an Information Retrieval System, *Report ISR-11* to the National Science Foundation, Section VI, Department of Computer Science, Cornell University, Ithaca, N.Y., June 1966.

[3] J. D. Broffitt, H. L. Morgan, and J. V. Soden, On Some Clustering Techniques for Information Retrieval, *Report ISR-11* to the National Science Foundation, Section IX, Department of Computer Science, Cornell University, Ithaca N.Y., June 1966.

[4] J. J. Rocchio, Jr., Document Retrieval Systems—Optimization and Evaluation, doctoral thesis, *Report ISR-10* to the National Science Foundation, Harvard Computation Laboratory, Cambridge, Mass., March 1966.

[5] G. Salton, Search Strategy and the Optimization of Retrieval Effectiveness, *Report ISR-12* to the National Science Foundation, Section V, Department of Computer Science, Cornell University, Ithaca, N.Y., June 1967; also Chapter 10 of this volume.

[6] R. T. Grauer and M. Messier, An Evaluation of Rocchio's Clustering Algorithm, *Report ISR-12* to the National Science Foundation, Section VI, Department of Computer Science, Cornell University, Ithaca, N.Y., June 1967; also Chapter 11 of this volume.

[7] R. T. Dattola, A Fast Algorithm for Automatic Classification, *Report ISR-14* to the National Science Foundation, Section V, Department of Computer Science, Cornell University, Ithaca, N.Y., October 1968.

[8] E. Ide, New Experiments in Relevance Feedback, *Report ISR-14* to the National Science Foundation, Section VIII, Department of Computer Science, Cornell University, Ithaca, N.Y., October 1968; also Chapter 16 of this volume.

APPENDIX

AIM, TARGET, AND REJECTION VALUES BY QUERY

(See tables on next 4 pages.)

Table A-1

DOCUMENTS CLUSTERED BY QUERY CLUSTERS, QUERIES 1–13

(Number of clusters expanded = 1)

QUERY NUMBER	NUMBER OF RELEVANT DOCUMENTS	TARGET CLUSTERS			AIM CLUSTERS			AIM TO TARGET RATIO	REJECTION
		Number of Relevant Documents in Cluster	Correlation Percentage†	Target Value	Number of Relevant Documents in Cluster	Correlation Percentage†	Aim Value		
1	3	3	29.2	1.0000	3	29.2	1.0000	1.0000	0.1765
2	10	7	40.3	0.7000	7	40.3	0.7000	1.0000	0.3889
3	10	10	40.3	1.0000	10	40.3	1.0000	1.0000	0.2439
4	10	10	29.2	1.0000	10	31.4	1.0000	1.0000	0.1282
5	6	4	34.9	0.6667	3	29.2	0.5000	0.7500	0.1905
6	5	4	35.4	0.8000	3	31.4	0.6000	0.7500	0.2000
7	4	4	34.9	1.0000	1	30.9	0.2500	0.2500	0.2352
8	5	5	40.3	1.0000	5	40.3	1.0000	1.0000	0.2941
9	3	2	31.4	0.6667	0	30.9	0.0000	0.0000	0.2500
10	6	5	34.9	0.8333	5	34.9	0.8333	1.0000	0.3571
11	5	4	35.1	0.8000	3	40.6	0.6000	0.7500	0.2500
12	6	6	21.0	1.0000	0	40.6	0.0000	0.0000	1.0000
13	4	4	40.3	1.0000	4	40.6	1.0000	1.0000	0.5000

†See text for explanation of these values.

Table A-2

DOCUMENTS CLUSTERED BY QUERY CLUSTERS, QUERIES 14–25

(Number of clusters expanded = 1)

QUERY NUMBER	NUMBER OF RELEVANT DOCUMENTS	TARGET CLUSTERS			AIM CLUSTERS			AIM TO TARGET RATIO	REJECTION
		Number of Relevant Documents in Cluster	Correlation Percentage†	Target Value	Number of Relevant Documents in Cluster	Correlation Percentage	Aim Value		
14	9	9	31.4	1.0000	5	21.0	0.5556	0.5556	0.4286
15	12	12	14.9	1.0000	10	30.9	0.8333	0.8333	0.2308
16	6	6	24.1	1.0000	6	24.1	1.0000	1.0000	0.5000
17	5	3	34.9	0.6000	0	30.9	0.0000	0.0000	0.2727
18	7	6	40.2	0.8571	3	40.6	0.4268	0.5000	0.3529
19	3	3	35.4	1.0000	0	21.0	0.0000	0.0000	0.5000
20	4	3	24.1	0.7500	3	24.1	0.7500	1.0000	0.6000
21	14	14	35.4	1.0000	14	35.4	1.0000	1.0000	0.3684
22	5	5	24.1	1.0000	1	21.0	0.2000	0.2000	0.6250
23	8	5	21.0	0.6250	2	34.9	0.2500	0.4000	0.2174
24	7	7	14.9	1.0000	7	14.9	1.0000	1.0000	0.5000
25	12	12	29.2	1.0000	12	21.0	1.0000	1.0000	0.2791
Averages	–	–	31.1	0.8920	–	31.2	0.6200	0.6796	0.3636

†See text for explanation of these values.

Table A-3

DOCUMENTS CLUSTERED BY DATTOLA'S ALGORITHM, QUERIES 1–13

(Number of clusters expanded = 1)

QUERY NUMBER	NUMBER OF RELEVANT DOCUMENTS	TARGET CLUSTERS			AIM CLUSTERS			AIM TO TARGET RATIO	REJECTION
		Number of Relevant Documents in Cluster	Correlation Percentage†	Target Value	Number of Relevant Documents in Cluster	Correlation Percentage†	Aim Value		
1	3	3	18.9	1.0000	0	13.7	0.0000	0.0000	0.1667
2	10	9	20.8	0.9000	1	14.7	0.1000	0.1111	0.4286
3	10	5	29.7	0.5000	5	29.7	0.5000	1.0000	0.1250
4	10	8	34.2	0.8000	3	13.7	0.3000	0.3750	0.1143
5	6	5	19.6	0.8333	1	13.7	0.1667	0.2000	0.1389
6	5	4	28.8	0.8000	2	32.6	0.4000	0.5000	0.1739
7	4	3	19.6	0.7500	3	29.7	0.7500	1.0000	0.1304
8	5	4	7.1	0.8000	0	35.7	0.0000	0.0000	0.3333
9	3	1	10.9	0.3333	1	35.7	0.3333	1.0000	0.2000
10	6	5	14.7	0.8333	5	14.7	0.8333	1.0000	0.6250
11	5	5	14.7	1.0000	5	14.7	1.0000	1.0000	0.8333
12	6	4	35.7	0.6667	2	17.5	0.3333	0.5000	0.4000
13	4	2	24.8	0.5000	0	17.5	0.0000	0.0000	0.3333

†See text for explanation of these values.

Table A-4

DOCUMENTS CLUSTERED BY DATTOLA'S ALGORITHM, QUERIES 14–25

(Number of clusters expanded = 1)

QUERY NUMBER	NUMBER OF RELEVANT DOCUMENTS	TARGET CLUSTERS			AIM CLUSTERS			AIM TO TARGET RATIO	REJECTION
		Number of Relevant Documents in Cluster	Correlation Percentage†	Target Value	Number of Relevant Documents in Cluster	Correlation Percentage†	Aim Value		
14	9	9	35.7	1.0000	0	10.9	0.0000	0.0000	0.5294
15	12	7	17.5	0.5833	7	17.5	0.5833	1.0000	0.5000
16	6	3	32.6	0.5000	2	17.5	0.3333	0.6667	0.1667
17	5	4	21.0	0.8000	1	13.7	0.2000	0.2500	0.1212
18	7	3	21.0	0.4286	3	35.7	0.4286	1.0000	0.1364
19	3	3	22.6	1.0000	0	35.7	0.0000	0.0000	0.1875
20	4	2	7.1	0.5000	1	28.5	0.2500	0.5000	0.2857
21	14	7	32.6	0.5000	3	10.9	0.2143	0.4286	0.1489
22	5	4	17.5	0.8000	4	17.5	0.8000	1.0000	0.2500
23	8	6	28.5	0.7500	2	10.9	0.2500	0.3333	0.2000
24	7	5	17.5	0.7143	5	17.5	0.7143	1.0000	0.4167
25	12	9	26.4	0.7500	9	26.4	0.7500	1.0000	0.1323
Averages	–	–	22.4	0.7217	–	21.1	0.3696	0.5546	0.2831

†See text for explanation of these values.

PART V

BASIC FEEDBACK RUNS

In evaluating the performance of a document retrieval system, the critical variables which determine system behavior must be isolated. For this purpose a model is introduced which identifies indexing, search request formulation, and request-document matching as the three primary functions of an automatic retrieval system. Search request formulation, the responsibility of the users of the system, is considered to be the variable with the greatest potential variance. In view of this, the idea of alteration and optimization of search requests is believed to constitute a primary possibility toward better control in evaluating indexing and request-document matching.

A process of request modifications called relevance feedback is developed based on a sequence of retrieval operations, such that after each operation the user is allowed to communicate his evaluation to the system. This information is used as a basis for altering the user's query. The modification algorithm is developed, and some preliminary results are presented.

14

RELEVANCE FEEDBACK IN INFORMATION RETRIEVAL †

J. J. ROCCHIO, JR.

14-1 SYSTEM MODEL

A document retrieval system is assumed in which the index transformation consists of mapping documents and requests from the natural language to multidimensional property vectors in an abstract space. The model is based on the SMART retrieval system, in which a text is represented as a numerical vector in a concept space. The index transformation is effected via a thesaurus mapping from word stems to concepts which may be augmented by several other text-processing techniques, for example, phrase identification and hierarchical transformations. The end product of the index transformation is, however, a vector in the concept space in which the weight of concept i (that is, the ith component of the vector) is indicative of the frequency of this concept in the original document.

The retrieval or searching process consists in matching a request image against the set of document images which constitute the store. Various matching strategies are possible; we shall assume here that the information contained in the index image of a text is represented by the orientation of the

†This study was issued originally as Section XXIII of *Scientific Report ISR-9*, August 1965.

313

concept vector in the concept space (that is, the matching process is assumed independent of the magnitude of the concept vector). Retrieval, therefore, consists in locating the set of documents having an orientation (angular position) similar to that of the request image.

14-2 REQUEST FORMULATION

The process of request formulation is complex and depends on particular attributes of the requestor, such as his knowledge of the contents of the store, his knowledge of the indexing and searching processes of the system, his familiarity with the topic matter being searched, his personal preferences as to vocabulary and style, and so on. In effect, the user must make a statistical decision based on his personal experience as to which request is most likely to produce results useful to him. Clearly the a priori likelihood of a request satisfying the user's needs varies over a wide range for any given retrieval system. For example, a user who needs to know whether a particular document is contained in the store can formulate a request which will satisfy this need with perfect certainty: for example, by submitting a request identical with the document in question. At the other end of the spectrum is the user who needs information on a topic unfamiliar to him. Clearly the probability of his being able to formulate a request which will retrieve the best set of documents satisfying his information needs is very small.

Operationally then, information requests submitted to a retrieval system vary over a wide spectrum of a priori likelihood of satisfying the user's needs. It is then pertinent to consider techniques of reducing this variance in two distinct contexts. First, in an operational sense one would like to process requests which are optimized with respect to the cost of retrieval, the cost of optimization, and the value of the information to the user. Second, in the evaluation of information retrieval systems, it is desirable to isolate the effect of the indexing process on retrieval performance from the effects due to request formulation. Thus the gross results of retrieval experiments carried out with a sample set of requests can be used to evaluate the indexing discipline with respect to that particular sample of requests. If it were possible, however, to define an optimal request corresponding to any given request (for some fixed index transformation), retrieval results based on optimal requests would provide a much clearer evaluation of the power of the indexing technique, since performance variations due to request malformation would be eliminated.

14-3 REQUEST OPTIMIZATION

To define an optimal request, it is necessary to operate with an explicit formulation of the request-document matching process. In accordance with the system model outlined above, an appropriate matching function is the cosine correlation of the request image and the set of document images in the store. The cosine correlation of two vectors is defined by

$$\rho(\mathbf{A}, \mathbf{B}) = \frac{\mathbf{A} \cdot \mathbf{B}}{|\mathbf{A}||\mathbf{B}|} = \cos(\mathbf{A}, \mathbf{B})$$

Since the vector images produced by the index transformation are limited to having nonnegative concept weights, this correlation induces a ranking on elements of the store, equivalent to their angular distance from the request vector (that is, $0 \leq \rho \leq 1$ corresponds to an angular separation of from 90 to 0 degrees).

Corresponding to any retrieval request $\mathbf{Q}$ we assume the existence of a subset D_R ($D_R \subset D$) of the set of documents contained in the store D. This set is the set of documents relevant to the request $\mathbf{Q}$ and must be specified outside the context of the retrieval system.

Having defined D_R, an *ideal* request may be defined as one which induces a ranking on the elements of D such that all members of D_R are ranked higher (that is, have a higher correlation) than all other elements of D.

Since relevance is a subjective attribute of a given request-document set pair determined in theory by the individual requester, there is no certainty that an ideal request (as defined above) in fact exists for a given request. In such a case one might say that the indexing is not defined from the point of view of the particular user, since it does not allow distinctions equivalent to those he can make. This of course will be the norm rather than the exception, since the indexing process is designed to reduce rather than preserve information. For this reason an unambiguous, optimal request is defined as a function of D_R, D, and the index transformation, which is unique for every nonempty unique subset D_R of D.

An *optimal* request corresponding to a given subset D_R of a store D, under an index transformation T, is that request which maximizes the difference between the mean of the correlations of the relevant documents (members of D_R) and the mean of the correlations of the nonrelevant documents (members of D not in D_R).

In mathematical terms the *optimal* request vector $\mathbf{Q}_0$ corresponding to a set $D_R \subset D$ is defined as that vector $\mathbf{Q}$ for which

$$C = \frac{1}{n_0} \sum_{D_i \in D_R} \rho(\mathbf{Q}, \mathbf{D}_i) - \frac{1}{n - n_0} \sum_{D_i \notin D_R} \rho(\mathbf{Q}, \mathbf{D}_i)$$

is maximum where $n_0 = n(D_R)$ the number of elements in D_R, and $n = n(D)$ the total number of elements in the store.

If we wish to consider only requests having nonnegative components (this corresponds to the assumption made originally about index images in the system under consideration), then the problem is modified to maximizing C subject to $\mathbf{Q}_i \geq 0$.

Substituting for $\rho(\mathbf{Q}, \mathbf{D}_i)$ and using vector notation results in

$$C = \frac{1}{n_0} \left(\frac{\mathbf{Q}}{|\mathbf{Q}|} \right) \cdot \sum_{D_i \in D_R} \frac{\mathbf{D}_i}{|\mathbf{D}_i|} - \frac{1}{n - n_0} \left(\frac{\mathbf{Q}}{|\mathbf{Q}|} \right) \cdot \sum_{D_i \notin D_R} \frac{\mathbf{D}_i}{|\mathbf{D}_i|},$$

or

$$C = \frac{\mathbf{Q}}{|\mathbf{Q}|} \cdot \left[\frac{1}{n_0} \sum_{D_i \in D_R} \frac{\mathbf{D}_i}{|\mathbf{D}_i|} - \frac{1}{n - n_0} \sum_{D_i \notin D_R} \frac{\mathbf{D}_i}{|\mathbf{D}_i|} \right].$$

Since this is equivalent to $C = \mathbf{Q}^* \cdot \mathbf{A}$, where $\mathbf{Q}^*$ is a unit vector, clearly $Q_{\mathrm{opt}} = k\mathbf{A}$ (k being an arbitrary scalar), or

$$\mathbf{Q}_{\mathrm{opt}} = \frac{1}{n_0} \sum_{D_i \in D_R} \frac{\mathbf{D}_i}{|\mathbf{D}_i|} - \frac{1}{n - n_0} \sum_{D_i \notin D_R} \frac{\mathbf{D}_i}{|\mathbf{D}_i|}.$$

Further, a simple proof shows that C is maximized subject to $\mathbf{Q}_i \geq 0$ (where i ranges over all coordinates of $\mathbf{Q}$) for the vector

$$\mathbf{Q}'_{\mathrm{opt}_i} = \begin{cases} \mathbf{Q}_{\mathrm{opt}_i}, & \text{for } Q_{\mathrm{opt}_i} \geq 0, \\ 0, & \text{for } Q_{\mathrm{opt}_i} < 0. \end{cases}$$

Hence, under the assumptions made, an unambiguous optimal (for the criterion stated) query exists corresponding to any nonempty subset D_R of D. In evaluating the effectiveness of automatic information retrieval systems, this formulation of an optimal request provides the ability to isolate the effects of indexing from variances due to request formulation. In effect, an optimal request measures the ability of the indexing transformation to differentiate a particular set of documents from all the others in the store, where the particular set in question is assumed to have some intrinsic association, specified independently of the system; that is, the set consists of the documents judged to be relevant to some particular topic.

14-4 RELEVANCE FEEDBACK

The formulation of the optimal query corresponding to a particular set of documents has no direct implication on operational information retrieval, since the set of documents in question is the object of the retrieval search. Thus there is no a priori way to make an optimal request, since having the ability to do so would eliminate the need for retrieval. This kind of circularity suggests a strong analogy to feedback control theory. Thus if we consider a sequence of retrieval operations starting with an initial query $\mathbf{Q}_0$, which is then modified on the basis of the output produced by the retrieval system (using $\mathbf{Q}_0$ as input) in such a way that the modified query $\mathbf{Q}_1$ is closer to the optimal query for this user, a precise analogy to a sequential feedback system can be drawn. Let the user specify which of the retrieved documents (resulting from the search using $\mathbf{Q}_0$) are relevant and which are not. This information constitutes an error signal to the retrieval system. On the basis of the error and the original input, it is then possible to produce a modified query (new command input) such that the retrieval output will be closer to what the user desires, or such that the modified query will in effect be closer to the optimal query for this user's needs. The effectiveness of this process will depend on how good the initial query is and on how fast the process of iteration converges to the optimal request.

On the basis of the formulation of request optimality, we then seek a procedure for using the relevance feedback from an initial retrieval operation to produce an improved query. Let Q_0 be the original retrieval request, and let the results of the retrieval operation be a list in correlation order of the documents whose images are most closely related to Q_0. The user examines this list and specifies which of the documents in the list are relevant and which are not. Since the modification is to be based only on a sample of the relevant documents (assuming that some are missing from the retrieved list associated with Q_0), the modified request will be formed by adding to the original query Q_0 an optimal query vector based on the feedback information. The resultant vector (the new query) should thus be a better approximation to the optimal query than Q_0, and should therefore produce better retrieval when resubmitted.

Hence we seek a relation of the form

$$Q_1 = f(Q_0, R, S),$$

where Q_0 is the original query, R is the subset of the retrieved set which the user deems relevant, and S is the subset of the retrieved set (based on Q_0) which the user deems nonrelevant. The form suggested immediately by the above is

$$Q_1 = Q_0 + \frac{1}{n_1} \sum_{i=1}^{n_1} R_1 - \frac{1}{n_2} \sum_{i=1}^{n_2} S_i,$$

where $n_1 = n(R)$, $n_2 = (S)$, $R = \{R_1, R_2, \ldots, R_{n_1}\}$, $S = \{S_1, S_2, \ldots, S_{n_2}\}$, and all vectors are unit vectors. Thus Q_1 is the vector sum of the original query vector plus the optimal vector to differentiate the members of the set R from those of the set S. In other words, Q_1 is the vector sum of Q_0 plus the optimal vector for the subset of the store for which the user has provided relevance information.

The above equation may be rewritten in the form

$$Q_1 = n_1 n_2 Q_0 + n_2 \sum_{R_i \in R} R_i - n_1 \sum_{S_i \in S} S_i.$$

Q_1 may be restricted to having nonnegative components by setting

$$Q'_{1_i} = \begin{cases} Q_{1_i}, & \text{for } Q_{1_i} \geq 0, \\ 0 & \text{for } Q_{1_i} < 0. \end{cases}$$

The above represents the basic relation for request modification using relevance feedback. This relation can be modified in various ways by imposing additional constraints. For example, the weighting of the original query (Q_0) could be a function of the amount of feedback, such that with large amounts of feedback the original query has less effect on the resultant than with small amounts of feedback. Another constraint, for example, might be to regulate the number of nonzero components of the modified query on the basis of the degree of overlap of a component among the relevant set which is fed back. Clearly there are a large number of variations to this basic relation which might be tried.

The modification process described is of course amenable to iteration and hence can be written in the general form

$$\mathbf{Q}_{i+1} = f(\mathbf{Q}_i, R_i, S_i),$$

where $\mathbf{Q}_i$ is the ith query of a sequence, and R_i and S_i are the relevant and nonrelevant subsets, respectively, identified in response to retrieval with query $\mathbf{Q}_i$. It is expected that the rate of convergence of such a sequence to a near optimal query will be rapid enough to make the process economical; however, this must be investigated experimentally. In any case, the convergence rate can be estimated by the user, since it is reflected in the stability of the retrieved output.

The user's original query serves to identify a region in the index space which should contain relevant documents. Since he has no detailed knowledge about the characteristics of the document images in the store, it is unlikely that the vector image of his query is located optimally. By identifying relevant documents in the region, the user provides the system with sufficient information to attempt to produce a modified query which is positioned centrally with respect to the relevant documents, while maintaining maximum distance from the nonrelevant documents. This is possible, however, only insofar as the index images of the relevant set are differentiable from those of the nonrelevant set.

In a theoretical framework, the request optimization process focuses on the power of the index transformation to distinguish sets of associated documents within the store by eliminating variances due to particular query formulations. In an operating context, relevance feedback provides a technique whereby the system user can extract the full power of the index transformation to his retrieval problem, at the cost of iterating the search (possibly on a sample collection from a large store).

14-5   INITIAL EXPERIMENTAL RESULTS

To test the effectiveness of the technique of relevance feedback as outlined above, a few experiments have been conducted using the SMART retrieval system. A set of 17 requests available with the SMART system was used as a test sample. For each request the output resulting from a cosine correlation run using the SMART thesaurus (version 2) was examined. From the initial portion of the retrieved list (source documents having high correlations), two sets of documents were selected, one containing relevant documents and one containing nonrelevant documents. The vector images of the documents (given by the SMART thesaurus) together with the image of the request were used as input to a FORTRAN program used to produce a modified vector suitable for input to SMART. The first step of the request modification algorithm was applied directly to the initial query to produce

$$\mathbf{Q}_1 = n_1 n_2 \mathbf{Q}_0 + n_2 \sum_{i=1}^{n_1} \mathbf{R}_i - n_1 \sum_{i=1}^{n_2} \mathbf{S}_i,$$

where $\mathbf{R}_i (i = 1, n_1)$ constituted the relevant subset identified and $\mathbf{S}_i (i = 1, n_2)$ the nonrelevant subset (the $\mathbf{R}_i$'s and $\mathbf{S}_i$'s being normalized vector images of the documents in question under the index transformation). Since the SMART system is designed to operate on document and query images having nonnegative components only, the vector $\mathbf{Q}_1$ was modified by setting

$$\mathbf{Q}'_{1_i} = \begin{cases} \mathbf{Q}_{1_i}, & \text{for } \mathbf{Q}_{1_i} \geq 0, \\ 0, & \text{for } \mathbf{Q}_{1_i} < 0. \end{cases}$$

A further modification was introduced to keep the modified query from becoming too specialized to the relevant set which was fed back. This modification was incorporated because relatively small amounts of feedback were to be tested. Specifically, a nonzero component was allowed in the resultant query image if and only if it occurred in $\mathbf{Q}_1$ and was either (1) in $\mathbf{Q}_0$ or (2) occurred in at least $n_1/2$ of the images of the relevant set, and in more relevant vectors than nonrelevant vectors.

The amount of feedback, that is, the number of relevant and nonrelevant documents returned varied from request to request, the two sets being kept roughly equivalent. In some cases, when only a few relevant documents were available for a particular request, only the relevant documents were identified to see what would happen under these circumstances. Tables 14-1, 14-2, and 14-3 show the results of one iteration of the search request modification process for three different queries. In the first two cases there is substantial improvement in both the recall and precision evaluation measures (shown for the original and modified query), while in the third case only the precision measure is increased. It is important to note that while the query modification process improves the performance with respect to the relevant documents identified by the user, as one would expect, it also in general improves performance

Table 14-1(a)

QUERY PROCESSING USING RELEVANCE FEEDBACK

(Retrieval results using original query "I–R Indexing"
including user feedback)

Document Rank	Document Number	Correlation	User Feedback
1	167	0.46	not relevant
2	166	0.43	not relevant
3	188	0.40	–
4	221	0.38	relevant
5	314	0.38	–
6	75	0.37	–
7	79	0.36	relevant

Table 14-1(b)

QUERY PROCESSING USING RELEVANCE FEEDBACK

(Comparison of search results using original
and modified queries)

RETRIEVAL RESULTS USING ORIGINAL QUERY			RESULTS USING QUERY MODIFIED BY USER FEEDBACK		
Ranks of Relevant Documents	*Document Number*	*Correlation*	*Ranks of Relevant Documents*	*Document Number*	*Correlation*
4	221	0.38	1	79	0.54
7	79	0.36	2	221	0.47
13	3	0.26	4	3	0.33
15	80	0.26	5	126	0.31
17	48	0.25	6	80	0.30
23	126	0.21	25	48	0.17

Normalized Recall 0.976	Normalized Recall 0.991
Normalized Precision 0.728	Normalized Precision 0.928

with respect to other relevant documents. This is illustrated in Figs. 14-1 and 14-2, which show precision versus recall averaged over a sample of 17 search requests. Figure 14-1 is the result of averaging the interpolated precision for each request at

Table 14-2(a)

QUERY PROCESSING USING RELEVANCE FEEDBACK

(Retrieval results using original query for "Pattern Recognition"
including user feedback)

Document Rank	*Document Number*	*Correlation*	*User Feedback*
1	351	0.65	relevant
2	353	0.42	relevant
3	350	0.41	relevant
4	163	0.36	–
5	82	0.35	–
6	1	0.32	–
7	208	0.27	not relevant
8	225	0.25	not relevant
9	54	0.24	–
10	335	0.21	not relevant

recall values of $0.1k$, for integral values of k from 1 to 10. Figure 14-2 is a precision versus recall curve for the same set of 17 queries produced in a different way. This plot is obtained by choosing a cutoff after m consecutive nonrelevant documents

Table 14-2(b)

QUERY PROCESSING USING RELEVANCE FEEDBACK

(Comparison of search results using original
and modified queries)

RETRIEVAL RESULTS USING ORIGINAL QUERY			RESULTS USING QUERY MODIFIED BY USER FEEDBACK		
Ranks of Relevant Documents	*Document Number*	*Correlation*	*Ranks of Relevant Documents*	*Document Number*	*Correlation*
1	351	0.65	1	351	0.66
2	353	0.42	2	350	0.60
3	350	0.41	3	353	0.55
4	163	0.36	5	163	0.37
6	1	0.32	6	1	0.32
9	54	0.24	7	54	0.29
26	205	0.17	11	314	0.23
27	224	0.17	16	205	0.19
33	314	0.16	17	39	0.19
34	39	0.12	30	224	0.16

Normalized Recall 0.972   Normalized Recall 0.989
Normalized Precision 0.864   Normalized Precision 0.923

Table 14-3(a)

QUERY PROCESSING USING RELEVANCE FEEDBACK

(Retrieval results using original query "Analog-Digital"
including relevance feedback)

Document Rank	*Document Number*	*Correlation*	*User Feedback*
1	157	0.42	relevant
2	165	0.40	relevant
3	362	0.39	not relevant
4	296	0.37	relevant
5	308	0.37	not relevant
6	307	0.37	not relevant
7	226	0.36	–
8	88	0.36	–

Table 14-3(b)

QUERY PROCESSING USING RELEVANCE FEEDBACK

(Comparison of search results using original
and modified queries)

RETRIEVAL RESULTS USING ORIGINAL QUERY			RESULTS USING QUERY MODIFIED BY USER FEEDBACK		
Ranks of Relevant Documents	*Document Number*	*Correlation*	*Ranks of Relevant Documents*	*Document Number*	*Correlation*
1	157	0.42	1	296	0.58
2	165	0.40	2	157	0.56
4	296	0.37	3	165	0.53
19	42	0.27	4	42	0.42
21	46	0.26	40	46	0.20

Normalized Recall 0.984
Normalized Precision 0.870

Normalized Recall 0.983
Normalized Precision 0.918

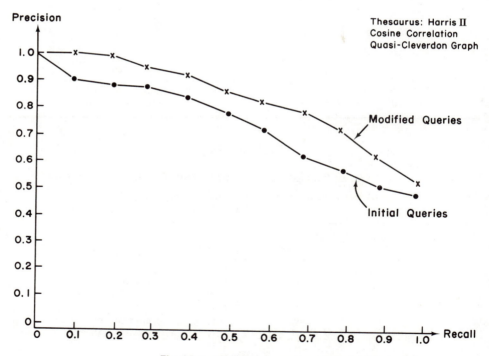

Fig. 14-1 Precision versus recall for initial queries and queries
modified by relevance feedback (averaged over 17 search requests).

(*m* ranging from 1 to 20), and averaging the precision and recall values for each request at each cutoff point to get a single average point which is plotted.

The general conclusion which can be tentatively drawn at present is that relevance feedback provides a powerful tool for improving performance at the cost of iteration of a request through the system.

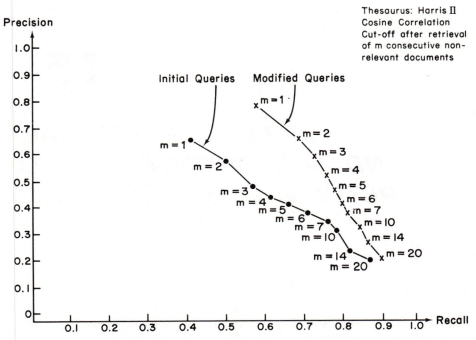

Fig. 14-2 Precision versus recall for initial queries and queries modified by relevance feedback (averaged over 17 search requests).

Various methods can be used in an attempt to have the customer participate in the information search process. These procedures range from relatively simple dictionary printout routines, where a display of dictionary excerpts serves as an aid in rephrasing poorly worded search requests, to more sophisticated methods in which the reformulation of the requests is performed automatically based on feedback information obtained from the user population. Such an automatic "relevance feedback" process is described in the present study, and evaluation results are included for document collections in several subject fields.

15

RELEVANCE FEEDBACK AND THE OPTIMIZATION OF RETRIEVAL EFFECTIVENESS†

G. SALTON

15-1 RELEVANCE FEEDBACK

The *relevance feedback* operation is an automatic process for the modification of search requests based on relevance assessments provided by the user population for previously retrieved documents. The process is particularly well suited to a time-sharing computer organization and to the simple console equipment likely to be available to the customers, since it requires only a minimum of interaction with the user and places most of the burden on internally stored routines. Specifically, an initial search is first performed for each request received, and a small amount of output, consisting of some of the highest-scoring documents, is presented to the user. Some of the retrieved output is then examined by the user who identifies each document as being either relevant (R) or not relevant (N) to his purpose. These relevance judgments are later returned to the system and used automatically to adjust the initial search request in such a way that query terms or concepts present in the relevant documents are promoted (by increasing their weight), whereas

†An earlier version of this study was included in *Mechanized Information Storage, Retrieval and Dissemination*, K. Samuelson, ed., North-Holland Publishing Co., Amsterdam 1968. It was also issued as Section V in *Scientific Report ISR-12*, June 1967.

terms occurring in the documents designated as nonrelevant are similarly demoted [1,] [2,] [3]. This process produces an altered search request which may be expected to exhibit greater similarity with the relevant document subset and greater dissimilarity with the nonrelevant set.

The altered request can be submitted next to the system, and a second search can be performed using the new request formulation. If the system performs as expected, additional relevant material may then be retrieved, or in any case, the relevant items may produce higher correlations with the altered request than with the original. The newly retrieved items can be examined again by the user, and new relevance assessments can be used to obtain a second reformulation of the request. This process can be continued over several iterations, until such time as the user is satisfied with the results obtained.

The actual method used for the request alteration consists in picking, at each point, that request formulation which maximizes the difference in request-document correlation between relevant and nonrelevant document subsets. Specifically, if D_R is the nonempty document subset designated as relevant, then an optimal query is the one which provides the maximum discrimination of the subset D_R from the rest of the collection $(D - D_R)$. More formally, if $\rho(\mathbf{q}, \mathbf{d})$ is the distance function (correlation method) used in the matching process between query $\mathbf{q}$ and document $\mathbf{d}$, then the optimal query $\mathbf{q}_0$ may be defined as that query which maximizes the function

$$F = \sum_{\mathbf{d}^{(i)} \in D_R} \bar{\rho}[\mathbf{q}, \mathbf{d}^{(i)}] - \sum_{\mathbf{d}^{(i)} \notin D_R} \bar{\rho}[\mathbf{q}, \mathbf{d}^{(i)}],$$

where $\bar{\rho}$ is the average distance function, and decreasing distance implies stronger query-document correlation [2].

In practice, the preceding equation is of no immediate use, even assuming that the optimal query $\mathbf{q}_0$ can be determined as a function of D and D_R, since knowledge of the set D_R (the relevant document subset) obviates the need for retrieval. Instead of producing the optimal query $\mathbf{q}_0$ directly, it is then necessary to generate a series of approximations to $\mathbf{q}_0$, starting with some initial query which identifies a part of the set D_R. As new relevant documents are identified, the subset of known relevant documents approaches D_R, and the sequence of modified queries comes close to $\mathbf{q}_0$. One may hope that in practice only a few iterations will suffice for the average user; in any case, the rate of convergence is reflected in the stability of the retrieved set.

The query modification algorithm, which produces an optimal query to differentiate the *partial* set of relevant documents identified by the user from the remaining documents, may be written in the form:

$$\mathbf{q}_{i+1} = n_1 n_2 \mathbf{q}_i + n_2 \sum_{i=1}^{n_1} \frac{\mathbf{r}_i}{|\mathbf{r}_i|} - n_1 \sum_{i=1}^{n_2} \frac{\mathbf{s}_i}{|\mathbf{s}_i|} \tag{1}$$

where $\mathbf{q}_i$ is the *i*th query of the sequence, $R = \{\mathbf{r}_1, \mathbf{r}_2, \ldots, \mathbf{r}_{n_1}\}$ is the set of relevant documents retrieved in response to query $\mathbf{q}_i$, and $S = \{\mathbf{s}_1, \mathbf{s}_2, \ldots, \mathbf{s}_{n_2}\}$ is the set of nonrelevant document vectors retrieved in response to $\mathbf{q}_i$ [2]. The specification of the sets R and S constitute the feedback from the user after the ith iteration of the process.

The programmed experimental feedback system uses a somewhat more general modification algorithm which allows additional variations in several parameters, as follows:

$$\mathbf{q}_{i+1} = \alpha \mathbf{q}_i + \beta \mathbf{q} + \gamma \sum_{i=1}^{n_1} \mathbf{c}_i \mathbf{r}_i + \delta \sum_{i=1}^{n_2} \mathbf{c}_i \mathbf{s}_i, \qquad (2)$$

where α, β, γ, and δ are variable weighting parameters; $\mathbf{q}$ is the initial query before any alteration; $\mathbf{c}_i$ is either set equal to 1 for all i, or to the magnitude of the correlation coefficient between query $\mathbf{q}$ and document $\mathbf{d}^{(i)}$, depending on the setting of an additional variable parameter. The first two terms on the right-hand side of equation (2) permit the generation of $\mathbf{q}_{i+1}$ either from $\mathbf{q}_i$ or from $\mathbf{q}$, and the parameters $\mathbf{c}_i$ present in the last two terms are used to alter more heavily concepts which are derived from relevant documents exhibiting a high correlation with the query than others included in documents which are further removed from the original query.

Evaluation results for the feedback procedure are given in the next section.

15-2 FEEDBACK EVALUATION

An example of the request modification process is shown in Table 15-1 for request Q147 processed against a collection of 200 documents in aerodynamics. The concept numbers and weights derived for the original request by the machine process are given in Table 15-1(a). Following a search with the original request, the user identifies document no. 94 as relevant. The altered request produced by the addition of new terms from document 94 is shown in Table 15-1(b). Several of the original concepts are reinforced in the process (for example, concept 2558), while many others appear for the first time in Table 15-1(b). When this altered request is processed, the user next identifies as relevant documents 94, 90, and 95, thereby producing a new altered query represented in Table 15-1(c). When this last query is used, the set of relevant documents increases to four, consisting of documents 95, 94, 91, and 90. This gener-

Table 15-1(a)

REQUEST MODIFICATION PROCESS

(Initial query vector Q_0 for query Q147)

Concept Numbers	Weights	Concept Numbers	Weights	Concept Numbers	Weights	Concept Numbers	Weights
1282	12	1307	12	1534	12	1597	12
1626	12	2308	12	2450	12	2547	12
2552	12	2558	12	2576	12		

Table 15-1(b)

REQUEST MODIFICATION PROCESS

(Query vector Q_1 after identification of relevant document no. 94)

Concept Numbers	Weights	Concept Numbers	Weights	Concept Numbers	Weights	Concept Numbers	Weights
60	12	224	12	358	12	411	12
633	12	639	12	1010	12	1109	12
1263	12	1282	12	1307	12	1308	12
1534	12	1545	48	1597	12	1626	12
1662	12	1663	12	1665	24	1794	12
1894	12	1915	12	1930	24	1936	12
1950	12	1981	12	1986	24	2011	48
2034	12	2068	36	2100	12	2163	12
2173	12	2209	12	2226	12	2278	48
2300	12	2308	12	2313	12	2335	24
2346	84	2363	48	2364	24	2370	12
2380	24	2388	12	2390	24	2393	12
2394	12	2411	36	2422	12	2450	12
2457	12	2473	12	2479	60	2496	24
2506	24	2507	12	2510	24	2521	12
2530	24	2536	24	2545	48	2547	36
2552	12	2577	48	2558	48	2566	24
2567	12	2571	60	2575	12	2576	48
2585	12	2586	48	2589	48	2594	24
2596	12	2597	12	2601	48	2603	60
2607	72	2619	72	2621	12	2622	24
2624	24	2626	120	2627	24		

ates the third modification of the original query, reproduced in Table 15-1(d). A comparison of Table 15-1(a) to Table 15-1(d) reveals a considerable increase in the number of concepts used, as well as a large increase in the concept weights.

The recall-precision plot produced by the feedback process for query Q147 is shown in Fig. 15-1 for the original query (represented by *F*'s and asterisks), as well as for the three subsequent iterations (1's and single hyphens, 2's and double hyphens, and 3's and triple hyphens). It is seen in Fig. 15-1 how the recall and precision values improve from one iteration to the next, until a near perfect output is produced for the last iteration.

This same phenomenon can be observed in more detail in the tables of Fig. 15-2, which contain a complete record of the process for query Q147. For each of the four iterations, an output ranking is given for the whole document collection. The documents are listed in decreasing correlation order together with the respective correlation coefficients, as well as recall and precision figures. The relevant document set, determined manually outside of the system, consists of documents 90, 91, 93, 94, and 95. For the original query, these relevant documents, identified by an *R* in Fig.

Table 15-1(c)

REQUEST MODIFICATION PROCESS

(Query vector Q_2 after identification
of relevant documents 94, 90, and 95)

Concept Numbers	Weights	Concept Numbers	Weights	Concept Numbers	Weights	Concept Numbers	Weights
60	36	115	24	157	24	168	24
224	36	290	24	358	60	411	36
522	24	633	36	639	36	826	24
1010	36	1109	36	1200	24	1203	24
1206	24	1218	48	1221	48	1259	24
1263	36	1282	12	1307	12	1308	36
1534	12	1545	144	1597	36	1626	12
1644	48	1662	60	1663	60	1665	72
1750	24	1763	72	1765	24	1794	36
1818	72	1836	24	1888	24	1894	36
1915	36	1930	72	1936	36	1950	36
1981	36	1986	72	2011	144	2018	48
2034	36	2068	108	2100	36	2134	48
2163	26	2171	24	2173	60	2191	48
2192	24	2198	24	2209	36	2220	96
2224	72	2226	36	2278	240	2283	24
2300	108	2308	12	2313	36	2320	24
2335	72	2337	48	2346	252	2363	144
2364	72	2370	36	2380	72	2388	36
2390	72	2393	36	2394	36	2396	24
2399	96	2409	24	2410	24	2411	108
2422	36	2444	48	2450	36	2457	60
2465	24	2473	36	2477	24	2479	180
2496	192	2498	24	2501	24	2506	96
2507	84	2510	72	2514	24	2519	24
2521	36	2528	24	2530	72	2536	72
2542	48	2545	144	2547	84	2552	12
2557	216	2558	168	2566	96	2567	60
2571	276	2575	84	2576	144	2580	24
2581	24	2585	60	2586	168	2589	240
2594	96	2595	24	2596	60	2597	60
2599	96	2601	168	2603	228	2607	288
2611	48	2619	240	2621	36	2622	120
2623	96	2624	96	2626	408	2627	192

15-2, receive ranks of 22, 76, 21, 14, and 41, respectively, for the sample collection of 200 documents.

The user is now assumed to look at the top 15 documents retrieved, thereby identifying document 94 with rank 14 as relevant. This leads to the first modification with improved rankings of the relevant set. The top 15 now include three relevant items: 94, 90, and 95 with ranks 1, 7, and 10, respectively. A second iteration leads to

Table 15-1(d)

REQUEST MODIFICATION PROCESS

(Query vector Q_3 after identification
of relevant documents 95, 94, 91 and 90)

Concept Numbers	Weights	Concept Numbers	Weights	Concept Numbers	Weights	Concept Numbers	Weights
60	72	115	60	157	60	168	60
224	72	290	60	358	168	411	72
522	60	633	72	639	72	826	60
852	36	1010	72	1109	72	1200	60
1203	60	1206	60	1218	120	1221	120
1259	60	1263	72	1282	12	1307	12
1308	72	1534	12	1545	288	1558	36
1579	108	1597	72	1626	12	1631	36
1644	120	1656	36	1662	132	1663	132
1665	144	1750	60	1763	180	1765	60
1794	72	1818	252	1836	60	1888	60
1894	72	1915	72	1930	144	1936	72
1950	72	1981	72	1986	144	2011	288
2018	120	2034	72	2068	216	2094	72
2100	72	2133	36	2134	120	2163	72
2171	60	2173	132	2187	36	2191	120
2192	60	2198	60	2209	72	2220	312
2224	216	2226	72	2241	36	2278	564
2283	60	2300	288	2308	12	2313	72
2320	60	2335	144	2337	120	2346	504
2363	288	2364	144	2370	72	2378	72
2380	144	2388	72	2390	144	2393	72
2394	72	2396	60	2399	240	2409	60
2410	60	2411	216	2422	72	2423	36
2444	120	2450	72	2457	132	2465	60
2467	36	2473	72	2477	60	2479	360
2496	444	2498	60	2501	60	2504	72
2506	204	2507	228	2510	144	2514	60
2519	60	2521	72	2528	60	2530	144
2536	144	2542	120	2545	288	2547	156
2552	12	2557	540	2558	348	2566	240
2567	132	2571	636	2575	192	2576	324
2580	60	2581	60	2585	132	2586	384
2589	600	2594	240	2595	60	2596	132
2597	132	2599	240	2601	348	2603	480
2607	648	2608	36	2611	156	2619	492
2621	72	2622	264	2623	240	2624	204
2626	840	2627	480				

further improvements in the rankings of the relevant set and to the addition of relevant document 91 to the top 15. This generates the last query form, which in turn produces the near perfect ranking of the relevant document set (ranks 1, 2, 3, 5, and 11).

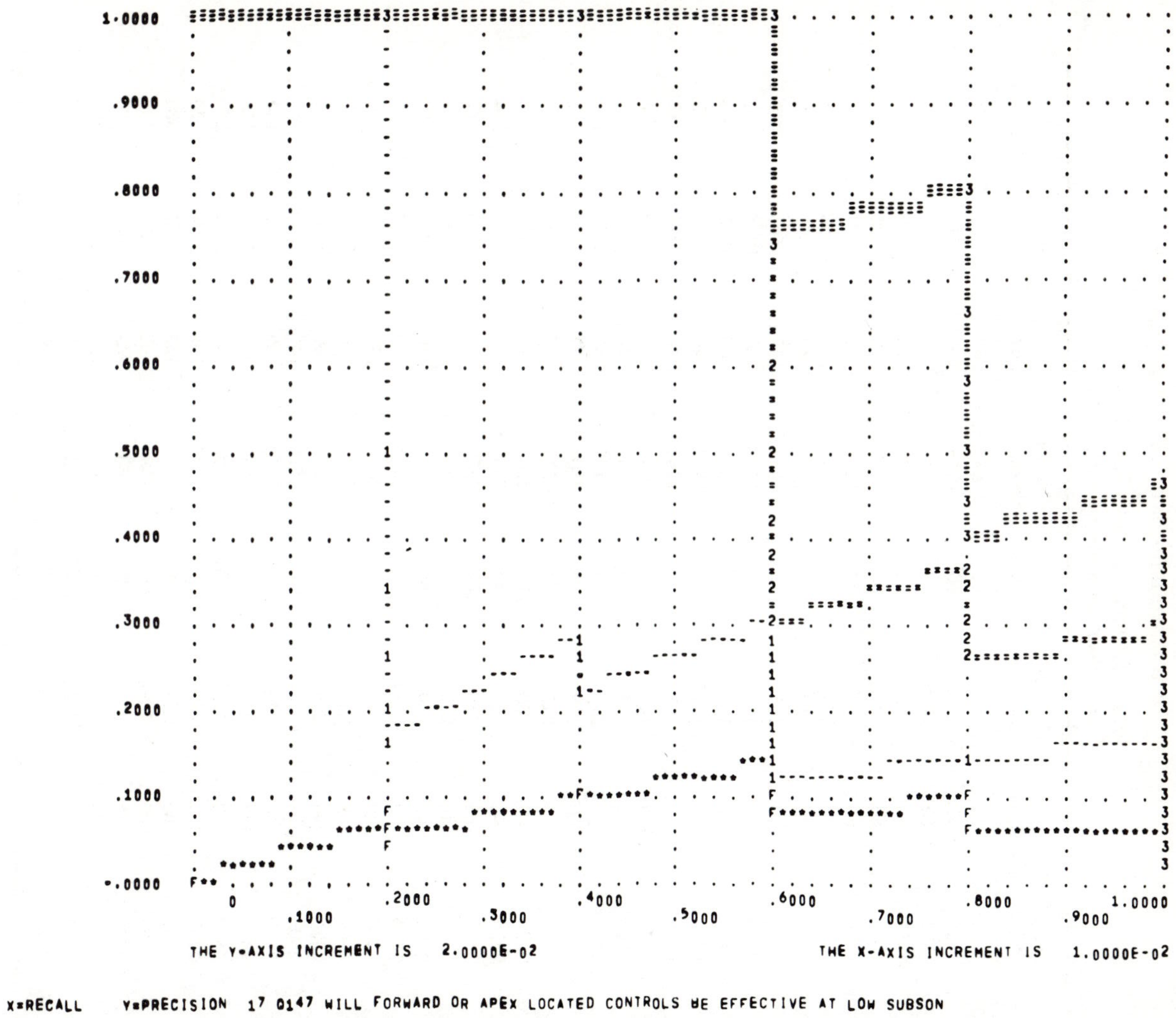

X=RECALL   Y=PRECISION 17 Q147 WILL FORWARD OR APEX LOCATED CONTROLS BE EFFECTIVE AT LOW SUBSON

THE Y-AXIS INCREMENT IS   2.0000E-02   THE X-AXIS INCREMENT IS   1.0000E-02

Fig. 15-1   Recall-precision plot for query Q147 (original query and three alterations).

17 Q147 WILL FORWARD OR APEX LOCATED CONTROLS BE EFFECTIVE AT LOW SUBSON

INITIAL SEARCH AND 3 FEEDBACK ITERS. THE 5 RELEVANT DOCUMENTS BEING 90 91 93 94 95

	INITIAL		FEEDBACK ITERATIONS 1		2		3		RECALL				PRECISION			
RANK	DOC	CORR	DOC	CORR	DOC	CORR	DOC	CORR	INIT	1	2	3	INIT	1	2	3
1	109	.2224	94R	.9914	94R	.9348	94R	.8954	0	.2000	.2000	.2000	0	1.0000	1.0000	1.0000
2	60	.1928	81	.4909	95R	.6190	95R	.6675	0	.2000	.4000	.4000	0	.5000	1.0000	1.0000
3	121	.1570	195	.4802	90R	.5449	90R	.5881	0	.2000	.6000	.6000	0	.3333	1.0000	1.0000
4	192	.1388	123	.4233	195	.5023	195	.4929	0	.2000	.6000	.6000	0	2500	.7500	.7500
5	193	.1359	80	.4144	81	.4494	91R	.4632	0	.2000	.6000	.8000	0	.2000	.6000	.8000
6	119	.1226	114	.3781	80	.3969	81	.4199	0	.2000	.6000	.8000	0	.1667	.5000	.6667
7	82	.1212	90R	.3742	114	.3850	80	.3808	0	.4000	.6000	.8000	0	.2857	.4286	.5714
8	24	.1177	193	.3685	193	.3795	111	.3787	0	.4000	.6000	.8000	0	.2500	.3750	.5000
9	86	.1151	122	.3394	123	.3778	114	.3758	0	.4000	.6000	.8000	0	.2222	.3333	.4444
10	123	.1149	95R	.3371	111	.3776	193	.3735	0	.6000	.6000	.8000	0	.3000	.3000	.4000
11	100	.1115	111	.3309	91R	.3557	93R	.3541	0	.6000	.8000	1.0000	0	.2727	.3636	.4545
12	146	.1044	64	.3201	109	.3378	123	.3538	0	.6000	.8000	1.0000	0	.2500	.3333	.4167
13	18	.0992	102	.3181	159	.3348	192	.3369	0	.6000	.8000	1.0000	0	.2308	.3077	.3846
14	94R	.0992	109	.3177	103	.3314	109	.3368	.2000	.6000	.8000	1.0000	.0714	.2143	.2857	.3571
15	167	.0930	82	.3077	192	.3281	159	.3329	.2000	.6000	.8000	1.0000	.0667	.2000	.2667	.3333
16	125	.0906	103	.3033	82	.3260	155	.3287	.2000	.6000	.8000	1.0000	.0625	.1875	.2500	.3125
17	163	.0900	78	.2936	93R	.3143	103	.3262	.2000	.6000	1.0000	1.0000	.0588	.1765	.2941	.2941
18	114	.0848	125	.2933	78	.3104	82	.3196	.2000	.6000	1.0000	1.0000	.0556	.1667	.2778	.2778
19	65	.0848	20	.2851	172	.3069	78	.3014	.2000	.6000	1.0000	1.0000	.0526	.1579	.2632	.2632
20	177	.0844	192	.2736	102	.2992	110	.2891	.2000	.6000	1.0000	1.0000	.0500	.1500	.2500	.2500
21	93R	.0836	124	.2714	64	.2986	122	.2884	.4000	.6000	1.0000	1.0000	.0952	.1429	.2381	.2381
22	90R	.0836	159	.2711	155	.2969	153	.2874	.6000	.6000	1.0000	1.0000	.1364	.1364	.2273	.2273
23	19	.0811	194	.2709	110	.2894	11	.2874	.6000	.6000	1.0000	1.0000	.1304	.1304	.2174	.2174
24	153	.0794	196	.2659	11	.2878	76	.2859	.6000	.6000	1.0000	1.0000	.1250	.1250	.2083	.2083
25	181	.0778	86	.2634	153	.2822	64	.2820	.6000	.6000	1.0000	1.0000	.1200	.1200	.2000	.2000
26	58	.0775	63	.2578	76	.2813	92	.2818	.6000	.6000	1.0000	1.0000	.1154	.1154	.1923	.1923
27	22	.0772	66	.2524	196	.2677	102	.2804	.6000	.6000	1.0000	1.0000	.1111	.1111	.1852	.1852
28	172	.0771	91R	.2496	20	.2668	152	.2783	.6000	.8000	1.0000	1.0000	.1071	.1429	.1786	.1786
29	200	.0726	110	.2485	194	.2657	161	.2670	.6000	.8000	1.0000	1.0000	.1034	.1379	.1724	.1724
30	64	.0726	93R	.2457	132	.2648	132	.2644	.6000	1.0000	1.0000	1.0000	.1000	.1667	.1667	.1667
31	3	.0715	11	.2426	152	.2637	196	.2601	.6000	1.0000	1.0000	1.0000	.0968	.1613	.1613	.1613
32	195	.0713	61	.2376	92	.2623	96	.2584	.6000	1.0000	1.0000	1.0000	.0938	.1563	.1563	.1563
33	144	.0696	77	.2362	125	.2618	29	.2568	.6000	1.0000	1.0000	1.0000	.0909	.1515	.1515	.1515
34	122	.0693	76	.2245	124	.2590	133	.2553	.6000	1.0000	1.0000	1.0000	.0882	.1471	.1471	.1471
35	63	.0671	132	.2236	86	.2585	194	.2537	.6000	1.0000	1.0000	1.0000	.0857	.1429	.1429	.1429
36	184	.0663	104	.2235	161	.2505	20	.2523	.6000	1.0000	1.0000	1.0000	.0833	.1389	.1389	.1389
37	34	.0657	153	.2194	61	.2491	86	.2489	.6000	1.0000	1.0000	1.0000	.0811	.1351	.1351	.1351
38	74	.0652	74	.2178	133	.2482	104	.2469	.6000	1.0000	1.0000	1.0000	.0789	.1316	.1316	.1316
39	113	.0639	69	.2055	29	.2480	61	.2436	.6000	1.0000	1.0000	1.0000	.0769	.1282	.1282	.1282
40	17	.0635	177	.2030	104	.2474	125	.2429	.6000	1.0000	1.0000	1.0000	.0750	.1250	.1250	.1250
41	95R	.0626	144	.2028	63	.2448	176	.2424	.8000	1.0000	1.0000	1.0000	.0976	.1220	.1220	.1220
42	75	.0626	67	.2004	96	.2401	124	.2413	.8000	1.0000	1.0000	1.0000	.0952	.1190	.1190	.1190
43	67	.0600	29	.1988	83	.2384	121	.2410	.8000	1.0000	1.0000	1.0000	.0930	.1163	.1163	.1163
44	140	.0599	60	.1976	77	.2347	83	.2374	.8000	1.0000	1.0000	1.0000	.0909	.1136	.1136	.1136
76	91R	.0389	19	.1436	160	.1745	160	.1793	1.0000	1.0000	1.0000	1.0000	.0658	.0658	.0658	.0658

1 03/22/67 25.12.41

Fig. 15-2 Recall-precision tables for Q147 showing improvements in the rankings of the revelant documents.

The recall-precision figures included in Fig. 15-2 reflect the excellent performance of query Q147.

Average performance characteristics are shown in the recall-precision plot of Fig. 15-3 for the relevance feedback process, using 42 search requests with a collection of 200 documents in aerodynamics. In each case, it is assumed that the user looks at the top 15 documents produced by the computer search and identifies those that are relevant. This information is used to update the request using equation (2) with $\alpha = 1$; $\beta = 0$; $\gamma = 1, 2, 3$ for the first, second, and third alterations, respectively; all $c_i = 1$; $\delta = 0$. The increase in the value of γ from one iteration to the next is motivated by the thought that the user becomes increasingly more informed as he sees more output, and that his relevance judgments should therefore be weighted increasingly more heavily.

Figure 15-3 shows the large increase in precision for each given recall value between initial searches and first feedback runs. A smaller increase is present between the first and second feedback runs, with very little increase thereafter. The same large-scale improvements are noted also for document collections in other subject areas. Figure 15-4 shows relevance feedback data for three collections in computer science, aerodynamics, and documentation, averaged over 24, 42, and 35 requests, respectively. In each case, the increase between initial requests and first feedback runs is very large and diminishes thereafter. The output of Fig. 15-4 suggests that if low-recall, high-precision performance is desired, a single feedback step may be sufficient; in the high-recall region, additional iterative steps may be useful.

The output shown in Figs. 15-3 and 15-4 is produced with a single feedback strategy. Many of the changes suggested by the variable parameters of equation (2) still remain to be tested. Procedures must also be devised to cover the case where the user finds no relevant material to be returned, or where he finds only nonrelevant items. Finally, requests may have to be handled which cover several distinct subject areas. In that case, the feedback algorithm may not perform satisfactorily, since it is not then possible to approach a well-specified subject area in an optimal way.

15-3 ADAPTIVE USER-CONTROLLED MULTILEVEL SEARCH

In a real-time environment, fast, partial searches of the collection and feedback techniques may be combined into a single overall search scheme based on cluster searches for fast turnaround and on relevance feedback for the optimization of retrieval effectiveness. A possible systems design is suggested in Fig. 15-5 [2], [4].

First an attempt is made to perform a query cluster search for each incoming search request, since this type of search may be expected to require the smallest number of comparison operations [5]. If the request cluster process reveals relevant items, the relevance feedback process is used next. If no relevant items are found, however, a document cluster search is tried next, followed again by the relevance feedback method. Eventually, a full search may be tried, assuming that a high recall

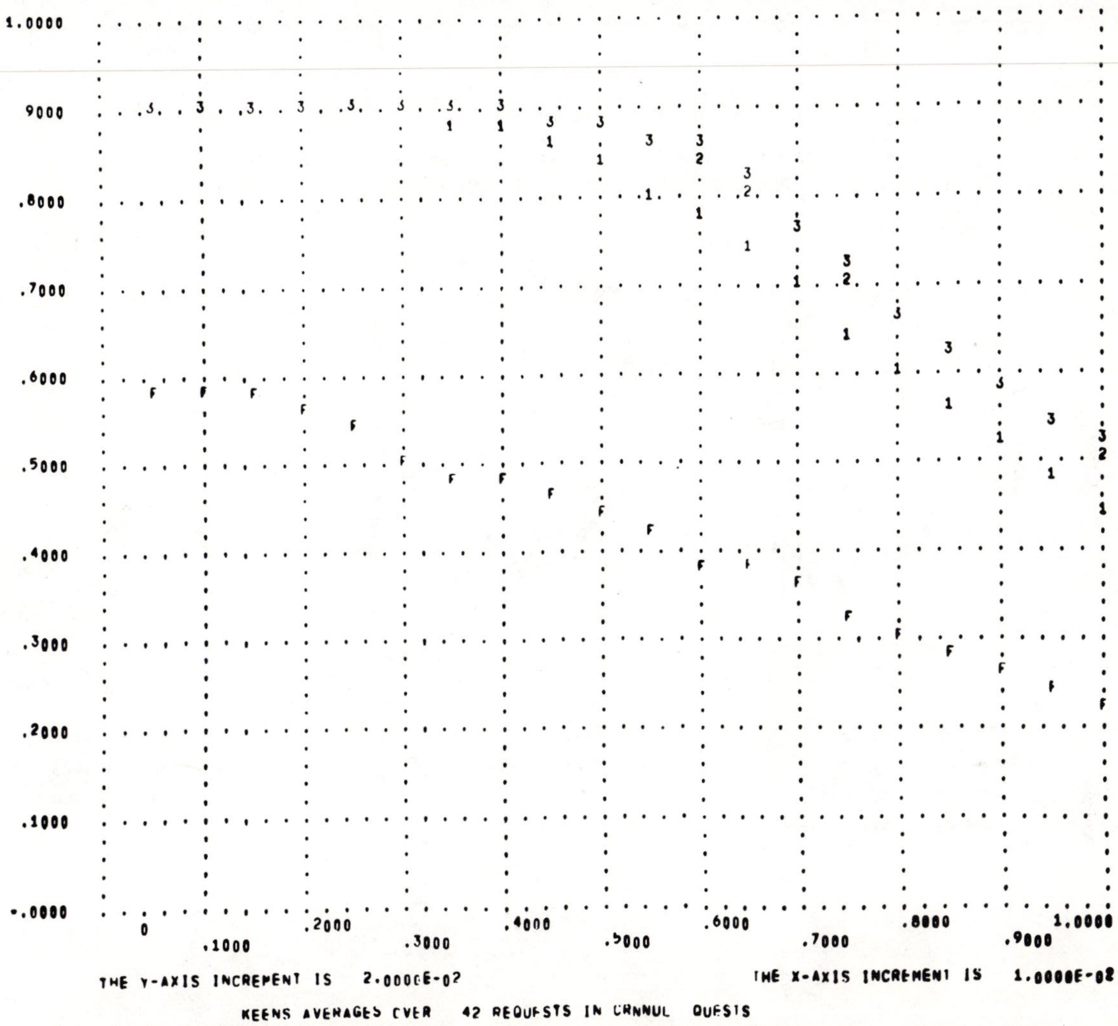

Fig. 15-3 Averaged recall-precision plot for relevance feedback process (averages over 42 search requests—200 documents in aerodynamics).

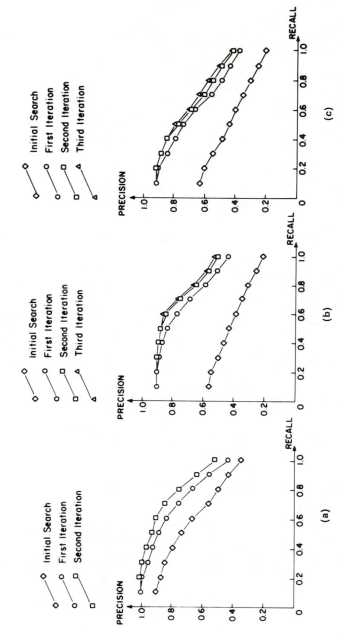

Fig. 15-4 Comparison of initial search with iterated search process using relevance feedback: (a) IRE-2, 24 requests; (b) Cranfield-1, abstracts stem, 42 requests; (c) ADI, abstracts thesaurus, 35 requests.

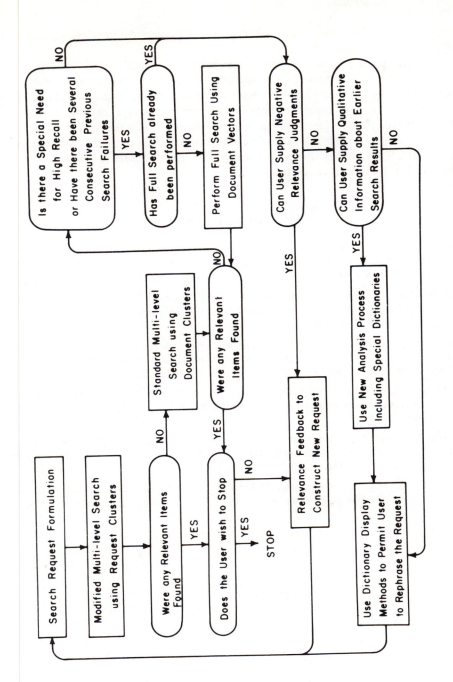

Fig. **15-5** Sample search strategy using multi-level searches and relevance feedback.

335

need exists, and that the two cluster searches are not successful in retrieving relevant material.

If only negative relevance judgments are available, a negative feedback algorithm may be used. Finally, if all else fails, qualitative information may be available from the user, suggesting the use of phrase procedures or hierarchical expansions of the type included in the SMART system to broaden or narrow the area covered by a given request. Dictionary display methods may also be used to help the user in rephrasing his request if the automatic relevance feedback method does not produce the desired results [1], [6]. This proposed real-time search strategy and others like it remain to be tested under operational conditions.

REFERENCES

[1] J. J. Rocchio, Jr. and G. Salton, Information Search Optimization and Iterative Retrieval Techniques, *Proceedings of the AFIPS Fall Joint Computer Conference*, Las Vegas, Nev., November 1965, Spartan Books, New York, 1965, pp. 293–305.

[2] J. J. Rocchio, Jr., Document Retrieval Systems—Optimization and Evaluation, *Report ISR-10* to the National Science Foundation, Section III, Harvard Computation Laboratory, Cambridge, Mass., March 1966.

[3] W. Riddle, T. Horwitz, and R. Dietz, Relevance Feedback in an Information Retrieval System, *Report ISR-11* to the National Science Foundation, Section VI, Department of Computer Science, Cornell University, Ithaca, N.Y., June 1966.

[4] E. M. Keen, User Controlled Search Strategies, *Proceedings of the Fourth Annual National Colloquium on Information Retrieval*, A. B. Tonik, ed., Int. Information Inc., Philadelphia, 1967, pp. 141–154.

[5] S. Worona, Query Clustering in a Large Document Space, Scientific *Report ISR-16*, Section XV, Department of Computer Science, Cornell University, Ithaca, N.Y., October 1969, also Chap. 13 of this volume.

[6] R. M. Curtice and V. Rosenberg, Optimizing Retrieval Results with Man-machine Interaction, *Center for the Information Sciences Report*, Lehigh University, Bethlehem, Pa., 1965.

New results are given for interactive user-controlled retrieval strategies, using relevance feedback. Search strategies are described which depend on the identification by the user of a fixed or variable number of relevant or nonrelevant documents. The evaluation results are based on experiments using 200 documents and 42 queries in the field of aerodynamics.

16

NEW EXPERIMENTS IN RELEVANCE FEEDBACK†

E. IDE

16-1 THE RELEVANCE FEEDBACK PROCEDURE

Automated information retrieval systems, like most mechanical processes, suffer from unavoidable inflexibility. The needs of users of a large information collection, especially a document collection, are too varied to be satisfied with any one exhaustive automatic retrieval algorithm. Users whose needs best match the assumptions built into the system are satisfied; others are not.

One suggested way to overcome this limitation is to employ feedback information from the user during the retrieval process. In a document retrieval situation, this could be accomplished as follows:

(a) The user poses a request to the retrieval system.

(b) The retrieval system returns some information (perhaps abstracts) about a specified number of documents judged relevant to the user's request.

(c) The user selects from this set of initially retrieved items those documents

---

†This study was published originally as Section VIII in *Scientific Report ISR-14*, October 1968.

which *he* deems relevant to the request and feeds this information to the retrieval system.

(d) Another retrieval search is performed incorporating these user judgments.

Steps (c) and (d) are iterated as often as desired.

Such an interactive process was proposed by Rocchio, who called it "relevance feedback" [1], [2], [3]. He showed that, in a document retrieval system based on classification and using the cosine correlation function, the theoretically optimum query for retrieving a set of documents $R = \{\mathbf{r}_i\}$ is given by the formula:

$$\mathbf{Q}_{\text{opt}} = \frac{1}{n_r} \sum_1^{n_r} \frac{\mathbf{r}_i}{|\mathbf{r}_i|} - \frac{1}{n_s} \sum_1^{n_s} \frac{\mathbf{s}_i}{|\mathbf{s}_i|},$$

where

$R = \{\mathbf{r}_i\}$, the descriptor vectors of all documents in the collection which are relevant, according to the user, to the request,

$S = \{\mathbf{s}_i\}$, the descriptor vectors of all other documents in the collection, that is, of all nonrelevant documents,

n_r = number of relevant documents in the collection,

n_s = number of nonrelevant documents,

$|\mathbf{r}_i|$ and $|\mathbf{s}_i|$ = length of the document descriptor vectors $\mathbf{r}_i$ and $\mathbf{s}_i$.

Of course, the sets R and S are not known to the system. On each iteration, however, the user feedback supplies information about two subsets, $R' \in R$ and $S' \in S$, where $R' = \{\mathbf{r}'_i\}$ is the subset of relevant documents retrieved, and $S' = \{\mathbf{s}'_i\}$ is the subset of nonrelevant documents retrieved. Therefore, the formula actually used by Rocchio to construct a new query from the query of the previous iteration is as follows:

$$\mathbf{Q}_{i+1} = \mathbf{Q}_i + \frac{1}{n'_r} \sum_1^{n'_r} \frac{\mathbf{r}'_i}{|\mathbf{r}'_i|} - \frac{1}{n'_s} \sum_1^{n'_s} \frac{\mathbf{s}'_i}{|\mathbf{s}'_i|}, \tag{1}$$

where $n'_r(n'_s)$ is the number of relevant (nonrelevant) documents retrieved for feedback in the previous iteration.

Rocchio investigated relevance feedback using the above formula and 17 queries in the field of computer science and found that his algorithm does improve retrieval results [1], [2], [3].

Another investigation of a relevance feedback system was based on the ADI collection, a collection of 82 documents presented at a conference on documentation. Thirty-five queries were constructed for this collection, and the documents considered relevant to those requests were specified by the two originators of the queries. The investigation of relevance feedback in the ADI collection was conducted by

Riddle, Horwitz, and Dietz [4]. They used 22 of the 35 queries and studied a slightly different algorithm for modifying the search query using the following method of query modification:

$$\mathbf{Q}_{i+1} = \mathbf{Q}_i + \alpha \sum_{1}^{n_r} \mathbf{r}'_i.$$

16-2 THE EXPERIMENTAL ENVIRONMENT

The document collection used in this study (the Cranfield collection) contains 200 documents from the field of aerodynamics, chosen from a library of 1400 documents. For this collection, there exist at present 42 queries, constructed by some of the authors of the 1400 documents; these requestors are also responsible for the relevance judgments.

The concept vectors describing documents and queries are quite sparse for this collection. The maximum number of concepts used to describe one document is 85 out of a possible 552 concepts. The largest weight given to any concept in any document descriptor is 288. The query description vectors are sparser by one order of magnitude and shorter than the document descriptors. The maximum number of concepts used in a single query vector is 13; the largest weight in any query vector is 24. The largest number of documents relevant to a single query is 12, or 6% of the collection. The comparative brevity of the query vectors in this collection is typical for technical document retrieval and provides a strong argument for the use of relevance feedback techniques. With relevance feedback, the user in effect provides a much more detailed query merely by citing a document; the document descriptor itself is used as the query.

The relevance feedback system being studied uses the following query update formula:

$$\mathbf{Q}_{i+1} = \pi\mathbf{Q}_i + \omega\mathbf{Q}_0 + \alpha \sum_{1}^{\min(n_a,\,n'_r)} \mathbf{r}_i + \mu \sum_{1}^{\min(n_b,\,n'_s)} \mathbf{s}_i, \tag{2}$$

where $n'_r + n'_s$ (see equation (1) Sec. 16-1) equals N, the number of documents retrieved for feedback.

The experimental variables are α, ω, π, μ, n_a, n_b, and N. The parameter α is positive and weights all incoming relevant documents relative to the other contributors to the query (previous query, initial query, and nonrelevant documents). The parameter π permits the previous query to be increased in weight relative to the incoming documents. Q_0 is the initial query, as opposed to the query of the previous iteration; ω permits the initial query to be used as part of the new query. The parameter μ should be negative theoretically, as it permits some significance to be attached to the nonrelevant documents retrieved. The parameter $n_a(n_b)$ permits some specific number of relevant (nonrelevant) documents to be used in the query, even if $n'_r(n'_s)$

is larger. It is assumed that the r_i' and s_i' are indexed in order of decreasing relevance (as determined by the system) to the query; that is, the n_a-relevant documents (or n_b-non-relevant documents) used in the new query will be those closest in the descriptor space to the previous query. The flexibility of this formula permits the investigation of several feedback strategies.

The system also provides the following formula to simulate Rocchio's algorithm:

$$\mathbf{Q}_{i+1} = \pi n_r' n_s' \mathbf{Q}_i + \omega \mathbf{Q}_0 + n_s' \sum_1^{\min(n_{r_i}', n_a)} \mathbf{r}_i - n_r \sum_1^{\min(n_{s_i}', n_b)} \mathbf{s}_i. \tag{3}$$

Formula (3) does not however, normalize the vector lengths as does Rocchio's algorithm. The document and query description vectors for both collections were constructed using a SMART thesaurus dictionary on the document abstracts and the queries [3]. The cosine correlation function is used to determine the order of retrieval.

16-3 EARLIER RESULTS IN THE SAME ENVIRONMENT

An earlier study [5] uses the Cranfield 200-document collection and the relevance feedback system described in Sec. 16-2. Three major variations in relevance feedback strategy are investigated:

1. The parameters π, ω, and α in formula (2) of Sec. 16-2 are varied, holding μ equal to 0. This strategy is similar to the type investigated by Riddle, Horwitz, and Dietz [4]. The variation in results obtained when π, ω, and α are changed is slight; in fact, it is less than the variation found by Riddle, Horwitz, and Dietz, who used a different document collection.

2. The number of documents retrieved for feedback (N) is varied. N is set to 5, 10, and 15 documents. The improvement obtained by feeding back 10 documents instead of 5 is impressive; the further improvement obtained with 15 documents is less so. In addition, a "variable feedback" strategy is investigated, in which documents are retrieved until 1 relevant document is found, or until 15 documents have been retrieved. This strategy provides greatly improved precision at low recall but only slightly better precision at high recall than does the $N = 5$ strategy.

3. Two strategies using the information in retrieved nonrelevant documents are studied. In formula (2) (Sec. 16-2), μ is set to minus 1, and n_b is set to 1 and 2. That is, the first nonrelevant document (the first *two* nonrelevant in the second strategy) is subtracted from the query. The strategy in which $n_b = 1$ (called *Dec Hi*), with $N = 5$, produces a performance comparable to that of a strategy using only relevant documents with $N = 10$.

The following conclusions may be reached from the results of the earlier study. The investigation supports relevance feedback as an information retrieval strategy.

It also shows that varying the parameters in a query update formula which uses relevant documents only is not a promising way to produce significant improvement in performance. The most promising strategies investigated, variable feedback and nonrelevant document feedback, require further study before they can be recommended firmly. The variable feedback strategy and the suggested combination of fixed and variable feedback should be investigated in a suitable evaluation system. The nonrelevant feedback strategies should be studied in a system which permits normalizing as in Rocchio [1]. Eventually, some combination of fixed and variable feedback may prove optimal in similar information retrieval environments.

16-4 EVALUATION OF RETRIEVAL PERFORMANCE

16-4-A The Feedback Effect in Evaluation

The investigation described in Sec. 16-3 uses a retrieval and evaluation method that has been assessed by Hall and Weiderman [6]. After each iteration, all documents in the collection are ranked, and the top-ranked N documents are used for feedback. Hall and Weiderman point out that evaluation of this retrieval technique takes into account two effects, which they call *ranking effect* and *feedback effect*.

Relevance feedback in effect uses information from one or more document descriptors to modify the query descriptor. The relevant documents used for this purpose will be ranked higher by the modified query than previously, and the nonrelevant documents used will be ranked lower. The effect of these rank changes in "retrieved" documents is termed the "ranking effect". If the ranking effect is included in an overall performance measure, the measured change in performance between feedback iterations is quite impressive, as is seen in the results included in the earlier report described in Sec. 16-3 [5]. This large change in "total performance" (including both ranking and feedback effect) indicates the extent to which the initial query has been perturbed toward the centroid of the relevant documents and strongly supports Rocchio's theory.

Hall and Weiderman state that in an environment where the user must actively supply relevance judgments for feedback, changes in the ranks of documents which the user has already seen are of no interest to him. The user in such an environment is concerned primarily with the "feedback effect", that is, the effectiveness of the modified query in bringing new relevant documents to his attention. They conclude that, though total performance is a valid measure of the effectiveness of relevance feedback in approaching the "ideal query", the feedback effect should be isolated and examined as well.

The present study evaluates feedback performance in the manner suggested by Hall and Weiderman by discarding the ranking effect and preserving only the feedback effect. The ranks of the top N documents retrieved in each iteration (the documents used for feedback) are "frozen" in all subsequent iterations, and only the remainder of the collection is searched using the modified query. Thus, in the present investigation, the N documents retrieved on any iteration are guaranteed to be N *new* documents, that is, documents *not* used for feedback on any previous iteration. Moreover, the performance measures for the first (second, third) iteration are calculated from a ranked document list in which the top N $(2N, 3N)$ documents are the same as those retrieved previously. Only the changes in the ranks of documents not yet seen by the user are measured.

The evaluation described gives overall results that are deceptively low. Because the top ranks are frozen, no newly retrieved document can achieve a rank higher than that of any previously retrieved document. With a constant feedback strategy, therefore, on the first (second, third) iteration, the highest possible rank for a new document is $N + 1$ $(2N + 1, 3N + 1)$. For this reason, the feedback effect evaluation is a misleading measure of the performance of the retrieval system and should be used in conjunction with other evaluation methods. Isolation of the feedback effect is primarily useful to compare different feedback strategies from the viewpoint of a user in an interactive retrieval environment.

16-4-B   Performance Measures

Several average measures of the performance of the tested retrieval algorithms on the 42 Cranfield queries are used in this report. Each measure is based on the concepts of "recall" and "precision". In evaluating an information retrieval system, an arbitrary cutoff is often employed, and documents above this cutoff are termed "retrieved". With such a cutoff, "recall" is the percentage of documents relevant to the user that is retrieved, and "precision" is the percentage of retrieved documents that is relevant. The average measures used in this study do not employ a cutoff but evaluate the retrieval performance over the entire document collection. A discussion of the generalization of the concepts of recall and precision to such an overall evaluation is found in reference [7].

The average measures used herein are rank recall, log precision, normalized recall, normalized precision, and a curve reflecting average precision at each 10% of recall. The first four of these measures are defined in reference [7]. The recall-precision curve used here differs from any used in previous studies.

Both the quasi-Cleverdon curve, used in the earlier study (Sec. 16-3), and the new curve used here are average plots of precision at each 5% or 10% of recall. Each query is averaged into each point of the plot. To accomplish this averaging process, an interpolation procedure is needed, since for example, a query with two relevant documents can only achieve uninterpolated recall levels of 50% and 100%. The quasi-Cleverdon curve and new curve are distinguished by the method of interpolation used.

Figures 16-1 and 16-2 show two graphs for a hypothetical query having 4 relevant documents. The relevant documents are assumed to be retrieved with ranks of 4, 6, 12, and 20. Thus, at 25% recall the precision is 25%, at 50% recall the precision is 33%, and so on. However, these values correspond actually to the highest possible precision points because they are calculated just after a relevant document is retrieved.

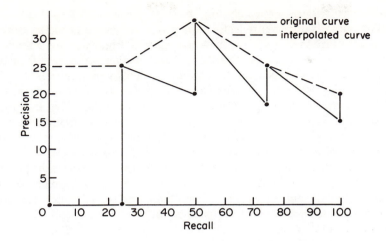

Fig. 16-1 An illustration of the interpolation method used for the quasi-Cleverdon recall-precision averages.

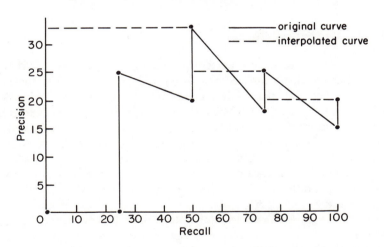

Fig. 16-2 An illustration of the interpolation method used for the new recall-precision averages.

In this example, after three documents are retrieved, the precision is 0%, after five documents, the precision is 20%, and so on. This range of precision for each recall level is indicated by the top and bottom points in Figs. 16-1 and 16-2 at 25%, 50%, 75%, and 100% recall. The solid sawtooth line connecting these points is not used for interpolation; rather it is intended to indicate the drop in precision between the actual recall levels for this query as more nonrelevant documents are retrieved.

The quasi-Cleverdon averages use a straight-line interpolation between peak points of precision, as indicated by the dashed line in Fig. 16-1. It has been argued that this interpolation is artificially high because it lies at all points above the saw-tooth curve and thus does not reflect, in any way, the precision drop as more nonrelevant documents are retrieved. The new averages of Fig. 16-2 use an interpolation that projects a horizontal line leftward from each peak point of precision and stops when a higher point of precision is encountered. This new interpolation curve (the dashed line in Fig. 16-2) does *not* lie above the sawtooth curve at all points. When the precision drops from one recall level actually achieved to the next, an immediate drop in precision after the first point to the level of the next point is indicated. For example, in Fig. 16-2 the precision value at 50% recall is 33%, but at 55% recall, the interpolated value used for the new averages is 25% precision. When the precision rises from one recall level to the next, however, the first precision point actually achieved is ignored for purposes of interpolation. The achieved precision of 25% at 25% recall in the example of Fig. 16-2 is ignored, and for all recall levels from 0 to 50%, an interpolated precision of 33% is used for the new averages. The proponents of the new interpolation argue that this method indicates in all cases a precision that the user could actually achieve, if he were to use hindsight by retrieving exactly the right number of documents. Both the new averages are used now at Harvard and Cornell in evaluating the SMART system.

16-4-C Statistical Tests

Several statistical tests are reported here using as input rank recall, log precision, normalized recall, normalized precision, and ten points from the new recall-precision curve. The statistical tests are intended to measure the "significance" of the average difference in values of these measures obtained for two iterations or two distinct search algorithms. The test results are expressed as the probability that the two sets of values obtained from two separate runs are actually drawn from samples which have the same characteristics. Thus a small probability value indicates that the two curves are actually significantly different. If this probability for one measure is, for example 5%, the difference in the two average values of that measure is said to be "significant at the 5% level".

Choice of a statistical method for calculating this probability is important. The present study uses two statistical tests, the familiar *t* test and the Wilcoxon signed rank test (WSR) [8]. The *t* test takes into account the magnitude of the differences and assumes that the measures tested are distributed normally. The WSR test does not make this assumption. Instead, the WSR test takes account of only the *ranks* of the differences, ignoring their magnitude. Because this test does not assume normality of the input and because it ignores some information (magnitudes of differences), the WSR test is more conservative than the *t* test. It is therefore less prone to the error of calling a result "significant" when it is not. Because information retrieval provides discrete rather than continuous data and because only 42 data points (42 queries) are provided, the more conservative WSR test is preferable in the present evaluation.

16-5 EXPERIMENTAL RESULTS

Results of three major areas of investigation are presented:

(a) A comparison of two strategies that use only R', the set of relevant documents retrieved, to modify the query vector.

(b) An investigation of the retrieval effect of the number of documents used for relevance feedback on each iteration.

(c) An investigation of strategies using the set S', that is, the nonrelevant documents retrieved, to modify the query.

The statistical significance of the average results obtained is tested in each case.

16-5-A Two Strategies Using Relevant Documents Only

In the earlier report, summarized in Sec. 16-3 [5], several strategies using relevant documents only are compared. The differences in total performance found among these strategies were very slight. A feedback effect comparison of two "relevant only" strategies is made here. The strategies chosen are

1. The straightforward strategy of setting α equal to 1, π equal to 1, and the other constants equal to 0 in formula (2) (Sec. 16-2). The feedback formula in effect for this strategy is therefore

$$\mathbf{Q}_{i+1} = \mathbf{Q}_i + \sum_1^{n'_r} \mathbf{r}_i.$$

This formula is not equivalent to any strategy used in the earlier study because the feedback effect evaluation provides new documents for feedback on each iteration (Sec. 16-4-A), while the total performance evaluation does not. The nearest comparable strategy from the previous study is the so-called "Q_0 strategy" (also called "increment only").

2. A strategy that gives added weight to the user's original query: $\pi = 1$, $\alpha = 1$, and $\omega = 4$. This strategy is intended to compensate for the large difference in magnitude between document vector weights and query vector weights (Sec. 16-2).

The difference in feedback effect between these two methods is trivial. For all average measures, the differences observed are less than 1.25%. The recall level averages for the second strategy, called "$Q_0 +$", are presented in Fig. 16-5 to be described later. This result is hardly surprising, since for several "relevant only" strategies the total performance results reported in the earlier study are nearly identical.

16-5-B   Varying the Amount of Feedback

In the earlier study (Sec. 16-3), the improvement in total performance achieved by feeding back ten rather than five documents to the user is impressive. This difference, however, is due primarily to the ranking effect. The feedback effect results, shown in Fig. 16-3, are actually better at medium recall levels when only five docu-

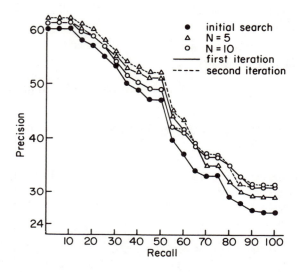

Fig. 16-3   Increment only feedback of five or ten documents.

ments are used for feedback. At high recall levels, the performance achieved by feeding back five documents twice is roughly equal to that obtained by feeding back ten documents once. The average improvement in feedback effect gained by feeding back more documents on each iteration does not seem worth the cost of asking the user to make more relevance judgments.

It must be noted, however, that the feedback effect evaluation gives an unfair advantage to runs using few documents for feedback. When five documents are used for feedback, ranks 1–5 are frozen on the first iteration and ranks 1–10 on the second. When ten documents are fed back, however, ranks 1–10 are frozen on the first iteration and ranks 1–20 on the second. The difference in results caused by increasing the number of documents fed back is therefore minimized by the evaluation process.

A variable feedback strategy is tested in the earlier study. The user is asked to search the retrieved list from the top until he finds 1 relevant document or has seen 15 documents. The total performance reported indicates that the user who does not require high recall (50% recall or less) reaps considerable benefit from this strategy, but that high recall performance is very little better than that obtained by a constant feedback with $N = 5$. The feedback effect evaluation produces a different picture. In

Fig. 16-4 one iteration of variable feedback is compared to one iteration feeding back five documents. The "average user" must look at four documents from the initial search to find one relevant document. The feedback effect performance at 10% recall is better for the variable feedback strategy. At 20% recall, the two strategies are the same, at 30% variable, feedback is worse. At medium recall levels, the two strategies are again approximately the same. At recall levels above 70%, however, the variable feedback strategy gives higher precision.

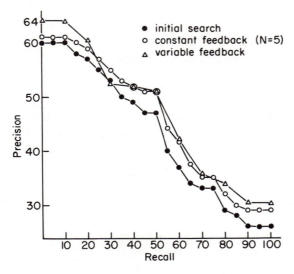

Fig. 16-4 Constant feedback compared to variable feedback—first iteration.

The variable feedback results are also affected by the feedback effect measure. Since for 75% of the queries five or fewer documents are used for feedback, variable feedback receives the "unfair advantage" noted earlier. This advantage should, however, be most evident at low recall, whereas the major improvement observed here is at high recall.

The apparent inconsistency of a large total performance improvement (from constant feedback to variable feedback) at low recall, with a feedback effect improvement at high recall, is easily explained. As was mentioned in Sec. 16-4-A, the feedback effect evaluation prevents a document retrieved by feedback from achieving a higher rank than any document retrieved earlier. The total performance improvement at low recall indicates that relevant documents retrieved early (including the first relevant document retrieved which is used for feedback) make larger jumps in rank with variable feedback than with constant feedback. These jumps are inhibited by the artificial rank ceiling imposed by the feedback method of evaluation. The feedback effect shows improvement at high recall, indicating that even at high recall levels new relevant documents appear sooner in the retrieved list with variable feedback than with constant feedback. The total performance results favor variable feedback primarily for the user who does not require high recall. The feedback effect results support this type of variable feedback as a strategy to be *generally* recommended in an interactive environment.

Two further investigations must, however, be considered. First, the performance of several iterations of the variable feedback strategy should be investigated using the feedback effect evaluation. Second, the results presented here are valid for a hypothetical "average" user. An examination of subgroups of queries would show whether or not certain types of users achieve better results with the constant feedback strategy.

16-5-C Strategies Using Nonrelevant Documents

In the earlier report (Sec. 16-3), a strategy using nonrelevant documents displays a total performance similar to that achieved using relevant documents only and using twice as many documents for feedback. This nonrelevant document strategy, called Dec Hi in both the earlier and the present reports, uses the retrieval formula

$$\mathbf{Q}_{i+1} = \mathbf{Q}_i + \sum_1^{n'_r} \mathbf{r}_i - \mathbf{s}_1,$$

where $\mathbf{s}_1$ is the first nonrelevant document retrieved.

In the previous study, it was recommended that Rocchio's relevance feedback strategy, a strategy using all documents retrieved, be tested. The present study tests Rocchio's strategy but without normalizing the lengths of the documents used to modify the query. Since the cosine correlation is used to rank documents for retrieval, this normalization is a theoretical necessity [2].

The results of the significance tests on the three strategies, $Q_0 +$ (see Sec. 16-5), Rocchio (Rocchio's algorithm without normalization), and Dec Hi, are given in Table 16-1. Table 16-1 shows the significance levels of the differences among the three strategies for two iterations, using the less conservative t test. It is evident that the differences in averages among the three strategies described are not significant.

Two comparisons are of particular importance: (1) the differences in normalized recall between the "relevant only" strategy $Q_0 +$, and (2) the two nonrelevant document strategies, Rocchio and Dec Hi, on the first iteration. The 5% difference between $Q_0 +$ and Dec Hi is significant at the 6% level; the 6% difference between $Q_0 +$ and Rocchio is significant at the 3% level, according to the t test. However, the Wilcoxon signed rank test (WSR) indicates that the two algorithms do not give significantly different results. The significance level comparing $Q_0 +$ and Dec Hi is 46%, and that comparing $Q_0 +$ and Rocchio is 48%.

These different significance levels must be considered in the light of the characteristics of the two significance tests. The t test takes account of magnitude, the WSR test considers only rank. Evidently, differences favoring Q_0+ and differences favoring the nonrelevant document strategy are mixed in rank, producing "insignificant"

Table 16-1

COMPARING THREE FEEDBACK STRATEGIES, FIRST AND SECOND ITERATIONS, DIFFERENCES, AND SIGNIFICANCE LEVELS

STRATEGIES	ROCCHIO VERSUS Q_0+				DEC HI VERSUS Q_0+				DEC HI VERSUS ROCCHIO			
	ITERATION 1		ITERATION 2		ITERATION 1		ITERATION 2		ITERATION 1		ITERATION 2	
	Diff.	Sign.	Diff.	Sign.	Diff.	Sign.	Diff.	Sign.	Diff.	Sign.	Diff.	Sign.
Rank recall	−0.1	99.8	0.1	96.1	0.3	76.8	−0.4	81.3	0.4	61.3	−0.5	55.9
Log precision	−0.4	61.7	−0.2	81.0	0.0	93.3	0.3	83.7	0.4	32.9	0.0	94.8
Normed recall	−6.1	3.4†	−4.4	17.7†	5.4	5.7†	−7.0	9.4†	0.6	75.8	−2.6	36.4
Normed precision	−2.9	15.4	−2.0	43.0	−2.1	31.4	−3.0	29.6	0.8	55.0	−1.0	53.8
Recall level: 10%	0.0	99.4	−0.2	87.9	0.2	84.2	−0.2	89.0	0.2	66.1	0.0	96.6
20%	0.3	83.4	0.3	83.5	0.6	57.4	0.3	81.4	0.4	48.9	0.0	93.8
30%	0.1	94.7	0.2	89.1	0.6	61.3	0.3	83.8	0.5	49.8	0.1	85.0
40%	−0.1	93.6	0.4	78.9	0.7	58.1	0.9	56.1	0.5	29.2	0.5	40.8
50%	0.1	92.3	0.6	69.8	0.9	48.5	0.8	60.7	0.8	24.7	0.2	71.8
60%	−0.5	95.4	−1.2	63.7	0.8	55.5	0.8	62.2	1.3	39.7	2.0	11.3
70%	0.7	68.0	1.0	54.6	0.4	61.4	0.7	51.2	−0.3	92.3	−0.3	94.6
80%	1.1	42.5	0.9	50.8	1.1	42.7	0.5	70.0	−0.1	98.3	−0.5	47.6
90%	0.7	55.8	0.0	95.1	0.6	67.9	−0.1	50.9	−0.2	77.4	−1.1	16.2
100%	0.6	66.4	0.0	92.3	0.5	72.5	−0.8	60.3	−0.1	89.5	−0.8	31.3

Q_0+: $Q_{i+1} = Q_i + \sum \mathbf{r}_i + 4\mathbf{Q}_0,$

Rocchio: $Q_{i+1} = n_r' n_s' \mathbf{Q}_i + n_s' \sum \mathbf{r}_i - n_r' \sum \mathbf{s}_i,$

Dec Hi: $Q_{i+1} = \mathbf{Q}_i + \sum \mathbf{r}_i - \mathbf{s}_1.$

†Significance of normalized recall for WSR test: Rocchio versus Q_0+ gives Iteration 1 = 24.1, Iteration 2 = 48.9, and Dec Hi versus Q_0+ gives Iteration 1 = 98.5, Iteration 2 = 45.6.

results for the WSR test. Yet, some of the results favoring Q_0+ (not *all*, because the ranks are mixed) must be very large in magnitude, to give "significant" indications on the t test. Thus, for a few queries, the Rocchio and Dec Hi algorithms must be much less effective than Q_0+ as measured by normalized recall.

The total performance normalized recall measured in the previous study (Sec. 16-3) was also low for Dec Hi, compared with a "relevant only" strategy. The explanation given in the earlier report is equally valid for the feedback effect results reported here. In brief, the use of nonrelevant documents for feedback seems to raise the ranks of fairly high-ranking relevant documents and, at the same time, lower the ranks of some low-ranking relevant documents.

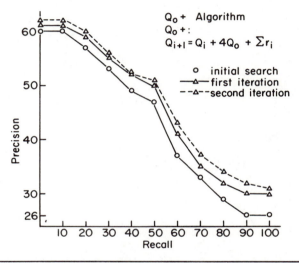

| | FIRST ITER. VS. INITIAL SEARCH | | SECOND ITER. VS. INITIAL SEARCH | |
	Percent Difference	*Percent Significance*	*Percent Difference*	*Percent Significance*
Rank Recall	4.1	3.8	5.1	1.9
Log Precision	2.3	4.1	2.8	1.2
Normalized Recall	3.1	0.6	3.7	0.1
Normalized Precision	2.7	1.8	3.6	0.5
Recall Level 10%	1.0	6.8	1.8	1.3
20%	1.8	4.3	2.5	0.8
30%	2.2	1.5	3.0	0.9
40%	3.0	0.5	3.7	0.4
50%	3.1	0.8	3.7	1.1
60%	3.5	5.7	5.7	2.8
70%	2.4	29.2	4.4	19.5
80%	3.2	18.3	4.9	4.5
90%	3.6	6.1	5.6	2.4
100%	3.6	6.1	5.2	2.6

Fig. 16-5 Comparison of first and second iterations to initial search differences and significance levels—Q_0+ algorithm.

The significance levels obtained by comparing the first and second iteration results to the initial search result, *within* each of the three strategies, are very informative. Figures 16-5, 16-6, and 16-7 show the performance of algorithms Q_0+, Rocchio, and Dec Hi, respectively. The significance of the gap between the initial search and each iteration is tested, using the more conservative WSR test.

Looking at the three recall-precision graphs, the average performance of the three algorithms seems quite similar. Table 16-1 shows that, in fact, the differences in average performance are not significant. Yet the significance levels displayed in Fig. 16-5 differ greatly from those displayed in Figs. 16-6 and 16-7.

For the Q_0+ strategy, the differences between the initial search and each feed-

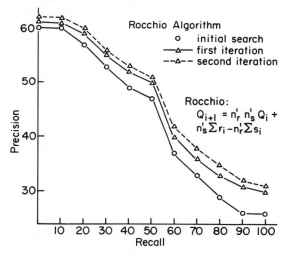

	FIRST ITER. VS. INITIAL SEARCH		SECOND ITER. VS. INITIAL SEARCH	
	Percent Difference	*Percent Significance*	*Percent Difference*	*Percent Significance*
Rank Recall	4.0	19.1	5.3	5.4
Log Precision	1.8	32.6	2.6	8.2
Normalized Recall	−3.0	60.0	−0.8	23.5
Normalized Precision	−0.1	55.5	1.6	20.8
Recall Level 10%	1.0	51.8	1.6	30.7
20%	2.1	25.8	2.8	12.4
30%	2.3	14.9	3.2	5.3
40%	2.9	10.4	4.1	2.2
50%	3.2	8.8	4.3	3.0
60%	3.1	47.7	4.5	28.7
70%	3.1	43.2	5.4	12.0
80%	4.3	22.1	5.8	8.5
90%	4.4	19.1	5.1	5.7
100%	4.2	21.1	5.3	7.4

Fig. 16-6 Comparison of first and second iterations to initial search differences and significance levels—Rocchio algorithm.

back iteration are significant. On the first iteration, the four overall measures and the precision differences from 20% through 50% recall are significant at the 5% level or less, and only at 70% and 80% recall are the precision differences not significant at the 10% level.† On the second iteration, the performance difference is significant at the 5% level for all points except 70% recall. For the Rocchio strategy, however, only

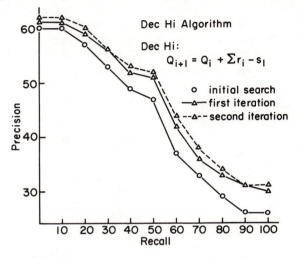

Dec Hi Algorithm

Dec Hi:

$$Q_{i+1} = Q_i + \Sigma r_i - s_l$$

○ initial search
△ first iteration
△ second iteration

| | FIRST ITER. VS. INITIAL SEARCH | | SECOND ITER. VS. INITIAL SEARCH | |
	Percent Difference	*Percent Significance*	*Percent Difference*	*Percent Significance*
Rank Recall	4.3	13.6	4.8	9.5
Log Precision	2.3	14.5	2.6	9.2
Normalized Recall	−2.3	45.1	−3.3	19.6
Normalized Precision	1.5	25.9	0.6	14.1
Recall Level 10%	1.2	30.9	1.6	21.5
20%	2.4	13.3	2.9	8.4
30%	2.8	8.3	3.3	7.1
40%	3.7	5.5	4.7	1.8
50%	4.0	4.1	4.5	2.3
60%	4.4	14.5	6.5	5.2
70%	2.8	39.1	5.1	16.7
80%	4.3	16.7	5.4	8.5
90%	4.2	17.3	4.6	10.5
100%	4.1	17.9	4.5	10.9

Fig. 16-7 Comparison of first and second iterations to initial search differences and significance levels—Dec Hi algorithm.

†For these comparisons, a one-tailed significance level is appropriate, since performance is expected to improve. To obtain one-tailed values, the reported two-tailed values must be divided by two. That is, the probability that the first iteration is *no better* than the initial search is 5% or less except at 70% and 80% recall.

one measure (precision at 50% recall) shows a significant difference between the first iteration and initial search at the 10% level or less. Even on the second iteration, only 8 of the 14 differences are significant at the 10% level or less and 2 at the 5% level or less. The significance of the corresponding differences for the Dec Hi strategy are similar.

This difference between strategies in the significance of the improvement obtained by feedback leads to a general conclusion. Performance on all measures is less consistent for the nonrelevant document strategies than for the $Q_0 +$ strategy. However, since the average magnitude of this improvement is equal for the three algorithms (from the significance results presented in Table 16-1), it must be true that the Rocchio and Dec Hi strategies are better for some queries and worse for others than is the more consistent $Q_0 +$ strategy.

Therefore the greater variance of nonrelevant document strategies is demonstrated not only by the normalized recall but by all performance measures. The results given here seem to indicate that for some types of queries nonrelevant documents should be used for feedback, but for others, only relevant documents should be used. If the queries appropriate to each strategy could be distinguished easily *before* the retrieval operation, performance of the system could be improved by choosing the appropriate strategy for each query. Procedures for distinguishing such subgroups of queries must be investigated.

16-6 SUMMARY AND RECOMMENDATIONS

The isolation of the feedback effect adds to an understanding of relevance feedback in an automatic interactive retrieval system. The present investigation supports the earlier finding [5] that changing the constant formula parameters in the simplest algorithm—using only relevant documents—has little effect on retrieval. This study contradicts the earlier conclusion concerning the optimum amount of feedback. Looking only at the feedback effect, returning ten rather than five documents no longer seems worth the extra user effort. However, feedback effect evaluation tends to minimize differences caused by varying the number of documents used for feedback.

The combination of the results for total performance and feedback effect favors the general use of "variable feedback", in which the user searches the retrieval list only until one relevant document is found. In feedback effect, strategies using nonrelevant documents no longer display an average performance superior to strategies using relevant documents only. Significance tests indicate that "relevant only" strategies are superior for some queries and nonrelevant document strategies for others.

Several areas of investigation are recommended. At least one more iteration of variable feedback and at least two iterations of the "combination strategy" recommended in the earlier total performance study [5] should be investigated using feedback effect evaluation. Significance tests on the variable feedback results should also be obtained. Rocchio's strategy *with* normalization should be investigated.

Results of comparing relevant only and nonrelevant document strategies suggest strongly that an investigation be made of subgroups of queries. These types of algorithms seem appropriate to different groups of queries. It would be useful to be able to choose the appropriate strategy for a query before retrieval, by examination of the query. For variable feedback, an investigation of query subgroups should be performed to determine whether or not some identifiable group of users is shortchanged by this strategy.

The use of query subgroups, however, raises questions of sample adequacy. Even if the 200 documents and 42 queries of the Cranfield 200 collection are representative of a typical retrieval environment, the statistical dangers of dividing 42 queries into small subgroups must be considered. Investigation of relevance feedback should therefore be continued in a more adequate environment. The Cranfield 1400-document collection, available to the SMART system, would provide significantly larger samples of documents and queries.

REFERENCES

[1] J. J. Rocchio, Jr., Relevance Feedback in Information Retrieval, *Report ISR-9* to the National Science Foundation, Section III, Harvard Computation Laboratory, Cambridge, Mass., August 1965; also Chap. 14 of this volume.

[2] J. J. Rocchio, Jr., Document Retrieval Systems—Optimization and Evaluation, doctoral thesis, *Report ISR-10* to the National Science Foundation, Harvard Computation Laboratory, Cambridge, Mass., March 1966.

[3] J. J. Rocchio, Jr. and G. Salton, Search Optimization and Iterative Retrieval Techniques, *Proceedings of the AFIPS Fall Joint Computer Conference*, Nov., 1965, Spartan Books, New York, 1965.

[4] W. Riddle, T. Horwitz, and R. Dietz, Relevance Feedback in Information Retrieval Systems, *Report ISR-11* to the National Science Foundation Section VI, Department of Computer Science, Cornell University, Ithaca, N.Y., June 1966.

[5] E. Ide, User Interaction with an Automated Information Retrieval System, *Report ISR-12* to the National Science Foundation, Section VIII, Department of Computer Science, Cornell University, Ithaca, N.Y., June 1967.

[6] H. A. Hall and N. H. Weiderman, The Evaluation Problem in Relevance Feedback Systems, *Report ISR-12* to the National Science Foundation, Section XII, Department of Computer Science, Cornell University, Ithaca, N.Y., June 1967.

[7] G. Salton, The Evaluation of Automatic Retrieval Processes, Selected Test Results using the SMART System, *American Documentation*, Vol. 16, No. 3, July 1965.

[8] F. Wilcoxon, *Some Rapid Approximate Statistical Procedures*, American Cyanamid Company, Stamford, Conn., 1949.

Three methods of feedback evaluation are described: modified freezing, residual collection, and test and control groups. Feedback runs are performed using each method with the SMART system, and results are compared against the previously used evaluation methods of total performance and full freezing, with respect to improvements of "feedback effect" evaluation.

17

EVALUATION OF FEEDBACK RETRIEVAL USING MODIFIED FREEZING, RESIDUAL COLLECTION, AND TEST AND CONTROL GROUPS†

Y. K. CHANG, C. CIRILLO, and J. RAZON

17-1 INTRODUCTION

The two most common methods of evaluation of feedback retrieval systems both have weaknesses: total performance and feedback effect (full freezing) evaluation limit the attainable performance in later iterations. In total performance the evaluation after feedback is biased because relevant documents, already seen by the user, are moved to the top of the ranking, thereby distorting the feedback evaluation by making it appear better than it really is, while most of the improvement is gained by a reranking of documents already seen. This is known as the "ranking effect." The goal in feedback evaluation is to eliminate this ranking effect and to develop a method based on only the "feedback effect," that is, on the improvement of the new query over the old query due to the number and rank of *new* relevant documents retrieved.

Three methods of feedback evaluation, suggested by Ide in *Report ISR-15*, are evaluated in this study [1]. The first is known as the modified-freezing technique. This is a method similar to the full freezing used by SMART except that certain nonrelevant documents are not frozen, in an attempt to give a

†This study appeared originally as Section X in *Scientific Report ISR-16*, October 1969.

more accurate picture of the "feedback effect." The second method is that of residual collection evaluation. Here both the ith and $(i + 1)$st iteration queries are used to search the $(i + 1)$st iteration residual collection, thereby isolating the "feedback effect" for the residual collection. The third examines the test and control group method. A document collection is split into two halves—feedback runs are done on the test group, and the resulting modified queries are run on the control group, thus eliminating the "ranking effects" on the control group. This produces an accurate evaluation of only the "feedback effect."

17-2   THE MODIFIED-FREEZING EVALUATION

The full-freezing evaluation method used in the SMART system freezes the ranks of all documents presented to the user on earlier feedback iterations and assigns to the first document retrieved on the ith iteration a rank $iN + 1$, where N documents are presented to the user (used for feedback) on each iteration. This measure of the "feedback effect" is fairly accurate for the first iteration. However, after that, any documents retrieved cannot be ranked higher than $2N + 1$ and hence will have very little effect on the precision-recall curve.

A method suggested by Ide to evaluate these later iteration feedback improvements somewhat more effectively is the use of a *modified-freezing* technique [1]. Modified freezing differs from full freezing in the following way. In modified freezing, all *relevant* documents retrieved on the ith iteration and used for feedback on the $(i + 1)$st iteration have their ranks frozen, and all nonrelevant documents ranked above the last-ranked relevant document used for feedback are also frozen. Nonrelevant documents ranked below the last relevant are not frozen. Hence the number of documents frozen on each iteration may vary, while in full freezing a specified number N are frozen on each iteration. In both methods, however, N new documents are retrieved (used for feedback) on each iteration.

The modified-freezing algorithm is not implemented at present in the SMART system. In order to evaluate feedback by using the modified-freezing method, the method is simulated by manually reranking the output from a previous search which uses the full-freezing evaluation technique. A specific example should indicate exactly how this reranking is done.

Consider query 25 of the ADIABTH collection with three relevant documents. The initial query ranks the document as follows:

Rank	1	2	3	4	5	$\cdots$	15
Document	13R	53R	60	37	40	$\cdots$	24R

Using feedback and full freezing, the results on the first iteration are:

Rank	Document	Correlation
1	13R	0.8772
2	53R	0.8103
3	60	0.2902
4	37	0.2770
5	40	0.2834
6	24R	0.5092
7	26	0.3707
8	56	0.3601
9	74	0.3156
10	5	0.2989

The first five (N) documents are frozen in this case, regardless of whether they are relevant or not. Document 24 moves up from rank 15 to rank 6 ($1N + 1$). This is the best possible improvement and should be reflected in a sizable increase in the precision-recall curve for the first iteration over that of the initial query.

A reranking using the modified-freezing technique would freeze the documents only up to rank 2 (the last-ranked relevant document retrieved in this case). For the example the following rankings are produced:

Rank	Document	Correlation
1	13R	0.8772
2	53R	0.8103
3	24R	0.5092
4	26	0.3707
5	56	0.3601
6	74	0.3156
7	5	0.2989
8	60	0.2902
9	40	0.2834
10	52	0.2829

Ranks 3–5 are not frozen because they were nonrelevant documents ranked below the last retrieved relevant document. Document 24 moves up from rank 15 to rank 3. Once again this is the best possible improvement in the feedback iteration. In this example the modified-freezing process would be superior to full freezing as a method of evaluating the "feedback effect."

Consider, however, the case where a relevant document is initially ranked fifth. Then if the feedback effect moves another relevant document up from rank 15 to rank 6, it will still be ranked 6 by the modified-freezing technique, and the precision-recall curves will be identical. However, because the rank freezing normally produces lower evaluation output, it will seem as if the full-freezing output actually reflects better feedback output than the modified-freezing evaluation, although in reality the feedback improvements in both cases are identical. This is a minor side effect of the modified-freezing method.

If no relevant documents are retrieved with the initial query on the first iteration, one looks at the first ten documents (the first five will be identical to those retrieved on the first iteration, providing positive feedback is used), following the identical rules spelled out earlier.

17-3 MODIFIED-FREEZING EVALUATION RESULTS

In this section, copies of the output for searches of two document collections using feedback and full freezing are examined (the ADIABTH and the CRN-200 collections). Simulation of the modified-freezing technique was accomplished by reranking the documents by hand, using the correlations listed in the output as explained earlier.

For the ADIABTH collection, all 35 queries are used, and full freezing is compared to modified freezing on the first and second iterations. The resulting precision-recall curves turn out to be almost identical, with the modified-freezing curves slightly higher than the full-freezing curves. This is expected, since the relevant documents can only receive higher and not lower ranks using modified freezing. Two arguments can explain why the average curves are so close together. First, the feedback for the ADIABTH collection is not as effective as for the CRN-200. Second, all queries are used in the evaluation, even though for about half of the ADI queries the statistics using modified freezing and those using full freezing are identical. The following cases arise in particular:

(a) The feedback result is not good enough to enable any relevant documents to have higher correlations than the unfrozen, previously retrieved nonrelevant documents.

(b) All relevant documents are retrieved by the initial query.

(c) No relevant documents are retrieved by the initial query.

(d) A relevant document is the last retrieved item in any iteration.

For the CRN- 200 collection, only the queries with different statistics for the modified- and full-freezing rankings are considered. This is done in order to isolate the advantages of modified freezing over full freezing. Only 24 out of the 42 queries yield different results for the two methods. The resulting precision-recall curve appears in Fig. 17-1. In the graph of Fig. 17-1, the area between curves 0 and 2 represents the feedback gain between the first and second iterations using full freezing, and the area between curves 1 and 3 does the same using modified freezing. The latter area is considerably greater than the former. Because both isolate the "feedback effect," the higher curves give a more reasonable picture of the improvement gained, in view of the absence of the damping due to the freezing of so many nonrelevant documents. In fact, modified-

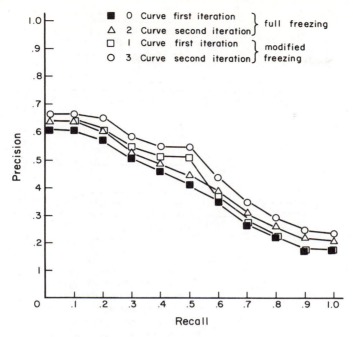

Fig. 17-1 Modified freezing evaluation (200 documents, 24 queries).

freezing evaluation seems superior to that of full freezing even on the first iteration. The modified-freezing curves exhibit a wider range than the full-freezing curves and hence can show more distinctly the difference between good and average feedback (because of the decrease in the damping effect mentioned earlier). Hence the conclusion that modified freezing is superior to full freezing on a query-by-query basis.

The present method of modified freezing can only be used with a positive feed-back algorithm, since in negative feedback, the nonrelevant documents are used to modify the query. If these are not frozen, they may be used again to modify the query, thus biasing the results. A small change in the algorithm can remedy this problem.

To summarize, modified freezing does seem to produce an improvement over full freezing as a method of evaluating the "feedback effect," especially on an individual query basis. However, the improvement tends to be swamped (as shown by the results on the ADI collection) by queries in which no difference appears between the two methods. It would seem worthwhile to include a modified-freezing algorithm in the SMART system to be used as an option for individual query comparisons.

17-4 THE RESIDUAL COLLECTION METHOD

A measure of effectiveness of a relevance feedback system should reflect the number of newly retrieved relevant documents due to the feedback process, as

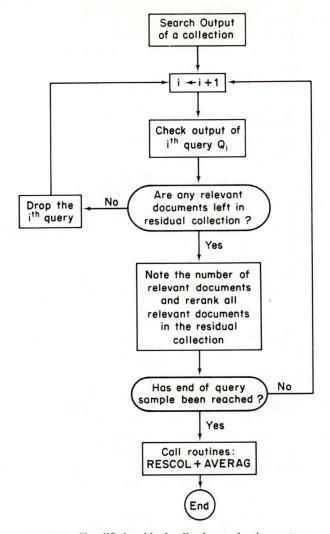

Fig. 17-2 Simplified residual collection evaluation system.

stated by Hall and Weiderman [2]. In other words, the question to be answered should be "how close is the modified query to the optimum query for the documents not yet presented to the user?" Although this question is important for the evaluation of feedback strategies, neither the ordinary freezing method nor the modified-freezing evaluation can be used to answer it directly. The residual collection evaluation method is used in an attempt to solve the problem [1]. For each feedback iteration, this method treats the remainder of the document collection, excluding those documents used for feedback, as a complete collection and the remainder of the relevant documents as a complete set of relevant documents. Then it carries out a total performance evaluation of the modified query in this new environment.

Initially, one obtains the output of a search of a document collection using three iterations of full freezing, including the ranks of all the relevant documents for each query. To calculate the performance of the ith iteration query in the $(i + 1)$st iteration residual collection, all relevant documents not used for feedback retrieval on the $(i + 1)$st iteration are to be reranked in the following way. The relevant documents in the ith iteration are reranked by subtracting the number of documents used for feedback retrieval on the $(i + 1)$st iteration from the original rank of these documents. If no relevant documents remain, the query is not used in the evaluation. Using these new ranks for the relevant documents, and the size of the $(i + 1)$st iteration residual collection as the size of the document collection, the SMART routines, RESCOL and AVERAG, are called to calculate all measures and to plot recall-precision graphs. A simplified flowchart of the process is given in Fig. 17-2.

Consider as a specific example the evaluation of the second iteration query with respect to the third iteration residual collection in the ADIABTH collection (82 documents, 35 queries):

1. Obtain a copy of ADIABTH relevance feedback search output (five new documents are presented to the user and are frozen on each iteration).

2. Since five documents are presented on each iteration, the size of the third iteration residual collection is $82 - 3 \times 5 = 67$, and all relevant documents with ranks larger than 15 as seen from the second iteration output are decreased by 15. For example, Q7 has originally four relevant documents numbered 7, 9, 19, and 40. On the second iteration, the following output is obtained:

Rank	Document	New Rank
1	19R	–
.	.	
.	.	
.	.	
13	40R	–
.	.	
.	.	
.	.	
15	69	–
16	7R	$1 (= 16 - 15)$
17	9R	$2 (= 17 - 15)$
.	.	
.	.	
.	.	

The number of relevant documents to be used is 2, since there are only two relevant documents, 7 and 9, with ranks larger than 15. They are reranked, and new ranks $16 - 15 = 1$ and $17 - 15 = 2$, respectively, are obtained.

3. If no relevant document remains for a given query, the query is dropped from the query sample. For instance, Q6 has only two relevant documents, 71 and 12, with ranks 3 and 11, respectively. Since both ranks are less than 15, no relevant document remains in the third iteration residual collection, and the query Q6 is dropped.

4. After reranking the original search output for each of the 35 queries, the RESCOL and AVERAG routines are called, and the recall-precision curve labeled 0 is generated.

5. In order to compare the performances between the second and the third iteration queries, both with respect to the third iteration residual collection, those relevant documents in the residual collection of the third iteration are reranked similarly, and curve 1 is obtained.

6. The original performance curves for the second and third iterations with respect to the original 82-document collection are included in the same plot, labeled 2 and 3, respectively.

17-5 RESIDUAL COLLECTION EVALUATION RESULTS AND CONCLUSIONS

In examining the output results, the following details must be kept in mind:

(a) When all relevant documents are retrieved before all requested iterations are completed, the query is dropped from the query sample.

(b) Difficulties may arise in averaging the performance of different queries because each query may have a different-sized residual collection. In this project the number of documents used for feedback is the same for all queries on a given iteration. Therefore the size of the residual collection is fixed, and no trouble arises. Otherwise recall and precision could be averaged after a specific number of documents or after a certain percentage of the document collection had been retrieved.

(c) A further difficulty occurs in comparing two methods of feedback when, for a given query, different generality numbers are obtained for the residual collections. As subsequent searches are made, the queries will be searching collections that include a different number of relevant items, and hence direct comparison (or averaging) of the results may not be valid.

The output for four computer runs is given in Figs. 17-3 through 17-6. From the figures, several conclusions can be drawn:

(a) In the *R-P* curves for the initial and first iteration queries, curve 1 is found to be quite a bit higher than curve 0 in both Fig. 17-3 and Fig. 17-5. This is as expected because the modified query improves the results in the first iteration significantly.

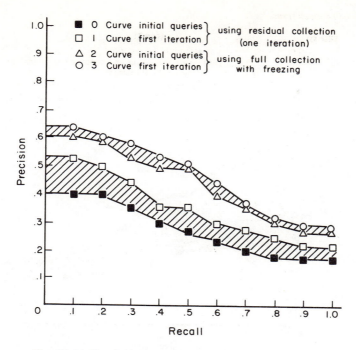

Fig. 17-3 Cranfield collection—residual collection evaluation.

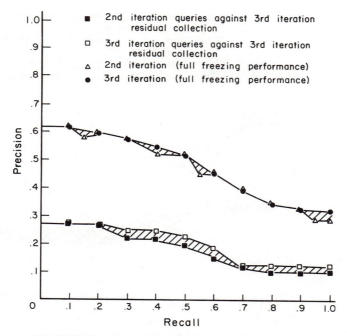

Fig. 17-4 Cranfield collection—residual collection evaluation.

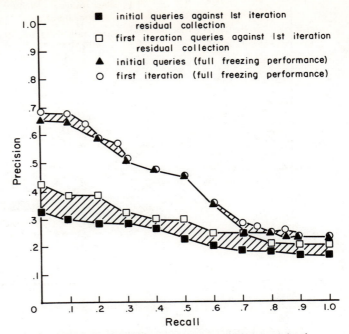

Fig. 17-5   ADI collection—residual collection evaluation.

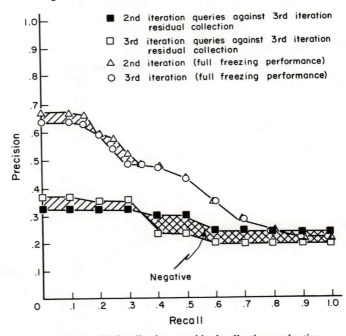

Fig. 17-6   ADI collection—residual collection evaluation.

The residual collection evaluation method thus shows that a further iteration is worthwhile to obtain additional relevant documents.

(b) A comparison of the *R-P* curves for the second and third iteration queries (Fig. 17-4 and Fig. 17-6) demonstrates that in Fig. 17-4 curve 1 is almost the same as curve 0, and in Fig. 17-6 curve 1 is lower than curve 0. This can be explained by noting that after two iterations, the relevant documents are mostly already retrieved; the query could then be modified by weighting in the wrong direction, especially for the not-well-formed ADIABTH collection. Thus for higher recall, curve 1 produces a worse performance than curve 0, as shown in Fig. 17-6. These results imply that no further iteration is recommended; that is, the user should look at more retrieved items on the second iteration, instead of performing a third iteration feedback.

(c) The difference between curve 1 and curve 0 is much larger than that between curve 3 and curve 2 (original freezing performance curves). Further, no ranking and freezing effects are involved in this evaluation method. It appears that the residual collection evaluation method produces better results than either the full-freezing and modified-freezing methods. However the reranking job must be done for each iteration, and the problems discussed previously must be considered.

(d) The relevance feedback searching algorithm appears to operate well since, within two or three iterations, almost all relevant documents are normally retrieved.

(e) Since the CRN2TH-200 documents and 42 queries are better formed and selected than the ADIABTH collection, the performance curves are smoother than those for the ADIABTH collection.

17-6 THE TEST AND CONTROL METHOD

A third method of feedback retrieval evaluation which avoids the ranking effect problems is being used experimentally. The general scheme is as follows. A given collection is split randomly into two halves. One group is used to run an initial search and to modify the queries based on user relevance judgments, and the other group, which has not been utilized to modify the queries, is used to evaluate the performance of the feedback retrieval. Figure 17-7 represents this process schematically.

The collection CRN4S which includes 424 documents and 155 queries was used experimentally. Two collections were created based on odd and even document numbers. The odd collection is used as the test group, while the even collection is used as the control group.

The reason for splitting the collection by using odd and even document numbers is the simplicity of the process. It is assumed that this process is sufficiently random to generate evenly distributed collections. From the original set of queries, two queries were deleted because no relevant documents were found for them in the test collection. Two query collections were then created, each one including the same num-

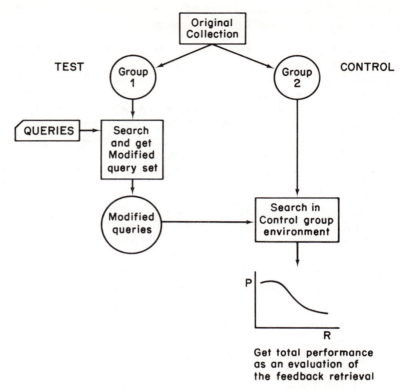

Fig. 17-7   General flow chart of the test and control process.

ber of queries (153) but with relevance decisions adjusted to interact with the test and control groups (see details in Sec. 17-7).

Figure 17-8 shows the generality distribution of the original CRN-400 collection along with that for the two subcollections. The collections are quite balanced from the point of view of relevant documents (508 relevant documents in the even collection and 483 in the odd). The discrepancy between number of relevant documents per query in the odd and even collections is also small as shown in Fig. 17-9. Attention should be paid to the fact that the difference between the generality of the even collection and the odd collection, as represented by the dashed curve in Fig. 17-8, is due to 14 queries from the odd collection *centered* at a range of 3–6 relevant documents against 15 queries from the even collection *spread* over the rest of the whole range. This uneven distribution might cause discrepancies in the performance of the two collections.

The following steps are now carried out:

(a) An initial full search (0 and 1 iteration) of the query sets against the test and control groups is performed, and averages are computed. The results of these runs are preserved.

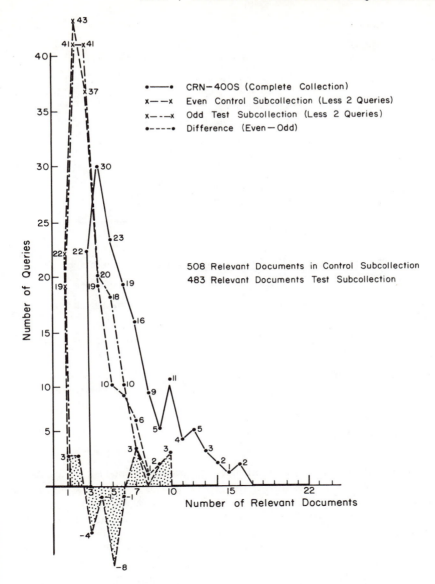

Fig. 17-8 Generality distribution of CRN4S against the split test and control collections.

(b) The results of the zeroth iteration between the two groups are compared, and the similarity of the two subcollections is evaluated.

(c) The relevance decisions of the queries which have been modified by the odd-test collection are changed by inserting the identifications of the relevant documents

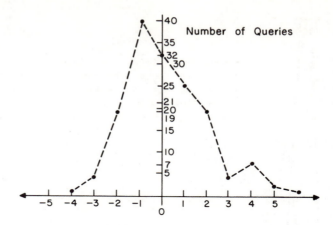

Fig. 17-9   Discrepancy between number of relevant documents per query.

of the even-control collection as the relevant documents for the modified query collection.

(d) The feedback evaluation search is performed using the modified query collection and the control group.

(e) The results are evaluated.

17-7   TEST AND CONTROL RESULTS AND EVALUATION

Figure 17-10 represents the recall-precision graph obtained by the test and control evaluation. Observing the results for the zeroth iteration on original test and control collections, the two subcollections do not seem to be on the average entirely equivalent. For lower recall the control collection performs better than the test collection. This means that the split of the collection using odd and even document numbers was not good enough, at least in this case; care must be taken that the differences in generality between the two subcollections remain small and evenly distributed. This could be done by shifting some documents back and forth until the proper distribution is found. A better way would be to identify queries that perform much worse in one group compared to the second group and to drop them. No attempt was made in the present test to correct the collection groups.

After executing steps (c) and (d) of Sec. 17-6, the curve drawn with white circles in the output of Fig. 17-10 is produced; this represents the true evaluation of the feedback retrieval. This curve is obtained as a result of a zero iteration full search of the queries which have been modified by the test collection, and thus it is free from

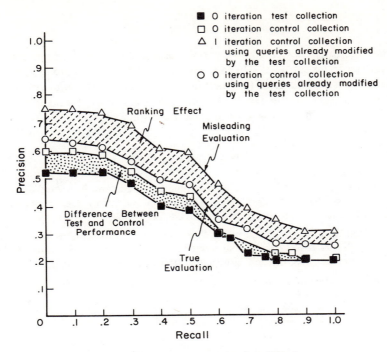

Fig. 17-10 True test and control evaluation (212 documents—153 queries).

any ranking effects. At the same time, ranks are assigned beginning from rank 1. The last curve, identified by white triangles in Fig. 17-10 is the recall-precision curve obtained after the first iteration in the control group. This curve reflects the total performance of the feedback retrieval which includes feedback effect as well as ranking effect.

Because of the differences in performance for the two subcollections, it may be assumed that the differences between the two zero iteration curves using the control collection may be greater for balanced collections. It is interesting to note that the difference between true and misleading evaluation curves (white circles and triangles) is quite even (it is bigger in the 0.0–0.6 recall range and then drops down). This can be explained by the fact that the ranking effects are on the average constant, and the differences between the two curves are due to this effect.

Another interesting phenomenon is the fact that the misleading evaluation curve of Fig. 17-10 (first iteration control collection using queries already modified by the test collection) is almost identical to the first iteration search result using the original queries with the control collection. The fact that both of them are raised to the same level means that the performance of the queries modified by the different collections is on the average almost the same.

17-8 CONCLUSIONS

The experiment described does show that test and control groups can be used for evaluating feedback retrieval. The fact that different collections are used for the evaluation is the main advantage of this method, since this permits the use of total performances as a measure of the feedback retrieval. Care must be taken in splitting the original collection in order to ensure accurate results.

REFERENCES

[1] E. Ide, Relevance Feedback in an Automatic Document Retrieval System, Master's thesis, *Report ISR-15* to the National Science Foundation, Department of Computer Science, Cornell University, Ithaca, N.Y., January 1969.

[2] H. A. Hall and N. H. Weiderman, The Evaluation Problem in Relevance Feedback Systems, *Report ISR-12* to the National Science Foundation, Section XII, Department of Computer Science, Cornell University, Ithaca, N.Y., June 1967.

[3] G. Salton, *Automatic Information Organization and Retrieval*, Chap. 8, McGraw-Hill, Inc., New York, 1968.

PART VI

FEEDBACK REFINEMENTS

*A great deal of effort has been devoted in recent years to the evaluation of
automatic or semiautomatic information retrieval systems. Recent evaluation results
indicate that the search effectiveness presently achieved, or likely to be achieved in the
foreseeable future, is much smaller than expected by a majority of the potential user
population. Furthermore, theoretical advances in language analysis and data
organization promise only relatively modest future improvements.*

*The most significant advances in retrieval effectiveness are likely to be obtained
by adaptive interaction techniques which extract information from the user during
the search process to improve the organization of the data space, thereby providing
more effective search and retrieval operations. The various user feedback techniques
described either modify the user queries in such a way as to bring these queries closer
to existing groups of relevant documents or modify the document space to bring
relevant documents closer to the corresponding search requests.*

18

INTERACTIVE SEARCH STRATEGIES AND DYNAMIC FILE ORGANIZATION IN INFORMATION RETRIEVAL†

E. IDE and G. SALTON

18-1 RETRIEVAL SYSTEM PERFORMANCE

Over the past few years, the design of improved information storage and
retrieval systems has become important to an increasing segment of the technically trained population. As a result, considerable attention has been paid
to the development of automatic or semiautomatic hardware and software
systems designed to store ever increasing amounts of information and to
make the stored data available to selected user classes. As the interest has
grown in the development of automatic information systems, procedures for
evaluating the performance of information systems have also become increasingly important, since the large investments necessarily required in a mechanization of information-handing procedures would not be justified without
some assurance that the resulting systems could render reasonably effective
services.

†This study was published originally as Section XI of *Scientific Report ISR-16*, and
a shorter version is included in the *Proc. of the ASIS National Meeting*, San Francisco,
October 1969.

Evaluation studies of information system performance are often carried out by choosing some subset of the information requests submitted to a given system and identifying as "relevant" to each query a list of items that have been hand-selected by the user or by a subject expert. The effectiveness of the search and retrieval system is then measured by determining the extent to which the selected items have been retrieved and other items have been rejected in answer to the query sample.

Two standard retrieval measures have been used widely to evaluate retrieval effectiveness: *recall*, the proportion of relevant items actually retrieved, and *precision*, the proportion of retrieved items actually relevant. A perfect system, achieving both maximum recall and maximum precision, is not generally achieved in actual practice. In fact, recall is found to vary inversely with precision, that is, as the recall of a system goes up because more relevant items are retrieved, precision goes down because more irrelevant items are also retrieved. Therefore, the user must choose between obtaining either high recall and low precision or high precision and low recall.

The average search results obtained in several recent retrieval evaluation studies vary between a recall of 0.1 at a high precision of 0.9, for specific and narrow search statements, and a recall of 0.9 at a low precision of 0.2, when the search statement is interpreted broadly [1], [2], [3]. Operational systems normally compromise by operating in the middle ranges where neither the recall nor the precision are very low. In fact, the Medlars system of the National Library of Medicine is said to operate at an average recall of 0.58 and an average precision of 0.50, thus producing the correct retrieval of about 60% of what is wanted, while keeping the amount of useless material also retrieved to about 50% [3].

Two pragmatic approaches are being pursued actively in an attempt to improve the retrieval effectiveness of existing or proposed information systems. The first consists of using more refined information analysis procedures designed to generate query and document identifiers which are more reflective of information content. For example, the experimental automatic SMART document retrieval system, which provides fully automatic document and query analysis, includes procedures for automatic synonym recognition using stored dictionaries and thesauri, for the assignment of phrase identifiers instead of simple terms, for the refinement or broadening of information identifiers using stored hierarchical subject arrangements, and for the use of statistical and syntactic language analysis methods [4], [5].

The second, more recently used method of improving retrieval effectiveness, utilizes automatic information displays during on-line search procedure in an attempt to encourage the user into submitting viable search statements. Excerpts of stored dictionaries or term lists can be displayed, as well as term frequency information, lists of related words, and titles or abstracts of stored documents [6], [7], [8].

While both advanced language analysis methods and on-line interactive display techniques appear to improve retrieval effectiveness, the increment of improvement generated is relatively small, generally from 5% to 15% [2], [7]. Thus it appears that by methods which are well understood and seem reasonable economically, recall and precision figures of 0.60 to 0.65 are presently achievable at least in experimental environments.

Whether more dramatic improvements may be expected in the future—for example by the use of more refined grammatical models such as transformational language analysis—remains to be seen. Some evidence exists to suggest that presently obtainable results are only about 25% lower than those produced by an "ideal" search system, where human subject experts conduct exhaustive manual searches through the complete stored collection [9]. Therefore, recall and precision results of about 0.75 may constitute an upper bound to the performance of both automatic and manual retrieval system. Whether any automatic system can achieve such results depends to some extent on the ability of the system to adapt to the expectations of the particular user population being serviced. Heuristic methods for this purpose are described in the remainder of this study.

18-2 REQUEST SPACE MODIFICATIONS

18-2-A Relevance Feedback

A principal technique for improving the performance of automatic information retrieval consists of using information supplied by the customer in order to alter the request to correspond to the user's need. Specifically, the query representation—consisting in many retrieval systems of weighted sets of terms or concepts—can be changed by adding or stressing concepts which appropriately identify the user's information need and by minimizing or even deleting concepts which are not representative of the user's need. The altered query should then be more similar to the stored representations of documents relevant to the user and less similar to the representations of nonrelevant documents.

One way this can be accomplished is by performing an initial search of the collection, using the original query, and retrieving for the user's attention a small amount of output, consisting of some of the highest-scoring documents (those most similar to the query). These documents are examined by the user who identifies each retrieved item as either relevant (reflective of his information needs) or irrelevant. Then the stored representations of these judged documents are used automatically to adjust the queries in such a way that terms present in the relevant documents are promoted, whereas terms occurring in documents designated as nonrelevant are demoted. In a somewhat simplified form, a typical query-updating procedure is represented by the following equation:†

$$\mathbf{q}_{i+1} = \mathbf{q}_i + \alpha \sum_{i=1}^{n_r} \mathbf{r}_i - \beta \sum_{i=1}^{n_s} \mathbf{s}_i, \tag{1}$$

where $\mathbf{q}_{i+1}$ represents the updated query vector, $\mathbf{q}_i$ is the original query vector, $\mathbf{r}_i$ is one of n_r document representations identified as relevant, and $\mathbf{s}_i$ is one of n_s nonrelevant documents [10], [11].

†In the experimental system discussed here, terms having negative weights are deleted from the query (given zero weight).

Two major variants of the *relevance feedback* process described above are discussed in Sec. 18-2-B. The simpler algorithm, *positive feedback*, uses only the retrieved documents judged relevant to alter the query [equation (1), $\beta = 0$]. The second variant uses both the relevant and nonrelevant documents retrieved to modify the query [equation (1), $\beta > 0$]. A study of the differences in performance between these two strategies reveals an important characteristic of the space of document representations and leads to a proposal for several new techniques designed to improve retrieval in similar environments.

18-2-B Positive and Negative Strategies

A typical *positive* query alteration process, where concepts may be added to the query but none are deleted, is illustrated in the examples of Tables 18-1 and 18-2.

Table 18-1

POSITIVE FEEDBACK ILLUSTRATION

(Query Q146: What information is available for dynamic response
of airplanes to gusts or blasts in subsonic regime?)

Vector Type	Illustration

(a) Initial query vector	airplane available blast dynamic
	  12 12 12 12
	gust information regime response
	  12 12 12 12
	subsonic
	  12

(b) Relevant document 102
retrieved with rank 2
(partial vector)
	gust lift oscillating penetration
	  48 48 12 12
	response subsonic sudden
	   24 12 12

(c) Query modified by
document 102
	airplane available blast dynamic
	  12 12 12 12
	gust information lift oscillating
	  60 12 48 12
	penetration regime response subsonic
	     12 12 36 24
	sudden
	  12

(d) Relevant document 80 (improves from rank 14 to rank 7; partial vector)	gust lift penetration sudden 24 72 12 12
(e) Relevant document 81 (improves from rank 137 to rank 6; partial vector)	lift oscillating sudden 84 12 12

Table 18-2

POSITIVE FEEDBACK STRATEGY FOR QUERY Q147 SHOWING
IMPROVEMENTS IN RELEVANT DOCUMENT RANKS

(Query Q147: Will forward or apex-located controls
be effective at low subsonic speeds?)

INITIAL		FEEDBACK ITERATIONS			ITEMS
		1	*2*	*3*	
Rank	*Document*	*Document*	*Document*	*Document*	
1	109	94R	94R	94R	
2	60	81	95R	95R	
3	121	195	90R	90R	
4	192	123	195	195	
5	193	80	81	91R	
6	119	114	80	81	
7	82	90R	114	80	
8	24	193	193	111	Retrieved
9	86	122	123	114	
10	123	95R	111	193	
11	100	111	91R	93R	
12	146	64	109	123	
13	18	102	159	192	
14	94R	109	103	109	
15	167	82	192	159	
16	125	103	82	155	
17	163	78	93R	103	
18	114	125	78	82	
19	65	20	122	78	
20	177	192	102	110	
21	93R	124	64	122	
22	90R	159	155	153	
23	19	194	110	111	
24	153	196	11	76	
25	181	86	153	64	Not retrieved
26	58	63	76	92	
27	22	66	196	102	
28	172	91R	20	152	
29	200	10	194	161	
30	64	93R	132	132	
31	3	11	152	196	
32	195	61	92	96	
33	144	77	125	29	
34	122	76	124	133	
35	63	132	86	194	
36	184	104	161	20	
37	34	153	61	86	
38	74	54	133	104	
39	113	49	29	61	
40	17	177	104	125	
41	95R	144	63	176	
42	75	67	96	124	
43	67	29	83	121	
44	140	60	77	83	
76	91R	19	160	160	

An original query statement is given in Table 18-1, as well as the analyzed query "vector" in terms of a weighted term list. Following the addition of terms from document no. 102, identified previously as relevant, the revised query vector retrieves two more relevant documents, 80 and 81, with ranks 7 and 6, respectively (for retrieval purposes, documents are always ranked in decreasing order of similarity with the query). These two documents were originally assigned ranks 14 and 137, using the unaltered query vector.

Table 18-2 shows a typical retrieval output list, giving the ranks of retrieved documents in decreasing correlation order with the query. Relevant document numbers are identified by *R*. The identified relevant document number 94 retrieved originally with rank 14) is used first to update the query. This pulls up relevant documents 90 and 95 to ranks 7 and 10, respectively. When these two new documents are used in turn to update the query, additional relevant items are retrieved, until finally all five relevant documents are retrieved within the top 12 items following feedback run 3.

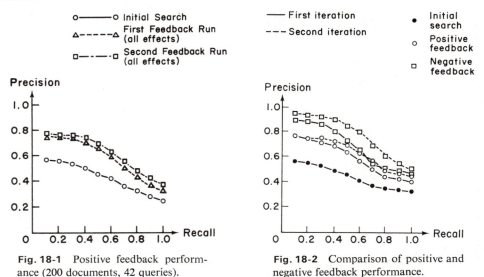

Fig. 18-1 Positive feedback performance (200 documents, 42 queries).

Fig. 18-2 Comparison of positive and negative feedback performance.

A typical recall-precision graph for positive feedback is shown in Fig. 18-1, giving averages over the 42 queries for initial runs and two feedback iterations. The curves closest to the upper right-hand corner of the graph (where recall and precision are equal to 1) represent improved performance. It is seen that the updated queries produced by the feedback operations exhibit a precision average 10% to 20% better than the original queries for all recall points.†

Although positive feedback is often successful (for example, for query 147 of Table 18-2), it fails to aid the retrieval performance of some queries. This occurs

†The recall-precision output in this study includes both the ranking and the feedback effects.

notably when no relevant items are retrieved, or when the retrieved relevant items are dissimilar. Performance may be improved even under these unfavorable conditions by a negative strategy that moves the queries away from those items specifically *not* wanted by the user.

An illustration of the potential usefulness of the negative feedback strategy is given in Table 18-3, showing positive and negative performance for query 3. Here the positive strategy produces no improvement on the first iteration and then promotes relevant documents 57, 31, 4, 30, and 32, while demoting item 33 which goes down from rank 124 to 194. The negative strategy, on the other hand, retrieves documents 4, 57, 30, and 32 on the first iteration by moving away from the nonrelevant initially retrieved (documents 179, 42, 112, 39, and 117).

A thorough experimental comparison between positive and negative feedback strategies in a collection of 200 documents reveals the following differences in performance [12]:

(a) The overall average differences in performance measured by the changes in rank of *all* documents strongly favor negative feedback, as is seen in Fig. 18-2.

Table 18-3

EXAMPLE OF IMPROVEMENTS OBTAINABLE WITH
NEGATIVE FEEDBACK (QUERY 3)

RANK	POSITIVE STRATEGY ITERATION			RANK	NEGATIVE STRATEGY ITERATION		
	0	*1*	*2*		*0*	*1*	*2*
1	179	179	57R	1	179	4R	4R
2	42	42	31R	2	42	71	57R
3	112	112	179	3	112	57R	32R
4	39	39	4R	4	39	30R	30R
5	117	117	112	5	117	32R	31R
6	181	181	30R	6	181	182	200
7	57R	45	42	7	57R	152	189
8	45	57R	182	8	45	43	184
9	152	152	117	9	152	3	34
10	62	62	39	10	62	199	0
11	182	182	45	11	182	0	0
12	153	153	189	12	153	0	0
13	31R	31R	181	13	31R	0	0
14	43	43	0	14	43	0	0
15	116	116	0	15	116	0	0
16	0	0	32R	20	30R	0	0
20	30R	30R	0	22	0	31R	0
23	32R	32R	0	23	32R	0	0
25	4R	4R	0	25	4R	0	0
124	33R	33R	0	27	0	0	33R
194	0	0	33R	115	0	33R	0
				124	33R	0	0

(b) The overall average differences measured by rank changes of *unretrieved* documents only are not statistically significant.

(c) However, the variance in the performance is always greater for negative feedback than for positive, indicating that for some queries negative feedback is better and for other queries it is worse than positive feedback.

(d) Queries retrieving no relevant document in an initial search (which therefore cannot be updated on the first iteration by any positive strategy) are helped by the negative procedure.

(e) On the average, the performance of queries that *do* retrieve relevant items in the initial search is not hindered by the negative strategy.

(f) The negative strategy changes the query vector much more than the positive strategy (the average correlation between initial and updated queries is about 0.85 for the positive strategy, but only 0.50 for the negative strategy).

(g) A plot of the average recall and precision differences between positive and negative feedback strategies is shown in Fig. 18-3; the following distinctions are apparent for the collection of 200 documents:

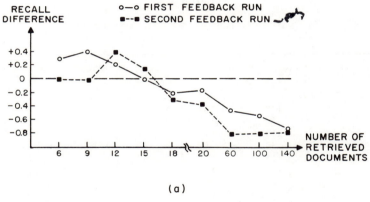

(a)

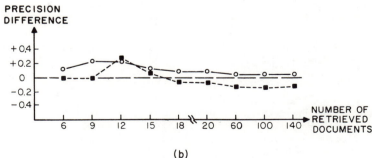

(b)

Fig. 18-3 Differences between negative and positive feedback (averages 200 documents, 42 queries): (a) recall differences; (b) precision differences.

   i.   If recall and precision are measured after the retrieval of about 15 documents, the negative strategy is better by about 5% in recall and about 3% in precision.
  ii.   After the retrieval of 20 to 30 items, the two strategies are about equal.
 iii.   After 40 retrieved items, the positive strategy is better by about 10% in recall and 20% in precision.

This indicates that negative feedback retrieves more relevant documents within the top 10% of the document collection than positive feedback, but that the relevant documents remaining in the lower 70% of the collection are assigned much lower ranks by the negative strategy than by the positive strategy. Thus, in general, the query produced by negative feedback is closer to some relevant documents and at the same time further from other relevant documents than the positive feedback query.

The evidence summarized above supports the following conclusion concerning the vector space of document representations:

> . . . the documents selected by the user as relevant to his query are often found in two or more distinct groups in the document vector space; and these groups are separated from one another by nonrelevant documents. For a significant number of queries, this separation of relevant document groups effectively prevents the retrieval of some relevant documents by conventional feedback strategies [12].

Consider as an illustration the document space of Fig. 18-4. Here documents and queries are shown by points in the plane and the distance between two points represents closeness of the corresponding subject matter.† Each query is assumed to retrieve all documents lying in a sphere around the query. The positive feedback illustration of Fig. 18-4(a) shows that the original query, identified by a circled zero, retrieves two relevant documents, one to the right of the query and one to the left, as well as six nonrelevant documents. The expanded query, represented by a circled 1, retrieves additional documents, including a relevant one located to the left of the original circle. The new relevant item is used in a second updating operation to pull the query over to the left. The final updated query, represented by a circled 2, retrieves the three relevant items located on the left side of the picture; at the same time, two of the three relevant items on the right side are unfortunately lost.

The same document space and query are processed by a negative feedback strategy in Fig. 18-4(b). Here the three nonrelevant items located just left of center move the original query over to the right, away from the nonrelevant group. A new updating operation then moves the query further away from the original position in the general direction of the relevant document group on the right. The negative feedback strategy thus retrieves the relevant items on the right side of the picture but "loses" two of the relevant ones on the left.

---

†In actual fact each document or query must be represented by a *t*-dimensional vector, where *t* is the number of distinct allowable identifying terms; the two-dimensional picture of Fig. 18-4 is thus a simplified analogy of the actual *t*-dimensional space.

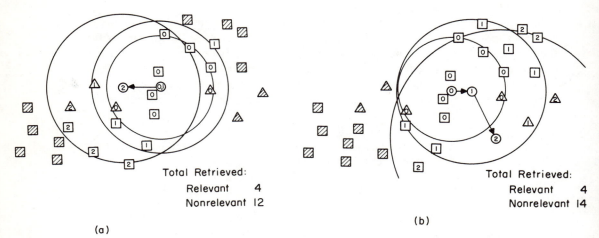

△ Relevant Document
□ Nonrelevant Document
Ⓝ Query on Iteration N

Total Retrieved:
Relevant   4
Nonrelevant 12

(a)

Total Retrieved:
Relevant   4
Nonrelevant 14

(b)

Fig. 18-4 Positive and negative feedback; (a) positive feedback; (b) positive and negative feedback.

Table 18-4

Positive and Negative Feedback Strategies

(Query 9 with separate relevant document clusters)

RANK	POSITIVE STRATEGY ITERATION			RANK	NEGATIVE STRATEGY ITERATION		
	0	*1*	*2*		*0*	*1*	*2*
1	179	179	116R	1	179	25	25
2	112	112	179	2	112	71	71
3	39	39	62	3	39	41	41
4	42	42	102	4	42	64	3
5	181	181	181	5	181	3	98
6	45	45	39	6	45	85	178
7	62	62	42	7	62	88	82R
8	116R	116R	117	8	116R	23	160
9	97	97	3	9	97	101	64
10	188	188	45	10	188	17	101
11	31	31	115	11	31	82R	0
12	57	57	2	12	57	0	0
13	117	117	158	13	117	116R	0
14	2	2	0	14	2	0	0
15	25	25	0	15	25	0	116R
33	82R	82R	0	33	82R	0	0
54	0	0	82R				

This type of retrieval behavior is illustrated for the example of query 9 in Table 18-4, where the positive strategy moves the query away from relevant document 82 when relevant document 116 is used for feedback. The negative strategy retrieves document 82 by using nonrelevant documents for feedback, but simultaneously, the query is moved away from document 116.

If the high retrieval performance sometimes achieved by human subject experts is to be duplicated in an automatic environment, new retrieval strategies must be designed specifically to select separated groups of relevant documents. Each of the techniques proposed in the following sections exhibits some advantages over conventional retrieval methods in the type of document vector space depicted in Fig. 18-4.

18-2-C Selective Negative Feedback

The discussion in Sec. 18-2-B indicates that the use of retrieved nonrelevant documents for feedback often lowers further the ranks assigned to low-ranking relevant documents. This suggests that a more selective process might be devised in applying the negative strategy in order to improve overall performance. Under the present procedure, *all* terms included in the identified set of nonrelevant documents are automatically deleted from the query or reduced in weight. This process may lead to the effective loss of important query terms, particularly terms which may have more than one meaning in the document collection. The illustration of Table 18-5, de-

Table 18-5

EXAMPLE OF INADEQUATE NEGATIVE FEEDBACK

(Query: Please give specification for all currently available data sets.)

Type of Vector	Illustration				
(a) Initial query vector	available 12	current 12	data set 12	specification 12	
(b) Sum of retrieved nonrelevant documents	access 48	data set 60	file 24	list 24	structure 84
(c) Standard negative feedback result	available 12	current 12	specification 12		

scribing a query dealing with data sets, shows that the crucial term "data set" is eventually deleted from the query.†

Two selective negative procedures are proposed. The first one, illustrated in Table 18-6, consists of assigning negative weights to terms extracted from nonrelevant documents while leaving the original query terms unchanged. Thus, in the example, the term data set is still present in the final query, but the related terms derived from

---

†"Data set" is an ambiguous term denoting both a communications device (the meaning assumed in the query) and a "set of data" (the meaning derived from the nonrelevant document set).

Table 18-6

SELECTIVE NEGATIVE WEIGHTING

Type of Vector	Illustration
(a) Initial query vector	available current data set specification 12 12 12 12
(b) Sum of retrieved nonrelevant documents	access data set file list structure 48 60 24 24 84
(c) Negative context vector (query concepts deleted)	access file list structure 48 24 24 84
(d) Selective negative feedback result (b − c)	access available current data set −48 12 12 12 file list specification structure −24 −24 12 −84

Table 18-7

NEGATIVE FEEDBACK WITH RELATED CONCEPTS

Type of Vector	Illustration
(a) Initial query vector	available current data set specification 12 12 12 12
(b) Concepts related to "data set" with correlation strength	access bandwidth file interface line list 77 28 50 58 52 47 retrieval sort structure transmission 49 50 19 30
(c) Related concept vector (top 5 concepts with weight of 24)	access file interface line structure 24 24 24 24 24
(d) Query vector with related concepts	access available current data set file 24 12 12 12 24 interface line specification structure 24 24 12 24
(e) Sum of retrieved nonrelevant documents	access data set file list structure 48 60 24 24 84
(f) Feedback result with related concepts	available current interface line specification 12 12 24 24 12
(g) Related concepts and selective negative weighting	access available current data set interface −24 12 12 12 24 line list specification structure 24 −24 12 −60

the nonrelevant document set which suggest sets of data are assigned negative weights.

The other selective procedure, illustrated in Table 18-7, uses a synonym dictionary or thesaurus (or alternatively, an associative indexing procedure) to provide a set of related terms for each term. First these related dictionary terms are added to the query statement, after which the terms obtained from the nonrelevant documents are subtracted out. In the example of Table 18-7, the thesaurus provides contextual information for the term data set used both in the sense of a communications device and in the sense of sets of data; the latter context is then eliminated by the negative feedback operation.

Both of the suggested selective negative feedback strategies are intended to retain in the query the terms that might lead to the eventual retrieval of relevant documents separated from the query by nonrelevant documents. Since the intervening nonrelevant documents are also retrieved, it remains to be seen whether these strategies improve performance for a significant number of queries.

18-3 DOCUMENT CLUSTERING

When relevant documents are separated from each other by nonrelevant documents, no conceivable strategy which uses a *single* query to search the complete document space can identify the separate sets of relevant items, while properly rejecting the nonrelevant documents located between them. A multiple query set might then be used, instead of a single query, in such a way that each "subquery" searches a distinct part of the document space. This, in turn, suggests that the documents in a collection be grouped into "clusters" of similar documents, and that each document cluster be searched separately. Then it may be easier to discriminate between relevant and nonrelevant items within a given document cluster than in the document collection as a whole.

Several methods exist for producing document clusters automatically in such a way that items sufficiently similar to each other are placed in the same group [13], [14], [15]. Such clustered document collections can be used conveniently in a retrieval environment to reduce the search to a small portion of the document space by comparing the query against only those documents located within a specified subset of clusters [16], [17].

Cluster searching can be performed in several distinct ways. The *combined cluster search* of Fig. 18-5(a) operates in such a way that all documents in the cluster set to be searched are ranked according to their distance from the query. Thus, the initial query of Fig. 18-5(a) first retrieves 6 documents all located in the left-hand cluster, including one relevant item; a second search operation is then used to retrieve 13 more items. Alternatively, a *separate cluster search* can be performed, as shown in Fig. 18-5(b), where the documents are ranked separately within each cluster relative to other documents in the same cluster. The query then retrieves the highest-ranking documents from each cluster searched. In the illustration the 6 relevant items are retrieved more efficiently in the separate cluster search than in the combined search, since the number of unwanted items obtained is only 10 for the separate compared with 13 for the combined strategy.

The cluster searches shown in Fig. 18-5 compare all documents in all selected clusters with the same initial query. In order to generate a distinct query for each

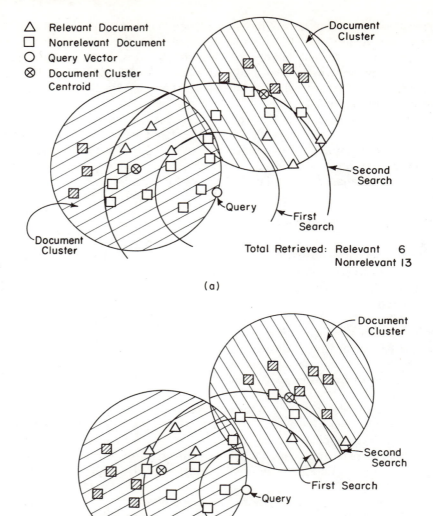

Fig. 18-5 Single query cluster searches; (a) combined cluster search; (b) separate cluster search.

cluster to be searched, it is possible to combine the notion of the cluster search with the query alteration methods used in relevance feedback. Specifically, a query alteration procedure can be utilized in which retrieved documents from separate clusters generate distinct queries, each of which operates within a distinct document cluster.

The *cluster feedback* process illustrated in Fig. 18-6(a) is a partial search method of this type. The following principal steps are required:

(a) The original query (designated in Fig. 18-6 by a circled 0) is compared first with the centers (centroids) of all document clusters.

(b) The clusters whose centroids are closest to the original query are then selected, and the individual document vectors within the selected clusters are compared to the query.

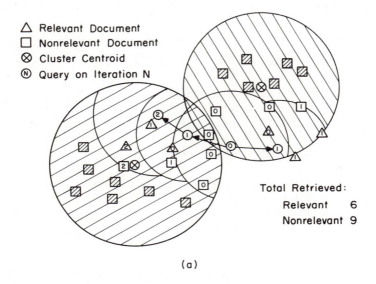

(a)

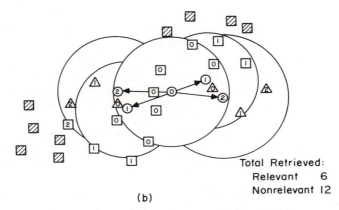

(b)

Fig. 18-6   Multiple query searches: (a) cluster feedback; (b) split queries.

(c) Relevance judgments are obtained for those documents found to be closest to the query.

(d) A *new* query is constructed for *each* cluster, using the original query as well as the relevant (or nonrelevant) documents from that particular cluster only—in the example of Fig. 18-6(a) the original query (circled 0) leads to two distinct new queries (circled 1) obtained by using the relevant documents from the right-hand and from the left-hand cluster, respectively.

(e) Each new query is now matched only against the documents in its own cluster, and only the documents retrieved by a given query are used to modify that query in further feedback iterations.

(f) All documents retrieved from all selected clusters may be used to generate from the initial query a new centroid search query to select additional clusters to be searched.†

(g) Since more than one query is generated, some means of discarding queries that seem unlikely to retrieve additional relevant items would be desirable. Several possible criteria for eliminating such queries are suggested elsewhere [12].†

In the illustration of Fig. 18-6(a), only nine nonrelevant items are retrieved together with the six relevant.

The cluster feedback algorithm described above is equally feasible in combination with a technique called *request clustering*. This suggested alternative to document clustering assumes that documents formerly retrieved in answer to similar previous queries should be considered in processing a new query. In step (*a*) the request cluster feedback algorithm would compare the new query to the centroids of clusters of previous *queries* submitted to the system. The clusters of documents searched in steps (*b*), (*c*), (*d*), and (*e*) would then include documents judged relevant to the queries in the query clusters nearest the new query. Request clustering allows documents which are adjacent in the document space to be placed into different clusters and nonadjacent documents to be placed into the same cluster. This may turn out to be advantageous in an environment containing separated groups of relevant documents.

If the cluster search is to operate successfully, the retrieval problem (that is, the separation of relevant from nonrelevant) within each cluster must be simpler than the problem in the space as a whole; furthermore, the cluster selection method must pick few unproductive clusters to be searched. Should separated clusters of relevant documents still occur within one or more of the clusters, it may be necessary to construct multiple queries all of which search the same set of documents.

A "query-splitting" process designed to do this has been investigated with some success on a small test collection [18]. A query is split into two subqueries whenever the correlation between two relevant documents previously retrieved is small compared to the average interdocument correlation between the first five retrieved documents. An alternative strategy might be to split the query whenever a retrieved nonrelevant document is located between two retrieved relevant ones; that is, relevant documents

†Steps (f) and (g) are not illustrated in Fig. 18-6(a).

r and **v** are used to generate distinct (split) queries whenever, for some nonrelevant item **n**,

$$\text{Correlation } (\mathbf{n}, \mathbf{v}) > \text{Correlation } (\mathbf{r}, \mathbf{v}),$$

and

$$\text{Correlation } (\mathbf{n}, \mathbf{r}) > \text{Correlation } (\mathbf{r}, \mathbf{v}).$$

An illustration of the query-splitting concept is shown in Fig. 18-6(b). First the original query (circled 0) retrieves two relevant items, one to the right and one to the left, whose interdocument correlation is small compared with the correlation of each relevant item to one of the nonrelevant in the middle. This leads to a split of the initial query into two pieces (circled 1), and to two additional queries (circled 2) after one more iteration. The subqueries on the right retrieve the rightmost relevant, and the left subqueries handle the relevant on the left. Both of the multiple query strategies illustrated in Fig. 18-6 remain to be tried out in a realistic document environment.

18-4 DOCUMENT SPACE MODIFICATION

The feedback procedures described up to now all produce a modification of the query space in such a way that queries are moved close to certain identified relevant documents or away from identified nonrelevant ones. The strategies suggested in this section attack the problem directly by permanently changing the *document* vector space. Specifically, the vector representations of documents judged relevant to a query are moved closer to the query vector. This strategy is more radical than query modification, since it implies that the queries are more fundamental as subject indicators than the original document identifying terms.

Two different document space modification methods are illustrated in Fig. 18-7. In the first one [Fig. 18-7(a)], the previously identified relevant documents are modified by addition of query terms as follows:

$$\mathbf{d}_{i+1} = (1 - \alpha) \, \mathbf{d}_i + \alpha \mathbf{q}_0 \qquad\qquad (2)$$

where $\mathbf{d}_{i+1}$ is the modified document, $\mathbf{d}_i$ the original document, and $\mathbf{q}_0$ the original query.

A test was performed for this document modification process using a collection of 425 documents in aerodynamics and a set of 125 queries to effect the space modification. A new set of 30 additional queries not used previously for space modification was then processed with the modified document space, and improvements in both recall and precision of 10% to 15% were detected, compared with the use of these same queries in conjunction with the original, unmodified document space. These relatively large improvements appear to indicate that new customers, whose relevance criteria play no part in the space modification, profit directly from the query-document associations derived from previous system users.

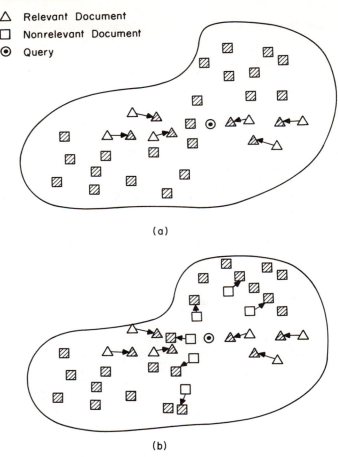

Fig. 18-7   Document space modification: (a) relevant document modification; (b) adaptive document modification.

A second document space modification procedure, illustrated in Fig. 18-7(b), is based on strategies tried previously in adaptive pattern recognition [12]. The basic idea is to pair each retrieved relevant document with a nonrelevant document not modified previously; if the nonrelevant item happens to be located closer to the query than the relevant one, an interchange procedure is used to move the relevant forward (closer to the query) and the nonrelevant backward (away from the query). More formally, the process is as follows:

(a) If for *all* $\mathbf{d}_i$, such that $\mathbf{d}_i$ is relevant to query $\mathbf{q}_0$ and for all $\mathbf{d}_j$ such that $\mathbf{d}_j$ is nonrelevant,

$$\text{Correlation } (\mathbf{d}_i, \mathbf{q}_0) > \text{Correlation } (\mathbf{d}_j, \mathbf{q}_0) + \theta,$$

then no adjustment is made.

(b) Otherwise, each vector $\mathbf{d}_i$ denoting relevant document i is processed *in order* with $\mathbf{q}_0$; if there is a document k, *not yet* adjusted by $\mathbf{q}_0$, and $\mathbf{d}_k$ is not relevant to $\mathbf{q}_0$, and

$$\text{Correlation } (\mathbf{d}_k, \mathbf{q}_0) + \theta \geq \text{Correlation } (\mathbf{d}_i, \mathbf{q}_0),$$

then

$$\mathbf{d}'_i = (1 - \alpha)\mathbf{d}_i + \alpha\mathbf{q}_0,$$

and

$$\mathbf{d}'_k = (1 - \alpha)\mathbf{d}_k - \alpha\mathbf{q}_0,$$

where $\mathbf{d}_k$ is that previously unmodified nonrelevant item having the highest correlation with $\mathbf{q}_0$, and $\mathbf{d}'_i$ and $\mathbf{d}'_k$ are the new adjusted document vectors.

(c) If no nonrelevant document k exists which has not been previously adjusted, the modification of the relevant item $\mathbf{d}_i$ is still performed.

This procedure is intended to produce a document space which groups all the relevant items around the corresponding queries, while moving the nonrelevant items further away. Moreover, the space alteration is controlled in the sense that a different nonrelevant item is subtracted out each time.

The basic differences between the two suggested modification procedures is similar to the distinction between positive and negative feedback. The first technique adjusts only relevant documents, while the second alters both relevant and nonrelevant documents. A comparison of the two strategies in the 425-document collection shows the superiority of the second method when α [modifier in equation (2)] is relatively small (0.05 to 0.10). The advantage in precision of "negative modification" over "positive modification" is greatest at relatively low recall levels, reaching 4% at 20% recall.

Both document space modification algorithms can be combined easily with the relevance feedback methods in an operating retrieval system to provide a continual adjustment of the document identifiers in accordance with the user's expectations. The simplest procedure consists in modifying only the retrieved documents. This modification could take place after the relevance judgments are rendered by the user. Only the vector representation of the user's initial query would be used to alter the document representations. The proposed combined query and document space modification has not yet been tested in a retrieval environment.

18-5 CONCLUSION

In this chapter several search and retrieval strategies are described that use feedback information supplied by the user during the retrieval process to modify the query or document spaces. In each case, the space modification is intended to increase the correlation between queries and relevant documents while decreasing the query correlation with nonrelevant items. Experimental evidence indicates that the improvements in retrieval effectiveness obtainable with these heuristic search strategies are much larger than the improvements immediately derivable from the more formal deterministic methods based on better document and query analyses and more sophisticated linguistic normalization tools.

REFERENCES

[1] C. W. Cleverdon and E. M. Keen, Factors Determining the Performance of Indexing Systems, *Test Results*, Vol. 2, Aslib–Cranfield Research Project, Cranfield, England, 1966.

[2] G. Salton and M. E. Lesk, Computer Evaluation of Indexing and Text Processing, *Journal of the ACM*, Vol. 15, No. 1, January 1968; also Chap. 7 of this volume.

[3] F. W. Lancaster, Evaluating the Operating Efficiency of Medlars, Final Report, National Library of Medicine, Washington, D.C., January 1968.

[4] G. Salton, *Automatic Information Organization and Retrieval*, McGraw-Hill, Inc., New York, 1968.

[5] G. Salton and M. E. Lesk, The SMART Automatic Document Retrieval System— An Illustration, *Communications of the ACM*, Vol. 8, No. 6, June 1965.

[6] J. L. Bennett, On-line Computer Aids for the Indexer, *Proceedings of the 1968 Meeting of the American Society for Information Science*, Columbus, Ohio, October 1968.

[7] M. E. Lesk and G. Salton, Interactive Search and Retrieval Methods Using Automatic Information Displays, *Report ISR-14* to the National Science Foundation, Section IX, Department of Computer Science, Cornell University, Ithaca, N.Y., October 1968; also in *Proceedings of the 1969 AFIPS Spring Joint Computer Conference*, Afips Press, Montvale, N. J., May 1969.

[8] H. Borko, *Utilization of On-line Interactive Displays*, in *Information Systems Science and Technology*, D. Walker, ed., Thompson Book Co., Washington, D.C., 1967.

[9] M. E. Lesk and G. Salton, Relevance Assessments and Retrieval System Evaluation, *Report ISR-14* to the National Science Foundation, Section III, Department of Computer Science, Cornell University, Ithaca, N.Y., October 1968; also Chap. 26 of this volume.

[10] J. J. Rocchio, Jr. and G. Salton, Information Search Optimization and Interactive Retrieval Techniques. *Proceedings of the AFIPS Fall Joint Computer Conference*, Las Vegas, Nev., November 1965, Spartan Book Co., New York, 1965.

[11] G. Salton, Search and Retrieval Experiments in Real-Time Information Retrieval, *Proceedings IFIP Congress 68*, Edinburgh, August 1968, North-Holland Publishing Co., Amsterdam, 1969.

[12] Eleanor Ide, Relevance Feedback in an Automatic Document Retrieval System, Master's thesis, *Report ISR-15* to the National Science Foundation, Department of Computer Science, Cornell University, Ithaca, N.Y., January 1969.

[13] R. E. Bonner, On Some Clustering Techniques, *IBM Journal of Research and Development*, Vol. 8, No. 1, January 1964.

[14] H. Borko and M. D. Bernick, Automatic Document Classification, *Journal of the ACM*, Vol. 10, No. 2, April 1963.

[15] R. M. Needham and K. Sparck Jones, Keywords and Clumps, *Journal of Documentation*, Vol. 20, No. 1, March 1964.

[16] J. J. Rocchio, Jr., Document Retrieval Systems—Optimization and Evaluation, Harvard University doctoral thesis, *Report ISR-10* to the National Science Foundation, Harvard Computation Laboratory, Cambridge, Mass., March 1966.

[17] G. Salton, Search Strategy and the Optimization of Retrieval Effectiveness, *Proceedings of the FID/IFIP Conference on Mechanized Information Storage, Retrieval and Dissemination*, North-Holland Publishing Co., Amsterdam, 1968.

[18] A. Borodin, L. Kerr, and F. Lewis, Query Splitting in Relevance Feedback Systems, *Report ISR-14* to the National Science Foundation, Section XII, Department of Computer Science, Cornell University, Ithaca, N.Y., October 1968; also Chap. 19 of this volume.

[19] T. L. Brauen, R. C. Holt, and T. R. Wilcox, Document Indexing Based on Relevance Feedback, *Report ISR-14* to the National Science Foundation, Section XI, Department of Computer Science, Cornell University, Ithaca, N.Y., October 1968.

A modification of normal relevance feedback is introduced which, instead of simply modifying a query on each iteration, actually creates two or more new queries from an originally available query. Evaluation of experimental results shows that this method produces some improvement. A new evaluation measure is introduced which permits extrapolation of the results presented here to large document collections. Using this measure for evaluation purposes, it appears that query splitting is best suited for large systems.

19

QUERY SPLITTING IN RELEVANCE FEEDBACK SYSTEMS†

A. BORODIN, L. KERR, and F. LEWIS

19-1 INTRODUCTION

Query splitting is an extension of the standard relevance feedback procedure. Instead of simply modifying a query on each iteration, two or more new queries may be formed. Such a procedure often provides improved results. Consider the example shown in Fig. 19-1.

Q is the original query. If a simple feedback algorithm moves the query toward one of the groups of relevant documents, then the relevant documents in the other group will not be retrieved. In fact, the query may not move significantly toward either group. Ideally, one would like to replace Q with two queries Q_1 and Q_2. Then the user would make relevance judgments on the documents retrieved by Q_1 and Q_2, and a relevance feedback algorithm can be applied to Q_1 and Q_2 separately, producing new queries Q_3 and Q_4.

Query splitting is beneficial when the relevant documents are located in distinct groups in the document space. This may occur when user requests are not very specific and actually deal with more than one topic. Moreover, the structure of the document space is based on predetermined correlation

†This study was published originally as Section XII of *Scientific Report ISR-14,* October 1968.

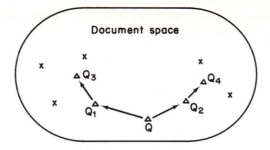

x   Represents relevant documents
△   Represents queries

Fig. 19-1   Query-splitting example.

judgments which do not necessarily reflect the user's conception of relevance. Query splitting is not always required, of course, and indiscriminate use of the method may lead to inefficiencies. An important part of the query-splitting strategy, therefore, consists in deciding when a query should be split.

19-2 THE QUERY-SPLITTING ALGORITHM

As stated in Chapter 18, the query-splitting algorithm is assumed to be embedded within a relevance feedback system. The system first reads in the user's initial query, Q_0. New queries are then formed iteratively, as follows:

1. The documents in the collection are ranked according to their correlation with Q_i.
2. The five highest-ranking documents, not previously retrieved, are presented to the user for relevance assessment.
3. The user indicates to the system which of the retrieved documents are relevant to his purposes.
4. The system examines these relevant documents to see if they form distinct groups. This decision is based on the document-document correlations of the relevant documents, relative to the average correlation between Q_i and the first five documents retrieved by Q_i. If a document-document correlation does not exceed a constant (TP) times the average query-document correlation, then the two documents are considered to belong to separate groups. In this way, the system clusters the relevant documents into zero (if no relevant documents are retrieved), one, or several groups.
5. For each group j, a new query Q_{i+1}^j is formed according to the relevance feedback formula

$$Q_{i+1}^j = Q_i + \sum_k \mathbf{r}_k - \sum_k \mathbf{n}_k,$$

where $\mathbf{r}_k$ represents the relevant documents in the group, and $\mathbf{n}_k$ represents the two highest-ranking nonrelevant documents retrieved by Q_i. If Q_i retrieves no new relevant documents, then just one new query is formed, using the negative feedback formula

$$Q_{i+1} = Q_i - \sum_k \boldsymbol{n}_k,$$

where $\mathbf{n}_k$ again represents the two top nonrelevant documents.

6. The above steps are then repeated for each of the new queries separately, with the exception that in step 2 only three documents are retrieved from each split query. This avoids a proliferation of retrieved documents when query splitting occurs.

The query-splitting algorithm used in the experimental analysis was not as specific as the one presented here. It allowed for more extensive query splitting as well as for a more general feedback formula. The algorithm described here is derived by using the strategy which gave the best results after trying a number of different parameter values.

19-3   EVALUATION AND RESULTS

In order to implement and test the query-splitting strategy, a program was written to simulate the feedback portion of the SMART system. The Cranfield thesaurus collection of 200 documents and 42 queries was used to compare various strategies. Final evaluation is provided by a comparison of the performance of relevance feedback with and without the query-splitting strategy.

Twenty-four of the 42 queries in the Cranfield collection produced some query splitting (i.e., two or more relevant documents were retrieved on some iteration). Evaluation is restricted to these 24 queries, since for the other queries, regular feedback and query splitting perform identically. The following methods were compared:

1. Regular feedback.
2. Query splitting with the threshold parameter $TP = 1.5$.
3. Query splitting with $TP = 0.75$ (results in fewer splits).

One possible measure of performance is a "user measure" in which recall and precision values are determined from the order in which the user receives the documents. Conventions for such ordering are not difficult to establish. Table 19-1 exhibits the improvement over regular feedback in the number of relevant documents retrieved by query splitting, as a function of the number of retrieved documents. Only the queries for which such differences appear are listed. These results tend to favor query splitting, especially for larger numbers of retrieved documents.

Another measure, better suited for evaluating overall system performance, is

Table 19-1

IMPROVEMENT IN THE RETRIEVAL OF RELEVANT ITEMS
DUE TO QUERY SPLITTING

QUERY NUMBER	INCREASE IN NUMBER OF RELEVANT DOCUMENTS RETRIEVED									
	Number of Documents Retrieved TP = 1.5					*Number of Documents Retrieved TP = 0.75*				
	5	*10*	*15*	*20*	*25*	*5*	*10*	*15*	*20*	*25*
3	–	–	–	–	+1	–	–	–	–	–
5	–	−1	−1	−1	−1	–	–	–	–	–
7	–	+1	+2	+2	+2	–	+1	+2	+2	+2
13	–	−1	–	–	–	–	–	–	–	–
15	–	–	−2	–	–	–	–	−1	−1	–
16	–	–	−1	–	–	–	–	–	–	–
28	–	–	−1	–	–	–	–	–	–	–
31	–	–	+1	+1	+1	–	–	–	–	–
35	–	−1	–	–	–	–	–	–	–	–
36	–	−1	–	–	–	–	−1	–	–	–
38	–	+1	–	–	–	–	–	–	–	–
Total improvement	0	−2	−2	+2	+3	0	0	+1	+1	+2

obtained as follows. Recall and precision values are computed for the ranked set of documents in each iteration, considering previously retrieved documents to be removed from the document space. The recall-precision curves averaged over 24 search requests are shown in Figs. 19-2 and 19-3. Once again, general improvement for 0.75

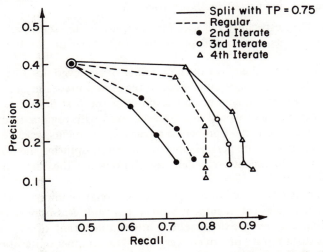

Fig. 19-2 Query splitting ($TP = 0.75$) vs. regular feedback (averages over 24 queries).

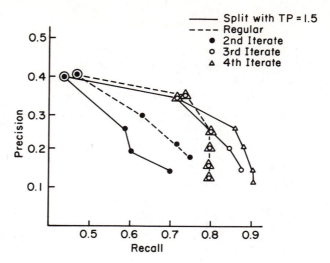

Fig. 19-3 Query splitting $(TP = 1.5)$ vs. regular feedback (averages over 24 queries).

query splitting is illustrated, while improvement for 1.5 query splitting is restricted to the higher recall range.

Two arguments tend to support the notion that the results presented here tend to be meaningful:

1. The Cranfield 200 is a small homogeneous collection which provides neither the diversification of document space nor the user population which leads to the type of general request mentioned in the introduction.

2. The measures used, especially the user measure, are quite "sensitive" to the large number of documents retrieved in proportion to the size of the document space.

Figure 19-4 illustrates the effect of the number of retrieved documents per iteration for query 7. Relatively large differences in recall and precision occur depending on whether five or ten documents are retrieved after the first iteration. Figure 19-4 also shows that document 95 would never be retrieved with regular feedback procedures in a large collection if the number of retrieved documents were kept relatively small. This is in contrast to the performance of the query-splitting method illustrated in Fig. 19-4(b). The document-document correlations for the relevant documents of query 7 are shown in Fig. 19-5.

A new measure is introduced designed to reflect "relative improvement" between iterations. Consider a relevant document with initial rank R. Suppose one iteration of relevance feedback causes the document to attain a new rank of $R/3$. Then if subsequent iterations sustain this "rate of convergence," the number of iterations required to retrieve the document is the least i which satisfied

$$(\tfrac{1}{3})^i R \leq n,$$

Rank	Iteration Number			
	1	2	3	4
1	41*R	41R	100	90R
2	100*	90R	127*	42*R
3	90*R	156*	187*	11
4	111*	91*	41R	41R
5	11*	96*	196*	199
6	45	199*	24*	156
7	110	29*	128*	188*
8	127	60	72R	45*
9	104	23	103	111
10	192	109	39	100
11	71	72R	26	29
12	159	95R	17	173*
13	42R	193	170	39*
14	76	42R	99	104
15	133	56	84	192
16	185	155	154	71
17	176	11	104	159
18	83	188	158	176
19	196	141	83	184
20	156	184	69	76
35	72R	0	0	0
38	0	0	0	72R
44	95R	0	0	0
50	0	0	95R	0
66	0	0	0	95R
92	0	0	42R	0
130	0	0	90R	0

(a)

Rank	Iteration	Split Subqueries	
	1	2	3
1	41*R	41R	90R
2	100*	100	91*
3	90*R	71*	11
4	111*	111	111
5	11*	39*	95*R
6	45	83*	93*
7	110	25	110
8	127	84	94
9	104	110	192
10	192	29	195
11	71	155	159
12	159	127	109
13	42R	45	104
14	76	156	100
15	133	92	76
16	185	114	96
17	176	153	121
18	83	23	199
19	196	192	176
20	156	90R	82
24	0	72R	0
25	0	0	0
29	0	0	41R
35	72R	0	0
37	0	95R	42R
44	95R	0	0
59	0	42R	0
60	0	0	72R
79	0	0	0
86	0	0	0
89	0	0	0
102	0	0	0
137	0	0	0

(b)

*Indicates retrieved document.

Fig. 19-4 Rankings of retrieved documents for regular and split query relevance feedback (query 7): (a) regular feedback; (b) query splitting ($TP = 0.75$).

where n is the number of documents given to the user. For this example, the rate of convergence r is $\frac{1}{3}$.

In the case of query splitting, the descendents become independent queries, each with its own rate of convergence for any previously unseen relevant document. The largest of these rates is taken to be the true rate of convergence. This is justifiable, since query splitting is designed to iterate towards individual groups, and the document need only be retrieved by one of the split queries. However, to be consistent with

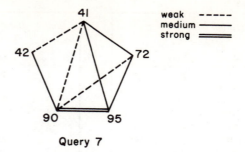

Fig. 19-5   Correlations between relevant documents of Fig. 19-4.

regular feedback, a document is considered to be retrieved only when its rank becomes less than n/S, where S is the number of queries into which the original query was split.

Formally, let $\hat{r}$ be the expected rate of convergence and assume that $\hat{r}$ is maintained throughout all iterations. This assumption may not be completely valid. But it was found, experimentally, that $\hat{r}$ is maintained at least as well for query splitting as it is with regular feedback. A document with initial rank R will be retrieved within i iterations if

$$(\hat{r})^i \cdot R \le \frac{n}{\hat{S}},$$

where $\hat{S}$ is the expected number of queries generated in the splitting process. Algebraic manipulation yields

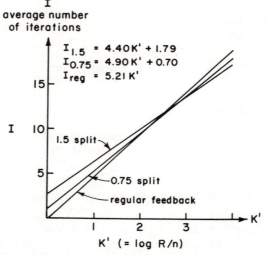

Fig. 19-6   Expected iterations required for relevant document retrieval.

$$i \geq \frac{\log{(R/n)} + \log{\hat{S}}}{-\log{\hat{r}}}$$

Since $\hat{r} < 1$, $\log{\hat{r}}$ is negative. This motivates the definition of $\hat{M}$; the rate of improvement is $\hat{M} = -\log{\hat{r}}$.

From the experimental results, values of $\hat{r}$ and $\hat{S}$ were obtained for each query for the three methods. Then i was computed in terms of a parameter $K' = \log{(R/n)}$. The values of i were averaged over the 17 queries of the original 24 which did not retrieve all relevant documents on the first iteration, and the average I was plotted against K' for each method. The results are shown in Fig. 19-6.

Since I (the average number of iterations) is an indication of retrieval effort, the best method is the one which yields minimal values of I. The curves of Fig. 19-6 show that query splitting is not beneficial unless $K' > 2.2$, that is, $R/n > 150$. Since R is of the same order of magnitude as the size of the document collection, it is apparent that in large collections, query splitting would probably produce better results than those obtained with the Cranfield 200, for which $K' \approx 1$.

19-4 CONCLUSIONS AND SUGGESTIONS FOR FURTHER RESEARCH

As in all systems, one must weigh expected gains against the cost of a proposed improvement. Although the query-splitting algorithm is easy to implement, the cost of the increased computing time may prove prohibitive. However, the algorithm can be modified readily for use with clustered document spaces. In this form, the query-splitting method should be realistically considered for use with the large collections for which query splitting appears to be most appropriate.

The following topics are suggested for further research:

1. A scheme for dropping nonproductive queries would produce improved precision and a reduction in computing time.

2. A potentially useful modification would consist of generating, by negative feedback, an additional query on each iteration. Such a strategy might retrieve documents which could not be retrieved in any other way. These queries would have a higher probability of being nonproductive, however, so that this modification should be implemented in conjunction with suggestion 1.

3. A better understanding of the topology of relevant documents in the document space might lead to more complex but more efficient query-splitting strategies.

REFERENCES

[1] S. Friedman, J. Maceyak, and S. Weiss, A Relevance Feedback System Based on Document Transformation, *Information Storage and Retrieval, Report ISR-12* to the

National Science Foundation, Section X, Department of Computer Science, Cornell University, Ithaca, N.Y., June 1967; also Chapter 23 of this volume.

[2] H. A. Hall and N. H. Weiderman, The Evaluation Problem in Relevance Feedback Systems, Information Storage and Retrieval, *Report ISR-12* to the National Science Foundation, Section XII, Department of Computer Science, Cornell University, Ithaca, N.Y., June 1967.

[3] E. Ide, User Interaction with an Automated Information Retrieval System, Information Storage and Retrieval, *Report ISR-12* to the National Science Foundation, Section VIII, Department of Computer Science, Cornell University, Ithaca, N.Y., June 1967.

[4] J. Kelly, Negative Response Relevance Feedback, Information Storage and Retrieval, *Report ISR-12* to the National Science Foundation, Section IX, Department of Computer Science, Cornell University, Ithaca, N.Y., June 1967, also Chapter 20 of this volume.

[5] G. Salton, Search and Retrieval Experiments in Real-Time Information Retrieval, *Proceedings IFIP Congress 68*, Edinburgh, August 1968, North-Holland Publishing Co., Amsterdam, 1969.

In this chapter a relevance feedback method is presented capable of retrieving relevant documents as a result of the feedback operations even when the original query does not succeed in retrieving any relevant items. The query modification process is described, and evaluation results are presented based on the manipulation of randomly generated document and query vectors.

20

NEGATIVE RESPONSE RELEVANCE FEEDBACK†

J. KELLY

20-1 INTRODUCTION

Relevance feedback is a method for improving the performance of an automatic information retrieval system so that the system better satisfies the needs of its users [1], [2]. Such a method is required for at least two reasons. First, because of unfamiliarity with the system on the part of many users, the initial queries are often misstated and hence do not reflect the user's true needs. Second, because of the particular indexing scheme employed by the system, an initial query may not properly distinguish concepts which the user is capable of distinguishing.

Previous research [1], [2] has concentrated on the case in which at least one relevant document is retrieved initially, and the goal is to retrieve additional relevant items. The results obtained previously show that a few feedback iterations significantly increase the precision and recall of most queries. However, a significant number of initial queries exists which fails to retrieve any relevant documents. This makes it useful to design a query modification algorithm capable of handling these cases effectively. The purpose of

†This study was contained originally as Section IX of *Scientific Report ISR-12*, June 1967.

this study then, is to determine and test a query modification procedure capable of retrieving a relevant document in as few iterations as possible whenever the initial query retrieves only nonrelevant documents.

20-2 PRINCIPAL ALGORITHM

A document or query is represented by a t-component vector in which the value of the ith component gives the importance or weight for the document or query of the ith concept. The weights are nonnegative, and a weight of zero represents absence of the corresponding concept. Let $\mathbf{d}^j$ represent the jth document vector, $\mathbf{q}^i$ the query vector of the ith iteration ($i = 1$ for the initial query), and $\mathbf{v}_k$ the kth component of vector $\mathbf{v}$. Throughout this study all vectors are assumed to be normalized to unit length unless stated otherwise, that is,

$$\sum_{k=1}^{t} (\mathbf{v}_k)^2 = 1.$$

Let D be the set of integers from 1 to the number of documents d such that each document has a unique integer assigned to it. It is assumed that the user designates all retrieved documents as either relevant or nonrelevant. Hence, let D^i be the set of documents retrieved by $\mathbf{q}^i$, R^i those designated relevant, and N^i those not relevant, where $D^i \leq D$, $R^i \leq D^i$, and $N^i \leq D^i$. Finally, each concept k is assigned a weight reflected by the magnitude of the corresponding components $\mathbf{v}_k$ in the various document vectors (for example, concept k may occur in ten of the d documents). The concept frequencies may be ranked in descending order, and $f(k)$ may then be used to represent the concept number, $1 \leq f(k) \leq t$, with the kth highest frequency.

The set D^i is determined by the matching function $p(\mathbf{d}^j, \mathbf{q}^i)$, which correlates $\mathbf{d}^j$ and $\mathbf{q}^i$, and by the number s of new documents sent to the user. A useful matching function is the cosine correlation

$$p(\mathbf{d}, \mathbf{q}) = \mathbf{d} \cdot \mathbf{q} = \sum_{k=1}^{t} \mathbf{d}_k \mathbf{q}_k = \cos (\mathbf{d}, \mathbf{q}).$$

As usual, $\mathbf{q}^i$ may be correlated with each $\mathbf{d}^j$, $j = 1, 2, \ldots, d$, and the correlations may be ranked in decreasing order. In addition, a list may be maintained which contains the document numbers and the user's responses for those documents sent to him on previous iterations. After the second search iteration, D^i consists of the r most highly correlated documents (with $\mathbf{q}^i$), including s documents ($r \geq s$) not previously retrieved by any earlier search. The s new documents are sent to the user and added to the list along with his responses.

Assuming that the user wishes to perform another search of the document collection, the modified query $\mathbf{q}^{i+1}$ is computed from $\mathbf{q}^i$, N^i, and R^i by the following algorithm. Two sums of document vectors are formed, one over R^i and one over N^i. Should either set be empty, its sum is set to zero. Let $g(j) = r + 1 - h(j)$, where $h(j)$ is the rank of the jth document as determined by the correlations with $\mathbf{q}^i$. Then

$$\mathbf{S}_R = \sum_{j \in R^i} g(j)\mathbf{d}^j \quad \text{and} \quad \mathbf{S}_N = \sum_{j \in N^i} g(j)\mathbf{d}^j.$$

In addition, two sums of document weights may be formed as follows:

$$W_R = \sum_{j \in R^i} g(j) \quad \text{and} \quad W_N = \sum_{i \in N^i} g(j).$$

Now $\mathbf{S}_R/W_R$ and $\mathbf{S}_N/W_N$ form the weighted means of the documents in R^i and N^i.

The new query $\mathbf{q}^{i+1}$ is computed in three steps. First, if N^i is nonempty, one forms $\mathbf{q}' = \mathbf{q}^i - a_N \mathbf{S}_N/W_N$, where a_N is an arbitrary weighting factor determined by experience with the system. In forming $\mathbf{q}'$, any element $\mathbf{q}'_k$ less than zero is set to zero. The second step, taken when R^i is nonempty, is to form $\mathbf{q}^{i+1} = \mathbf{q}' + a_R \mathbf{S}_R/W_R$, where a_R is another arbitrary weighting factor. The third step, taken when R^i is empty, is to add an arbitrary weight W to the ith most frequent concept $f(i)$; that is, $\mathbf{q}^{i+1} = \mathbf{q}'_k$ for $k \neq f(i)$, and $\mathbf{q}^{i+1}_{f(i)} = \mathbf{q}'_{f(i)} + W$. Finally, $\mathbf{q}^{i+1}$ is normalized to unit length.

The two factors a_N and a_R control the amount of feedback used in forming $\mathbf{q}^{i+1}$. Since $\mathbf{S}_N/W_N$ and $\mathbf{S}_R/W_R$ are mean vectors of N^i and R^i, their component values are approximately of the same order of magnitude as those of $\mathbf{q}^i$. Hence, a reasonable range for a_N and a_R is 0.5 to 2.0. The added weight W is designed to cause the successive queries $\mathbf{q}^i$, $i = 1, 2, \ldots$, to sweep through the document space until a relevant document is retrieved. Thus, W should be large enough to cause a significant change in the query. On the other hand, $\mathbf{q}^i$ and in particular $\mathbf{q}^1$ may be fairly close to a relevant document, so that W should not be too large. A reasonable choice for W is thus $W \approx \frac{1}{2}(\max q'_k)$ for $k = (1, \ldots, t)$.

20-3 EXPERIMENTAL METHOD

The algorithm outlined above has been tested on a simulation of the ADI collection (82 documents, 35 queries, and 601 concepts, which was produced by a thesaurus run on abstracts and titles), that is, on a document collection with approximately the same characteristics as the ADI collection already used with SMART but with a larger number of documents and a smaller number of concepts. Two important characteristics must be simulated. The first is the concept frequency introduced earlier and used in the algorithm; the other is the concept weight frequency, that is, the probability that a nonzero concept weight has a particular value. For example, the nonzero weight 12 occurs with a frequency of 0.656 in the ADI collection. Because concept numbers are assigned arbitrarily in the experimental collection, the ranking function $f(i)$ becomes unnecessary if the concept numbers in the new collection are assigned in decreasing frequency order, so that concept one occurs most often. Both frequencies are independent of d while the weight frequency is also independent of t. The concept frequency becomes approximately independent of t by appropriate scaling. For example, if one sixth as many concepts are desired as originally available, then every sixth concept of the original collection is used (after the concepts are ranked by frequency).

A new random document collection with arbitrary d (number of documents) and t (number of concepts), but with the same frequency characteristics, may be generated by means of a uniform random number generator which generates numbers with equal probability in the range 0 to 1. The frequencies are now simply probabilities and thus need only be normalized to the interval $(0,1)$. Hence, the nonzero concept weights are assigned to distinct successive subintervals of (0,1) so that the length of a subinterval equals the probability of that weight being selected. For example, weights 12, 24, and 36 with frequencies $\frac{1}{2}$, $\frac{1}{3}$, and $\frac{1}{6}$, respectively, would be assigned intervals $(0, \frac{1}{2})$, $(\frac{1}{2}, \frac{5}{6})$, and $(\frac{5}{6}, 1)$. The concept frequencies are already normalized. The value of each concept within each document is then determined by two random numbers. If the first number is larger than the concept frequency, the value is set to zero. Otherwise, the second number selects that weight within whose subinterval it lies. For instance, $\frac{2}{3}$ selects 24 in the above example. Finally, the vectors are normalized to unit length. Note that typical initial queries may be generated in the same manner, the characteristic frequencies then being those of a collection of queries for the document collection.

The use of a random document collection rather than an actual collection brings with it one main advantage: flexibility. Thus d and t may be adjusted so that the collection of vectors fills exactly the main memory of a computer. By storing vectors in such a way that one concept occupies one word of memory, the program for implementing and testing the algorithm becomes easily modifiable. The described query modification algorithm is the result of trial and error experimentation in which the ease of alteration has proved worthwhile. Finally, since actual document collections vary widely in their characteristics, the simulation may not need to be very accurate.

The following procedure was used for testing the feedback algorithm. First a document collection is generated. Next, a query is generated to be used as the target or goal of the modification process. The relevant documents are those most highly correlated with the target query. This defines the set of relevant items as a relatively tight cluster of documents, implying that if a given document is retrieved, then the others will also usually be retrieved within one or two more iterations. Furthermore, the query must lie within one small sector of the document space to retrieve any relevant documents. In practical applications, the relevant documents often occupy larger areas of the document space, thereby increasing the chance of finding at least one relevant document while simultaneously decreasing the likelihood of retrieving all of them. The third step consists in generating an initial query whose correlation with the target (TIQ correlation) lies within a specified range, for example, 0.500 to 0.800. The final step is to begin the iterations of search, retrieval, response, and query modification.

20-4   RESULTS

An experiment consists in the application of the above procedure for one target-initial query pair. The following list specifies the parameters used in the experiments, all of which were performed on the same document collection using the cosine correlation function.

> 150 documents.
> 100 concepts.
> 3 documents selected as relevant.
> 2 new documents sent to user per iteration.

The tables in the Appendix contain the results of 89 experiments using the principal algorithm and six modifications of it. Method 1 is the principal algorithm with $a_N = 0.9$, $a_R = 1$, and $W = \frac{1}{2} \max (\mathbf{q}'_k)$. In all other methods, rank weighting does not occur; that is, $g(j) = 1$ for all j. In Methods 2, 3, 4, and 7, $a_N = 1$. Methods 2, 3, and 7 utilize W's of 0, (1/10) min $(\mathbf{q}'_k)$, and $\frac{1}{2} \max (\mathbf{q}'_k)$, respectively, while Method 4 allows the concept weights to be negative and uses $W = \frac{1}{2} \max (\mathbf{q}'_k)$. Finally Methods 5 and 6 add $W = \frac{1}{2} \max (\mathbf{q}'_k)$ into two concepts, namely i and $i + 5$ for Method 5, and i and $i + 4$ for Method 6, where i is the iteration number.

Because the goal is to retrieve a relevant document when the initial query fails, suitable measures of performance are the percentage of successful experiments (relevant document found) and the average number of iterations required to succeed. Precision and recall measures are not appropriate because both are zero until a relevant document is found. Table 20-1 summarizes these measures for the seven methods.

Table 20-1

SUMMARIZATION OF EVALUATION RESULTS

Method	Number of Successes	Number of Failures	Percent Success	Percent Failure	Average Number Iterations for Success	TIQ Correlation Range
1	30	12	71	29	3.0	0.0–0.8
2	5	5	50	50	12.4	0.0–0.7
3	1	2	33	67	5.0	0.0–0.1
4	1	2	33	67	25.0	0.0–0.1
5	3	3	50	50	4.0	0.2–0.7
6	4	8	33	67	2.8	0.5–0.8
7	4	5	44	56	4.5	0.0–0.7

Clearly, the principal method (Method 1) gives the best overall results. Examination of Table 20-2 in the Appendix shows that this method works well over the entire TIQ collection range from 0 to 0.8. When the added concept weight W is zero or small (Methods 2 and 3), success usually occurs only because a large portion of the document collection has been retrieved. Allowing query concept weights to become negative (Method 4) also fails because in only a few iterations most of the weights will become negative, producing a query well outside the document space. Double insertion of W (Methods 5 and 6) fails because the added concepts overpower the query by forcing too many of the concept weights to approximately the same value (the maximum value). However, the low success of Method 7 $[g(j) = 1]$ is due to a lack of experiments in the 0.5–0.8 TIQ correlation range. Methods with large W sweep through the document space and retrieve new documents only in 70–90% of the iterations.

20-5 CONCLUSION

The use of the nonrelevant documents retrieved and the insertion of extra concept weights as described in the principal algorithm appear to be effective methods of query modification for retrieving relevant documents in a few iterations, even if the initial query retrieves nothing useful. It is recommended that the method be tested on several actual document collections, in particular, the ADI collection. In addition, Method 7 should be tested further because it may give equally good results with less computation. Another untested possibility consists in using only the one or two highest-ranked nonrelevant documents rather than all of those retrieved. In any case, the insertion of large concept weights into successively ranked concepts is vital to the success of the algorithm. Without it, a query is restricted to the concepts of the initial query, and these are often eliminated because of their prominence in the retrieved nonrelevant documents. Finally, it is suggested that the use of concept weight insertion to locate widely separated relevant documents not retrievable by a single query be investigated.

REFERENCES

[1] J. J. Rocchio, Jr., Document Retrieval Systems—Optimization and Evaluation, *Report ISR-10* to the National Science Foundation, March 1966.

[2] W. Riddle, T. Horwitz, and R. Dietz, Relevance Feedback in an Information Retrieval System, *Report ISR-11* to the National Science Foundation, Section VI, June 1966.

[3] D. J. Wilde, *Optimum Seeking Methods*, Prentice-Hall, Inc., Englewood Cliffs, N.J., 1964.

APPENDIX

The next seven tables list the experiments performed for each of the seven methods tested. The column headings carry the following meanings:

Expt. No. = Experiment number.

TIQ Corr. = Target-initial query correlation.

Target Terms = Generated nonzero target query concepts (boldface concept numbers indicate larger weights).

IQ Terms = Initial query concepts.

SF = Succeeded or failed in finding a relevant document (IS means the initial query succeeded).

No. Iter. = Number of iterations to find a relevant document if successful, otherwise the number of iterations performed before arbitrarily stopping.

Table 20-2

EXPERIMENT PERFORMED FOR METHOD 1

Expt. No.	TIQ Corr.	Target Terms	IQ Terms	SF	No. Iter.
44	0.707	1	1, 3	F	20
45	0.500	1, 3	1, 2	S	4
46	0.500	1, 5	1, 13	F	20
47	0.500	1, 13	1, 11	S	2
48	0.500	1, 8	1, 4	S	2
49	0.500	1, 2	1, 8	S	3
50	0.707	1, 10	1	S	2
51	0.707	2	1, 2	S	3
52	0.707	1	1, 3	F	20
53	0.500	2, 3	1, 2	IS	1
54	0.707	1, 2	2	S	2
55	0.500	1, 7	1, 3	F	20
56	0.500	9, 10	1, 10	S	2
57	0.500	1, 3	1, 11	S	5
58	0.500	1, 5	1, 3	F	20
59	0.500	1, 13	1, 4	S	2
60	0.500	1, 8	1, 2	S	12
61	0.500	1. 2	1, 13	S	3
62	0.707	1, 10	1	S	2
63	0.577	2	1, 2, 13	S	2
64	0.707	6	1, 6	IS	1
65	0.707	2, 3	2	S	2
66	0.707	1, 2	1	S	3
67	0.500	1, 7	1, 2	S	2
68	0.707	1, 10	1	S	2
69	0.707	1, 6	1	F	10
70	0.577	1, 4	2, 3, **4**	IS	1
71	0.707	5	1, 5	S	3
72	0.707	1, 11	1	F	10
73	0.500	2, 3	1, 3	S	2
74	0.707	2	1, 2	S	3
75	0.500	1, 2, 7, 14	1	F	10
76	0.700	1, **4**	1, 3, 4	S	2
77	0.707	1	1, 7	S	2
78	0.500	1, 2	1, 10	S	3
79	0.671	**1**, 5	1, 11	S	2
80	0.577	1, 2, 4	1	S	3
81	0.707	1, 3	3	IS	1
82	0.500	1, 11	1, 6	F	15
83	0.577	1	1, 3, 10	F	15
84	0.408	8	1, **4**, 8	S	2
85	0.577	1	1, 3, 7	F	15
86	0.000	1	2	F	15
87	0.000	3	1, 2, 6, 7	S	5
88	0.000	2	1, 11	S	4
89	0.000	1	9	S	3

Table 20-3

EXPERIMENTS PERFORMED FOR METHOD 2

Expt. No.	TIQ Corr.	Target Terms	IQ Terms	SF	No. Iter.
1	0.000	1	3, 13	F	25
2	0.000	1	2	F	25
3	0.000	1, 3	5, 10	S	22
4	0.000	1, 5	2	S	15
20	0.577	1	1, 2, 11	F	25
21	0.500	1, 3	1, 11	F	2
22	0.408	1, 5	1, 3, 12	S	8
23	0.500	1, 13	1, 8	S	2
24	0.500	1, 8	1, 2	F	25
25	0.500	1, 5	1, 2	S	15

Table 20-4

EXPERIMENTS PERFORMED FOR METHOD 3

Expt. No.	TIQ Corr.	Target Terms	IQ Terms	SF	No. Iter.
5	0.000	1	2	F	25
6	0.000	1, 3	5, 10	S	5
7	0.000	1, 5	2	F	25

Table 20-5

EXPERIMENTS PERFORMED FOR METHOD 4

Expt. No.	TIQ Corr.	Target Terms	IQ Terms	SF	No. Iter.
11	0.000	1	2	S	25
12	0.000	1, 3	5, 10	F	25
13	0.000	1, 5	11	F	25

Table 20-6

EXPERIMENTS PERFORMED FOR METHOD 5

Expt. No.	TIQ Corr.	Target Terms	IQ Terms	SF	No. Iter.
26	0.577	1	1, 2, 11	F	25
27	0.500	1, 3	1, 11	F	25
28	0.408	1, 5	1, 3, 12	F	25
29	0.500	1, 13	1, 8	S	2
30	0.500	1, 8	1, 2	S	6
31	0.500	1, 2	1, 3	S	4

Table 20-7

EXPERIMENTS PERFORMED FOR METHOD 6

Expt. No.	TIQ Corr.	Target Terms	IQ Terms	SF	No. Iter.
32	0.707	1	1, 3	F	20
33	0.500	1, 3	1, 2	F	20
34	0.500	1, 5	1, 13	F	20
35	0.500	1, 13	1, 11	S	2
36	0.500	1, 8	1, 4	S	2
37	0.500	1, 2	1, 8	F	20
38	0.707	1, 10	1	F	20
39	0.707	2	1, 2	S	4
40	0.671	**1**, 11	1, 3	F	20
41	0.500	1	1, 3, 5, 12	F	20
42	0.707	1, 2	2	S	3
43	0.500	1, 7	1, 3	F	20

Table 20-8

EXPERIMENTS PERFORMED FOR METHOD 7

Expt. No.	TIQ Corr.	Target Terms	IQ Terms	SF	No. Iter.
8	0.000	1	2	S	3
9	0.000	1, 3	5, 10	S	5
10	0.000	1, 5	11	F	25
14	0.577	1	1, 2, 11	F	25
15	0.408	1, 3	1, 2, 11	S	5
16	0.408	1, 5	1, 2, 11	F	25
17	0.333	1, 3, 12	1, 2, 11	S	5
18	0.577	1	1, 2, 11	F.	25
19	0.577	1	1, 2, 11	F	21

A new approach to relevance feedback, the statistically significant concept (SSC) approach, is presented. Feedback iteration queries are constructed using concepts shown to be statistically significant in differentiating relevant from nonrelevant documents rather than in using entire document and query vectors as entities. Three new query types for testing the SSC are presented, and the results of testing these queries are given. The experimental queries are found to be approximately equivalent to Rocchio-type methods in the results produced, regardless of the evaluation criterion [including a newly developed frozen exponential ranking factor (FERF)] used, but future study is recommended, and courses of investigation are outlined.

21

THE USE OF STATISTICAL SIGNIFICANCE IN RELEVANCE FEEDBACK†

J. STEVEN BROWN and PAUL D. REILLY

21-1 INTRODUCTION

One of the major problems which an information retrieval system must solve is the determination of the correspondence between a given query and the information which the user really wishes to obtain. Often the user supplies a request which is too inaccurate, too brief, or too poorly worded for precise retrieval of the documents relevant to his needs. One method for improving the performance of a document retrieval system is to display items found during a preliminary search of the document files and to ask the user to score these documents as either relevant or nonrelevant to his query. The system then generates a new query by combining the information from these judgments and from the known characteristics (words used, ideas expressed, bibliographic entries, etc.) of the documents retrieved. Several algorithms, among them that of J. J. Rocchio [1], [2], [3] and that of R. Crawford and H. Melzer [4], have been developed to address this technique of relevance feedback.

Nearly all of the relevance feedback experimentation to date has utilized the general query update formula cited by Crawford and Melzer [4]:

†This study was published originally as Section IX in *Scientific Report ISR-16*, October 1969.

412

$$\mathbf{Q}_{i+1} = \alpha\mathbf{Q}_i + \beta\mathbf{Q}_0 + \gamma\sum_{i=1}^{N_1}\mathbf{R}_i + \delta\sum_{i=1}^{N_2}\mathbf{N}_i + \sum_{i=1}^{N_3}\mathbf{w}_i\cdot\mathbf{d}_i + \sum_{i=1}^{N_4}\mathbf{v}_i\cdot\mathbf{c}_i, \tag{1}$$

where

$\mathbf{Q}_i$ = query at ith iteration,

$\mathbf{R}_i$ = relevant documents returned,

$\mathbf{N}_i$ = nonrelevant documents returned,

$\mathbf{d}_i$ = vectors of a set of documents considered as "environment,"

$\mathbf{c}_i$ = vectors of concepts showing imposed relationships,

$\alpha, \beta, \gamma, \delta, \mathbf{w}_i, \mathbf{v}_i$ = weights.

Table 21-1 details the conditions of some of the experiments previously carried out. In each approach, a combination of vectors considered as indivisible entities (that is, the entire vector is used in each case with no instance of using only certain vector elements) is utilized.

Table 21-1

EXPERIMENTAL CONDITIONS FOR PREVIOUS STUDIES

References	α	β	γ	δ	w_i	v_i
Ide [5]	1	0	1	0	0	0
Riddle, Horwitz, Dietz [6]	0	1	1	0	0	0
Crawford, Melzer [4]	0	0	1	0	0	0
Rocchio [1], [2], [3]	1	0	$\frac{1}{N_1}$	$-\frac{1}{N_2}$	0	0

The investigation reported in this chapter considers the effect of using statistical tests to select concepts to be manipulated individually in relevance feedback algorithms. Concepts shown to be significant in differentiating between relevant and nonrelevant documents are used to construct one of three different query forms (Table 21-2) whose retrieval performance is then tested. The rationale for this statistically significant concept (SSC) approach to relevance feedback is based on the following hypotheses:

1. The user bases his relevance judgments on only a few of the concepts present in each document.

Table 21-2

QUERY DEFINITIONS

Query	Positively Significant and Negatively Significant Concepts	Nonsignificant Concepts
Concept correlated	Mean of relevant document concept values	Mean of concept values for all documents
Nonsignificant elements	0	Remaining elements of original query (if any)
Strictly significant	Mean of relevant document concept values	0

2. The small set of concepts which the user employs in his selection represents more accurately the information in which he is interested than does the total set of concepts in the search query.

3. Those concepts which the user considers important can be determined by a statistical analysis.

Therefore the present study is concerned with procedures for finding a statistical method which will satisfy step (3).

The basic SSC approach developed in this study depends on the correlation between the (user-judged) relevance of a document to a given query and the weights a particular concept has in each retrieved (relevant or nonrelevant) document. The construction of Table 21-3 explains the process. As is evident, the document vectors $\mathbf{d}_i$ are padded with zero weights as necessary so that each vector has the same number of elements. The vectors are then aligned so that the element $\mathbf{d}_{ij} = \mathbf{w}_{ij}$ represents the weight in document i of concept j (which numbering is determined from an enumeration of all concepts in $C = \{c \mid c \in \mathbf{d}_i, i = 1, \dots, n\}$, where C has n elements). The column vector $\mathbf{S}_i$ then contains as entries w_{ji} the weights of concept c_i in each document retrieved. The relevance vector $\mathbf{R}$ includes either binary or spectral (graded) relevance judgments for each $\mathbf{d}_i$, the latter being included to ascertain whether the type of relevance judgment materially affects the correlation.

For each $i = 1, 2, \dots, m$, $\mathbf{S}_i$ is correlated against $\mathbf{R}$ using the Pearson product moment:

$$P_{xy} = \frac{\sum_{i=1}^{n}(x_i - \mu_1)(y_i - \mu_2)}{\sqrt{\sum_{i=1}^{n}(x_i - \mu_i)^2 \sum_{i=1}^{n}(y_i - \mu_2)^2}}, \tag{2}$$

where

$$\mu_1 = \frac{1}{n}\sum_{i=1}^{n} x_i \quad \text{and} \quad \mu_2 = \frac{1}{n}\sum_{i=1}^{n} y_i.$$

Table 21-3

CORRELATION BETWEEN CONCEPTS AND RELEVANCE WEIGHTS

Correlation vector **V**:

		v_j	

Correlation between
R and S_j

R	S_1	S_2	S_3		S_j		S_m	
r_1	w_{11}	w_{12}	w_{13}	$\cdots$	w_{1j}	$\cdots$	w_{1m}	$\mathbf{d}_1$
r_2	w_{21}	w_{22}	w_{23}	$\cdots$	w_{2j}	$\cdots$	w_{2m}	$\mathbf{d}_2$
r_3	w_{31}	w_{32}	w_{33}	$\cdots$	w_{3j}	$\cdots$	w_{3m}	$\mathbf{d}_3$
.				.				.
.				.				.
.				.				.
r_n	w_{n1}	w_{n2}	w_{n3}	$\cdots$	w_{nj}	$\cdots$	w_{nm}	$\mathbf{d}_n$

Column vectors: S_i = concept vectors,
Column vector: **R** = relevance vector of user judgments,
Vector entry: w_{ij} = weight of jth concept in document i,
Row vectors: $\mathbf{d}_i$ = document vectors.

A correlation vector $\mathbf{V} = (v_1, v_2, \ldots, v_m)$ is then formed using the relation

$$v_i - P_{RS_i}. \tag{3}$$

This coefficient of correlation differs from the cosine value

$$q_{xy} = \frac{\sum_{i=1}^{n} x_i \cdot y_i}{\sqrt{\sum_{i=1}^{n} x_i^2 \sum_{i=1}^{n} y_i^2}} \tag{4}$$

in that each occurrence of a vector element x_i or y_i in the cosine coefficient formula is replaced by the term $x_i - \mu_1$ or $y_i - \mu_2$, as appropriate, where μ_i is the mean of the entries of the particular vector. The Pearson moment thus provides values ranging from -1 to $+1$ regardless of the signs of the vector elements; the cosine correlation, on the other hand, will be strictly nonnegative if all vector entries are nonnegative.

As an example of the difference between the two coefficients, one can consider the following two-element vectors:

$$\mathbf{A} = (1,10), \quad \mathbf{B} = (1,10) \quad \text{and} \quad \mathbf{C} = (10,1). \tag{5}$$

The cosine correlation coefficients for these vectors are $q_{\mathbf{AB}} = 1.0$ and $q_{\mathbf{AC}} = q_{\mathbf{BC}} = 0.20$, while the Pearson correlations are $P_{\mathbf{AB}} = 1.0$ and $P_{\mathbf{AC}} = P_{\mathbf{BC}} = -0.98$. The latter value of -0.98 in the Pearson set is indicative of a strong magnitude of association between vectors $\mathbf{A}$ and $\mathbf{C}$ and vectors $\mathbf{B}$ and $\mathbf{C}$. This association is nearly as strong as that between $\mathbf{A}$ and $\mathbf{B}$, but the "direction" of association is reversed. (That is, a high value of the first component of $\mathbf{A}$ implies that the first component of $\mathbf{B}$ will also have a high value, but that the first component of $\mathbf{C}$ will have a low value, if the associations are assumed to hold among $\mathbf{A}$, $\mathbf{B}$, and $\mathbf{C}$ in general.) The Pearson moment thus distinguishes the three cases of high negative correlation (in information retrieval, an indication of active user disinterest is a concept), values near zero (a sign of user unconcern regarding a concept), and high positive correlation (an indication of active interest in a concept). These categories correspond to the intuitive ideas of positive and negative relationships, and they provide a basis for a possible extension of the present study to include some variety of negative feedback.

For either correlation method, there exists a test based on Student's t test (see Spiegel [9]) for significance of the difference of the correlation vector component v_i from zero:

$$t = \frac{r_{xy}}{\sqrt{(1 - r_{xy}^2)/(N - 2)}}. \tag{6}$$

where $N - 2$ represents the number of degrees of freedom of the experiment, and r_{xy} represents the correlation.

In the case for which $N = 10$ (ten documents retrieved), one finds that for a one-tailed t distribution, the confidence level correlation cutoff values shown in Table 21-4 obtain:

Table 21-4

CORRELATION CUTOFF

Confidence Level	Cutoff x ($|r| < x$)
$p = 0.10$	0.4436
$p = 0.05$	0.5495
$p = 0.01$	0.7159

Cutoff levels of 0.8000, 0.6000, and 0.4000 were chosen for investigation because these values cover the confidence level range fairly well, giving low and high confidence points as well as an average (0.6000) figure.

The above discussion then indicates that after the correlations are performed, the cutoff can be used to determine which concepts are significant in the determination of the relevance of the documents retrieved. Those v_i for which $v_i > x$ ($x = $ cutoff value) are called *positively significant concepts*, while those for which $v_i < -x$ are called *negatively significant concepts*. Other v_i are called *nonsignificant concepts*.

In summary, the basic idea underlying the SSC approach to relevance feedback is that document and query vectors are treated as strings of components (the individual concept-weight pairs) rather than as inseparable units. As noted earlier, both the Rocchio and Crawford–Melzer strategies deal with whole vectors, whereas the SSC-oriented methods break the relevance determinantion into finer levels.

21-2   QUERY CONSTRUCTION

The investigation as executed used the query definitions outlined in Table 21-2, though other combinations of the information obtained by the methods described above are readily apparent. The queries investigated were chosen heuristically as being likely to yield fruitful results.

The first of the three query types, the concept-correlated query, is formed by using the mean of relevant document weights for positively significant concepts and the mean of concept values for all retrieved documents otherwise. This construction is similar to the iteration query proposed by Crawford and Melzer [4] but differs by the component approach described above and by the application of significance tests in determining weights. Clearly, the concept-correlated query may be farther from the original query (in document space) than desirable; a possible future investigation might lessen this movement by using the vector composed of the mean of relevant document weights for positively significant concepts and the remaining (i.e., nonsignificant) concepts of the original query.

The nonsignificant elements query is intended as a possible means for handling the difficulty (pointed out by Ide [7]) of mixed relevant and nonrelevant documents within the document space as illustrated in the example of Fig. 21-1. In this situation,

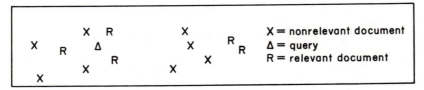

Fig. 21-1   Separated groups of relevant items.

exemplified by the classic sample query requesting information about the aerodynamics of birds, certain concepts of the query (aerodynamics) may greatly overshadow others (birds) in influencing the search. The nonsignificant elements query is thus constructed using only those elements of the original query which the significance test has shown to be overshadowed (nonsignificant). It seems feasible that this type of query might be useful in a query-splitting algorithm or in the final stages of an iterative search (in an effort to boost the recall as high as possible).

The third query type, the strictly significant query, is the diametric opposite of the nonsignificant elements query, since the former includes only those concepts of the original query shown to be positively significant (the mean of the concept weight of relevant retrieved documents is used as the entry for each element). The use of such a query in an iteration will clearly produce a shift toward the items which the user judged relevant on the previous iteration and will thus effectively block the retrieval of separated (in document space) new material. As Crawford and Melzer [4] have noted, however, this characteristic has value if the user is highly pleased with the results of the previous retrieval runs.

In general the last two methods will produce sparse query vectors and hence cannot always be used effectively. This quality of sparseness (depending on the generality of the concepts and the correlation cutoff level) may cause either the retrieval of a great many documents or the return of a very small number of documents and the disappearance of the vector on successive iterations. A further study, however, may indicate that the set sum (or possibly intersection in the case of high retrieval from the nonsignificant elements query) of those documents retrieved under the strictly significant query and under the nonsignificant elements query may produce better results than either method taken alone.

21-3   CONDUCT OF THE EXPERIMENT

The present study has been carried out using the word form Cranfield 200 collection [8] and the accompanying 42 queries because this grouping provides a reasonably (and manageably) large number of documents and queries. The collection has the additional advantage of being composed of documents which have been ranked against queries on a five grade relevance scale; this graded information was used rather than the binary judgments in an effort to test whether the use of finer relevance distinctions would appreciably improve the performance of the queries.

The form of each experimental run, which was conducted within the general context of the SMART information retrieval system, was that of a three iteration search. The zeroth iteration consisted of a full search, while iterations 1, 2, and 3 were performed using one of the previously described vectors (the same in all iterations) as the iteration query. Interfacing with the SMART system occurred at four main points: (1) parameter entry, (2) initialization, (3) acquisition and storage of vectors of retrieved documents, and (4) computation of the new query vector. The first three were handled by trivial mechanical routines, while the fourth was accomplished by the routine OURCON, which effectively assumed the role of the SMART subprogram MODQUE in creating queries.

In this context, then, several runs of the three query types were made in an effort to determine (1) the effects of the parametric variation of the correlation cutoff level, (2) the effect of the use of spectral relevance judgments as opposed to binary decisions, and (3) the performance of each of the three query types shown in Table 21-2.

21-4 *EXPERIMENTAL RESULTS*

With regard to the cutoff level, it was observed that, for the computing facilities available, the 0.60 figure (corresponding, as noted in Table 21-4, to a confidence level of about 0.05) was most suitable regardless of the query type investigated. Experimental runs made using a 0.40 cutoff in all cases produced queries with several hundred concepts, so that the core storage required for continuation of processing soon exceeded the available limits. The 0.80 level, on the other hand, caused the query to shrink noticeably, so that 7 out of the 42 queries vanished entirely during the first iteration (the attempt to construct the first experimental query vector) of the search.

Because of this situation then, the 0.60 cutoff was used in all production runs. The query types were checked for performance using both the binary and the spectral relevance schemes (the Appendix contains a summary of the spectral scores), and as shown in Table 21-5, no appreciable difference between the types of judgments was detected. Queries 11 and 24 show the most consistent differences in performance, and in each of these cases, the binary method provided better final ranking than did the spectral approach. In cases in which the spectral method might be judged superior (queries 13, 16, and 28), the differences were confined to changes of two or less in the rank of a single document.

Table 21-5

PERFORMANCE DIFFERENCE BETWEEN SPECTRAL
AND BINARY RELEVANCE

Query Type	Number of Differences in Final Ranks of Relevant Documents Between Binary and Spectral Schemes	Number of Differences Affecting Order of Presentation of Document (Iteration Level) to User
Strictly significant	0	0
Concept correlated	8 (Q11, 13, 15, 16, 24, 26, 28, 42)	2 (Q11, 24)
Nonsignificant elements	2 (Q11, 24)	1 (Q24)

The principal results are shown in the document level recall and precision graphs of Fig. 21-2. Figure 21-2(a) shows the performance of the Rocchio-type method characterized by equation (7).

$$\mathbf{Q}_{i+1} = \mathbf{Q}_i + \sum_{i=1}^{N_1} \mathbf{R}_i \qquad (7)$$

where $\alpha = 1$, $\gamma = 1$, and all other coefficients $= 0$ in equation (1).

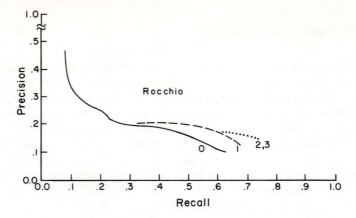

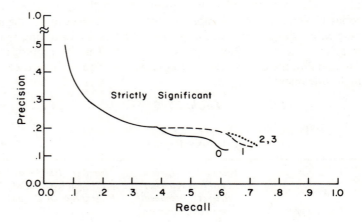

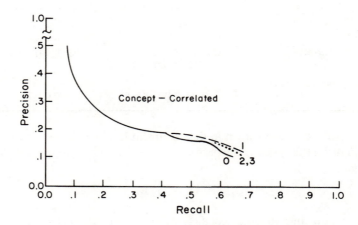

Fig. 21-2   Recall precision graphs.

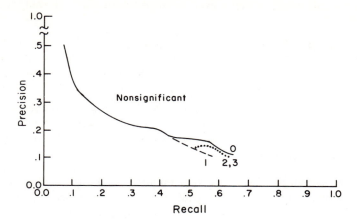

Fig. 21-2—*Cont.* Recall precision graph.

Figure 21-2(b) illustrates the behavior of the strictly significant queries, Fig. 21-2(c) shows the curve for the concept-correlated queries, and Fig. 21-2(d) details the performance of the nonsignificant elements queries. All plots are for information obtained from averaged results over 30 queries (excluding queries 6, 9, 12, 14, 21, 23, 25, 32, 33, 35, and 36 in which all relevant documents were retrieved in the zeroth iteration).

In the graphs, a solid line denotes performance on the zeroth iteration (full search), a dashed line indicates performance on the first iteration, and a dotted line shows results of the second and third iterations (grouped together). Where two iterations map to the same point, the lower-numbered iteration key predominates.

The conclusion that the spectral relevance scheme is not advantageous agrees with what one might expect because if binary relevance cannot be rendered consistently by different individuals (this fact has been observed by Cleverdon, Mills, and Keen [8]) then the more subjective factors involved in judging degrees of relevance would provide a shaky basis indeed for feedback modification.

For these reasons the general evaluation of the three query types is carried out in the context of a 0.60 correlation cutoff level and binary relevance grades. In addition, in 12 cases (Q6, 9, 12, 14, 21, 23, 25, 29, 32, 33, 35, and 36) all relevant documents were returned to the user on the zeroth iteration (the full search), and in accordance with procedures used by other investigators (e.g., Ide [7]), these queries are excluded from the evaluation.

The output of Fig. 21-2 indicates that the best results are obtained with the Rocchio-type output of Fig. 21-2(a). Three points, however, should be noted:

1. The experiment was conducted in such a way that if at any time an iteration query failed to return any new relevant documents in the group of ten documents shown to the user, that query was discarded, and the original query was used in its place

until either the iteration count was satisfied or another relevant document was retrieved.

2. If the original full search retrieved no relevant documents before position j ($j > 10$), the original query continued to be used until position j was reached in the return to the user; thus the number of iterations in which the experimental query was used was reduced.

3. The search comparisons were accomplished using a cosine correlation between query and document vectors taken as entities. A procedure more parallel to the SSC approach might have used a concept-wise correlation dealing only with those concepts appearing in the query.

The first characteristic leads to what might be called the "roller coaster" effect, in which postsearch analysis shows that previously unfetched relevant documents moved up sharply during an iteration of the experimental query but were lost when a return was made to the original query. Examples of this effect are shown in Table 21-6.

The second observation shows that the results are biased somewhat by the fact that in several cases (for example, Q10, 11, 20, and 26) the experimental query was first used on iteration 2. For query 1 the results were outstandingly bad in all efforts—the original query had a zero correlation with all relevant documents, and no experimental method was ever applied at all. For future studies, a wiser action in the situation in which no relevant documents are returned would probably be to utilize a variant of equation (1), perhaps with $\alpha = 1$, $\gamma = 1$, $\delta = 1$, with all other coefficients $= 0$, in order to move the query in the document space. Alternatively, the inclusion of a negative feedback strategy into the experimental queries might be used.

With regard to the performance of specific query types, it was discovered that in all of the 30 user queries in the analysis, the nonsignificant elements query produced final rankings lower than either the strictly significant, the concept-correlated, or the Rocchio-type [formulated as in equation (7)] queries, thus indicating either that the type query for which it is effective is not present in this collection or that the method is generally inapplicable.

One should note, however, that the experimental nonsignificant elements queries (first iteration) contained an average of 8.0 concepts, as compared to an average of 9.1 concepts for the original queries. This finding corroborates hypothesis (2) of Sec. 21-1, which states that only a very few ideas in the original request are really important in determining the user's needs. This last conclusion is noteworthy for its possible application to the interpretation of an original natural language request, since it may imply that a detailed analysis of the query is not necessary because some quick method might be developed to abstract the discriminatory ideas.

The strictly significant query performed in general very similarly to the Rocchio-type query of equation (7). Table 21-7 details examples in which either method surpassed the other, thus lending support to the feeling that perhaps the key to more successful retrieval is the development of a strategy by which queries can be classified into groups for which a particular method is appropriate. One should note that experimental results confirm the pretest projections in that the strictly significant query

Table 21-6

"ROLLER COASTER" EFFECT DUE TO DISCARDING
OF EXPERIMENTAL ITERATION QUERY

(STRICTLY SIGNIFICANT QUERY, BINARY JUDGMENTS, 0.6000 CUTOFF)

	QUERY 18					QUERY 22			
RANK	ITERATION				RANK	ITERATION			
	0†	1	2†	3†		0†	1	2†	3†
1	96R	96R	96R	96R	1	163	163	163	163
2	140	140	140	140	2	179	179	179	179
3	97R	97R	97R	97R	3	167	167	167	167
4	199R	199R	199R	199R	4	200	200	200	200
5	46	46	46	46	5	112	112	112	112
6	64	64	64	64	6	130R	130R	130R	130R
7	68	68	68	68	7	150	150	150	150
8	52	52	52	52	8	125	125	125	125
9	47	47	47	47	9	166	166	166	166
10	42	42	42	42	10	164	164	164	164
11	141	90	90	90	11	14	10	10	10
12	108	119	119	119	12	57	137	137	137
13	49	120	120	120	13	184	129	129	129
14	178	117	117	117	14	58	14	14	14
15	161	18	18	18	15	31	142	142	142
16	21	27	27	27	16	42	160	160	160
17	85	95	95	95	17	102	106	106	106
18	171	99	99	99	18	30	136	136	136
19	40	194	194	194	19	198	143	143	143
20	100	193	193	193	20	189	135	135	135
21	10	153	141	141	21	109	140	57	57
22	44	89	108	108	22	147	108	184	184
23	61	104	49	49	23	39	107	58	58
24	54	72	178	178	24	142	139	31	31
25	112	155R	161	161	25	32	11	42	42
26	187	141	21	21	26	60	153	102	102
27	55	121	85	85	27	178	24	30	30
28	181	173	171	171	28	145	83	198	198
29	157	134	40	40	29	103	184	189	189
30	143	93	100	100	30	129	149	109	109
					55		128R		
					69	128R			
					74			128R	
					75				128R
					110		131R		
					128	127R			
					132		127R	127R	
					134				127R
					187	131R			
					188			131R	
					189				131R

†Original query used.

Table 21-7

FINAL RANKS OF RELEVANT DOCUMENTS
FOR SELECTED QUERIES

Query	Strictly Significant Query		Concept-Correlated Query		Rocchio-Type Method	
Query 3	10	32R	10	32R	10	32R
(strictly	14	33R	16	30R	18	30R
significant)†	15	30R	18	33R	21	4R
	20	4R	26	4R	22	57R
	21	57R	27	31R	24	31R
	22	31R	32	57R	124	33R
Query 5	1	59R	1	59R	1	59R
(strictly	4	58R	4	58R	4	58R
significant)	11	13R	15	200R	12	200R
	14	60R	32	60R	17	60R
	15	200R	134	13R	56	13R
	144	8R	141	8R	82	8R
Query 11	12	92R	12	92R	12	92R
(concept	14	45R	14	45R	14	45R
correlated)	40	16R	40	16R	61	44R
	119	44R	115	44R	72	16R
Query 17	5	94R	5	94R	5	94R
(Rocchio)	22	90R	22	90R	20	95R
	24	93R	24	93R	21	91R
	32	91R	32	91R	22	90R
	33	95R	38	95R	25	93R
Query 18	1	96R	1	96R	1	96R
(Rocchio)	3	97R	3	97R	3	97R
	4	199R	4	199R	4	199R
					18	155R
Query 39	1	154R	1	154R	1	154R
(strictly	3	17R	3	17R	3	17R
significant)	14	136R	15	135R	12	135R
	16	135R	51	157R	20	157R
	20	157R	140	136R	39	136R

†Method judged best by FERF criterion over three iterations (Sec. 21-3). All ranks less than 10 were set by the initial full search.

moved decidedly closer to the previously retrieved documents, so that in some cases relevant documents were actually pushed down in the ranked list.

The concept-correlated query followed the same general pattern as the Rocchio-type method but in general performed noticeably less well than either the Rocchio query or the strictly significant query. If rankings are made using the FERF coefficient (defined below), the concept-correlated query never surpasses the Rocchio method (the two are tied for queries 16, 27, 28, and 31) and surpasses the strictly significant query only for queries 11, 16, 26, 27, 28, and 31. In addition, for some queries such as queries 5 and 39 (Table 21-7), the concept-correlated method performs considerably worse than does either the Rocchio or the strictly significant type. The most probable explanation for this behavior is that the noise introduced by the entries for nonsignificant concepts (Table 21-2) is adversely affecting the discrimination of the search.

In an effort to gain a more solid quantitative measure of the performance of an iteration method in a frozen feedback situation (in which the documents retrieved have their ranks locked, so that the highest ranking a document can receive on iteration i is $i * N$, where N documents are returned to the user on each iteration), the *frozen exponential ranking factor* (FERF) has been developed as follows:

$$g_r = T - \sum_{j=0}^{r-1} n_j, \quad r = 1, 2, \ldots, i. \tag{9}$$

$$f_r = \begin{cases} 0, & \text{if } g_r = 0, \\ \dfrac{n_r}{g_r}, & \text{otherwise,} \end{cases} \tag{10}$$

$$p = \text{FERF} = \sum_{j=0}^{i-1} [10 ** (i - j)] * f_{j+1}, \tag{11}$$

where

> $T =$ total number of documents relevant to a query,
>
> $n_k =$ number of relevant documents retrieved on the kth iteration,
>
> $i =$ number of iterations (not counting initial full search) performed.

The quantity p, which always lies in the range $[0, 10 ** i]$, has been introduced as a possible answer to the evaluation problem pointed out by Hall and Weiderman [10]. The FERF is not affected by the number of relevant documents retrieved in the full search (provided all are not found, in which case the evaluation breaks down), and it does assign a higher coefficient to a method which retrieves new material promptly than to a method which retrieves the same material in a later iteration. Furthermore, the FERF is in some sense "normalized" because it is independent of the number of documents relevant to a query.

One should note that the FERF is a rather gross measure of desirability in that it makes no evaluation of rank within an iteration group shown to the user. This limitation, however, is not one of major consequence because the user will presumably examine the entire group returned in any case. Goodness of result has for these reasons been associated directly with the magnitude of the FERF (an assignment which is intuitively pleasing, as seen in the example below). An illustration of the FERF is given in Table 21-8.

Following these ideas, the rankings of Table 21-9 obtain the various types of

Table 21-8

AN ILLUSTRATION OF THE FERF APPROACH

GLOBAL CONDITIONS: QUERY Q, $i = 2$, $N = 5$, AND $T = 7$.
(NOTATION IS IDENTICAL TO THAT IN BODY OF THE PAPER.)

Approach	Method A	Method B	Method C
Full Search	1	1	1
	2 R†	2 R	2 R
	3	3	3
	4 R	4 R	4 R
	5	5	5
Iteration 1	6 R	6 R	6
	7 $\quad g_1 = 5$	7 $\quad g_1 = 5$	7 $\quad g_1 = 5$
	8 R	8	8 R
	9 R $f_1 = 0.6$	9 $\quad f_1 = 0.4$	9 R $f_1 = 0.6$
	10	10 R	10 R
Iteration 2	11	11 R	11
	12 $\quad g_2 = 2$	12 R $g_2 = 3$	12 $\quad g_2 = 2$
	13	13 R	13
	14 $\quad f_2 = 0.0$	14 $\quad f_2 = 1.0$	14 $\quad f_2 = 0.5$
	15	15	15 R
	FERF = 60	FERF = 50	FERF = 65

†Indicates position of a relevant document.

Table 21-9

OVERALL SIGNIFICANCE EVALUATION

Query Type	FERF
Rocchio [equation (7)]	547
Strictly significant	475
Concept correlated	398
Nonsignificant elements	291

experimental queries in this study when averages over the 30 user queries are taken. This measure also shows that the experimental queries do not surpass the simple Rocchio-type query performance.

The SSC method, as tested in this investigation, does require a sizeable amount of time beyond that necessary for an ordinary Rocchio-type relevance feedback search. The information fetches, significance calculations, and query construction increase the machine time of a search by approximately 15%, and the time (and effort) required by the user to judge the relevance of ten documents (a quantity which is probably necessary to provide a defensible base for the statistical calculations) is markedly greater than in unembellished methods. Consequently, the SSC approach must be proved capable of producing substantially better results than do existing strategies before the increased resource expenditure necessary to utilize the SSC ideas can be justified.

21-5 CONCLUSIONS AND RECOMMENDATIONS

The investigations conducted with the queries of Table 21-2 have not been outstandingly successful in obtaining better methods of relevance feedback. However, the writers feel that because of the impossibility of testing all aspects of the broad concept of the SSC feedback approach in a single rather limited experiment, some of the ideas on which the present study is based should be investigated further before being dropped from consideration. In particular, the approach of treating documents and queries as strings of concept beads which can be broken apart, rather than as indivisible bars which must be added, subtracted, and weighted as entities, seems to have value because it allows the investigator to be more selective in filtering out the noise introduced by irrelevant information contained in parts of a document or query vector. The use of statistical tests to identify those concepts which are important in distinguishing relevant from nonrelevant documents should be investigated further, and additional query types should be developed, perhaps along the lines suggested previously, in which the characteristics of the SSC approach can be fully exploited. For example, one could investigate a modified concept-correlated query in which positively significant concepts are entered with the mean of the weight in relevant documents, and each remaining (unused) concept of the original (or ith) query is entered with its weight unchanged. Similarly, procedures to handle the situation in which the iteration query retrieves no further relevant documents for a particular iteration and means for introducing negative feedback into the SSC approach should be considered.

Another possible area of future research is the extension of the concept-wise procedure to the actual retrieval of documents, as outlined in the third evaluative point in Sec. 21-4. Further work could also be done in the area of checking correlation cutoff levels; it is now known, for instance, that for the type of feedback reported here coefficients of 0.40 and 0.80 are beyond the effective workable range, but smaller perturbations in the cutoff from 0.60 have not been studied.

REFERENCES

[1] J. J. Rocchio, Jr., Relevance Feedback in Information Retrieval, *Report ISR-9* to the National Science Foundation, Section III, Harvard Computation Laboratory, Cambridge, Mass., August 1965; also Chap. 14 of this volume.

[2] J. J. Rocchio, Jr., Document Retrieval System Optimization and Evaluation, Doctoral thesis, *Report ISR-10* to the National Science Foundation, Harvard Computation Laboratory, Cambridge, Mass., March 1966.

[3] J. J. Rocchio, Jr., and G. Salton, Search Optimization and Iterative Retrieval Techniques, *Proceedings of the AFIPS Fall Joint Computer Conference*, Las Vegas, Nev., November 1965, Spartan Books, New York, 1965.

[4] R. G. Crawford and H. Z. Melzer, The Use of Relevant Documents Instead of Queries in Relevance Feedback, *Report ISR-14* to the National Science Foundation, Section XIII, Department of Computer Science, Cornell University, Ithaca, N.Y., October 1968.

[5] W. Riddle, T. Horwitz, and R. Dietz, Relevance Feedback in an Information Retrieval System, *Report ISR-11* to the National Science Foundation, Section VI, Department of Computer Science, Cornell University, Ithaca, N.Y., June 1966.

[6] E. Ide, User Interaction with an Automated Retrieval System, Report ISR-12 to the National Science Foundation, Section XII, Department of Computer Science, Cornell University, Ithaca, N.Y., June 1967.

[7] E. Ide, "Relevance Feedback in an Automatic Document Retrieval System", Master's thesis, *Report ISR-15* to the National Science Foundation, Department of Computer Science, Cornell University, Ithaca, N.Y., January 1969.

[8] C. Cleverdon, J. Mills, and M. Keen, *Factors Determining the Performance of Indexing Systems, Aslib–Cranfield Research Project*, Cranfield, England, 1966.

[9] M. R. Spiegel, *Statistics*, Schaum Publishing Co., New York, 1961, p. 247.

[10] H. A. Hall and N. H. Weiderman, The Evaluation Problem in Relevance Feedback Systems, *Report ISR-12* to the National Science Foundation, Section XII, Department of Computer Science, Cornell University, Ithaca, N.Y., June 1967.

APPENDIX

ORIGINS OF THE SPECTRAL RELEVANCE JUDGMENTS

FOR THE

CRANFIELD 200 DOCUMENT COLLECTION

Method of Retrieving Documents

(Abstracted from Cleverdon, Mills, and Keen [8], Vol. 1, p. 79)

Stage 1. Authors of documents in the collection construct search questions (queries) and make a relevance assessment of items listed in the bibliographic citations of their own documents which are included in the collection.

Stage 2. Using the document collection and questions from Stage 1, technically competent people examine every document in relation to every question to find any additional (to the bibliographic citations noted in Stage 1) relevant documents.

Stage 3. The document authors receive the additional documents produced by Stage 2 and make a final assessment of relevance.

Method of Marking Relevance

(Abstracted from Cleverdon, Mills, and Keen [8], Vol. 2, p. 123; codes changed to conform to the usage in the present experiment.)

Grade 4. References which are a complete answer to the question.

Grade 3. References which are of a high degree of relevance, the lack of which would have made the research (to answer the query) impracticable or would have resulted in a considerable amount of extra work.

Grade 2. References which are useful, either as general background to the work or as suggesting methods of tackling certain aspects of the work.

Grade 1. References which are of minimum interest (for example, those that have been included from a historical viewpoint).

Grade 0. References which are of no interest.

In order to determine whether bibliographic information provides a useful tool for relevance feedback, parallel retrieval and feedback searches are made with and without bibliographic information within the framework of the SMART retrieval system. Bibliographic material operating as a sole source of feedback is shown to be comparable in efficiency to subject material alone. Recommendations are made for further investigation.

22

AN EXPERIMENT IN THE USE OF BIBLIOGRAPHIC DATA AS A SOURCE OF RELEVANCE FEEDBACK IN INFORMATION RETRIEVAL†

D. MICHELSON, M. AMREICH, G. GRISSOM and E. IDE

22-1 INTRODUCTION

If the processes of storing documents for future use and of retrieving appropriate stored documents in response to given user queries are to be automated, the normal limitations in storage capacity and search time dictate that a concise but meaningful representation of the document be used instead of the full-length natural language text.

Such representations consist generally of subject indicators of some type, comparable to the subject identifiers contained normally in a library catalog. These subject indices may be assigned on the basis of a human judgment of the relevance of each document to the given subject or on the basis of some mechanical procedure approximating such a process. One such mechanical procedure is the assignment of indices based on keywords extracted from a document and judged indicative of content. Extracted keywords can be used directly for content identification, or a thesaurus can be used in such a way

†This study was published originally as Section XI in *Scientific Report ISR-12*, June 1967.

430

that the same index is assigned to words sharing some common property, for example synonymous expressions, words differing only by a suffix, and so on. In practice, these sets of "concepts" often turn out to be either insufficiently refined or sensitive to small differences in the wording of a user's request. These shortcomings of the standard content identifiers motivate the present attempt to evaluate the utility of a second type of information, bibliographic data, as an additional factor in the generation of document identifications useful in information retrieval.

22-2   THE BIBLIOGRAPHIC ASSUMPTIONS

The underlying assumptions implicit in the use of bibliographic information as a classificatory device are the following: [1]

1. A document cites a work if and only if that work has contributed information (facts, methodology, etc.) to the subject area treated in the document; furthermore, since both the work and the document deal with that same contributed information, they must share at least that much common subject matter.

2. By extension, two documents citing the same work frequently share some common subject matter or tend to deal with the same subject. Note that no claim is made for the converse; that is, it is not assumed that all documents dealing with a given subject need to be linked bibliographically.

3. Documents by one author tend to deal with similar or related subjects.

22-3   THE PROBLEM AND METHOD

An experiment is described which attempts to combine normal subject indicators with bibliographic information for content analysis purposes. No attempt is made to classify documents uniquely by the bibliographic information; rather, the bibliographic data are used only as a supplementary indication of content. The method employed to generate the bibliographic information is a form of feedback starting with documents already known to be relevant. The basic test then consists of a comparison, within a controlled framework, of the retrieval capacities using documents with and without the use of bibliographic data [2].

The tripartite framework consists of a retrieval system, a document collection, and a set of requests for information from that collection, along with human judgments of the relevance or nonrelevance of each document to each query. The following framework is used for the proposed experiment:

(a) The SMART retrieval system, as implemented at Cornell University.

(b) The ADI document collection (already coded on SMART except for bibliographic information), consisting of 82 abstracts from short papers given at the 1963 meeting of the American Documentation Institute [3].

(c) The set of 35 queries associated with the ADI collection.

Detailed knowledge of the method of investigation is important in order to understand the structure of the experiment. Although the initial queries used in a keyword search system could contain bibliographic information (e.g., "What has X written on the subject of Y?"), the queries available with the ADI collection are based on subject information only. To introduce bibliographic information into the system, a procedure called relevance feedback is used [2]. Following an initial retrieval operation, the user's request is modified to reflect the *contents* of those documents which were retrieved and declared relevant by the user. In the present experiment, this modification includes *bibliographic information* from the documents declared relevant. The value of bibliographic information for retrieval is then judged by its usefulness in a relevance feedback environment, rather than in initial retrieval. Relevance feedback provides a valid test of the assumptions of Sec. 22-2.

The ADI collection, the only available SMART document collection which includes bibliographic information, is atypical in two respects. First, since the collection consists of short conference papers, there is a paucity of bibliographic citations. Slightly over 20% of the documents have no bibliography, and several others name no authors for the works they cite. Second, since the entire collection was published simultaneously, there exist no cases of document i citing work j, where both i and j are in the collection.

The SMART representation of the ADI collection is based on the abstracts of the papers, with concept numbers assigned by a thesaurus. Each document is stored as a vector so that the entire collection may be viewed as a matrix of terms (concepts) against documents. Thus, for concept i and document j, the matrix entry C_j^i has an assigned value, known as the weight of concept i in document j. To save space in the actual machine representation, only those values of C_j^i greater than zero are stored. To indicate the position of the weight of concept i in document C_j, the code number (i) for the concept is paired with the corresponding weight.

An extension of the notion of "concept number" allows the inclusion of proper nouns, that is, authors' names and titles of cited works. The addition of bibliographic data to the document vector is carried out in the following manner:

1. Dictionaries are constructed manually to assign concept identifiers to the authors (both of documents in the collection and of works cited by documents in the collection) and to the titles of the works cited.

2. The completed dictionaries are used to generate triplets (D, N, W), where D is the number of the document in which author or title concept N occurs with a weight of W.

3. These triplets are sorted by document number D. For each document, the pairs (N, W) are then sorted by ascending value of N, since the particular implementation of SMART used in the present experiment requires that the concept numbers be

stored in the vector in strict ascending order. These ordered additions of bibliographic information are then added to the original concept vector.

Each document is thus represented by a three-part vector **OAC** where **O** is the original vector of subject information, **A** represents the authors of the document or of the works cited by the document, and **C** represents the citations.

Note that little information is lost by grouping the authors of the documents in the collection together with the authors of the works cited by documents because of a weighting scheme which distinguishes among different types of author and citation information. Relative weights of 3, 2, and 1 are assigned, respectively, to authors of documents, citations made by documents, and authors of those citations. (When a citation is listed in the document by title only, the author of the citation is not added to the vector.) The following arguments explain the assignment of these relative values. When the author of a cited work is entered into a document vector, the connection with the citing document is often quite removed. However, the cited document generally provides a stronger subject indication; for example, two documents citing the same work are likely to be related. Finally, the author of the document has presumably contributed more to his own document than the cited references. These basic weights are combined by simple addition when necessary. Thus, the author of two works both cited by a given document receives a relative weight of 2 in the vector of that document. Note that a citation of three works by the same author renders the weight of the cited author identical to that of the author of the document itself. Note also that if an author cites his own works, his weight is strongly increased [1].

The SMART system operates in such a way that all the documents are ranked in decreasing order of the correlations between query and documents. The user is then first presented with documents which exhibit a high correlation with the query. The correlations of query vector with document vector may be done in various ways. Of the several correlation coefficients programmed into SMART, two in particular invite consideration for present purposes: the "overlap" and the "cosine"

$$\text{Cosine:} \quad R_j^i = R_i^j = \frac{\sum_{k=1}^{m} C_k^i \, C_k^j}{\sqrt{\sum_{k=1}^{m} (C_k^i)^2 \sum_{k=1}^{m} (C_k^j)^2}},$$

and

$$\text{Overlap:} \quad R_j^i = R_i^j = \frac{\sum_{k=1}^{m} C_k^i C_k^j}{\min\left(\sum_{k=1}^{m} C_k^i, \sum_{k=1}^{m} C_k^j\right)},$$

where m is the number of distinct concept numbers in the system. Each of these coefficients has a serious drawback. As seen in the formula, the denominator of the cosine coefficient is sensitive to document vector length (or more precisely, to the number of nonzero weights regardless of match with request). On the other hand, the numerator of the overlap coefficient is insufficiently sensitive to varying weights above the minimum. In view of the reliance on a relative weighting scheme described previously, the overlap coefficient becomes distinctly undesirable. Furthermore, the earlier relevance feedback experiments performed with SMART (using only subject material) do not use the overlap correlation; thus the cosine provides a better basis for comparison.

The choice of the cosine is not, however, made without reservation. The ADI collection is typical, in the sense that the number of nonzero weights varies from one document to another. Furthermore, the revised document vectors **OAC** all exhibit greater lengths than the original document vectors **O** but not by any fixed amount or in proportion to the length of **O**. Since the present experiment operates only with the *feedback* capabilities of bibliographic information, the set of initial queries associated with the old ADI collection remains unaltered and contains therefore only subject **O** information. Therefore the initial query can match only on **O** information, and the cosine correlation of a given query matched against the longer **OAC** representation of a document will necessarily be lower than that of the same query matched against the **O** representation of the same document.

Because this lowering of the cosine coefficient could affect the document ranks, two parallel classes of initial and feedback retrieval searches are made. In the first class (denoted by the symbol K) all query sets, initial and feedback, are matched with a constant set of document vectors containing all types of information **OAC**, regardless of the type(s) of information in the query set. In the other class (denoted by V), the set of document subvector searches is allowed to vary appropriately, each type of query set being matched only with those sections of the document vector containing the same type(s) of information as the query set.

22-4 QUERY ALTERATION IN FEEDBACK

The standard procedure in feedback is to exhibit for the user a limited number n of documents which the system retrieves after an initial search (in SMART, the n top-ranking documents) and to alter the query in favor of those documents which the user designates as relevant. The parameter n may vary, and any relevant documents above this arbitrary cutoff are considered to be retrieved and become the source of the feedback information. It follows that if no relevant documents are retrieved on the initial search, a positive feedback procedure based on relevant items only cannot be employed. To minimize this possibility, a cutoff of 15 is used in the present experiments. Such a high cutoff increases the risk of retrieving all relevant documents on the first search, in which case the application of feedback techniques can produce no additional relevant documents. In practice, it is found that the cutoff at 15 leaves 3 out of 5 of the ADI queries in the ideal range for feedback, retrieving some, but not all, of the relevant documents.

The results of this study are presented as average Quasi-Cleverdon curves [4] of precision plotted at each 0.05 of recall. For purposes of comparison with other studies, all 35 queries are averaged in the recall-precision plots, although not all of these queries can be improved by relevance feedback.

22-5 EVALUATION RESULTS

Three iterations of standard relevance feedback are applied to both the original **O** document vectors, which include only subject information, and to the augmented vectors **OAC** with added bibliographic information. Both sets of vectors are searched by starting with the same set of 35 queries containing only subject information.

It is seen in Fig. 22-1 that the initial search with the given query set yields different results for the two vector representations of the same document collection, differing only in length (see the discussion of the cosine coefficient in Sec. 22-3). The application of the three feedback iterations produces for each initial search comparable improvement in performance. From this result alone, it is unclear to what degree the bibliographic data furnished material for feedback. In particular, it is uncertain if

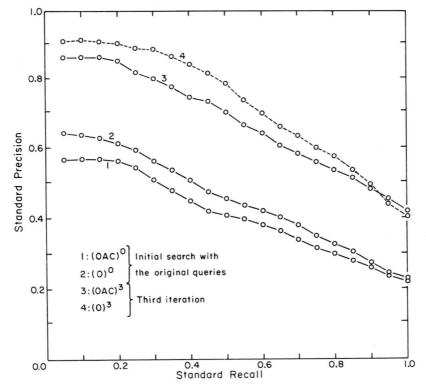

Fig. 22-1   Standard feedback process (initial search and third iteration) on original and augmented **OAC** vectors.

the improvement in the case of the augmented vectors can be attributed to the subject **O** material alone, or in part to the author **A** and citation **C** material.

To answer this question it becomes necessary to abandon the standard relevance feedback technique of treating the entire vector uniformly and to feed back only certain types of information. Two new feedback strategies are employed:

(a) Only author and citation information are added to the original query (symbolized as $O^0A^1C^1$ for the first iteration and $O^0A^2C^2$ for the second).

(b) The bibliographic feedback is examined further in complete isolation from the initial query. That is, the initial query O^0 is discarded, and A^1C^1, or A^1 and C^1 separately, are used as feedback query sets.

In order to answer some of the previously raised questions concerning the effect of the cosine coefficient on the search results (Sec. 22-3), parallel K and V searches are made using each of the feedback strategies mentioned earlier. K indicates that the full length **OAC** document vectors are used consistently, while V indicates that for each initial or feedback search, the query is correlated only with those document

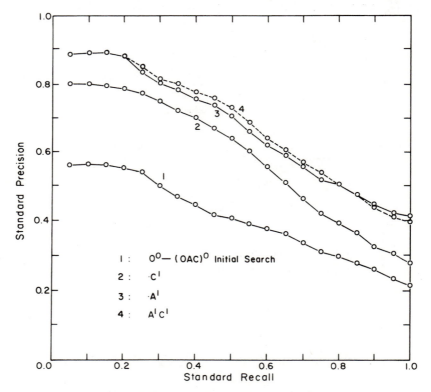

Fig. 22-2 First iteration feedback of citation **C** and author **A** queries alone, with full length document vectors **OAC**.

vector segments with which a match is possible. For example, the initial query (O^0) in a *V* search is correlated with only the **O** segment of the document vectors, and A^1C^1 queries [using strategy (b) described above] are correlated only with the bibliographic segment **AC**. The results of these searches are shown in Figs. 22-2 to 22-5.

Comparison of Fig. 22-1, where the original **O** subject information is used for feedback, with Figs. 22-2 to 22-5, where no **O** data are fed back, shows that the same type of improvement over the initial searches occurs with each of the various query sets. The runs using citation information C^1 alone show the least improvement, since over 20% of the documents include no citations. However, even there the improvement is sufficient to indicate that bibliographic data alone, even in a citation-poor collection, can be used as a successful feedback tool, either in the complete absence of subject information or in conjunction with the original query.

A direct comparison of the feedback results in Fig. 22-1 with those in Figs. 22-2 to 22-5 is misleading because Fig. 22-1 shows the result of three iterations, while Figs. 22-2 to 22-5, except for one second iteration $O^0A^2C^2$, include only one iteration of feedback. Figure 22-6, however, which presents selected comparisons at the same iteration level between the runs of Fig. 22-1 and those of Figs. 22-3 and 22-5, shows

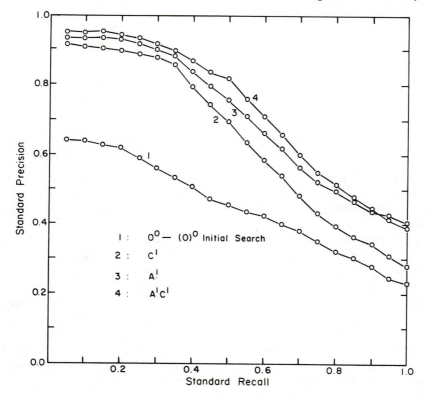

Fig. 22-3 First iteration feedback of citation **C** and author **A** information alone, with variable document vector segments *V*.

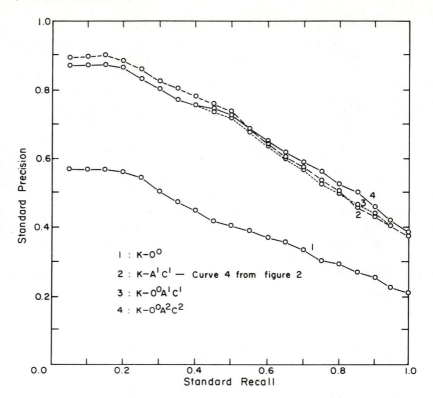

Fig. 22-4   First and second iteration feedback of author **A** and citation **C** information retaining the original (subject) query, with full length document **OAC**.

differences smaller than 4% applicable to the feedback of subject data **O** only, compared with the feedback of bibliographic data **AC** only. This implies that the usefulness of bibliographic data for feedback is of the same order as that of subject descriptors.

The difference between the $(\mathbf{OAC})^3$ and $\mathbf{O}^3$ results in Fig. 22-1 is, therefore, not due to any lack of merit of the bibliographic information. It appears, then, that this difference is attributable primarily to the difference in initial search results caused by the sensitivity of the cosine coefficient to vector length. Since the initial searches are different, different documents are available for first iteration feedback; the discrepancy in performance is propagated similarly to the third iteration.

Figure 22-7 shows difference curves which compare results from Figs. 22-2 and 22-4 (*K*) with those from Figs. 22-3 and 22-5 (*V*). It is obvious that the *V* runs produce consistently better results than the *K* runs regardless of the type of feedback information used. The forms of these difference curves are so similar that a single cause is indicated. The only constant difference between all *V* and *K* runs is the initial search, which for all *K* runs is $(\mathbf{OAC})^0$ and for all *V* runs is $\mathbf{O}^0$.

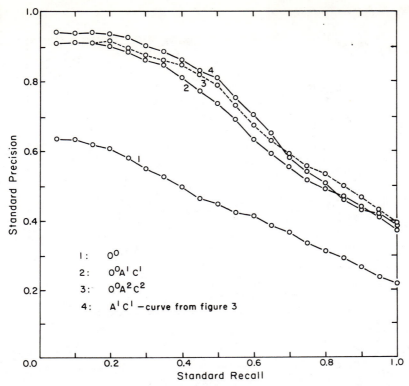

Fig. 22-5 First and second iteration feedback of author **A** and citation **C** information retaining the original query, with variable document vector segments *V*.

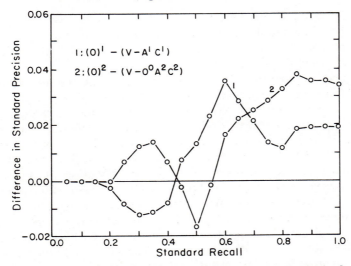

Fig. 22-6 First and second iteration comparisons of feedback of subject **O** and bibliographic **AC** information.

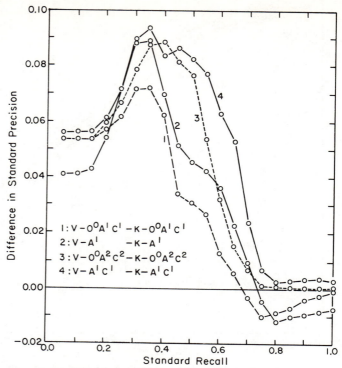

Fig. 22-7 Differences between corresponding V and K curves (V–K.)

Figure 22-8 shows the difference curve for $\mathbf{O}^3$ minus $(\mathbf{OAC})^3$ from Fig. 22-1. This curve has the same shape and magnitude as the difference curves in Fig. 22-7. This also indicates that the difference between **OAC** and **O** feedback is attributable to the differences in initial search results.

Two important questions remain in connection with the use of different types of content information in a retrieval system. First, to what extent is an observed relationship between document vector length and relevance to the query set true of other types of information than bibliographic. K and V difference curves of $\mathbf{A}^1\mathbf{C}^1 - \mathbf{O}^0\mathbf{A}^1\mathbf{C}^1$ are shown in Fig. 22-9. The K curve differences are very small, with no differences above 2%. The V curves, however, differ by as much as 7%. A relationship between vector length and document relevance probably causes the difference between the V and K curves. Both K runs and the $V - \mathbf{O}^0\mathbf{A}^1\mathbf{C}^1$ run use the full length document vectors. However, the $V - \mathbf{A}^1\mathbf{C}^1$ run is correlated using only the bibliographic document subvectors ($\mathbf{A}^1\mathbf{C}^1$). Twelve of the highly relevant documents, identified by longer subject subvectors, have relatively higher cosine coefficients in the $V - \mathbf{A}^1\mathbf{C}^1$ run which does not use the subject subvectors. This effect of adding subject to bibliographic information is similar to but weaker than that observed in Figs. 22-7 and 22-8, where bibliographic information is added to subject information.

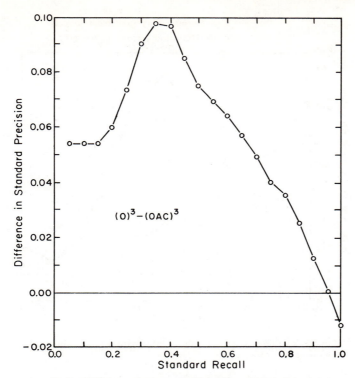

Fig. 22-8   Difference between feedback based on original vector and on augmented vectors **OAC**.

The second remaining question concerns the likelihood of observing relevance relationships found for the ADI query-document set in other retrieval environments as well. This question deserves more investigation. It seems reasonable, however, that in a typical document collection, items covering a wider subject range, which by the assumptions in Sec. 22-2 should also contain larger bibliographies, are likely, to be relevant to a wider range of requests than items dealing with narrower topics. In the ADI collection, only 12 such documents out of 82 caused significant changes in retrieval performance. In most retrieval environments, a similar or greater proportion of such general documents might be expected. Thus, relationships between document length and relevance are likely to be important in any attempt to use more than one type of content information in a retrieval system with the cosine correlation.

22-6 CONCLUSIONS AND RECOMMENDATIONS

This study indicates that bibliographic information can be used effectively in a mechanized retrieval system as a source of feedback information. In fact, bibliographic

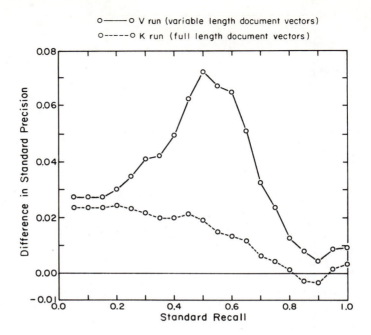

○———○ V run (variable length document vectors)

○-----○ K run (full length document vectors)

Fig. 22-9   Effect of adding subject information to a bibliographic vector $(A^1C^1-O^0C^1)$.

information alone seems as valuable as subject information alone in the retrieval environment studied. Since the bibliographic information is useful for relevance feedback, it should also prove valuable for initial retrieval searches.

A direct relationship between document vector length and relevance of the document to the query set is observed in the ADI collection of 82 documents and 35 queries. Documents relevant to more queries tend to have longer bibliographic description vectors and, less strongly, longer subject descriptor vectors. This length-relevance relationship lowers retrieval performance when a query containing only one type of information is correlated (using the cosine coefficient) with document vectors containing both types. This situation may be observable in most retrieval environments.

These conclusions support the following recommendations for keyword retrieval systems using the cosine correlation coefficient:

(a) Bibliographic information (the author of the document, citation titles, and citation authors, each treated in this study as single concepts) should be used as well as subject descriptors to classify the documents.

(b) The user should be permitted to use bibliographic information in his initial request.

(c) Whenever a request (initial *or* feedback) contains only subject or only bibliographic information, the request should be correlated only with the appropriate subvector of each document description vector.

Several topics remain for further investigation:

(a) Joint subject and bibliographic feedback should be attempted in the present retrieval environment using the retrieval order of the initial subject search $(V - O^0)$ for first iteration feedback. This procedure will provide a more valid comparison of subject and joint feedback than does Fig. 22-1.

(b) Other document-query collections should be investigated to see if length-relevance relationships are observed.

(c) The document collection used for this study (ADI) is citation poor. The value of bibliographic information should be investigated in more normal collections.

(d) Only one relative weighting of the four types of keywords (subject, document author, citation, and citation author) is used in this study. Some other relative weighting schemes might improve retrieval.

(e) Initial queries using bibliographic information should be utilized.

REFERENCES

[1] G. Salton, Associative Document Retrieval Techniques Using Bibliographic Information, *Journal of the ACM*, Vol. 10, No. 4, October 1963, pp. 445–447.

[2] W. Riddle, T. Horwitz, and R. Dietz, Relevance Feedback in an Information Retrieval System, *Report ISR-11* to the National Science Foundation, Section VI, Department of Computer Science, Cornell University, Ithaca, N.Y., June 1966.

[3] H. P. Luhn, ed., Automation and Scientific Communication, Part 2. Short papers contributed to the *26th Annual Meeting of the American Documentation Institute*, October 1963.

[4] G. Salton, The Evaluation of Automatic Retrieval Procedures—Selected Test Results Using the SMART System, *American Documentation*, Vol. 16, No. 3, July 1965, pp. 209–222.

PART VII

DOCUMENT SPACE TRANSFORMATIONS

An information retrieval system using relevance feedback to modify the document space is proposed. A suitable algorithm is exhibited that achieves high precision and recall.

23

A RELEVANCE FEEDBACK SYSTEM BASED ON DOCUMENT TRANSFORMATIONS†

S. R. FRIEDMAN, J. A. MACEYAK, and S. F. WEISS

23-1 THE PROBLEM

An information retrieval system can be viewed as consisting of a document collection together with procedures for accessing and retrieving the documents in the collection. For evaluation purposes, the main goal of such a system can be taken to be the retrieval of all documents in the collection relevant to a request presented by a user. Hence, the problem of retrieval is to relate the user's need to an available collection of information. How efficiently this relation can be generated depends in general on how the document collection is organized.

In traditional retrieval systems, that is, in libraries, books are grouped by subject matter according to some classification system such as the Dewey Decimal System or the Library of Congress System. The virtue of all such classification systems is that books similar in content will often be located physically close to each other on the library shelves.

Libraries in general represent *static* document spaces in the sense that documents are assigned permanent positions in the space. Static document

†The present study was published originally as Section X in *Scientific Report ISR-12*, June 1967.

spaces suffer from two major weaknesses. First, given a classification system, it is possible to construct a request such that documents relevant to that request may not be located close to each other. For example, the topic "aerodynamics of birds" might be discussed in books which are concerned primarily with aerodynamics and concerned only slightly with birds, or alternatively, in books which are concerned primarily with birds and only tangentially with their aerodynamics. Second, given a classification system, it is possible to imagine a document which is inherently difficult to classify. For example, Church's *Calculi of Lambda-Conversion* might be placed with computing texts or with pure mathematics texts because it relates to both areas.

In general, static document spaces impose a classification system on the user which may not always suit his needs. The user's success with such a system varies as a function of how much his needs agree with the subject categories determined by the classification. Most automated retrieval systems have inherited the static document space. These systems are normally more flexible than libraries, in that subject categories are permitted to overlap. However, the fact remains that documents are assigned permanent positions in the space. Hence, as in most libraries, documents relevant to a given request might lie far away from each other in the space.

In the SMART system, the classification of a document is based on the importance of certain concepts in the document. A document or query is then represented by a vector whose elements are the relative weights of these concepts. The query vector can then be thought of as positioned in the document space with access to all documents located in close proximity to it. Since the user might not phrase his original query in the best possible manner, relevance feedback systems have been suggested to improve system operations. Most of these systems are based on successive modifications of the *query vector* using feedback information obtained from the user. One such system described by Salton and Rocchio [4] has been implemented by Riddle, Horwitz, and Dietz [2]. The main weakness of the system lies in its inability to retrieve all documents relevant to a query when these documents do not lie close together in the document space.

The present study addresses itself to the question of whether a relevance feedback system can be devised that will retrieve such documents. The solution proposed is based on the use of a *dynamic document space*. Every user who submits a search request is given access to the standard document space. Subsequently, the document space is distorted in response to feedback information received from the user in an attempt to bring relevant documents closer to the query. Hence, the query is kept static, and the document space is altered. The standard document space is then no longer viewed as an absolute structure but as an initial structure which can be altered to better suit the personal classification scheme of the user.

An implementation of such a relevance feedback system is described here. The system has been tested for the 82-document ADI collection using queries for which a priori relevance judgments were available.

23-2 THE IMPLEMENTATION

The initial task in implementing a relevance feedback system based on document modification is to devise an algorithm that distorts the document space to bring relevant documents close to the query. The algorithm actually used is based on the assumption that concepts which are strong (highly weighted) in the documents judged relevant by the user and weak in the documents judged nonrelevant tend to characterize relevant documents. Hence, the weights of these concepts should be raised in all documents in which they occur so as to increase the correlation between these documents and the query. Similarly, it is assumed that concepts which are strong in the nonrelevant documents and weak in the relevant documents tend to characterize nonrelevant documents and should be decreased in all documents in which they occur in order to lower the correlations.

The problem remains of how the concept weights should be raised or lowered. It seems natural that the amount of alteration for a concept should depend on how much that concept characterizes the relevant or nonrelevant documents already seen by the user. That is, if a concept is judged to be a good positive discriminator (i.e., strong in relevant documents, weak in nonrelevant documents), it should be raised by an amount proportional to how strong it is in the relevant documents. Similarly, concepts judged to be good negative discriminators (i.e., strong in nonrelevant documents, weak in relevant documents), should be lowered by an amount proportional to how strong they are in the nonrelevant documents. It also seems desirable to insist that the amount of alteration of a concept weight for a document should be proportional to that weight. That is, if a concept which is marked as a good discriminator is very weak for a particular document, then it should not be altered much because it does not strongly characterize that document. On the other hand, if it is strong in the document, then it should be altered more because it provides a better characterization of the document.

These considerations were used to determine the final form of the algorithm:

(a) Enter request. Retrieve the ten documents having highest correlation with the query.

(b) Use a priori relevance judgments to determine relevant and nonrelevant documents.

(c) Compute R_i, N_i, and D_i, where

$$R_i = \frac{\text{Sum over all relevant documents of the weights of concept } i}{\text{Number of relevant documents}},$$

$$N_i = \frac{\text{Sum over all nonrelevant documents of the weights of concept } i}{\text{Number of nonrelevant documents}},$$

$$D_i = R_i - N_i = \text{Discrimination value of concept } i.$$

(d) Choose those concepts which seem to be good discriminators between relevant and nonrelevant documents, that is, those i for which $|D_i| > \delta$. To these concepts, add all concepts which occur in the query.

(e) For the concepts i obtained in Step (d), compute F_i^1, F_i^2, and F_i^3, where

$$F_i^1 = \frac{\text{Weight of concept } i \text{ in query}}{\text{Sum of the weights of all concepts in query}},$$

$$F_i^2 = \frac{\text{Sum of the weights of concept } i \text{ in relevant documents}}{\text{Sum of the weights of all concepts in relevant documents}},$$

$$F_i^3 = \frac{\text{Sum of the weights of concept } i \text{ in nonrelevant documents}}{\text{Sum of the weights of all concepts in nonrelevant documents}}.$$

These three parameters are measures of the importance of concept i in the query, the relevant documents, and the nonrelevant documents, respectively.

(f) For the concepts i obtained in Step (d), compute T_i where

$$T_i = \alpha_1 F_i^1 + \alpha_2 F_i^2, \quad \text{if } D_i > \delta \text{ or if the query contains concept } i.$$
$$T_i = -\alpha_2 F_i^3, \qquad\quad \text{if } D_i < \delta \text{ and if the query does not have concept } i.$$

(g) Alter the document space by changing the weights of the concepts i obtained in Step (d) as follows:
   i. If document j has not been judged nonrelevant

$$W_i^j \longleftarrow W_i^j + W_i^j T_i,$$

   where W_i^j is the weight of concept i in document j.
   ii. If document j has been judged nonrelevant, all its concept weights are set equal to zero. This step has the effect of moving documents judged nonrelevant as far from the query as possible.

(h) Return to Step (a) using the same query and the altered document space. Actually Step (g) is performed during the search in Step (a). This loop is continued until the user is satisfied with his results, or until he gives up.

The algorithm makes use of three parameters: δ, α_1, and α_2. δ is the cutoff point for discrimination values. High values for δ lower the number of good discriminators. α_1 and α_2 are the respective weights given to the query and to the relevant and nonrelevant documents to denote their importance in adjusting the document space.

The algorithm was intended originally to use the cosine correlation function for correlating the query to documents. However, experiments with the algorithm gave better results with a modified version of the cosine function. In this version, the denominator is kept constant (i.e., equal to its value in the initial search) through all updates of the document space. This modification has the effect of magnifying all changes to the document vectors. It was decided to experiment with each of these correlation functions in the algorithm.

The algorithm was implemented by modifying existing relevance feedback programs used for query altering. Queries from the ADI collection were processed using various choices for α_1, α_2, and δ. After processing 11 queries, the program obtains precision-recall curves averaged over all 11 queries.

23-3 EXPERIMENTAL RESULTS

In general, modification of the document space using relevance feedback information leads to significantly better results than modification of the query. The highest averages of normalized precision and normalized recall achieved by Riddle, Horwitz, and Dietz using query modification are 0.7554 and 0.8386, respectively. Corresponding averages using document modication are 0.8576 and 0.8871 for the modified cosine correlation function and 0.7987 and 0.8806 for the standard cosine correlation function. This improvement can be ascertained by comparing Figs. 23-1 and 23-2.

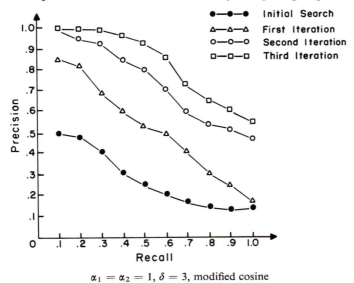

$\alpha_1 = \alpha_2 = 1$, $\delta = 3$, modified cosine

Fig. 23-1 Document space modification. ADI collection— averages over 11 requests.

Figure 23-1 gives recall-precision curves averaged over 11 requests using document space modification. Figure 23-2 gives typical corresponding curves for query modification.

The information in Tables 23-1 and 23-2 provides an explanation for this improvement. Table 23-1 lists the relevant documents retrieved by query modification and by document modification. For queries 11, 12, 14, and 15, document modification techniques retrieve more relevant documents. Table 23-2 contains the documents

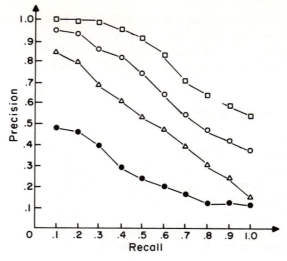

$\alpha_1 = \alpha_1 = 1$, $\delta = 3$, modified cosine

Fig. 23-2 Query modification.

Table 23-1

COMPARISON OF RELEVANT DOCUMENTS RETRIEVED BY
QUERY MODIFICATION AND DOCUMENT MODIFICATION

Query Number	DOCUMENT NUMBERS			
	QUERY MODIFICATION		DOCUMENT MODIFICATION	
	Retrieved	*Not Retrieved*	*Retrieved*	*Not Retrieved*
9	50, 82		50, 82	
10	29, 39, 2	50, 11	50, 2, 39	11, 29
11	43	79, 81, 8	43, 79	81, 8
12	4	42, 9, 25, 7	4, 25, 7, 42, 9	
13	1, 14, 37, 27	80, 65	1, 37, 65	14, 27, 80
14	20	33	20, 33	
15	11, 37	36, 6, 32, 67	11, 37, 6	32, 36, 67
26	5		5	
28	69, 9, 48, 70		69, 9, 48, 70	

retrieved by both techniques for these queries as well as the number of concepts each such document has in common with the relevant documents retrieved by only document modification techniques. In most cases, this number is 1, indicating very little similarity between the documents retrieved by both techniques and those retrieved only by document modification. Hence, the improved results achieved by document

Table 23-2

RELATIONSHIP BETWEEN DOCUMENTS RETRIEVED BY
BOTH TECHNIQUES AND THOSE RETRIEVED ONLY
BY DOCUMENT MODIFICATION

Query Number	Retrieved by Query and Document Modification	Retrieved Only by Document Modification	Number of Concepts in Common
11	43	79	1
12	4	25	1
	4	7	1
	4	9	3
	4	42	2
14	20	33	1
15	11	6	1
	37	6	3

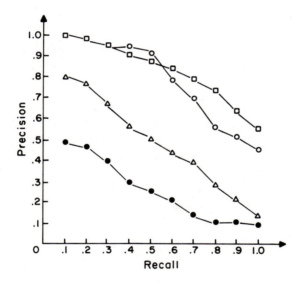

$\alpha_1 = \alpha_2 = 1$, $\delta = 11$, modified cosine

Fig. 23-3 Document space modification.

modification are due to its ability to retrieve documents unlike each other but relevant to the query.

The graphs in Figs. 23-1, 23-3, 23-4, and 23-5 show the effect of different values of δ on recall-precision curves averaged over 11 requests. The curves for the third iteration for δ equal to 3 and 5 are almost identical and are better than the third iteration curves for δ equal to 11. Also, the curves for the second iteration for δ equal to 3 are better than the curves for the second iteration for δ equal to 5. Hence, smaller values of δ cause the relevant documents to converge faster to the query.

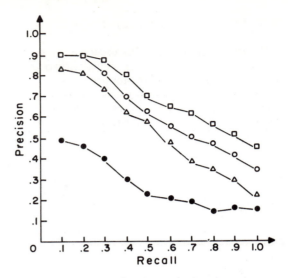

$\alpha_1 = \alpha_2 = 1, \delta = 3$, standard cosine

Fig. 23-4   Document space modification.

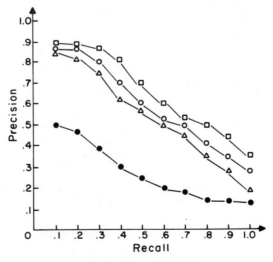

$\alpha_1 = \alpha_2 = 1, \delta = 5$, standard cosine

Fig. 23-5   Document space modification.

Figure 23-5 contains average recall-precision curves achieved by using the standard cosine correlation function. Comparison with Fig. 23-1 shows that the modified cosine correlation function yields much better results. In fact, as can be seen from the graphs, the modified cosine achieves, on the average, better recall and precision after two iterations than standard cosine achieves after three.

Experiments performed on the effect of varying α_1 and α_2 are disappointing. The results are erratic and do not seem to yield any general conclusions about the effects of α_1 and α_2. In particular, the use of different values of α_1 and α_2 for each iteration causes undesirable instabilities, such as relevant documents being very nearly retrieved on the second iteration and then being moved far from the query on the third iteration. The results for α_1 and α_2 equal to 1 are the best ones obtained in this investigation.

23-4 CONCLUSIONS

The effectiveness of relevance feedback is enhanced by the use of a dynamic document space. Such a space enables relevant documents to be brought close to each other and close to the query. Moreover, this study exhibits a relevance feedback algorithm based on document modification that consistently achieves better recall and precision than the algorithm based on query alteration suggested by Salton and Rocchio, and implemented by Riddle, Horwitz, and Dietz.

These conclusions lead to further areas for investigation. First, there is a definite need for a theoretical study of document modification. This study presents a particular algorithm that works well. However, this algorithm is not necessarily optimal. Theoretical investigation might uncover such an algorithm.

Second, a study should be made of the efficiency of document modification. It is clearly more time consuming than query modification, since changes are made to the entire document collection as opposed to being made only to the query. Further investigation might show that a selective document modification can be implemented without too great a loss in efficiency over query modification. In that case, the improved results achieved by document modification would justify the extra expenditure of computing time.

Third, an investigation should be made into the possibility of using both query and document modification. The results achieved in the present study might be further improved by such a hybrid technique.

REFERENCES

[1] E. M. Keen, Evaluation of Relevance Feedback Methods, *Report ISR-11* to the National Science Foundation, Section VI, Appendix, Cornell University, Ithaca, N.Y. June 1966.

[2] T. Horwitz, R. Dietz, and O. W. Riddle, Relevance Feedback in an Information Retrieval System, *Report ISR-11* to the National Science Foundation, Section VI, Cornell University, Ithaca, N.Y., June 1966.

[3] J. J. Rocchio, Jr., Document Retrieval Systems—Optimization and Evaluation, Doctoral Thesis, *Report ISR-10* to the National Science Foundation, Harvard Computation Laboratory, Cambridge, Mass., June 1965.

[4] G. Salton and J. J. Rocchio, Jr., Information Search Optimization and Iterative Retrieval Techniques, *AFIPS Conference Proceedings*, Vol. 27, Spartan Books, New York, 1965.

[5] G. Salton, *Automatic Information Organization and Retrieval*, McGraw-Hill, Inc., New York, 1968.

Numerous methods have been developed for using the feedback information supplied by the customers of a retrieval system to improve system effectiveness. The present study is concerned with methods for utilizing feedback information obtained from old searches to improve the performance of new searches to be carried out in the future. In particular, strategies are proposed for the modification of document surrogates based on previously submitted queries. The proposed methods are tested, and the evaluation results are given.

24

DOCUMENT VECTOR MODIFICATION†

T. L. BRAUEN

24-1 INTRODUCTION

Information retrieval systems have been developed which provide bibliographic references in answer to user information requests. The basic processes included in many of the retrieval systems may be summarized as follows:

1. A collection of documents is transformed into a collection of document vectors. Each vector consists of a set of concept numbers with weights. The concept numbers represent the subject identifiers assigned to the document, while the weights denote the relative importance of each concept within the document.

2. A natural language query specifying the type of subject material useful to the user is translated similarly into a query vector.

3. The document collection is searched by comparing the query vector against some or all of the document vectors.

†This study is a shortened version of a master's thesis submitted at Cornell University and published as *Scientific Report ISR-17*, September 1969.

456

4. The document vectors are ranked in decreasing order of the query-document correlation.

5. The top five or ten ranked documents are listed and brought to the user's attention.

6. The query vector is modified by relevance feedback, and steps 3–5 are repeated until some modified query vector retrieves a satisfactory list of documents.

It should be noted that step 1 is executed only once for a given document collection, whereas steps 2 through 6 are executed for each submitted query.

Several different user feedback strategies have been devised in an attempt to improve the performance of retrieval systems. Most of these strategies involve one or more of steps 2, 3, and 6. The query transformations which are produced by these feedback methods are not, however, permanent. Thus, even though these strategies may improve the system performance for individual queries, they cannot improve the system itself over time. It would seem potentially useful, then, to consider adding a seventh step whose purpose would be to effect useful permanent changes of retrieval systems. As the only permanent structure within any retrieval system, the set of document vectors would seem to be a logical point of attack.

Permanent changes in the document vector space may serve several purposes. First, given a group of users knowledgeable in some field and given that these users submit a set of roughly similar queries, one might expect that similar sets of documents will satisfy all these queries. This effect follows from the basic standardization of scientific terminology. A strategy designed to "group" relevant document vectors about the original query vectors applicable to them may then aid the retrieval performance of similar query vectors submitted in the future. Each document relevant to a given query will then correlate more highly with future similar queries, and fewer relevance feedback iterations may be needed to secure all of these documents. Since documents judged relevant for an initial query will tend to satisfy future similar queries, retrieval performance may be enhanced.

Secondly, even though the vocabulary in many scientific fields is essentially standardized, it does not remain constant over time. Vocabulary in fact changes with new developments, new personnel, and other factors. As a result, document vectors, which are reasonably well defined at one time, may appear to be ill-defined five years later. At present no obvious method is available, short of reindexing entire document vectors, to keep document vector concepts contemporary with field vocabulary. A method of document vector modification which uses information requests to introduce new concepts into the document vectors would however continuously update the vocabulary in these document vectors.

A third useful effect of document vector modification may be produced by allowing the concept weights in the document vectors to fluctuate. Concept weights in new document vectors are presently assigned according to the frequency of occurrence of the concepts in the given document abstracts. This amounts to a mechanical counting process. However, it is not always an accurate assumption that the most important concepts in a document are those repeated most often in the abstract.

The use of subjective user opinion to update the weights of the several concepts in a document may produce document vectors which reflect document content more accurately.

24-2 STANDARD DOCUMENT VECTOR MODIFICATION

Several strategies designed to aid retrieval system performance through document vector modification have been proposed earlier. Of these, only two have produced good test results and are practically implementable.

The first strategy proposed by Brauen, Holt, and Wilcox [1] modifies *all relevant* document vectors to increase their correlations with the corresponding original query vector. Modifications are carried out in two steps. First the length of the original query vector, defined as the sum of all concept weights included in the vector, is normalized to the length of the document vector being modified. If $A\mathbf{q}_0$ designates the length of the query vector, and $A\mathbf{d}_n$ is the length of the corresponding document vector, then the normalization formula is given as:

$$\hat{\mathbf{q}}_0 = \mathbf{q}_0 \cdot \left(\frac{A\mathbf{d}_n}{A\mathbf{q}_0}\right). \tag{1}$$

Following the query normalization, the modification of the document vector is carried out in a second step by formula (2):

$$\hat{\mathbf{d}}_n = \mathbf{d}_n + \alpha(\mathbf{q}_0 - \mathbf{d}_n). \tag{2}$$

Normalization of the query vector ensures that the length of the document vector is maintained during modification. The changes made to individual concepts are rounded to the nearest integer.

Tests of this method were made with the Cranfield collection of 424 documents and 155 queries. Several values of α were tried, and a value of 0.20 has produced the best results so far. Test queries processed in the modified document vector spaces have shown significantly higher normalized recall, normalized precision, and recall-level averages than the same queries processed in the original Cranfield document vector space.

A second document space modification strategy was suggested by Ide [2]. This method modifies relevant documents to increase their correlation with the original query vector; in addition it also modifies high-ranking nonrelevant documents to decrease their correlation with the original query vector. As in the earlier Brauen, Holt, and Wilcox strategy, the method by Ide normalizes the original query vector to the length of the document vector to be modified. Formulas (3) and (4) are then used to modify relevant and nonrelevant document vectors, respectively:

$$\hat{\mathbf{d}}_n = \mathbf{d}_n + \alpha(\mathbf{q}_0 - \mathbf{d}_n), \tag{3}$$

and

$$\hat{\mathbf{d}}_n = \mathbf{d}_n + \alpha(\mathbf{d}_n - \mathbf{q}_0). \tag{4}$$

An adaptation of a pattern-matching technique is used to determine which relevant and nonrelevant document vectors are to be modified.

Tests of Ide's proposal have been conducted with the Cranfield collection, and the results show retrieval performance improvements very similar to those given by the Brauen, Holt, and Wilcox method. The tests also indicate that an alpha value of about 0.20 yields the best retrieval performance improvements. Higher values may lead to erratic results.

24-3 ANALYSIS OF STANDARD DOCUMENT VECTOR MODIFICATION

Both the Brauen, Holt, and Wilcox strategy and the Ide proposal will yield improvements in information retrieval performance. Some of the implications inherent in these methods are, however, subject to question. First, both strategies normalize the original query vector to the length of the document vector being modified, the purpose being to retain document vector length during modification. The retention of document vector length, however, has never been shown to be useful or justifiable. Maintaining *individual* concept weights at a reasonable size is useful, but this can be achieved without query vector normalization. Proposals are made later in this chapter which limit concept weight sizes without using normalization.

Secondly, there is not enough discrimination between different types of concepts in applying the modification strategies. In particular three types of concepts arise during modification. A concept may be:

1. Present only in the query vector.

2. Present only in the document vector.

3. Present in both the query vector and the document vector.

The previous strategies handle all three cases using a single formula and a single adjustable parameter. It may, however, be more appropriate to use distinct procedures for each of the individual cases in order to achieve the best results. Proposals for this purpose are made in the remaining sections of this study.

24-4 A FIRST PROPOSAL FOR IMPROVED DOCUMENT SPACE MODIFICATION

24-4-A The Method

Both the Brauen, Holt, and Wilcox strategy and the Ide strategy for document vector modification lead to significant improvements in retrieval system performance. In Sec. 24-3 some weaknesses of these strategies were discussed. The purpose of the present section is to define and test a different and possibly more effective document vector modification strategy.

A choice must be made immediately between a strategy modifying only relevant document vectors (as in the Brauen, Holt, and Wilcox method) and a strategy modifying *both* relevant *and* nonrelevant document vectors (as in the Ide method). Two arguments make it appear that initial consideration should be given to a strategy modifying only relevant document vectors. First, this is the simpler method. Any decision needed to identify the document vectors to be modified is straightforward, and fewer document vectors must be modified. Thus a strategy modifying only relevant document vectors will be easier to implement and cheaper to run. Second, a comparison of the test results produced for the earlier standard document space modification favors slightly the method modifying only relevant document vectors. The greatest improvements in retrieval performance were found for an alpha of 0.20. For this value of alpha the Brauen, Holt, and Wilcox method was found to produce better results than the Ide method.

The new document vector modification strategy described in this section operates as follows:

1. An initial query vector $\mathbf{q}_0$ is submitted and processed. Relevance feedback iterations are performed until some modified query vector $\mathbf{q}_n$ returns a list of documents satisfactory to the user.

2. *Each relevant* document vector identified by the user during the feedback processing is then modified as follows:

    (a) Any concept i present in the *original* query vector $\mathbf{q}_0$ and absent from relevant document vector $\mathbf{d}_n$ is added to $\mathbf{d}_n$ with weight

    $$\hat{\mathbf{d}}_n^i = \beta. \tag{5}$$

    (b) The weight of concept i present in both the original query vector $\mathbf{q}_0$ and relevant document vector $\mathbf{d}_n$ is modified according to equation (6) as follows:

    $$\hat{\mathbf{d}}_n^i = \mathbf{d}_n^i + \gamma(120 - \mathbf{d}_n^i). \tag{6}$$

    (c) Any concept i present in relevant document $\mathbf{d}_n$ but absent from the *original* query vector $\mathbf{q}_0$ receives a decreased weight as follows:

    $$\hat{\mathbf{d}}_n^i = \mathbf{d}_n^i - \left(\frac{\mathbf{d}_n^i}{\delta} + 1\right). \tag{7}$$

Thus procedures 2(a), 2(b), and 2(c) produce a different modification process according to the type of concept involved, and each process is controlled by a parameter (β, γ, or δ) that allows for optimization. No normalization of the original query vector occurs. Since more than 96% of all query vector concepts carry an initial weight of 12, the weights of the query vector concepts are ignored in the modification procedure; that is, all modifications are based solely on concepts present in the original query vector. Formula (6) ensures that no document vector concept weight will exceed 120. As in the previous methods, all weight adjustments are rounded to the nearest integer.

24-4-B Testing Procedure

A number of tests of the strategy outlined above, called Strategy 1, were run for various values of β, γ, and δ. The collection used in testing is an updated version of the Cranfield collection of 424 documents in aerodynamics and 155 queries with known relevance judgments. Each document in this collection is relevant to at least one query, and each query has at least *three* relevant documents. All tests were conducted in the following manner:

1. A *test set* of 30 queries was chosen from the 155 queries available. A *modification set* was then defined as the remaining 125 queries *not included* in the test set.

2. Test values for β, γ, and δ were established for the run.

3. A modified document vector space was created by modifying some or all of the relevant document vectors for each of the 125 queries in the modification set according to Strategy 1.

4. A *single full search* was run through the modified document vector space for *each* of the 30 queries in the test set. Average retrieval performance figures were calculated over the set of searches.

5. A comparison was then made between the performance of the 30 test queries using the original document space and their performance using the modified document space. Since the test queries were not used in any way during the document space modification, the differences of performance of the test queries represents an accurate measurement of the value of the document space modification.

Two different test sets (and hence two different modification sets) of queries were established for testing. Each experimental case considered (i.e., each set of values for β, γ, and δ) was later processed using Test Set 1 and Modification Set 1, *and* using Test Set 2 and Modification Set 2. This duplication of effort was undertaken to prevent experimental results based on insufficient data. Thus all experimental cases using Test Set 1 and Modification Set 1 are directly comparable; the same cases, using Test Set 2 and Modification Set 2, are again directly comparable.

It is useful at this point to state explicitly what the test runs measure. For each experimental case, the original Cranfield document vector space is modified on the basis of relevancy decisions for the 125 queries. One full search is then run for each of the 30 queries in the corresponding test set, and average retrieval performance figures are calculated. The standard against which the document space modification is to be compared is the average retrieval performance for one full search of the same test set queries in the *unmodified* space of document vectors. Comparisons of the various experimental cases with the standard indicate the magnitude of the *first search* retrieval improvement provided by the document vector modification.

Experience has shown that no retrieval system can operate adequately by doing a single search for each query submitted; several feedback iterations are usually needed to retrieve a suitable set of documents. On the other hand, it is also the case that every relevance feedback iteration necessary for a query carries an associated "cost"; the retrieval system cost is relatively small, but the cost of time and effort to a user can be significant. Clearly, if the first search performance of modified document vectors is significantly better than that of the unmodified document vectors, fewer relevance feedback iterations may be necessary to retrieve a suitable set of documents. Thus document vector modification may lead directly to greater retrieval system efficiency, particularly from the standpoint of a user.

Two precautions were taken in the present tests to prevent possible errors. Previous experiments in document vector modification have always been carried out by modifying *all* relevant document vectors for *each* query in the modification set. This was done because all the relevant documents for any query were known a priori. In the present tests, however, only some of the relevant document vectors were modified for each query in the modification set. All 155 queries of the Cranfield collection were processed through the SMART information retrieval system using relevance feedback techniques. For each query a list was prepared of the top 30 ranked documents obtained after an initial run *and three* relevance feedback iterations. For any query in the modification set, only those relevant documents that ranked 30 or better on the SMART output list were actually modified.† This precaution was taken to keep the experimental runs close to a realistic situation by ensuring that only those relevant documents that a user would actually see if he were using a terminal to process the query would be modified.

In order to determine whether the query type had any influence on the results of the document space modification, test results were compiled separately for test queries that were similar to queries in the modification set and for test queries not similar to the modification set queries. The following definitions of similarity are used in the present study:

1. Given queries q and q', if $q \cap q'$ consists of zero, one, or two concepts, the query vectors are said to be nonsimilar.

2. If $q \cap q'$ consists of three, four, or five concepts, the query vectors are said to be similar.

3. If $q \cap q'$ consists of six or more concepts, the query vectors are said to be very similar.

Note. The number of concepts in q or q' consists typically of nine concepts.

As mentioned previously, two different test sets and modification sets of queries were used throughout the present tests. Although most of the queries in each test set were chosen randomly, both test sets were ordered so as to provide information

---

†The initial search produced a list of 5 documents. These documents were *frozen*, and the first relevance feedback search produced a list containing the 5 frozen documents plus 10 more items (total of 15). These 15 documents were frozen, and the second relevance feedback search produced a list containing the 15 frozen documents plus 15 more (total of 30). Using the same query vector as the second relevance feedback search, the third relevance feedback search produced the 30 documents previously retrieved in *fluid* order. The set of 30 documents in fluid order was used to determine which relevant documents could be modified for each modification set query.

about the retrieval performance for similar and nonsimilar test set and modification set queries. In particular, the first 15 queries of Test Set 1 are similar to *none* of the 125 queries in Modification Set 1, while the second 15 queries are similar to *one or more* queries in Modification Set 1; the same conditions hold for Test Set 2 and Modification Set 2. As a result of the composition of the test sets, the following three types of retrieval performance figures are calculated for each test run:

1. Average retrieval performance over the 30-query test set.

2. Average retrieval performance over the 15 queries not similar to queries in the modification set.

3. Average retrieval performance over the 15 queries similar to queries in the modification set.

If the document vector modification process is to produce convincing improvements in retrieval performance, then all three of the following criteria must be met:

1. The average retrieval performance figures for an entire test set should be significantly better for the test set queries processed in a modified document vector space than for the unmodified space.

2. The average retrieval performance figures for test set queries not similar to modification set queries should not be substantially lower in the modified document vector space than in the unmodified space.

3. The average retrieval performance figures for test set queries similar to modification set queries should be significantly higher in the modified document vector space than in the unmodified space.

Two measures of retrieval performance are calculated for each test. The first measure is the recall-level averaged recall-precision graph. This measure shows average precision obtained at recall levels of 0.1, 0.2, . . ., 1.0. The second measure utilized is the normalized recall and precision. For a *single query* with R relevant documents in a total collection of T documents, where r_i denotes the rank of the ith relevant document, these measures are given by:

$$R_{\text{norm}} = 1 - \frac{1}{R} \cdot \frac{\sum\limits_{i=1}^{R}(r_i - i)}{T - R} \tag{8}$$

and

$$P_{\text{norm}} = 1 - \frac{\sum\limits_{i=1}^{R}\log r_i - \sum\limits_{i=1}^{R}\log i}{\log[T!/(T-R)!R!]} \tag{9}$$

For each test, figures are also computed representing average normalized recall and average normalized precision for sets of either 15 or 30 queries. Table 24-1 summarizes all test runs for Strategy 1.

Table 24-1

SUMMARY OF TEST CASES FOR STRATEGY 1

Run	β	γ	δ	Test Set	Modification Set
1–0	–	–	–	1	–
2–0	–	–	–	2	–
1–1	24	0.10	12	1	1
2–1	24	0.10	12	2	2
1–2	24	0.15	12	1	1
2–2	24	0.15	12	2	2
1–3	30	0.20	8	1	1
2–3	30	0.20	8	2	2
1–4	30	0.25	8	1	1
2–4	30	0.25	8	2	2
1–5	30	0.33	8	1	1
2–5	30	0.33	8	2	2

24-4-C   Test Results

Runs 1–0 and 2–0 represent the standard runs for Test Sets 1 and 2. Both utilize a single full search for the test set queries in the *original* Cranfield document space. Runs 1–1 through 1–5 and 2–1 through 2–5 are the tests conducted for Strategy 1. Each pair of runs (e.g., runs 1–1 and 2–1) represents a single experimental condition tested on two different test sets and modification sets. The runs are listed in increasing order according to the amount of modification done to the document vectors. Runs

Table 24-2

AVERAGE NORMALIZED RECALL AND PRECISION
FOR ALL QUERIES

Run	R_{norm}	Percent Change from Standard	P_{norm}	Percent Change from Standard
1–0	0.8975	–	0.6500	–
2–0	0.8739	–	0.6595	–
1–1	0.9079	+2.8	0.7220	+7.2
2–1	0.9055	+3.2	0.7082	+4.9
1–2	0.9085	+2.9	0.7247	+7.5
2–2	0.9053	+3.1	0.7109	+5.1
1–3	0.9077	+2.8	0.7309	+8.1
2–3	0.9058	+3.2	0.7138	+5.4
1–4	0.9081	+2.9	0.7334	+8.3
2–4	0.9052	+3.1	0.7164	+5.7
1–5	0.9083	+2.9	0.7342	+8.4
2–5	0.9046	+3.0	0.7220	+6.3

Table 24-3

AVERAGE NORMALIZED RECALL AND PRECISION
FOR NONSIMILAR QUERIES

Run	R_{norm}	Percent Change from Standard	P_{norm}	Percent Change from Standard
1–0	0.8894	–	0.6901	–
2–0	0.8650	–	0.6301	–
1–1	0.9043	+1.5	0.7177	+2.8
2–1	0.9118	+4.7	0.6995	+6.9
1–2	0.9050	+1.6	0.7211	+3.1
2–2	0.9124	+4.7	0.7047	+7.5
1–3	0.9038	+1.4	0.7242	+3.4
2–3	0.9139	+4.9	0.7147	+8.5
1–4	0.9039	+1.4	0.7241	+3.4
2–4	0.9139	+4.9	0.7197	+9.0
1–5	0.9045	+1.5	0.7261	+3.6
2–5	0.9148	+5.0	0.7314	+10.1

Table 24-4

AVERAGE NORMALIZED RECALL AND PRECISION
FOR SIMILAR QUERIES

Run	R_{norm}	Percent Change from Standard	P_{norm}	Percent Change from Standard
1–0	0.8697	–	0.6099	–
2–0	0.8828	–	0.6890	–
1–1	0.9115	+4.2	0.7262	+11.6
2–1	0.8993	+1.7	0.7160	+2.7
1–2	0.9120	+4.2	0.7284	+11.9
2–2	0.8981	+1.5	0.7172	+2.8
1–3	0.9116	+4.2	0.7376	+12.8
2–3	0.8977	+1.5	0.7129	+2.4
1–4	0.9122	+4.3	0.7428	+13.3
2–4	0.8964	+1.4	0.7131	+2.4
1–5	0.9121	+4.2	0.7424	+13.3
2–5	0.8945	+1.2	0.7127	+2.4

1–1 and 2–1 represent the smallest amount of document vector modification, while runs 1–5 and 2–5 produce the greatest changes.

For *all* runs, Tables 24-2, 24-3, and 24-4 present average normalized recall and precision figures. Table 24-2 shows R_{norm} and P_{norm} over 30 queries; Table 24-3 lists R_{norm} and P_{norm} for the 15 nonsimilar queries; Table 24-4 shows R_{norm} and P_{norm} for the 15 similar queries. Tables 24-5 through 24-10 include the recall-level averages for the tests. For the six runs utilizing Test Set 1 and Modification Set 1, Table 24-5 lists

Table 24-5

RECALL-LEVEL AVERAGES FOR TEST SET 1—ALL QUERIES

Recall Level	Run 1–0	Run 1–1	Run 1–2	Run 1–3	Run 1–4	Run 1–5
0.10	0.7009	0.7215	0.7197	0.7247	0.7285	0.7286
0.20	0.6121	0.6732	0.6714	0.6750	0.6818	0.6803
0.30	0.4760	0.5663	0.5677	0.5831	0.5905	0.5987
0.40	0.3932	0.5217	0.5289	0.5604	0.5576	0.5744
0.50	0.3764	0.5063	0.5160	0.5469	0.5472	0.5571
0.60	0.2877	0.4530	0.4590	0.5037	0.5003	0.4937
0.70	0.2205	0.3702	0.3971	0.4056	0.4186	0.4270
0.80	0.1963	0.3152	0.3234	0.3512	0.3686	0.3668
0.90	0.1336	0.2243	0.2290	0.2368	0.2515	0.2549
1.00	0.1273	0.2078	0.2134	0.2251	0.2468	0.2515

Table 24-6

RECALL-LEVEL AVERAGES FOR
TEST SET 1—NONSIMILAR QUERIES

Recall Level	Run 1–0	Run 1–1	Run 1–2	Run 1–3	Run 1–4	Run 1–5
0.10	0.7622	0.7603	0.7618	0.7661	0.7593	0.7612
0.20	0.6568	0.6683	0.6698	0.6668	0.6660	0.6646
0.30	0.5155	0.5194	0.5272	0.5550	0.5517	0.5660
0.40	0.4733	0.4823	0.4902	0.5204	0.5184	0.5526
0.50	0.4508	0.4722	0.4814	0.5059	0.5086	0.5439
0.60	0.3599	0.4518	0.4671	0.4949	0.4940	0.4866
0.70	0.3042	0.4054	0.4173	0.4503	0.4619	0.4635
0.80	0.2717	0.3744	0.3848	0.3953	0.4124	0.4195
0.90	0.1775	0.2622	0.2728	0.2627	0.2697	0.2810
1.00	0.1773	0.2415	0.2509	0.2508	0.2675	0.2773

Table 24-7

RECALL-LEVEL AVERAGES FOR TEST SET 1—SIMILAR QUERIES

Recall Level	Run 1–0	Run 1–1	Run 1–2	Run 1–3	Run 1–4	Run 1–5
0.10	0.6395	0.6827	0.6777	0.6832	0.6976	0.6960
0.20	0.5674	0.6780	0.6729	0.6832	0.6976	0.6960
0.30	0.4365	0.6133	0.6083	0.6112	0.6293	0.6314
0.40	0.3131	0.5610	0.5677	0.6004	0.5969	0.5962
0.50	0.3019	0.5404	0.5505	0.5880	0.5858	0.5703
0.60	0.2156	0.4542	0.4509	0.5125	0.5067	0.5008
0.70	0.1368	0.3350	0.3408	0.3608	0.3753	0.3906
0.80	0.1208	0.2559	0.2620	0.3071	0.3248	0.3141
0.90	0.0897	0.1864	0.1851	0.2110	0.2333	0.2289
1.00	0.0813	0.1741	0.1759	0.1995	0.2261	0.2256

Table 24-8

RECALL-LEVEL AVERAGES FOR TEST SET 2—ALL QUERIES

Recall Level	Run 2–0	Run 2–1	Run 2–2	Run 2–3	Run 2–4	Run 2–5
0.10	0.6093	0.6472	0.6544	0.6547	0.6881	0.7292
0.20	0.5114	0.6120	0.6187	0.6219	0.6347	0.6401
0.30	0.4287	0.5469	0.5527	0.5633	0.5691	0.5924
0.40	0.3747	0.4989	0.5155	0.5266	0.5373	0.5536
0.50	0.3489	0.4342	0.4515	0.4721	0.4746	0.4785
0.60	0.3172	0.3881	0.3988	0.4048	0.4008	0.3855
0.70	0.2638	0.3310	0.3362	0.3563	0.3551	0.3445
0.80	0.2233	0.2859	0.2887	0.3060	0.3092	0.3138
0.90	0.1656	0.2097	0.2159	0.2197	0.2217	0.2228
1.00	0.1471	0.1781	0.1868	0.1895	0.1900	0.1925

Table 24-9

RECALL-LEVEL AVERAGES FOR
TEST SET 2—NONSIMILAR QUERIES

Recall Level	Run 2–0	Run 2–1	Run 2–2	Run 2–3	Run 2–4	Run 2–5
0.10	0.5185	0.5825	0.5939	0.6021	0.6316	0.6713
0.20	0.4709	0.5669	0.5784	0.5846	0.6079	0.6113
0.30	0.3915	0.4806	0.4957	0.5219	0.5229	0.5588
0.40	0.3407	0.4473	0.4623	0.4953	0.5062	0.5366
0.50	0.3367	0.4163	0.4342	0.4840	0.4835	0.4862
0.60	0.3073	0.3782	0.4015	0.4203	0.4196	0.3985
0.70	0.2599	0.3221	0.3404	0.3605	0.3651	0.3489
0.80	0.2269	0.2702	0.2764	0.2899	0.3001	0.3116
0.90	0.2080	0.2449	0.2563	0.2529	0.2564	0.2626
1.00	0.1918	0.2352	0.2535	0.2499	0.2535	0.2597

Table 24-10

RECALL-LEVEL AVERAGES FOR TEST SET 2—SIMILAR QUERIES

Recall Level	Run 2–0	Run 2–1	Run 2–2	Run 2–3	Run 2–4	Run 2–5
0.10	0.7001	0.7118	0.7149	0.7073	0.7446	0.7872
0.20	0.5520	0.6572	0.6590	0.6592	0.6615	0.6690
0.30	0.4659	0.6132	0.6098	0.6046	0.6154	0.6260
0.40	0.4087	0.5506	0.5686	0.5580	0.5685	0.5706
0.50	0.3611	0.4521	0.4688	0.4603	0.4657	0.4708
0.60	0.3271	0.3979	0.3962	0.3893	0.3821	0.3725
0.70	0.2678	0.3399	0.3320	0.3522	0.3451	0.3400
0.80	0.2197	0.3016	0.3010	0.3220	0.3184	0.3160
0.90	0.1233	0.1745	0.1754	0.1865	0.1870	0.1829
1.00	0.1024	0.1210	0.1201	0.1291	0.1265	0.1252

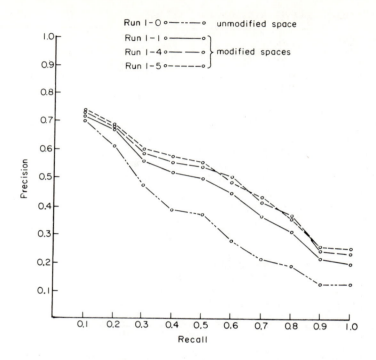

Fig. 24-1   Recall-level averages, Strategy 1, Test Set 1—all queries.

recall-level averages over the 30 queries, Table 24-6 shows averages over the 15 nonsimilar queries, and Table 24-7 lists averages over the 15 similar queries. For the six runs utilizing Test Set 2 and Modification Set 2, Tables 24-8, 24-9, and 24-10 are analogous to Tables 24-5, 24-6, and 24-7. To aid in reading Tables 24-5 through 24-10, the run showing the *greatest* improvement over the standard at each recall level is underlined.

Figures 24-1 and 24-2 represent the actual recall-precision graphs produced by Test Sets 1 and 2, respectively, averaged over all queries. Runs 1–0 and 2–0 represent the standard performance for the unmodified document spaces for the two test sets.

24-4-D   Discussion

The experimental results outlined in the previous subsection raise a number of interesting questions. The first concerns the overall effect of Strategy 1. Formula (5) provides for the addition of query concepts to relevant document vectors not originally containing these concepts. Over a short space of time, this permits the addition of synonyms to document vectors. Particularly in those cases where the synonymous

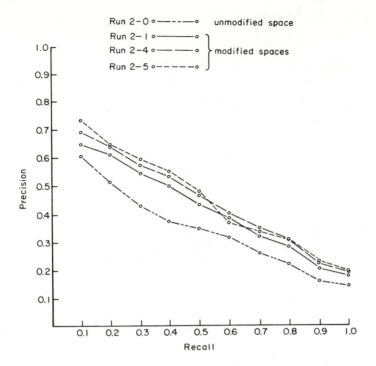

Fig. 24-2   Recall-level averages, Strategy 1, Test Set 1—all queries.

concepts are represented by a stem different from that used in document abstracts, and where vectors are defined by word-stem or word-form techniques, this adds flexibility to the document indexing. In the long run, the addition of concepts allows for an expansion of the field vocabulary applicable to the existing document vectors.

Formulas (6) and (7) allow a concept weight to fluctuate within a document vector. Two advantages may result. First, inappropriate concepts and concepts seldom used in seeking a document will be assigned lower weights in the document vector. This may help in refining ill-defined document vectors. Moreover, document vector concepts will no longer merely reflect the original contents of the documents; they will also reflect the user judgments of the importance of the various contents.

The expected effects of Strategy 1 on individual document-document correlations and on the concept weights are also of interest. Consider the following sample vectors and conditions:

1. A query vector q with nine concepts all of weight 12.

2. A query vector q' with nine concepts of weight 12.

3. $q \cap q'$ consisting of three concepts.

4. A document vector *d* with
     40 concepts of weight 12,
     10 concepts of weight 24,
     3 concepts of weight 36,
     1 concept of weight 48.

5. $q \cap d$ consisting of three concepts, all having weight 12 in both *q* and *d*.

6. $q' \cap d$ consisting of zero concepts.

7. $\beta = 30$, $\gamma = 0.225$, and $\delta = 8$.

The initial correlation of query vector *q* with document vector *d* is 0.0875. After modification, the new document vector (denoted $\hat{d}$) contains the following concept distribution:

Concepts	Weight	Distribution
45	10	12 − 2
10	20	24 − 4
6	30	Added
3	31	36 − 5
3	36	12 + 24
1	41	48 − 7

The correlation of *q* with $\hat{d}$ is now 0.6420. While this increase in correlation will surely retrieve $\hat{d}$ in response to a future query exactly like *q*, the more interesting effect concerns the correlation of *q'* with $\hat{d}$. (Note: *q'* is similar to *q*.) The correlation of *q'* with *d* was originally equal to zero. However, after modification, $\hat{d}$ shows a correlation of 0.2040 with *q'*. This new correlation is large enough so that $\hat{d}$ will generally rank among the top ten documents for *q'*.

For collections similar in nature to the Cranfield collection, the values assumed for β, γ, and δ will generally produce the following results:

1. Depending on the size of the document vector *d*, each concept *i* added to *d* with weight β for a query vector *q* will increase the correlation of $\hat{d}$ with a query *q'* similar to *q* by 0.07.

2. For $\gamma = 0.225$, 17 *successive* queries, all containing concept *i*, would be required to increase the weight of concept *i* in *d* from 12 to 119. Only five successive queries are required, however, to increase the weight from 12 to 90. Thus concepts used frequently in queries seeking a document will gain relatively high weights in the document vector fairly rapidly.

3. For $\delta = 8$, document vector concept weights decrease reasonably quickly when the concepts are not used in queries seeking the document. For example, five successive

queries not utilizing concept i will cause the document vector weight of that concept to drop from 30 to 13.

The fluctuations of document vector concept weights may then be expected to follow a pattern. The weights for concepts used occasionally in queries seeking a document will usually oscillate in the range from 20 to 60. Considering the effects of δ, however, most of these weights at any given time will tend toward the lower range values. Similarly, infrequently used concepts may be expected to have weights oscillating in the range 0–30; most of these concept weights will again have low range values at any given time.

Another topic that may be considered is the amount of first search retrieval performance improvement shown by the tests of Strategy 1. Three criteria were given in Sec 24-4-B as a basis for determining whether the improvements are significant. Criterion 1 requires significant improvement over all 30 queries in a test set. The 30 queries of Test Set 1 show normalized recall improvements of up to 2.9% and normalized precision improvements of up to 8.4%. Table 24-5 shows average precision improvements of 0.10 to 0.20 at many recall levels. The 30 queries of Test Set 2 show normalized recall increases of up to 3.2% and normalized precision increases of up to 6.3%. Table 24-8 resembles Table 24-5, showing average precision improvements of 0.10 to 0.18 at many recall levels.

Criterion 2 requires that the retrieval performance should not decrease for test set queries not similar to modification set queries. A glance at Tables 24-3, 24-6, and 24-9 shows that this condition is met. In fact, performance actually improves for these nonsimilar queries. This improvement stems primarily from two conditions:

1. Test set queries may have up to two concepts in common with a modification set query while still being termed nonsimilar.

2. The nonsimilar test set queries have some relevant documents in common with some of the modification set queries.

The combination of a small concept overlap and a small overlap in relevant documents between test set and modification set queries then leads to some improvements in retrieval performance.

Criterion 3 of Sec. 24-4-B requires that test set queries similar to modification set queries show a significant improvement in first search retrieval performance. Test Set 1 similar queries show normalized recall improvements of up to 4.3% and normalized precision improvements of up to 13.3%. The recall-level curves for Test Set 1 are far better than the standard curve; run 1–3 shows an improvement of 0.2969 at recall level 0.60 over the standard. The performance of Test Set 2 similar queries, while not as outstanding as that of Test Set 1, still represents a significant improvement for the modified document vector spaces. R_{norm} and P_{norm} show increases of up to 1.7% and 2.8%, respectively. More importantly, Table 24-10 shows average precision values which are higher by 0.08 to 0.16 in comparison with the standard at many recall levels. Since all criteria of Sec. 24-4-B have been met in the present tests, the case for retrieval performance improvement under document vector modification must be considered as established.

It is interesting to see if the improvement produced by document vector modification in first search retrieval performance is as great as the improvements generated by one or more relevance feedback iterations. It was noted earlier in this connection that the 155 queries of the Cranfield collection were run under the SMART information retrieval system using an initial search and three relevance feedback iterations. Recall-level averages, R_{norm}, and P_{norm} were calculated over the 155 queries after the initial run. After the second search (i.e., after the use of one relevance feedback iteration for each query), these figures were recomputed. Normalized recall and normalized precision showed improvements of 4.01% and 4.29%, respectively; average precision was 0.01 to 0.06 higher at various recall levels. Similarly, after the second relevance feedback search, R_{norm} was 5.21% higher than after the initial search, and P_{norm} was 5.23% higher; average precision increases at various recall levels were 0.01 to 0.08 higher than after the initial search. The third relevance feedback search is not considered here.

For the tests of Strategy 1, runs 1–5 and 2–5 showed the most marked retrieval performance improvements for queries in Test Sets 1 and 2. Averaging the performance figures for these two runs shows that, over 60 queries, document vector modification increased first search R_{norm} and P_{norm} by 3.1% and 7.3%, respectively; average precision showed increases of 0.09 and 0.20 at various recall levels. It would appear, then, that the first search retrieval improvement produced by the document vector modification is greater than the improvements shown by both the first and second relevance feedback iterations. The fact that normalized recall shows smaller improvement under Strategy 1 than under relevance feedback is of no consequence because it is generally more important to place *most* relevant documents for a query in high ranks than to place *all* relevant documents in high ranks. Normalized precision as well as recall-level averages are the important measures in this respect.

Unhappily, the performance figures just cited for relevance feedback and for document vector modification are not completely comparable. The searching under Strategy 1 was entirely fluid; that is, *all* document vectors were ranked in decreasing order of their correlations with the query vector. In the first relevance feedback search, the top five ranked documents were, however, frozen after the initial search, and only ranks 6 and below could reflect rank changes for the new correlations with the once-modified query vector. Similarly, in the second relevance feedback search, the top 15 ranked documents were frozen after the initial search and the first relevance feedback search. To be directly comparable to Strategy 1, then, both relevance feedback searches would have to be entirely fluid.

Still, an approximate comparison can be made between the first search improvements of Strategy 1 and the improvements of relevance feedback. Consider the first relevance feedback search. Of the five documents frozen after the initial search, one or (more commonly) two will be relevant to the query. If the search *were* fully fluid, and assuming that any relevant document in the frozen top five would remain in the top five in a fluid search, relevant documents ranked 6 or below could only shift upward by three ranks at best. Not all relevant documents would shift upward, of course; the three nonrelevant documents presently frozen in the top five may still be expected to retain high ranks in a fluid search. Thus, even if the first relevance feedback search were entirely fluid, the retrieval performance improvement shown over the initial search could only be moderately better than the improvement presently shown.

The same considerations do not apply to the second relevance feedback search. Presently 15 documents are frozen in the second search. If this search were entirely fluid, a drastic revision of ranks could occur. In fact, it may be expected that performance figures for a fully fluid second relevance feedback search would be much higher than the present figures indicate for a search with 15 frozen documents.

It is assumed that the first relevance feedback search will produce a retrieval performance moderately better than the SMART first search, and that the second relevance feedback search will exhibit a considerably better retrieval performance than the SMART second search. One may then expect that the retrieval performance for the first search under the document vector modification procedure will be roughly equivalent to the performance of an initial search in an unmodified space, plus one relevance feedback iteration. Thus, the document vector modification may be expected to eliminate the system time, the user time, and the effort necessary for one complete relevance feedback iteration. This is an important advantage in terms of systems efficiency.

A final question to be considered relates to the values of β, γ, and δ which produce optimal retrieval performance. In this discussion the term "optimal" designates the best results obtainable by using the least effort. In the perfect case, then, a small effort will yield results better than all larger efforts. In a more typical case, suppose effort X yields result A, and effort Y yields result B. Suppose further that X is much smaller than Y, but A is only a little less than B. The present definition of the term "optimal" will then pick X over Y as the recommended effort. This definition of optimal fits best with permanent changes to an information retrieval system. If only temporary changes were being considered, it might be better to make large efforts in order to secure maximum results.

It might be argued that the values of β, γ, and δ used for runs 1–1 and 2–1 are optimal. Surely they produce the smallest modifications and show the greatest single increase in retrieval performance. However, a close look at the averages in Tables 24-5 through 24-10 is sufficient to eliminate this possibility. Runs 1–1 and 2–1 produce usually significantly lower figures (often by about 0.05 or 0.06 in the middle recall levels) than the maximum results obtained. Four specific observations derived from Tables 24-5 through 24-10 are now useful:

1. With the exception of the similar queries in Test Set 1 (Table 24-7), runs 1–5 and 2–5 generally dominate retrieval improvement.

2. With only a few exceptions, runs 1–4 and 2–4 show retrieval results that are within 0.005 of the results of runs 1–5 and 2–5 at all recall levels. For most of the exceptions, the results differ by less than 0.01.

3. With only a few exceptions, runs 1–3 and 2–3 show retrieval results that are within 0.01 of the results obtained for runs 1–4 and 2–4 at all recall levels. Most of the exceptions differ by less than 0.02.

4. Runs 1–2 and 2–2 show significantly lower results than runs 1–3 and 2–3. Particularly in the middle recall levels, differences of 0.03 to 0.05 are not uncommon.

It is apparent that runs 1–3 and 2–3 through 1–5 and 2–5 must be studied to obtain information concerning the optimal values for β, γ, and δ; the average precision difference at all recall levels for these runs almost always lies within a range of 0.015 to 0.03. The values of β and δ for all these runs are the same, namely 30 and 8. The values of γ, however, vary significantly; runs 1–3 and 2–3 use a $\gamma = 0.20$; runs 1–4 and 2–4 have $\gamma = 0.25$; runs 1–5 and 2–5 have $\gamma = 0.33$. Consider a typical modification for a concept with weight 12. Runs 1–3 and 2–3 will increase the weight by 22, runs 1–4 and 2–4 by 27, and runs 1–5 and 2–5 by 36. Obviously $\gamma = 0.33$ makes large changes in concept weights while yielding little increase in retrieval performance over the other two values of γ. The best value of γ may in fact lie between 0.20 and 0.25. Such a value would utilize only $\frac{2}{3}$ of the effort shown by $\gamma = 0.33$ and would produce retrieval results within 0.01 to 0.02 of the maximum at all recall levels. For Strategy 1, then, values of $\beta = 30$, $\gamma = 0.225$, and $\delta = 8$ are suggested as optimal for document collections similar to the Cranfield collection.

In conclusion, Strategy 1 has been shown to fulfill the objectives specified in Sec. 24-1. The strategy serves to facilitate the document vector indexing, and retrieval performance does improve substantially with its use. It is worth noting, however, that the *specific* measurements included in these discussions are directly applicable to the Cranfield collection and similar collections. Collections with document abstracts that are much longer than the average Cranfield abstract length, or with document vectors not defined initially by the word form technique, may show somewhat different results. One may expect, however, that the main trends exhibited in the present tests will be maintained.

24-5   A SECOND PROPOSAL FOR IMPROVED DOCUMENT SPACE MODIFICATION

24-5-A   The Method

In Sec. 24-4 a proposal was introduced which would modify the *relevant* document vectors for queries submitted to an information retrieval system. The next logical step is to see if further improvements in retrieval performance can be obtained by modifying both *relevant* and *nonrelevant* document vectors.† Such a procedure is outlined in the present section.

†The modification of relevant document vectors to increase their correlations with the original query vector is occasionally called positive modification. Similarly, the modification of nonrelevant document vectors is sometimes called negative modification.

The only strategy advanced to date for modifying both relevant and nonrelevant document vectors is the one developed by Ide. Although the theory behind this method appears sound, and test runs so far have shown good results, one possible weakness may hinder its usefulness when incorporated into an on-line retrieval system. To understand this weakness, it is necessary to briefly consider the process as well as the characteristics of on-line query processing. Ide suggests that the final list of documents accepted by the user be evaluated, that all (or almost all) relevant documents be modified to increase their correlations with the original query vector, and that at the same time a number of nonrelevant documents be modified to decrease their correlations with the original query vector. The number of nonrelevant document vectors modified is always less than or equal to the number of relevant document vectors modified.

In on-line query processing, a user typically submits a query and receives in return a *small* list of documents (usually about five), representing the output of a first search effort using the original query vector. The user may then submit feedback information including, for example, the identification of relevant documents previously retrieved, and based on the user's comments, the system modifies the original query vector and returns a second list of different documents (perhaps ten in number) correlating highly with the new query vector. This is the process known as relevance feedback, which continues until the user has seen a satisfactory number of relevant documents. The intent of Ide's negative modification is to move several nonrelevant document vectors that correlate highly with the *original* query vector away from the *original* query vector. However, by utilizing the *final* list of retrieved documents (i.e., actually a union of all intermediate lists), most negative modifications are made based on correlations with a *modified* query vector. Only the *first* list of five retrieved documents actually represents retrieval based on correlations with the original query vector. Hence, only nonrelevant documents found in this first list should be moved away from the original query vector. Experiments with the Cranfield collection have shown that of the five documents retrieved on first lists an average of between one and two are relevant to the user's query. Thus, to apply Ide's strategy accurately, a somewhat difficult decision process must be utilized to negatively modify only one or two nonrelevant document vectors per query. A simpler procedure which modifies a larger number of nonrelevant document vectors might be more effective.†

The modification strategy tested in the present section is called Strategy 2 and operates as follows:

1. An initial query vector q_0 is submitted, and a first list is returned. Relevance feedback iterations are then run until the user is satisfied with the union of all retrieval lists.

---

†One reason why previous testings of Ide's method have shown good results is that only one search was conducted for the modification set queries before the modification procedure was carried out. Large first lists were printed for these searches. All (or most) of the relevant documents found in these large first lists were modified, thus allowing the modification of several nonrelevant documents for each query.

2. *Any relevant* document that has appeared in *any* retrieval list (i.e., first list, second list after one relevance feedback iteration, . . ., nth list after $n - 1$ relevance feedback iterations) is processed according to Strategy 1 to increase its correlation with the original query vector.

3. *Each nonrelevant* document that has appeared in the *first* retrieval list is processed as follows:

   (a) If concept i appears in the original query vector $\mathbf{q}_0$ but is absent from non-relevant document $\mathbf{d}_n$, no action is taken.

   (b) If concept i appears in both nonrelevant document $\mathbf{d}_n$ and the original query vector $\mathbf{q}_0$, its weight in $\mathbf{d}_n$ is decreased as follows:

$$\hat{\mathbf{d}}_n^i = \mathbf{d}_n^i - \left[\left(\frac{\mathbf{d}_n^i}{\theta} \right) + 1 \right] \tag{10}$$

   (c) If concept i appears in nonrelevant document $\mathbf{d}_n$ but is absent from the original query vector $\mathbf{q}_0$, its weight in $\mathbf{d}_n$ is increased as shown:

$$\hat{\mathbf{d}}_n^i = \mathbf{d}_n^i + \varepsilon \, (120 - \mathbf{d}_n^i). \tag{11}$$

The procedures outlined above for modifying nonrelevant document vectors strongly resemble those of Strategy 1. The three concept categories used [3(a), 3(b), and 3(c)] are precisely the same, but the actions taken are the inverse of the actions taken for Strategy 1. This results from the desire to decrease document-query correlations rather than to increase them. All weight changes are rounded to the nearest integer. Concept category 3(a) produces no action. In an operational system, it might be useful to add concept i to $\mathbf{d}_n$ with a negative weight; for the present, however, it is best to avoid the complications of negative weighting. As in Strategy 1, no normalization of the query vector occurs, and formula (11) maintains 120 as an upper bound for concept weights. All modifications ignore query vector concept weights. Procedure 3 states that *each* nonrelevant document vector in the first list should be modified negatively. The assumption is that the first list consists of five documents.

24-5-B Testing Procedure

Several tests of Strategy 2 were performed using various values for θ and ε. The Cranfield collection of 424 documents and 155 queries was used for these tests. The following procedure was utilized:

1. A test set of 30 queries was chosen from the 155 queries available. A modification set was then defined as the 125 queries not included in the test set.

2. Test values for θ and ε were established for the run.

3. A modified document vector space was created by modifying relevant and non-relevant document vectors for each query in the modification set according to Strategy 2.

4. A single full search was run through the modified document vector space for each of the 30 queries in the test set. Average retrieval performance figures were calculated for the set of searches.

The same two test sets and modification sets already used in Sec. 24-4-C were used in the present series of tests. As in Sec. 24-4 all tests were run using both Test Set 1 and Modification Set 1 *and* Test Set 2 and Modification Set 2. Again the purpose of the tests was to compare first search retrieval performance of modified document vector spaces and unmodified spaces. Both test sets still consisted of 15 queries not similar to the 125 queries of the corresponding modification sets and 15 queries similar to one or more modification set queries. Thus for each test run, the following three types of retrieval performance figures were calculated:

1. Average performance over the entire 30-query test set.

2. Average performance over the 15 nonsimilar queries.

3. Average performance over the 15 similar queries.

As for Strategy 1, both recall-level averages and average normalized recall and precision were calculated to indicate retrieval performance.

The retrieval performance results of Strategy 2 tests were compared to two standards. Tests utilizing Test Set 1, for example, were compared against the following two runs made previously:

1. Run 1–0: The retrieval performance of Test Set 1 queries in the original Cranfield document vector space.

2. Run 1–00: The retrieval performance generated by run 1–4 of Strategy 1, which produced results close to those believed to be optimal (see Sec. 24-4-D).

Run 1–00 (and also run 2–00) represents a progress standard. It has already been shown in Sec. 24-4 that Strategy 1 aids document vector indexing and leads to significantly improved retrieval performance. Strategy 2 is equally attractive for document vector indexing as Strategy 1, but is somewhat more costly to operate. Therefore, if Strategy 2 is to be justified as a modification method, the resulting retrieval performance improvements must be significantly greater than those shown for Strategy 1. Runs 1–4 and 2–4 for Strategy 1 produced results close to the optimal and are therefore included in the present tests for comparison 2. The values of β, γ, and δ in the test runs are the optimal values discussed in Sec. 24-4-D. Table 24-11 summarizes all test runs performed for Strategy 2.

24-5-C Test Results

Runs 1–1 through 1–3 and 2–1 through 2–3 are the actual tests conducted for Strategy 2. Each pair of runs (e.g., runs 1–1 and 2–1) represents a single experimental

Table 24-11

SUMMARY OF TESTS FOR STRATEGY 2

Run	β	γ	δ	θ	ε	Test Set	Modification Set
1–0	–	–	–	–	–	1	–
2–0	–	–	–	–	–	2	–
1–00	30	0.250	8	–	–	1	1
2–00	30	0.250	8	–	–	2	2
1–1	30	0.225	8	36	0.05	1	1
2–1	30	0.225	8	36	0.05	2	2
1–2	30	0.225	8	24	0.10	1	1
2–2	30	0.225	8	24	0.10	2	2
1–3	30	0.225	8	24	0.15	1	1
2–3	30	0.225	8	24	0.15	2	2

condition tested with both test sets and modification sets. The runs are numbered in increasing order by the amount of modification to nonrelevant document vectors; the modifications performed on the relevant document vectors are standardized in all tests.

Tables 24-12, 24-13, and 24-14 show average normalized recall and precision for all runs. Table 24-12 lists the averages over the 30 queries in the test sets, Table 24-13 shows averages over the nonsimilar queries, and Table 24-14 presents averages for the similar queries. Recall-level averages are listed in Tables 24-15 through 24-20. For the five runs utilizing Test Set 1 and Modification Set 1, Table 24-15 lists averages over the 30 queries, Table 24-16 presents averages for the 15 nonsimilar queries, and Table 24-17 lists the averages for the 15 similar queries. For the five runs utilizing Test Set 2 and Modification Set 2, Table 24-18, 24-19, and 24-20 are analogous to Tables 24-15,

Table 24-12

AVERAGE NORMALIZED RECALL AND PRECISION
FOR ALL QUERIES

Run	R_{norm}	*Percent Change from Standard*	P_{norm}	*Percent Change from Standard*
1–0	.8795	–	.6500	–
2–0	.8739	–	.6595	–
1–00	.9081	+2.9	.7334	+8.3
2–00	.9052	+3.1	.7164	+5.7
1–1	.9096	+3.0	.7306	+8.1
2–1	.9073	+3.3	.7174	+5.8
1–2	.9092	+3.0	.7203	+7.0
2–2	.9068	+3.3	.7081	+4.9
1–3	.9082	+2.9	.7130	+6.3
2–3	.9049	+3.1	.6993	+4.0

Table 24-13

AVERAGE NORMALIZED RECALL AND PRECISION
FOR NONSIMILAR QUERIES

Run	R_{norm}	Percent Change from Standard	P_{norm}	Percent Change from Standard
1–0	0.8894	–	0.6901	–
2–0	0.8650	–	0.6301	–
1–00	0.9039	+1.5	0.7241	+3.4
2–00	0.9139	+4.9	0.7191	+8.9
1–1	0.9048	+1.5	0.7192	+2.9
2–1	0.9157	+5.1	0.7257	+9.5
1–2	0.9039	+1.5	0.7130	+2.3
2–2	0.9152	+5.0	0.7142	+8.4
1–3	0.9025	+1.3	0.7091	+1.9
2–3	0.9136	+4.9	0.7031	+7.3

Table 24-14

AVERAGE NORMALIZED RECALL AND PRECISION
FOR SIMILAR QUERIES

Run	R_{norm}	Percent Change from Standard	P_{norm}	Percent Change from Standard
1–0	0.8697	–	0.6099	–
2–0	0.8828	–	0.6890	–
1–00	0.9122	+4.3	0.7428	+13.3
2–00	0.8964	+1.4	0.7131	+2.4
1–1	0.9145	+4.5	0.7421	+13.2
2–1	0.8990	+1.6	0.7095	+2.1
1–2	0.9146	+4.5	0.7276	+11.8
2–2	0.8984	+1.6	0.7020	+1.3
1–3	0.9138	+4.4	0.7170	+10.7
2–3	0.8961	+1.3	0.6955	+0.7

Table 24-15

RECALL-LEVEL AVERAGES FOR TEST SET 1—ALL QUERIES

Recall Level	Run 1–0	Run 1–00	Run 1–1	Run 1–2	Run 1–3
0.10	0.7009	0.7285	0.7228	0.7135	0.7130
0.20	0.6121	0.6818	0.6795	0.6520	0.6345
0.30	0.4760	0.5905	0.5945	0.5777	0.5660
0.40	0.3932	0.5576	0.5740	0.5327	0.5124
0.50	0.3764	0.5472	0.5651	0.5144	0.4993
0.60	0.2877	0.5003	0.4646	0.4234	0.4022
0.70	0.2205	0.4186	0.3686	0.3219	0.3019
0.80	0.1963	0.3686	0.3144	0.2648	0.2364
0.90	0.1336	0.2515	0.2449	0.2144	0.1936
1.00	0.1273	0.2468	0.2425	0.2111	0.1871

Table 24-16

RECALL-LEVEL AVERAGES FOR
TEST SET 1—NONSIMILAR QUERIES

Recall Level	Run 1–0	Run 1–00	Run 1–1	Run 1–2	Run 1–3
0.10	0.7622	0.7593	0.7399	0.7350	0.7366
0.20	0.6568	0.6660	0.6644	0.6582	0.6598
0.30	0.5155	0.5517	0.5472	0.5437	0.5448
0.40	0.4733	0.5184	0.5179	0.5087	0.5083
0.50	0.4508	0.5086	0.5001	0.4918	0.4928
0.60	0.3599	0.4940	0.4400	0.4097	0.4031
0.70	0.3042	0.4619	0.3677	0.3223	0.3018
0.80	0.2717	0.4124	0.3471	0.2833	0.2628
0.90	0.1775	0.2697	0.2620	0.2271	0.2104
1.00	0.1773	0.2675	0.2601	0.2237	0.2008

Table 24-17

RECALL-LEVEL AVERAGES FOR TEST SET 1—SIMILAR QUERIES

Recall Level	Run 1–0	Run 1–00	Run 1–1	Run 1–2	Run 1–3
0.10	0.6395	0.6976	0.7057	0.6920	0.6895
0.20	0.5674	0.6976	0.6946	0.6459	0.6092
0.30	0.4365	0.6293	0.6418	0.6118	0.5873
0.40	0.3131	0.5969	0.6302	0.5567	0.5165
0.50	0.3019	0.5858	0.6302	0.5370	0.5058
0.60	0.2156	0.5067	0.4893	0.4370	0.4012
0.70	0.1368	0.3753	0.3696	0.3215	0.3021
0.80	0.1208	0.3248	0.2813	0.2462	0.2100
0.90	0.0897	0.2333	0.2279	0.2017	0.1767
1.00	0.0813	0.2261	0.2250	0.1984	0.1733

Table 24-18

RECALL-LEVEL AVERAGES FOR TEST SET 2—ALL QUERIES

Recall Level	Run 2–0	Run 2–00	Run 2–1	Run 2–2	Run 2–3
0.10	0.6093	0.6881	0.6621	0.6609	0.6580
0.20	0.5114	0.6347	0.6440	0.6077	0.6018
0.30	0.4287	0.5691	0.5811	0.5412	0.5277
0.40	0.3747	0.5373	0.5224	0.5041	0.4936
0.50	0.3489	0.4746	0.4655	0.4431	0.4132
0.60	0.3172	0.4008	0.3919	0.3768	0.3534
0.70	0.2638	0.3551	0.3395	0.3152	0.2892
0.80	0.2233	0.3092	0.2910	0.2622	0.2355
0.90	0.1656	0.2217	0.2244	0.2151	0.1999
1.00	0.1471	0.1900	0.2011	0.1915	0.1739

Table 24-19

RECALL-LEVEL AVERAGES FOR
TEST SET 2—NONSIMILAR QUERIES

Recall Level	Run 2–0	Run 2–00	Run 2–1	Run 2–2	Run 2–3
0.10	0.5185	0.6316	0.6121	0.5800	0.5675
0.20	0.4709	0.6079	0.6097	0.5800	0.5509
0.30	0.3915	0.5229	0.5447	0.5051	0.4869
0.40	0.3407	0.5062	0.5169	0.4767	0.4546
0.50	0.3367	0.4835	0.4595	0.4335	0.4115
0.60	0.3073	0.4196	0.4009	0.3785	0.3476
0.70	0.2599	0.3651	0.3638	0.3402	0.3091
0.80	0.2269	0.3001	0.3132	0.2912	0.2637
0.90	0.2080	0.2564	0.2675	0.2503	0.2256
1.00	0.1918	0.2535	0.2620	0.2436	0.2090

Table 24-20

RECALL-LEVEL AVERAGES FOR TEST SET 2—SIMILAR QUERIES

Recall Level	Run 2–0	Run 2–00	Run 2–1	Run 2–2	Run 2–3
0.10	0.7001	0.7446	0.7120	0.7419	0.7484
0.20	0.5520	0.6615	0.6783	0.6354	0.6527
0.30	0.4659	0.6154	0.6176	0.5774	0.5684
0.40	0.4087	0.5685	0.5480	0.5315	0.5326
0.50	0.3611	0.4657	0.4714	0.4528	0.4149
0.60	0.3271	0.3821	0.3829	0.3752	0.3592
0.70	0.2678	0.3451	0.3152	0.2902	0.2693
0.80	0.2197	0.3184	0.2687	0.2332	0.2073
0.90	0.1233	0.1870	0.1812	0.1799	0.1742
1.00	0.1024	0.1265	0.1401	0.1395	0.1389

24-16, and 24-17. At each recall level in Tables 24-15 through 24-20, the run showing the highest average precision is underscored.

The actual recall-precision graphs produced by Test Sets 1 and 2, respectively, are presented averaged over all queries in Figs. 24-3 and 24-4. Runs 1–0 and 2–0 again represent standard performance for unmodified document spaces, and runs 1–00 and 2–00 reflect the best output obtainable by the positive space modification of Strategy 1.

24-5-D   Discussion

As noted in Sec. 24-5-B, Strategy 1 has already proved useful in document vector indexing and information retrieval performance. Furthermore, since Strategy 2 can

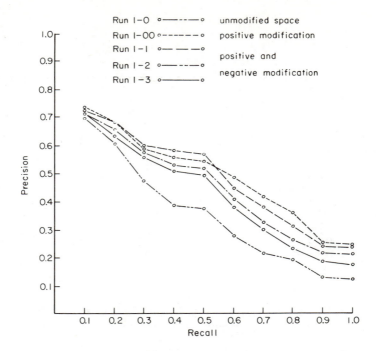

Fig. 24-3   Recall-level averages, Strategy 2, Test Set 1—all queries.

also be used to add new concepts to document vectors and to alter concept weights in the same manner as Strategy 1, it provides exactly the same benefits to vector indexing as Strategy 1. At the same time Strategy 2 is more expensive to operate. It must show significantly better retrieval performance than Strategy 1 to justify its extra cost. The test results listed in Sec. 24-5-C reveal that this condition is not met.

A constant pattern of retrieval performance emerges from the tests for Strategy 2. Consider the results for the 30 queries of Test Set 1. Table 24-15 clearly reveals that run 1–00, which represents the optimal performance for Strategy 1, has a performance equal to or better than all tests for Strategy 2. Furthermore, as the amount of negative modification increases for Strategy 2, the retrieval performance decreases. Thus run 1–1, which makes the smallest changes in nonrelevant document vectors, is the best run of Strategy 2; run 1–3, which produces the most marked changes in nonrelevant document vectors, is the poorest run. Normalized recall for the Strategy 2 tests is within 0.1 % of the normalized recall for run 1–00. Normalized precision for run 1–1 is close to that for run 1–00, but runs 1–2 and 1–3 show progressively lower normalized precision values. This same pattern occurs for experiments with both Test Set 1 and Test Set 2 and for similar queries, nonsimilar queries, as well as all 30 queries of the Test Sets. In those few cases where Strategy 2 performs better than the Strategy 1 standard, the increases are not large enough to be termed significant, and they are surely not large enough to warrant the extra expense of Strategy 2.

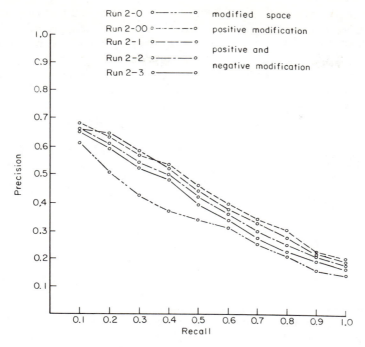

Fig. 24-4   Recall-level averages, Strategy 2, Test Set 2—all queries.

Thus, under the present conditions, the modification of nonrelevant document vectors does not appear to aid retrieval performance. Two possible improvements might lead to better performance for Strategy 2. Consider, first, that the best runs for Strategy 2 are invariably those which produce the least modification to nonrelevant document vectors. It might be argued that still smaller modifications would lead to better retrieval performance. On the other hand, since the increase produced by formula (11) for a concept with weight 12 is only five (if $\varepsilon = 0.05$ as in runs 1–1 and 2–1), and since for $\theta = 36$, the weight decreases produced by formula (10) are usually only one or two for a single modification, it is possible that smaller changes would border too closely on a zero change.

A second possible method would be to increase the number of nonrelevant document vectors modified per query vector. Unfortunately, a drawback to this solution exists also. The only nonrelevant document vectors that can be modified legitimately are those that have some relationship (e.g., high correlation) with the *original* query vector.† This limits the choice of nonrelevant documents to some subset of the documents which appear in the first list. If more nonrelevant document vectors are to be modified, then the number of documents in the first list must be increased.

†The purpose of document vector modification is to introduce user vocabulary and judgment into the document vectors. If modifications are allowed which are not based on the user's query, this purpose is subverted.

First lists, however, do not typically produce good retrieval performance. Poorly phrased queries, nonfamiliarity with the retrieval system, inappropriate document concept weights, and other factors combine to hinder the retrieval performance for initial queries. Thus, first lists are generally kept small in order to allow a user to scan and comment on only a *few* documents. The system can then modify the query and produce a new output list with a greater expectation of good retrieval performance. Longer first lists will only add to the number of documents to be considered by the user in order to find the first few relevant ones. It is not necessarily a good idea to tie negative modification to such extra user efforts.

The tests of Strategy 2 indicate that the modification of nonrelevant documents in the manner envisioned presently is not worth the effort. This is not to say, however, that a profitable method of modifying nonrelevant document vectors does not exist. A new method of attacking the problem is probably required.

24-6 *CONCLUSIONS*

The tests and discussions presented for Strategy 1 in Sec. 24-4 suggest strongly that document vector modification may be a useful technique in information retrieval. It is apparent that both retrieval performance and document vector indexing may benefit from such strategies. Further research effort in this area is indicated. More comprehensive discussions of these questions are included in the previously cited papers by Brauen, Holt, and Wilcox, and by Ide, and in *Report ISR-17* to the National Science Foundation.

REFERENCES

[1] T. L. Brauen, R. C. Holt, and T. R. Wilcox, Document Indexing Based on Relevance Feedback, *Report ISR-14* to the National Science Foundation, Section XI, Department of Computer Science, Cornell University, Ithaca, N.Y., June 1968.

[2] E. Ide, Relevance Feedback in an Automatic Document Retrieval System, *Report ISR-15* to the National Science Foundation, Cornell University, Ithaca, N.Y., January 1969, pp. VII-81 through VII-85.

PART VIII

OPERATIONAL COMPARISONS

Information storage and retrieval systems which are presently available do not produce retrieval results which will satisfy the information needs of all potential users. Interactive search methods using console displays and conversational computing methods promise to furnish retrieval results which are far superior to those achievable by conventional procedures. In the present study, various interactive search strategies are used in conjunction with the automatic SMART document retrieval system, and an attempt is made to evaluate the effectiveness of each method as part of a retrieval system.

In particular, the usefulness of each method in retrieving wanted and rejecting unwanted items is discussed, as well as the cost of the user-system interaction in terms of additional user effort and computer time. It is found that for all but the most experienced users, automatic methods requiring little user effort are preferable to more sophisticated procedures which may produce somewhat better retrieval results at somewhat higher cost.

25

INTERACTIVE SEARCH AND RETRIEVAL METHODS USING AUTOMATIC INFORMATION DISPLAYS†

M. E. LESK and G. SALTON

25-1 INTRODUCTION

Throughout the world, the design and operation of large-scale information systems has become of concern to an ever-increasing segment of the scientific and professional population. Furthermore, as the amount and complexity of the available information has continued to grow, the use of mechanized or partly mechanized procedures for various information storage and retrieval tasks has also become more widespread. While a number of retrieval systems are already in operation, in which the search operations needed to compare the incoming information requests with the stored items are performed automatically, no systematic study has ever been made of the use of man–machine interaction as a part of a mechanized text analysis and information processing system. Specifically, the recent development of high capacity random-access storage mechanisms and conversational input–output con-

†This study was issued as Section IX in *Scientific Report ISR-14*, October 1968, and is also included in the *AFIPS Conference Proceedings*, Vol. 34, Afips Press, Montvale, N.J., 1969.

soles should permit a rapid interchange of information between users and system. Such an interchange can then be used to produce improved search formulations, resulting in a more effective retrieval service.

The present report describes and evaluates the performance of a variety of such interactive search and retrieval procedures in which information supplied by the user population is considered in an attempt to achieve improved system responses. Several basic approaches to user–system interaction are possible. On the one hand, an attempt can be made to construct refined query formulations, using dictionary displays and similar methods, *before* any file search is actually attempted. On the other hand, an original query can be processed when it is first received, and a query reformulation attempted *after* the results of an initial search are actually available. These two procedures, called *presearch* and *postsearch* respectively, can in turn be executed in several different ways. Either the system assumes most of the burden of the query reformulation through an automatic query alteration process, or the users themselves can rephrase their queries using the available automatic displays. In the latter case, the skill of the user population becomes a more important factor. The stored data most important in the presearch methods might include synonym dictionaries, thesauri, word frequency statistics, and lists of significant words; the postsearch information, on the other hand, consists of the titles, abstracts, or texts of documents retrieved by a previous search process.

The investigation of the various interactive search and retrieval methods is carried out with the help of the automatic SMART document retrieval system [1], [2]. The SMART system is a large computer-based retrieval system capable of performing a variety of different text analysis, search, and retrieval operations. Completely automatic text analysis and information searches are made using several different analysis methods and search strategies. Among the main text analysis procedures are synonym recognition, word disambiguation, phrase recognition, statistical term association, and hierarchical text expansion methods.

The effectiveness of the various analysis and search methods may be evaluated by using for this purpose the familiar *recall* and *precision* measures, representing respectively the proportion of relevant material actually retrieved, and the proportion of retrieved material actually relevant. Ideally, all relevant items should be retrieved for the user, while at the same time, all nonrelevant items should be rejected, thus leading to a system where both recall and precision are equal to 1. The performance effectiveness of an operating system can then be estimated by averaging recall and precision figures over many searches and comparing the results with the ideal situation where recall and precision are equal to 1. The SMART system automatically generates for each search a set of recall-precision graphs first introduced by Cleverdon [3] and also includes procedures for performing computations of the statistical significance of the results. Evaluation data for a wide variety of automatic text-processing, search, and retrieval methods have been published previously [4].

In addition to the recall-precision data which reflect the capability of the system to deliver to the user the information he requests, it is also important in an interactive computing environment to take into account the amount of effort required from the user to obtain satisfactory results. Thus, the standard performance of fully automatic search and retrieval operations must be compared against the improvements obtainable through interactive procedures at additional cost in user effort and computer time.

In the remainder of this study, the effectiveness of various types of interactive search methods is examined, including both presearch and postsearch methods, and semiautomatic or fully automatic query reformulation procedures. The results are compared using, in each case, the evaluation methods incorporated into the SMART system. Construction principles are then derived for future information services designed to use man–machine interaction during the search process.

25-2 FULLY AUTOMATIC RETRIEVAL

In the SMART system, various fully automatic language analysis procedures are used to normalize the text of incoming search requests and of stored documents. The normalized, reduced forms of the information items, consisting generally of weighted "concept" numbers, are then compared, and the document representations which are most similar to the request representations are extracted from the file as answers to the queries. The language normalization procedures incorporated into the SMART system range from simple word-stem matching methods to more sophisticated processes using stored synonym dictionaries and hierarchies, as well as statistical and syntactic analysis methods [1], [2].

Three of the simplest language analysis methods known respectively, as *word form*, *word stem*, and *thesaurus* processes, may be described as follows:

(a) In the word form, or suffix "*s*," process, no word normalization in the proper sense is used at all, and the original words with only the final "*s*" removed (to confound, for example, "book" and "books") are compared directly.

(b) In the word-stem method, the original text words are reduced to word stems by a suffix cutoff process to confound words like "analyzer," "analysis," "analyzed," and so on, before the comparison between queries and documents.

(c) In the thesaurus process, each word stem is looked up in a synonym dictionary, or thesaurus, where it is replaced by one or more so-called concept numbers, representing synonym classes; the concepts extracted from the thesaurus are then matched instead of the original word forms or word stems.

In all analysis methods, the terms are weighted normally, using word frequency and other criteria, before a comparison is made between stored documents and search requests.

An excerpt from a typical, manually constructed thesaurus is shown in Table 25-1. Three of the synonym classes defined by the thesaurus mapping are shown in the right-hand side of Table 25-1. Concept class 346, for example, contains words

Table 25-1

THESAURUS EXCERPT

ALPHABETIC ORDER			NUMERIC ORDER	
Word	Concept Code	Syntax Code	Concept Code	Word
Wide	438	001 043 040	344	obstacle
Will	32032	009 070 043 044 049		target
Wind	345 233	070 043	345	atmosphere
Winding	233	070 136 137		weather
Wipe	403	043 070		meteorolog
Wire	232 105	070 043		wind
Wire-wound	233	001	346	aircraft
				airplane
				bomber
				craft
				helicopter
				missile
				plane

specifying objects that fly; concept class 345 lists words associated with weather. If a request were made, asking

> Do planes fly when the weather is bad?

the system would retrieve a document stating

> Proper meteorological conditions are necessary for the successful piloting of air-craft,

since both document and query would be assigned the concepts 345 and 346.

The handling of ambiguous words in the thesaurus is exemplified by the entry for "wind", which could be either the noun, referring to weather, or the verb, indicating a method of constructing loops or coils. The table shows that "wind" is in two categories, 345 and 233. Category 345, containing also "weather" and "atmosphere", represents the noun, and category 233, which contains such words as "winding", "wire-wound", and "solenoid", represents the verbal meaning. Whenever "wind" appears, both 345 and 233 will be entered into the concept vector. Because the word is considered ambiguous, the weight will be divided between these two categories; each will receive half of the weight assigned to "wind".

It should be noted that the thesaurus entries may consist of word stems, so that "meteorolog" suffices to look up "meteorology" and "meteorological". If desired, however, suffixed forms of a word may be entered in the thesaurus; this has been done with "winding" because, if only "wind" were in the dictionary, "winding" would also be treated as ambiguous, but the presence of "winding" in the thesaurus makes it possible to identify "winding" in the text with category 233 only.

The high concept number identifies "will" as a so-called common word, not to be used for content identification. The syntax codes shown with the thesaurus entries in Table 25-1 are not used in the simple automatic thesaurus process.

Since the fully automatic thesaurus process based on concept number matching is often an effective analysis tool, more sophisticated language normalization methods may not be required normally in an operational retrieval system.

25-3 USER INTERACTION THROUGH PRESEARCH METHODS

One of the main hopes in obtaining a retrieval performance which exceeds that reached presently under normal operating conditions is to include the customer in the search process. In particular, fewer errors are likely to be made if the information obtained from the users is not restricted to the search request proper but is supplemented by a variety of special user indications, or by evaluation data about the acceptability of items previously retrieved by the system in answer to the search requests. User–system interaction is now current for many computer applications often implemented by special input–output console devices, with the help of operating systems which enable the system to render more or less simultaneous service to a large class of users.

In an information retrieval environment, user interaction may take the form of simple dictionary display routines which can be used to present the user with selected dictionary excerpts to aid in formulating the original search requests or in reformulating queries which were originally inadequate [5], [6]. Alternatively, more sophisticated methods may be used in which the reformulation of the search requests is performed automatically based on feedback information obtained from the user population [7], [8].

The conceptually simpler methods are the *presearch procedures*, based on term and dictionary displays of previously stored information. In each case, a user would look at the displayed information and, based on the available data, would decide before any file search is actually attempted how his query could best be reformulated in order to reflect his information needs properly. The following types of presearch information could be displayed for this purpose:

(a) Lists of terms included in the user's original search formulation together with word frequency information giving the frequency of use of each word in one or more of the stored document collections.

(b) Thesaurus excerpts corresponding to the terms included in the user's search formulation and consisting, for each of the originally available terms, of a complete thesaurus class, which includes synonyms and other terms related to the original.

(c) Titles and abstracts of *source documents*, that is, of documents known originally to the user as relevant to his search query (the intent of the user is then to retrieve new documents similar to the source items).

The principal differences between fully automatic retrieval and retrieval using presearch interaction are summarized in the flow charts of Figs. 25-1(a) and 25-1(b). The presearch requires the generation of a computer display followed by a manual choice of terms on the part of the user during the query formulation process.

The display of word frequency information is designed to inform the user of the characteristics of the vocabulary which may be used to express his information needs. Thus, if a user notices that many of the terms included in his search request are general terms with a very high frequency of occurrence in the stored document collection (for example, terms such as "computer" and "automatic" in a collection on computer science), he may decide that it is wise to delete these terms from his query so as to prevent the generation of high query-document correlations for many nonrelevant documents. On the other hand, the user may decide to emphasize many highly specific low-frequency terms by repeating them in the query formulation.

A thesaurus display can be used for *manual* query updating by requesting a printout of the complete thesaurus classes corresponding to each term included in the original query. Consider, as an example, a query dealing with the "contraction of satellite orbits," and assume that the user signifies that he is interested in the "satellite" class. The computer might then type out terms such as

> Discoverer, Sputnik, Vanguard, Cosmos, Moon, rocket,
> trajectory, countdown, drag, telemetry, and so on.

After studying the display, the user might decide that his original query formulation had been insufficiently specific, and the query might then be altered by addition of the terms "Discoverer", "Sputnik", "Vanguard", "Cosmos", "drag", and "telemetry". The other displayed terms would, however, be rejected as not being germane to the search topic. A second expansion might begin by typing in the term "drag" and then considering the new display of terms related to "drag".

Thesaurus displays are also occasionally useful for the removal from the query formulation of incorrectly used and ambiguous terms. For example, a user interested in information retrieval, who identifies his search topic as "IR", might discover that the thesaurus display produces a list of synonyms in the area of "infra-red spectroscopy". As a result, the term "IR" would, of course, be removed from the search formulation.

The use of thesaurus displays for manual query updating provides an opportunity for a selective choice of synonym and related terms. That is, the user can choose some terms to be added to the original query and others to replace already existing ones in an attempt to improve search *precision*. On the other hand, the automatic thesaurus process operates less selectively and provides synonym recognition by the standard process of automatically replacing the word stems included originally in the search requests and documents by the corresponding concept class numbers extracted from the thesaurus. The automatic thesaurus process is thus designed to normalize query and document statements by generalizing the respective formulations rather than by making them more specific. Such a process may be expected to improve *recall*,

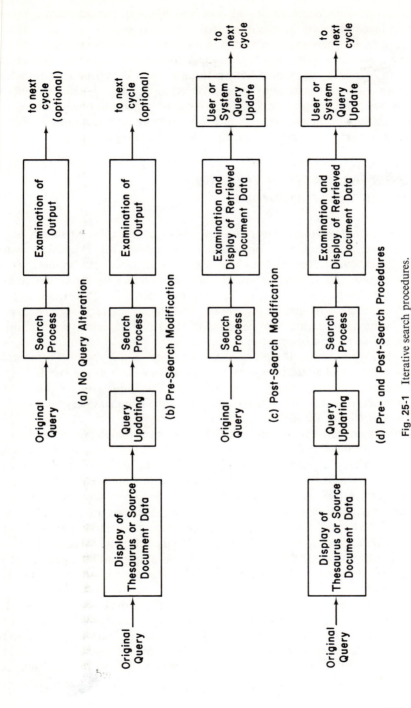

(a) No Query Alteration

(b) Pre-Search Modification

(c) Post-Search Modification

(d) Pre- and Post-Search Procedures

Fig. 25-1   Iterative search procedures.

since more relevant documents could now match the query statements and could thus be retrieved in answer to the respective search requests.

Obviously, the manual query updating methods using thesaurus displays place a considerable burden on the user because he is forced to consider a large number of alternative possibilities before eventually making a move. Moreover, the choice must be made before a search has actually been performed, at a time when he cannot know as yet how well the machine will perform with any potential query formulation.

A comparison of the effectiveness of manual and automatic thesaurus procedures is contained in Sec. 25-5 together with the other evaluation output.

25-4 USER INTERACTION THROUGH POSTSEARCH METHODS

The postsearch methods are those applicable after an initial search has been performed first. In such a case, one or more documents will already be available, including in particular those items which were judged initially to be most similar to the search requests. These items can now be used in a manner analogous to that utilized previously for the thesaurus displays. Specifically, the titles, or abstracts, of the first few retrieved documents can be examined, and document terms which appear to reflect the wanted subject area can be added to the query statement, while ambiguous and unwanted terms can be removed.

Consider, for example, the previously cited query dealing with the "contraction of satellite orbits" and assume that the first two retrieved items are entitled "Discoverer satellite and South Pacific splashdown", and "The moon and the tides". A user could now proceed to add "Discoverer satellite" to the original query but could avoid the addition of "South Pacific".

The document feedback expansion may be even more difficult to carry out than the dictionary display procedure, since the user is forced to make sophisticated decisions using relatively large text excerpts. Thus, while the dictionary display procedure can often be performed in less than one minute per query, approximately four minutes are required on the average for the use of five typical document abstracts. Furthermore, the document expansion process also entails a higher cost in machine time and storage space than the dictionary display, since document abstracts in natural language form constitute a much greater bulk than dictionary excerpts. In addition, an initial retrieval run must be made first before document feedback can be used. On the other hand, a stored dictionary need not be available, of course, for the document feedback method.

Another postsearch method is designed particularly for those users who do not wish to assume the burden of query reformulation themselves. For such users, an automatic *relevance feedback* method is available which requires only a minimum of interaction with the user, since most of the burden is placed on internally stored routines [7], [8], [9], [10]. Specifically, an initial search is performed first for each request received, and a small amount of output consisting of some of the highest-scoring documents is presented to the user. Some of the retrieved output is then examined by the user who identifies each document as being either relevant *R* or not relevant *N* to his purpose. These relevance judgments are later returned to the system and are used automatically to adjust the initial search request in such a way that query terms, or concepts, present in the relevant documents are promoted (by increasing their weight), whereas terms occurring in the documents designated as nonrelevant are similarly demoted.

If the terms from the relevant items are added to the search requests, while terms from nonrelevant items are subtracted, the first query-updating operation can be represented by the equation:

$$\mathbf{q}_1 = \mathbf{q}_0 + \sum_i \mathbf{r}_i - \sum_i \mathbf{s}_i$$

where $\mathbf{q}_0$ is the original query formulation, $\mathbf{q}_1$ is the updated query, $\mathbf{r}_i$ is the set of terms identifying the *i*th document specified as relevant by the user, and $\mathbf{s}_i$ is the set of terms identifying the *i*th nonrelevant document. This process produces an altered search request which may be expected to exhibit greater similarity with the relevant document subset and greater dissimilarity with the nonrelevant set.

Next the altered request can be submitted to the system, and a second search can be performed using the new request formulation. If the system performs as expected, additional relevant material may then be retrieved, or in any case, the relevant items may produce a greater similarity with the altered request than with the original. The newly retrieved items can be examined again by the user, and new relevance assessments can be used to obtain a second reformulation of the request. This process can be continued over several iterations, until such time as the user is satisfied with the results obtained. Since the method makes very few demands on the user, the automatic relevance feedback process may be expected to be preferred by users unfamiliar with the system operations. On the other hand, the process is not likely to be effective if the user is unable to identify for the system at least one document which is clearly relevant to his needs.

The postsearch methods as well as the combined methods making use of presearch as well as postsearch information are illustrated in the bottom half of Fig. 25-1. A summary of all the query-updating methods is given in Table 25-2.

25-5 EVALUATION RESULTS AND DISCUSSION

The experimental results included in this section are based on the manipulation of a collection of 200 abstracts of documents in aerodynamics, together with 42 search requests proposed by scientists active in aerodynamics. Complete relevance judgments, prepared by these same scientists, were available which identify for each query the set of relevant documents. The aerodynamics collection has been used previously for test purposes by the Aslib–Cranfield project [3] and by the SMART system [4].

Table 25-2

TYPICAL QUERY UPDATING METHODS

Query Alteration Process	Explanation
Presearch	
1. Repeated concepts	User chooses query terms to be repeated for emphasis.
2. Thesaurus display	User chooses terms obtained from thesaurus display to update query (with or without time restrictions).
3. Word frequency	User looks at display of word frequency information before updating query.
4. Source document	User looks at display of source document before updating.
Postsearch	
5. Title display	User looks at titles of first five retrieved documents before updating.
6. Abstract display	User looks at abstracts of first five retrieved documents.
7. Relevance feedback	Query is updated automatically using relevance judgments supplied by user following an initial search.
Combined Methods	
8. Abstract plus thesaurus	User looks at presearch and postsearch information.

The thesaurus used for both the manual and automatic query expansion operations contains 3230 word stems and 736 thesaurus classes. This thesaurus was constructed by SMART staff members using text concordances, word frequency lists, standard dictionaries and reference works, and word lists obtained earlier from the Cranfield project. An attempt was made to time the query expansion operations by restricting the use of the thesaurus display to either one minute, two minutes, or more than two minutes. While the output of Table 25-3 shows that increasingly more terms can be added to the queries as more time becomes available for the updating operations, the differences in retrieval effectiveness are small, and the evaluation output shown represents the output obtained for a display time of two minutes. The main results are presented first in terms of recall-precision graphs and then in terms of cost and user effort.

25-5-A   Recall-Precision Results

The evaluation output is presented in Figs. 25-2 to 25-7 using the standard recall-precision graphs, in each case averaged over the 42 queries used with the collection of 200 documents. The curves are, as usual, monotonically decreasing, reflecting the

Table 25-3

VARIATION IN QUERY LENGTH

Query Type	Average Number of Significant Terms Per Query
Original Query	8.3
Terms added: in 1 minute	3.6
in 2 minutes	2.0
later	1.0

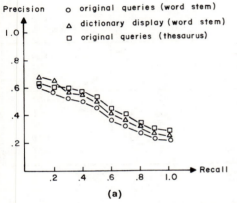

Precision
- o original queries (word stem)
- △ dictionary display (word stem)
- □ original queries (thesaurus)

Recall	Precision			t-test Significance	
	○	△	□	△ ○	□ ○
0.1	.634	.691	.669	.580	.798
0.3	.534	.594	.605	.203	.339
0.5	.462	.510	.541	.199	.168
0.7	.343	.376	.411	.138	.181
0.9	.253	.292	.314	.061	.252

(a)   (b)

Fig. 25-2 Effectiveness of dictionary display compared with stored thesaurus: (a) recall–precision graph; (b) recall–precision tables and statistical significance output.

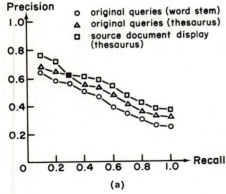

Precision
- o original queries (word stem)
- △ original queries (thesaurus)
- □ source document display (thesaurus)

Recall	Precision			t-test Significance	
	○	△	□	△ ○	□ △
0.1	.634	.669	.748	.798	.327
0.3	.534	.605	.603	.339	.869
0.5	.462	.541	.585	.168	.523
0.7	.343	.411	.470	.181	.767
0.9	.292	.314	.362	.252	.770

(a)   (b)

Fig. 25-3 Effectiveness of source document display (averages over 200 documents and 42 queries): (a) recall–precision graph; (b) recall–precision tables and statistical significance output.

fact that as more relevant items are retrieved (as recall goes up), more irrelevant items are also retrieved (causing the precision to go down). Increasingly more effective retrieval performance is reflected by recall-precision curves close to the upper right-hand corner of the graph where both recall and precision take on ideal values of 1. Next to the graphs, some of the numeric values are presented in terms of recall-precision tables, giving the average precision values at certain selected recall values.

Significance values, computed by a standard t-test, are also included in the output figures, representing in each case the probability that the performance values for two specified processing methods are in fact derived from the same distribution. Thus, if the computed probability value is high, the two methods are assumed to be statis-

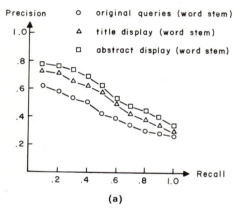

Recall	Precision			t-test Significance	
	○	△	□	△ / ○	□ / ○
0.1	.634	.767	.799	.002	.003
0.3	.534	.627	.714	.002	.001
0.5	.462	.564	.627	.007	.001
0.7	.343	.377	.423	.014	.001
0.9	.253	.275	.328	.035	.001

(a) (b)

Fig. 25-4 Comparison of title and abstract display: (a) recall–precision graph; (b) recall–precision tables and statistical significance output.

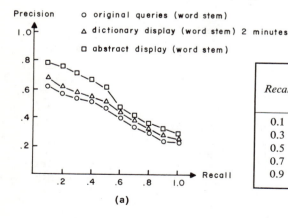

Recall	Precision			t-test Significance	
	○	△	□	△ / ○	□ / ○
0.1	.634	.691	.799	.580	.003
0.3	.534	.594	.714	.203	.001
0.5	.462	.510	.627	.199	.001
0.7	.343	.376	.423	.138	.001
0.9	.253	.292	.328	.061	.001

(a) (b)

Fig. 25-5 Comparison of dictionary and text display: (a) recall–precision graph; (b) recall–precision tables and statistical significance output.

tically indistinguishable; on the other hand, if the probability value is low—perhaps 0.05 or less—the likelihood that the evaluation results could have been derived from the same data set is very small, and the differences in performance can then be assumed to be statistically significant.

The following principal conclusions can be drawn from the output of Figs. 25-2 through 25-7:

(a) Automatic thesaurus versus presearch using thesaurus display (Fig. 25-2). Both the automatic thesaurus expansion and the manual expansion using presearch thesaurus display produce an improvement in performance over the word stem matching process. Overall, the automatic thesaurus (which requires no user

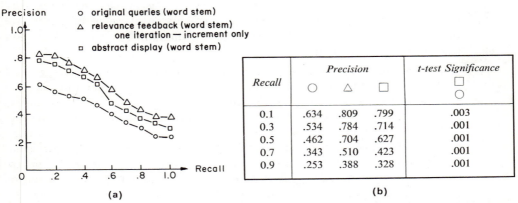

| Recall | Precision | | | t-test Significance |
	○	△	□	□ / ○
0.1	.634	.809	.799	.003
0.3	.534	.784	.714	.001
0.5	.462	.704	.627	.001
0.7	.343	.510	.423	.001
0.9	.253	.388	.328	.001

(a)   (b)

Fig. 25-6 Comparison of abstract display and relevance feedback: (a) recall–precision graph; (b) recall–precision tables and statistical significance output.

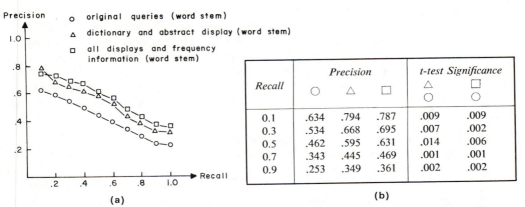

| Recall | Precision | | | t-test Significance | |
	○	△	□	△ / ○	□ / ○
0.1	.634	.794	.787	.009	.009
0.3	.534	.668	.695	.007	.002
0.5	.462	.595	.631	.014	.006
0.7	.343	.445	.469	.001	.001
0.9	.253	.349	.361	.002	.002

(a)   (b)

Fig. 25-7 Comparison of combined methods (word-stem process): (a) recall–precision graph; (b) recall–precision tables and statistical significance output.

intervention) is superior. At high precision, however, the greater selectivity of the words chosen by the manual process produces better results. The superiority of the automatic thesaurus at medium and high recall is attributed to the previously mentioned difficulty of selecting appropriate terms from the thesaurus display.

(b) Automatic thesaurus versus presearch using source document display (Fig. 25-3). The source document display produces a precision improvement of up to 10% over and above the automatic thesaurus process; however, the table appearing with Fig. 25-3 shows that the improvement is not statistically significant. The relatively modest increase in performance may be due to the fact that the source documents and queries used in the experiment originated with the same authors, so that the source documents contain many of the terms already included in the query statements; also, some of the source documents appear only marginally relevant to the actual queries. Both of the interactive presearch methods therefore turn out to be not substantially superior to the full automatic thesaurus method (except at high precision).

(c) Postsearch procedures using displays of titles or abstracts of previously retrieved items (Figs. 25-4 and 25-5). Title and abstract postsearch displays are superior to both of the presearch displays, as shown in Figs. 25-4 and 25-5. Improvement with title display is limited to the high precision regions, since the titles are so short that words not in the query are rarely included. Therefore the query alterations due to title display are limited to deletion of unnecessary concepts, improving mostly the precision. Abstract displays produce both precision and recall improvements, at the cost of greatly increased work on the user's part. The amount of text examined during an abstract display process is about 1,000 words, from which five to ten may be selected for query expansion.

(d) Automatic thesaurus versus postsearch updating using abstract display and relevance feedback (Fig. 25-6). Both the manual postsearch method with abstract display and the automatic relevance feedback process are superior to the standard word-stem process; the abstract display is best in the very high precision ranges. The performance differences between the two postsearch methods are not significant at high precision, although the improvements obtained with both methods over the standard word-stem process are significant. In each case, the relevance feedback output included in Fig. 25-6 is obtained by retrieving five documents at a time, asking the user to identify any relevant items and adding the corresponding terms to the search request.

(e) Combined presearch dictionary and postsearch abstract display (Fig. 25-7). Figure 25-7 shows that a combination of abstracts and thesaurus displays offers an overall improvement of about 20% over the standard word-stem process and of 10% to 15% over the thesaurus process; in both cases, the improvement is statistically significant. When word frequency information is added to the display, a further improvement results for the word-stem procedure, since the user can now ensure that all parts of the query are properly weighted. The output of Fig. 25-7 is approximately equivalent to the automatic relevance feedback process

(Fig. 25-6); however, the combined presearch and postsearch process requires much more user effort and experience than the relevance feedback method before it can operate successfully.

25-5-B Overall Evaluation

The performance of the various interactive procedures is summarized in Table 25-4. The first column reflects computer demands; the second reflects user effort; the last two columns reflect search effectiveness in terms of recall and precision improvements over and above the normal word-stem matching method.

Table 25-4

PERFORMANCE SUMMARY

PROCESSING METHOD	DEMANDS ON COMPUTER	DEMANDS ON USER	PRECISION IMPROVEMENT OVER WORD-STEM MATCH (%)	
			Low Recall	*High Recall*
Fully automatic				
Word-stem match	Normal	None	–	–
Automatic thesaurus	Normal	None	+4	+6
Presearch interaction				
Thesaurus display	Normal +	Medium–high	+6	+4
Source document display	Normal +	Medium	+8	+5
Postsearch interaction				
Title display	High	Medium	+13	+2
Abstract display	High	Very high	+17	+7
Relevance feedback	High	Low	+10	+7

Since the postsearch methods require two separate file-searching operations—one prior to the interactive process and one following it—the computer demands are comparatively higher for postsearch than for the other methods. Thus, when search time may be expected to be considerable—for example, for very large collection sizes—the presearch procedures may become mandatory.

From the user's viewpoint, when less information is displayed, the interactive process will be normally easier. Thus the relevance feedback procedure is simplest because the user must merely identify one or another document as either relevant or nonrelevant. The presearch thesaurus displays and the postsearch abstract displays are hardest, since complicated decisions are required to update the search requests.

Turning now to the performance parameters, it is seen in Table 25-4 that, everything else being equal, the postsearch methods are more powerful than the presearch procedures. (Unfortunately, those are also the methods which put the highest demands on the computer.) One obvious reason why the postsearch methods operate more reliably is that a computer search has already been performed before the user is asked to update the query. Thus, the query alteration process is undertaken with prior knowledge of how well the original query has performed. Then the postsearch alteration can be used to initiate small changes for queries requiring only little improvement and more massive changes for the others. For the presearch methods, no such prior information is available. Of the postsearch methods, the best performance is obtained with abstract display; however this method also makes the greatest demands on the user. The relevance feedback method is superior and much preferable from the user's viewpoint.

To summarize the performance and cost indications, the following search strategy would appear to be useful under most circumstances:

(a) Normally, use the standard automatic thesaurus method without user interaction.

(b) If improvement is needed and search time is not excessive, use relevance feedback.

(c) If search time is at a premium, use presearch source document or thesaurus display.

(d) On the other hand, if high retrieval performance is mandatory, try postsearch abstract display.

The difficulties of the manual query-updating methods may be illustrated by the example of query 317, reproduced in Table 25-5. The original word-stem retrieval run produces the two relevant documents in rank positions 4 and 10. From the thesaurus display, the following words were selected: "elastic", "resilient", "unstiffened", "modulus", "aeroelastic", "laminar-boundary layer". This promotes the two relevant documents to rank positions 2 and 5; however, the automatic thesaurus run yields rank positions 2 and 4, without any user interaction. When the postsearch displays are used, the results are similar. Title display is not very effective for this particular query, yielding only an indication that "theoretical" should be increased in weight, which raises the rank positions of the relevant from 4 and 10 (in the original word-stem run) to 4 and 9. Abstract display is more fruitful, adding "elastic" and "resilient" as well. This increases the ranks of the relevant documents to 1 and 6. However, the same query, now processed through the automatic thesaurus (abstract display and automatic thesaurus run) yields perfect performance, as does the automatic thesaurus run with relevance feedback.

To achieve perfect performance using only manual updating methods and word-stem matches, it is necessary to utilize a combined thesaurus display, abstract display, and word frequency information, which yield the following rather complex set of changes. Delete "anyone" and "investigate"; increase the weight on "theoretical" and "flexibility" by a factor of two; add with weight of one the words "analytic", "resilient", "calculate", "unstiffened", "aeroelastic", and "laminar-boundary"; add with weight of two "flexure"; add with weight of three "elastic". These changes produce a word-stem run with perfect performance but at far greater time and trouble than the automatic thesaurus with abstract display run. The exact adjustment of the

Table 25-5

TYPICAL MANUAL QUERY UPDATING

(Query 317: Has anyone investigated theoretically whether surface flexibility can stabilize a laminar-boundary layer?)

Processing Method	Terms Added† or Deleted‡	Ranks of Relevant Documents
Fully automatic		
Word-stem match	–	4, 10
Automatic thesaurus	–	2, 4
Improved searches		
Word stem plus thesaurus display (presearch)	"unstiffened", "modulus", "elastic", "resilient", "aeroelastic"	2, 5
Word stem plus title display (postsearch)	"theoretical"	4, 9
Word stem plus abstract display (postsearch)	"elastic", "resilient", "theoretical"	1, 6
Perfect searches		
Automatic thesaurus plus relevance feedback	–	1, 2
Word stem plus abstract display plus automatic thesaurus	"elastic", "resilient"	1, 2
Thesaurus display plus abstract display plus word frequency display	*anyone*, *investigate*, "theoretical", "flexibility", "analytic", "resilient", "calculate", "unstiffened", "aeroelastic", "laminar-boundary", "flexure", "elastic"	1, 2

†In quotes.
‡In italics.

term weights is normally performed more accurately and more easily by the automatic thesaurus. The manual methods are thus best reserved for users with the skill and interest to consult lengthy displays and to make complex decisions.

A meaningful cost analysis is difficult to make without the use of an operational time-sharing system to perform the experiments. Table 25-6 contains an estimated cost summary based on running times for the IBM 7094. Machine and user costs are assumed to be $75.00 and $10.00 per hour, respectively. Scanning time is 5 milliseconds per document, and additional central processor time is ignored. Table 25-6 shows that the postsearch methods are clearly the most expensive (they also are the most effective) with relevance feedback relatively cheaper than abstract displays. In general, the automatic procedures appear better suited economically and operationally to the retrieval operations than the manual methods. Since the cost of human time may be expected to continue to increase relative to the cost of machine time, the automatic procedures may grow even more attractive in the future.

The bottom part of Table 25-6 shows that processing cost decreases drastically

Table 25-6

ESTIMATED COST FIGURES†

PROCESSING METHOD	ESTIMATED COST PER QUERY ($)	
	50,000 documents	*100,000 documents*
Fully Automatic		
Word-stem match	5.00	10.00
Automatic thesaurus	5.00	10.00
Interactive presearch		
Thesaurus display	6.00	11.00
Source document display	5.50	10.50
Interactive postsearch		
Title display	10.50	20.50
Abstract display	13.00	23.00
Relevance feedback	10.50	20.50
Partial search		
Cluster searches (one tenth of collection)	0.50	1.00
Cluster search plus relevance feedback	6.00	11.50
Cluster search plus abstract display	8.50	14.00

†Assumptions: machine cost = $75.00 per hour; document scan = 5 milliseconds per document; central processing cost = 0; human time = $10.00 per hour.

if *partial* rather than full searches of the collection are performed. Such partial "cluster" searches are implemented with the SMART system; however, the cluster searches cannot be used if a recall performance higher than about 50% is required [11].

25-6   CONCLUSION

The best overall process for precision purposes is the abstract display used in conjunction with a word-stem matching procedure. For recall purposes, a combination of abstract display with thesaurus word normalization appears best. The automatic relevance feedback approximates the abstract display method while requiring much less user effort. Considering the complexity of the abstract display system, a sensible set of recommendations for high performance real-time retrieval would be the following:

(a) For highest precision, use title display and word-stem matching.

(b) For highest recall with normal users, use the automatic thesaurus followed by automatic relevance feedback; with experienced and patient users, use abstract display and dictionary display plus frequency information.

(c) For maximum cost reduction at lower performance, use partial searches of the document collection.

These rules provide a graded set of feedback methods, ranging from automatic procedures which make only minimal demands on the user and are suitable for novices (automatic thesaurus expansion and relevance feedback) to methods permitting sophisticated user–system interaction which combine the best features of manual and automatic query adjustment (thesaurus and abstract display). One may expect that a suitable mix of user feedback procedures can be found to produce optimal retrieval under many different conditions over many types of user classes.

REFERENCES

[1] G. Salton and M. E. Lesk, The SMART Automatic Document Retrieval System—An Illustration, *Communications of the ACM*, Vol. 8, No. 6, June 1965.

[2] G. Salton et al., Scientific Reports on the SMART System to the National Science Foundation, *ISR-11, ISR-12, ISR-13*, Department of Computer Science, Cornell University, Ithaca, N.Y., June 1966, June 1967, and January 1968.

[3] C. W. Cleverdon, J. Mills, and E. M. Keen, Factors Determining the Performance of Indexing Systems, *Design*, Vol. 1, Aslib–Cranfield Research Project, Cranfield, England, 1966.

[4] G. Salton and M. E. Lesk, Computer Evaluation of Indexing and Text Processing, *Journal of the ACM*, Vol. 15, No. 1, January 1968; also Chap. 7 of this volume.

[5] R. M. Curtice and V. Rosenberg, Optimizing Retrieval Results with Man–Machine Interaction, *Center for the Information Sciences Report*, Lehigh University, Bethlehem, Pa., 1965.

[6] H. Borko, Utilization of On-Line Interactive Displays, in *Information Systems Science and Technology*, D. Walker, ed., Thompson Book Co., Washington, D.C., 1967.

[7] J. J. Rocchio, Jr., Document Retrieval Systems—Optimization and Evaluation, Doctoral thesis, *Report ISR-10* to the National Science Foundation, Harvard Computation Laboratory, Cambridge, Mass., March 1966.

[8] J. J. Rocchio, Jr. and G. Salton, Information Search Optimization and Iterative Retrieval Techniques, *Proceedings of the AFIPS Fall Joint Computer Conference*, Las Vegas, Nev., 1965, Spartan Books, New York, 1965.

[9] G. Salton, Search and Retrieval Experiments in Real-Time Information Retrieval, *Proceedings IFIP Congress 68*, Edinburgh, August 1968, North-Holland Publishing Co., Amsterdam, 1969.

[10] E. Ide, User Interaction with an Automated Information Retrieval System, *Report ISR-12* to the National Science Foundation, Section VIII, Department of Computer Science, Cornell University, Ithaca, N.Y., June 1967.

[11] R. T. Grauer and M. Messier, An Evaluation of Rocchio's Clustering Algorithm, *Report ISR-12* to the National Science Foundation, Section VI, Department of Computer Science, Cornell University, Ithaca, N.Y., June 1967; also Chap. 11 of this volume.

Two widely used criteria for evaluating the effectiveness of information retrieval systems are, respectively, recall and precision. Since the determination of these measures is dependent on a distinction between documents which are relevant, and documents which are not relevant to a given query set, it has sometimes been claimed that an accurate, generally valid evaluation cannot be based on recall and precision.

A study was made to determine the effect of variations in relevance assessments on the average recall and precision values used to measure retrieval effectiveness. Using a collection of 1200 documents in information science for test purposes, it is found that large scale differences in the relevance assessments do not produce significant variations in average recall and precision. Thus it appears that properly computed recall and precision data may represent effectiveness indicators which are generally valid for many distinct user classes.

26

RELEVANCE ASSESSMENTS AND RETRIEVAL SYSTEM EVALUATION†

M. E. LESK and G. SALTON

26-1 INTRODUCTION

Over the last few years, the interest in the design of automatic information-handling systems has increased steadily. At the same time, it has become necessary to devote a good deal of attention to the evaluation of information systems in an attempt to identify those factors which contribute to system effectiveness. Many criteria can be used in such an evaluation process; furthermore, the factors which may be most appropriate in one circumstance may not be in another. In particular, different effectiveness indicators might be generated depending on whether one's viewpoint is the user's, the manager's, or the operator's. The manager, for example, may be most concerned about system costs, while the operator may be interested primarily in the characteristics of the equipment used in the process. The user, however, is not normally interested in the equipment and may be only peripherally concerned with costs. He does, however, want to make certain that the system is responsive to user needs.

Many recent efforts at retrieval system evaluation have been based

†This study was published originally as Section III in *Scientific Report ISR-14*, October 1968; it is also included in *Information Storage and Retrieval*, Vol. 4, pp. 343–359, 1969.

mainly on user criteria, and while several possible criteria are available—including, for example, the type of presentation of the output, the amount of user effort needed during a search, the time lag between submission of a query and the presentation of search results, and the coverage of the collection being searched—it is generally agreed that the two most important user-oriented measures are the ability of the system to retrieve wanted information and at the same time to reject unwanted informations. As a result, several of the more recent evaluation studies have used a test methodology based mainly on the computation of the *recall* and *precision* values applicable to a set of test queries [1], [2], [3].

Recall and precision are defined, respectively, as the proportion of relevant material actually retrieved and the proportion of retrieved material actually relevant. In an ideal system, it may be assumed that everything relevant to a user's query is in fact retrieved (thus producing a recall of 1), while everything not relevant is rejected (producing a precision of 1). In real life, conditions are not so perfect, and generally, it is not possible to achieve a high recall and a high precision at the same time.

In order to generate recall and precision values, first it is necessary to differentiate retrieved from nonretrieved documents and then to separate documents termed relevant to a query from those termed nonrelevant. The second of these partitions must obviously depend on a personal judgment either by the author of a given query, by a system operator, or by an outside expert. In any case, once a decision is reached about the relevance of each document to each query, it is possible, by examining the set of retrieved and nonretrieved documents, to compute unique recall and precision values. Unfortunately, relevance assessments tend to vary depending on who renders the judgment, and the recall and precision values obtained by using these assessments may then turn out to be inherently unstable. This question is investigated further in the remainder of this chapter.

26-2 THE RELEVANCE PROBLEM

In a recent study of the relevance-judging process, Cuadra and Katter recognize four main types of variables which potentially affect the outcome of a relevance judgment [4]. First, the type of document being judged, including its subject matter, level of difficulty, level of condensation, style, and so on; second, the conditions under which the judgments must be rendered, that is, the time available, the order of presentation and size of the document set, the type of task specification, and so on; third, the statement specifying the information requirement which determines relevance; fourth, the type of judge used to render the judgments, that is, his experience, background, attitude, and so on. These variables are summarized in the chart of Fig. 26-1. Additional variables may enter into the process if the judgment to be rendered is not expressible as a simple yes–no decision.

Because of the obvious complexity of the judgment process, numerous authors have stated that it is impossible to obtain stable relevance judgments from individual informants. Fairthorne, for example, has suggested that individual relevance judg-

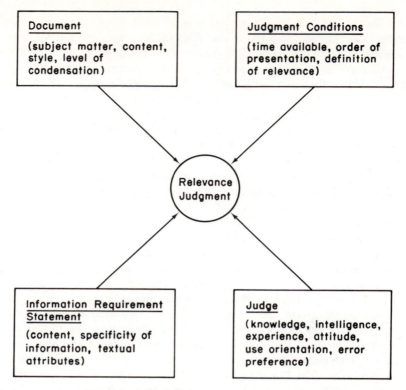

Fig. 26-1   Variables related to relevance judgments (adapted from Cuadra and Katter [4]).

ments should be replaced by global judgments representing a consensus of ideas by several independent judges [5]. O'Connor and Doyle have pointed out that the expression of a user's information need can take many different forms, and that it is not possible in consequence simply to claim that "document A is relevant to query B" without appropriate qualifying statements [6], [7], [8]. Taube has drawn the conclusion that recall and precision are not concepts which can be defined properly or used in retrieval systems evaluation [9].

A number of studies have also been conducted to show that different sets of relevance judgments are actually obtained under different judgment conditions. Thus, distinctions are made between "motivated" and "unmotivated" judges [10] and between judgments based on an examination of full as compared with partial document excerpts [11]. Furthermore, in the two most extensive studies of the judgment process by Cuadra and Katter [4], and [12], and Rees [13], and [14], a large number of factors are varied, and the effect on the resulting relevance judgments is observed.

The conclusion sometimes drawn from studies such as the preceding is that the existing methodology in systems evaluation must be revised, and that evaluation results based on recall and precision are unreliable and must be viewed with great caution. Cuadra and Katter state in particular [4]:

... the first and most obvious implication is that one cannot legitimately view "precision" and "recall" scores as precise and stable bases for comparison between systems or systems components, unless ... (appropriate controls are introduced) ...

Rees voices similar misgivings in a somewhat different context [13]:

... the lack of replication (that is experimental control permitting duplication of the experiments) of the results of either the SMART [3] or the Cranfield studies [1] must necessarily introduce a note of caution to the existence of "rules" and generalizability of results.

While these sentiments appear to be perfectly justified at first, since obviously, the subjectiveness and variability of individual relevance judgments cannot be contested, the jump which is necessary to reach the conclusion that recall and precision results are unreliable because relevance judgments are unstable has never been proved or substantiated adequately. Indeed, there exists some evidence that such a conclusion cannot be drawn from the available evidence. Giuliano and Jones, for example, made a small study using a panel of three relevance judges. Their findings are summarized as follows [2]:

... for purposes of comparing retrieval performance curves for two or more search options, it does not appear to matter much whether the curves are for any one of the single judges, or whether they are the averaged curves for a panel of three judges; the differences are primarily ones of scale, and the relative positions of the curves for the different search options tend to be the same in all cases.

Rees and Schultz also find that the judgment groups used in their study agree substantially as to the relative positioning (i.e., ordering in decreasing order of relevance to a search request) of the documents, although the judges tend to assign different numerical ratings to the documents [14].

The experimental evidence cited above may indicate that, contrary to expectations, recall and precision results do not vary as widely as the relevance judgments used to generate them. Several reasons can be cited further to support such an opinion:

(a) Recall and precision data are normally given as *averages* over many search requests; these averages may not be sensitive to small variations in the results for individual queries.

(b) Recall and precision data depend mainly on the relative positions of relevant and nonrelevant documents, when the documents are arranged in decreasing or increasing relevance order; individual changes in the composition of the relevant and nonrelevant document sets may have only a minor effect on the ordering of the sets as a whole.

(c) Disagreements among relevance judges may affect mostly the borderline cases, while preserving a general consensus for a large set of items definitely identified as either relevant or nonrelevant; such borderline cases normally receive a low position in the relevance ordering, and their effect on the recall and precision values may be expected to be negligible.

(d) Recall-precision results are often given as relative differences between sets of different search and retrieval methods; the recall and precision results may vary in such a way that differences between methods are preserved even though the values for the individual methods may change.

These questions are further examined in an experiment to be described in the remaining sections of this chapter.

26-3   THE EXPERIMENT

The evaluation procedures incorporated into the SMART document retrieval system lend themselves to a pair-wise comparison of the effectiveness of two or more processing methods. Specifically, a number of evaluation parameters are computed for each of the processing methods under investigation. Then a comparison of the corresponding measures for two or more methods can be used to produce a ranking of the methods in decreasing order of retrieval effectiveness.

The following evaluation measures are generated by the SMART system for each processing run [3]:

(a) A recall-precision graph reflecting the average precision value at ten discrete recall points (from a recall of 0.1 to a recall of 1.0 in intervals of 0.1).

(b) Two global measures, known as normalized recall and normalized precision, which together reflect the overall performance level of the system.

(c) Two simplified global measures, known as rank recall and log precision, respectively.

The experiments described in the present chapter were designed to determine the degree of sensitivity of the SMART evaluation output to variations in the relevance assessments used to compute the evaluation measure. If the recall-precision output obtained by SMART turns out to be unstable because of the instability of the relevance judgments used, then an extrapolation of the results to other user populations and different retrieval environments may not be possible. On the other hand, if the evaluation output remains stable, then the significance of the results appears to be confirmed.

A collection of 1,268 abstracts in the field of documentation and library science comprising about 131,500 English text words (the Ispra collection) was used for experimental purposes. The collection includes most of the articles published in 1963 and 1964 in *American Documentation* and several other journals in the information retrieval area. Eight different persons were used to generate a total of 48 different search requests in the documentation field; each person was familiar with the library science field, either as a librarian or as a student in library science, and each one was asked to produce six requests that actually might be asked by library science students. To aid in the query generation, a detailed and carefully drawn set of instructions was distributed to the group of query authors. The main criteria proposed for the query formulation are reproduced in Table 26-1.

Table 26-1

PRINCIPAL CRITERIA FOR QUERY FORMULATION

Positive Criteria for Query Formulation	*Negative Criteria for Query Formulation*
1. Generate queries of real interest to a potential researcher or student.	Avoid "exotic" topics and doubtful subject matter.
2. Formulate queries in clear, coherent, grammatically correct sentences.	Avoid metaphors, jokes, and allusions.
3. Use from 50 to 100 words and up to 3 sentences to formulate queries.	Do not submit queries corresponding to the contents of a specific document; do not rephrase specific document contents.
4. Use positive formulations stating what subject areas are actually wanted.	Avoid negative formulations and clauses introduced by "except", "other than", "not", and so on.
5. Use homogeneous query formulations representing a single topic.	
6. Use only common abbreviations.	

Each query was expected to represent a real information need and had to be expressed in grammatically correct and hopefully unambiguous English. As usual for queries processed by the SMART system, positive formulations were required, and the queries were to be generated independently from the document collection. In particular, no "source" document was to be used for the formulation of any of the queries.

Following receipt of the query formulations from each of the eight authors, the texts of the document abstracts comprising the collection were distributed, and each author was asked to assess the relevance of each document abstract with respect to each of *his* six queries. Dichotomous relevance judgments were to be used, asserting either the relevance or the nonrelevance of each item for each query. Furthermore, the relevance criterion to be used was a strict one, in the sense that relevance of a document was to be specified only

> . . . if it is directly stated in the abstract as printed, or can be directly deduced from the printed abstract, that the document contains information on the topic asked for in the query.

Since each query presumably represented an information need, an abstract would be called relevant if the author felt that, given the abstract, he would with great probability wish to consult the complete document.

After receipt of the relevance judgments from each of the authors (the *A* judgments), a second and independent set of relevance judgments (the *B* judgments) was obtained by asking each person in the test group to judge for relevance six additional queries originated by six *different* people, not including himself. The same relevance criteria were used for the second relevance judgments as for the original ones; the only difference was that the *A* judgments were rendered by query authors, while the *B* judgments were nonauthor judgments. In order to preserve independence, the *B* judges were not informed of the *A* judgments obtained previously, nor was there any interaction between assessors either before or during the judging process.

Thus for each of the 48 queries, a set of four different document sets became available, each consisting of the items termed relevant by a different set of people as follows:

A set.   Relevance assessed by query author.

B set.   Relevance assessed by outside subject expert.

C set.   Relevance asserted by either *A* or *B* assessor.

D set.   Relevance asserted by both *A* and *B*.

The situation is summarized in Table 26-2.

A measure of agreement in the relevance judgments can be obtained for the query set from the material of Table 26-3. For each query, the number of items is given for sets *A* and *B*, respectively, as well as the total number of distinct items (set *C*) and the total number of items common to both sets *A* and *B* (set *D*). Each query number listed

Table 26-2

RELEVANCE JUDGMENT GROUPINGS

Group of Judges	Explanation
A	Original group of query authors. Each person in *A* group made relevance judgments for his six queries.
B	Nonauthor judges. Each person in *B* group made relevance judgments for six queries corresponding to six *different* authors from *A* group.
C	Document is relevant to a given query if *either* the *A* judge *or* the *B* judge termed it relevant.
D	Document is relevant to a given query if both *A* and *B* judges termed it relevant.

Table 26-3

AGREEMENT OF RELEVANCE JUDGMENTS

QUERY NUMBER		NUMBER OF RELEVANT				AGREEMENT $\frac{A \cap B}{A \cup B} = \frac{D}{C}$	AVERAGE AGREEMENT WITH AUTHOR
First Judge	Second Judge	A	B	C (A ∪ B)	D (A ∩ B)		
12		17	18	26	9	0.3462	
13		3	4	4	3	0.7500	
14		19	6	21	4	0.1905	Author 1
15		22	25	37	10	0.2703	0.3611
16		7	9	14	2	0.1429	
17		9	13	15	7	0.4667	
21		20	25	37	8	0.2162	
23		32	8	39	1	0.0256	
25		20	7	25	2	0.0800	Author 2
26		19	8	23	4	0.1739	0.1757
27		14	17	23	8	0.3478	
28		7	16	19	4	0.2105	
31		4	3	5	2	0.4000	
32		6	18	22	2	0.0909	
34		27	20	45	2	0.0444	Author 3
35		27	27	35	19	0.5429	0.1838
36		34	8	41	1	0.0244	
37		5	6	11	0	0	
41		14	8	17	5	0.2941	
42		19	20	26	13	0.5000	
45		8	41	42	7	0.1667	Author 4
46		10	8	12	6	0.5000	0.4298
47		8	10	10	8	0.8000	
48		25	33	44	14	0.3182	
51		10	11	16	5	0.3125	
52		72	16	78	10	0.1282	
53		31	14	42	3	0.0714	Author 5
54		13	9	19	3	0.1579	0.2167
56		34	25	47	12	0.2553	
58		33	22	40	15	0.3750	
61		6	10	11	5	0.4545	
63		23	49	61	11	0.1803	
64		12	12	17	7	0.4118	Author 6
65		7	6	9	4	0.4444	0.5297
67		11	10	11	10	0.9091	
68		7	9	9	7	0.7777	
71		14	28	31	11	0.3548	
72		9	14	15	8	0.5333	
73		19	11	23	7	0.3043	Author 7
74		9	22	24	7	0.2917	0.4557
75		6	5	6	5	0.8333	
78		12	22	24	10	0.4167	
81		22	6	24	4	0.1667	
82		37	32	54	15	0.2778	
83		34	4	35	3	0.0857	Author 8
84		21	10	28	3	0.1071	0.1067
86		18	0	18	0	0	
87		17	8	25	0	0	
Totals		853	713	1260	306	Overall average	0.3074

in Table 26-3 is coded in such a way that the number *ij* is assigned to the query authored by person *i*, with the second (*B*) relevance judgment being obtained from person *j*.

The agreement among the relevance sets is measured as usual by dividing the total number of common items by the total number of distinct items $(A \cap B)/(A \cup B)$. The numerical values are given in column 6 of Table 26-3. An average agreement score is given for each author in column 7 of Table 26-3. This score is seen to vary from a high of 0.53 for Author 6 to a low of 0.11 for Author 8. The overall agreement for all eight authors is seen to be slightly higher than 30% (0.3074). This figure is believed to be typical of the consistency which can be obtained under independent conditions from different assessors. It also agrees with comparable figures contained elsewhere in the literature. It remains to show how such a relatively low consistency level is reflected in the evaluation output. This is described further in the next section.

26-4 EXPERIMENTAL RESULTS

Three of the principal automatic language analysis procedures incorporated into the SMART system are used with the Ispra collection under study. The methods known as word form, word stem, and thesaurus, respectively, may be described as follows:

(a) Word form. Texts of document abstracts and queries are reduced by removal of common words and final "s" endings, and weights are assigned to the remaining word forms; the reduced texts are then matched to obtain document-query correlation coefficients.

(b) Word stem. Texts are treated as above, except that complete suffixes are removed from text words to reduce the texts to weighted word stems; the query-document matching process remains the same as in process (a).

(c) Thesaurus. Each word stem produced by procedure (b) is looked up in a thesaurus providing synonym recognition, and the resulting weighted concept identifiers assigned to queries and documents are compared (instead of word forms or word stems).

The output produced by the SMART system consists of superimposed recall-precision graphs exhibiting averages over a complete query set for several processing methods [3]. The method which generates the curve closest to the upper right-hand corner of the graph (where recall and precision are equal to 1) exhibits the best performance. Under normal circumstances, an evaluation of performance for a variety of processing methods does not require a detailed comparison of the actual recall and precision values, but only an examination of the *ranking* of the corresponding recall-precision curves. Thus, to show that the performance measures are insensitive to changes in the relevance judgments, it is sufficient to observe a consistent ranking of the recall-precision graphs obtained from the several processing methods. The data for the four types of relevance judgments (*A, B, C,* and *D*) are shown averaged over the 48 queries in Fig. 26-2.

The following conclusions may be drawn from the output of Fig. 26-2:

(a) All four sets of relevance judgments produce the same ranking of the processing methods; in particular, the word-form process is always much less powerful than the other two procedures, and the thesaurus process is slightly better than the word-stem match.

(b) The main difference in the output produced by the *A* and *B* judgments is the somewhat closer agreement between word-stem and thesaurus runs for the *B* judgments than for *A*.

(c) The best results in terms of recall and precision are obtained for the *D* judgments which represent the agreement between both *A* and *B* relevance judges; for low recall, the precision is about 20% higher for *D* than for *A, B,* or *C*.

While it is clear from the output of Fig. 26-2 that the SMART evaluation output does not vary with variations in the relevance judgments, it may be of interest to examine the data in somewhat more detail. Table 26-4 contains the numeric values corresponding to the curves of Fig. 26-2. The average precision is given for each of five recall points for the four curves of Fig. 26-2. In addition, the numeric precision difference is given at these same recall points between the *A* and *B* curves (in column 4 or Table 26-4) and between the *C* and *D* curves (in column 7 of the table). It may be seen that the maximum difference between the averaged *A* and *B* output occurs for the word-form process at very low recall (precision difference of 0.06). The normal precision difference for the two sets of relevance judgments is about 1% to 2%. For the thesaurus run, which exhibits the best performance, the maximum precision difference is only 0.015 at low recall, with a normal difference of less than 1%.

From the output of Table 26-4 and Fig. 26-2, it appears reasonable to conclude not only that the performance methods are ranked in the same order, no matter which of the four sets of relevance judgments is used, but also that the actual performance differences resulting from differences between author and nonauthor judgments are negligible. This point can also be made by looking at the individual performance differences for each of the eight query authors as shown in Table 26-5.

Table 26-5 exhibits the average rank recall [in Table 26-5(a)] and average normalized precision [Table 26-5(b)] for the six queries originated by each of the eight authors. In each case, the average obtained by using the author relevance judgments is shown (case *A*), followed by the average for the same six queries using the nonauthor judgments, followed finally by the difference of the measures between *A* and *B*. It may be seen once again that the processing methods are ranked identically by seven out of eight authors from the best method (thesaurus) to the worst (word form). Only for the queries of Author 6 (nos. 61–68) does the word-stem process produce slightly better results than the thesaurus method; however, the word-form process is

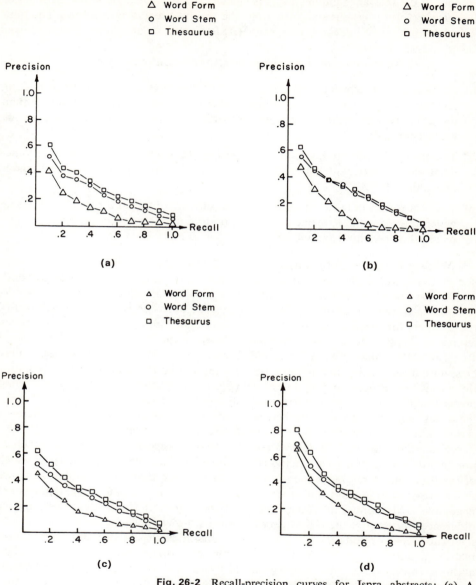

Fig. 26-2 Recall-precision curves for Ispra abstracts: (a) A judgments; (b) B judgments; (c) C judgments; (d) D judgments.

inferior even for that author. When the *B* relevance judgments are used, the same ranking is again obtained for seven out of eight query sets. For queries 61–68 the word-stem process is again superior to the thesaurus, while for queries 31–37 and 51–58, the *B* judgments produce approximately equal performance for word stem and

Table 26-4(a)

AVERAGE STANDARD RECALL AND PRECISION VALUES
FOR THREE ANALYSIS METHODS
AND FOUR TYPES OF RELEVANCE JUDGMENTS

(Word-Form Process)

RECALL	AVERAGE PRECISION VALUES					
	A	*B*	*A — B*	*C*	*D*	*D — C*
0.1	0.405	0.467	−0.062	0.448	0.664	0.216
0.3	0.196	0.206	−0.010	0.235	0.322	0.087
0.5	0.102	0.081	+0.021	0.128	0.165	0.037
0.7	0.039	0.028	+0.011	0.058	0.070	0.012
0.9	0.023	0.018	+0.005	0.029	0.023	−0.006

Table 26-4(b)

AVERAGE STANDARD RECALL AND PRECISION VALUES
FOR THREE ANALYSIS METHODS
AND FOUR TYPES OF RELEVANCE JUDGMENTS

(Word-Stem Process)

RECALL	AVERAGE PRECISION VALUES					
	A	*B*	*A — B*	*C*	*D*	*D — C*
0.1	0.514	0.524	−0.010	0.503	0.693	0.190
0.3	0.363	0.375	−0.012	0.376	0.434	0.058
0.5	0.243	0.283	−0.040	0.266	0.308	0.042
0.7	0.162	0.182	−0.020	0.167	0.196	0.029
0.9	0.095	0.093	+0.002	0.056	0.111	0.055

Table 26-4(c)

AVERAGE STANDARD RECALL AND PRECISION VALUES
FOR THREE ANALYSIS METHODS
AND FOUR TYPES OF RELEVANCE JUDGMENTS

(Thesaurus Dictionary)

RECALL	AVERAGE PRECISION VALUES					
	A	*B*	*A — B*	*C*	*D*	*D — C*
0.1	0.612	0.627	−0.015	0.604	0.801	0.197
0.3	0.406	0.398	+0.008	0.433	0.485	0.052
0.5	0.293	0.307	−0.014	0.315	0.319	0.004
0.7	0.204	0.199	+0.005	0.213	0.227	0.014
0.9	0.112	0.106	+0.006	0.113	0.119	0.006

Table 26-5(a)

AVERAGE RANK RECALL AND NORMALIZED PRECISION FOR EACH OF EIGHT QUERY AUTHORS

Average Rank Recall Differences (Three Analysis Methods)

METHODS		QUERY NUMBERS								
		12–17	*21–28*	*31–37*	*41–48*	*51–58*	*61–68*	*71–78*	*81–87*	*All*
Word form	A	0.011	0.023	0.016	0.028	0.034	0.013	0.021	0.018	0.021
	B	0.013	0.014	0.015	0.026	0.016	0.019	0.023	0.010	0.017
	A − B	−0.002	0.009	0.001	0.002	0.018	−0.006	−0.002	0.008	0.004
Word stem	A	0.077	0.056	0.087	0.162	0.103	0.271	0.063	0.038	0.108
	B	0.085	0.037	0.115	0.165	0.057	0.256	0.065	0.048	0.104
	A − B	−0.008	0.019	−0.028	−0.003	0.045	0.015	−0.002	−0.010	0.004
Thesaurus	A	0.133	0.078	0.091	0.254	0.125	0.156	0.134	0.067	0.120
	B	0.122	0.079	0.114	0.236	0.052	0.108	0.162	0.074	0.118
	A − B	0.011	−0.001	−0.013	0.018	0.073	0.048	−0.028	−0.007	0.002

Table 26-5(b)

AVERAGE RANK RECALL AND NORMALIZED PRECISION FOR EACH OF EIGHT QUERY AUTHORS

Average Normalized Precision Differences (Three Analysis Methods)

METHODS		QUERY NUMBERS								
		12–17	*21–28*	*31–37*	*41–48*	*51–58*	*61–68*	*71–78*	*81–87*	*All*
Word form	A	0.172	0.243	0.279	0.481	0.342	0.363	0.437	0.215	0.209
	B	0.289	0.228	0.176	0.406	0.258	0.499	0.307	0.236	0.300
	A − B	−0.117	0.015	0.103	0.075	0.084	−0.136	0.130	−0.021	−0.091
Word stem	A	0.511	0.416	0.358	0.659	0.385	0.760	0.663	0.256	0.469
	B	0.489	0.432	0.524	0.632	0.432	0.768	0.566	0.299	0.518
	A − B	0.022	−0.016	−0.166	0.027	−0.047	−0.008	0.097	−0.043	−0.049
Thesaurus	A	0.673	0.507	0.391	0.717	0.472	0.739	0.764	0.366	0.557
	B	0.641	0.562	0.504	0.659	0.445	0.655	0.720	0.533	0.590
	A − B	0.032	−0.055	−0.113	0.058	0.027	0.084	0.044	−0.167	−0.033

thesaurus. The differences in rank recall and normalized precision obtained for the two sets of relevance judgments (*A* and *B*) are shown in row 3 of Table 26-5 for each dictionary. The differences are again exceedingly small.

In Sec. 26-5, performance results are given for individual queries, and an attempt is made to explain why the relatively large differences in the relevance judgments do not lead to substantial differences in the performance parameters.

26-5 JUDGMENT CONSISTENCY
AND PERFORMANCE MEASURES

In order to explain why the average recall and precision data exhibited previously are relatively insensitive to differences in the relevance assessments, it is necessary to look at the performance characteristics for some individual queries.

First consider the data of Table 26-6 giving normalized recall and normalized pre-

Table 26-6

NORMALIZED RECALL AND PRECISION AVERAGES FOR
THREE ANALYSIS METHODS AND
FOUR TYPES OF RELEVANCE JUDGMENTS
(COSINE CORRELATION, NUMERIC VECTORS)

GROUP	NORMALIZED RECALL			NORMALIZED PRECISION		
	Word Form	*Word Stem*	*Thesaurus*	*Word Form*	*Word Stem*	*Thesaurus*
A	0.5289	0.8340	0.8858	0.2090	0.4690	0.5570
B	0.5249	0.8452	0.8904	0.2473	0.5104	0.5850
C	0.6234	0.8249	0.8777	0.1804	0.3655	0.4885
D	0.5493	0.8759	0.9212	0.3492	0.5777	0.6403

cision figures averaged over the 48 queries for the four sets of relevance assessments. It may be seen that with the sole exception of the word-form normalized recall, the highest performance is obtained in each case using the *D* judgments followed by *B*, *A*, and finally *C*. The *D* judgments, however, represent the agreement in the relevance assessments between authors and nonauthors, and the corresponding relevance sets are therefore produced under reasonably stringent conditions (at least two independent people must agree before an item is termed relevant). On the other hand, the *C* judgments are produced by relatively free criteria, since an item is called relevant if either one of two independent judges calls it relevant. It appears then from the output of Table 26-6 that the *D* judgments which are designed to select those documents most certainly relevant to each query also select those documents most efficiently retrieved by the computer system. That is, the query-document pairs which are most closely and unarguably related are exactly the pairs on which the retrieval performance is best.

This result is confirmed by the output of Table 26-7, where those queries are selected which exhibit the best agreement between the relevance assessors. Such queries represent relatively unambiguous, closely related query-document sets. It is found, just as with the *D* judgments, that these closely related pairs produce the best retrieval performance.

Table 26-7

CORRELATION OF JUDGMENT CONSISTENCY WITH PERFORMANCE

RELEVANCE JUDGMENT CONSISTENCY†	PERFORMANCE MEASURE‡					
	TOP 12		MIDDLE 24		BOTTOM 12	
	B Better	*A Better*	*B Better*	*A Better*	*B Better*	*A Better*
Top 12	4	5	1	2	0	0
Middle 24	1	2	6	11	4	0
Bottom 12	0	0	0	4	5	3

†Relevance judgment consistency $= \dfrac{\text{No. of relevant items in } D}{\sqrt{(\text{No. of relevant in } A)(\text{No. relevant in } B)}}$

‡Performance measure $= \dfrac{(NP \text{ for } A) + (NP \text{ for } B) + (NR \text{ for } A) + (NR \text{ for } B)}{4}$

Table 26-7 contains a plot of performance effectivenesss versus consistency in the relevance judgments. Specifically, a single performance measure and a single measure of relevance consistency are computed for each query as follows:

$$\text{Performance measure} = \frac{(NP \text{ for } A) + (NP \text{ for } B) + (NR \text{ for } A) + (NR \text{ for } B)}{4},$$

and

$$\text{Judgment consistency} = \frac{\text{No. of relevant items in } D}{\sqrt{(\text{No. of relevant in } A)(\text{No. of relevant in } B)}},$$

where NP and NR are normalized precision and normalized recall, respectively. The 48 queries are then arranged into three groups for performance (the top 12, the middle 24, and the bottom 12) and into three groups for relevance judgment consistency. Table 26-7 shows how relevance consistency correlates with performance.

It may be seen that performance is best for those queries with the best relevance consistency. Indeed, 9 of the 12 queries in each top group are also in the other top group. Conversely, not a single query from the bottom 12 in judgment consistency is in the top 12 for performance, and not a single query from the bottom 12 in performance is in the top 12 for judgment consistency.

The performance indicators of Table 26-7 are subdivided further into queries for which the B judgments provide the better performance and those for which the A judgments are superior. In the former case, the nonauther judgments proved more useful than the author judgments, indicating possibly that these queries are ambiguous or poorly formulated. It may be seen from the table that this is the case for a total of $5 + 7 + 9 = 21$ queries out of 48, of which 9 are ranked in the bottom 12 for performance.

It is now possible to explain why the recall-precision output is basically invariant for the collection under study, even though the agreement among relevance judgments is relatively low:

(a) On the one hand, the performance is best for those queries with the best consistency in the relevance judgments.

(b) On the other hand, the recall and precision measures are most sensitive to documents (both relevant and nonrelevant) retrieved early in the search, that is, documents with low rank.

The conclusion then is obvious that, although there may be a considerable difference in the document sets termed relevant by different judges, *there is in fact a considerable amount of agreement for those documents which appear most similar to the queries and which are retrieved early in the search process* (assuming retrieval is in decreasing correlation order with the queries). Since it is precisely these documents which largely determine retrieval performance, it is not surprising to find that the evaluation output is substantially invariant for the different sets of relevance judgments.

The situation is illustrated by a typical query (number 12) in Fig. 26-3. The first row of Table 26-3 shows that for this particular query, the number of relevant items identified by A was 17, while the B judge identified 18 relevant documents. The total number of distinct relevant items was 26 of which 9 were chosen in common by the A and B judges. The agreement score is 0.3462. The ranks of all 26 relevant documents are given in Fig. 26-3(a), with the common items being shown underlined. It may be seen that of the 8 relevant items with the lowest rank (from rank 1 to rank 25) there was agreement between the judges for 6 items; on the other hand, of the 8 relevant items retrieved with highest rank (ranks 178 to 832) there was not a single agreement between the A and B judges. The two recall-precision graphs for query 12 are shown in Fig. 26-3(b); they are seen to be remarkably similar, reflecting the fact that, for the top 25 documents retrieved, the differences in relevance judgments between the A and B judges are very small indeed.

In conclusion, it can be stated that, if the relevance assessments obtained from the query authors used in the present study are typical of what can be expected from general user populations of retrieval systems, then the resulting average recall-precision figures appear to be stable indicators of system performance which do in fact reflect actual retrieval effectiveness.

26-6 MACHINE-SEARCH EFFECTIVENESS

It has been said elsewhere [17] that the retrieval effectiveness obtained with the automatic text-processing methods incorporated into the SMART system appears to be roughly equivalent to the effectiveness obtainable with presently operating manual or semiautomatic retrieval systems. It may be of interest to ask how this presently achievable performance compares with the performance of the best possible imaginable delegated search system. The differences between present performance and such an optimum delegated search system may then give an indication of the amount of improvement in performance which may eventually result from future developments.

It is not completely unreasonable to assume that the best possible delegated search system is one in which a subject expert completely reads through an entire document collection and ranks each document in decreasing similarity order with a given search query. Such a system, which for obvious reasons is not operationally implementable, should in theory be superior to any search system based on indexing or on other reduced document representations. The set of *B* searchers used in the present experiment then can be assumed to constitute such an ideal search system, since they in fact were asked to search through the complete document collection for each query.

RANK	1	2	9	11	15	18	20	25	30	44	54	60	61	69	72	88	105	133	178	179	196	199	277	298	322	832
A	x	x	x	x	x		x	x	x	x	x		x		x	x	x	x		x			x			
B	x	x		x	x	x	x	x			x	x	x	x	x		x		x		x	x			x	x
A∩B	x	x		x	x		x	x			x				x			x								

(a)

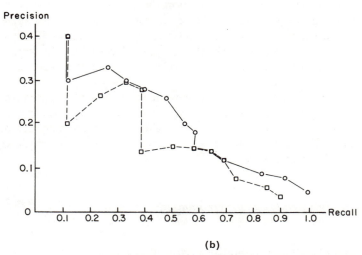

(b)

Fig. 26-3 Sample performance (Query 12): (a) ranks of relevant documents for Query 12 (agreement score 0.3462); (b) recall-precision graph for Query 12 (cutoff after 5, 10, 15, 20, 25, etc. retrieved items).

A comparison has been made between the amount of material "retrieved" by the *B* searcher (that is the number of documents termed relevant by *B*), and the number of relevant items retrieved by the machine search using the same cutoff as the *B* searcher. In both cases, relevance is determined by using the author (*A*) judgments as criteria. Specifically, "optimum recall" and "optimum precision" figures are computed for each query by evaluating the performance of the *B* searcher (in comparison with the *A* relevance judgments) as follows:

$$\text{Optimum } (B) \text{ recall} = \frac{\text{No. of relevant in } (A \cap B)}{\text{No. of relevant in } A},$$

and

$$\text{Optimum } (B) \text{ precision} = \frac{\text{No. of relevant in } (A \cap B)}{\text{No. of relevant in } B}.$$

Then these optimum recall and precision figures are compared with the machine performance, using the thesaurus dictionary for analysis purposes. To permit a fair comparison, the number of items retrieved in the machine search must be the same as the number of items "retrieved" by the *B* searcher; the cutoff in the machine search is therefore set at the number of relevant items identified by *B*. The machine recall and precision are defined as follows:

$$\text{Machine recall} = \frac{\text{No. of relevant in } A \text{ retrieved before cutoff}}{\text{No. of relevant in } A},$$

and

$$\text{Machine precision} = \frac{\text{No. of relevant in } A \text{ retrieved before cutoff}}{\text{Total no. of relevant in } B \text{ (cutoff)}}.$$

The output of Table 26-8 shows that the overall machine-search results are about 25% lower on the average than the *B* results. For some query sets (for example, 41–48 and 71–78), the results are approximately equivalent, and for five queries out of the set of 48, the machine performance is in fact better than that of the *B* searcher. It is seen in Table 26-8 that the average recall and precision for the *B* searcher are about 0.46, while the comparable machine figures are 0.32. Once again these figures demonstrate that the improvements obtainable by refinements in the search and analysis techniques (from 0.32 to 0.46) are relatively modest, in comparison with the desirable perfect system where recall and precision are close to 1. The gap between the complete human search and a perfect search (from 0.46 to 1) appears to be due to ambiguities inherent in the query formulation process and to the difficulties of reconciling the user's view of a subject area with the subject analysis provided for a given document collection. This latter gap may well never be bridged by any search and retrieval system likely to come into existence in the foreseeable future.

Table 26-8(a)

COMPARISON OF OPTIMUM WITH MACHINE
(THESAURUS) PERFORMANCE†

Average Optimum and Machine Recall

Performance	12–17	21–28	31–37	41–48	51–58	61–68	71–78	81–87	All
Optimum search	0.51	0.50	0.35	0.34	0.59	0.25	0.54	0.68	0.46
Machine search (thesaurus)	0.36	0.19	0.17	0.43	0.16	0.40	0.48	0.11	0.32
Difference	0.15	0.31	0.18	−0.09	0.43	−0.15	0.06	0.57	0.14

Table 26-8(b)

COMPARISON OF OPTIMUM WITH MACHINE
(THESAURUS) PERFORMANCE†

Average Optimum and Machine Precision

Performance	12–17	21–28	31–37	41–48	51–58	61–68	71–78	81–87	All
Optimum search	0.52	0.49	0.45	0.38	0.54	0.35	0.47	0.52	0.46
Machine search (thesaurus)	0.40	0.24	0.17	0.33	0.23	0.31	0.35	0.27	0.32
Difference	0.12	0.25	0.28	0.05	0.31	0.04	0.12	0.25	0.14

$$\dagger \text{Optimum } (B) \text{ recall} = \frac{\text{Relevant in } D}{\text{Relevant in } A},$$

$$\text{Optimum } (B) \text{ precision} = \frac{\text{Relevant in } D}{\text{Relevant in } B},$$

$$\text{Machine recall} = \frac{\text{Relevant in } A \text{ before cutoff}}{\text{Relevant in } A},$$

$$\text{Machine precision} = \frac{\text{Relevant in } A \text{ before cutoff}}{\text{Relevant in } B \text{ (cutoff)}},$$

To summarize, several sets of relevance judgments are used in the present study in conjunction with a document collection of over 1,200 items in library science and documentation. The retrieval results in terms of recall and precision obtained for the various relevance sets are substantially identical, even though the overall agreement among the relevance assessments is only about 30%. This fact is explained, and the conclusion is drawn that there appears to be no reason to reject previously published evaluation results for manual or automatic searches, because of uncertainties and instabilities in the computation of the performance measures. It is pointed out again that the absolute performance achievable under present conditions, or likely to be achieved in the future, is much lower than the theoretically desirable optimum.

REFERENCES

[1] C. W. Cleverdon, J. Mills, and E. M. Keen, Factors Determining the Performance of Indexing Systems, *Test Results*, Vol. 2, Aslib–Cranfield Research Project, Cranfield, England 1966.

[2] V. E. Giuliano and P. E. Jones, Study and Test of a Methodology for Laboratory Evaluation of Message Retrieval Systems, *Report ESD-TR-66-405*, Little, Brown & Company, Boston, August 1966.

[3] G. Salton and M. E. Lesk, Computer Evaluation of Indexing and Text Processing, *Journal of the ACM*, Vol. 15, No. 1, January 1968, pp. 8–36; also Chap. 7 of this volume.

[4] C. A. Cuadra and R. V. Katter, Experimental Studies of Relevance Judgments: Final Report, *Report TM-3520*, Vol. 1, *Project Summary*, Vol. 2, *Description of Individual Studies*, System Development Corp., Santa Monica, Calif., June 1967.

[5] R. A. Fairthorne, Implications of Test Procedures, in *Information Retrieval in Action*, Western Reserve University Press, Cleveland, Ohio, 1963, pp. 109–113.

[6] J. O'Connor, Relevance Disagreements and Unclear Request Forms, *American Documentation*, Vol. 18, No. 3, July 1967.

[7] J. O'Connor, Some Questions Concerning Information Need, *American Documentation*, Vol. 19, No. 2, April 1968.

[8] L. B. Doyle, Is Relevance an Adequate Criterion in Retrieval System Evaluation, *Proceedings of the 26th Annual Meeting*, American Documentation Institute, Chicago, October 1963.

[9] M. Taube, A Note on the Pseudomathematics of Relevance, *American Documentation*, Vol. 16, No. 2, April 1965, pp. 69–72.

[10] E. D. Dym, Relevance Predictability—Investigation, Background and Procedures, in *Electronic Handling of Information: Testing and Evaluation*, A. Kent et. al., eds., Thompson Book Co., Washington, D.C., pp. 175–185.

[11] D. L. Shirey and M. Kurfeerst, Relevance Predictability—Data Reduction, in *Electronic Handling of Information: Testing and Evaluation*, A. Kent et. al., eds., Thompson Book Co., Washington, D.C., pp. 187–198.

[12] C. A. Cuadra and R. V. Katter, Opening the Black Box of Relevance, *Journal of Documentation*, Vol. 23, No. 4, December 1967.

[13] A. M. Rees, Evaluation of Information Systems and Services, in *Annual Review of Information Science and Technology*, C. Cuadra, ed., Vol. 2, Interscience Publishers, New York, 1967.

[14] A. M. Rees and D. G. Schultz, A Field Experimental Approach to the Study of Relevance Assessments in Relation to Document Searching, *Final Report to the National Science Foundation*, Center for Documentation and Communication Research, Case Western Reserve University, Cleveland, Ohio, October 1967.

[15] G. Salton et al., Scientific Reports on the SMART System to the National Science

Foundation, *ISR-11, ISR-12, ISR-13*, Department of Computer Science, Cornell University, Ithaca, N.Y., June 1966, June 1967, and January 1968.

[16] G. Salton, Search and Retrieval Experiments in Real-Time Information Retrieval, *Proceedings IFIP Congress 68*, Edinburgh, August 1968, North-Holland Publishing Co., Amsterdam, 1969.

[17] G. Salton, A Comparison Between Manual and Automatic Indexing Methods, *American Documentation*, Vol. 20, No. 1, January 1969, p. 61–71; also Chap. 27 of this volume.

APPENDIX

This appendix shows that the ranking in decreasing order of performance for several processing methods stays constant under conditions of considerable generality, assuming that the performance order is defined by the usual recall and precision measurements.

A perfect relevance judge can be characterized by the fact that he will call a relevant document in fact "relevant" with a probability equal to 1.0, while calling a nonrelevant item "relevant" with a probability equal to 0.0. A somewhat slipshod judge who makes random errors in judgment can be characterized by probabilities p_r and p_{nr}, where p_r is the probability that he will call a relevant document "relevant", and p_{nr} is the probability that he will call a nonrelevant document "relevant". As p_r decreases from 1.0 and p_{nr} increases from 0.0, the judge becomes increasingly inaccurate.

Consider a retrieval system which operates with procedure a, at a recall R_a and precision P_a, measured by the perfect judge. Call the number of documents retrieved n, the total number of documents in the collection N, and the total number of relevant items G. The performance of this system can be evaluated using judgments made by a slipshod judge. The total number of relevant retrieved is $P_a \cdot n$; of these $P_a \cdot n \cdot p_r$ are called relevant. Furthermore, $(1 - P_a) \cdot n$ nonrelevant are retrieved; of these $p_{nr} \cdot (1 - P_a) \cdot n$ are called relevant. The apparent precision using the slipshod judge for evaluation therefore is:

$$P'_a = \frac{[P_a n p_r + (1 - P_a) n p_{nr}]}{n} = P_a(p_r - p_{nr}) + p_{nr}.$$

Similarly, the apparent recall turns out to be

$$R'_a = \frac{[R_a G(p_r - p_{nr}) + n p_{nr}]}{G(p_r - p_{nr}) + N p_{nr}}.$$

It is obvious that if $p_r > p_{nr}$, P'_a is monotonically increasing with P_a; also R'_a is linearly increasing with R_a. That is, any judge with $p_n > p_{nr}$ ranks retrieval methods in the same order of performance as does the ideal judge, and any two inaccurate judges for whom this criterion is satisfied therefore produce identical performance rankings. Furthermore, if $p_{nr} \ll p_r$, the above transformations are equivalent to changes of scale and even percentage changes in the measures will be reproduced accurately. In practice, p_{nr} is expected to be very small, so that this condition is likely to be fulfilled. Of course, the statistical expectations derived here do not imply that random variations may not produce individual queries for which an inaccurate order is apparently indicated. If a reasonable number of queries is averaged, however, the above results are expected to hold.

It should be noted that the constraints placed on the relevance judgments are very weak; it is necessary only that a judge be more likely to label relevant material as "relevant" than he is to label nonrelevant material as "relevant." It does not matter if only a small fraction of the relevant material is identified as relevant, so long as less than that fraction of the nonrelevant material is called relevant. It does not matter either if the total number of documents called relevant is greater than the true number relevant, less than the true number, or equal to it; nor does it matter if the majority of the documents labeled relevant are actually nonrelevant. Because of the weakness of the constraints, it is therefore most unlikely that any misranking of the performance of retrieval methods can result from inferior relevance judgments.

The effectiveness of conventional document indexing is compared with that achievable by fully automatic text-processing methods. Evaluation results are given for a comparison between the MEDLARS search system used at the National Library of Medicine and the experimental SMART system, and conclusions are reached concerning the design of future automatic information systems.

27

A COMPARISON BETWEEN MANUAL AND AUTOMATIC INDEXING METHODS†

G. SALTON

27-1 INTRODUCTION

The design and operations of large-scale information systems has become of concern to an ever increasing segment of the scientific and professional world. Furthermore, as the amount and complexity of the available information has continued to grow, the use of mechanized or partly mechanized procedures for various information storage and retrieval tasks has also become more widespread. As a result, a number of large information systems are now in operation in which at least the search operation—that is, the comparison of incoming search requests with stored information—is carried out automatically. Typical examples in the United States are the NASA Scientific and Technical Information Facility, and the MEDLARS system at the National Library of Medicine.

While these operational information systems are thus able rapidly to search vast storage files, often containing many hundreds of thousands of items, most of the operations other than the search itself are performed manually with the help of human experts. In particular, all the content

†This study appeared originally as Section VI of *Scientific Report ISR-14*, October 1968; it is also included in *American Documentation*, Vol. 20, No. 1, January 1969.

analysis and indexing operations, which lead to the assignment of suitably chosen combinations of index terms to the stored documents and to incoming search requests, are performed normally by specialists who know the given subject area as well as the performance characteristics of the retrieval environment within which they operate.

Many of the information systems which base their operations on manual indexing with, for the most part, automatic search methods are quite successful in isolating, from the mass of largely irrelevant stored material, many of the items which prove pertinent to the users' information needs. Nevertheless, the feeling that manual systems and procedures should be replaced by suitably chosen automatic methods has continued to grow, and a number of fully automatic information storage and retrieval systems have been designed and put into operation, at least on an experimental basis. The SMART system represents one such effort to replace the intellectual indexing by sophisticated automatic text analysis procedures and thereby to produce a retrieval environment in which all document- and query-handling procedures are performed automatically [1], [2], [3].

In the next few paragraphs, some typical evaluation results obtained with the SMART system are given. Thereafter, the design of the SMART–MEDLARS test is examined, and evaluation results are given for the comparison between SMART and MEDLARS searches, using a variety of different analysis and search methods. Suggestions are made for improving the performance of presently operating information systems and for the design of future automatic retrieval services.

27-2 THE EVALUATION OF INFORMATION SYSTEMS

Many different criteria may suggest themselves for measuring the performance of an information system. In the evaluation work carried out with the SMART system, the effectiveness of an information system is assumed to depend on its ability to satisfy the users' information needs by retrieving wanted material, while rejecting unwanted items. Two measures have been used widely for this purpose: *recall* and *precision*. They represent, respectively, the proportion of relevant material actually retrieved and the proportion of retrieved material actually relevant [4], [5]. (Ideally, all relevant items should be retrieved, while at the same time, all nonrelevant items should be rejected, as reflected by perfect recall and precision values equal to 1.)

It should be noted that both the recall and precision figures which can be achieved by a given system are adjustable, in the sense that a relaxation of the search conditions often leads to high recall, while a tightening of the search criteria leads to high precision. Unhappily, experience has shown that, *on the average*, recall and precision tend to vary inversely because the retrieval of more relevant items also leads normally to the retrieval of more irrelevant ones. In practice, a compromise is usually made, and a performance level is chosen such that much of the relevant material is retrieved, while the number of nonrelevant items which are also retrieved is kept within tolerable limits.

In the SMART evaluation system, these various possible operating ranges are taken into account by computing for each search request and for each processing method a variety of different statistics related to recall and precision. Specifically, four global statistics are generated—rank recall, log precision, normalized recall, and normalized precision respectively—as well as ten local statistics, consisting of the standard precision at ten different recall levels. The global statistics are used to represent the overall performance of a given search, whereas the local statistics furnish individual recall-precision pairs for specific operating ranges of the system. Normally paired comparisons are presented, consisting of the *average* performance over many search requests of two given search and retrieval systems [5].

One of the document collections used for evaluation purposes with the SMART system over the last few years is the set of 200 documents and 42 search requests in the field of aerodynamics used earlier as part of the well-known Aslib–Cranfield experiments [4]. This collection is attractive for test purposes because a number of actual user queries were available, as well as sets of relevance judgments obtained from the scientists constituting the user population. Furthermore, English abstracts were furnished with each document, and thus it became possible to compare the effectiveness of the conventional retrieval operations based on a matching of the index term sets—manually assigned by trained indexers at Cranfield—with the performance of the fully automatic language-processing devices based on the manipulation of document abstracts used by the SMART programs. Such a comparison could then produce evidence to indicate whether document identifiers generated automatically by language analysis methods, such as suffix cutoff procedures, thesaurus lookup, phrase generation methods, statistical term associations, syntactic analysis, and others, would perform equally well as manually assigned index terms.

A typical comparison between the Cranfield indexing and an automatic word-stem matching process based on a matching of weighted word stems extracted from document abstracts and search requests, respectively, is shown in Fig. 27-1, averaged over the 42 Cranfield queries. The recall-precision graph of Fig. 27-1(a) and the corresponding tables of Fig. 27-1(b) indicate that the manual indexing is slightly superior to the simple automatic word-stem process. However, the statistical significance computations, included in Fig. 27-1(c), show that the differences in performance between the two systems are not significant. Specifically, each of the values shown in Fig. 27-1(c) represents the probability—computed by using either a standard t-test, or a sign test—that if the performance of the two systems (manual indexing and automatic word-stem matching) were in fact equally high, then a test value as large as the one actually observed would occur in practice [5]. A probability of 0.05 is usually taken as an upper bound in judging whether a deviation in test values is significant or not. The probability values included in Fig. 27-1(c) are seen to be much higher than 0.05, and the assumption that the two systems are approximately comparable in effectiveness cannot be rejected safely.

The results of the SMART–Cranfield comparisons seem to indicate that even

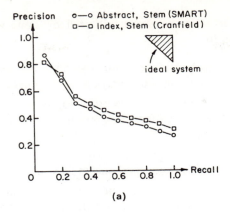

(a)

SMART *Word Stem*		*Cranfield Indexing*	
R	*P*	*R*	*P*
0.1	0.8239	0.1	0.8045
0.2	0.6518	0.2	0.6581
0.3	0.5578	0.3	0.5908
0.4	0.5093	0.4	0.5498
0.5	0.4522	0.5	0.5171
0.6	0.4143	0.6	0.4506
0.7	0.3800	0.7	0.4035
0.8	0.3431	0.8	0.3649
0.9	0.3005	0.9	0.3233
1.0	0.2551	1.0	0.2799
RNK REC = 0.2998		RNK REC = 0.3122	
LOG PRE = 0.4655		LOG PRE = 0.4674	
NOR REC = 0.8644		NOR REC = 0.8897	
NOR PRE = 0.6704		NOR PRE = 0.6831	

(b)

Evaluation Measures	*Probabilities*	
	t-Test	*Sign Test*
	(Indexing over Abstract)	
Precision at		
$R = 0.1$	0.5151	0.7011
$R = 0.3$	0.4358	0.7283
$R = 0.5$	0.1163	1.0000
$R = 0.7$	0.3682	0.8679
$R = 0.9$	0.4044	0.2559
RNK REC	0.6622	0.0470
LOG PRE	0.9341	1.0000
NOR REC	0.1491	0.1081
NOR PRE	0.7268	1.0000
Combined	0.0415	0.0465

(c)

Fig. 27-1 Recall-precision comparison for Cranfield indexing and SMART word-stem process (averages 42 queries, 200 document abstracts, cosine numeric): (a) recall-precision graph; (b) recall-precision tables; (c) significance output.

simple automatic text analysis procedures do not necessarily produce retrieval results that are much inferior to those obtained in a system based on manual indexing. In fact, the benefits of the index language control supplied in the conventional retrieval situation by the human indexers appears to be balanced by a deeper and more complex type of analysis available in the automatic environment, including selective term weighting and the use of relatively large sections of text to ensure a high degree of indexing exhaustivity.

While the results of the SMART–Cranfield test are in line with many other evaluation figures obtained by SMART with different document collections in other subject fields [5], the test nevertheless has been criticized by some writers. In particular, it has been claimed that [6]:

(a) The use of the standard recall-precision measures is questionable, since other possible criteria (cost, waiting time, etc.) are disregarded.

(b) The relevance of a document with respect to a search query is not a stable criterion but varies with the user population, thus presumably producing different evaluation results for different sets of users.

(c) The experimental controls used to identify the Cranfield user population, the query set, and the sets of relevance judgments may have been deficient.

(d) The sources of variation affecting systems performance are not pinpointed, and no indication is given to permit a generalization of the test results to large, operational situations.

Certain recent experiments appear to indicate that some of these objections may be groundless—for example, different user populations seem to agree on the relative *ordering* of a set of documents in decreasing order of relevance with respect to a search request, thereby producing constant recall and precision values [7]. However, further comparisons between manual and automatic indexing systems are certainly of interest. The experiments carried out with a small subset of the MEDLARS collection were undertaken in an attempt to obtain further evidence in the ongoing comparison of conventional and automatic information systems.

27-3   THE TEST DESIGN

27-3-A   The MEDLARS Evaluation Study

The SMART–MEDLARS experiments to be described are based on a small portion of a much larger systems evaluation study undertaken over the last few years within the National Library of Medicine [8], [9]. In this larger study, 302 search requests actually processed by MEDLARS were carefully chosen to reflect both a stratified sample of the MEDLARS-user population and a representative proportion of the subject fields covered by MEDLARS. For these 302 searches, the help of the users was enlisted in order to obtain careful value judgments, made on a sample of the search output for each query. Specifically, a *precision base* (PB) was constructed by judging for relevance a sample of the documents retrieved by MEDLARS in response to each query; similarly, a *recall base* (RB) was obtained by taking documents from a variety of sources which were identified in advance as being relevant to the query. The recall and precision base documents were then used to compute for each search the recall and precision actually achieved during the search of the MEDLARS collection.

While the design of the complete in-house MEDLARS test cannot be covered here, it is of interest to examine briefly some of the principal results. The overall average recall figure for MEDLARS was found to be approximately 0.58, while the overall precision was 0.50, thus indicating that, on the average, a typical search would retrieve almost 60% of the relevant material included in the collection, while only about half of the documents handed to the user in response to a search request would be nonrelevant. If one considers that the MEDLARS collection consists of 500,000 documents and that only a few hundred will, on the average, prove relevant to a given query, it is seen that the search system rejects consistently and properly many hundreds of thousands of nonrelevant items which the user obviously does not care to see, while retrieving a large proportion of the useful items at the same time.

The operating ranges for the present MEDLARS system are shown in the recall-precision graph of Fig. 27-2. In practice, the system operates in the center of

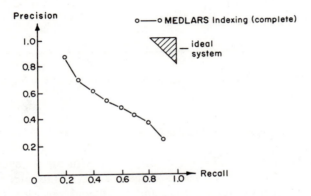

Fig. 27-2 MEDLARS recall-precision range for complete test (302 queries, 500,000 documents).

the curve, since that is the area where neither recall nor precision are unreasonably low. Other operating areas are, of course, possible by sliding up and down the curve of Fig. 27-2. However, most users are not likely to prefer either the high precision–low recall or the low precision–high recall ends, particularly since all points within easy reach of the presently implemented system are quite far away from the ideal operating range in the upper right-hand corner of the curve.

An indication of the recall and precision failures identified during the complete MEDLARS test is given in Table 27-1. It is seen that over 30% of both the recall and the precision failures are due to the fact that the manual query formulation does not reflect the real user need adequately. In addition, the indexing language in use produces many precision failures, and the document indexing is responsible for many recall failures. Finally, the lack of communication between user and system personnel during the search also causes a large number of errors. A comparison of these test

Table 27-1

TYPICAL RECALL AND PRECISION FAILURES FOR
COMPLETE MEDLARS TEST
(302 QUERIES, 500,000 DOCUMENTS)

Source of Failure	*797 Recall Failures (%)*	*3038 Precision Failures (%)*
Index language (lack of specific term or false coordination of terms)	10	36
Searching (search formulation too exhaustive or too specific)	35	32
Indexing (document indexing insufficiently exhaustive or too exhaustive, or omission of important term)	37	13
Lack of user-system interaction	25	17
Miscellaneous	1	2

results with those applicable to the SMART runs is made following the exposition of the test design actually used.

27-3-B   Design of the SMART Test

For a variety of reasons, having to do mostly with input keypunching, it was necessary to restrict the SMART tests to a small subset of the total MEDLARS test environment (300 queries, several thousand recall and precision base items, and over 500,000 documents to be searched). Specifically, 18 queries were obtained from the National Library of Medicine, together with 273 of their associated RB and PB documents. The 273 documents actually used were chosen as follows:

Documents	*Number*
Total evaluated by MEDLARS for the 18 queries in SMART subcollection (including 149 RB and 369 PB items)	518
Number unusable for SMART experiment because abstract or summary was not easily available	245
Total used in SMART subcollection	273

For the remaining 18 queries and 273 documents, the English abstracts were keypunched, and the SMART runs were carried out in accordance with the standard SMART methods [1], [2], [3], [5].

In order to make a comparison with the MEDLARS system possible, it was necessary, in addition, to choose a cutoff in the number of retrieved documents equivalent to that which MEDLARS would have obtained, had the SMART subcollection been used during the MEDLARS search. A typical cutoff computation is shown as an example in Table 27-2. Consider a typical request for which MEDLARS

Table 27-2

SAMPLE SMART–MEDLARS CUTOFF COMPUTATION

Recall Computation	*Number of Documents*
Retrieved by MEDLARS	3 RB (out of 6)†
	30 PB‡
	180 unassessed
Documents contained in SMART subset	all RB
	20 PB
SMART cutoff	20 PB + 3RB = 23
Assuming 4 RB retrieved (out of 23 items)	Recall $\frac{4}{6} = 0.66$

Precision Computation	*Number of Documents*
Initial cutoff	23
Intermediate cutoff (after removal of RB)	23 − 3 = 20
Number retrieved by SMART in top 20	4 RB, 9 PB relevant
Final cutoff	20 (remove 4 RB and replace by 4 new items)
SMART retrieval 9 relevant out of 16 1 relevant out of 4 new items	Precision $= \frac{9 + 1}{20} = 0.50$

†RB = Recall base documents.
‡PB = Precision base documents.

would have retrieved a total of 213 documents, including 3 RB items out of a total of 6, 30 PB items, and 180 items retrieved but unassessed for relevance with respect to the given query. If it is assumed that the SMART subset contains all of the RB items and 20 out of 30 PB items, then the retrieval cutoff is set at 23 documents for the recall calculations. (Since the SMART system ranks documents in decreasing correlation order with the search request, it is always possible to retrieve exactly the n highest-ranking items.) For the precision calculations, an additional adjustment is necessary because recall-base documents which are retrieved by MEDLARS are normally excluded from the MEDLARS precision calculations. For the example of

Table 27-2, 3 such RB items had to be removed, the final cutoff being then 20 for precision purposes.

This procedure for determining the number of documents to be retrieved by SMART permits a direct comparison with the MEDLARS searches for the 18 queries being processed. The following differences in the test environments, however, must be noted:

(a) The original MEDLARS searches were conducted using the complete MEDLARS document collection, whereas the SMART searches were made with the subset for which keypunched abstracts were available. The possible effect of this reduction in collection size is discussed in the concluding section of this chapter.

(b) The recall and precision bases used for the 18 queries were larger for MEDLARS (518 items) than for SMART (273 items). The average MEDLARS recall-precision results of Table 27-4(c) show, however, that the MEDLARS performance for the two document subsets is comparable—indeed, MEDLARS obtains somewhat better results with the smaller set of 273 items—so that no further bias is introduced by the reduction in the size of recall and precision bases.

(c) Since the MEDLARS *precision* calculations are based on the exact set of documents retrieved by Medlars in response to each search request, *a comparison with the precision obtained by SMART can be made directly only if SMART retrieves exactly the same items as Medlars;* in that case, the precision values are the same for the two systems. Under all other circumstances, SMART retrieves items not also retrieved by MEDLARS, in which case the corresponding documents are not normally assessed for relevance by MEDLARS, and a direct precision comparison becomes impossible. A precision adjustment must then be made before the respective values are comparable.

The precision adjustment actually made is based on the following argument. The apparent precision obtained by SMART takes into account only those documents which are retrieved by MEDLARS. But, MEDLARS does not retrieve *all* relevant items in its searches—in fact, the MEDLARS recall for the 18 test queries is only 0.64. Thus, the apparent SMART precision is based on the availability of only 64% of the relevant documents. Then the assumption is made that the SMART precision would remain the same, were the full set of relevant documents to enter into the computation instead of the 64% actually used; that is, it is conjectured that the proportion of relevant items retrieved would be the same for the unavailable relevant items (those not in the MEDLARS precision base) as for the available ones. Since

$$\frac{\text{Adjusted } P}{100 \text{ percent}} = \frac{\text{Apparent } P}{64 \text{ percent}},$$

the adjusted precision is obtained by multiplying the apparent precision by the factor 1.56. The complete argument is summarized in Table 27-3.

To summarize, the search results obtained by MEDLARS and SMART for the 18 queries are compared in the following manner. The cutoff value used by SMART

Table 27-3

EXPLANATION FOR PRECISION ADJUSTMENT

Precision Adjustment

---

1. SMART can reach MEDLARS precision value only if it retrieves *exactly the same* items as MEDLARS (since calculations are based on PB).

2. SMART PB base consists only of items retrieved by MEDLARS, and MEDLARS does *not* retrieve all relevant (MEDLARS recall on SMART subset = 0.64).

3. SMART and MEDLARS are independent systems, and assuming *all* relevant were available in SMART collection, some of them would be retrieved by SMART.

4. Assuming that the percentage of relevant retrieved were to remain the same if *all* relevant were available to SMART

$$\frac{\text{Apparent precision}}{\text{Percent relevant in SMART collection (64\%)}} = \frac{\text{Adjusted precision}}{\text{All relevant (100\%)}}.$$

5. Adjustment

$$\text{Adjusted } P = \text{Apparent } P \cdot \frac{100}{64}.$$

---

to distinguish retrieved from nonretrieved items is exactly the one used in the corresponding MEDLARS search for the subset of 273 items; the recall calculations are based on the retrieval of the complete set of known relevant items, and the output values which result are directly comparable. The apparent precision calculations are based on an average MEDLARS recall of only 64%, and a suitable adjustment is made to account for the lack of relevance assessments in that part of the colleton which is not retrieved by MEDLARS.

27-4 SMART-MEDLARS *COMPARISON*

The average recall and precision values obtained for the SMART and MEDLARS systems are shown in Table 27-4. The corresponding statistical significance calculations are given in Table 27-5. Tables 27-4(a) and 27-4(b) include, respectively, average recall and average precision values for the SMART runs for each of three different language analysis systems: (1) the *word form* dictionary, which makes it possible to match text words differing only in a final "s" (that is, singular and plural forms of the same word); (2) the *word stem* dictionary, which includes a single entry for all words exhibiting the same word stem; (3) the *thesaurus*, which is used to recognize also words included within a single thesaurus class (such as synonyms and other related items).

For each dictionary system, three different SMART query sets are used for

Table 27-4(a)

SMART RECALL AVERAGES (18 QUERIES, 273 DOCUMENTS)

AVERAGE	SMART (STANDARD)			SMART (NEGATIVE DELETE)			SMART (UPWEIGHT)		
	Word Form	*Thesaurus*	*Word Stem*	*Word Form*	*Thesaurus*	*Word Stem*	*Word Form*	*Thesaurus*	*Word Stem*
Micro	0.644	0.632	0.655	0.667	0.644	0.667	0.770	0.690	0.770
Macro	0.704	0.695	0.718	0.665	0.700	0.718	0.802	0.692	0.799

Table 27-4(b)

SMART PRECISION AVERAGES (18 QUERIES, 273 DOCUMENTS)

AVERAGE	SMART (STANDARD)			SMART (NEGATIVE DELETE)			SMART (UPWEIGHT)		
	Word Form	*Thesaurus*	*Word Stem*	*Word Form*	*Thesaurus*	*Word Stem*	*Word Form*	*Thesaurus*	*Word Stem*
Micro (apparent)	0.395	0.410	0.389	0.355	0.395	0.385	0.445	0.440	0.430
Macro (apparent)	0.368	0.393	0.367	0.353	0.394	0.342	0.431	0.430	0.421
Micro (adjusted)	0.583	0.605	0.574	0.524	0.583	0.568	0.656	0.649	0.634
Macro (adjusted)	0.571	0.611	0.570	0.549	0.613	0.531	0.670	0.669	0.655

Table 27-4(c)

MEDLARS RECALL-PRECISION VALUES (18 QUERIES)

Average	*Recall*	*Precision*
273 Documents		
Micro	0.678	0.640
Macro	0.643	0.625
518 Documents		
Micro	0.671	0.568
Macro	0.558	0.573

experimental purposes—"standard run", "negative delete", and "upweight", respectively. The results for the last two runs are examined in Sec. 27-5. In each case, *micro averages* are given as well as *macro averages*. The former represent the averages obtained by comparing the total number of relevant retrieved over all 18 queries, to the total relevant or the total retrieved for all the queries; the latter are the actual per query averages and are normally more representative of the performance experienced by the average user [10].

Table 27-5

SIGNIFICANCE COMPUTATIONS FOR
SMART–MEDLARS COMPARISONS
(18 QUERIES, 273 DOCUMENTS, STANDARD RUNS)

ANALYSIS METHODS BEING COMPARED	PROBABILITIES (A OVER B)		COMPARISONS FAVORING A, B, EVEN
	t-test	*sign test*	
MEDLARS search (*A*) SMART word stem (*B*)			
Recall	0.5676	1.0000	*A* = 11
Precision (apparent)	0.0001	0.0002	*B* = 13
Precision (adjusted)	0.2706	0.6291	Even = 12
MEDLARS search (*A*) SMART thesaurus (*B*)			
Recall	0.6883	1.0000	*A* = 9
Precision (apparent)	0.0004	0.0005	*B* = 15
Precision (adjusted)	0.8139	1.0000	Even = 12
MEDLARS search (*A*) SMART word form (*B*)			
Recall	0.5675	1.0000	*A* = 12
Precision (apparent)	0.0001	0.0002	*B* = 13
Precision (adjusted)	0.2911	0.6291	Even = 11

A comparison of the average *recall* values for the 18 queries [Tables 27-4(a) and 27-4(c)] indicates that the micro averages slightly favor MEDLARS, whereas the macro averages slightly favor SMART. That is, MEDLARS is able to retrieve slightly more relevant documents overall, but SMART exhibits the better average recall per query. An examination of the recall values obtained for the individual queries listed in Table 27-6, reveals that MEDLARS may do very well, or very badly, in retrieving relevant documents, whereas SMART is more consistent in obtaining a

Table 27-6

QUERY DISTRIBUTION IN VARIOUS RECALL RANGES

RECALL RANGE	NUMBER OF QUERIES IN RANGE	
	MEDLARS	*SMART* (*stem*)
1.0	10	7
0.99–0.50	1	7
0.49–0.01	3	4
0.0	4	0

performance which is generally neither perfect nor very poor. Thus, perfect recall is obtained ten times by MEDLARS, but only seven times by SMART. In exchange, MEDLARS retrieves not a single relevant document in four instances, while this never happens for the SMART searches.

These figures point to a fundamental difference between manual-indexing systems and the automatic text-processing schemes used in SMART. Often, the human intermediary charged with the formulation of the search statement in the manual system is exceptionally clever in determining the user's information needs; at other times, however, these needs are misunderstood, thus accounting for the searches with zero recall. In addition, the manual-indexing system is, of course, highly dependent on the richness and completeness of the indexing language and on the thoroughness and accuracy with which the document indexing is performed.

In the automatic text analysis, on the other hand, the complete text of a document abstract is normally used for analysis purposes, and it is very rare indeed that the resulting content identifiers do not reflect the actual document content at least to some extent. In addition, the automatic environment makes it possible to use complex weighting and matching procedures designed to increase the effect of certain important content identifiers at the expense of others that are less crucial. At the same time, the basic dependence on the initial vocabulary is also responsible for the fact that some relevant items are difficult to retrieve, thus accounting for the less-than-perfect performance of the SMART searches.

The statistical significance output of Table 27-5 shows clearly that the recall differences between SMART and MEDLARS are *not* statistically significant; indeed, the sign test probabilities are equal to 1 for each dictionary. Thus, the average recall performance is just about identical for the two systems.

The precision figures for the standard SMART runs and the MEDLARS searches are contained in Tables 27-4(b) and 27-4(c), respectively. As expected, the apparent SMART precision is much smaller than the corresponding MEDLARS precision. However, when the adjustment factor is included, it is seen that the adjusted precision is only slightly lower for SMART than for MEDLARS, the differences in performance being again not statistically significant. Overall, the average performance data of Table 27-4 lead to the conclusion that the MEDLARS and SMART performances are comparable for the 18 queries, with SMART showing a slightly better recall while MEDLARS exhibits a somewhat higher precision.

One factor, not taken into account in the average performance figures of Table 27-4, is the ability of the SMART system to rank the documents in decreasing correlation order with the search requests. Thus, in the comparison with MEDLARS, no distinction is made between different rankings of relevant documents that are retrieved.† Such a ranking is, however, important to a user interested in retrieving the relevant items ahead of the nonrelevant ones.

To test the ranking ability of the automatic SMART process, a separate test was

---

†Actually, a limited system of nested ranking on three levels is available in MEDLARS by constructing three increasingly refined formulations of each search query, thereby producing three nested sets of output documents.

made by comparing the "rank recall" measure [10] computed from the SMART ranks, with the rank recall obtained from a hand-ranked output list produced manually within the National Library of Medicine for test purposes. The hand-ranked output lists were available for 14 of the 18 queries, shown in the evaluation output of Table 27-7. Here again it is seen that the performance of the two ranking systems—manual ranking with MEDLARS and automatic ranking with SMART—is about equally effective, the average rank recall being slightly better for SMART than for MEDLARS. A number of conclusions to be drawn from the foregoing test results are examined following the comparison of the various SMART runs.

Table 27-7

RANK RECALL COMPARISON FOR HAND-RANKED MEDLARS
WITH SMART WORD STEM PROCESS
(14 QUERIES USING PB DOCUMENTS ONLY)

QUERY NUMBERS	NUMBER OF PB RELEVANT	RANK RECALL		NUMBER OF QUERIES FAVORING		
		MEDLARS	*SMART*	*MEDLARS*	*SMART*	*Neither*
02	5	0.88	0.94		X	
04	13	0.91	0.83	X		
05	10	0.92	0.98		X	
06	8	0.40	0.76		X	
07	3	0.43	1.0		X	
09	11	0.97	0.93	X		
10	11	0.90	0.83	X		
13	10	0.97	0.63	X		
14	2	1.0	1.0			X
16	4	0.71	0.71			X
18	2	0.60	1.0		X	
32	15	0.75	0.75			X
40	3	1.0	1.0			X
187	9	0.70	0.69	X		
Average rank recall		0.80	0.86	5	5	4

27-5 COMPARISON OF SMART ANALYSIS METHODS

Several different language analysis procedures were used for the SMART runs conducted with the MEDLARS subcollection. Specifically, runs were made using document titles only or full document abstracts, and three different dictionaries—known, respectively, as the word form, word stem, and thesaurus dictionaries—were used for language normalization. The first two dictionaries were generated by machine using for this purpose the standard SMART procedures; the thesaurus was generated by hand [11].

The differences in the dictionary makeup account, in general, for the differences in performance observed in the recall and precision measures of Table 27-4. Both the recall and precision values are nearly the same for word form and word stem dictionaries in the standard SMART runs. The thesaurus dictionary, on the other hand, which would be expected normally to produce better results than either of the suffix dictionaries produces only slightly better precision but slightly worse recall. The thesaurus groupings were actually constructed by a staff member without special knowledge of the medical terminology, and so the corresponding performance is not

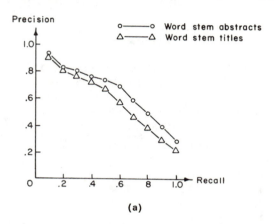

(a)

Word Stem Abstracts		*Word Stem Titles*	
R	*P*	*R*	*P*
0.1	0.9167	0.1	0.8973
0.2	0.8132	0.2	0.8154
0.3	0.8008	0.3	0.7610
0.4	0.7646	0.4	0.7178
0.5	0.7311	0.5	0.6718
0.6	0.6947	0.6	0.5694
0.7	0.5893	0.7	0.4683
0.8	0.4904	0.8	0.3904
0.9	0.3962	0.9	0.2909
1.0	0.2814	1.0	0.2319
RNK REC = 0.4092		RNK REC = 0.3023	
LOG PRE = 0.6926		LOG PRE = 0.6446	
NOR REC = 0.9104		NOR REC = 0.7508	
NOR PRE = 0.8199		NOR PRE = 0.7169	

(b)

Evaluation Measures	*Probabilities*	
	t-Test	*Sign Test*
	(Abstracts over Titles)	
Precision at		
$R = 0.1$	0.5066	1.0000
$R = 0.3$	0.3076	0.2266
$R = 0.5$	0.2311	1.0000
$R = 0.7$	0.0438	0.0213
$R = 0.9$	0.1305	0.1435
RNK REC	0.1446	0.0042
LOG PRE	0.4790	0.0127
NOR REC	0.0005	0.0074
NOR PRE	0.0085	0.0127
Combined	0.0000	0.0000

(c)

Fig. 27-3 Recall-precision data for abstract-title comparisons (MEDLARS collection, 18 queries, 273 documents): (a) recall-precision graph; (b) recall-precision tables; (c) significance output.

typical of the thesaurus results obtained by SMART with document collections in different subject fields [5].

The results obtained by using document titles instead of full abstracts for analysis purposes are, however, fully in accord with comparable data obtained previously for different subject areas. The graph of Fig. 27-3(a) shows, in particular, that titles are much less effective than abstracts, particularly at the high recall end of the curve. Furthermore, the significance output of Fig. 27-3(c) indicates that the performance differences are, in fact, statistically significant, at least for the global measures.

Two additional minor modifications were made in the query set for test purposes. The first consisted of removing all negative phrases from the query statements included to denote what the user did *not* wish to retrieve. Such negative phrases are not recognized presently by the standard SMART analysis methods, with the result that negative statements are actually interpreted as positive subject descriptions. The second query modification consisted of repeating certain technical words in the query statements occurring in the collection with low frequency. This modification produces an increased weight for the corresponding document identifiers and thereby may generate a query statement which matches the user's interests more closely than the original. The several types of query formulations resulting from the modification procedure are shown for three queries in Table 27-8.

Both of the query alterations were performed manually, although machine programs might have been written to accomplish the same tasks. The new queries represent formulations that could occur realistically in an environment of informed users who would be instructed not to use negative subject descriptions, and who would emphasize the important technical terms in their query formulation.

Table 27-8

SAMPLES OF QUERY MODIFICATION BY NEGATIVE
PHRASE DELETION AND UPWEIGHTING

Query Number	Original Query	Negative Phrase Delete	With Term Upweighting
01	The crystalline lens in vertebrates, including humans, but not drug therapy or surgery.	The crystalline lens in vertebrates, including humans.	Original query: crystalline lens, crystalline lens.
03	Electron microscopy of lung or bronchi. Pleura or pleural diseases may be excluded.	Electron microscopy of lung or bronchi.	Original query: electron, electron, lung, bronchi.
13	Blood or urinary steroids in human breast or prostatic neoplasms. Drug therapy, toxicology, etc., to be excluded.	Blood or urinary steroids in human breast or prostatic neoplasm.	Original query: steroids, steroids, breast, prostate.

The evaluation results for "negative deletion" and "upweighting" are included in Table 27-4 for the recall and precision averages corresponding to the MEDLARS searches: in Fig. 27-4 they are included in the form of recall-precision graphs. It is seen that the upweighting process improves both recall and precision by 5–10% over the complete range of the recall-precision curve. The negative phrase deletion does not, however, exhibit the same uniformly beneficial effects, although some improvement in precision is noticeable at the low recall end of the curve. The significance data of Fig. 27-4(c) show that the changes in search effectiveness between original and altered queries are not sufficiently pronounced to be statistically significant.

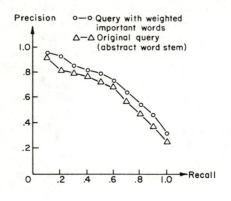 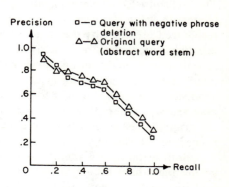

(a)

Measures	Original	Upweight	Negative
Precision at			
R = 0.1	0.9167	0.9627	0.9288
R = 0.3	0.8008	0.8500	0.7939
R = 0.5	0.7311	0.8004	0.7246
R = 0.7	0.5893	0.6441	0.5794
R = 0.9	0.3962	0.4776	0.3898
RNK REC	0.4092	0.4546	0.3973
LOG PRE	0.6926	0.7260	0.6874
NOR REC	0.9104	0.9200	0.8294
NOR PRE	0.8199	0.8476	0.7674

(b)

Evaluation Measures	Upweight over Original (Sign Test)	Original over Negative (Sign Test)
Precision at		
R = 0.1	0.6875	1.0000
R = 0.3	1.0000	1.0000
R = 0.5	0.7539	1.0000
R = 0.7	1.0000	0.7266
R = 0.9	0.0574	0.7539
RNK REC	0.4545	0.7539
LOG PRE	0.1796	0.5078
NOR REC	0.4240	0.7539
NOR PRE	0.3018	0.7539
Combined	0.0011	0.1215

(c)

Fig. 27-4 Recall-precision comparisons for original queries and altered queries by negative phrase deletion and upweighting (MEDLARS collection, 18 queries, 273 documents, abstract stem process): (a) recall-precision graphs for comparison of original queries with altered queries; (b) recall-precision tables; (c) significance output.

An examination of the search results for the individual queries shows that the negative phrase deletion does not perform equally well for all queries. In particular, the procedure fails to improve the retrieval if the deletion process reduces the query to only a very short statement, which is no longer representative of user needs. It may also fail in cases where a given thesaurus grouping includes a variety of different concepts, with some of the concepts occurring in a negative phrase, while others occur in a positive sense within the same query. In that case, the deletion of the negative phrases produces a decrease in the weight of important terms, which consequently may reduce the search effectiveness.

The upweighting process for important technical terms generally produces an improvement in search effectiveness. However, the improvement may be less uniform than expected. For some queries, it is easy to select appropriate terms whose weight should be increased; for example, in query 01, listed in Table 27-8, the term "lens" may be expected to be much more essential for the subject description than, for example, the term "vertebrate." Other query statements may, however, occur for which the important terms are much more difficult to locate; in such cases, the search improvements due to upweighting may remain small or may be nonexistent.

The two query modification procedures incorporated into the SMART system are only two possible methods which may improve the result of the automatic searches. Similar methods can, of course, also be used for the semimanual MEDLARS searches. The prospects for such potential improvements in retrieval effectiveness are discussed in the concluding section.

27-6   CONCLUSIONS

The MEDLARS test comparisons which are described in this study lead to the same conclusions reached previously in other test environments with the SMART evaluation system [5]. Fully automatic text analysis and search systems do not appear to produce a retrieval performance which is inferior to that obtained by conventional systems using manual document indexing and manual search formulations. While the manual indexing and search formulations can lead to exceptionally fine results when the indexer and/or the searcher are completely aware of the relationships between the stored collection and the user needs, the search results may also be very poor when these conditions are not met. The automatic process, on the other hand, with its exhaustive input data and complex analysis methods, rarely performs very poorly and may often produce completely satisfactory retrieval action.

Two important questions may be asked concerning the practical implications of the foregoing test results. First, is it reasonable to expect that identical results would hold if the automatic text-processing methods were applied to the operational MEDLARS environment comprising 500,000 or more documents; second, can anything be done to improve the search effectiveness of presently existing automatic and manual information systems beyond those reflected in the recall-precision graphs of Figs. 27-1 to 27-4.

The first question cannot be answered with full certainty, since it is obviously not likely that keypunched abstracts should ever become available for the full MEDLARS collection. To what extent the present results can be extrapolated safely to searches performed with the full MEDLARS collection depends to a large extent on whether the set of properly rejected nonrelevant documents included in the MEDLARS collection falls into subject categories which are clearly far away from the query subjects. Obviously, if the nonrelevant documents not included in the SMART subset but included in the full collection could be assumed to be easier to reject than the nonrelevant actually included in the subset, then the SMART results for the full collection should be the same as those obtained for the subset alone. If, on the other hand, there are many more hard-to-reject nonrelevant items in the full collection than in the subset, the results obtained by SMART on the subcollection may not be directly transferable to those obtainable on the full collection. An estimate for the amount of degradation to be expected in such a case may be obtained by adding to the SMART subset new documents which are nearly—but not quite—relevant to the search requests and repeating the searches with the augmented collection. Based on the previous test results obtained with the SMART system in other subject areas, it is this writer's guess that the degradation, if any, will be small. This assertion, however, remains to be tested.

The problem relating to the fundamental improvements of both the SMART and MEDLARS searches is easier to treat. The originators of the internal MEDLARS test have, in fact, some pertinent suggestions to make concerning possible changes to be implemented in the search formulations, indexing language, and user–system interaction:

(a) Concerning an appropriate query formulation "... the prime requirement is a complete statement of what the requester is looking for in the requester's own natural language, narrative form; [the query formulation must *not*] be deliberately phrased ... in a form that the requester believes will approximate a MEDLARS search strategy." (Lancaster [9], p. 117.)

(b) Concerning the indexing language to be used "we recommend a shift in emphasis away from the external advisory committee on terminology and towards the continued analysis of the terminological requirements of MEDLARS users as reflected in the demands placed upon the system." (Lancaster [9], p. 193.)

(c) Concerning user-system interaction during the search "... the greatest potential for improvement in MEDLARS exists at the interface between user and system; a significant improvement in the statement of requests can raise both the recall and the precision ...." (Lancaster [9], p. 193.)

That these suggestions are all well taken has been shown by the retrieval comparisons made previously with the SMART system [5]. Indeed, the search formulations suggested as ideal for MEDLARS are exactly the ones already used for all SMART searches. Furthermore, the dictionary construction principles derived for the SMART system also point in the direction of greater responsiveness to collection makeup and user needs and away from committee control [12]. Finally, user-controlled iterative searches have been implemented successfully with the SMART system for several years [13], [14], [15].

It is difficult to predict exactly how much improvement in search effectiveness may result from the introduction of these various search and retrieval aids. The test results obtained under experimental conditions with the SMART system appear to indicate that the potential improvement will not exceed 10–15%, leading to a recall and precision performance of 0.70 or 0.75, instead of the present 0.50 to 0.60. Such a performance would still be far short of what is desirable. However, it is encouraging to note that the present situations are understood well enough to make it reasonable to suggest avenues for the design of future improved systems, including viable automatic search and analysis procedures in place of some of the uncertain manual ones now in use.

REFERENCES

[1] G. Salton and M. E. Lesk, The SMART Automatic Document Retrieval System— An Illustration, *Communications of the ACM*, Vol. 8, No. 6, June 1965.

[2] M. E. Lesk, Operating Instructions for the SMART Text Processing and Document Retrieval System, *Report ISR-11* to the National Science Foundation, Section II, Department of Computer Science, Cornell University, Ithaca, N.Y., June 1966.

[3] G. Salton et al., Information Storage and Retrieval, Scientific Reports to the National Science Foundation, *ISR-11, ISR-12, ISR-13*, Department of Computer Science, Cornell University, Ithaca, N.Y., June 1966, June 1967, and January 1968.

[4] C. W. Cleverdon and E. M. Keen, Factors Determining the Performance of Indexing Systems, *Test Results*, Vol. 2, Aslib–Cranfield Research Project, Cranfield, England, 1966.

[5] G. Salton and M. E. Lesk, Computer Evaluation of Indexing and Text Processing, *Journal of the ACM*, Vol. 15, No. 1, January 1968; also Chap. 7 of this volume.

[6] A. M. Rees, Evaluation of Information Systems and Services, in *Annual Review of Information Science and Technology*, C. Cuadra, ed., Vol. 2, Interscience Publishers, New York, 1967.

[7] A. M. Rees and D. G. Schultz, A Field Experimental Approach to the Study of Relevance Assessments in Relation to Document Searching, *Final Report to the National Science Foundation*, Center for Documentation and Communication Research, Case Western Reserve University, Cleveland, Ohio, October 1967.

[8] F. W. Lancaster, Evaluating the Performance of a Large Operating Information Retrieval System, *Proceedings of the Second Electronic Information Handling Conference*, Thompson Book Company, Washington, D.C., 1967.

[9] F. W. Lancaster, Evaluation of the MEDLARS Demand Search Service, Final Report, National Library of Medicine, Washington, D.C., January 1968.

[10] G. Salton, The Evaluation of Computer-Based Information Retrieval Systems, *Proceedings* 1965 *International FID Congress*, Spartan Books, New York, 1966.

[11] E. M. Keen, Suffix Dictionaries and Thesaurus, Phrase, and Hierarchy Dictionaries, Information Storage and Retrieval, *Report ISR-13* to the National Science Foundation, Sections VI and VII, Department of Computer Science, Cornell University, Ithaca, N.Y., January 1968.

[12] G. Salton, Information Dissemination and Automatic Information Systems, *Proc. IEEE*, Vol. 54, No. 12, December 1966.

[13] J. J. Rocchio, Jr., Document Retrieval Systems—Optimization and Evaluation, Doctoral thesis, *Report ISR-10* to the National Science Foundation, Harvard Computation Laboratory, Cambridge, Mass., March 1966.

[14] J. J. Rocchio, Jr. and G. Salton, Information Search Optimization and Iterative Retrieval Techniques, *Proceedings of the AFIPS Fall Joint Computer Conference*, Las Vegas, Nev., November 1965, Spartan Books, New York, 1965.

[15] G. Salton, Search and Retrieval Experiments in Real-Time Information Retrieval, *Proceedings IFIP Congress 68*, Edinburgh, August 1968, North-Holland Publishing Co., Amsterdam, 1969.

AUTHOR INDEX

549

SUBJECT INDEX